PAUL MICHAEL

THE ACADEMY AWARDS: A PICTORIAL HISTORY

HUMPHREY BOGART: THE MAN AND HIS FILMS

MOVIE GREATS

The Players, Directors, Producers

PAUL MICHAEL
Editor in Chief

JAMES ROBERT PARISH
Associate Editor

JOHN ROBERT COCCHI • RAY HAGEN • JACK EDMUND NOLAN
Contributing Editors

GARLAND BOOKS / 95 MADISON AVENUE / NEW YORK 10016

ACKNOWLEDGMENTS

The editors wish to extend their thanks to the following for their generous help in the preparation of this volume: Entertainment Copyright Research Co., Inc., 225 West 57th Street, New York, New York, for making available their most complete files on the motion picture industry, for without the extensive library and research facilities of this organization, the book would not have been possible; Lennard DeCarl, for making available his detailed files on all available screen credits of over 1,500 performers, gathered over a period of nearly two decades; Jerry Vermilye, whose career studies of such performers as Jean Arthur, Ida Lupino and Maria Montez have appeared in *Films in Review* and *Screen Facts*, for his tremendous help in the verification of material; Ken Jones, Mrs. Peter Smith, Charles Stumpf, Charles Smith and Harry Wilkinson, for opening their superb collections of photographs for use in all chapters; Marc Ricci, for opening the doors of The Memory Shop and allowing the selection of hundreds of photographs for use in the book.

The editors would also like to thank: William Breen, Samuel Goldwyn Productions; Ted McInerney; Martin A. Grove, American Broadcasting Company; Judith L. Bly, The Walter Reade Organization; Paul Kamey, Universal Pictures Corporation; Harvey Stewart; Leonard Brown, Collectors Book Shop; Jonas Rosenfield, Jr. and Jerry Anderson, 20th Century-Fox; Perry Mandel, Vitaprint; Michael Linden and Joseph Infantino, Motion Picture Association of America; Harold Danziger, Columbia Pictures; Charles Alicoate and Gloria Kravitz, *Film Daily;* Arthur Freed, former President of The Academy of Motion Picture Arts and Sciences; Lorraine Burdick; Mary Fiore and Mark J. Greenberg, *Photoplay* magazine; Florence Solomon; Peter Miglierini; Samuel M. Sherman; Robert Seger, Harshe-Rotman and Druck; Barney Pitkin; Phil Moshcovitz, Famous Fantasy Films; Sig Shore, Video Artists Features; David Bloom, Hollywood Television Service; Erwin Ezzes and Helen Killeen, United Artists Television; Paul Lazarus and Albert Stefanic, National Screen Service; Lou Valentino; Peter Rogers and Ruth Robinson, National Telefilm Associates; Hank Warner, CBS-TV; Marvin Korman, Screen Gems; Phil Saltman, MCA-TV; Emery Austin and Norman Kaphan, Metro-Goldwyn-Mayer; A. Morgan Maree and Earl R. Beaman, The Selznick Company; David Cantor, Magna Pictures Corporation; Lou Edelman, Embassy Film Corporation; Jack Goldstein, Allied Artists Corporation; Leonard Maltin, *Film Fan Monthly;* Albert B. Manski; Jeanne Stein; Mike Berman, Paramount Pictures; Jonas Mekas, *Film Culture* magazine; Henry Hart, *Films in Review;* Homer Dickens; William K. Everson; Jane Gordon, Seven Arts Associated Corporation; Robert W. Fouse, The American Humane Association; Mrs. Rose Cocchi; Lillian Schwartz and her staff at the Academy of Motion Pictures Arts and Sciences, Barbara Browning, Joyce Foreman, Midori Martin, Mildred Simpson; Don Koll; Hilary Knight; Victor Sanjuro; Hanna Henner; the late Walt Disney; Apco Apeda Photos; Diane Giddis, my very patient editor, and hundreds of others in and out of the motion picture industry.

KEY TO ABBREVIATIONS OF PRODUCTION COMPANIES

AA	Allied Artists
AIP	American International
BIP	British International Pictures
BV	Buena Vista
Col.	Columbia Pictures
DCA	Distributing Corporation of America
EL	Eagle Lion Classics
Fox	Fox Picture Corporation
GN	Grand National Pictures
Lip.	Lippert Pictures
MGM	Metro-Goldwyn-Mayer, Inc.
Mon.	Monogram Pictures
Par.	Paramount Pictures
PRC	Producers Releasing Corporation
PRO	Producers Releasing Organization
Rank	J. Arthur Rank
Rep.	Republic Pictures
RKO	RKO Radio Pictures
Tif.	Tiffany
20th	20th Century-Fox Film Corporation
UA	United Artists
Univ.	Universal Pictures, Universal-International
WB	Warner Brothers Pictures and First National Pictures

CONTENTS

Here, in alphabetical order, are over 600 actors and actresses who have made their mark in American sound films — not only the top stars and award-winners, but the character men and women, Western stars and sidekicks, mobsters and gun molls, B-picture heroes and heroines — all the players who have given their talents to the medium. For each player there is a brief biography, a complete listing of all his English-language films, and a still from one of the films.

Films have been called "the director's medium" — and here are over 50 of the top directors of American sound films. For each director there is a complete chronological listing of his English-language sound feature films, as well as a still from one of the films.

The art of film producing is much misundertstood, for every producer contributes in a different way. Some are in complete command of the production while others act only as business managers. Here are more than 50 top film producers with a listing of their productions, accompanied by a still from one of their great films.

CHAPTER I

THE PLAYERS

Nat Pendleton, Bud Abbott and Lou Costello in *Buck Privates*.

ABBOTT AND COSTELLO

BUD ABBOTT (William A. Abbott) Born October 2, 1895, Asbury Park, New Jersey. Married Betty Pratt (1918), children: Bud, Vickie.

LOU COSTELLO (Louis Francis Cristillo) Born March 6, 1908, Paterson, New Jersey. Married Anne Balter (1934), children: Patricia, Carole, Christine. Died March 3, 1959.

Sound Feature Films: *One Night in the Tropics* (Univ., 1940), *Buck Privates* (Univ., 1941), *In the Navy* (Univ., 1941), *Hold That Ghost* (Univ., 1941), *Keep 'Em Flying* (Univ., 1941), *Ride 'Em Cowboy* (Univ., 1942), *Rio Rita* (MGM, 1942), *Pardon My Sarong* (Univ., 1942), *Who Done It?* (Univ., 1942), *It Ain't Hay* (Univ., 1943), *Hit the Ice* (Univ., 1943), *Lost in a Harem* (Univ., 1944), *In Society* (Univ., 1944), *Here Come the Co-eds* (Univ., 1945), *The Naughty Nineties* (Univ., 1945), *Bud Abbott and Lou Costello in Hollywood* (MGM, 1945), *Little Giant* (Univ., 1946), *The Time of Their Lives* (Univ., 1946), *Buck Privates Come Home* (Univ., 1947), *The Wistful Widow of Wagon Gap* (Univ., 1947), *The Noose Hangs High* (EL, 1948), *Abbott and Costello Meet Frankenstein* (Univ., 1948), *Mexican Hayride* (Univ., 1948), *Africa Screams* (UA, 1949), *Abbott and Costello Meet the Killer* (Univ., 1949), *Abbott and Costello in the Foreign Legion* (Univ., 1950), *Abbott and Costello Meet the Invisible Man* (Univ., 1951), *Comin' Round the Mountain* (Univ., 1951), *Jack and the Beanstalk* (WB, 1952), *Lost in Alaska* (Univ., 1952), *Abbott and Costello Meet Captain Kidd* (WB, 1952), *Abbott and Costello Go to Mars* (Univ., 1953), *Abbott and Costello Meet Dr. Jekyll and Mr. Hyde* (Univ., 1953), *Abbott and Costello Meet the Keystone Kops* (Univ., 1955), *Abbott and Costello Meet the Mummy* (Univ., 1955), *Dance With Me, Henry* (UA, 1956), *The 30 Foot Bride of Candy Rock* (Col., 1959).*

*Without Bud Abbott.

WALTER ABEL Born June 6, 1898, St. Paul, Minnesota. Married Marietta Bitter (1926).

Sound Feature Films: *The Three Musketeers* (RKO, 1935), *The Lady Consents* (RKO, 1936), *Two in the Dark* (RKO, 1936), *The Witness Chair* (RKO, 1936), *Fury* (MGM, 1936), *We Went to College* (MGM, 1936), *Second Wife* (RKO, 1936), *Portia on Trial* (Rep., 1937), *Wise Girl* (RKO, 1937), *Law of the Underworld* (RKO, 1938), *Racket Busters* (WB, 1938), *Men With Wings* (Par., 1938), *King of the Turf* (UA, 1939), *A Miracle on Main Street* (Col., 1940), *Dance, Girl, Dance* (RKO, 1940), *Arise, My Love* (Par., 1940), *Michael Shayne, Private Detective* (20th, 1940), *Who Killed Aunt Maggie?* (Rep., 1940), *Hold Back the Dawn* (Par., 1941), *Skylark* (Par., 1941), *Glamour Boy* (Par., 1941), *Beyond the Blue Horizon* (Par., 1942), *Holiday Inn* (Par., 1942), *Wake Island* (Par., 1942), *Star Spangled Rhythm* (Par., 1942), *So Proudly We Hail!* (Par., 1943), *Fired Wife* (Univ., 1943), *Mr. Skef-*

Shirley Temple, Walter Abel and Katharine Alexander in *Kiss and Tell*.

Iris Adrian, Barry Norton and Betty Blythe in *Murder at Glen Athol*.

fington (WB, 1944), *An American Romance* (MGM, 1944), *The Affairs of Susan* (Par., 1945), *The Hitler Grang* (narrator; Par., 1944), *Duffy's Tavern* (Par., 1945), *Kiss and Tell* (Col., 1945), *The Kid From Brooklyn* (RKO, 1946), *13 Rue Madeleine* (20th, 1946), *The Hal Roach Comedy Carnival* (UA, 1947), *Dream Girl* (Par., 1948), *That Lady in Ermine* (20th, 1948), *So This Is Love* (WB, 1953), *Night People* (20th, 1954), *The Indian Fighter* (UA, 1955), *The Steel Jungle* (WB, 1956), *Bernardine* (20th, 1957), *Raintree County* (MGM, 1957), *Handle With Care* (MGM, 1958), *Mirage* (Univ., 1965).

IRIS ADRIAN (Iris Adrian Hostetter) Born May 29, 1913, Los Angeles, California. Married Charles Over (1935); divorced 1936. Married George Jay.

Feature Films: *Paramount on Parade* (Par., 1930), *Gay Deception* (Fox, 1935), *Rumba* (Par., 1935), *Stolen Harmony* (Par., 1935), *Murder at Glen Athol* (Invincible, 1935), *Our Relations* (MGM, 1936), *Stage Struck* (WB, 1936), *A Message to Garcia* (20th, 1936), *Mister Cinderella* (MGM, 1936), *Lady Luck* (Chesterfield, 1936), *One Rainy Afternoon* (UA, 1936), *Gold Diggers of 1937* (WB, 1936), *One Third of a Nation* (Par., 1939), *Back Door to Heaven* (Par., 1939), *Meet the Wildcat* (Univ., 1940), *Go West* (MGM, 1940), *Road to Zanzibar* (Par., 1941), *Horror Island* (Univ., 1941), *Meet the Chump* (Univ., 1941), *The Lady From Cheyenne* (Univ., 1941), *Wild Geese Calling* (20th, 1941), *New York Town* (Par., 1941), *Too Many Blondes* (Univ., 1941), *Hard Guy* (PRC, 1941), *I Killed That Man* (Mon., 1941), *Sing Another Chorus* (Univ., 1941), *Swing It Soldier* (Univ., 1941), *Roxie Hart* (20th, 1942), *To the Shores of Tripoli* (20th, 1942), *Rings on Her Fingers* (20th, 1942), *Juke Box Jenny* (Univ., 1942), *Broadway* (Univ., 1942), *Fingers at the Window* (MGM, 1942), *Moonlight Masquerade* (Rep., 1942), *Orchestra Wives* (20th, 1942), *Ladies' Day* (RKO, 1943), *The Crystal Ball* (UA, 1943), *Taxi, Mister* (UA, 1943), *Lady of Burlesque* (UA, 1943), *Action in the North Atlantic* (WB, 1943), *Calaboose* (UA, 1943), *Hers to Hold* (Univ., 1943), *Submarine Base* (PRC, 1943), *Spotlight Scandals* (Mon., 1943), *Career Girl* (PRC, 1944), *Million Dollar Kid* (Mon., 1944), *Shake Hands With Murder* (PRC, 1944), *The Singing Sheriff* (Univ., 1944), *Bluebeard* (PRC, 1944), *Alaska* (Mon., 1944), *I'm From Arkansas* (PRC, 1944), *Swing Hostess* (PRC, 1944), *Once Upon a Time* (Col., 1944), *The Woman in the Window* (RKO, 1944), *It's a Pleasure* (RKO, 1945), *Steppin' in Society* (Rep., 1945), *Road to Alcatraz* (Rep., 1945), *The Stork Club* (Par., 1945), *Boston Blackie's Rendezvous* (Col., 1945), *The Bamboo Blonde* (RKO, 1946), *Vacation in Reno* (RKO, 1946), *Cross My Heart* (Par., 1946), *Fall Guy* (Mon., 1947), *Philo Vance Returns* (PRC, 1947), *The Trouble With Women* (Par., 1947), *Smart Woman* (AA, 1948), *Out of the Storm* (Rep., 1948), *The Paleface* (Par., 1948), *Flamingo Road* (WB, 1949), *The Lovable Cheat* (Film Classics, 1949), *Sky Dragon* (Mon., 1949), *Miss Mink of 1949* (20th, 1949), *Trail of the Yukon* (Mon., 1949), *Always Leave Them Laughing* (WB, 1949), *There's a Girl in My Heart* (AA, 1949), *Tough Assignment* (Lip., 1949), *Mighty Joe Young* (RKO, 1949), *My Dream Is Yours* (WB, 1949), *Woman on Pier 13* (RKO, 1949), *Hi-Jacked* (Lip., 1950), *Once a Thief* (UA, 1950), *Blondie's Hero* (Col., 1950), *Joe Palooka in*

Humphrey Takes a Chance (Mon., 1950), *Sideshow* (Mon., 1950), *Stop That Cab* (Lip., 1951), *My Favorite Spy* (Par., 1951), *Varieties on Parade* (Lip., 1951), *G. I. Jane* (Lip., 1951), *The Racket* (RKO, 1951), *Carson City* (WB, 1952), *Take the High Ground* (MGM, 1953), *The Fast and Furious* (American Releasing Corp., 1954), *Crime Wave* (WB, 1954), *Devil's Harbor* (20th, 1954), *Carnival Rock* (Howco, 1957), *The Buccaneer* (Par., 1958), *Blue Hawaii* (Par., 1961), *The Errand Boy* (Par., 1961), *Fate Is the Hunter* (20th, 1964), *That Darn Cat* (BV, 1965).

BRIAN AHERNE (Brian de Lacy Aherne) Born May 2, 1902, King's Norton, Worcestershire, England. Married Joan Fontaine (1939); divorced 1943. Married Eleanor Labrot (1946).

Feature Films: *Song of Songs* (Par., 1933), *What Every Woman Knows* (MGM, 1934), *The Fountain* (RKO, 1934), *The Constant Nymph* (Fox, 1934), *Sylvia Scarlet* (RKO, 1935), *I Live My Life* (MGM, 1935), *Beloved Enemy* (UA, 1936), *The Great Garrick* (WB, 1937), *Merrily We Live* (MGM, 1938), *Captain Fury* (UA, 1939), *Juarez* (WB, 1939), *Lady in Question* (Col., 1940), *Hired Wife* (Univ., 1940), *My Son, My Son* (UA, 1940), *The Man Who Lost Himself* (Univ., 1941), *Skylark* (Par., 1941), *Smilin' Through* (MGM, 1941), *My Sister Eileen* (Col., 1942), *Forever and a Day* (RKO, 1943), *A Night to Remember* (Col., 1943), *First Comes Courage* (Col., 1943), *What a Woman!* (Col., 1943), *The Locket* (RKO, 1946), *Smart Woman* (AA, 1948), *Angel on the Amazon* (Rep., 1948), *I Confess* (WB, 1953), *Titanic* (20th, 1953), *Prince Valiant* (20th, 1954), *A Bullet Is Waiting* (Col., 1954), *The Swan* (MGM, 1956), *The Best of Everything* (20th, 1959), *Susan Slade* (WB, 1961), *Sword of Lancelot* (Univ., 1963), *The Cavern* (20th, 1965), *Rosie!* (Univ., 1968).

Brian Aherne and Louis Hayward in *My Son, My Son*.

Rosemary Lane, Eddie Albert and May Robson in *Four Wives*.

EDDIE ALBERT (Edward Albert Heimberger) Born April 22, 1908, Rock Island, Illinois. Married Margo (1945), children: Edward, Maria.

Feature Films: *Brother Rat* (WB, 1938), *On Your Toes* (WB, 1939), *Four Wives* (WB, 1939), *Brother Rat and a Baby* (WB, 1940), *An Angel From Texas* (WB, 1940), *My Love Came Back* (WB, 1940), *A Dispatch From Reuters* (WB, 1940), *Four Mothers* (WB, 1941), *The Wagons Roll at Night* (WB, 1941), *Thieves Fall Out* (WB, 1941), *Out of the Fog* (WB, 1941), *The Great Mr. Nobody* (WB, 1941), *Treat 'Em Rough* (Univ., 1942), *Eagle Squadron* (Univ., 1942), *Ladies' Day* (RKO, 1943), *Lady Bodyguard* (RKO, 1943), *Bombardier* (RKO, 1943), *Strange Voyage* (Mon., 1945), *Rendezvous With Annie* (Rep., 1946), *The Perfect Marriage* (Par., 1946), *Smash-Up—The Story of a Woman* (Univ., 1947), *Time Out of Mind* (Univ., 1947), *Hit Parade of 1947* (Rep., 1947), *The Dude Goes West* (AA, 1948), *You Gotta Stay Happy* (Univ., 1948), *The Fuller Brush Girl* (Col., 1950), *You're in the Navy Now* (20th, 1951), *Meet Me After the Show* (20th, 1951), *Actors and Sin* (UA, 1952), *Carrie* (Par., 1952), *Roman Holiday* (Par., 1953), *The Girl Rush* (Par., 1955), *Oklahoma!* (Magna, 1955), *I'll Cry Tomorrow* (MGM, 1955), *Attack!* (UA, 1956), *The Teahouse of the August Moon* (MGM, 1956), *The Sun Also Rises* (20th, 1957), *The Joker Is Wild* (Par., 1957), *The Gun Runners* (UA, 1958), *The Roots of Heaven* (20th, 1958), *Orders to Kill* (United Motion Pictures Organization, 1958), *Beloved Infidel* (20th, 1959), *The Young Doctors* (UA, 1961), *The Two Little Bears* (20th, 1961), *Madison Avenue* (20th, 1962), *The Longest Day* (20th, 1962), *Who's Got the Action?* (Par., 1962), *Miracle of the White Stallions* (BV, 1963), *Captain Newman, M.D.* (Univ., 1963), *7 Women* (MGM, 1965), *The Party's Over* (AA, 1968).

LOUISE ALLBRITTON Born July 3, 1920, Oklahoma City, Oklahoma. Married Charles Collingwood (1946).

Robert Paige and Louise Albritton in *Her Primitive Man*.

Feature Films: *Parachute Nurse* (Col., 1942), *Danger in the Pacific* (Univ., 1942), *Not a Ladies' Man* (Col., 1942), *Who Done It?* (Univ., 1943), *Pittsburgh* (Univ., 1942), *It Comes Up Love* (Univ., 1943), *Good Morning, Judge* (Univ., 1943), *Fired Wife* (Univ., 1943), *Son of Dracula* (Univ., 1943), *Follow the Boys* (Univ., 1944), *This Is the Life* (Univ., 1944), *Her Primitive Man* (Univ., 1944), *San Diego, I Love You* (Univ., 1944), *Bowery to Broadway* (Univ., 1944), *The Men in Her Diary* (Univ., 1945), *That Night With You* (Univ., 1945), *Tangier* (Univ., 1946), *The Egg and I* (Univ., 1947), *Sitting Pretty* (20th, 1948), *Walk a Crooked Mile* (Col., 1948), *Don't Trust Your Hasband* (UA, 1948), *The Doolins of Oklahoma* (Col. 1949).,

Sara Allgood and Ginger Rogers in *Roxie Hart*.

SARA ALLGOOD Born October 31, 1883, Dublin, Ireland. Married Gerald Hanson (1917); widowed. Died September 13, 1950.

Feature Films: *Blackmail* (Sono Art-World Wide, 1929), *Riders to the Sea* (Flanagan-Hurst, 1935), *The Passing of the Third Floor Back* (Gaumont-British, 1935), *It's Love Again* (Gaumont-British, 1936), *Storm in a Teacup* (UA, 1937), *Kathleen* (Hoffberg, 1938), *On the Night of the Fire* (GFD, 1939), *That Hamilton Woman* (UA, 1941), *Dr. Jekyll and Mr. Hyde* (MGM, 1941), *Lydia* (UA, 1941), *How Green Was My Valley* (20th, 1941), *Roxie Hart* (20th, 1942), *This Above All* (20th, 1942), *It Happened in Flatbush* (20th, 1942), *The War Against Mrs. Hadley* (MGM, 1942), *Life Begins at 8:30* (20th, 1942), *City Without Men* (Col., 1943), *The Lodger* (20th, 1944), *Jane Eyre* (MGM, 1944), *Between Two Worlds* (WB, 1944), *Keys of the Kingdom* (20th, 1945), *The Strange Affair of Uncle Harry* (Univ., 1945), *Kitty* (Par., 1945), *The Spiral Staircase* (RKO, 1946), *Cluny Brown* (20th, 1946), *The Fabulous Dorseys* (UA, 1947), *Ivy* (Univ., 1947), *Mother Wore Tights* (20th, 1947), *Mourning Becomes Electra* (RKO, 1947), *My Wild Irish Rose* (WB, 1947), *The Girl From Manhattan* (UA, 1948), *One Touch of Venus* (Univ., 1948), *The Man From Texas* (EL, 1948), *The Accused* (Par., 1948), *Challenge to Lassie* (MGM, 1949), *Cheaper by the Dozen* (20th, 1950), *Sierra* (Univ., 1950).

JUNE ALLYSON (Ella Geisman) Born October 7, 1923, Bronx, New York. Married Dick Powell (1945), children: Pamela, Richard; widowed 1963. Married Alfred Glenn Maxwell (1963); divorced 1965. Remarried 1966.

Feature Films: *Best Foot Forward* (MGM, 1943), *Girl Grazy* (MGM, 1943), *Thousands Cheer* (MGM, 1943), *Two Girls and a Sailor* (MGM, 1944), *Meet the People* (MGM, 1944), *Music For Millions* (MGM, 1945), *Her Highness and the Bellboy* (MGM, 1945), *The Sailor Takes a Wife* (MGM, 1945), *Two Sisters From Boston* (MGM, 1946), *Till the Clouds Roll By* (MGM, 1946), *The Secret Heart* (MGM, 1946), *High Barbaree* (MGM, 1947), *Good News* (MGM, 1947), *The Bride Goes Wild* (MGM, 1948), *The Three Musketeers* (MGM, 1948), *Words and Music* (MGM, 1948), *Little Women* (MGM, 1949), *The Stratton Story* (MGM, 1949), *The Reformer and the Redhead* (MGM, 1950),

Right Cross (MGM, 1950), *Too Young to Kiss* (MGM, 1951), *The Girl in White* (MGM, 1952), *Battle Circus* (MGM, 1953), *Remains to Be Seen* (MGM, 1953), *The Glenn Miller Story* (Univ., 1954), *Executive Suite* (MGM, 1954), *Woman's World* (20th, 1954), *Strategic Air Command* (Par., 1955), *The McConnell Story* (WB, 1955), *The Shrike* (Univ., 1955), *The Opposite Sex* (MGM, 1956), *You Can't Run Away From It* (Col., 1956), *Interlude* (Univ., 1957), *My Man Godfrey* (Univ., 1957), *Stranger in My Arms* (Univ., 1959).

Robert Sterling and June Allyson in *The Secret Heart*.

Arleen Whelan and Don Ameche in *Gateway*.

DON AMECHE (Dominic Felix Amici) Born May 31, 1910, Kenosha, Wisconsin. Married Honore Prendergast (1932), children: Ronald, Dominic, Thomas, Lonnie, Bonnie, Connie.

Feature Films: *Sins of Man* (20th, 1936), *Ramona* (20th, 1936), *Ladies in Love* (20th, 1936), *One in a Million* (20th, 1936), *Love Is News* (20th, 1937), *Fifty Roads to Town* (20th, 1937), *You Can't Have Everything* (20th, 1937), *Love Under Fire* (20th, 1937), *In Old Chicago* (20th, 1938), *Happy Landing* (20th, 1938), *Josette* (20th, 1938), *Alexander's Ragtime Band* (20th, 1938), *Gateway* (20th, 1938), *The Three Musketeers* (20th, 1939), *Midnight* (Par., 1939), *The Story of Alexander Graham Bell* (20th, 1939), *Hollywood Cavalcade* (20th, 1939), *Swanee River* (20th, 1939), *Little Old New York* (20th, 1939), *Lillian Russell* (20th, 1940), *Four Sons* (20th, 1940), *Down Argentine Way* (20th, 1940), *That Night in Rio* (20th, 1941), *Moon Over Miami* (20th, 1941), *Kiss the Boys Goodbye* (Par., 1941), *The Feminine Touch* (MGM, 1941), *Confirm or Deny* (20th, 1941), *The Magnificent Dope* (20th, 1942), *Girl Trouble* (20th, 1942), *Heaven Can Wait* (20th, 1943), *Happy Land* (20th, 1943), *Something to Shout About* (Col., 1943), *Wing and a Prayer* (20th, 1944), *Greenwich Village* (20th, 1944), *It's in the Bag* (UA, 1945), *Guest Wife* (UA, 1945), *So Goes My Love* (Univ., 1946), *That's My Man* (Rep., 1947), *Sleep, My Love* (UA, 1948), *Slightly French* (Col., 1949), *A Fever in the Blood* (WB, 1961), *Rings Around the World* (Col., 1966), *Picture Mommy Dead* (Embassy, 1966).

LEON AMES (Leon Waycoff) Born January 20, 1903, Portland, Indiana. Married Christine Gossett (1938), children: Shelley, Leon.

Feature Films:

as **Leon Waycoff** *Murders in the Rue Morgue* (Univ., 1932), *13 Women* (RKO, 1932), *Cannonball Express* (World-Wide, 1932), *Uptown New York* (World-Wide, 1932), *Parachute Jumper* (WB, 1933), *Alimony Madness* (Mayfair, 1933), *The Man Who Dared* (Fox, 1933), *Forgotten* (Invincible, 1933), *Ship of Wanted Men* (Showmen's Pictures, 1933), *The Count of Monte Cristo* (UA, 1934), *I'll Tell the World* (Univ., 1934), *Now I'll Tell You* (Fox, 1934), *Reckless* (MGM, 1935).

as **Leon Ames** *Strangers All* (RKO, 1935), *Mutiny Ahead* (Majestic, 1935), *Get That Man* (Empire, 1935), *Stowaway* (20th, 1936), *Dangerously Yours* (20th, 1937), *Murder in Greenwich Village* (Col., 1937), *Charlie Chan on Broadway* (20th, 1937), *45 Fathers* (20th, 1937), *International Settlement* (20th, 1938), *Walking Down Broadway* (20th, 1938), *The Spy Ring* (Univ., 1938), *Island in the Sky* (20th, 1938), *Come On Leathernecks* (Rep., 1938), *Mysterious Mr. Moto* (20th, 1938), *Strange Faces* (Univ., 1938), *Cipher Bureau* (GN, 1938), *Suez* (20th, 1938), *Secrets of a Nurse* (Univ., 1938), *Risky Business* (Univ., 1939), *I Was a Convict* (Rep., 1939), *Mr. Moto in Danger Island* (20th, 1939), *Panama Patrol* (GN, 1939), *Man of Conquest* (Rep., 1939), *Fugitive at Large* (Col., 1939), *Code of the Streets* (Univ., 1939), *Legion of Lost Flyers* (Univ., 1939), *Calling All Marines* (Rep., 1939), *Thunder Afloat* (MGM, 1939), *East Side Kids* (Mon., 1940), *Marshal of Mesa City* (RKO, 1940), *No Greater Sin* (University Film Products, 1941), *Ellery Queen and the Murder Ring* (Col., 1941), *Crime Doctor* (Col., 1943), *The Iron Major* (RKO, 1943), *Meet Me in St. Louis* (MGM, 1944), *Thirty Seconds Over Tokyo* (MGM, 1944), *The Thin Man Goes Home* MGM, 1944), *Son of Lassie* (MGM, 1945), *Weekend at the Waldorf* (MGM, 1945), *Yolanda and the Thief* (MGM, 1945), *They Were Expendable* (MGM, 1945), *The Postman Always Rings Twice* (MGM,

Fay Wray and Leon Ames in *Murder in Greenwich Village.*

1946), *No Leave, No Love* (MGM, 1946), *The Show-off* (MGM, 1946), *The Cockeyed Miracle* (MGM, 1946), *Undercover Maisie* (MGM, 1947), *Song of the Thin Man* (MGM, 1947), *Merton of the Movies* (MGM, 1947), *Alias a Gentleman* (MGM, 1948), *On an Island With You* (MGM, 1948), *A Date With Judy* (MGM, 1948), *The Velvet Touch* (RKO, 1948), *Little Women* (MGM, 1949), *Any Number Can Play* (MGM, 1949), *Scene of the Crime* (MGM, 1949), *Battleground* (MGM, 1949), *Ambush* (MGM, 1949), *The Big Hangover* (MGM, 1950), *The Skipper Surprised His Wife* (MGM, 1950), *The Happy Years* (MGM, 1950), *Crisis* (MGM, 1950), *Cattle Drive* (Univ., 1951), *On Moonlight Bay* (WB, 1951), *It's a Big Country* (MGM, 1951), *Angel Face* (RKO, 1952), *By the Light of the Silvery Moon* (WB, 1953), *Let's Do It Again* (Col., 1953), *Sabre Jet* (UA, 1953), *Peyton Place* (20th, 1957), *From the Terrace* (20th, 1960), *The Absent-Minded Professor* (BV, 1961), *Son of Flubber* (BV, 1963), *The Misadventures of Merlin Jones* (BV, 1964), *The Monkey's Uncle* (BV, 1965).

Stanley Ridges and Dana Andrews in *Canyon Passage*.

DANA ANDREWS (Carver Dan Andrews) Born January 1, 1912, Collins, Mississippi. Married Janet Murray (1932), child: David; widowed 1935. Married Mary Todd (1939), children: Kathryn, Stephen, Susan.

Feature Films: *The Westerner* (UA, 1940), *Lucky Cisco Kid* (20th, 1940), *Sailor's Lady* (20th, 1940), *Kit Carson* (UA, 1940), *Tobacco Road* (20th, 1941), *Belle Starr* (20th, 1941), *Swamp Water* (20th, 1941), *Ball of Fire* (RKO, 1941), *Berlin Correspondent* (20th, 1942), *Crash Dive* (20th, 1943), *The Ox-Bow Incident* (20th, 1943), *The North Star* (RKO, 1943), *The Purple Heart* (20th, 1944), *Wing and a Prayer* (20th, 1944), *Up in Arms* (RKO, 1944), *Laura* (20th, 1944), *State Fair* (20th, 1945), *Fallen Angel* (20th, 1945), *A Walk in the Sun* (20th, 1945), *Canyon Passage* (Univ., 1946), *The Best Years of Our Lives* (RKO, 1946), *Boomerang* (20th, 1947), *Night Song* (RKO, 1947), *Daisy Kenyon* (20th, 1947), *The Iron Curtain* (20th, 1948), *Deep Waters* (20th, 1948), *No Minor Vices* (MGM, 1948), *The Forbidden Street* (20th, 1949), *Sword in the Desert* (Univ., 1949), *My Foolish Heart* (RKO, 1949), *Where the Sidewalk Ends* (20th, 1950), *Edge of Doom* (RKO, 1950), *The Frogmen* (20th, 1951), *Sealed Cargo* (RKO, 1951), *I Want You* (RKO, 1951), *Assignment Paris* (Col., 1952), *Elephant Walk* (Par., 1954), *Duel in the Jungle* (WB, 1954), *Three Hours to Kill* (Col., 1954), *Smoke Signal* (Univ., 1955), *Strange Lady in Town* (WB, 1955), *Comanche* (UA, 1956), *While the City Sleeps* (RKO, 1956), *Beyond a Reasonable Doubt* (RKO, 1956), *Curse of the Demon* (Col., 1957), *Spring Reunion* (UA, 1957), *Zero Hour* (Par., 1957), *The Fearmakers* (UA, 1958), *Enchanted Island* (WB, 1958), *The Crowded Sky* (WB, 1960), *Madison Avenue* (20th, 1962), *Crack in the World* (Par., 1965), *The Satan Bug* (UA, 1965), *In Harm's Way* (Par., 1965), *Brainstorm* (WB, 1965), *Town Tamer* (Par., 1965), *The Loved One* (MGM, 1965),

Battle of the Bulge (WB, 1965), *Johnny Reno* (Par., 1966), *Spy in Your Eye* (AIP, 1966), *Hot Rods to Hell* (MGM, 1967), *The Frozen Dead* (WB-7 Arts, 1967), *Cobra* (AIP, 1967), *Ten Million Dollar Grab* (RKO, 1968).

Julie Andrews and Max Von Sydow in *Hawaii*.

JULIE ANDREWS (Julia Welles) Born October 1, 1934, Walton-on-the-Thames, England. Married Tony Walton (1959), child: Emma Kate; divorced 1968.

Feature Films: *Mary Poppins* (BV, 1964), *The Americanization of Emily* (MGM, 1964), *The Sound of Music* (20th, 1965), *Torn Curtain* (Univ., 1966), *Hawaii* (UA, 1966), *Thoroughly Modern Millie* (Univ., 1967), *The Singing Princess* (voice only; Larry Joachim Prod., 1967), *Star* (20th, 1968).

THE ANDREWS SISTERS (Patty, Maxene, LaVerne)
    PATRICIA Born February 16, 1920, Minneapolis, Minnesota. Married Marty Melcher; divorced. Married Wally Wechsler.
    MAXENE Born January 3, 1918, Minneapolis, Minnesota. Married Lou Levy (1941), children: Aleda, Peter; divorced 1950.
    LAVERNE Born July 6, 1915, Minneapolis, Minnesota. Married Louis A. Rogers (1948). Died May 8, 1967.

Feature Films: *Argentine Nights* (Univ., 1940), *In the Navy* (Univ., 1941), *Buck Privates* (Univ., 1941), *Hold That Ghost* (Univ., 1941), *Give Out, Sisters* (Univ., 1942), *Private Buckaroo* (Univ., 1942), *What's Cookin'?* (Univ., 1942), *Always a Bridesmaid* (Univ., 1943), *How's About It?* (Univ., 1943), *Follow the Boys* (Univ., 1944), *Hollywood Canteen* (WB, 1944), *Moonlight and Cactus* (Univ., 1944), *Swingtime Johnny* (Univ., 1944), *Her Lucky Night* (Univ., 1945), *Make Mine Music* (RKO, 1946), *Road to Rio* (Par., 1947), *Melody Time* (RKO, 1948).

LaVerne, Patti and Maxene Andrews in *Follow the Boys.*

Evelyn Ankers and Lon Chaney, Jr., in *The Frozen Ghost*.

EVELYN ANKERS Born August 17, 1918, Valparaiso, Chile. Married Richard Denning, child: Diana.

Feature Films: *Villiers Diamond* (British), *Second Thoughts* (British), *Land Without Music* ("Forbidden Music"—Capitol Films, 1936), *Rembrandt* (London Films, 1936), *Fire Over England* (UA, 1937), *Knight Without Armour* (UA, 1937), *Wings of the Morning* (20th, 1937), *Murder In the Family* (20th, 1937), *Claydon Treasure Mystery* (20th, 1938), *Over the Moon* (London Films, 1939), *Hold That Ghost* (Univ., 1941), *Hit the Road* (Univ., 1941), *Bachelor Daddy* (Univ., 1941), *Burma Convoy* (Univ., 1941), *Sandy Steps Out* (Univ., 1941), *The Wolf Man* (Univ., 1941), *The Ghost of Frankenstein* (Univ., 1942), *North to the Klondike* (Univ., 1942), *Eagle Squadron* (Univ., 1942), *Pierre of the Plains* (MGM, 1942), *Sherlock Holmes and the Voice of Terror* (Univ., 1942), *The Great Impersonation* (Univ., 1942), *Keep 'Em Slugging* (Univ., 1943), *The Mad Ghoul* (Univ., 1943), *You're a Lucky Fellow, Mr. Smith* (Univ., 1943), *All By Myself* (Univ., 1943), *Hers to Hold* (Univ., 1943), *Captive Wild Woman* (Univ., 1943), *Son of Dracula* (Univ., 1943), *His Butler's Sister* (Univ., 1943), *Follow the Boys* (Univ., 1944), *Ladies Courageous* (Univ., 1944), *Pardon My Rhythm* (Univ., 1944), *Invisible Man's Revenge* (Univ., 1944), *Jungle Woman* (Univ., 1944), *The Pearl of Death* (Univ., 1944), *Weird Woman* (Univ., 1944), *Bowery to Broadway* (Univ., 1944), *The Fatal Witness* (Rep., 1945), *The Frozen Ghost* (Univ., 1945), *Queen of Burlesque* (PRC, 1946), *The French Key* (Rep., 1946), *Black Beauty* (20th, 1946), *Spoilers of the North* (Rep., 1947), *The Last of the Redmen* (Col., 1947), *The Lone Wolf in London* (Col., 1947), *Tarzan's Magic Fountain* (RKO, 1949), *Parole, Inc.* (EL, 1949), *The Texan Meets Calamity Jane* (Col., 1950), *No Greater Love* (Brandon Films, 1960).

Ann-Margret and John Forsythe in *Kitten With a Whip*.

ANN-MARGRET (Ann Margret Olson) Born April 28, 1941, Stockholm, Sweden. Married Roger Smith, 1967.

Feature Films: *Pocketful of Miracles* (20th, 1961), *State Fair* (20th, 1962), *Bye Bye Birdie* (Col., 1962), *Viva Las Vegas* (MGM, 1964), *Kitten With a Whip* (Univ., 1964), *Bus Riley's Back in Town* (Univ., 1965), *The Pleasure Seekers* (20th, 1965), *Once a Thief* (MGM, 1965), *Cincinnati Kid* (MGM, 1965), *Made in Paris* (MGM, 1966), *The Swinger* (Par., 1966), *Stagecoach* (20th, 1966), *Murderers' Row* (Col., 1966), *The Tiger and the Pussycat* (Embassy, 1967), *Maggie* (Fairfilm, 1968).

Barton MacLane and Eve Arden in *Big Town Czar*.

EVE ARDEN (Eunice Quedens) Born April 30, 1912, Mill Valley, California. Married Ned Bergen (1939), children: Liza, Constance; divorced (1947). Married Brooks West (1951), children: Duncan, Douglas.

Feature Films:

as **Eunice Quedens** *Song of Love* (Col., 1929), *Dancing Lady* (MGM, 1933).

as **Eve Arden** *Oh, Doctor* (Univ., 1937), *Stage Door* (RKO, 1937), *Cocoanut Grove* (Par., 1938), *Letter of Introduction* (Univ., 1938), *Having Wonderful Time* (RKO, 1938), *Women in the Wind* (WB, 1939), *Big Town Czar* (Univ., 1939), *The Forgotten Women* (Univ., 1939), *Eternally Yours* (UA, 1939), *At the Circus* (MGM, 1939), *A Child Is Born* (WB, 1940), *Slightly Honorable* (UA, 1940), *Comrade X* (MGM, 1940), *No, No, Nanette* (RKO, 1940), *Ziegfeld Girl* (MGM, 1941), *That Uncertain Feeling* (UA, 1941), *She Couldn't Say No* (WB, 1941), *She Knew All the Answers* (Col., 1941), *San Antonio Rose* (Univ., 1941), *Sing for Your Supper* (Col., 1941), *Manpower* (WB, 1941), *Whistling in the Dark* (MGM, 1941), *Last of the Duanes* (20th, 1941), *Obliging Young Lady* (RKO, 1941), *Bedtime Story* (Col., 1941), *Hit Parade of 1943* (Rep., 1943), *Let's Face It* (Par., 1943), *Cover Girl* (Col., 1944), *The Doughgirls* (WB, 1944), *Pan Americana* (RKO, 1945), *Patrick the Great* (Univ., 1945), *Earl Carroll's Vanities* (Rep., 1945), *Mildred Pierce* (WB, 1945), *My Reputation* (WB, 1946), *The Kid From Brooklyn* (RKO, 1946), *Night and Day* (WB, 1946), *Song of Scheherazade* (Univ., 1947), *The Arnelo Affair* (MGM, 1947), *The Unfaithful* (WB, 1947), *The Voice of the Turtle* (WB, 1947), *One Touch of Venus* (Univ., 1948), *Whiplash* (WB, 1948), *My Dream Is Yours* (WB, 1949), *The Lady Takes a Sailor* (WB, 1949), *Paid in Full* (Par., 1950), *Curtain Call at Cactus Creek* (Univ., 1950), *Tea for Two* (WB, 1950), *Three Husbands* (UA, 1950), *Goodbye, My Fancy* (WB, 1951), *We're Not Married* (20th, 1952), *The Lady Wants Mink* (Rep., 1953), *Our Miss Brooks* (WB, 1956), *Anatomy of a Murder* (Col., 1959), *The Dark at the Top of the Stairs* (WB, 1960), *Sgt. Deadhead* (AIP, 1965).

Clancy Cooper, Mary Beth Hughes, Richard Arlen, June Havoc and Edmund MacDonald in *Timber Queen*.

RICHARD ARLEN (Richard Van Mattemore) Born September 1, 1900, Charlottesville, Virginia. Married Jobyna Ralston (1927), child: Richard; divorced 1945.

Sound Feature Films: *The Man I Love* (Par., 1929), *Thunderbolt* (Par, 1929), *Dangerous Curves* (Par., 1929), *The Virginian* (Par., 1929), *Burning Up* (Par., 1930), *Dangerous Paradise* (Par., 1930), *Light of Western Stars* (Par., 1930), *Paramount on Parade* (Par., 1930), *Border Legion* (Par., 1930), *Sea God* (Par., 1930), *Santa Fe Trail* (Par., 1930), *Only Saps Work* (Par., 1930), *The Conquering Horde* (Par., 1931), *Gun Smoke* (Par., 1931), *The Lawyer's Secret* (Par., 1931), *The Secret Call* (Par., 1931), *Caught* (Par., 1931), *Touchdown* (Par., 1931), *Wayward* (Par., 1932), *The Sky Bride* (Par., 1932), *Guilty as Hell* (Par., 1932), *Tiger Shark* (WB, 1932), *The All American* (Univ., 1932), *Island of Lost Souls* (Par., 1933), *Song of the Eagle* (Par., 1933), *College Humor* (Par., 1933), *Three-Cornered Moon* (Par., 1933), *Golden Harvest* (Par., 1933), *Alice in Wonderland* (Par., 1933), *Hell and High Water* (Par., 1933), *Come On Marines* (Par., 1934), *She Made Her Bed* (Par., 1934), *Ready for Love* (Par., 1934), *Helldorado* (Fox, 1935), *Let 'Em Have It* (UA, 1935), *Three Live Ghosts* (MGM, 1935), *The Calling of Dan Matthews* (Col., 1936), *The Mine With the Iron Door* (Col., 1936), *Secret Valley* (20th, 1936), *Silent Barriers* (Gaumont-British, 1937), *Artists and Models* (Par., 1937), *Murder in Greenwich Village* (Col., 1937), *No Time to Marry* (Col., 1938), *Call of the Yukon* (Rep., 1938), *Straight, Place and Show* (20th, 1938), *Missing Daughters* (Col., 1939), *Mutiny on the Blackhawk* (Univ., 1939), *Tropic Fury* (Univ., 1939), *Legion of Lost Flyers* (Univ., 1939), *The Man From Montreal* (Univ., 1940), *Danger on Wheels* (Univ., 1940), *Hot Steel* (Univ., 1940), *The Leather Pushers* (Univ., 1940), *Black Diamonds* (Univ., 1940), *The Devil's Pipeline* (Univ., 1940), *A Dangerous Game* (Univ., 1941), *Lucky Devils* (Univ., 1941), *Mutiny in the Arctic* (Univ., 1941), *Men of the Timberland* (Univ., 1941), *Raiders of the Desert* (Univ., 1941), *Forced Landing* (Par., 1941), *Power Dive* (Par., 1941), *Flying Blind* (Par., 1941), *Torpedo Boat* (Par., 1942), *Wildcat* (Par., 1942), *Wrecking Crew* (Par., 1942), *Alaska Highway* (Par., 1943), *Aerial Gunner* (Par., 1943), *Submarine Alert* (Par., 1943), *Minesweeper* (Par., 1943), *Timber Queen* (Par., 1944), *The Lady and the Monster* (Rep., 1944), *Storm Over Lisbon* (Rep., 1944), *That's My Baby!* (Rep., 1944), *The Big Bonanza* (Rep., 1945), *Identity Unknown* (Rep., 1945), *The Phantom Speaks* (Rep., 1945), *Accomplice* (PRC, 1946), *The French Key* (Rep., 1946),* *Speed to Spare* (Par., 1948), *When My Baby Smiles at Me* (20th, 1948), *Return Of Wildfire* (Screen Guild, 1948), *Grand Canyon* (Screen Guild, 1949), *Kansas Raiders* (Univ., 1950), *Flaming Feather* (Par., 1952), *Silver City* (Par., 1952), *Hurricane Smith* (Par., 1952), *The Blazing Forest* (Par., 1952), *Sabre Jet* (UA, 1953), *Devil's Harbor* (20th, 1954), *Stolen Time* (British Lion, 1955), *Hidden Guns* (Rep., 1956), *The Mountain* (Par., 1956), *Blonde Blackmailer* (AA, 1958), *Warlock* (20th, 1959), *Raymie* (AA, 1960), *The Last Time I Saw Archie* (UA, 1961), *The Young and the Brave* (MGM, 1963), *Thunder Mountain* ("Shepherd of the Hills"—Howco, 1963), *Cavalry Command* (Pano-

rama, 1963), *Law of the Lawless* (Par., 1964), *The Best Man* (UA, 1964), *Young Fury* (Par., 1965), *Black Spurs* (Par., 1965), *The Bounty Killer* (Embassy, 1965), *Town Tamer* (Par., 1965), *The Human Duplicator* (AA, 1965), *Apache Uprising* (Par., 1966), *Johnny Reno* (Par., 1966), *Waco* (Par., 1966), *To the Shores of Hell* (Robert Patrick-SR, 1966), *Red Tomahawk* (Par., 1967), *Fort Utah* (Par., 1967), *Huntsville* (Par., 1967), *Arizona Bushwhackers* (Par., 1968), *Rogue's Gallery* (Par., 1968), *The Frontiersman* (Par., 1968), *Buckskin* (Par., 1968).

*Unbilled guest appearance.

Marjorie Gateson, George Arliss and Patricia Ellis in *The King's Vacation*.

GEORGE ARLISS Born April 10, 1868. Married Florence Montgomery (1899). Died February 5, 1946.

Sound Feature Films: *Disraeli* (WB, 1929), *The Green Goddess* (WB, 1930), *Old English* (WB, 1930), *Millionaire* (WB, 1931), *Alexander Hamilton* (WB, 1931), *The Man Who Played God* (WB, 1932), *Successful Calamity* (WB, 1932), *King's Vacation* (WB, 1933), *Working Man* (WB, 1933), *Voltaire* (WB, 1933), *House of Rothschild* (UA, 1934), *Last Gentleman* (UA, 1934), *Cardinal Richelieu* (UA, 1935), *Iron Duke* (Gaumont-British, 1935), *The Guv'nor* ("Mister Hobo"—Gaumont-British, 1935), *East Meets West* (Gaumont-British, 1936), *Man of Affairs* (Gaumont-British, 1937), *Dr. Syn* (Gaumont-British, 1937).

EDWARD ARNOLD (Guenther Schneider) Born February 18, 1890, New York, New York. Married Harriet Marshall (1917), children: Elizabeth, Jane, William; divorced 1927. Married Olive Emerson (1929); divorced 1948. Married Cleo McClain (1951). Died April 26, 1956.

Sound Feature Films: *Rasputin and the Empress* (MGM, 1932), *Okay America!* (Univ., 1932), *Afraid to Talk* (Univ., 1932), *Whistling in the Dark* (MGM, 1933), *The White Sister* (MGM, 1933), *The Barbarian* (MGM, 1933), *Jennie Gerhardt* (Par., 1933), *Her Bodyguard* (Par., 1933), *Secret of the Blue Room* (Univ., 1933), *I'm No Angel* (Par.,

Purnell Pratt, Edward Arnold and Harry C. Bradley in *Diamond Jim*.

1933), *Roman Scandals* (UA, 1933), *Madame Spy* (Univ., 1934), *Sadie McKee* (MGM, 1934), *Thirty Day Princess* (Par., 1934), *Unknown Blonde* (Majestic, 1934), *Hide-Out* (MGM, 1934), *Million Dollar Ransom* (Univ., 1934), *The President Vanishes* (Par., 1934), *Wednesday's Child* (RKO, 1934), *Biography of a Bachelor Girl* (MGM, 1935), *Cardinal Richelieu* (UA, 1935), *The Glass Key* (Par., 1935), *Diamond Jim* (Univ., 1935), *Crime and Punishment* (Col., 1935), *Remember Last Night?* (Univ., 1935), *Sutter's Gold* (Univ., 1936), *Meet Nero Wolf* (Col., 1936), *Come and Get It* (UA, 1936), *John Meade's Woman* (Par., 1937), *The Toast of New York* (RKO, 1937), *Easy Living* (Par., 1937), *Blossoms on Broadway* (Par., 1937), *The Crowd Roars* (MGM, 1938), *You Can't Take It With You* (Col., 1938), *Let Freedom Ring* (MGM, 1939), *Idiot's Delight* (MGM, 1939), *Man About Town* (Par., 1939), *Mr. Smith Goes to Washington* (Col., 1939), *Slightly Honorable* (UA, 1940), *The Earl of Chicago* (MGM, 1940), *Johnny Apollo* (20th, 1940), *Lillian Russell* (20th, 1940), *The Penalty* (MGM, 1941), *The Lady From Cheyenne* (Univ., 1941), *Meet John Doe* (WB, 1941), *Nothing But the Truth* (Par., 1941), *Unholy Partners* (MGM, 1941), *Design for Scandal* (MGM, 1941), *Johnny Eager* (MGM, 1941), *All That Money Can Buy* (RKO, 1941), *The War Against Mrs. Hadley* (MGM, 1942), *Eyes in the Night* (MGM, 1942), *The Youngest Profession* (MGM, 1943), *Standing Room Only* (Par., 1944), *Janie* (WB, 1944), *Kismet* (MGM, 1944), *Mrs. Parkington* (MGM, 1944), *Main Street After Dark* (MGM, 1944), *Weekend at the Waldorf* (MGM, 1945), *The Hidden Eye* (MGM, 1945), *Ziegfeld Follies* (MGM, 1946), *Janie Gets Married* (WB, 1946), *Three Wise Fools* (MGM, 1946), *No Leave, No Love* (MGM, 1946), *The Mighty McGurk* (MGM, 1946), *My Brother Talks to Horses* (MGM, 1946), *Dear Ruth* (Par., 1947), *The Hucksters* (MGM, 1947), *Three Daring Daughters* (MGM, 1948), *The Big City* (MGM, 1948), *Wallflower* (WB, 1948), *Command Decision* (MGM, 1948), *John Loves Mary* (WB, 1949), *Take Me Out to the Ball Game* (MGM, 1949), *Big Jack* (MGM, 1949), *Dear Wife* (Par., 1949), *The Yellow Cabman* (MGM, 1950), *Annie Get Your Gun* (MGM, 1950), *The Skipper Surprised His Wife* (MGM, 1950), *Dear Brat* (Par., 1951), *Belles on Their Toes* (20th, 1952), *The City That Never Sleeps* (Rep., 1953), *Man of Conflict* (Atlas, 1953), *Living It Up* (Par., 1954), *The Houston Story* (Col., 1956), *The Ambassador's Daughter* (UA, 1956), *Miami Exposé* (Col., 1956).

JEAN ARTHUR (Gladys Georgianna Greene) Born October 17, 1905, New York, New York. Married Julian Anker (1928); divorced 1928. Married Frank Ross (1932); divorced 1949.

Sound Feature Films: *Easy Come, Easy Go* (Par., 1928), *The Canary Murder Case* (Par., 1929), *The Mysterious Dr. Fu Manchu* (Par., 1929), *The Greene Murder Case* (Par., 1929), *The Saturday Night Kid* (Par., 1929), *Half Way to Heaven* (Par., 1929), *Street of Chance* (Par., 1930), *Young Eagles* (Par., 1930), *Paramount on Parade* (Par., 1930), *The Return of Dr. Fu Manchu* (Par., 1930), *Danger Lights* (RKO, 1930), *The Silver Horde* (RKO, 1930), *The Gang Buster* (Par., 1931), *Virtuous Husband* (Univ., 1931), *The Lawyer's Secret* (Par., 1931), *Ex-Bad Boy* (Univ., 1931), *Get That Venus* (Regent, 1933), *The Past of Mary*

Charles Arnt, Lee Bowman and Jean Arthur in *The Impatient Years.*

Holmes (RKO, 1933), *Whirlpool* (Col., 1934), *The Defense Rests* (Col., 1934), *Most Precious Thing in Life* (Col., 1934), *The Whole Town's Talking* (Col., 1935), *Public Hero Number One* (MGM, 1935), *Party Wire* (Col., 1935), *Diamond Jim* (Univ., 1935), *The Public Menace* (Col., 1935), *If You Could Only Cook* (Col., 1935), *Mr. Deeds Goes to Town* (Col., 1936), *The Ex-Mrs. Bradford* (RKO, 1936), *Adventure in Manhattan* (Col., 1936), *The Plainsman* (Par., 1936), *More Than a Secretary* (Col., 1936), *History Is Made at Night* (UA, 1937), *Easy Living* (Par., 1937), *You Can't Take It With You* (Col., 1938), *Only Angels Have Wings* (Col., 1939), *Mr. Smith Goes to Washington* (Col., 1939), *Too Many Husbands* (Col., 1940), *Arizona* (Col., 1940), *The Devil and Miss Jones* (RKO, 1941), *The Talk of the Town* (Col., 1942), *The More the Merrier* (Col., 1943), *A Lady Takes a Chance* (RKO, 1943), *The Impatient Years* (Col., 1944), *A Foreign Affair* (Par., 1948), *Shane* (Par., 1953).

Bing Crosby, Joan Caulfield and Fred Astaire in *Blue Skies.*

FRED ASTAIRE (Frederick Austerlitz) Born May 10, 1899, Omaha, Nebraska. Married Phyllis Potter (1933), children: Fred, Ava; widowed 1954.

Feature Films: *Dancing Lady* (MGM, 1933), *Flying Down to Rio* (RKO, 1933), *Roberta* (RKO, 1935), *Top Hat* (RKO, 1935), *Follow the Fleet* (RKO, 1936), *Swing Time* (RKO, 1936), *Shall We Dance* (RKO, 1937), *A Damsel in Distress* (RKO, 1937), *Carefree* (RKO, 1938), *The Story of Vernon and Irene Castle* (RKO, 1939), *Broadway Melody of 1940* (MGM, 1940), *Second Chorus* (Par., 1940), *You'll Never Get Rich* (Col., 1941), *Holiday Inn* (Par., 1942), *You Were Never Lovelier* (Col., 1942), *The Sky's the Limit* (RKO, 1943), *Yolanda and the Thief* (MGM, 1945), *Ziegfeld Follies of 1946* (MGM, 1946), *Blue Skies* (Par., 1946), *Easter Parade* (MGM, 1948), *The Barkleys of Broadway* (MGM, 1949), *Three Little Words* (MGM, 1950), *Let's Dance* (Par., 1950), *Royal Wedding* (MGM, 1951), *The Belle of New York* (MGM, 1952), *The Band Wagon* (MGM, 1953), *Deep in my Heart* (MGM, 1954), *Daddy Long Legs* (20th, 1955), *Funny Face* (Par., 1957), *Silk Stockings* (MGM, 1957), *On the Beach* (UA, 1959), *The Notorious Landlady* (Col., 1962), *Finian's Rainbow* (WB-7 Arts, 1968).

MARY ASTOR (Lucille Vasconcells Langhanke) Born May 3, 1906, Quincy, Illinois. Married Kenneth Hawks (1928); widowed 1930. Married Franklyn Thorpe (1931), child: Marylyn; divorced 1935. Married Manuel del Campo (1936), child: Anthony; divorced 1941. Married Thomas Wheelock (1945); divorced 1955.

Sound Feature Films: *Ladies Love Brutes* (Par., 1930), *The Runaway Bride* (RKO, 1930), *Holiday* (Pathé, 1930), *The Lash* (WB, 1930), *The Sin Ship* (RKO, 1930), *The Royal Bed* (RKO, 1930), *Other Men's Women* (WB, 1931), *Behind Office Doors* (RKO, 1931), *White Shoulders* (RKO, 1931), *Smart Woman* (RKO, 1931), *Men of Chance* (RKO,

Mary Astor and Van Heflin in *Act of Violence*.

1931), *The Lost Squadron* (RKO, 1932), *A Successful Calamity* (WB, 1932), *Those We Love* (World Wide, 1932), *Red Dust* (MGM, 1932), *The Little Giant* (WB, 1933), *Jennie Gerhardt* (Par., 1933), *The Kennel Murder Case* (WB, 1933), *Convention City* (WB, 1933), *The World Changes* (WB, 1933), *Easy to Love* (WB, 1934), *The Man With Two Faces* (WB, 1934), *Return of the Terror* (WB, 1934), *Upper World* (WB, 1934), *The Case of the Howling Dog* (WB, 1934), *I Am a Thief* (WB, 1934), *Man of Iron* (WB, 1935), *Red Hot Tires* (WB, 1935), *Straight From the Heart* (Univ., 1935), *Dinky* (WB, 1935), *Page Miss Glory* (WB, 1935), *The Murder of Dr. Harrigan* (WB, 1935), *The Lady From Nowhere* (Col., 1936), *And So They Were Married* (Col., 1936), *Dodsworth* (UA, 1936), *Trapped by Television* (Col., 1936), *The Prisoner of Zenda* (UA, 1937), *The Hurricane* (UA, 1937), *Paradise for Three* (MGM, 1938), *No Time to Marry* (Col., 1938), *There's Always a Woman* (Col., 1938), *Woman Against Woman* (MGM, 1938), *Listen, Darling* (MGM, 1938), *Midnight* (Par., 1939), *Turnabout* (UA, 1940), *Brigham Young* (20th, 1940), *The Great Lie* (WB, 1941), *The Maltese Falcon* (WB, 1941), *Across the Pacific* (WB, 1942), *In This Our Life* (WB, 1942)* *Young Ideas* (MGM, 1943), *Meet Me in St. Louis* (MGM, 1944), *Blonde Fever* (MGM, 1944), *Claudia and David* (20th, 1946), *Desert Fury* (Par., 1947), *Cynthia* (MGM, 1947), *Fiesta* (MGM, 1947), *Act of Violence* (MGM, 1948), *Cass Timberlane* (MGM, 1948), *Little Women* (MGM, 1949), *Any Number Can Play* (MGM, 1949), *A Kiss Before Dying* (UA, 1956), *The Power and the Prize* (MGM, 1956), *The Devil's Hairpin* (Par., 1957), *This Happy Feeling* (Univ., 1958), *Stranger in My Arms* (Univ., 1959), *Return to Peyton Place* (20th, 1961), *Youngblood Hawke* (WB, 1964), *Hush . . . Hush, Sweet Charlotte* (20th, 1964).

*Unbilled guest appearance

LIONEL ATWILL Born March 1, 1885, Croydon, England. Married Phyllis Ralph (1917); divorced 1919. Married Elsie Mackay (1919),

Lon Chaney, Jr., Anne Nagel and Lionel Atwill in *Man-Made Monster*.

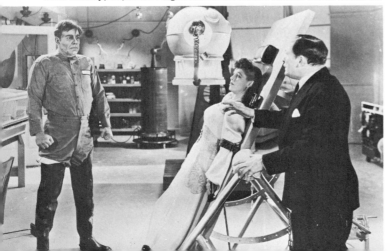

child: John; divorced 1928. Married Louise Stolesbury (1930); divorced 1943. Married Mary Shelstone (1944), child: Lionel. Died April 22, 1946.

Sound Feature Films: *Silent Witness* (Fox, 1932), *Dr. X* (WB, 1932), *Vampire Bat* (Majestic, 1933), *Secret of Madame Blanche* (MGM, 1933), *Mystery of the Wax Museum* (WB, 1933), *Murders in the Zoo* (Par., 1933), *The Sphinx* (Mon., 1933), *Song of Songs* (Par., 1933), *Solitaire Man* (MGM, 1933), *Secret of the Blue Room* (Univ., 1933), *Beggars in Ermine* (Mon., 1934), *Nana* (UA, 1934), *Stamboul Quest* (MGM, 1934), *One More River* (Univ., 1934), *Age of Innocence* (RKO, 1935), *Firebird* (WB, 1934), *The Man Who Reclaimed His Head* (Univ., 1935), *Mark of the Vampire* (MGM, 1935), *The Devil Is a Woman* (Par., 1935), *Murder Man* (MGM, 1935), *Rendezvous* (MGM, 1935), *Captain Blood* (WB, 1935), *Lady of Secrets* (Col., 1936), *Absolute Quiet* (MGM, 1936), *Till We Meet Again* (Par., 1936), *The Road Back* (Univ., 1937), *Last Train From Madrid* (Par., 1937), *Lancer Spy* (20th, 1937), *The Wrong Road* (Rep., 1937), *The Great Garrick* (WB, 1937), *High Command* (GN, 1938), *Three Comrades* (MGM, 1938), *The Great Waltz* (MGM, 1938), *The Three Musketeers* (20th, 1939), *Son of Frankenstein* (Univ., 1939), *The Hound of the Baskervilles* (20th, 1939), *The Mad Empress* (WB, 1939), *The Gorilla* (20th, 1939), *The Sun Never Sets* (Univ., 1939), *Mr. Moto Takes a Vacation* (20th, 1939), *The Secret of Dr. Kildare* (MGM, 1939), *Balalaika* (MGM, 1939), *Charlie Chan in Panama* (20th, 1940), *Johnny Apollo* (20th, 1940), *Charlie Chan's Murder Cruise* (20th, 1940), *The Girl in 313* (20th, 1940), *Boom Town* (MGM, 1940), *The Great Profile* (20th, 1940), *Man-Made Monster* (Univ., 1941), *Junior G-Men of the Air* (Univ. serial, 1942), *Ghost of Frankenstein* (Univ., 1942), *Strange Case of Dr. RX*, (Univ., 1942), *Pardon My Sarong* (Univ., 1942), *Cairo* (MGM, 1942), *Night Monster* (Univ., 1942), *Sherlock Holmes and the Secret Weapon* (Univ., 1942), *Mad Doctor of Market Street* (Univ., 1942), *Captain America* (Rep. serial, 1943), *Frankenstein Meets the Wolf Man* (Univ., 1943), *Raiders of Ghost City* (Univ. serial, 1944), *Lady in the Death House* (PRC, 1944), *Secrets of Scotland Yard* (Rep., 1944), *House of Frankenstein* (Univ., 1945), *Fog Island* (PRC, 1945), *Crime, Inc.*, (PRC, 1945), *House of Dracula* (Univ., 1945), *Genius at Work* (RKO, 1946), *Lost City of the Jungle* (Univ. serial, 1946).

GENE AUTRY Born September 29, 1907, Tioga, Texas. Married Ina Spivey (1932).

Feature Films: *In Old Santa Fe* (Mascot, 1934), *Mystery Mountain* (Mascot serial, 1934), *The Phantom Empire* (Mascot serial, 1935), *Tumbling Tumble-weeds* (Rep., 1935), *Melody Trail* (Rep., 1935), *The Sagebrush Troubadour* (Rep., 1935), *The Singing Vagabond* (Rep., 1935), *Red River Valley* (Rep., 1936), *Comin' Round the Mountain* (Rep., 1936), *The Singing Cowboy* (Rep., 1936), *Guns and Guitars* (Rep., 1936), *Oh, Susannah!* (Rep., 1936), *Ride, Ranger, Ride* (Rep., 1936), *The Old Corral* (Rep., 1936), *Round-up Time in Texas* (Rep., 1937), *Git Along, Little Dogies* (Rep., 1937), *Rootin' Tootin' Rhythm* (Rep., 1937),

Smiley Burnette, Charles King, Gene Autry, Tom London, J.P. McGowan, Earle Hodgins and Dorothy Dix in *Guns and Guitars*.

Yodelin' Kid From Pine Ridge (Rep., 1937), *Public Cowboy No. 1* (Rep., 1937), *Boots and Saddles* (Rep., 1937), *Manhattan Merry-Go-Round* (Rep., 1937), *Springtime in the Rockies* (Rep., 1937), *The Old Barn Dance* (Rep., 1938), *Gold Mine in the Sky* (Rep., 1938), *Man from Music Mountain* (Rep., 1938), *Prairie Moon* (Rep., 1938), *Rhythm of the Saddle* (Rep., 1938), *Western Jamboree* (Rep., 1938), *Home on the Prairie* (Rep., 1939), *Mexicali Rose* (Rep., 1939), *Blue Montana Skies* (Rep., 1939), *Mountain Rhythm* (Rep., 1939), *Colorado Sunset* (Rep., 1939), *In Old Monterey* (Rep., 1939), *Rovin' Tumbleweeds* (Rep., 1939), *South of the Border* (Rep., 1939), *Rancho Grande* (Rep., 1940), *Shooting High* (20th, 1940), *Gaucho Serenade* (Rep., 1940), *Carolina Moon* (Rep., 1940), *Ride, Tenderfoot, Ride* (Rep., 1940), *Melody Ranch* (Rep., 1940), *Ridin' on a Rainbow* (Rep., 1941), *Back in the Saddle* (Rep., 1941), *The Singing Hills* (Rep., 1941), *Sunset in Wyoming* (Rep., 1941), *Under Fiesta Stars* (Rep., 1941), *Down Mexico Way* (Rep., 1941), *Sierra Sue* (Rep., 1941), *Cowboy Serenade* (Rep., 1942), *Heart of the Rio Grande* (Rep., 1942), *Home in Wyomin'* (Rep., 1942), *Stardust on the Sage* (Rep., 1942), *Call of the Canyon* (Rep., 1942), *Bells of Capistrano* (Rep., 1942), *Sioux City Sue* (Rep., 1946), *Trail to San Antone* (Rep., 1947), *Twilight on the Rio Grande* (Rep., 1947), *Saddle Pals* (Rep., 1947), *Robin Hood of Texas* (Rep., 1947), *The Last Round-up* (Col., 1947), *The Strawberry Roan* (Col., 1948), *Loaded Pistols* (Col., 1949), *The Big Sombrero* (Col., 1949), *Riders of the Whistling Pines* (Col., 1949), *Rim of the Canyon* (Col., 1949), *The Cowboy and the Indians* (Col., 1949), *Riders in the Sky* (Col., 1949), *Sons of New Mexico* (Col., 1950), *Mule Train* (Col., 1950), *Cow Town* (Col., 1950), *Beyond the Purple Hills* (Col., 1950), *Indian Territory* (Col., 1950), *The Blazing Hills* (Col., 1950), *Gene Autry and the Mounties* (Col., 1951), *Texans Never Cry* (Col., 1951), *Whirlwind* (Col., 1951), *Silver Canyon* (Col., 1951), *Hills of Utah* (Col., 1951), *Valley of Fire* (Col., 1951), *The Old West* (Col., 1952), *Night Stage to Galveston* (Col., 1952), *Apache Country* (Col., 1952), *Barbed Wire* (Col., 1952), *Wagon Team* (Col., 1952), *Blue Canadian Rockies* (Col., 1952), *Winning of the West* (Col., 1953), *On Top of Old Smoky* (Col., 1953), *Goldtown Ghost Riders* (Col., 1953), *Pack Train* (Col., 1953), *Saginaw Trail* (Col., 1953), *Last of the Pony Riders* (Col., 1953), *Silent Treatment* (Ralph Andrews, 1968).

LEW AYRES (Lewis Ayres) Born December 28, 1908, Minneapolis, Minnesota. Married Lola Lane; divorced 1933. Married Ginger Rogers (1933); divorced 1940. Married Diana Hall (1964).

Sound Feature Films: *The Sophomore* (Pathé, 1929), *All Quiet on the Western Front* (Univ., 1930), *Common Clay* (Fox, 1930), *Doorway to Hell* (WB, 1930), *East Is West* (Univ., 1930), *Iron Man* (Univ., 1931),

Up for Murder (Univ., 1931), *Many a Slip* (Univ., 1931), *Spirit of Notre Dame* (Univ., 1931), *Heaven on Earth* (Univ., 1931), *Impatient Maiden* (Univ., 1932), *Night World* (Univ., 1932), *Okay America!* (Univ., 1932), *State Fair* (Fox, 1933), *Don't Bet on Love* (Univ., 1933), *My Weakness* (Fox, 1933), *Cross Country Cruise* (Univ., 1934), *Let's Be Ritzy* (Univ., 1934), *She Learned About Sailors* (Fox, 1934), *Servants' Entrance* (Fox, 1934), *Lottery Lover* (Fox, 1935), *Silk Hat Kid* (Fox, 1935), *The Leathernecks Have Landed* (Rep., 1936), *Panic on the Air* (Col., 1936), *Shakedown* (Col., 1936), *Lady Be Careful* (Par., 1936), *Murder With Pictures* (Par., 1936), *The Crime Nobody Saw* (Par., 1937), *Last Train From Madrid* (Par., 1937), *Hold 'Em Navy* (Par., 1937), *King of the Newsboys* (Rep., 1938), *Scandal Street* (Par., 1938), *Holiday* (Col., 1938), *Rich Man—Poor Girl* (MGM, 1938), *Young Dr. Kildare* (MGM, 1938), *Spring Madness* (MGM, 1938), *Ice Follies of 1939* (MGM, 1939), *Broadway Serenade* (MGM, 1939), *Calling Dr. Kildare* (MGM, 1939), *These Glamour Girls* (MGM, 1939), *Remember?* (MGM, 1939), *Secret of Dr. Kildare* (MGM, 1939), *Dr. Kildare's Strange Case* (MGM, 1940), *The Golden Fleecing* (MGM, 1940), *Dr. Kildare Goes Home* (MGM, 1940), *Dr. Kildare's Crisis* (MGM, 1940), *Maisie Was a Lady* (MGM, 1941), *The People vs. Dr. Kildare* (MGM, 1941), *Dr. Kildare's Wedding Day* (MGM, 1942), *Dr. Kildare's Victory* (MGM, 1942), *Fingers at the Window* (MGM,1942), *The Dark Mirror* (Univ., 1946), *The Unfaithful* (WB, 1947), *Johnny Belinda* (WB, 1948), *The Capture* (RKO, 1950), *New Mexico* (UA, 1951), *No Escape* (UA, 1953), *Donovan's Brain* (UA, 1953), *Advise and Consent* (Col., 1962), *The Carpetbaggers* (Par., 1964).

Lauren Bacall and Humphrey Bogart in *Dark Passage*.

LAUREN BACALL (Betty Joan Perske) Born September 16, 1924, New York, New York. Married Humphrey Bogart (1945), children: Stephen, Leslie; widowed 1957. Married Jason Robards, Jr. (1961), child: Sam.

Feature Films: *To Have and Have Not* (WB, 1944), *Confidential Agent* (WB, 1945), *Two Guys From Milwaukee* (WB, 1946),* *The Big Sleep* (WB, 1946), *Dark Passage* (WB, 1947), *Key Largo* (WB, 1948), *Young Man With a Horn* (WB, 1950), *Bright Leaf* (WB, 1950), *How to Marry a Millionaire* (20th, 1953), *Woman's World* (20th, 1954), *The Cobweb* (MGM, 1955), *Blood Alley* (WB, 1955), *Written on the Wind* (Univ., 1956), *Designing Woman* (MGM, 1957), *The Gift of Love* (20th, 1958), *Flame Over India* (20th, 1960), *Shock Treatment* (20th, 1964), *Sex and the Single Girl* (WB, 1965), *Harper* (WB, 1966).

*Unbilled guest appearance

FAY BAINTER Born December 7, 1892, Los Angeles, California. Married Reginald Venable (1922), child: Reginald; widowed 1964. Died April 16, 1968.

Feature Films: *This Side of Heaven* (MGM, 1934), *Quality Street* (RKO, 1937), *The Soldier and the Lady* (RKO, 1937), *Make Way for Tomorrow* (Par., 1937), *Jezebel* (WB, 1938), *White Banners* (WB,

Lionel Barrymore and Lew Ayres in *Young Dr. Kildare.*

Judy Garland and Fay Bainter in *Presenting Lily Mars*.

1938), *Mother Carey's Chickens* (RKO, 1938), *The Arkansas Traveler* (Par., 1938), *The Shining Hour* (MGM, 1938), *Yes, My Darling Daughter* (WB, 1939), *The Lady and the Mob* (Col., 1939), *Daughters Courageous* (WB, 1939), *Our Neighbors, the Carters* (Par., 1939), *Young Tom Edison* (MGM, 1940), *A Bill of Divorcement* (RKO, 1940), *Our Town* (UA, 1940), *Maryland* (20th, 1940), *Babes on Broadway* (MGM, 1941), *Woman of the Year* (MGM, 1942), *The War Against Mrs. Hadley* (MGM, 1942), *Mrs. Wiggs of the Cabbage Patch* (Par., 1942), *Journey for Margaret* (MGM, 1942), *The Human Comedy* (MGM, 1943), *Presenting Lily Mars* (MGM, 1943), *Salute to the Marines* (MGM, 1943), *Cry Havoc* (MGM, 1943), *The Heavenly Body* (MGM, 1943), *Dark Waters* (UA, 1944), *Three Is a Family* (UA, 1944), *State Fair* (20th, 1945), *The Kid From Brooklyn* (RKO, 1946), *The Virginian* (Par., 1946), *Deep Valley* (WB, 1947), *The Secret Life of Walter Mitty* (RKO, 1947), *Give My Regards to Broadway* (20th, 1948), *June Bride* (WB, 1948), *Close to My Heart* (WB, 1951), *The President's Lady* (20th, 1953), *The Children's Hour* (UA, 1962).

Carroll Baker, Hanna Landy and Red Buttons in *Harlow*.

CARROLL BAKER Born May 28, 1931, Johnstown, Pennsylvania. Married Jack Garfein (1955), children: Blanche, Herschel.

Feature Films: *Easy to Love* (MGM, 1953), *Giant* (WB, 1956), *Baby Doll* (WB, 1956), *The Big Country* (UA, 1958), *The Miracle* (WB, 1959), *But Not for Me* (Par., 1959), *Something Wild* (UA, 1961), *Bridge to the Sun* (MGM, 1961), *How the West Was Won* (MGM, 1963), *Station Six—Sahara* (AA, 1964), *The Carpetbaggers* (Par., 1964), *Cheyenne Autumn* (WB, 1964), *The Greatest Story Ever Told* (UA, 1965), *Sylvia* (UA, 1965), *Mr. Moses* (UA, 1965), *Harlow* (Par., 1965), *Jack of Diamonds* (MGM, 1967), *Her Harem* (Sancro, 1968).

LUCILLE BALL Born August 6, 1910, Jamestown, New York. Married Desi Arnaz (1940), children: Lucie, Desi; divorced 1960. Married Gary Morton (1961).

Feature Films: *Roman Scandals* (UA, 1933), *Blood Money* (UA, 1933), *Moulin Rouge* (UA, 1934), *Nana* (UA, 1934), *Hold That Girl* (Fox, 1934), *Jealousy* (Col., 1934), *Fugitive Lady* (Col., 1934), *Men of the Night* (Col., 1934), *Bottoms Up* (Fox, 1934), *Broadway Bill* (Col., 1934), *Bulldog Drummond Strikes Back* (UA, 1934), *Kid Millions* (UA, 1934), *Affairs of Cellini* (UA, 1934), *Roberta* (RKO, 1935), *Old Man Rhythm* (RKO, 1935), *Carnival* (Col., 1935), *I Dream Too Much* (RKO, 1935), *Top Hat* (RKO, 1935), *Chatterbox* (RKO, 1936), *Winterset* (RKO, 1936), *Follow the Fleet* (RKO, 1936), *The Farmer in the Dell* (RKO, 1936), *Bunker Bean* (RKO, 1936), *That Girl From Paris* (RKO, 1936), *Don't Tell the Wife* (RKO, 1937), *Stage Door* (RKO, 1937), *Joy of Living* (RKO, 1938), *Go Chase Yourself* (RKO, 1938), *Having Wonderful Time* (RKO, 1938), *The Affairs of Annabel* (RKO, 1938), *Room Service* (RKO, 1938), *Next Time I Marry* (RKO, 1938), *Annabel Takes a Tour* (RKO, 1938), *Beauty for the Asking* (RKO, 1939), *Twelve Crowded Hours* (RKO, 1939), *Panama Lady* (RKO, 1939), *Five Came Back* (RKO, 1939), *That's Right, You're Wrong* (RKO, 1939), *The Marines Fly High* (RKO, 1940), *You Can't Fool Your Wife* (RKO, 1940), *Dance, Girl, Dance* (RKO, 1940), *Too Many Girls* (RKO, 1940), *A Girl, a Guy and a Gob* (RKO, 1941), *Look Who's Laughing* (RKO, 1941), *Valley of the Sun* (RKO, 1942), *The Big Street* (RKO, 1942), *Seven Days' Leave* (RKO, 1942), *Du Barry Was a Lady* (MGM, 1943), *Best Foot Forward* (MGM, 1943), *Thousands Cheer* (MGM, 1943), *Meet the People* (MGM, 1944), *Abbott and Costello in Hollywood* (MGM, 1945), *Without Love* (MGM, 1945), *Ziegfeld Follies of*

Agnes Moorehead, Eugene Pallette, Henry Fonda and Lucille Ball in *The Big Street*.

1946 (MGM, 1946), *The Dark Corner* (20th, 1946), *Lover Come Back* (Univ., 1946), *Easy to Wed* (MGM, 1946), *Two Smart People* (MGM, 1946), *Lured* (UA, 1947), *Her Husband's Affairs* (Col., 1947), *Miss Grant Takes Richmond* (Col., 1949), *Sorrowful Jones* (Par., 1949), *Easy Living* (RKO, 1949), *Fancy Pants* (Par., 1950), *A Woman of Distinction* (Col., 1950),* *The Fuller Brush Girl* (Col., 1950), *The Magic Carpet* (Col., 1951), *The Long, Long Trailer* (MGM, 1954), *Forever Darling* (MGM, 1956), *The Facts of Life* (UA, 1960), *Critic's Choice* (WB, 1963), *A Guide for the Married Man* (20th, 1967), *Yours, Mine and Ours* (UA, 1968).

*Unbilled guest appearance.

10

Martin Balsam and Paul Newman in *Hombre*.

MARTIN BALSAM (Martin Henry Balsam) Born November 4, 1919, New York, New York. Married Pearl Somner (1952); divorced 1954. Married Joyce Van Patten (1959), child: Talia; divorced 1962. Married Irene Miller (1963).

English-Language Feature Films: *On the Waterfront* (Col., 1954), *12 Angry Men* (UA, 1957), *Time Limit* (UA, 1957), *Marjorie Morningstar* (WB, 1958), *Al Capone* (AA, 1959), *Middle of the Night* (Col., 1959), *Psycho* (Par., 1960), *Ada* (MGM, 1961), *Breakfast at Tiffany's* (Par., 1961), *Cape Fear* (UA, 1962), *Who's Been Sleeping in My Bed?* (Par., 1963), *The Carpetbaggers* (Par., 1964), *Youngblood Hawke* (WB, 1964), *Seven Days in May* (Par., 1964), *Harlow* (Par., 1965), *The Bedford Incident* (Col., 1965), *A Thousand Clowns* (UA, 1965), *After the Fox* (UA, 1966), *Hombre* (20th, 1967), *2001: A Space Odyssey* (MGM, 1968).

Steven Hill and Anne Bancroft in *The Slender Thread*.

ANNE BANCROFT (Anna Maria Italiano) Born September 17, 1931, Bronx, New York. Married Martin May (1953); divorced 1957. Married Mel Brooks (1964).

Feature Films: *Don't Bother to Knock* (20th, 1952), *Tonight We Sing* (20th, 1953), *Treasure of the Golden Condor* (20th, 1953), *The Kid From Left Field* (20th, 1953), *Demetrius and the Gladiators* (20th, 1954), *The Raid* (20th, 1954), *Gorilla at Large* (20th, 1954), *A Life in the Balance* (20th, 1955), *New York Confidential* (WB, 1955), *The Naked Street* (UA, 1955), *The Last Frontier* (Col., 1955), *Walk the Proud Land* (Univ., 1956), *Nightfall* (Col., 1956), *The Restless Breed* (20th, 1957), *The Girl in Black Stockings* (UA, 1957), *The Miracle Worker* (UA, 1962), *The Pumpkin Eater* (UA, 1964), *The Slender Thread* (Par., 1965), *Seven Women* (MGM, 1965), *The Graduate* (Embassy, 1967).

Gordon Westcott, Gary Cooper, Tallulah Bankhead and Charles Laughton in *Devil and the Deep*.

TALLULAH BANKHEAD Born January 31, 1902, Huntsville, Alabama. Married John Emery (1937); divorced 1941.

Sound Feature Films: *Tarnished Lady* (Par., 1931), *My Sin* (Par., 1931), *The Cheat* (Par., 1931), *Thunder Below* (Par., 1932), *Make Me a Star* (Par., 1932),* *Devil and the Deep* (Par., 1932), *Faithless* (Par., 1932), *Stage Door Canteen* (UA, 1943), *Lifeboat* (20th, 1944), *A Royal Scandal* (20th, 1945), *Main Street to Broadway* (MGM, 1953), *Die! Die! My Darling!* (Col., 1965), *The Daydreamer* (voice only; Embassy, 1966).

   *Unbilled guest appearance.

LYNN BARI (Marjorie Schuyler Fisher) Born December 18, 1917, Roanoke, Virginia. Married Walter Kane (1938), divorced 1943. Married Sid Luft (1943), child: John; divorced 1950. Married Nathan Rickles (1955).

Feature Films: *Dancing Lady* (MGM, 1933), *Meet the Baron* (MGM, 1933), *Coming Out Party* (Fox, 1934), *Stand Up and Cheer* (Fox, 1934), *Search for Beauty* (Par., 1934), *George White's Scandals* (Fox, 1935), *Caravan* (Fox, 1934), *Spring Tonic* (Fox, 1935), *My Marriage* (20th, 1935), *The Man Who Broke the Bank at Monte Carlo* (Fox, 1935), *Redheads on Parade* (Fox, 1935), *Thanks a Million* (Fox, 1935), *Music is Magic* (Fox, 1935), *Everybody's Old Man* (20th, 1936), *Ladies in Love* (20th, 1936), *The Song and Dance Man* (20th, 1936), *Crack-Up* (20th, 1936), *Pigskin Parade* (20th, 1936), *Sing, Baby, Sing* (20th, 1936), *36 Hours to Kill* (20th, 1936), *Wee Willie Winkie* (20th, 1937), *This Is My Affair* (20th, 1937), *Sing and Be Happy* (20th, 1937), *Love Is News* (20th, 1937), *Lancer Spy* (20th, 1937), *Wife, Doctor and Nurse* (20th, 1937), *On the Avenue* (20th, 1937), *I'll Give a Million* (20th, 1938), *Rebecca of Sunnybrook Farm* (20th, 1938), *Josette* (20th, 1938), *Speed to Burn* (20th, 1938), *The Baroness and the Butler* (20th, 1938), *Walking Down Broadway* (20th, 1938), *Mr. Moto's Gamble* (20th, 1938), *Battle of Broadway* (20th, 1938), *Always Goodbye* (20th, 1938), *Sharpshooters*

Lynn Bari and Edward G. Robinson in *Tampico*.

(20th, 1938), *Meet the Girls* (20th, 1938), *Return of the Cisco Kid* (20th, 1939), *Chasing Danger* (20th, 1939), *News Is Made at Night* (20th, 1939), *Pack Up Your Troubles* (20th, 1939), *Elsa Maxwell's Hotel for Women* (20th, 1939), *Charlie Chan in City in Darkness* (20th, 1939), *Hollywood Cavalcade* (20th, 1939), *Pardon Our Nerve* (20th, 1939), *City of Chance* (20th, 1940), *Free, Blonde and 21* (20th, 1940), *Lillian Russell* (20th, 1940), *Earthbound* (20th, 1940), *Pier 13* (20th, 1940), *Kit Carson* (UA, 1940), *Charter Pilot* (20th, 1940), *Sleepers West* (20th, 1941), *Blood and Sand* (20th, 1941), *We Go Fast* (20th, 1941), *Sun Valley Serenade* (20th, 1941), *Moon Over Her Shoulder* (20th, 1941), *The Perfect Snob* (20th, 1941), *Secret Agent of Japan* (20th, 1942), *Night Before the Divorce* (20th, 1942), *The Falcon Takes Over* (RKO, 1942), *The Magnificent Dope* (20th, 1942), *Orchestra Wives* (20th, 1942), *China Girl* (20th, 1942), *Hello, Frisco, Hello* (20th, 1943), *The Bridge of San Luis Rey* (UA, 1944), *Tampico* (20th, 1944), *Sweet and Lowdown* (20th, 1944), *Captain Eddie* (20th, 1945), *Shock* (20th, 1946), *Home Sweet Homicide* (20th, 1946), *Margie* (20th, 1946), *Nocturne* (RKO, 1946), *The Man From Texas* (EL, 1948), *The Spiritualist* (EL, 1948), *The Kid From Cleveland* (Rep., 1949), *I'd Climb the Highest Mountain* (20th, 1951), *On the Loose* (RKO, 1951), *Sunny Side of the Street* (Col., 1951), *Has Anybody Seen My Gal* (Univ., 1952), *I Dream of Jeannie* (Rep., 1952), *Francis Joins the WACs* (Univ., 1954), *Abbott and Costello Meet the Keystone Kops* (Univ., 1955), *The Women of Pitcairn Island* (20th, 1956), *Damn Citizen* (Univ., 1958), *Trauma* (Parade, 1964).

Brenda Joyce, Lex Barker and Evelyn Ankers in *Tarzan's Magic Fountain.*

LEX BARKER (Alexander Crichlow Barker) Born May 8, 1919, Rye, New York. Married Constance Thurlow (1942), children: Lynne Alexander; divorced 1951. Married Arlene Dahl (1951); divorced 1952. Married Lana Turner (1953); divorced 1957. Married Irene Labhart (1959), child: Christopher; widowed 1962. Married Maria Cervera (1965).

English-Language Feature Films: *Doll Face* (20th, 1945), *Do You Love Me?* (20th, 1946), *Two Guys From Milwaukee* (WB, 1946), *Farmer's Daughter* (RKO, 1947), *Dick Tracy Meets Gruesome* (RKO, 1947), *Crossfire* (RKO, 1947), *Under the Tonto Rim* (RKO, 1947), *Unconquered* (Par., 1947), *Mr. Blandings Builds His Dream House* (RKO, 1948), *Return of the Bad Men* (RKO, 1948), *The Velvet Touch* (RKO, 1948), *Tarzan's Magic Fountain* (RKO, 1949), *Tarzan and the Slave Girl* (RKO, 1950), *Tarzan's Peril* (RKO, 1951), *Tarzan's Savage Fury* (RKO, 1952), *Battles of Chief Pontiac* (Realart, 1952), *Tarzan and the She-Devil* (RKO, 1953), *Thunder Over the Plains* (WB, 1953), *The Yellow Mountain* (Univ., 1954), *The Man From Bitter Ridge* (Univ., 1955), *Duel on the Mississippi* (Col., 1955), *Mystery of the Black Jungle* (Rep., 1955), *The Price of Fear* (Univ., 1956), *Away All Boats* (Univ., 1956), *The Girl in the Kremlin* (Univ., 1957), *War Drums* (UA, 1957), *Jungle Heat* (UA, 1957), *The Deerslayer* (20th, 1957), *The Girl in Black Stockings* (UA, 1957), *Strange Awakening* (Merton Park Studios, 1958), *Mission in Morocco* (Venus Enterprises, 1959), *Code 7, Victim 5* (Col., 1964), *24 Hours to Kill* (7 Arts, 1966), *Woman Times Seven* (Embassy, 1967), *Devil May Care* (Feature Film Corp. of America, 1968).

BINNIE BARNES (Gitelle Enoyce Barnes) Born March 25, 1906, London, England. Married Samuel Joseph (1932); divorced 1936. Married Mike Frankovich (1940), children: Michael, Michelle, Peter.

Janet Blair, Joan Blondell and Binnie Barnes in *Three Girls About Town.*

Feature Films: *Night in Montmartre* (Gaumont-British, 1931), *Love Lies* (British International, 1931), *Dr. Josser, K. C.* (British International, 1931), *Out of the Blue* (British International, 1931), *Down Our Street* (Par., 1931), *Murder at Covent Garden* (Twickenham, 1931), *Strip Strip Hooray* (British International, 1932), *Partners, Please* (PDC, 1932), *The Last Coupon* (British International, 1932), *Old Spanish Customs* (British International, 1932), *Innocents in Chicago* (British International, 1932), *Council's Opinion* (London Films, 1933), *Heads We Go* (British International, 1933), *The Private Life of Henry VIII* (UA, 1933), *The Private Life of Don Juan* (UA, 1934), *The Lady Is Willing* (Col., 1934), *Gift of Gab* (Univ., 1934), *There's Always Tomorrow* (Univ., 1934), *One Exciting Adventure* (Univ., 1934), *No Escape* (British, 1934), *Diamond Jim* (Univ., 1935), *Rendezvous* (MGM, 1935), *Small Town Girl* (MGM, 1936), *Sutter's Gold* (Univ., 1936), *The Last of the Mohicans* (UA, 1936), *The Magnificent Brute* (Univ., 1936), *Breezing Home* (Univ., 1937), *Three Smart Girls* (Univ., 1937), *Broadway Melody of 1938* (MGM, 1937). *The First Hundred Years* (MGM, 1938), *The Adventures of Marco Polo* (UA, 1938), *Holiday* (Col., 1938), *Always Goodbye* (20th, 1938), *Gateway* (20th, 1938), *Tropic Holiday* (Par., 1938), *Three Blind Mice* (20th, 1938), *Thanks for Everything* (20th, 1938), *The Divorce of Lady X* (UA, 1939), *Wife, Husband and Friend* (20th, 1939), *The Three Musketeers* (20th, 1939), *Man About Town* (Par., 1939), *Frontier Marshal* (20th, 1939), *Day-Time Wife* (20th, 1939), *Till We Meet Again* (WB, 1940), *New Wine* (UA, 1941), *This Thing Called Love* (Col., 1941), *Angels With Broken Wings* (Rep., 1941), *Tight Shoes* (Univ., 1941), *Skylark* (Par., 1941), *Three Girls About Town* (Col., 1941), *Call Out the Marines* (RKO, 1942), *I Married an Angel* (MGM, 1942), *In Old California* (Rep., 1942), *The Man From Down Under* (MGM, 1943), *Barbary Coast Gent* (MGM, 1944), *The Hour Before the Dawn* (Par., 1944), *Up in Mabel's Room* (UA, 1944), *It's in the Bag* (UA, 1945), *The Spanish Main* (RKO, 1945), *Getting Gertie's Garter* (UA, 1945), *The Time of Their Lives* (Univ., 1946), *If Winter Comes* (MGM, 1947), *The Dude Goes West* (AA, 1948), *My Own True Love* (Par., 1948), *The Pirates of Capri* (Film Classics, 1949), *Fugitive Lady* (Rep., 1951), *Decameron Nights* (RKO, 1953), *Fire Over Africa* (Col., 1954), *Shadow of the Eagle* (UA, 1955), *The Trouble With Angels* (Col., 1966), *Where Angels Go . . . Trouble Follows* (Col., 1968).

ETHEL BARRYMORE (Ethel Mae Barrymore) Born August 15, 1879, Philadelphia, Pennsylvania. Married Russell Colt (1909), children: Samuel, John, Ethel; divorced 1923. Died June 18, 1959.

Sound Feature Films: *Rasputin and the Empress* (MGM, 1932), *None But the Lonely Heart* (RKO, 1944), *The Spiral Staircase* (RKO, 1946), *The Farmer's Daughter* (RKO, 1947), *Moss Rose* (20th, 1947), *Night Song* (RKO, 1947), *The Paradine Case* (Selznick, 1948), *Moonrise* (Rep., 1948), *Portrait of Jennie* (Selznick, 1948), *The Great Sinner* (MGM, 1949), *That Midnight Kiss* (MGM, 1949), *The Red Danube* (MGM, 1949), *Pinky* (20th, 1949), *Kind Lady* (MGM, 1951), *The Secret of Convict Lake* (20th, 1951), *It's a Big Country* (MGM, 1951), *Deadline, U.S.A.* (20th, 1952), *Just for You* (Par., 1952), *The Story of Three Loves* (MGM, 1953), *Main Street to Broadway* (MGM, 1953), *Young at Heart* (WB, 1954), *Johnny Trouble* (WB, 1957).

Maurice Evans, Betsy Blair, Ethel Barrymore, Keenan Wynn and Angela Lansbury in *Kind Lady*.

John Barrymore and Lionel Barrymore in *Arsene Lupin*.

Peter Holden, John Barrymore, Virginia Weidler and Katharine Alexander in *The Great Man Votes*.

JOHN BARRYMORE Born Feb. 15, 1882, Philadelphia, Pennsylvania. Married Katherine Harris (1910); divorced 1917. Married Mrs. Leonard Thomas (1917), child: Diana; divorced 1928. Married Dolores Costello (1928); divorced 1935. Married Elaine Barrie (1936); divorced 1940. Died May 29, 1942.

Sound Feature Films: *Show of Shows* (WB, 1929), *General Crack* (WB, 1929), *The Man From Blankley's* (WB, 1930), *Moby Dick* (WB, 1930), *Svengali* (WB, 1931), *Mad Genius* (WB, 1931), *Arsene Lupin* (MGM, 1932), *Grand Hotel* (MGM, 1932), *State's Attorney* (RKO, 1932), *A Bill of Divorcement* (RKO, 1932), *Rasputin and the Empress* (MGM, 1932), *Topaze* (RKO, 1933), *Reunion in Vienna* (MGM, 1933), *Dinner at Eight* (MGM, 1933), *Night Flight* (MGM, 1933), *Counsellor at Law* (Univ., 1933), *Long Lost Father* (RKO, 1934), *Twentieth Century* (Col., 1934), *Romeo and Juliet* (MGM, 1936), *Maytime* (MGM, 1937), *Bulldog Drummond Comes Back* (Par., 1937), *Night Club Scandal* (Par., 1937), *True Confession* (Par., 1937), *Bulldog Drummond's Revenge* (Par., 1937), *Bulldog Drummond's Peril* (Par., 1938), *Romance in the Dark* (Par., 1938), *Spawn of the North* (Par., 1938), *Marie Antoinette* (MGM, 1938), *Hold That Co-ed* (20th, 1938), *The Great Man Votes* (RKO, 1939), *Midnight* (Par., 1939), *The Great Profile* (20th, 1940), *The Invisible Woman* (Univ., 1941), *World Premiere* (Par., 1941), *Playmates* (RKO, 1941).

LIONEL BARRYMORE Born April 28, 1878, Philadelphia, Pennsylvania. Married Doris Rankin (1904); divorced 1922. Married Irene Fenwick (1932); widowed 1936. Died November 15, 1954.

Sound Feature Films: *Alias Jimmy Valentine* (MGM, 1928), *Mysterious Island* (MGM, 1929), *Hollywood Revue of 1929* (MGM, 1929), *Free and Easy* (MGM, 1930), *A Free Soul* (MGM, 1931), *Guilty Hands* (MGM, 1931), *Yellow Ticket* (Fox, 1931), *Mata Hari* (MGM, 1931), *Broken Lullaby* (Par., 1932), *Arsene Lupin* (MGM, 1932), *Grand Hotel* (MGM, 1932), *Washington Masquerade* (MGM, 1932), *Rasputin and*

the Empress (MGM, 1932), *Sweepings* (RKO, 1933), *Looking Forward* (MGM, 1933), *Dinner at Eight* (MGM, 1933), *Stranger's Return* (MGM, 1933), *Night Flight* (MGM, 1933), *One Man's Journey* (RKO, 1933), *Christopher Bean* (MGM, 1933), *Should Ladies Behave?* (MGM, 1933), *This Side of Heaven* (MGM, 1934), *Carolina* (Fox, 1934), *Treasure Island* (MGM, 1934), *Girl From Missouri* (MGM, 1934), *David Copperfield* (MGM, 1935), *Mark of the Vampire* (MGM, 1935), *Little Colonel* (Fox, 1935), *Public Hero Number One* (MGM, 1935), *The Return of Peter Grimm* (RKO, 1935), *Ah! Wilderness* (MGM, 1936), *The Voice of Bugle Ann* (MGM, 1936), *The Road to Glory* (20th, 1936), *The Devil Doll* (MGM, 1936), *The Gorgeous Hussy* (MGM, 1936), *Camille* (MGM, 1936), *Captains Courageous* (MGM, 1937), *A Family Affair* (MGM, 1937), *Saratoga* (MGM, 1937), *Navy Blue and Gold* (MGM, 1937), *Test Pilot* (MGM, 1938), *A Yank at Oxford* (MGM, 1938), *You Can't Take It With You* (Col., 1938), *Young Dr. Kildare* (MGM, 1938), *Let Freedom Ring* (MGM, 1939), *Calling Dr. Kildare* (MGM, 1939), *On Borrowed Time* (MGM, 1939), *Secret of Dr. Kildare* (MGM, 1939), *Dr. Kildare's Strange Case* (MGM, 1940), *Dr. Kildare Goes Home* (MGM, 1940), *Dr. Kildare's Crisis* (MGM, 1940), *The Bad Man* (MGM, 1941), *The Penalty* (MGM, 1941), *The People vs. Dr. Kildare* (MGM, 1941), *Lady Be Good* (MGM, 1941), *Dr. Kildare's Wedding Day* (MGM, 1941), *Dr. Kildare's Victory* (MGM, 1942), *Calling Dr. Gillespie* (MGM, 1942), *Dr. Gillespie's New Assistant* (MGM, 1942), *Tennessee Johnson* (MGM, 1942), *Thousands Cheer* (MGM, 1943), *Dr. Gillespie's Criminal Case* (MGM, 1943), *A Guy Named Joe* (MGM, 1943), *Three Men in White* (MGM, 1944), *Since You Went Away* (UA, 1944), *Valley of Decision* (MGM, 1945), *Between Two Women* (MGM, 1945), *Three Wise Fools* (MGM, 1946), *The Secret Heart* (MGM, 1946), *It's A Wonderful Life* (RKO, 1946), *Duel in the Sun* (Selznick, 1946), *Dark Delusion* (MGM, 1947), *Key Largo* (WB, 1948), *Down to the Sea in Ships* (20th, 1949), *Malaya* (MGM, 1949), *Right Cross* (MGM, 1950), *Bannerline* (MGM, 1951), *Lone Star* (MGM, 1952), *Main Street to Broadway* (MGM, 1953).

RICHARD BARTHELMESS (Richard Semler Barthelmess) Born May 9, 1895, New York, New York. Married Mary Hay (1920), child: Mary; divorced 1926. Married Jessica Sargeant (1928). Died August 17, 1963.

Richard Barthelmess, Clyde Cook, Douglas Fairbanks, Jr., and Edmund Breon in *Dawn Patrol*.

Sound Feature Films: *Weary River* (WB, 1929), *Drag* (WB, 1929), *Young Nowheres* (WB, 1929), *The Show of Shows* (WB, 1929), *Son of the Gods* (WB, 1930), *The Dawn Patrol* (WB, 1930), *The Lash* (WB, 1930), *The Finger Points* (WB, 1931), *The Last Flight* (WB, 1931), *Alias the Doctor* (WB, 1932), *Cabin in the Cotton* (WB, 1932), *Central Airport* (WB, 1933), *Heroes for Sale* (WB, 1933), *Massacre* (WB, 1934), *A Modern Hero* (WB, 1934), *Midnight Alibi* (WB, 1934), *Four Hours to Kill* (Par., 1935), *Spy of Napoleon* (Twickenham-Unity Prod., 1936), *Only Angels Have Wings* (Col., 1939), *The Man Who Talked Too Much* (WB, 1940), *The Mayor of 44th Street* (RKO, 1942), *The Spoilers* (Univ., 1942).

Freddie Bartholomew and Victor McLaglen in *Professional Soldier*.

FREDDIE BARTHOLOMEW (Frederick Llewellyn) Born March 28, 1924, London, England. Married Maely Daniele (1946); divorced 1953. Married Aileen Paul (1953), children: Kathleen, Frederick.

Feature Films: *David Copperfield* (MGM, 1935), *Anna Karenina* (MGM, 1935), *Professional Soldier* (MGM, 1935), *Little Lord Fauntleroy* (MGM, 1936), *The Devil Is a Sissy* (MGM, 1936), *Lloyds of London* (20th, 1936), *Captains Courageous* (MGM, 1937), *Kidnapped* (20th, 1938), *Lord Jeff* (MGM, 1938), *Listen, Darling* (MGM, 1938), *Spirit of Culver* (Univ., 1938), *Two Bright Boys* (Univ., 1939), *Swiss Family Robinson* (RKO, 1940), *Tom Brown's School Days* (RKO, 1940), *Naval Academy* (Col., 1941), *Cadets on Parade* (Col., 1942), *A Yank at Eton* (MGM, 1942), *The Town Went Wild* (PRC, 1944), *Sepia Cinderella* (Herald Pictures, 1947), *St. Benny the Dip* (UA, 1951).

FLORENCE BATES (Florence Rabe) Born April 15, 1888, San Antonio, Texas. Married 1909, child: Ann; divorced. Married Will Jacoby (1929); widowed 1951. Died January 31, 1954.

Feature Films: *The Man in Blue* (Univ., 1937), *Rebecca* (UA, 1940), *Calling All Husbands* (WB, 1940), *The Son of Monte Cristo* (UA, 1940), *Hudson's Bay* (20th, 1940), *Kitty Foyle* (RKO, 1940), *Road*

Raymond Hatton and Florence Bates in *County Fair*.

Show (UA, 1941), *Strange Alibi* (WB, 1941), *Love Crazy* (MGM, 1941), *The Devil and Miss Jones* (RKO, 1941), *The Chocolate Soldier* (MGM, 1941), *Mexican Spitfire at Sea* (RKO, 1942), *The Tuttles of Tahiti* (RKO, 1942), *We Were Dancing* (MGM, 1942), *The Moon and Sixpence* (UA, 1942), *My Heart Belongs to Daddy* (Par., 1942), *They Got Me Covered* (RKO, 1943), *Slightly Dangerous* (MGM, 1943), *Mister Big* (Univ., 1943), *Mr. Lucky* (RKO, 1943) *Heaven Can Wait* (20th, 1943), *His Butler's Sister* (Univ., 1943), *The Mask of Dimitrios* (WB, 1944), *Since You Went Away* (UA, 1944), *Kismet* (MGM, 1944), *The Belle of the Yukon* (RKO, 1944), *Tahiti Nights* (Col., 1945), *Tonight and Every Night* (Col., 1945), *Out of This World* (Par., 1945), *San Antonio* (WB, 1945), *Saratoga Trunk* (WB, 1945), *Whistle Stop* (UA, 1946), *The Diary of a Chambermaid* (UA, 1946), *Cluny Brown* (20th, 1946), *Claudia and David* (20th, 1946), *The Time, the Place and the Girl* (WB, 1946), *The Brasher Doubloon* (20th, 1947), *Love and Learn* (WB, 1947), *The Secret Life of Walter Mitty* (RKO, 1947), *Desire Me* (MGM, 1947), *The Inside Story* (Rep., 1948), *I Remember Mama* (RKO, 1948), *Winter Meeting* (WB, 1948), *River Lady* (Univ., 1948), *Texas, Brooklyn and Heaven* (UA, 1948), *My Dear Secretary* (UA, 1948), *Portrait of Jennie* (UA, 1948), *A Letter to Three Wives* (20th, 1949), *The Judge Steps Out* (RKO, 1949), *The Girl From Jones Beach* (WB, 1949), *On the Town* (MGM, 1949), *Belle of Old Mexico* (Rep., 1950), *County Fair* (Mon., 1950), *The Second Woman* (UA, 1951), *The Lullaby of Broadway* (WB, 1951), *Father Takes the Air* (Mon., 1951), *The Tall Target* (MGM, 1951), *Havana Rose* (Rep., 1951), *The San Francisco Story* (WB, 1952), *Les Miserables* (20th, 1952), *Main Street to Broadway* (MGM, 1953), *Paris Model* (Col., 1953).

Anne Baxter and Dana Andrews in *Swamp Water*.

ANNE BAXTER Born May 7, 1923, Michigan City, Indiana. Married John Hodiak (1946), child: Katrina; divorced 1953. Married Randolph Galt (1960), children: Maginal, Melissa; divorced 1968.

Feature Films: *Twenty Mule Team* (MGM, 1940), *The Great Profile* (20th, 1940), *Charley's Aunt* (20th, 1941), *Swamp Water* (20th, 1941), *The Magnificent Ambersons* (RKO, 1942), *The Pied Piper* (20th, 1942), *Crash Dive* (20th, 1943), *Five Graves to Cairo* (Par., 1943), *The North Star* (RKO, 1943), *The Sullivans* (20th, 1944), *The Eve of St. Mark* (20th, 1944), *Guest in the House* (UA, 1944), *Sunday Dinner for a Soldier* (20th, 1944), *A Royal Scandal* (20th, 1945), *Smoky* (20th, 1946), *Angel on My Shoulder* (UA, 1946), *The Razor's Edge* (20th, 1946), *Mother Wore Tights* (narrator; 20th, 1947), *Blaze of Noon* (Par., 1947), *Homecoming* (MGM, 1948), *The Luck of the Irish* (20th, 1948), *The Walls of Jericho* (20th, 1948), *Yellow Sky* (20th, 1949), *You're My Everything* (20th, 1949), *A Ticket to Tomahawk* (20th, 1950), *All About Eve* (20th, 1950), *Follow the Sun* (20th, 1951), *Outcasts of Poker Flat* (20th, 1952), *My Wife's Best Friend* (20th, 1952), *O. Henry's Full House* (20th, 1952), *I Confess* (WB, 1953), *The Blue Gardenia* (WB, 1953), *Carnival Story* (RKO, 1954), *Bedevilled* (MGM, 1955), *One Desire* (Univ., 1955), *The Spoilers* (Univ., 1955), *The Come-On* (AA, 1956), *The Ten Commandments* (Par., 1956), *Three Violent People*

(Par., 1957), *Chase a Crooked Shadow* (WB, 1958), *Cimarron* (MGM, 1960), *Mix Me a Person* (Blackton, 1961), *Season of Passion* (UA, 1961), *Walk on the Wild Side* (Col., 1962), *The Family Jewels* (Par., 1965),* *Tall Women* (AA, 1967), *The Busy Body* (Par., 1967).

*Unbilled guest appearance

J. Carroll Naish, Carlos De Valdez, Ann Loring and Warner Baxter in *Robin Hood of El Dorado*.

Louise Beavers, Betty Roadman and Evelyn Venable in *The Headleys at Home*.

WARNER BAXTER Born March 29, 1892, Columbus, Ohio. Married Winifred Bryson (1917). Died May 7, 1951.

Sound Feature Films: *In Old Arizona* (Fox, 1929), *Through Different Eyes* (Fox, 1929), *Behind That Curtain* (Fox, 1929), *Romance of the Rio Grande* (Fox, 1929), *Happy Days* (Fox, 1930), *Such Men Are Dangerous* (Fox, 1930), *Arizona Kid* (Fox, 1930), *Renegades* (Fox, 1930), *Doctor's Wives* (Fox, 1931), *Squaw Man* (MGM, 1931), *Daddy Long Legs* (Fox, 1931), *Their Mad Moment* (Fox, 1931), *Cisco Kid* (Fox, 1931), *Surrender* (Fox, 1931), *Amateur Daddy* (Fox, 1932), *Man About Town* (Fox, 1932), *Six Hours to Live* (Fox, 1932), *Dangerously Yours* (Fox, 1933), *42nd Street* (WB, 1933), *I Loved You Wednesday* (Fox, 1933), *Paddy the Next Best Thing* (Fox, 1933), *Penthouse* (MGM, 1933), *As Husbands Go* (Fox, 1934), *Stand Up and Cheer* (Fox, 1934), *Such Women Are Dangerous* (Fox, 1934), *Grand Canary* (Fox, 1934), *Broadway Bill* (Col., 1934), *Hell in the Heavens* (Fox, 1934), *One More Spring* (Fox, 1935), *Under the Pampas Moon* (Fox, 1936), *King of Burlesque* (Fox, 1935), *Robin Hood of El Dorado* (MGM, 1936), *The Prisoner of Shark Island* (20th, 1936), *The Road to Glory* (20th, 1936), *To Mary—With Love* (20th, 1936), *White Hunter* (20th, 1936), *Slave Ship* (20th, 1937), *Vogues of 1938* (UA, 1937), *Wife, Doctor and Nurse* (20th, 1938), *Kidnapped* (20th, 1938), *I'll Give a Million* (20th, 1938), *Wife, Husband and Friend* (20th, 1939), *Return of the Cisco Kid* (20th, 1939), *Barricade* (20th, 1939), *Earthbound* (20th, 1940), *Adam Had Four Sons* (Col., 1941), *Crime Doctor* (Col., 1943), *Crime Doctor's Strangest Case* (Col., 1943), *Lady in the Dark* (Par., 1944), *Shadows in the Night* (Col., 1944), *The Crime Doctor's Courage* (Col., 1945), *Just Before Dawn* (Col., 1946), *The Crime Doctor's Man Hunt* (Col., 1946), *The Millerson Case* (Col., 1947), *The Crime Doctor's Gamble* (Col., 1947), *A Gentleman From Nowhere* (Col., 1948), *Prison Warden* (Col., 1949), *The Devil's Henchman* (Col., 1949), *The Crime Doctor's Diary* (Col., 1949), *State Penitentiary* (Col., 1950).

LOUISE BEAVERS Born 1902, Cincinnati, Ohio. Married Le Roy Moore. Died October 26, 1962.

Sound Feature Films: *Coquette* (UA, 1929), *Barnum Was Right* (Univ., 1929), *Glad Rag Doll* (Univ., 1929), *Nix on Dames* (Fox, 1929), *Wall Street* (Col., 1929), *Wide Open* (WB, 1930), *She Couldn't Say No* (WB, 1930), *Back Pay* (WB, 1930), *Safety in Numbers* (Par., 1930), *Party Husbands* (WB, 1931), *Annabelle's Affairs* (Fox, 1931), *Girls About Town* (Par., 1931), *Sundown Trail* (RKO, 1931), *Good Sport* (Fox, 1931), *Six Cylinder Love* (Fox, 1931), *The Expert* (WB, 1932), *Freaks* (MGM, 1932), *Night World* (Univ., 1932), *Ladies of the Big House*

(Par. 1932), *It's Tough to be Famous* (WB, 1932), *Young America* (Fox, 1932), *Street of Women* (WB, 1932), *What Price Hollywood* (RKO, 1932), *Unashamed* (MGM, 1932), *Divorce in the Family* (MGM, 1932), *Wild Girl* Fox, (1932), *Too Busy to Work* (Fox, 1932), *Pick Up* (Par., 1933), *She Done Him Wrong* (Par., 1933), *Girl Missing* (WB, 1933), *What Price Innocence* (Col., 1933), *A Shriek in the Night* (Allied, 1933), *Her Bodyguard* (Par., 1933), *Notorious But Nice* (Chesterfield, 1933), *Bombshell* (MGM, 1933), *Her Splendid Folly* (Progressive, 1933), *Bedside* (WB, 1934), *In the Money* (Chesterfield, 1934), *I've Got Your Number* (WB, 1934), *Cheaters* (Liberty, 1934), *Glamour* (Univ., 1934), *The Merry Frinks* (WB, 1934), *Imitation of Life* (Univ., 1934), *West of the Pecos* (RKO, 1934), *I Believed in You* (Fox, 1934), *I Give My Love* (Univ., 1934), *Merry Wives of Reno* (WB, 1934), *A Modern Hero* (WB, 1934), *Registered Nurse* (WB, 1934), *Annapolis Farewell* (Par., 1935), *Bullets or Ballots* (WB, 1936), *Wives Never Know* (Par., 1936), *General Spanky* (MGM, 1936), *Rainbow on the River* (RKO, 1936), *Make Way for Tomorrow* (Par., 1937), *Wings Over Honolulu* (Univ., 1937), *Love in a Bungalow* (Univ., 1937), *The Last Gangster* (MGM, 1937), *Scandal Street* (Par., 1938), *Life Goes On* (Million Dollar Productions, 1938), *Brother Rat* (WB, 1938), *Reckless Living* (Univ., 1938), *The Headleys at Home* (Standard, 1938), *Peck's Bad Boy With the Circus* (RKO, 1938), *Made for Each Other* (UA, 1939), *The Lady's From Kentucky* (Par., 1939), *Reform School* (Million Dollar Productions, 1939), *Women Without Names* (Par., 1940), *Parole Fixer* (Par., 1940), *No Time for Comedy* (WB, 1940), *I Want a Divorce* (Par., 1940), *Virginia* (Par., 1941), *Belle Starr* (20th, 1941), *Sign of the Wolf* (Mon., 1941), *Shadow of the Thin Man* (MGM, 1941), *The Vanishing Virginian* (MGM, 1941), *Reap the Wild Wind* (Par., 1942), *Young America* (20th, 1942), *Holiday Inn* (Par., 1942), *The Big Street* (RKO, 1942), *Tennesse Johnson* (MGM, 1942), *Seven Sweethearts* (MGM, 1942), *Good Morning, Judge* (Univ., 1943), *Du Barry Was a Lady* (MGM, 1943), *Top Man* (Univ., 1943), *All by Myself* (Univ., 1943), *Jack London* (UA, 1943), *There's Something About a Soldier* (Col., 1943), *Follow the Boys* (Univ., 1944), *South of Dixie* (Univ., 1944), *Dixie Jamboree* (PRC, 1944), *Barbary Coast Gent* (MGM, 1944), *Delightfully Dangerous* (UA, 1945), *Lover Come Back* (Univ., 1946), *Banjo* (RKO, 1947), *Good Sam* (RKO, 1948), *Mr. Blandings Builds His Dream House* (RKO, 1948), *For the Love of Mary* (Univ., 1948), *Tell It to the Judge* (Col., 1949), *Girls' School* (Col., 1950), *The Jackie Robinson Story* (EL, 1950), *Colorado Sundown* (Rep., 1952), *I Dream of Jeannie* (Rep., 1952), *Never Wave at a WAC* (RKO, 1952), *Goodbye, My Lady* (WB, 1956), *You Can't Run Away From It* (Col., 1956), *Teenage Rebel* (20th, 1956), *Tammy and the Bachelor* (Univ., 1957), *The Goddess* (Col., 1958), *The Facts of Life* (UA, 1960), *All the Fine Young Cannibals* (MGM, 1960).

WALLACE BEERY Born April 1, 1889, Kansas City, Missouri. Married Gloria Swanson (1916); divorced 1918. Married Areta Gillman (1924), child: Carol. Died April 1, 1949.

Wallace Beery and Leo Carrillo in *Wyoming*.

Sound Feature Films: *Chinatown Nights* (Par., 1929), *River of Romance* (Par., 1929), *Big House* (MGM, 1930), *Way for a Sailor* (MGM, 1930), *Billy the Kid* (MGM, 1930), *A Lady's Morals* (MGM, 1930), *Min and Bill* (MGM, 1930), *Secret Six* (MGM, 1931), *Hell Divers* (MGM, 1931), *The Champ* (MGM, 1931), *Grand Hotel* (MGM, 1932), *Flesh* (MGM, 1932), *Dinner at Eight* (MGM, 1933), *Tugboat Annie* (MGM, 1933), *The Bowery* (UA, 1933), *Viva Villa!* (MGM, 1934), *Treasure Island* (MGM, 1934), *The Mighty Barnum* (UA, 1934), *West Point of the Air* (MGM, 1935), *China Seas* (MGM, 1935), *O'Shaughnessy's Boy* (MGM, 1935), *Ah! Wilderness* (MGM, 1936), *A Message to Garcia* (20th, 1936), *Old Hutch* (MGM, 1936), *Good Old Soak* (MGM, 1937), *Slave Ship* (20th, 1937), *The Bad Man of Brimstone* (MGM, 1938), *Port of Seven Seas* (MGM, 1938), *Stablemates* (MGM, 1938), *Stand Up and Fight* (MGM, 1939), *Sergeant Madden* (MGM, 1939), *Thunder Afloat* (MGM, 1939), *The Man From Dakota* (MGM, 1940), *20 Mule Team* (MGM, 1940), *Wyoming* (MGM, 1940), *Barnacle Bill* (MGM, 1941), *The Bugle Sounds* (MGM, 1941), *Jackass Mail* (MGM, 1942), *Salute to the Marines* (MGM, 1943), *Rationing* (MGM, 1944), *Barbary Coast Gent* (MGM, 1944), *This Man's Navy* (MGM, 1945), *Bad Bascomb* (MGM, 1946), *The Mighty McGurk* (MGM, 1946), *Alias a Gentleman* (MGM, 1948), *A Date With Judy* (MGM, 1948), *Big Jack* (MGM, 1949).

Susan Hayward, Ed Begley and Jimmy Conlin in *Tulsa*.

ED BEGLEY (Edward James Begley) Born March 25, 1901, Hartford, Connecticut. Married Amada Huff (1922), children: Allene, Edward; widowed 1957. Married Dorothy Reeves (1961); divorced 1963. Married Helen Jordan (1963), child: Maureen.

Feature Films: *Big Town* (Par., 1947), *Boomerang* (20th, 1947), *Deep Waters* (20th, 1948), *Sitting Pretty* (20th, 1948), *Street With No Name* (20th, 1948), *Sorry, Wrong Number* (Par., 1948), *Tulsa* (EL, 1949), *It Happens Every Spring* (20th, 1949), *The Great Gatsby* (Par., 1949), *Backfire* (WB, 1950), *Stars in My Crown* (MGM, 1950), *Wyoming Mail* (Univ., 1950), *Convicted* (Col., 1950), *Saddle Tramp* (Univ., 1950),

Dark City (Par., 1950), *Lady From Texas* (Univ., 1951), *On Dangerous Ground* (RKO, 1951), *You're in the Navy Now* (20th, 1951), *Deadline, U.S.A.* (20th, 1952), *Boots Malone* (Col., 1952), *Turning Point* (Par., 1952), *What Price Glory* (20th, 1952), *Lone Star* (MGM, 1952), *Patterns* (UA, 1956), *12 Angry Men* (UA, 1957), *Odds Against Tomorrow* (UA, 1959), *The Green Helmet* (MGM, 1961), *Sweet Bird of Youth* (MGM, 1962), *The Unsinkable Molly Brown* (MGM, 1964), *The Oscar* (Par., 1966), *Warning Shot* (Par., 1967), *A Time to Sing* (MGM, 1968), *Hang 'Em High* (UA, 1968), *Firecreek* (WB-7 Arts, 1968).

David Holt and Ralph Bellamy in *Straight From the Shoulder*.

RALPH BELLAMY Born June 17, 1904. Married Alice Delbridge (1922); divorced 1930. Married Catherine Willard (1931), children: Lynn, Willard; divorced 1945. Married Ethel Smith (1945); divorced 1947. Married Alice Murphy (1949).

Feature Films: *The Secret Six* (MGM, 1931), *Magnificent Lie* (Par., 1931), *Surrender* (Fox, 1931), *West of Broadway* (MGM, 1932), *Forbidden* (Col., 1932), *Disorderly Conduct* (Fox, 1932), *Young America* (Fox, 1932), *The Woman in Room 13* (Fox, 1932), *Rebecca of Sunnybrook Farm* (Fox, 1932), *Almost Married* (Fox, 1932), *Wild Girl* (Fox, 1932), *Air Mail* (Univ., 1932), *Second Hand Wife* (Fox, 1933), *Parole Girl* (Col., 1933), *Destination Unknown* (Univ., 1933), *Picture Snatchers* (WB, 1933), *Below the Sea* (Col., 1933), *Narrow Corner* (WB, 1933), *Flying Devils* (RKO, 1933), *Headline Shooters* (RKO, 1933), *Ever in My Heart* (WB, 1933), *Blind Adventure* (RKO, 1933), *Ace of Aces* (RKO, 1933), *Spitfire* (RKO, 1934), *This Man Is Mine* (RKO, 1934), *Once to Every Woman* (Col., 1934), *Before Midnight* (Col., 1934), *One Is Guilty* (Col., 1934), *Girl in Danger* (Col., 1934), *Crime of Helen Stanley* (Col., 1934), *Woman in the Dark* (RKO, 1935), *Helldorado* (Fox, 1935), *Wedding Night* (UA, 1935), *Rendezvous at Midnight* (Univ., 1935), *Eight Bells* (Col., 1935), *Air Hawks* (Col., 1935), *The Healer* (Mon., 1935), *Gigolette* (RKO, 1935), *Navy Wife* (Fox, 1935), *Hands Across the Table* (Par., 1935), *Dangerous Intrigue* (Col., 1936), *Roaming Lady* (Col., 1936), *Straight From the Shoulder* Par., 1936), *The Final Hours* (Col., 1936), *Wild Brian Kent* (RKO, 1936), *The Man Who Lived Twice* (Col., 1936), *Counterfeit Lady* (Col., 1937), *Let's Get Married* (Col., 1937), *The Awful Truth* (Col., 1937), *The Crime of Dr. Hallet* (Univ., 1938), *Fools for Scandal* (WB, 1938), *Boy Meets Girl* (WB, 1938), *Carefree* (RKO, 1938), *Girls' School* (Col., 1938), *Trade Winds* (UA, 1938), *Let Us Live* (Col., 1939), *Smashing the Spy Ring* (Col., 1939), *Blind Alley* (Col., 1939), *Coast Guard* (Col., 1939), *His Girl Friday* (Col., 1940), *Flight Angels* (WB, 1940), *Brother Orchid* (WB, 1940), *Queen of the Mob* (Par., 1940), *Dance, Girl, Dance* (RKO, 1940), *Public Deb No. 1* (20th, 1940), *Ellery Queen, Master Detective* (Col., 1940), *Meet the Wildcat* (Univ., 1940), *Ellery Queen's Penthouse Mystery* (Col., 1941), *Footsteps in the Dark* (WB, 1941), *Affectionately Yours* (WB, 1941), *Ellery Queen and the Perfect Crime* (Col., 1941), *Dive Bomber* (WB, 1941), *Ellery Queen and the Murder Ring* (Col., 1941), *The Wolf Man* (Univ., 1941), *The Ghost of Frankenstein* (Univ., 1942), *Lady in a Jam* (Univ., 1942), *Men of Texas* (Univ.,

1942), *The Great Impersonation* (Univ., 1942), *Stage Door Canteen* (UA, 1943), *Guest in the House* (UA, 1944), *Delightfully Dangerous* (UA, 1945), *Lady on a Train* (Univ., 1945), *The Court-Martial of Billy Mitchell* (WB, 1955), *Sunrise at Campobello* (WB, 1960), *The Professionals* (Col., 1966), *Rosemary's Baby* (Par., 1968).

Alan Ladd and William Bendix in *The Blue Dahlia.*

WILLIAM BENDIX Born January 4, 1906, New York, New York. Married Therese Stefanotti (1928), children: Lorraine, Stephanie. Died December 14, 1964.

Feature Films: *Woman of the Year* (MGM, 1942), *Brooklyn Orchid* (UA, 1942), *Wake Island* (Par., 1942), *The Glass Key* (Par., 1942), *Who Done It?* (Univ., 1942), *Star Spangled Rhythm* (Par., 1942), *The Crystal Ball* (UA, 1943), *Taxi, Mister* (UA, 1943), *China* (Par., 1943), *Hostages* (Par., 1943), *Guadalcanal Diary* (20th, 1943), *Lifeboat* (20th, 1944), *The Hairy Ape* (UA, 1944), *Abroad With Two Yanks* (UA, 1944), *Greenwich Village* (20th, 1944), *It's in the Bag* (UA, 1945), *Don Juan Quilligan* (20th, 1945), *A Bell for Adano* (20th, 1945), *Sentimental Journey* (20th, 1946), *The Blue Dahlia* (Par., 1946), *The Dark Corner* (20th, 1946), *Two Years Before the Mast* (Par., 1946), *White Tie and Tails* (Univ., 1946), *I'll Be Yours* (Univ., 1947), *Blaze of Noon* (Par., 1947), *Calcutta* (Par., 1947), *The Web* (Univ., 1947), *Where There's Life* (Par., 1947), *Variety Girl* (Par., 1947), *The Time of Your Life* (UA, 1948), *Race Street* (RKO, 1948), *The Babe Ruth Story* (AA, 1948), *The Life of Riley* (Univ., 1949), *A Connecticut Yankee in King Arthur's Court* (Par., 1949), *Streets of Laredo* (Par., 1949), *Cover Up* (UA, 1949), *The Big Steal* (RKO, 1949), *Johnny Holiday* (UA, 1949), *Kill the Umpire* (Col., 1950), *Gambling House* (RKO, 1950), *Submarine Command* (Par., 1951), *Detective Story* (Par., 1951), *Macao* (RKO, 1952), *A Girl in Every Port* (RKO, 1952), *Blackbeard the Pirate* (RKO, 1952), *Dangerous Mission* (RKO, 1954), *Crashout* (Filmakers, 1955), *Battle Stations* (Col., 1956), *The Deep Six* (WB, 1958), *Idle on Parade* (Col., 1959), *Portrait of a Sinner* (AIP, 1961), *Boys' Night Out* (MGM, 1962), *The Young and the Brave* (MGM, 1963), *For Love or Money* (Univ., 1963), *Law of the Lawless* (Par., 1964), *The Phony American* (Signal International, 1964), *Young Fury* (Par., 1965), *Johnny Nobody* (Medallion, 1965).

CONSTANCE BENNETT (Constance Campbell Bennett) Born October 22, 1905, New York, New York. Married Chester Moorhead (1921); divorced 1924. Married Philip Plant (1925), child: Peter; divorced 1930. Married Henri de la Falaise (1932); divorced 1940. Married Gilbert Roland (1941), children: Linda, Gyl Christina; divorced 1945. Married John Coulter (1946). Died July 24, 1965.

Sound Feature Films: *This Thing Called Love* (Pathé, 1929), *Son of the Gods* (WB, 1930), *Rich People* (Pathé, 1930), *Common Clay* (Fox, 1930), *Three Faces East* (WB, 1930), *Sin Takes a Holiday* (Pathé, 1930), *The Easiest Way* (MGM, 1931), *Born to Love* (RKO, 1931), *The Common Law* (RKO, 1931), *Bought* (WB, 1931), *Lady With a Past* (RKO, 1932), *What Price Hollywood* (RKO, 1932), *Two Against the*

Tullio Carminati, Franchot Tone and Constance Bennett in *Moulin Rouge.*

World (WB, 1932), *Rockabye* (RKO, 1932), *Our Betters* (RKO, 1933), *Bed of Roses* (RKO, 1933), *After Tonight* (RKO, 1933), *Moulin Rouge* (UA, 1934), *Affairs of Cellini* (UA, 1934), *Outcast Lady* (MGM, 1934), *After Office Hours* (MGM, 1935), *Everything Is Thunder* (Gaumont-British, 1936), *Ladies in Love* (20th, 1936), *Topper* (MGM, 1937), *Merrily We Live* (MGM, 1938), *Service De Luxe* (Univ., 1938), *Topper Takes a Trip* (UA, 1938), *Tail Spin* (20th, 1939), *Escape to Glory* (Col., 1940), *Law of the Tropics* (WB, 1941), *Two-Faced Woman* (MGM, 1941), *Wild Bill Hickok Rides* (WB, 1941), *Sin Town* (Univ., 1942), *Madame Spy* (Univ., 1942), *Paris Underground* (UA, 1945), *Centennial Summer* (20th, 1946), *The Unsuspected* (WB, 1947), *Smart Woman* (AA, 1948), *Angel on the Amazon* (Rep., 1949), *As Young as You Feel* (20th, 1951), *It Should Happen to You* (Col., 1953), *Madame X* (Univ., 1966).

Francis Lederer and Joan Bennett in *The Man I Married.*

JOAN BENNETT Born February 27, 1910, Palisades, New Jersey. Married John Fox (1926), child: Diana; divorced 1928. Married Gene Markey (1932), child: Melinda; divorced 1937. Married Walter Wanger (1940), children: Stephanie, Shelley; divorced 1962.

Feature Films: *Power* (Pathé, 1928), *Bulldog Drummond* (UA, 1929), *Three Live Ghosts* (UA, 1929), *Disraeli* (WB, 1929), *Mississippi Gambler* (Univ., 1929), *Puttin' on the Ritz* (UA, 1930), *Crazy That Way* (Fox, 1930), *Moby Dick* (WB, 1930), *Maybe It's Love* (WB, 1930), *Scotland Yard* (Fox, 1930), *Many a Slip* (Univ., 1931), *Doctors'*

Jack Benny and Marie Dressler in *Chasing Rainbows*.

Wives (Fox, 1931), *Hush Money* (Fox, 1931), *She Wanted a Millionaire* (Fox, 1932), *Careless Lady* (Fox, 1932), *The Trial of Vivienne Ware* (Fox, 1932), *Weekends Only* (Fox, 1932), *Wild Girl* (Fox, 1932), *Me and My Gal* (Fox, 1932), *Arizona to Broadway* (Fox, 1933), *Little Women* (RKO, 1933), *The Pursuit of Happiness* (Par., 1934), *The Man Who Reclaimed His Head* (Univ., 1935), *Private Worlds* (Par., 1935), *Mississippi* (Par., 1935), *Two for Tonight* (Par., 1935), *The Man Who Broke the Bank at Monte Carlo* (Fox, 1935), *She Couldn't Take It* (Col., 1935), *13 Hours by Air* (Par., 1936), *Big Brown Eyes* (Par., 1936), *Two in a Crowd* (Univ., 1936), *Wedding Present* (Par., 1936), *Vogues of 1938* (UA, 1937), *I Met My Love Again* (UA, 1938), *The Texans* (Par., 1938), *Artists and Models Abroad* (Par., 1938), *Trade Winds* (UA, 1939), *Man in the Iron Mask* (UA, 1939), *The Housekeeper's Daughter* (UA, 1939), *Green Hell* (Univ., 1940), *The House Across the Bay* (UA, 1940), *The Man I Married* (20th, 1940), *Son of Monte Cristo* (UA, 1940), *She Knew All the Answers* (Col., 1941), *Man Hunt* (20th, 1941), *Wild Geese Calling* (20th, 1941), *Confirm or Deny* (20th, 1941), *Twin Beds* (UA, 1942), *The Wife Takes a Flyer* (Col., 1942), *Girl Trouble* (20th, 1942), *Margin for Error* (20th, 1943), *Woman in the Window* (RKO, 1944), *Nob Hill* (20th, 1945), *Scarlet Street* (Univ., 1945), *Col. Effingham's Raid* (20th, 1946), *The Macomber Affair* (UA, 1947), *Secret Beyond the Door* (Univ., 1947), *Woman on the Beach* (RKO, 1947), *Hollow Triumph* ("The Scar"—EL, 1948), *The Reckless Moment* (Col., 1949), *Father of the Bride* (MGM, 1950), *For Heaven's Sake* (20th, 1950), *Father's Little Dividend* (MGM, 1951), *The Guy Who Came Back* (20th, 1951), *Highway Dragnet* (AA, 1954), *We're No Angels* (Par., 1955), *There's Always Tomorrow* (Univ., 1956), *Navy Wife* (AA, 1956), *Desire in the Dust* (20th, 1960).

JACK BENNY (Benjamin Kubelsky) Born February 14, 1894, Waukegan, Illinois. Married Mary Livingston (1927).

Feature Films: *Hollywood Revue of 1929* (MGM, 1929), *Chasing Rainbows* (MGM, 1930), *Medicine Man* (Tif., 1930), *Transatlantic Merry-Go-Round* (UA, 1934), *Broadway Melody of 1936* (MGM, 1935), *It's in the Air* (MGM, 1935), *The Big Broadcast of 1937* (Par., 1936), *College Holiday* (Par., 1936), *Artists and Models* (Par., 1937), *Artists and Models Abroad* (Par., 1938), *Man About Town* (Par., 1939), *Buck Benny Rides Again* (Par., 1940), *Love Thy Neighbor* (Par., 1940), *Charley's Aunt* (20th, 1941), *To Be or Not to Be* (UA, 1942), *George Washington Slept Here* (WB, 1942), *The Meanest Man in the World* (20th, 1943), *Hollywood Canteen* (WB, 1944), *It's in the Bag* (UA, 1945), *The Horn Blows at Midnight* (WB, 1945), *Without Reservations* (RKO, 1946),* *The Great Lover* (Par., 1949),* *Somebody Loves Me* (Par., 1952),* *Susan Slept Here* (RKO, 1954),* *Beau James* (Par., 1957),* *Gypsy* (WB, 1962),* *It's A Mad, Mad, Mad, Mad World* (UA, 1963),* *A Guide For the Married Man* (20th, 1967).

*Unbilled guest appearance.

INGRID BERGMAN Born August 29, 1915, Stockholm, Sweden. Married Petter Lindstrom (1937), child: Pia; divorced 1950. Married Roberto Rossellini (1950), children: Renato, Isotta Ingrid, Isabella; annulled 1958. Married Lars Schmidt (1958).

English-Language Feature Films: *Intermezzo* (UA, 1939), *Adam Had Four Sons* (Col., 1941), *Rage in Heaven* (MGM, 1941), *Dr. Jekyll and Mr. Hyde* (MGM, 1941), *Casablanca* (WB, 1942), *For Whom the Bell Tolls* (Par., 1943), *Gaslight* (MGM, 1944), *Spellbound* (UA, 1945), *Saratoga Trunk* (WB, 1945), *The Bells of St. Mary's* (RKO, 1946), *Notorious* (RKO, 1946), *Arch of Triumph* (UA, 1948), *Joan of Arc* (RKO, 1948), *Under Capricorn* (WB, 1949), *Strangers* (Fine Arts, 1955), *Anastasia* (20th, 1956), *Indiscreet* (WB, 1958), *The Inn of the Sixth Happiness* (20th, 1958), *Goodbye Again* (UA, 1961), *The Visit* (20th, 1964), *The Yellow Rolls-Royce* (MGM, 1965), *Stimulantia* (Swedish, 1967), *Fugitive in Vienna* (WB, 1968).

Ingrid Bergman and Warner Baxter in *Adam Had Four Sons*.

CHARLES BICKFORD Born January 1, 1889. Cambridge, Massachusetts. Married Beatrice Loring (1919), children: Doris, Rex. Died November 9, 1967.

Feature Films: *Dynamite* (Par., 1929), *South Sea Rose* (Fox, 1929), *Hell's Heroes* (Univ., 1929), *Anna Christie* (MGM, 1930), *Sea Bat* (MGM, 1930), *Passion Flower* (MGM, 1930), *River's End* (WB, 1931), *Squaw Man* (MGM, 1931), *East of Borneo* (Univ., 1931), *Pagan Lady* (Col., 1931), *Men in Her Life* (Col., 1931), *Panama Flo* (RKO, 1932), *Thunder Below* (Par., 1932), *Scandal for Sale* (Univ., 1932), *Last Man* (Col., 1932), *Vanity Street* (Col., 1932), *No Other Woman* (RKO, 1933), *Song of the Eagle* (Par., 1933), *This Day and Age* (Par., 1933), *White Woman* (Par., 1933), *Little Miss Marker* (Par., 1934), *A Wicked Woman* (MGM, 1934), *A Notorious Gentleman* (Univ., 1935), *Under Pressure* (Fox, 1935), *The Farmer Takes a Wife* (Fox, 1935), *East of Java* (Univ., 1935), *The Littlest Rebel* (Fox, 1935), *Rose of the Rancho* (Par., 1936), *Pride of the Marines* (Col., 1936), *The Plainsman* (Par., 1936), *Night Club Scandal* (Par., 1937), *Thunder Trail* (Par., 1937),

Claire Trevor and Charles Bickford in *Valley of the Giants*.

Daughter of Shanghai (Par., 1937), *High, Wide and Handsome* (Par., 1937), *Gangs of New York* (Rep., 1938), *Valley of The Giants* (WB, 1938), *The Storm* (Univ., 1938), *Thou Shalt Not Kill* (Rep., 1940), *Girl From God's Country* (Rep., 1940), *South to Karanga* (Univ., 1940), *Queen of the Yukon* (Mon., 1940), *Riders of Death Valley* (Univ. serial, 1941), *Burma Convoy* (Univ., 1941), *Reap the Wild Wind* (Par., 1942), *Tarzan's New York Adventure* (MGM, 1942), *Mr. Lucky* (RKO, 1943), *The Song of Bernadette* (20th, 1943), *Wing and a Prayer* (20th, 1944), *Captain Eddie* (20th, 1945), *Fallen Angel* (20th, 1945), *Duel in the Sun* (Selznick, 1946), *The Farmer's Daughter* (RKO, 1947), *The Woman on the Beach* (RKO, 1947), *Brute Force* (Univ., 1947), *Four Faces West* (UA, 1948), *The Babe Ruth Story* (AA, 1948), *Johnny Belinda* (WB, 1948), *Command Decision* (MGM, 1948), *Roseanna McCoy* (RKO, 1949), *Whirlpool* (20th, 1949), *Guilty of Treason* (EL, 1949), *Branded* (Par., 1950), *Riding High* (Par., 1950), *Jim Thorpe—All American* (WB, 1951), *The Raging Tide* (Univ., 1951), *Elopement* (20th, 1951), *A Star Is Born* (WB, 1954), *Prince of Players* (20th, 1955), *Not as a Stranger* (UA, 1955), *The Court-Martial Of Billy Mitchell* (WB, 1955), *You Can't Run Away From It* (Col., 1956), *Mister Cory* (Univ., 1957), *The Big Country* (UA, 1958), *The Unforgiven* (UA, 1960), *Days of Wine and Roses* (WB, 1962), *Big Hand for the Little Lady* (WB, 1966).

Kay Francis, Gloria Warren and Sidney Blackmer in *Always in My Heart.*

SIDNEY BLACKMER Born July 13, 1898, Salisbury, North Carolina. Married Leonore Ulric (1928); divorced 1939. Married Suzanne Kaaren (1942).

Sound Feature Films: *A Most Immoral Lady* (WB, 1929), *The Love Racket* (WB, 1930), *Sweethearts and Wives* (WB, 1930), *Strictly Modern* (WB, 1930), *Bad Man* (WB, 1930), *Kismet* (WB, 1930), *Mothers Cry* (WB, 1930), *Lady Who Dared* (WB, 1931), *Woman Hungry* (WB, 1931), *It's a Wise Child* (MGM, 1931), *Daybreak* (MGM, 1931), *Once a Sinner* (Fox, 1931), *From Hell to Heaven* (Par., 1933), *Cocktail Hour* (Col., 1933), *The Wrecker* (Col., 1933), *The Deluge* (RKO, 1933), *This Man Is Mine* (RKO, 1934), *Goodbye Love* (RKO, 1934), *Count of Monte Cristo* (UA, 1934), *Down to Their Last Yacht* (RKO, 1934), *Transatlantic Merry-Go-Round* (UA, 1934), *The President Vanishes* (Par., 1934), *A Notorious Gentleman* (Univ., 1935), *The Great God Gold* (Mon., 1935), *Behind Green Lights* (Mascot, 1935), *The Little Colonel* (Fox, 1935), *Smart Girl* (Par., 1935), *The Girl Who Came Back* (Chesterfield, 1935), *The Firetrap* (Empire, 1935), *False Pretenses* (Chesterfield, 1935), *Streamline Express* (Mascot, 1935), *Forced Landing* (Rep., 1935), *Woman Trap* (Par., 1936), *Florida Special* (Par., 1936), *Early to Bed* (Par., 1936), *Heart of the West* (Par., 1936), *The President's Mystery* (Rep., 1936), *Missing Girls* (Chesterfield, 1936), *Girl Overboard* (Univ., 1937), *John Meade's Woman* (Par., 1937), *A Doctor's Diary* (Par., 1937), *Michael O'Halloran* (Rep., 1937), *This Is My Affair* (20th, 1937), *Wife, Doctor and Nurse* (20th, 1937), *Heidi* (20th, 1937), *Shadows of the Orient* (Mon., 1937), *Charlie Chan at*

Monte Carlo (20th, 1937), *Thank You, Mr. Moto* (20th, 1937), *The Last Gangster* (MGM, 1937), *In Old Chicago* (20th, 1938), *Speed to Burn* (20th, 1938), *Straight, Place and Show* (20th, 1938), *Orphans of the Street* (Rep., 1938), *Sharpshooters* (20th, 1938), *Trade Winds* (UA, 1938), *Suez* (20th, 1938), *Fast and Loose* (MGM, 1939), *Trapped in the Sky* (Col., 1939), *Within the Law* (MGM, 1939), *It's a Wonderful World* (MGM, 1939), *Unmarried* (Par., 1939), *Hotel for Women* (20th, 1939), *Law of the Pampas* (Par., 1939), *Framed* (Univ., 1940), *Maryland* (20th, 1940), *Dance, Girl, Dance* (RKO, 1940), *I Want a Divorce* (Par., 1940), *Cheers for Miss Bishop* (UA, 1941), *Murder Among Friends* (20th, 1941), *Rookies on Parade* (Rep., 1941), *The Great Swindle* (Col., 1941), *Love Crazy* (MGM, 1941), *Angels With Broken Wings* (Rep., 1941), *Ellery Queen and the Perfect Crime* (Col., 1941), *Down Mexico Way* (Rep., 1941), *The Feminine Touch* (MGM, 1941), *The Officer and the Lady* (Col., 1941), *Obliging Young Lady* (RKO, 1941), *The Panther's Claw* (PRC, 1942), *Always in My Heart* (WB, 1942), *Nazi Agent* (MGM, 1942), *Sabotage Squad* (Col., 1942), *Prison Girls* (PRC, 1942), *Quiet Please—Murder* (20th, 1942), *I Escaped From the Gestapo* (Mon., 1943), *Murder in Times Square* (Col., 1943), *In Old Oklahoma* (Rep., 1943), *Broadway Rhythm* (MGM, 1944), *Duel in the Sun* (Selznick, 1946), *My Girl Tisa* (WB, 1948), *A Song Is Born* (RKO, 1948), *People Will Talk* (20th, 1951), *Saturday's Hero* (Col., 1951), *The San Francisco Story* (WB, 1952), *The Washington Story* (MGM, 1952), *Johnny Dark* (Univ., 1954), *The High and the Mighty* (WB, 1954), *The View From Pompey's Head* (20th, 1955), *Accused of Murder* (Rep., 1956), *High Society* (MGM, 1956), *Beyond a Reasonable Doubt* (RKO, 1956), *Tammy and the Bachelor* (Univ., 1957), *How to Murder Your Wife* (UA, 1965), *Joy in the Morning* (MGM, 1965), *A Covenant With Death* (WB, 1967), *Rosemary's Baby* (Par., 1968).

VIVIAN BLAINE (Vivian S. Stapleton) Born November 21, 1921, Newark, New Jersey. Married Manuel "Manny" Frank (1945); divorced 1956. Married Milton Rackmil (1959); divorced 1961.

Feature Films: *Through Different Eyes* (20th, 1942), *Girl Trouble* (20th, 1942), *He Hired the Boss* (20th, 1943), *Jitterbugs* (20th, 1943), *Greenwich Village* (20th, 1944), *Something for the Boys* (20th, 1944), *Nob Hill* (20th, 1945), *State Fair* (20th, 1945), *Doll Face* (20th, 1945), *If I'm Lucky* (20th, 1946), *Three Little Girls in Blue* (20th, 1946), *Skirts Ahoy* (MGM, 1952), *Main Street to Broadway* (MGM, 1953), *Guys and Dolls* (MGM, 1955), *Public Pigeon No. One* (RKO, 1957).

JANET BLAIR (Martha Janet Lafferty) Born April 23, 1921, Altoona, Pennsylvania. Married Lou Bush (1943); divorced 1950. Married Nick Mayo (1952), children: Amanda, Andrew.

Perry Como, Martha Stewart, Vivian Blaine, Reed Hadley, Carmen Miranda and Dennis O'Keefe in *Doll Face.*

William Lundigan and Janet Blair in *The Fabulous Dorseys.*

Feature Films: *Three Girls About Town* (Col., 1941), *Blondie Goes to College* (Col., 1942), *Two Yanks in Trinidad* (Col., 1942), *Broadway* (Univ., 1942), *My Sister Eileen* (Col., 1942), *Something to Shout About* (Col., 1943), *Once Upon a Time* (Col., 1944), *Tonight and Every Night* (Col., 1945), *Tars and Spars* (Col., 1946), *Gallant Journey* (Col., 1946), *The Fabulous Dorseys* (UA, 1947), *I Love Trouble* (Col., 1948), *The Black Arrow* (Col., 1948), *The Fuller Brush Man* (Col., 1948), *Public Pigeon No. One* (RKO, 1957), *Boys' Night Out* (MGM, 1962), *Burn, Witch, Burn* (AIP, 1962), *The One and Only Genuine, Original Family Band* (BV, 1968).

JOAN BLONDELL Born August 30, 1909, New York, New York. Married George Barnes (1932); divorced 1935. Married Dick Powell (1936), children: Ellen, Norman; divorced 1944. Married Mike Todd (1947), child: Michael; divorced 1950.

Feature Films: *Office Wife* (WB, 1930), *Sinners' Holiday* (WB, 1930), *Illicit* (WB, 1931), *Millie* (RKO, 1931), *My Past* (WB, 1931), *Big Business Girl* (WB, 1931), *Public Enemy* (WB, 1931), *God's Gift to Women* (WB, 1931), *Other Men's Women* (WB, 1931), *The Reckless Hour* (WB, 1931), *Night Nurse* (WB, 1931), *Blonde Crazy* (WB, 1931), *The Greeks Had a Word for Them* (UA, 1932), *Union Depot* (WB, 1932), *The Crowd Roars* (WB, 1932), *Famous Ferguson Case* (WB, 1932), *Make Me a Star* (Par., 1932), *Miss Pinkerton* (WB, 1932), *Big City Blues* (WB, 1932), *Three on a Match* (WB, 1932), *Central Park* (WB, 1932), *Lawyer Man* (WB, 1932), *Broadway Bad* (Fox, 1933), *Blondie Johnson* (WB, 1933), *Gold Diggers of 1933* (WB, 1933), *Goodbye Again* (WB, 1933), *Footlight Parade* (WB, 1933), *Havana Widows* (WB, 1933), *Convention City* (WB, 1933), *I've Got Your Number* (WB, 1934), *Smarty* (WB, 1934), *He Was Her Man* (WB, 1934), *Dames* (WB, 1934), *Kansas City Princess* (WB, 1934), *Traveling Saleslady* (WB, 1935), *Broadway Gondolier* (WB, 1935), *We're in the Money* (WB, 1935), *Miss Pacific Fleet* (WB, 1935), *Colleen* (WB, 1936), *Sons o' Guns* (WB, 1936), *Bullets or Ballots* (WB, 1936), *Stage Struck* (WB, 1936), *Three Men on a Horse* (WB, 1936), *Gold*

Joan Blondell and Dick Powell in *I Want a Divorce.*

Diggers of 1937 (WB, 1936), *The King and the Chorus Girl* (WB, 1937), *Back in Circulation* (WB, 1937), *Perfect Specimen* (WB, 1937), *Stand-In* (UA, 1937), *There's Always a Woman* (Col., 1938), *Off the Record* (WB, 1939), *East Side of Heaven* (Univ., 1939), *The Kid From Kokomo* (WB, 1939), *Good Girls Go to Paris* (Col., 1939), *The Amazing Mr. Williams* (Col., 1939), *Two Girls on Broadway* (MGM, 1940), *I Want a Divorce* (Par., 1940), *Topper Returns* (UA, 1941), *Model Wife* (Univ., 1941), *Three Girls About Town* (Col., 1941), *Lady for a Night* (Rep., 1941), *Cry Havoc* (MGM, 1943), *A Tree Grows in Brooklyn* (20th, 1945), *Don Juan Quilligan* (20th, 1945), *Adventure* (MGM, 1945), *The Corpse Came C.O.D.* (Col., 1947), *Nightmare Alley* (20th, 1947), *Christmas Eve* (UA, 1947), *For Heaven's Sake* (20th, 1950), *The Blue Veil* (RKO, 1951), *The Opposite Sex* (MGM, 1956), *Lizzie* (MGM, 1957), *This Could Be the Night* (MGM, 1957), *Desk Set* (20th, 1957), *Will Success Spoil Rock Hunter?* (20th, 1957), *Angel Baby* (AA, 1961), *Advance to the Rear* (MGM, 1964), *The Cincinnati Kid* (MGM, 1965), *Ride Beyond Vengeance* (Col., 1966), *Paradise Road* (Syzygy, 1966), *Waterhole No. 3* (Par., 1967), *Kona Coast* (WB-7 Arts, 1968), *Stay Away, Joe* (MGM, 1968).

Barbara Stanwyck and Eric Blore in *Breakfast for Two.*

ERIC BLORE Born December 23, 1887, London, England. Married Clara Machin (1926); widowed. Married Viola Winter. Died March 1, 1959.

Feature Films: *Laughter* (Par., 1930), *My Sin* (Par., 1931), *Tarnished Lady* (Par., 1931), *Flying Down to Rio* (RKO, 1933), *Gay Divorcee* (RKO, 1934), *Limehouse Blues* (Par., 1934), *Behold My Wife* (Par., 1935), *Folies Bergère* (UA, 1935), *Casino Murder Case* (MGM, 1935), *The Good Fairy* (Univ., 1935), *Diamond Jim* (Univ., 1935), *Old Man Rhythm* (RKO, 1935), *I Live My Life* (MGM, 1935), *Top Hat* (RKO, 1935), *I Dream Too Much* (RKO, 1935), *To Beat the Band* (RKO, 1935), *Seven Keys to Baldpate* (RKO, 1935), *Two in the Dark* (RKO, 1936), *The Ex-Mrs. Bradford* (RKO, 1936), *Sons o' Guns* (WB, 1936), *Piccadilly Jim* (MGM, 1936), *Swing Time* (RKO, 1936), *Smartest Girl in Town* (RKO, 1936), *Quality Street* (RKO, 1937), *The Soldier and the Lady* (RKO, 1937), *Shall We Dance* (RKO, 1937), *It's Love I'm After* (WB, 1937), *Breakfast for Two* (RKO, 1937), *Hitting a New High* (RKO, 1937), *The Joy of Living* (RKO, 1938), *Swiss Miss* (MGM, 1938), *A Desperate Adventure* (Rep., 1938), *$1,000 a Touchdown* (Par., 1939), *Island of Lost Men* (Par., 1939), *The Man Who Wouldn't Talk* (Univ., 1940), *The Lone Wolf Strikes* (Col., 1940), *Music in My Heart* (Col., 1940), *Till We Meet Again* (WB, 1940), *The Lone Wolf Meets a Lady* (Col., 1940), *The Boys From Syracuse* (Univ., 1940), *Earl of Puddlestone* (Rep., 1940), *South of Suez* (WB, 1940), *Road to Zanzibar* (Par., 1941), *The Lone Wolf Keeps a Date* (Col., 1941), *The Lady Eve* (Par., 1941), *The Lone Wolf Takes a Chance* (Col., 1941), *Red Head* (Mon., 1941), *New York Town* (Par., 1941), *Lady Scarface* (RKO, 1941), *Three Girls About Town* (Col., 1941), *Confirm or Deny* (20th, 1941), *Sullivan's Travels* (Par., 1941), *The Shanghai Gesture* (UA, 1941), *Secrets of the Lone Wolf* (Col., 1941), *The Moon and Sixpence*

(UA, 1942), *Forever and a Day* (RKO, 1943), *Submarine Base* (PRC, 1943), *Holy Matrimony* (20th, 1943), *One Dangerous Night* (Col., 1943), *Passport to Suez* (Col., 1943), *The Sky's the Limit* (RKO, 1943), *San Diego, I Love You* (Univ., 1944), *Penthouse Rhythm* (Univ., 1945), *Easy to Look At* (Univ., 1945), *Kitty* (Par., 1945), *Men in Her Diary* (Univ., 1946), *The Notorious Lone Wolf* (Col., 1946), *Abie's Irish Rose* (UA, 1946), *Winter Wonderland* (Rep., 1947), *The Lone Wolf in London* (Col., 1947), *Romance on the High Seas* (WB, 1948), *Love Happy* (UA, 1949), *Fancy Pants* (Par., 1950), *Bowery to Bagdad* (AA, 1955).

Ann Blyth, Edmund Purdom and Fred Essler in *The Student Prince.*

ANN BLYTH (Ann Marie Blyth) Born August 16, 1928, Mt. Kisco, New York. Married James McNulty (1953), children: Timothy, Maureen, Kathleen, Terrence.

Feature Films: *Chip Off the Old Block* (Univ., 1944), *The Merry Monahans* (Univ., 1944), *Babes on Swing Street* (Univ., 1944), *Bowery to Broadway* (Univ., 1944), *Mildred Pierce* (WB, 1945), *Swell Guy* (Univ., 1946), *Brute Force* (Univ., 1947), *Killer McCoy* (MGM, 1947), *A Woman's Vengeance* (Univ., 1947), *Another Part of the Forest* (Univ., 1948), *Mr. Peabody and the Mermaid* (Univ., 1948), *Red Canyon* (Univ., 1949), *Once More, My Darling* (Univ., 1949), *Top o' the Morning* (Par., 1949), *Free For All* (Univ., 1949), *Our Very Own* (RKO, 1950), *The Great Caruso* (MGM, 1951), *Katie Did It* (Univ., 1951), *Thunder on the Hill* (Univ., 1951), *I'll Never Forget You* (20th, 1951), *The Golden Horde* (Univ., 1951), *The World in His Arms* (Univ., 1952), *One Minute to Zero* (RKO, 1952), *Sally and Saint Anne* (Univ., 1952), *All the Brothers Were Valiant* (MGM, 1953), *Rose Marie* (MGM, 1954), *The Student Prince* (MGM, 1954), *The King's Thief* (MGM, 1955), *Kismet* (MGM, 1955), *Slander* (MGM, 1957), *The Buster Keaton Story* (Par., 1957), *The Helen Morgan Story* (WB, 1957).

HUMPHREY BOGART (Humphrey De Forest Bogart) Born January 23, 1899, New York, New York. Married Helen Mencken (1926); divorced 1928. Married Mary Phillips (1928); divorced 1938. Married Mayo Methot (1938); divorced 1945. Married Lauren Bacall (1945), children: Stephen, Leslie. Died January 14, 1957.

Feature Films: *A Devil With Women* (Fox, 1930), *Up the River* (Fox, 1930), *Body and Soul* (Fox, 1931), *Bad Sister* (Univ., 1931), *Women of All Nations* (Fox, 1931), *A Holy Terror* (Fox, 1931), *Love Affair* (Col., 1932), *Three on a Match* (WB, 1932), *Midnight* (Univ., 1934), *The Petrified Forest* (WB, 1936), *Two Against the World* (WB, 1936), *Bullets or Ballots* (WB, 1936), *China Clipper* (WB, 1936), *Isle of Fury* (WB, 1936), *The Great O'Malley* (WB, 1937), *Black Legion* (WB, 1937), *San Quentin* (WB, 1937), *Marked Woman* (WB, 1937), *Kid Galahad* (WB, 1937), *Dead End* (UA, 1937), *Stand-In* (UA, 1937), *Swing Your Lady* (WB, 1938), *Men Are Such Fools* (WB, 1938), *The Amazing Dr. Clitterhouse* (WB, 1938), *Racket Busters* (WB, 1938),

Randolph Scott, Humphrey Bogart and George Regas in *Virginia City.*

Angels With Dirty Faces (WB, 1938), *King of the Underworld* (WB, 1939), *The Oklahoma Kid* (WB, 1939), *Dark Victory* (WB, 1939), *You Can't Get Away With Murder* (WB, 1939), *The Roaring Twenties* (WB, 1939), *The Return of Dr. X* (WB, 1939), *Invisible Stripes* (WB, 1939), *Virginia City* (WB, 1940), *It All Came True* (WB, 1940), *Brother Orchid* (WB, 1940), *They Drive by Night* (WB, 1940), *High Sierra* (WB, 1941), *The Wagons Roll at Night* (WB, 1941), *The Maltese Falcon* (WB, 1941), *All Through the Night* (WB, 1942), *The Big Shot* (WB, 1942), *In This Our Life* (WB, 1942)*, *Across the Pacific* (WB, 1942), *Casablanca* (WB, 1942), *Action in the North Atlantic* (WB, 1943), *Thank Your Lucky Stars* (WB, 1943), *Sahara* (Col., 1943), *To Have and Have Not* (WB, 1944), *Passage to Marseille* (WB, 1944), *Conflict* (WB, 1945), *The Big Sleep* (WB, 1946), *Two Guys From Milwaukee* (WB, 1946),* *The Two Mrs. Carrolls* (WB, 1947), *Dead Reckoning* (Col., 1947), *Dark Passage* (WB, 1947), *Treasure of the Sierra Madre* (WB, 1948), *Key Largo* (WB, 1948), *It's a Great Feeling* (WB, 1949), *Knock on Any Door* (Col., 1949), *Tokyo Joe* (Col., 1949), *Chain Lightning* (WB, 1950), *In a Lonely Place* (Col., 1950), *The Enforcer* (WB, 1951), *Sirocco* (Col., 1951), *The African Queen* (UA, 1952), *Deadline—U.S.A.* (20th, 1952), *Battle Circus* (MGM, 1953), *Beat the Devil* (UA, 1954), *The Caine Mutiny* (Col., 1954), *Sabrina* (Par., 1954), *The Barefoot Contessa* (UA, 1954), *Love Lottery* (Rank, 1954),* *We're No Angels* (Par., 1955), *The Left Hand of God* (20th, 1955), *The Desperate Hours* (Par., 1955), *The Harder They Fall* (Col., 1956).

 *Unbilled guest appearance

MARY BOLAND Born January 28, 1880, Philadelphia, Pennsylvania. Died June 23, 1965.

Sound Feature Films: *Personal Maid* (Par., 1931), *Secrets of a Secretary* (Par., 1931), *The Night of June 13th* (Par., 1932), *Trouble in Paradise* (Par., 1932), *Evenings for Sale* (Par., 1932), *If I Had a Million* (Par., 1932), *Mama Loves Papa* (Par., 1933), *Three-Cornered Moon* (Par., 1933), *The Solitaire Man* (MGM, 1933), *Four Frightened People* (Par., 1934), *Six of a Kind* (Par., 1934), *Melody in Spring* (Par., 1934), *Stingaree* (RKO, 1934), *Here Comes the Groom* (Par., 1934), *Down to Their Last Yacht* (RKO, 1934), *The Pursuit of Happiness* (Par., 1934),

Benny Bartlett, Mary Boland and Etienne Giradot in *Danger—Love at Work.*

John Boles and Loretta Young in *The White Parade*.

Ruggles of Red Gap (Par., 1935), *People Will Talk* (Par., 1935), *Two for Tonight* (Par., 1935), *The Big Broadcast of 1936* (Par., 1935), *Early to Bed* (Par., 1936), *Wives Never Know* (Par., 1936), *A Son Comes Home* (Par., 1936), *College Holiday* (Par., 1936), *Marry the Girl* (WB, 1937), *There Goes the Groom* (RKO, 1937), *Danger—Love at Work* (20th, 1937), *Mama Runs Wild* (Rep., 1937), *Little Tough Guys in Society* (Univ., 1938), *Artists and Models Abroad* (Par., 1938), *Boy Trouble* (Par., 1939), *The Magnificent Fraud* (Par., 1939), *Night Work* (Par., 1939), *The Women* (MGM, 1939), *He Married His Wife* (20th, 1940), *The New Moon* (MGM, 1940), *Pride and Prejudice* (MGM, 1940), *The Hit Parade of 1941* (Rep., 1940), *One Night in the Tropics* (Univ., 1940), *In Our Time* (WB, 1944), *Forever Yours* (Mon., 1944), *Nothing But Trouble* (MGM, 1944), *Julia Misbehaves* (MGM, 1948), *Guilty Bystander* (Film Classics, 1950).

JOHN BOLES Born October 27, 1899, Greenville, Texas. Married Marcellite Dobbs.

Sound Feature Films: *Desert Song* (WB, 1929), *Rio Rita* (RKO, 1929), *Song of the West* (WB, 1930), *King of Jazz* (Univ., 1930), *Captain of the Guard* (Univ., 1930), *Queen of Scandal* (UA, 1930), *One Heavenly Night* (UA, 1930), *Resurrection* (Univ., 1931), *Seed* (Univ., 1931), *Frankenstein* (Univ., 1931), *Good Sport* (Fox, 1931), *Careless Lady* (Fox, 1932), *Six Hours to Live* (Fox, 1932), *Back Street* (Univ., 1932), *Child of Manhattan* (Col., 1933), *My Lips Betray* (Fox, 1933), *Only Yesterday* (Univ., 1933), *I Believed in You* (Fox, 1934), *Beloved* (Univ., 1934), *Bottoms Up* (Fox, 1934), *Stand Up and Cheer* (Fox, 1934), *Life of Vergie Winters* (RKO, 1934), *Wild Gold* (Fox, 1934), *Age of Innocence* (RKO, 1934), *The White Parade* (Fox, 1934), *Orchids to You* (Fox, 1935), *Curly Top* (Fox, 1935), *Redheads on Parade* (Fox, 1935), *The Littlest Rebel* (Fox, 1935), *Rose of the Rancho* (Par., 1936), *A Message to Garcia* (20th, 1936), *Craig's Wife* (Col., 1936), *As Good as Married* (Univ., 1937), *Stella Dallas* (UA, 1937), *Fight for Your Lady* (RKO, 1937), *She Married an Artist* (Col., 1938), *Romance in the Dark* (Par., 1938), *Sinners in Paradise* (Univ., 1938), *Between Us Girls* (Univ., 1942), *Thousands Cheer* (MGM, 1943), *Babes in Bagdad* (UA, 1952).

Beulah Bondi and Burl Ives in *So Dear to My Heart*.

BEULAH BONDI (Beulah Bondy) Born May 3, 1892, Chicago, Illinois.

Feature Films: *Street Scene* (UA, 1931), *Arrowsmith* (UA, 1931), *Rain* (UA, 1932), *Stranger's Return* (MGM, 1933), *Christopher Bean* (MGM, 1933), *Finishing School* (RKO, 1934), *The Painted Veil* (MGM, 1934), *Two Alone* (RKO, 1934), *Registered Nurse* (WB, 1934), *Ready for Love* (Par., 1934), *Bad Boy* (Fox, 1935), *The Good Fairy* (Univ., 1935), *Invisible Ray* (Univ., 1936), *Trail of the Lonesome Pine* (Par., 1936), *The Moon's Our Home* (Par., 1936), *The Case Against Mrs. Ames* (Par., 1936), *Hearts Divided* (WB, 1936), *The Gorgeous Hussy* (MGM, 1936), *Maid of Salem* (Par., 1937), *Make Way for Tomorrow* (Par., 1937), *The Buccaneer* (Par., 1938), *Of Human Hearts* (MGM, 1938), *Vivacious Lady* (RKO, 1938), *The Sisters* (WB, 1938), *On Borrowed Time* (MGM, 1939), *Mr. Smith Goes to Washington* (Col., 1939), *The Under-Pup* (Univ., 1939), *Remember the Night* (Par., 1940), *Our Town* (UA, 1940), *The Captain Is a Lady* (MGM, 1940), *Penny Serenade* (Col., 1941), *Shepherd of the Hills* (Par., 1941), *One Foot in Heaven* (WB, 1941), *Tonight We Raid Calais* (20th, 1943), *Watch on the Rhine* (WB, 1943), *I Love a Soldier* (Par., 1944), *She's a Soldier, Too* (Col., 1944), *Our Hearts Were Young and Gay* (Par., 1944), *And Now Tomorrow* (Par., 1944), *The Very Thought of You* (WB, 1944), *The Southerner* (UA, 1945), *Back to Bataan* (RKO, 1945), *Breakfast in Hollywood* (UA, 1946), *Sister Kenny* (RKO, 1946), *It's a Wonderful Life* (RKO, 1946), *High Conquest* (Mon., 1947), *The Sainted Sisters* (Par., 1948), *The Snake Pit* (20th, 1948), *So Dear to My Heart* (RKO, 1948), *The Life of Riley* (Univ., 1949), *Reign of Terror* (EL, 1949), *Mr. Soft Touch* (Col., 1949), *The Baron of Arizona* (Lip., 1950), *The Furies* (Par., 1950), *Lone Star* (MGM, 1952), *Latin Lovers* (MGM, 1953), *Track of the Cat* (WB, 1954), *Back From Eternity* (RKO, 1956), *The Unholy Wife* (Univ., 1957), *The Big Fisherman* (BV, 1959), *A Summer Place* (WB, 1959), *Tammy, Tell Me True* (Univ., 1961), *The Wonderful World of the Brothers Grimm* (MGM, 1962), *Tammy and the Doctor* (Univ., 1963).

Shirley Booth and Shirley MacLaine in *Hot Spell*.

SHIRLEY BOOTH (Thelma Booth Ford) Born August 30, 1907, New York, New York. Married Ed Gardner (1929); divorced 1941. Married William Baker (1943); widowed 1951.

Feature Films: *Come Back, Little Sheba* (Par., 1952), *Main Street to Broadway* (MGM, 1953), *About Mrs. Leslie* (Par., 1954), *The Matchmaker* (Par., 1958), *Hot Spell* (Par., 1958).

VEDA ANN BORG Born January 11, 1915, Boston, Massachusetts. Married Paul Herrick (1942); divorced. Married Andrew McLaglen (1946), child: Andrew; divorced 1958.

Feature Films: *Three Cheers for Love* (Par., 1936), *Men in Exile* (WB, 1937), *Kid Galahad* (WB, 1937), *The Case of the Stuttering Bishop* (WB, 1937), *Public Wedding* (WB, 1937), *The Singing Marine* (WB, 1937), *Confession* (WB, 1937), *San Quentin* (WB, 1937), *Marry the*

Veda Ann Borg, Basil Rathbone, Kay Francis and Laura Hope Crews in *Confession.*

Ernest Borgnine, Lloyd Bridges and Lenore Lonergan in *The Whistle at Eaton Falls.*

Girl (WB, 1937), *It's Love I'm After* (WB, 1937), *Submarine D-1* (WB, 1937), *Varsity Show* (WB, 1937), *Alcatraz Island* (WB, 1937), *Missing Witness* (WB, 1937), *She Loved a Fireman* (WB, 1938), *Over the Wall* (WB, 1938), *Cafe Hostess* (Col., 1939), *The Law Comes to Texas* (Col., 1939), *A Miracle on Main Street* (Col., 1940), *The Shadow* (Col. serial, 1940), *I Take This Oath* (PRC, 1940), *Dr. Christian Meets the Women* (RKO, 1940), *Laughing at Danger* (Mon., 1940), *Glamour for Sale* (Col., 1940), *Bitter Sweet* (MGM, 1940), *Behind the News* (Rep., 1940), *The Arkansas Judge* (Rep., 1941), *The Penalty* (MGM, 1941), *The Get-Away* (MGM, 1941), *The Pittsburgh Kid* (Rep., 1941), *Honky Tonk* (MGM, 1941), *Down in San Diego* (MGM, 1941), *The Corsican Brothers* (UA, 1941), *Duke of the Navy* (PRC, 1942), *About Face* (UA, 1942), *She's in the Army* (Mon., 1942), *Two Yanks in Trinidad* (Col., 1942), *I Married an Angel* (MGM, 1942), *Lady in a Jam* (Univ., 1942), *Murder in Times Square* (Col., 1943), *The Isle of Forgotten Sins* (PRC, 1943), *Revenge of the Zombies* (Mon., 1943), *The Girl From Monterey* (PRC, 1943), *The Unknown Guest* (Mon., 1943), *False Faces* (Rep., 1943), *Something to Shout About* (Col., 1943), *Smart Guy* (Mon., 1944), *Standing Room Only* (Par., 1944), *Irish Eyes Are Smiling* (20th, 1944), *Detective Kitty O'Day* (Mon., 1944), *Marked Trails* (Mon., 1944), *The Girl Who Dared* (Rep., 1944), *The Big Noise* (20th, 1944), *The Falcon in Hollywood* (RKO, 1944), *Jungle Raiders* (Col., serial, 1945), *What a Blonde* (RKO, 1945), *Fog Island* (PRC, 1945), *Rough, Tough and Ready* (Col., 1945), *Bring On the Girls* (Par., 1945), *Don Juan Quilligan* (20th, 1945), *Scared Stiff* (Par., 1945), *Nob Hill* (20th, 1945), *Dangerous Intruder* (PRC, 1945), *Love, Honor and Goodbye* (Rep., 1945), *Mildred Pierce* (WB, 1945), *Life With Blondie* (Col., 1946), *Avalanche* (PRC, 1946), *Accomplice* (PRC, 1946), *Wife Wanted* (Mon., 1946), *The Fabulous Suzanne* (Rep., 1946), *The Pilgrim Lady* (Rep., 1947), *Big Town* (Par., 1947), *The Bachelor and the Bobby Soxer* (RKO, 1947), *Mother Wore Tights* (20th, 1947), *Blonde Savage* (EL, 1948), *Julia Misbehaves* (MGM, 1948), *Chicken Every Sunday* (20th, 1948), *Mississippi Rhythm* (Mon., 1949), *One Last Fling* (WB, 1949), *Forgotten Women* (Mon., 1949), *Rider From Tucson* (RKO, 1950), *The Kangaroo Kid* (Howard C. Brown Productions, 1950), *Aaron Slick From Punkin' Crick* (Par., 1952), *Big Jim McLain* (WB, 1952), *Hold That Line* (Mon., 1952), *A Perilous Journey* (Rep., 1953), *Mister Scoutmaster* (20th, 1953), *Hot News* (AA, 1953), *Three Sailors and a Girl* (WB, 1953), *Bitter Creek* (AA, 1954), *You're Never Too Young* (Par., 1955), *Guys and Dolls* (MGM, 1955), *Love Me or Leave Me* (MGM, 1955), *I'll Cry Tomorrow* (MGM, 1955), *Frontier Gambler* (Associated, 1956), *The Fearmakers* (UA, 1958), *Thunder in the Sun* (Par., 1959), *The Alamo* (UA, 1960).

ERNEST BORGNINE (Ermes Effron Borgnine) Born January 24, 1917, Hamden, Connecticut. Married Rhoda Kemins (1949), child: Nancy; divorced 1958. Married Katy Jurado (1959); divorced 1964. Married Ethel Merman (1964); divorced 1964. Married Donna Rancourt (1965), children: Sharon, Christopher.

Feature Films: *China Corsair* (Col., 1951), *Whistle at Eaton Falls* (Col., 1951), *The Mob* (Col., 1951), *From Here to Eternity* (Col., 1953), *The Stranger Wore a Gun* (Col., 1953), *Demetrius and the Gladiators* (20th, 1954), *The Bounty Hunter* (WB, 1954), *Johnny Guitar* (Rep.,

1954), *Vera Cruz* (UA, 1954), *Bad Day at Black Rock* (MGM, 1954), *Run for Cover* (Par., 1955), *Marty* (UA, 1955), *Violent Saturday* (20th, 1955), *The Last Command* (Rep., 1955), *The Square Jungle* (Univ., 1955), *Jubal* (Col., 1956), *The Catered Affair* (MGM, 1956), *The Best Things in Life Are Free* (20th, 1956), *Three Brave Men* (20th, 1957), *The Vikings* (UA, 1958), *The Badlanders* (MGM, 1958), *Torpedo Run* (MGM, 1958), *The Rabbit Trap* (UA, 1959), *Man on a String* (Col., 1960), *Pay or Die* (AA, 1960), *Go Naked in the World* (MGM, 1961), *Season of Passion* (UA, 1961), *Barabbas* (Col., 1962), *McHale's Navy* (Univ., 1964), *The Flight of the Phoenix* (20th, 1965), *The Oscar* (Par., 1966), *The Dirty Dozen* (MGM, 1967), *Chuka* (Par., 1967), *Ice Station Zebra* (MGM, 1968), *The Legend of Lylah Clare* (MGM, 1968).

STEPHEN BOYD Born July 4, 1928, Belfast, Ireland. Married Mariella de Sarzona (1958); divorced 1959.

English-Language Feature Films: *An Alligator Named Daisy* (Rank, 1955), *A Hill in Korea* (British Lion Films Ltd., 1956), *The Man Who Never Was* (20th, 1956), *Abandon Ship* (Col., 1957), *Island in the Sun* (20th, 1957), *Seven Thunders* (Rank, 1957), *The Night That Heaven Fell* (Kingsley-International, 1958), *The Bravados* (20th, 1958), *Ben-Hur* (MGM, 1959), *Woman Obsessed* (20th, 1959), *The Best of Everything* (20th, 1959), *The Big Gamble* (20th, 1961), *Lisa* (20th, 1962), *Billy Rose's Jumbo* (MGM, 1962), *Imperial Venus* (Rizzoli, 1963), *The Fall of the Roman Empire* (Par., 1964), *The Third Secret* (20th, 1964), *Genghis Khan* (Col., 1965), *The Oscar* (Par., 1966), *Fantastic Voyage* (20th,

Stephen Boyd and Gregory Ratoff in *The Big Gamble.*

1966), *The Bible* (20th, 1966), *The Caper of the Golden Bulls* (Embassy, 1967), *Assignment K* (Col., 1968).

WILLIAM BOYD Born June 5, 1898, Cambridge, Ohio. Married Ruth Miller (1921); divorced. Married Elinor Faire; divorced 1929. Married Dorothy Sebastian (1930); divorced 1936. Married Grace Bradley (1937).

William Boyd and Judith Allen in *Burning Gold*.

Sound Feature Films: *Flying Fool* (Pathé, 1929), *High Voltage* (Pathé, 1929), *Locked Door* (UA, 1929), *His First Command* (Pathé, 1930), *Officer O'Brien* (Pathé, 1930), *Painted Desert* (Pathé, 1931), *Beyond Victory* (Pathé, 1931), *Big Gamble* (Pathé, 1931), *Suicide Fleet* (Pathé, 1931), *Carnival Boat* (RKO, 1932), *Lucky Devils* (RKO, 1933), *Men of America* (RKO, 1933), *Emergency Call* (RKO, 1933), *Flaming Gold* (RKO, 1934), *Cheaters* (Bert Lubin, 1934), *Port of Lost Dreams* (Chesterfield, 1934), *Hop-A-Long Cassidy* (Par., 1935), *Racing Luck* (Rep., 1935), *Bar 20 Rides Again* (Par., 1935), *Eagle's Brood* (Par., 1935), *Call of the Prairie* (Par., 1936), *Three on the Trail* (Par., 1936), *Federal Agent* (Rep., 1936), *Burning Gold* (Rep., 1936), *Heart of the West* (Par., 1936), *Go Get 'Em Haines* (Rep., 1936), *Hopalong Cassidy Returns* (Par., 1936), *Trail Dust* (Par., 1936), *Borderland* (Par., 1937), *Hills of Old Wyoming* (Par., 1937), *North of the Rio Grande* (Par., 1937), *Rustler's Valley* (Par., 1937), *Hopalong Rides Again* (Par., 1937), *Texas Trail* (Par., 1937), *Partners of the Plains* (Par., 1937), *Cassidy of Bar 20* (Par., 1938), *Bar 20 Justice* (Par., 1938), *Heart of Arizona* (Par., 1938), *Pride of the West* (Par., 1938), *In Old Mexico* (Par., 1938), *The Frontiersman* (Par., 1938), *Sunset Trail* (Par., 1938), *Silver on the Sage* (Par., 1939), *Law of the Pampas* (Par., 1939), *Range War* (Par., 1939), *Renegade Trail* (Par., 1939), *Santa Fe Marshal* (Par., 1940), *Showdown* (Par., 1940), *Hidden Gold* (Par., 1940), *Stagecoach War* (Par., 1940), *Three Men From Texas* (Par., 1940), *Doomed Caravan* (Par., 1941), *In Old Colorado* (Par., 1941), *Pirates on Horseback* (Par., 1941), *Border Vigilantes* (Par., 1941), *Wide-Open Town* (Par., 1941), *Secrets of the Wasteland* (Par., 1941), *Stick to Your Guns* (Par., 1941), *Twilight on the Trail* (Par., 1941), *Outlaws of the Desert* (Par., 1941), *Riders of the Timberline* (Par., 1941), *Undercover Man* (UA, 1942), *Lost Canyon* (UA, 1943), *Leather Burners* (UA, 1943), *Hoppy Serves a Writ* (UA, 1943), *Border Patrol* (UA, 1943), *Colt Comrades* (UA, 1943), *Bar 20* (UA, 1943), *False Colors* (UA, 1943), *Riders of the Deadline* (UA, 1943), *Texas Masquerade* (UA, 1944), *Lumberjack* (UA, 1944), *Forty Thieves* (UA, 1944), *Mystery Man* (UA, 1944), *The Devil's Playground* (UA, 1946), *Fool's Gold* (UA, 1946), *Unexpected Guest* (UA, 1946), *Dangerous Venture* (UA, 1947), *Hoppy's Holiday* (UA, 1947), *The Marauders* (UA, 1947), *Silent Conflict*

Charles Boyer and Katharine Hepburn in *Break of Hearts*.

(UA, 1948), *The Dead Don't Dream* (UA, 1948), *Strange Gamble* (UA, 1948), *Sinister Journey* (UA, 1948), *False Paradise* (UA, 1948), *Borrowed Trouble* (UA, 1948), *The Greatest Show On Earth* (Par., 1952).*

*Unbilled guest appearance

CHARLES BOYER Born August 28, 1899, Figeac Lot, France. Married Pat Paterson (1934), child: Michael.

English-Language Sound Feature Films: *Red-Headed Woman* (MGM, 1932), *The Man From Yesterday* (Par., 1932), *The Only Girl* (Gaumont-British, 1933), *Caravan* (Fox, 1934), *Thunder in the East* (UA, 1934), *Private Worlds* (Par., 1935), *Shanghai* (Par., 1935), *Break of Hearts* (RKO, 1935), *The Garden of Allah* (UA, 1936), *Tovarich* (WB, 1937), *Conquest* (MGM, 1937), *History Is Made at Night* (UA, 1937), *Algiers* (UA, 1938), *Love Affair* (RKO, 1939), *When Tomorrow Comes* (Univ., 1939), *All This, and Heaven, Too* (WB, 1940), *Hold Back the Dawn* (Par., 1941), *Back Street* (Univ., 1941), *Appointment for Love* (Univ., 1941), *Tales of Manhattan* (20th, 1942), *The Heart of a Nation* (narrator; AFE, 1943), *The Constant Nymph* (WB, 1943), *Flesh and Fantasy* (Univ., 1943), *Gaslight* (MGM, 1944), *Together Again* (Col., 1944), *Confidential Agent* (WB, 1945), *Cluny Brown* (20th, 1946), *A Woman's Vengeance* (Univ., 1947), *Arch of Triumph* (UA, 1948), *The First Legion* (UA, 1951), *The Thirteenth Letter* (20th, 1951), *The Happy Time* (Col., 1952), *Thunder in the East* (Par., 1953), *The Cobweb* (MGM, 1955), *Around the World in 80 Days* (UA, 1956), *The Buccaneer* (Par., 1958), *Fanny* (WB, 1961), *The Four Horsemen of the Apocalypse* (MGM, 1962), *Love Is a Ball* (UA, 1963), *A Very Special Favor* (Univ., 1965), *How to Steal a Million* (20th, 1966), *Is Paris Burning?* (Par., 1966), *Casino Royale* (Col., 1967), *Barefoot in the Park* (Par., 1967), *The Day the Hot Line Got Hot* (AIP, 1968).

Eddie Bracken and June Preisser in *Sweater Girl*.

EDDIE BRACKEN (Edward Vincent Bracken) Born February 7, 1920, Astoria, New York. Married Connie Nickerson (1939), children: Judith, Caroline, Michael, Susan, David.

Feature Films: *Too Many Girls* (RKO, 1940), *Life With Henry* (Par., 1941), *Reaching for the Sun* (Par., 1941), *Caught in the Draft* (Par., 1941), *Sweater Girl* (Par., 1942), *The Fleet's In* (Par., 1942), *Star Spangled Rhythm* (Par., 1942), *Happy Go Lucky* (Par., 1943), *Young and Willing* (UA, 1943), *The Miracle of Morgan's Creek* (Par., 1944), *Hail the Conquering Hero* (Par., 1944), *Rainbow Island* (Par., 1944), *Out of This World* (Par., 1945), *Bring on the Girls* (Par., 1945), *Duffy's Tavern* (Par., 1945), *Hold That Blonde* (Par., 1945), *Ladies' Man* (Par., 1947), *Fun on a Weekend* (UA, 1947), *The Girl From Jones Beach* (WB, 1949), *Summer Stock* (MGM, 1950), *Two Tickets to Broadway* (RKO, 1951), *We're Not Married* (20th, 1952), *About Face* (WB, 1952), *A Slight Case of Larceny* (MGM, 1953).

Alice Brady and Conway Tearle in *Should Ladies Behave?*

ALICE BRADY Born November 2, 1892, New York, New York. Married James Crane (1919), child: Donald; divorced 1922. Died October 28, 1939.

Sound Feature Films: *When Ladies Meet* (MGM, 1933), *Broadway to Hollywood* (MGM, 1933), *Beauty for Sale* (MGM, 1933), *Stage Mother* (MGM, 1933), *Should Ladies Behave?* (MGM, 1933), *Miss Fane's Baby Is Stolen* (Par., 1934), *The Gay Divorcee* (RKO, 1934), *Let 'Em Have It* (UA, 1935), *Gold Diggers of 1935* (WB, 1935), *Lady Tubbs* (Univ., 1935), *Metropolitan* (20th, 1935), *The Harvester* (Rep., 1936), *My Man Godfrey* (Univ., 1936), *Go West, Young Man* (Par., 1936), *Mind Your Own Business* (Par., 1936), *Three Smart Girls* (Univ., 1937), *Call It a Day* (WB, 1937), *Mama Steps Out* (MGM, 1937), *Mr. Dodd Takes the Air* (WB, 1937), *100 Men and a Girl* (Univ., 1937), *Merry-Go-Round of 1938* (Univ., 1937), *In Old Chicago* (20th, 1937), *Joy of Living* (RKO, 1938), *Goodbye, Broadway* (Univ., 1938), *Zenobia* (UA, 1939), *Young Mr. Lincoln* (20th, 1939).

Marlon Brando, Pat Hingle, Sandra Church and Judson Pratt in *The Ugly American.*

MARLON BRANDO (Marlon Brando, Jr.) Born April 3, 1924, Omaha, Nebraska. Married Anna Kashfi (1957), children: Christian, Devi; divorced 1959. Married Movita Castenada (1960); divorced.

Feature Films: *The Men* (UA, 1950), *A Streetcar Named Desire* (WB, 1951), *Viva Zapata!* (20th, 1952), *Julius Caesar* (MGM, 1953), *The Wild One* (Col., 1954), *On the Waterfront* (Col., 1954), *Desiree* (20th, 1954), *Guys and Dolls* (MGM, 1955), *The Teahouse of the August Moon* (MGM, 1956), *Sayonara* (WB, 1957), *The Young Lions* (20th, 1958), *The Fugitive Kind* (UA, 1960), *One-Eyed Jacks* (Par., 1961), *Mutiny on the Bounty* (MGM, 1962), *The Ugly American* (Univ., 1962), *Bedtime Story* (Univ., 1964), *The Saboteur—Code Name Morituri* (20th, 1965), *The Chase* (Col., 1966), *The Appaloosa* (Univ., 1966), *The Countess From Hong Kong* (Univ., 1967), *Reflections in a Golden Eye* (WB, 1967), *The Night of the Following Day* (Univ., 1968), *Candy* (Cinerama, 1968).

Heather Sears, Joan Crawford and Rossano Brazzi in *The Story of Esther Costello.*

ROSSANO BRAZZI Born September 18, 1918, Bologna, Italy. Married Lydia Bertolina (1940).

English-Language Feature Films: *Little Women* (MGM, 1949), *Volcano* (UA, 1953), *The Barefoot Contessa* (UA, 1954), *Three Coins in the Fountain* (20th, 1954), *Angela* (20th, 1955), *Summertime* (UA, 1955), *Loser Takes All* (British Lion, 1956), *Interlude* (Univ., 1957), *The Story of Esther Costello* (Col., 1957), *Legend of the Lost* (UA, 1957), *South Pacific* (Magna, 1958), *A Certain Smile* (20th, 1958), *Count Your Blessings* (MGM, 1959), *Light in the Piazza* (MGM, 1962), *Rome Adventure* (WB, 1962), *Dark Purpose* (Univ., 1964), *The Battle of the Villa Fiorita* (WB, 1965), *The Christmas That Almost Wasn't* (Childhood Productions, 1966), *The Bobo* (WB, 1967), *Woman Times Seven* (Embassy, 1967), *East of Java* (Cinerama, 1968).

WALTER BRENNAN Born July 25, 1894, Swampscott, Massachusetts. Married Ruth Wells (1920), children: Arthur, Walter, Ruth.

Sound Feature Films: *The Long, Long Trail* (Univ., 1929) *The Shannons of Broadway* (Univ., 1929) *Smilin' Guns* (Univ., 1929) *King of Jazz* (Univ., 1930) *One Hysterical Night* (Univ., 1930) *Dancing Dynamite* (Capitol Film Exchange, 1931) *Neck and Neck* (Sono Art-World Wide, 1931), *Law and Order* (Univ., 1932), *Texas Cyclone* (Col., 1932) *Two-Fisted Law* (Col., 1932) *All American* (Univ., 1932) *Parachute Jumper* (WB, 1933), *Man of Action* (Col., 1933), *Fighting for Justice* (Col., 1933), *Sing, Sinner, Sing* (Majestic, 1933) *Strange People* (Chesterfield, 1933) *Silent Men* (Col., 1933), *One Year Later* (Alliance, 1933) *Good Dame* (Par., 1934), *Half a Sinner* (Univ., 1934), *Northern Frontier* (Ambassador, 1935), *The Wedding Night* (UA, 1935), *Law Beyond the Range* (Col., 1935), *Bride of Frankenstein* (Univ., 1935), *Lady Tubbs* (Univ., 1935), *Man on the Flying Trapeze* (Par., 1935) *Metropolitan* (Fox, 1935), *Barbary Coast* (UA, 1935), *Seven Keys to Baldpate* (RKO, 1935), *These Three* (UA, 1936), *The Three Godfathers* (MGM, 1936), *The Moon's Our Home* (Par., 1936), *Fury* (MGM, 1936), *The Prescott Kid* (Col., 1936), *Come and Get It* (UA, 1936), *Banjo on My Knee*

Jane Withers and Walter Brennan in *Wild and Wooly.*

(20th, 1936), *She's Dangerous* (Univ., 1937), *When Love Is Young* (Univ., 1937), *Affair of Cappy Ricks* (Rep., 1937), *Wild and Woolly* (20th, 1937), *The Adventures of Tom Sawyer* (UA, 1938), *The Buccaneer* (Par., 1938), *The Texans* (Par., 1938), *Mother Carey's Chickens* (RKO, 1938), *Kentucky* (20th, 1938), *The Cowboy and the Lady* (UA, 1938), *The Story of Vernon and Irene Castle* (RKO, 1939), *They Shall Have Music* (UA, 1939), *Stanley and Livingstone* (20th, 1939), *Joe and Ethel Turp Call on the President* (MGM, 1939), *Northwest Passage* (MGM, 1940), *Maryland* (20th, 1940), *The Westerner* (UA, 1940), *This Woman Is Mine* (Univ., 1941), *Nice Girl?* (Univ., 1941), *Meet John Doe* (WB, 1941), *Sergeant York* (WB, 1941), *Swamp Water* (20th, 1941), *Rise and Shine* (20th, 1941), *The Pride of the Yankees* (RKO, 1942), *Stand By for Action* (MGM, 1942), *Slightly Dangerous* (MGM, 1943), *Hangmen Also Die* (UA, 1943), *The North Star* (RKO, 1943), *Home in Indiana* (20th, 1944), *To Have and Have Not* (WB, 1944), *The Princess and the Pirate* (RKO, 1944), *Dakota* (Rep., 1945), *A Stolen Life* (WB, 1946), *Centennial Summer* (20th, 1946), *Nobody Lives Forever* (WB, 1946), *My Darling Clementine* (20th, 1946), *Driftwood* (Rep., 1947), *Scudda Hoo! Scudda Hay!* (20th, 1948), *Red River* (UA, 1948), *Blood on the Moon* (RKO, 1948), *The Green Promise* (RKO, 1949) *The Great Dan Patch* (UA, 1949), *Brimstone* (Rep., 1949), *Task Force* (WB, 1949), *Singing Guns* (Rep., 1950), *Ticket to Tomahawk* (20th, 1950), *Curtain Call at Cactus Creek* (Univ., 1950), *The Showdown* (Rep., 1950), *Surrender* (Rep., 1950), *Best of the Bad Men* (RKO, 1951), *Along the Great Divide* (RKO, 1951), *The Wild Blue Yonder* (Rep., 1951), *Return of the Texan* (20th, 1952), *Lure of the Wilderness* (20th, 1952), *Sea of Lost Ships* (Rep., 1953), *Drums Across the River* (Univ., 1954), *Four Guns to the Border* (Univ., 1954), *Bad Day at Black Rock* (MGM, 1954), *The Far Country* (Univ., 1955), *At Gunpoint* (AA, 1955), *Come Next Spring* (Rep., 1956), *Glory* (RKO, 1956), *Good-Bye, My Lady* (WB, 1956), *The Proud Ones* (20th, 1956), *Tammy and the Bachelor* (Univ., 1957), *Shoot-Out at Big Sag* (Parallel, 1962), *The Way to the Gold* (20th, 1957), *God Is My Partner* (20th, 1957), *Rio Bravo* (WB, 1959), *How the West Was Won* (MGM, 1962), *Those Calloways* (BV, 1964), *The Oscar* (Par., 1966), *Who's Minding the Mint?* (Col., 1967), *The Gnome-Mobile* (BV, 1967), *The One and Only Genuine, Original Family Band* (BV, 1968).

GEORGE BRENT (George B. Nolan.) Born March 15, 1904, Dublin, Ireland. Married Helen Campbell (1922); divorced 1922. Married Ruth Chatterton (1932); divorced 1934. Married Constance Worth (1939); divorced 1939. Married Ann Sheridan (1942); divorced 1943. Married Janet Michael (1947), children: Suzanne, Barry.

Sound Feature Films: *Under Suspicion* (Fox, 1930), *Lightning Warrior* (Mascot serial, 1931), *Once a Sinner* (Fox, 1931), *Fair Warning* (Fox, 1931), *Charlie Chan Carries On* (Fox, 1931), *Ex-Bad Boy* (Univ., 1931), *So Big* (WB, 1932), *The Rich Are Always With Us* (WB, 1932), *Week-End Marriage* (WB, 1932), *Miss Pinkerton* (WB, 1932), *Purchase Price*

Kay Francis and George Brent in *Living on Velvet.*

(WB, 1932), *The Crash* (WB, 1932), *They Call It Sin* (WB, 1932), *Luxury Liner* (Par., 1933), *42nd Street* (WB, 1933), *The Keyhole* (WB, 1933), *Lilly Turner* (WB, 1933), *Baby Face* (WB, 1933), *Female* (WB, 1933), *Stamboul Quest* (MGM, 1934), *Housewife* (WB, 1934), *Desirable* (WB, 1934), *The Painted Veil* (MGM, 1934), *Living on Velvet* (WB, 1935), *Stranded* (WB, 1935), *Front Page Woman* (WB, 1935), *The Goose and the Gander* (WB, 1935), *Special Agent* (WB, 1935), *In Person* (RKO, 1935), *The Right to Live* (WB, 1936), *Snowed Under* (WB, 1936), *The Golden Arrow* (WB, 1936), *The Case Against Mrs. Ames* (Par., 1936), *Give Me Your Heart* (WB, 1936), *More Than a Secretary* (Col., 1936), *God's Country and the Woman* (WB, 1936), *The Go-Getter* (WB, 1937), *Mountain Justice* (WB, 1937), *Submarine D-1* (WB, 1937), *Gold Is Where You Find It* (WB, 1938), *Jezebel* (WB, 1938), *Racket Busters* (WB, 1938), *Secrets of an Actress* (WB, 1938), *Wings of the Navy* (WB, 1939), *Dark Victory* (WB, 1939), *Old Maid* (WB, 1939), *The Rains Came* (20th, 1939), *The Man Who Talked Too Much* (WB, 1940), *South of Suez* (WB, 1940), *Honeymoon for Three* (WB, 1941), *The Great Lie* (WB, 1941), *They Dare Not Love* (Col., 1941), *International Lady* (UA, 1941), *In This Our Life* (WB, 1942), *Twin Beds* (UA, 1942), *The Gay Sisters* (WB, 1942), *You Can't Escape Forever* (WB, 1942), *Silver Queen* (UA, 1942), *The Affairs of Susan* (Par., 1945), *Experiment Perilous* (RKO, 1945), *My Reputation* (WB, 1946), *The Spiral Staircase* (RKO, 1946), *Tomorrow Is Forever* (RKO, 1946), *Lover Come Back* (Univ., 1946), *Temptation* (Univ., 1946), *Slave Girl* (Univ., 1947), *Out of the Blue* (EL, 1947), *The Corpse Came C.O.D.* (Col., 1947), *Christmas Eve* (UA, 1947), *Luxury Liner* (MGM, 1948), *Angel on the Amazon* (Rep., 1948), *Red Canyon* (Univ., 1949), *Illegal Entry* (Univ., 1949), *Kid From Cleveland* (Rep., 1949), *Bride for Sale* (RKO, 1949), *FBI Girl* (Lip., 1951), *Man Bait* (Lip., 1952), *Montana Belle* (RKO, 1952), *Tangier Incident* (AA, 1953), *Death of a Scoundrel* (RKO, 1956).

Francis McDonald, Lloyd Bridges and Lon Chaney, Jr., in *Strange Confession.*

LLOYD BRIDGES Born January 15, 1913, San Leandro, California. Married Dorothy Simpson (1938), children: Beau, Jeffrey.

Feature Films: *The Lone Wolf Takes a Chance* (Col., 1941), *Cadets on Parade* (Col., 1941), *Son of Davy Crockett* (Col., 1941), *Here Comes Mr. Jordan* (Col., 1941), *The Medico of Painted Springs* (Col., 1941), *Two Latins From Manhattan* (Col., 1941), *Harmon of Michigan* (Col., 1941), *Alias Boston Blackie* (Col., 1942), *Sing for Your Supper* (Col., 1942), *Stand By All Networks* (Col., 1942), *Blondie Goes to College* (Col., 1942), *Shut My Big Mouth* (Col., 1942), *Flight Lieutenant* (Col., 1942), *Atlantic Convoy* (Col., 1942), *Talk of the Town* (Col., 1942), *Riders of the Northland* (Col., 1942), *North of the Rockies* (Col., 1942), *The Spirit of Stanford* (Col., 1942), *Commandos Strike at Dawn* (Col., 1942), *Pardon My Gun* (Col., 1943), *Sahara* (Col., 1943), *Hail to the Rangers* (Col., 1943), *The Heat's On* (Col., 1943), *Passport to Suez* (Col., 1943), *Crime Doctor's Strangest Case* (Col., 1943), *She's a Soldier, Too* (Col., 1944), *Louisiana Hayride* (Col., 1944), *The Master Race*

Hillary Brooke and Robert Lowery in *Big Town*.

Cesar Romero and Phyllis Brooks in *Dangerously Yours*.

(RKO, 1944), *Saddle Leather Law* (Col., 1944), *A Walk in the Sun* (20th, 1945), *Miss Susie Slagle's* (Par., 1945), *Strange Confession* (Univ., 1945), *Abilene Town* (UA, 1946), *Canyon Passage* (Univ., 1946), *Ramrod* (UA, 1947), *The Trouble With Women* (Par., 1947), *Secret Service Investigator* (Rep., 1948), *16 Fathoms Deep* (Mon., 1948), *Red Canyon* (Univ., 1949), *Hide-Out* (Rep., 1949), *Home of the Brave* (UA, 1949), *Calamity Jane and Sam Bass* (Univ., 1949), *Trapped* (EL, 1949), *Colt .45* (WB, 1950), *Rocket Ship XM* (Lip., 1950), *The White Tower* (RKO, 1950), *The Sound of Fury* (UA, 1950), *Little Big Horn* (Lip., 1951), *Three Steps North* (UA, 1951), *The Whistle at Eaton Falls* (Col., 1951), *High Noon* (UA, 1952), *Plymouth Adventure* (MGM, 1952), *Last of the Comanches* (Col., 1952) *City of Bad Men* (20th, 1953) *The Kid From Left Field* (20th, 1953) *The Limping Man* (Lip., 1953) *Deadly Game* (Lip., 1954), *Pride of the Blue Grass* (AA, 1954), *Wichita* (AA, 1955), *Wetbacks* (Bob Banner Associates, 1956), *The Rainmaker* (Par., 1956), *Ride Out for Revenge* (UA, 1957), *The Goddess* (Col., 1958), *Around the World Under the Sea* (MGM, 1966), *Attack on the Iron Coast* (UA, 1968).

HILLARY BROOKE (Beatrice Peterson) Born Long Island, New York. Married Jack Vaughn; divorced. Married Raymond Klune, child: Donald.

Feature Films: *New Faces of 1937* (RKO, 1937), *Eternally Yours* (UA, 1939), *Florian* (MGM, 1940), *New Moon* (MGM, 1940), *The Philadelphia Story* (MGM, 1940), *Two Girls on Broadway* (MGM, 1940), *Dr. Jekyll and Mr. Hyde* (MGM, 1941), *Maisie was a Lady* (MGM, 1941), *Mr. and Mrs. North* (MGM, 1941), *Unfinished Business* (MGM, 1941), *Born to Sing* (MGM, 1942), *Ship Ahoy* (MGM, 1942), *Sleepytime Gal* (Rep., 1942), *Wake Island* (Par., 1942), *To the Shores of Tripoli* (20th, 1942), *Counter Espionage* (Col., 1942), *Sherlock Holmes and the Voice of Terror* (Univ., 1942), *Sherlock Holmes Faces Death* (Univ., 1943), *Lady in the Dark* (Par., 1944), *And the Angels Sing* (Par., 1944), *Practically Yours* (Par., 1944), *Jane Eyre* (20th, 1944), *Standing Room Only* (Par., 1944), *Ministry of Fear* (Par., 1944), *The Enchanted Cottage* (RKO, 1945), *The Crime Doctor's Courage* (Col., 1945), *The Woman in Green* (Univ., 1945), *Road to Utopia* (Par., 1945), *Up Goes Maisie* (MGM, 1946), *Strange Impersonation* (Rep., 1946), *Monsieur Beaucaire* (Par., 1946), *The Gentleman Misbehaves* (Col., 1946), *Earl Carroll's Sketchbook* (Rep., 1946), *Strange Journey* (20th, 1946), *The Strange Woman* (UA, 1946), *Big Town* (Par., 1947), *I Cover Big Town* (Par., 1947), *Big Town After Dark* (Par., 1947), *Big Town Scandal* (Par., 1948), *The Fuller Brush Man* (Col., 1948), *Let's Live Again* (20th, 1948), *Africa Screams* (UA, 1949), *Alimony* (EL, 1949), *Unmasked* (Rep., 1950), *The Admiral Was a Lady* (UA, 1950), *Beauty on Parade* (Col., 1950), *Bodyhold* (Col., 1950), *Vendetta* (RKO, 1950), *Lucky Losers* (Mon., 1950), *Insurance Investigator* (Rep., 1951), *Skipalong Rosenbloom* (UA, 1951), *The Lost Continent* (Lip., 1951), *Confidence Girl* (UA, 1952), *Abbott and Costello Meet Captain Kidd* (WB, 1952), *Never Wave at a WAC* (RKO, 1952), *Mexican Manhunt* (AA, 1953), *The Lady Wants Mink* (Rep., 1953), *Invaders From Mars* (20th, 1953), *The Maze* (AA, 1953), *Heat Wave* (Lip., 1954), *Dragon's Gold* (UA, 1954), *Bengazi* (RKO, 1955), *The Man Who Knew Too Much* (Par., 1956), *Spoilers of the Forest* (Rep., 1957).

PHYLLIS BROOKS (Phyllis Weiler) Born July 18, 1914, Boise, Idaho. Married Torbert MacDonald, child: Torbert.

Feature Films: *I've Been Around* (Univ., 1934), *McFadden's Flats* (Par., 1935), *Lady Tubbs* (Univ., 1935), *To Beat the Band* (RKO, 1935), *Another Face* (RKO, 1935), *You Can't Have Everything* (20th, 1937), *Dangerously Yours* (20th, 1937), *City Girl* (20th, 1937), *Rebecca of Sunnybrook Farm* (20th, 1938), *In Old Chicago* (20th, 1938), *Walking Down Broadway* (20th, 1938), *Straight, Place and Show* (20th, 1938), *Up the River* (20th, 1938), *Charlie Chan in Honolulu* (20th, 1938), *Charlie Chan in Reno* (20th, 1939), *Slightly Honorable* (UA, 1940), *The Flying Squad* (Associated British, 1940), *The Shanghai Gesture* (UA, 1941), *Silver Spurs* (Rep., 1943), *Hi'Ya, Sailor* (Univ., 1943), *No Place for a Lady* (Col., 1943), *Lady in the Dark* (Par., 1944), *The Unseen* (Par., 1945), *High Powered* (Par., 1945), *Dangerous Passage* (Par., 1945).

Judy Canova, John Hubbard, Joe E. Brown and Gus Schilling in *Chatterbox*.

JOE E. BROWN (Joseph Even Brown) Born July 28, 1892, Hogate, Ohio. Married Kathryn McGraw (1915), children: Don, Joe, Mary, Kathryn.

Sound Feature Films *On With the Show!* (WB, 1929), *Painted Faces* (Tif., 1930), *Song of the West* (WB, 1930), *Hold Everything* (WB, 1930), *Top Speed* (WB, 1930), *Lottery Bride* (UA, 1930), *Maybe It's Love* (WB, 1930), *Going Wild* (WB, 1931), *Sit Tight* (WB, 1931),

Broad-Minded (WB, 1931), *Local Boy Makes Good* (WB, 1931), *Fireman Save My Child* (WB, 1932), *The Tenderfoot* (WB, 1932), *You Said a Mouthful* (WB, 1932), *Elmer the Great* (WB, 1933), *Son of a Sailor* (WB, 1933), *A Very Honorable Guy* (WB, 1934), *Circus Clown* (WB, 1934), *Six Day Bike Rider* (WB, 1934), *Alibi Ike* (WB, 1935), *Bright Lights* (WB, 1935), *A Midsummer Night's Dream* (WB, 1935), *Sons o' Guns* (WB, 1936), *Earthworm Tractors* (WB, 1936), *Polo Joe* (WB, 1936), *When's Your Birthday?* (RKO, 1937), *Riding on Air* (RKO, 1937), *Fit for a King* (RKO, 1937), *Wide Open Faces* (Col., 1938), *The Gladiator* (Col., 1938), *Flirting With Fate* (MGM, 1938), *$1000 a Touchdown* (Par., 1939), *Beware Spooks!* (Col., 1939), *So You Won't Talk* (Col., 1940), *Shut My Big Mouth* (Col., 1942), *Joan of the Ozarks* (Rep., 1942), *Chatterbox* (Rep., 1943), *Casanova in Burlesque* (Rep., 1944), *Pin-Up Girl* (20th, 1944), *Hollywood Canteen* (WB, 1944), *The Tender Years* (20th, 1947), *Show Boat* (MGM, 1951), *Around the World in 80 Days* (UA, 1956), *Some Like It Hot* (UA, 1959), *The Comedy of Terrors* (AIP, 1963).

Nigel Bruce and Rosalind Ivan in *Pursuit to Algiers*.

NIGEL BRUCE (William Nigel Bruce) Born February 4, 1895, Ensenada, Mexico. Married Violet Shelton (1922), children: Jennifer, Pauline. Died October 8, 1953.

Sound Feature Films: *Red Aces* (British, 1929) *The Squeaker* (British Lion, 1931), *Escape* (ARP, 1931), *The Calendar* (British Lion-Gainsborough, 1931), *Lord Camber's Ladies* (BIP, 1932), *The Midshipmaid* (Gaumont-British, 1932), *Channel Crossing* (Gaumont-British, 1933), *I Was a Spy* (Gaumont-British, 1933), *Springtime for Henry* (Fox, 1934), *Stand Up and Cheer* (Fox, 1934), *Coming Out Party* (Fox, 1934), *Murder in Trinidad* (Fox, 1934), *The Lady Is Willing* (Col., 1934), *Treasure Island* (MGM, 1934), *The Scarlet Pimpernel* (UA, 1935), *Becky Sharp* (RKO, 1935), *Jalna* (RKO, 1935), *She* (RKO, 1935), *The Man Who Broke the Bank at Monte Carlo* (Fox, 1935), *The Trail of the Lonesome Pine* (Par., 1936), *Under Two Flags* (20th, 1936), *The White Angel* (WB, 1936), *The Charge of the Light Brigade* (WB, 1936), *Follow Your Heart* (Rep., 1936), *Make Way for a Lady* (RKO, 1936), *The Man I Marry* (Univ., 1936), *Thunder in the City* (Col., 1937), *The Last of Mrs. Cheyney* (MGM, 1937), *The Baroness and the Butler* (20th, 1938), *Kidnapped* (20th, 1938), *Suez* (20th, 1938), *The Hound of the Baskervilles* (20th, 1939), *The Adventures of Sherlock Holmes* (20th, 1939), *Rebecca* (UA, 1940), *Adventure in Diamonds* (Par., 1940), *The Bluebird* (20th, 1940), *Lillian Russell* (20th, 1940), *A Dispatch From Reuters* (WB, 1940), *Hudson's Bay* (20th, 1940), *Playgirl* (RKO, 1941), *Free and Easy* (MGM, 1941), *The Chocolate Soldier* (MGM, 1941), *This Woman Is Mine* (Univ., 1941), *Suspicion* (RKO, 1941), *Roxie Hart* (20th, 1942), *This Above All* (20th, 1942), *Eagle Squadron* (Univ., 1942), *Sherlock Holmes and the Voice of Terror* (Univ., 1942), *Journey For Margaret* (MGM, 1942), *Sherlock Holmes and the Secret Weapon* (Univ., 1942), *Sherlock Holmes in Washington* (Univ., 1943), *Forever and a Day* (RKO, 1943), *Sherlock Holmes Faces Death* (Univ., 1943), *Crazy House* (Univ., 1943),* *Follow the Boys* (Univ., 1944), *The Pearl of Death* (Univ., 1944), *Gypsy Wildcat* (Univ., 1944), *The Scarlet

Virginia Bruce, Edmund Lowe, Grant Mitchell and Nat Pendleton in *The Garden Murder Case*.

Claw (Univ., 1944), *Frenchman's Creek* (Par., 1944), *Son of Lassie* (MGM, 1945), *House of Fear* (Univ., 1945), *The Corn Is Green* (WB, 1945), *The Woman in Green* (Univ., 1945), *Pursuit to Algiers* (Univ., 1945), *Terror by Night* (Univ., 1946), *Dressed to Kill* (Univ., 1946), *The Two Mrs. Carrolls* (WB, 1947), *The Exile* (Univ., 1947), *Julia Misbehaves* (MGM, 1948), *Vendetta* (RKO, 1950), *Hong Kong* (Par., 1951), *Bwana Devil* (UA, 1952).

*Unbilled guest appearance

VIRGINIA BRUCE Born September 29, 1910, Minneapolis, Minnesota. Married John Gilbert (1932), child: Susan; divorced 1934. Married J. Walter Ruben, child: Christopher; widowed. Married Ali Apar; divorced 1940.

Feature Films: *Woman Trap* (Par., 1929), *Why Bring That Up?* (Par., 1929), *The Love Parade* (Par., 1929), *Lilies of the Field* (Par., 1930), *Only the Brave* (Par., 1930), *Slightly Scarlet* (Par., 1930), *Paramount on Parade* (Par., 1930), *Young Eagles* (Par., 1930), *The Love Parade* (Par., 1930), *Safety in Numbers* (Par., 1930), *Social Lion* (Par., 1930), *Hell Divers* (MGM, 1931), *Are You Listening?* (MGM, 1932), *The Wet Parade* (MGM, 1932), *The Miracle Man* (Par., 1932), *Sky Bride* (Par., 1932), *Winner Take All* (WB, 1932), *Downstairs* (MGM, 1932), *Kongo* (MGM, 1932), *A Scarlet Week-End* (MGM, 1932), *Jane Eyre* (Mon., 1934), *The Mighty Barnum* (UA, 1934), *Dangerous Corner* (RKO, 1934), *Times Square Lady* (MGM, 1935), *Society Doctor* (MGM, 1935), *Shadow of Doubt* (MGM, 1935), *Let 'Em Have It* (UA, 1935), *Escapade* (MGM, 1935), *Here Comes the Band* (MGM, 1935), *The Murder Man* (MGM, 1935), *Metropolitan* (20th, 1935), *The Garden Murder Case* (MGM, 1936), *The Great Ziegfeld* (MGM, 1936), *Born to Dance* (MGM, 1936), *Women of Glamour* (Col., 1937), *When Love Is Young* (Univ., 1937), *Between Two Women* (MGM, 1937), *Wife, Doctor and Nurse* (20th, 1937), *The First Hundred Years* (MGM, 1938), *Arsene Lupin Returns* (MGM, 1938), *Bad Man of Brimstone* (MGM, 1938), *Yellow Jack* (MGM, 1938), *Woman Against Woman* (MGM, 1938), *There's That Woman Again* (Col., 1938), *There Goes My Heart* (UA, 1938), *Let Freedom Ring* (MGM, 1939), *Society Lawyer* (MGM, 1939), *Stronger Than Desire* (MGM, 1939), *Flight Angels* (WB, 1940), *The Man Who Talked Too Much* (WB, 1940), *Hired Wife* (Univ., 1940), *The Invisible Woman* (Univ., 1941), *Adventure in Washington* (Col., 1941), *Butch Minds the Baby* (Univ., 1942), *Pardon My Sarong* (Univ., 1942), *Careful, Soft Shoulders* (20th, 1942), *Brazil* (Rep., 1944), *Action in Arabia* (RKO, 1944), *Love, Honor and Goodbye* (Rep., 1945), *The Night Has a Thousand Eyes* (Par., 1948), *State Dept.—File 649* (Film Classics, 1949), *The Reluctant Bride* (Gaumont-British, 1952), *Istanbul* (Turkish, 1953), *Three Grooms for a Bride* (20th, 1957), *Strangers When We Meet* (Col., 1960).

YUL BRYNNER Born July 11, 1915, Sakhalin, Russia. Married Virginia Gilmore (1944), child: Yul; divorced 1960. Married Doris Kleiner (1960), child: Victoria.

Feature Films: *Port of New York* (EL, 1949), *The King and I* (20th, 1956), *The Ten Commandments* (Par., 1956), *Anastasia* (20th, 1956), *The Brothers Karamazov* (MGM, 1958), *The Buccaneer* (Par., 1958),

Pat Hingle and Yul Brynner in *Invitation to a Gunfighter*.

The Journey (MGM, 1959), *The Sound and the Fury* (20th, 1959), *Solomon and Sheba* (UA, 1959), *Once More, With Feeling* (Col., 1960), *The Magnificent Seven* (UA, 1960), *Surprise Package* (Col., 1960), *Escape From Zahrain* (Par., 1962), *Taras Bulba* (UA, 1962), *Kings of the Sun* (UA, 1963), *Flight From Ashiya* (UA, 1964), *Invitation to a Gunfighter* (UA, 1964), *The Saboteur—Code Name Morituri* (20th, 1965), *Cast a Giant Shadow* (UA, 1966), *Is Paris Burning?* (Par., 1966), *Return of the Seven* (UA, 1966), *Triple Cross* (WB, 1967), *The Double Man* (WB-7 Arts., 1967), *The Long Duel* (Rank, 1967), *Villa Rides* (Par., 1968), *The Picasso Summer* (CBS Films, 1968).

Jane Darwell and Edgar Buchanan in *Red Canyon*.

EDGAR BUCHANAN Born March 21, 1903, Humansville, Missouri. Married Mildred Spence, child: Bucky.

Feature Films: *When the Daltons Rode* (Univ., 1940), *The Doctor Takes a Wife* (Col., 1940), *Too Many Husbands* (Col., 1940), *My Son Is Guilty* (Col., 1940), *Tear Gas Squad* (WB, 1940), *The Sea Hawk* (WB, 1940), *Arizona* (Col., 1940), *Three Cheers for the Irish* (WB, 1940), *Penny Serenade* (Col., 1941), *Submarine Zone* (Col., 1941), *Her First Beau* (Col., 1941), *Richest Man in Town* (Col., 1941), *Texas* (Col., 1941), *You Belong to Me* (Col., 1941), *Tombstone, the Town Too Tough To Die* (Par., 1942), *The Talk of the Town* (Col., 1942), *Destroyer* (Col., 1943), *City Without Men* (Col., 1943), *Good Luck, Mr. Yates* (Col., 1943), *Buffalo Bill* (20th, 1944), *Bride by Mistake* (RKO, 1944), *The Impatient Years* (Col., 1944), *Strange Affair* (Col., 1944), *The Fighting Guardsman* (Col., 1945), *Abilene Town* (UA, 1946), *The Bandit of Sherwood Forest* (Col., 1946), *Renegades* (Col., 1946), *Perilous Holiday* (Col., 1946). *The Walls Came Tumbling Down* (Col., 1946), *If I'm Lucky* (20th, 1946), *The Sea of Grass* (MGM, 1947), *Framed* (Col., 1947), *The Swordsman* (Col., 1947), *Coroner Creek* (Col., 1948), *The Black Arrow* (Col., 1948), *Adventures in Silverado* (Col., 1948), *Best Man Wins* (Col., 1948), *The Man From Colorado* (Col., 1948), *The Untamed Breed* (Col., 1948), *Red Canyon* (Univ., 1949), *The Wreck of the Hesperus* (Col., 1948), *The Walking Hills* (Col., 1949), *Any Number*

Can Play (MGM, 1949), *The Big Hangover* (MGM, 1950), *Cheaper by the Dozen* (20th, 1950), *Cargo to Capetown* (Col., 1950), *Devil's Doorway* (MGM, 1950), *The Great Missouri Raid* (Par., 1950), *Rawhide* (20th, 1951), *Silver City* (Par., 1951), *Cave of Outlaws* (Univ., 1951), *Flaming Feather* (Par., 1951), *The Big Trees* (WB, 1952), *Toughest Man in Arizona* (Rep., 1952), *Wild Stallion* (Mon., 1952), *Shane* (Par., 1953), *It Happens Every Thursday* (Par., 1953), *She Couldn't Say No* (RKO, 1954), *Make Haste to Live* (Rep., 1954), *Dawn at Socorro* (Univ., 1954), *Human Desire* (Col., 1954), *Destry* (Univ., 1954), *Rage at Dawn* (RKO, 1955), *Wichita* (AA, 1955), *Lonesome Trail* (Lip., 1955), *Come Next Spring* (Rep., 1956), *Spoilers of the* Forest (Rep., 1957), *Day of the Bad Man* (Univ., 1958), *The Sheepman* (MGM, 1958), *King of the Wild Stallions* (AA, 1959), *It Started With a Kiss* (MGM, 1959), *Hound-Dog Man* (20th, 1959), *Edge of Eternity* (Col., 1959), *Four Fast Guns* (Univ., 1959), *Chartroose Caboose* (Univ., 1960), *Cimarron* (MGM, 1960), *Tammy, Tell Me True* (Univ., 1961), *The Comancheros* (20th, 1961), *Ride the High Country* (MGM, 1962), *A Ticklish Affair* (MGM, 1963), *McLintock* (UA, 1963), *Move Over, Darling* (20th, 1963), *The Man From Button Willow* (voice only; United Screen Arts, 1965) *The Rounders* (MGM, 1965), *Gunpoint* (Univ., 1966), *Welcome to Hard Times* (MGM, 1967).

BILLIE BURKE (Ethelbert Appleton Burke) Born August 7, 1884, Washington, D.C. Married Florenz Ziegfeld (1914), child: Patricia; widowed 1932.

Sound Feature Films: *A Bill of Divorcement* (RKO, 1932), *Christopher Strong* (RKO, 1933), *Dinner at Eight* (MGM, 1933), *Only Yesterday* (Univ., 1933), *Finishing School* (RKO, 1934), *Where Sinners Meet* (RKO, 1934), *We're Rich Again* (RKO, 1934), *Forsaking All Others* (MGM, 1934), *Society Doctor* (MGM, 1935), *After Office Hours* (MGM, 1935), *Doubting Thomas* (Fox, 1935), *Becky Sharp* (RKO, 1935), *She Couldn't Take It* (Col., 1935), *Splendor* (UA, 1935), *A Feather in Her Hat* (Col., 1935), *Piccadilly Jim* (MGM, 1936), *My American Wife* (Par., 1936), *Craig's Wife* (Col., 1936), *Parnell* (MGM, 1937), *Topper* (MGM, 1937), *The Bride Wore Red* (MGM, 1937), *Navy Blue and Gold* (MGM, 1937), *Everybody Sing* (MGM, 1938), *Merrily We Live* (MGM, 1938), *The Young in Heart* (UA, 1938), *Topper Takes a Trip* (UA, 1939), *Zenobia* (UA, 1939), *Bridal Suite* (MGM, 1939), *The Wizard of Oz* (MGM, 1939), *Eternally Yours* (UA, 1939), *Remember?* (MGM, 1939), *Irene* (RKO, 1940), *And One Was Beautiful* (MGM, 1940), *The Captain Is a Lady* (MGM, 1940), *Dulcy* (MGM, 1940), *Hullabaloo* (MGM, 1940), *The Ghost Comes Home* (MGM, 1940), *Topper Returns* (UA, 1941), *The Wild Man of Borneo* (MGM, 1941), *One Night in Lisbon* (Par., 1941), *The Man Who Came to Dinner* (WB, 1941), *What's Cookin'?* (Univ., 1942), *In This Our Life* (WB, 1942), *They All Kissed the Bride* (Col., 1942), *Girl Trouble* (20th, 1942), *Hi Diddle Diddle* (UA, 1943), *Gildersleeve on Broadway* (RKO, 1943), *So's Your Uncle* (Univ., 1943), *You're a*

Frances Grant, Will Rogers and Bille Burke in *Doubting Thomas*.

George Burns, Gracie Allen and Wade Boteler in *Love in Bloom.*

Lucky Fellow, Mr. Smith (Univ., 1943), *Swing Out, Sister* (Univ., 1945), *The Cheaters* (Rep., 945), *Breakfast in Hollywood* (UA, 1946), *The Bachelor's Daughters* (UA, 1946), *The Barkleys of Broadway* (MGM, 1949), *And Baby Makes Three* (Col., 1950), *Father of the Bride* (MGM, 1950), *Boy From Indiana* (EL, 1950), *Three Husbands* (UA, 1950), *Father's Little Dividend* (MGM, 1951), *Small Town Girl* (MGM, 1953), *The Young Philadelphians* (WB, 1959), *Sergeant Rutledge* (WB, 1960), *Pepe* (Col., 1960).

BURNS AND ALLEN

GEORGE (Nathan Burnbaum) Born January 20, 1896, New York, New York. Married Gracie Allen (1926), children: Sandra, Ronald; widowed 1964.

GRACIE (Grace Ethel Cecile Rosalie Allen) Born July 26, 1902, San Francisco, California. Married George Burns (1926), children: Sandra, Ronald. Died August 28, 1964.

Feature Films: *The Big Broadcast* (Par., 1932), *International House* (Par., 1933), *College Humor* (Par., 1933), *Six of a Kind* (Par., 1934), *We're Not Dressing* (Par., 1934), *Many Happy Returns* (Par., 1934), *Love in Bloom* (Par., 1935), *Here Comes Cookie* (Par., 1935), *Big Broadcast Of 1936* (Par., 1935), *Big Broadcast Of 1937* (Par., 1936), *College Holiday* (Par., 1936), *A Damsel in Distress* (RKO, 1937), *College Swing* (Par., 1938), *Honolulu* (MGM, 1939), *The Gracie Allen Murder Case* (Par., 1939),* *Mr. and Mrs. North* (MGM, 1941),* *Two Girls and a Sailor* (MGM, 1944).

*Without George Burns

RICHARD BURTON (Richard Walter Jenkins, Jr.) Born November 10, 1925, Pontrhydyfen, South Wales. Married Sybil Williams (1949), children: Jessica, Kate; divorced 1963. Married Elizabeth Taylor (1964).

Feature Films: *The Last Days of Dolwyn* (London Films, 1948), *Now Barabbas Was a Robber* (WB, 1949), *Waterfront* (GFD, 1950), *The Woman With No Name* (Rank, 1952), *My Cousin Rachel* (20th, 1952), *The Desert Rats* (20th, 1953), *The Robe* (20th, 1953), *Prince of Players* (20th, 1955), *The Rains of Ranchipur* (20th, 1955), *Alexander*

Lana Turner and Richard Burton in *The Rains of Ranchipur.*

the Great (UA, 1956), *Sea Wife* (20th, 1957), *Bitter Victory* (Col., 1958), *Look Back in Anger* (WB, 1959), *Bramble Bush* (WB, 1960), *Ice Palace* (WB, 1960), *A Midsummer Night's Dream* (narrator; Czechoslovakian-British, 1961), *The Longest Day* (20th, 1962), *Cleopatra* (20th, 1963), *The V.I.P.'s* (MGM, 1963), *Becket* (Par., 1964), *Night of the Iguana* (MGM, 1964), *Hamlet* (WB, 1964), *The Sandpiper* (MGM, 1965), *What's New, Pussycat?* (UA, 1965),* *The Spy Who Came In From the Cold* (Par., 1966), *Who's Afraid Of Virginia Woolf?* (WB, 1966), *The Taming of the Shrew* (Col., 1967), *Dr. Faustus* (Col., 1968), *Boom* (Univ., 1968), *Candy* (Cinerama, 1968).

*Unbilled guest appearance

SPRING BYINGTON Born October 17, 1893, Colorado Springs, Colorado. Married Roy Chandler, children: Lois, Phyllis; divorced.

Feature Films: *Little Women* (RKO, 1933), *Werewolf of London* (Univ., 1935), *Orchids to You* (Fox, 1935), *Love Me Forever* (Col., 1935), *Mutiny on the Bounty* (MGM, 1935), *Way Down East* (20th, 1935), *Broadway Hostess* (WB, 1935), *Ah! Wilderness* (MGM, 1935), *The Great Impersonation* (Univ., 1935), *The Voice of Bugle Ann* (MGM, 1936), *Every Saturday Night* (20th, 1936), *Palm Springs* (Par., 1936), *Educating Father* (20th, 1936), *Stage Struck* (WB, 1936), *Back to Nature* (20th, 1936), *Dodsworth* (UA, 1936), *The Girl on the Front Page* (Univ., 1936), *Charge of the Light Brigade* (WB, 1936), *Theodora Goes Wild* (Col., 1936), *Clarence* (Par., 1937), *Green Light* (WB, 1937), *Off to the Races* (20th, 1937), *Penrod and Sam* (WB, 1937), *Big Business* (20th, 1937), *A Family Affair* (MGM, 1937), *The Road Back* (Univ., 1937), *Hotel Haywire* (Par., 1937), *It's Love I'm After* (WB, 1937), *Hot Water* (20th, 1937), *Borrowing Trouble* (20th, 1937), *Love on a Budget* (20th, 1938), *The Buccaneer* (Par., 1938), *Jezebel* (WB, 1938), *Penrod and His Twin Brother* (WB, 1938), *A Trip to Paris* (20th, 1938), *Safety in Numbers* (20th, 1938), *You Can't Take It With You* (Col., 1938), *The Jones Family in Hollywood* (20th, 1939), *The Story of Alexander Graham Bell* (20th, 1939), *Down on the Farm* (20th, 1939), *Everybody's Baby* (20th, 1939), *Chicken Wagon Family* (20th, 1939), *Quick Millions* (20th, 1939), *Too Busy to Work* (20th, 1939), *Young as You Feel* (20th, 1940), *The Blue Bird* (20th, 1940), *The Ghost Comes Home* (MGM, 1940), *A Child Is Born* (WB, 1940), *My Love Came Back* (WB, 1940), *On Their Own* (20th, 1940), *Lucky Partners* (RKO, 1940), *Laddie* (RKO, 1940), *Arkansas Judge* (Rep., 1941), *The Devil and Miss Jones* (RKO, 1941), *Meet John Doe* (WB, 1941), *Ellery Queen and the Perfect Crime* (Col., 1941), *When Ladies Meet* (MGM, 1941), *The Vanishing Virginian* (MGM, 1941), *Roxie Hart* (20th, 1942), *Rings on Her Fingers* (20th, 1942), *The Affairs of Martha* (MGM, 1942), *The War Against Mrs. Hadley* (MGM, 1942), *Presenting Lily Mars* (MGM, 1943), *Heaven Can Wait* (20th, 1943), *The Heavenly Body* (MGM, 1943), *I'll Be Seeing You* (UA, 1944), *Salty O'Rourke* (Par., 1945), *The Enchanted Cottage* (RKO, 1945), *Thrill of a Romance* (MGM, 1945), *Captain Eddie* (20th, 1945), *A Letter for Evie* (MGM, 1945), *Dragonwyck* (20th, 1946), *Meet Me on Broadway* (Col., 1946), *Little Mr. Jim* (MGM, 1946), *Faithful in My Fashion* (MGM, 1946), *My Brother Talks to Horses* (MGM, 1946), *Cynthia* (MGM, 1947), *Living in a Big Way* (MGM, 1947), *Singapore* (Univ., 1947), *It Had to Be You* (Col., 1947), *B. F.'s Daughter* (MGM, 1948), *In the Good Old Summertime* (MGM, 1949), *The Big Wheel* (UA, 1949), *Please Believe Me* (MGM, 1950), *Devil's Doorway* (MGM, 1950), *The Skipper Surprised His Wife* (MGM, 1950), *Louisa* (Univ., 1950), *Walk Softly, Stranger* (RKO, 1950), *The Reformer and the Redhead* (Voice only; MGM, 1950), *According to Mrs. Hoyle* (Mon., 1951), *Angels in the Outfield* (MGM, 1951), *Bannerline* (MGM, 1951), *No Room for the Groom* (Univ., 1952), *Because You're Mine* (MGM, 1952), *The Rocket Man* (20th, 1954), *Please Don't Eat the Daisies* (MGM, 1960).

JAMES CAGNEY (James Francis Cagney, Jr.) Born July 17, 1899, New York, New York. Married Frances Vernon (1920).

Feature Films: *Sinner's Holiday* (WB, 1930), *Doorway to Hell* (WB, 1930), *Other Men's Women* (WB, 1931), *The Millionaire* (WB, 1931), *Public Enemy* (WB, 1931), *Smart Money* (WB, 1931), *Blonde Crazy* (WB, 1931), *Taxi* (WB, 1932), *The Crowd Roars* (WB, 1932), *Winner Take All* (WB, 1932), *Hard to Handle* (WB, 1933), *Picture Snatcher*

Kenneth Howell, Florence Roberts, Jed Prouty, George Ernest and Spring Byington in *The Jones Family in Hollywood*.

Hobart Cavanaugh, Matt Willis, Minerva Urecal and Judy Canova in *Louisiana Hayride*.

(WB, 1933), *Mayor of Hell* (WB, 1933), *Footlight Parade* (WB, 1933), *Lady Killer* (WB, 1933), *Jimmy the Gent* (WB, 1934), *He Was Her Man* (WB, 1934), *Here Comes the Navy* (WB, 1934), *St. Louis Kid* (WB, 1934), *Devil Dogs of the Air* (WB, 1935), *G-Men* (WB, 1935), *The Irish in Us* (WB, 1935), *A Midsummer Night's Dream* (WB, 1935), *Frisco Kid* (WB, 1935), *Ceiling Zero* (WB, 1935), *Great Guy* (GN, 1936), *Something to Sing About* (GN, 1937), *Boy Meets Girl* (WB, 1938), *Angels With Dirty Faces* (WB, 1938), *Oklahoma Kid* (WB, 1939), *Each Dawn I Die* (WB, 1939), *The Roaring Twenties* (WB, 1939), *The Fighting 69th* (WB, 1940), *Torrid Zone* (WB, 1940), *City for Conquest* (WB, 1940), *Strawberry Blonde* (WB, 1941), *The Bride Came C.O.D.* (WB, 1941), *Captain of the Clouds* (WB, 1942), *Yankee Doodle Dandy* (WB, 1942), *Johnny Come Lately* (UA, 1943), *Blood on the Sun* (UA, 1945), *13 Rue Madeleine* (20th, 1946), *The Time of Your Life* (UA, 1948), *White Heat* (WB, 1949), *West Point Story* (WB, 1950), *Kiss Tomorrow Goodbye* (WB, 1950), *Come Fill the Cup* (WB, 1951), *Starlift* (WB, 1951), *What Price Glory* (20th, 1952), *A Lion Is in the Streets* (WB, 1953), *Run for Cover* (Par., 1955), *Love Me or Leave Me* (MGM, 1955), *Seven Little Foys* (Par., 1955), *Mister Roberts* (WB, 1955), *Tribute to a Bad Man* (MGM, 1956), *These Wilder Years* (MGM, 1956), *Man of a Thousand Faces* (Univ., 1957), *Never Steal Anything Small* (Univ., 1959), *Shake Hands With the Devil* (UA, 1959), *The Gallant Hours* (UA, 1960), *One, Two, Three!* (UA, 1961), *Arizona Bushwhackers* (narrator; Par., 1968).

Barton MacLane and James Cagney in *Frisco Kid*.

JUDY CANOVA (Juliet Canova) Born November 20, 1916, Jacksonville, Florida. Married William Burns (1936); divorced 1939. Married James Ripley (1941); annulled 1941. Married Chester England, child: Julietta; divorced 1949. Married Philip Rivero (1950), child: Diane.

Feature Films: *Going Highbrow* (WB, 1935), *In Caliente* (WB, 1935), *Artists and Models* (Par., 1937), *Thrill of a Lifetime* (Par., 1937),

Scatterbrain (Rep., 1940), *Sis Hopkins* (Rep., 1941), *Puddin' Head* (Rep., 1941), *Sleepytime Gal* (Rep., 1942), *True to the Army* (Par., 1942), *Joan of Ozark* (Rep., 1942), *Chatterbox* (Rep., 1943), *Sleepy Lagoon* (Rep. 1943), *Louisiana Hayride* (Col., 1944), *Hit the Hay* (Col., 1945), *Singin' in the Corn* (Col., 1946), *Honeychile* (Rep., 1951), *Oklahoma Annie* (Rep., 1952), *The WAC From Walla Walla* (Rep., 1952), *Untamed Heiress* (Rep., 1954), *Carolina Cannonball* (Rep., 1955), *Lay That Rifle Down* (Rep., 1955), *The Adventures of Huckleberry Finn* (MGM, 1960).

Louise Hovick (Gypsy Rose Lee) and Eddie Cantor in *Ali Baba Goes to Town*.

EDDIE CANTOR (Edward Israel Iskowitz) Born January 31, 1892, New York, New York. Married Ida Tobias (1914), children: Marjorie, Natalie, Edna, Marilyn, Janet; widowed 1962. Died October 10, 1964.

Sound Feature Films: *Glorifying the American Girl* (Par., 1929), *Whoopee* (UA, 1930), *Palmy Days* (UA, 1931), *The Kid From Spain* (UA, 1932), *Roman Scandals* (UA, 1933), *Kid Millions* (UA, 1934), *Strike Me Pink* (UA, 1936), *Ali Baba Goes to Town* (20th, 1937), *Forty Little Mothers* (MGM, 1940), *Thank Your Lucky Stars* (WB, 1943), *Hollywood Canteen* (WB, 1944), *Show Business* (RKO, 1944), *If You Knew Susie* (RKO, 1948), *The Story of Will Rogers* (WB, 1952), *The Eddie Cantor Story* (WB, 1953).

HARRY CAREY (Harry DeWitt Carey II) Born January 16, 1878, New York, New York. Married Olive Golden (1913), children: Harry, Jr., Ellen. Died September 21, 1947.

Sound Feature Films: *The Vanishing Legion* (Mascot serial, 1931), *Trader Horn* (MGM, 1931), *Bad Company* (Pathé, 1931), *Cavalier of*

Raymond Hatton and Harry Carey in *The Thundering Herd.*

the West (Artclass Pictures, 1931), *Devil Horse* (Mascot serial, 1932), *Last of the Mohicans* (Mascot serial, 1932), *Without Honor* (Artclass Pictures, 1932), *Law and Order* (Univ., 1932), *Border Devils* (Artclass Pictures, 1932), *Night Rider* (Artclass Pictures, 1932), *Sunset Pass* (Par., 1933), *Man of the Forest* (Par., 1933), *Thundering Herd* (Par., 1933), *Wagon Trail* (Ajax, 1935), *Barbary Coast* (UA, 1935), *Powder-smoke Range* (RKO, 1935), *Last of the Clintons* (Ajax, 1935), *Wild Mustang* (William Berke, 1935), *The Last Outpost* (Par., 1935), *The Man Behind the Mask* (British, 1936), *Ghost Town* (Commodore, 1936), *The Prisoner of Shark Island* (20th, 1936), *Sutter's Gold* (Univ., 1936), *Little Miss Nobody* (20th, 1936), *Valiant Is the Word for Carrie* (Par., 1936), *The Accusing Finger* (Par., 1936), *Souls at Sea* (Par., 1937), *Aces Wild* (Commodore, 1937), *Burn 'Em Up O'Connor* (MGM, 1939), *Street of Missing Men* (Rep., 1939), *Inside Information* (Univ., 1939), *Mr. Smith Goes to Washington* (Col., 1939), *My Son Is Guilty* (Col., 1940), *Outside the 3-Mile Limit* (Col., 1940), *Beyond Tomorrow* (RKO, 1940), *They Knew What They Wanted* (Col., 1940), *The Shepherd of the Hills* (Par., 1941), *Parachute Battalion* (RKO, 1941), *Among the Living* (Par., 1941), *Sundown* (UA, 1941), *The Spoilers* (Univ., 1942), *Air Force* (WB, 1943), *Happy Land* (20th, 1943), *The Great Moment* (Par., 1944), *China's Little Devils* (Mon., 1945), *Duel in the Sun* (Selznick, 1946), *Angel and the Badman* (Rep., 1947), *The Sea of Grass* (MGM, 1947), *Red River* (UA, 1948), *So Dear to My Heart* (RKO, 1948).

LESLIE CARON (Leslie Claire Margaret Caron) Born July 1, 1931, Paris, France. Married George Hormel (1951); divorced 1954. Married Peter Hall (1956), children: Christopher, Jennifer; divorced 1966.

English-Language Feature Films: *An American in Paris* (MGM, 1951), *The Man With a Cloak* (MGM, 1951), *Glory Alley* (MGM, 1952), *The Story of Three Loves* (MGM, 1953), *Lili* (MGM, 1953), *Daddy Long Legs* (20th, 1955), *The Glass Slipper* (MGM, 1955), *Gaby* (MGM, 1956), *Gigi* (MGM, 1958), *The Doctor's Dilemma* (MGM, 1958), *The Man Who Understood Women* (20th, 1959), *The Subterraneans*

Warren Beatty and Leslie Caron in *Promise Her Anything.*

(MGM, 1960), *Fanny* (WB, 1961), *Guns of Darkness* (WB, 1962), *The L-Shaped Room* (Col., 1963), *Father Goose* (Univ., 1964), *A Very Special Favor* (Univ., 1965), *Promise Her Anything* (Par., 1966), *Is Paris Burning?* (Par., 1966).

JOHN CARRADINE (Richmond Reed Carradine) Born February 5, 1906, New York, New York. Married Ardanelle Cosner, children: Bruce, David; divorced 1944. Married Sonia Sorel (1945), children: Christopher, John; divorced 1955.

English-Language Feature Films:
as John Peter Richmond *Tol'able David* (Col., 1930), *Heaven on Earth* (Univ., 1931), *Forgotten Commandments* (Par., 1932), *The Sign of the Cross* (Par., 1932), *The Invisible Man* (Univ., 1933), *This Day and Age* (Par., 1933), *Cleopatra* (Par., 1934), *The Black Cat* (Univ., 1934).
as John Carradine *Bride of Frankenstein* (Univ., 1935), *Les Miserables* (UA, 1935), *Clive of India* (UA, 1935), *The Crusades* (Par., 1935), *Cardinal Richelieu* (UA, 1935), *The Man Who Broke the Bank at Monte*

Amelita Ward, John Carradine, Charles Arnt and Margo in *Gangway for Tomorrow.*

Carlo (Fox, 1935), *She Gets Her Man* (Univ., 1935), *Dimples* (20th, 1936), *Anything Goes* (Par., 1936), *A Message to Garcia* (20th, 1936), *Under Two Flags* (20th, 1936), *Captain January* (20th, 1936), *The Prisoner of Shark Island* (20th, 1936), *Mary of Scotland* (RKO, 1936), *The Garden of Allah* (UA, 1936), *Daniel Boone* (RKO, 1936), *Ramona* (20th, 1936), *Winterset* (RKO, 1936), *Love Under Fire* (20th, 1937), *Nancy Steele Is Missing* (20th, 1937), *Captains Courageous* (MGM, 1937), *This Is My Affair* (20th, 1937), *The Last Gangster* (MGM, 1937), *Ali Baba Goesto Town* (20th, 1937), *Thank You, Mr. Moto* (20th, 1937), *The Hurricane* (UA, 1937), *Of Human Hearts* (MGM, 1938), *Four Men and a Prayer* (20th, 1938), *Gateway* (20th, 1938), *Alexander's Ragtime Band* (20th, 1938), *Kidnapped* (20th, 1938), *Submarine Patrol* (20th, 1938), *International Settlement* (20th, 1938), *Frontier Marshal* (20th, 1939), *Jesse James* (20th, 1939), *The Three Musketeers* (20th, 1939), *Captain Fury* (UA, 1939), *Drums Along the Mohawk* (20th, 1939), *Five Came Back* (RKO, 1939), *Stagecoach* (UA, 1939), *Chad Hanna* (20th, 1940), *The Return of Frank James* (20th, 1940), *Brigham Young—Frontiersman* (20th, 1940), *The Grapes of Wrath* (20th, 1940), *Western Union* (20th, 1941), *Blood and Sand* (20th, 1941), *Man Hunt* (20th, 1941), *Swamp Water* (20th, 1941), *Son of Fury* (20th, 1942), *Northwest Rangers* (MGM, 1942), *Whispering Ghosts* (20th, 1942), *Reunion in France* (MGM, 1942), *The Black Swan* (20th, 1942), *Hitler's Madman* (MGM, 1943), *I Escaped From the Gestapo* (Mon., 1943), *The Isle of Forgotten Sins* (PRC, 1943), *Silver Spurs* (Rep., 1943), *Gangway for Tomorrow* (RKO, 1943), *Voodoo Man* (Mon., 1944), *Adventures of Mark Twain* (WB, 1944), *Barbary Coast Gent* (MGM, 1944), *Alaska* (Mon., 1944), *Bluebeard* (PRC, 1944), *The Invisible Man's Revenge)* Univ., 1944), *It's in the Bag* (UA, 1945), *House of Frankenstein* (Univ., 1945), *Captain Kidd* (UA, 1945), *Fallen Angel* (20th, 1945), *House of Dracula* (Univ., 1945), *The Face of Marble* (Mon., 1946), *Down Missouri Way* (PRC, 1946), *The Private Affairs of Bel Ami* (UA, 1947), *C-Man* (Film Classics, 1949), *Casanova's Big Night* (Par., 1954), *Johnny Guitar* (Rep., 1954), *The Egyptian* (20th, 1954), *Thunder Pass* (Lip., 1954), *Stranger on Horseback* (UA, 1955), *The Kentuckian* (UA, 1955), *Desert Sands* (UA, 1955), *The Black Sleep* (UA, 1956), *Dark Venture* (WB, 1956), *Female Jungle* (AIP, 1956), *Around the World in 80 Days* (UA, 1956), *The Ten Commandments* (Par., 1956), *The Court Jester* (Par., 1956), *The True Story of Jesse James* (20th, 1957), *The Unearthly* (Rep., 1957), *The Story of Mankind* (WB, 1957), *Hell Ship Mutiny* (Rep., 1957), *Half Human* (DCA, 1957), *The Proud Rebel* (BV, 1958), *Showdown at Boot Hill* (20th, 1958), *The Last Hurrah* (Col., 1958), *The Cosmic Man* (AA, 1959), *Invisible Invaders* (UA, 1959), *The Oregon Trail* (20th, 1959), *The Adventures of Huckleberry Finn* (MGM, 1960), *Tarzan the Magnificent* (Par., 1960), *Sex Kittens Go to College* (AA, 1960), *The Incredible Petrified World* (Governor, 1960), *Invasion of the Animal People* (Jerry Warren Productions, 1962), *The Man Who Shot Liberty Valance* (Par., 1962), *The Patsy* (Par., 1964), *Cheyenne Autumn* (WB, 1964), *Wizard of Mars* (American Releasing Corp., 1964), *Billy the Kid vs. Dracula* (Embassy, 1966), *Munster Go Home* (Univ., 1966), *Hillbillies in a Haunted House* (Woolner, 1967), *The Hostage* (Crown International, 1967), *Dracula's Castle* (American Releasing, 1967), *Creatures of the Red Planet* (American Releasing, 1967), *Fiend With the Electronic Brain* (American Releasing, 1967), *Lonely Man* (American Releasing, 1967), *Dr. Terror's Gallery of Horrors* (Independent, 1967), *The Astro Zombies* (ATV Mikels Productions, 1968), *The Fakers* (East West International, 1968), *Genesis* (narrator; General Film Distributing Co., 1968).

LEO CARRILLO Born August 6, 1881, Los Angeles, California. Married Edith Haeselbarth (1940), child: Antoinette; widowed 1953. Died September 10, 1961.

Sound Feature Films: *Mr. Antonio* (Tif., 1929), *Hell Bound* (Tif., 1931), *Lasca of the Rio Grande* (Univ., 1931), *Homicide Squad* (Univ., 1931), *Guilty Generation* (Col., 1931), *Girl of the Rio* (RKO, 1932), *Broken Wing* (Par., 1932), *Parachute Jumper* (WB, 1933), *Deception* (Col., 1933), *Obey the Law* (Col., 1933), *Racetrack* (World Wide, 1933), *Men Are Such Fools* (RKO, 1933), *Moonlight and Pretzels* (Univ., 1933), *Before Morning* (Col., 1933), *Viva Villa!* (MGM, 1934), *Four Frightened People* (Par., 1934), *Manhattan Melodrama* (MGM, 1934), *Barretts of Wimpole Street* (MGM, 1934), *The Band Plays On* (MGM, 1934), *The Gay Bride* (MGM, 1934), *The Winning Ticket* (MGM, 1935), *In Caliente* (WB, 1935), *If You Could Only Cook* (Col., 1935), *Moonlight Murder* (MGM, 1936), *It Had to Happen* (20th, 1936), *The Gay Desperado* (UA, 1936), *History Is Made at Night* (UA, 1937), *I Promise to Pay* (Col., 1937), *Hotel Haywire* (Par., 1937), *52nd Street* (UA, 1937), *Manhattan Merry-Go-Round* (Rep., 1937), *The Barrier* (Par., 1937), *Girl of the Golden West* (MGM, 1938), *Little Miss Roughneck* (Col., 1938), *City Streets* (Col., 1938), *Too Hot to Handle* (MGM, 1938), *The Arizona Wildcat* (20th, 1938), *Flirting With Fate* MGM, 1938), *Fisherman's Wharf* (RKO, 1939), *Society Lawyer* (MGM, 1939), *Rio* (Univ., 1939), *Chicken Wagon Family* (20th, 1939), *20-Mule Team* (MGM, 1940), *Lillian Russell* (20th, 1940), *Captain Caution* (UA, 1940), *Wyoming* (MGM, 1940), *One Night in the Tropics* (Univ., 1940), *Horror Island* (Univ., 1941), *Riders of Death Valley* (Univ. serial, 1941), *Tight Shoes* (Univ., 1941), *Barnacle Bill* (MGM, 1941), *The Kid From Kansas* (Univ., 1941), *Road Agent* (Univ., 1941), *What's Cooking?* (Univ., 1942), *Unseen Enemy* (Univ., 1942), *Escape From Hong Kong* (Univ., 1942), *Men of Texas* (Univ., 1942), *Danger in the Pacific* (Univ., 1942), *Top Sergeant* (Univ., 1942), *Sin Town* (Univ., 1942), *American Empire* (UA, 1942), *Follow the Band* (Univ., 1943), *Larceny With Music* (Univ., 1943), *The Phantom of the Opera* (Univ., 1943), *Frontier Badmen* (Univ., 1943), *Crazy House* (Univ., 1943), *Ghost Catchers* (Univ., 1944), *Gypsy Wildcat* (Univ., 1944), *Bowery to Broadway* (Univ., 1944), *Moonlight and Cactus* (Univ., 1944), *Under Western Skies* (Univ., 1945), *Crime, Inc.* (PRC, 1945), *Mexicana* (Rep., 1945), *The Fugitive* (RKO, 1947), *The Valiant Hombre* (UA, 1948), *The Gay Amigo* (UA, 1949), *The Daring Caballero* (UA, 1949), *Satan's Cradle* (UA, 1949), *The Girl From San Lorenzo* (UA, 1950).

Armida, Duncan Renaldo and Leo Carrillo in *The Gay Amigo*.

MADELEINE CARROLL (Marie-Madeleine Bernadette O'Carroll) Born February 26, 1906, West Bromwich, England. Married Philip Astly (1931); divorced 1939. Married Sterling Hayden (1942) divorced 1946. Married Henri Lavorel (1946); divorced 1949. Married Andrew Heiskell (1950), child: Dianne; divorced 1965.

Feature Films: *Guns at Loos* (New Era, 1928), *What Money Can't Buy* (Par., 1929), *The American Prisoner* (British International, 1929), *Atlantic* (British International, 1930), *Young Woodley* (British International, 1930), *Escape* (ATP, 1930), *The "W" Plan* (Burlington, 1931), *Mme. Guillotine* (Fogwell, 1931), *Kissing Cup's Race* (Butchers, 1931), *French Leave* (Talking Picture Epics, 1931), *Fascination* (British International, 1932), *First Born* (Gainsborough, 1932), *School for Scandal* (Par., 1933), *Sleeping Car* (Gaumont-British, 1933), *I Was a Spy* (Fox, 1934), *The World Moves On* (Fox, 1934), *Loves of a Dictator* (Gaumont-British, 1935), *The 39 Steps* (Gaumont-British, 1935), *The Case Against Mrs. Ames* (Par., 1936), *Secret Agent* (Gaumont-British, 1936), *The General Died at Dawn* (Par., 1936), *Lloyds of London* (20th, 1936), *On the Avenue* (20th, 1937), *The Prisoner of Zenda* (UA, 1937), *It's All Yours* (Col., 1938), *Blockade* (UA, 1938), *Honeymoon in Bali* (Par., 1939), *Cafe Society* (Par., 1939), *My Son, My Son* (UA, 1940), *Safari* (Par., 1940), *North West Mounted Police* (Par., 1940), *Virginia* (Par., 1941), *One Night in Lisbon* (Par., 1941), *Bahama Passage* (Par., 1941), *My Favorite Blonde* (Par., 1942), *White Cradle Inn* ("High Fury"—UA, 1947), *An Innocent Affair* ("Don't Trust Your Husband"—UA, 1948), *The Fan* (Fox, 1949).

NANCY CARROLL (Ann Veronica LaHiff) Born November 19, 1906; New York, New York. Married Jack Kirkland (1924), child: Patricia; divorced 1931. Married Francis Bolton Mallory (1931); divorced 1935. Married C. H. J. Groen (1955). Died August 6, 1965.

Sound Feature Films: *The Shopworn Angel* (Par., 1929), *The Wolf of Wall Street* (Par., 1929), *Sin Sister* (Fox, 1929), *Close Harmony* (Par.,

Madeleine Carroll and Sterling Hayden in *Bahama Passage*.

Jack Benny, Nancy Carroll and Carlyle Moore, Jr., in *Transatlantic Merry-Go-Round.*

1929), *The Dance of Life* (Par., 1929), *Illusion* (Par., 1929), *Sweetie* (Par., 1929), *Dangerous Paradise* (Par., 1930), *Honey* (Par., 1930), *Paramount on Parade* (Par., 1930), *The Devil's Holiday* (Par., 1930), *Follow Through* (Par., 1930), *Laughter* (Par., 1930), *Stolen Heaven* (Par., 1931), *The Night Angel* (Par., 1931), *Personal Maid* (Par., 1931), *Broken Lullaby* (Par., 1932), *Wayward* (Par., 1932), *Scarlet Dawn* (WB, 1932), *Hot Saturday* (Par., 1932), *Under Cover Man* (Par., 1932), *Child of Manhattan* (Col., 1933), *The Woman Accused* (Par., 1933), *The Kiss Before the Mirror* (Univ., 1933), *I Love That Man* (Par., 1933), *Springtime for Henry* (Fox, 1934), *Transatlantic Merry-Go-Round* (UA, 1934), *Jealousy* (Col., 1934), *I'll Love You Always* (Col., 1935), *After the Dance* (Col., 1935), *Atlantic Adventure* (Col., 1935), *There Goes My Heart* (UA, 1938), *That Certain Age* (Univ., 1938).

JACK CARSON (John Elmer Carson) Born October 27, 1910, Carmen, Manitoba, Canada. Married Betty Lynn; divorced. Married Kay St. Germaine (1940), children: John, Germaine; divorced 1950. Married Lola Albright (1952); divorced 1958. Married Sandra Tucker (1961). Died January 3, 1963.

Fernando Lamas, Esther Williams and Jack Carson in *Dangerous When Wet.*

Feature Films: *You Only Live Once* (UA, 1937), *Too Many Wives* (RKO, 1937), *Music for Madame* (RKO, 1937), *It Could Happen To You* (Rep., 1937), *Stage Door* (RKO, 1937), *Stand-In* (UA, 1937), *High Flyers* (RKO, 1937), *Reported Missing* (Univ., 1937), *The Toast of New York* (RKO, 1937), *Crashing Hollywood* (RKO, 1938), *Bringing Up Baby* (RKO, 1938), *She's Got Everything* (RKO, 1938), *Quick Money* (RKO, 1938), *Everybody's Doing It* (RKO, 1938), *Night Spot*

(RKO, 1938), *Go Chase Yourself* (RKO, 1938), *Law of the Underworld* (RKO, 1938), *The Saint in New York* (RKO, 1938), *Vivacious Lady* (RKO, 1938), *This Marriage Business* (RKO, 1938), *Maid's Night Out* (RKO, 1938), *Having Wonderful Time* (RKO, 1938), *Carefree* (RKO, 1938), *The Kid From Texas* (MGM, 1939), *Mr. Smith Goes to Washington* (Col., 1939), *Legion of Lost Flyers* (Univ., 1939), *The Escape* (20th, 1939), *Destry Rides Again* (Univ., 1939), *The Honeymoon's Over* (20th, 1939), *I Take This Woman* (MGM, 1940), *Shooting High* (20th, 1940), *Young as You Feel* (20th, 1940), *Enemy Agent* (Univ., 1940), *Parole Fixer* (Par., 1940), *Typhoon* (Par., 1940), *Alias the Deacon* (Univ., 1940), *The Girl in 313* (20th, 1940), *Queen of the Mob* (Par., 1940), *Sandy Gets Her Man* (Univ., 1940), *Love Thy Neighbor* (Par., 1940), *Mr. and Mrs. Smith* (RKO, 1941), *The Strawberry Blonde* (WB, 1941), *Love Crazy* (MGM, 1941), *The Bride Came C.O.D.* (WB, 1941), *Navy Blues* (WB, 1941), *Blues in the Night* (WB, 1941), *Larceny, Inc.* (WB, 1942), *The Male Animal* (WB, 1942), *Wings for the Eagle* (WB, 1942), *The Hard Way* (WB, 1942), *Gentleman Jim* (WB, 1942), *Princess O'Rourke* (WB, 1943), *Thank Your Lucky Stars* (WB, 1943), *Arsenic and Old Lace* (WB, 1944), *The Doughgirls* (WB, 1944), *Hollywood Canteen* (WB, 1944), *Shine On, Harvest Moon* (WB, 1944), *Make Your Own Bed* (WB, 1944), *Roughly Speaking* (WB, 1945), *Mildred Pierce* (WB, 1945), *One More Tomorrow* (WB, 1946), *Two Guys From Milwaukee* (WB, 1946), *The Time, The Place and the Girl* (WB, 1946), *Love And Learn* (WB, 1947), *April Showers* (WB, 1948), *Romance on the High Seas* (WB, 1948), *Two Guys From Texas* (WB, 1948), *It's a Great Feeling* (WB, 1949), *My Dream Is Yours* (WB, 1949), *John Loves Mary* (WB, 1949), *Bright Leaf* (WB, 1950), *The Good Humor Man* (Col., 1950), *Mr. Universe* (EL, 1951), *The Groom Wore Spurs* (Univ., 1951), *Dangerous When Wet* (MGM, 1953), *Red Garters* (Par., 1954), *A Star Is Born* (WB, 1954), *Phffft* (Col., 1954), *Ain't Misbehavin'* (Univ., 1955), *The Bottom of the Bottle* (20th, 1956), *Magnificent Roughnecks* (AA, 1956), *The Tattered Dress* (Univ., 1957), *The Tarnished Angels* (Univ., 1957), *Cat on a Hot Tin Roof* (MGM, 1958), *Rally Round The Flag, Boys!* (20th, 1958), *The Bramble Bush* (WB, 1960), *King of the Roaring 20's—The Story of Arnold Rothstein* (AA, 1961).

JOAN CAULFIELD (Joan Beatrice Caulfield) Born June 1, 1922, Orange, New Jersey. Married Frank Ross (1950), child: Caulfield; divorced 1959. Married Robert Peterson (1960), child: John; divorced 1966.

Feature Films: *Miss Susie Slagle's* (Par., 1945), *Duffy's Tavern* (Par., 1945), *Blue Skies* (Par., 1946), *Monsieur Beaucaire* (Par., 1946), *Welcome Stranger* (Par., 1947), *Dear Ruth* (Par., 1947), *The Unsuspected* (WB, 1947), *Variety Girl* (Par., 1947), *The Sainted Sisters* (Par., 1948), *Larceny* (Univ., 1948), *Dear Wife* (Par., 1949), *The Petty Girl* (Col., 1950), *The Lady Says No* (UA, 1951), *The Rains of Ranchipur* (20th, 1955), *Cattle King* (MGM, 1963), *Red Tomahawk* (Par., 1967), *Buckskin* (Par., 1968).

George Reeves and Joan Caulfield in *The Sainted Sisters.*

Eugene Iglesias, Jeff Chandler, Earl Holliman and Charles Horvath in *East of Sumatra*.

JEFF CHANDLER (Ira Grossel) Born December 15, 1918, Brooklyn, New York. Married Marjorie Hoshelle (1946), children: Jamie, Dana; divorced 1959. Died June 17, 1961.

Feature Films: *Johnny O'Clock* (Col., 1947), *Invisible Wall* (20th, 1947), *Roses Are Red* (20th, 1947), *Mr. Belvedere Goes to College* (20th, 1949), *Sword in the Desert* (Univ., 1949), *Abandoned* (Univ., 1949), *Broken Arrow* (20th, 1950), *Two Flags West* (20th, 1950), *Deported* (Univ., 1950), *Bird of Paradise* (20th, 1951), *Smuggler's Island* (Univ., 1951), *Iron Man* (Univ., 1951), *Flame of Araby* (Univ., 1951), *Meet Danny Wilson* (Univ., 1952),* *Red Ball Express* (Univ., 1952), *Battle at Apache* Pass (Univ., 1952), *Yankee Buccaneer* (Univ., 1952), *Because of You* (Univ., 1952), *Great Sioux Uprising* (Univ., 1953), *East of Sumatra* (Univ., 1953), *War Arrow* (Univ., 1953), *Yankee Pasha* (Univ., 1954), *Taza, Son of Cochise* (Univ., 1954),* *Sign of the Pagan* (Univ., 1954), *Foxfire* (Univ., 1955), *Female on the Beach* (Univ., 1955), *The Spoilers* (Univ., 1956), *Toy Tiger* (Univ., 1956), *Away All Boats* (Univ., 1956), *Pillars of the Sky* (Univ., 1956), *Drango* (UA, 1957), *Jeanne Eagles* (Col., 1957), *Man in the Shadow* (Univ., 1958), *The Lady Takes a Flyer* (Univ., 1958), *Raw Wind in Eden* (Univ., 1958), *Stranger in my Arms* (Univ., 1959), *Thunder in the Sun* (Par., 1959), *Ten Seconds To Hell* (UA, 1959), *The Jayhawkers* (Par., 1959), *Story of David* (WB, 1960), *The Plunderers* (AA, 1960), *Return to Peyton Place* (20th, 1961), *Merrill's Marauders* (WB, 1961).

*Unbilled guest appearance

LON CHANEY, JR. (Creighton Chaney) Born 1907. Married, children: Lon, Ronald; divorced. Married Patsy Beck (1937).

English-Language Feature Films:

as **Creighton Chaney** *The Last Frontier* (RKO serial, 1932), *Girl Crazy* (RKO, 1932), *Bird of Paradise* (RKO, 1932), *Lucky Devils* (RKO, 1933), *Scarlet River* (RKO, 1933), *Son of the Border* (RKO, 1933), *Sixteen Fathoms Deep* (Mon., 1934), *The Life of Vergie Winters* (RKO, 1934), *Girl o' My Dreams* (Mon., 1934).

as **Lon Chaney, Jr.** *Captain Hurricane* (RKO, 1935), *Accent on Youth* (Par., 1935), *Hold 'Em Yale* (Par., 1935), *Shadow of Silk Lennox* (Commodore, 1935), *The Marriage Bargain* (Hollywood Exchange, 1935), *Scream in the Night* (Commodore, 1935), *Ace Drummond* (Univ. serial, 1936), *Undersea Kingdom* (Rep. serial, 1936), *The Singing Cowboy* (Rep., 1936), *Killer at Large* (Col., 1936), *The Old Corral* (Rep., 1936), *Secret Agent X-9* (Univ. serial, 1937), *Midnight Taxi* (20th, 1937), *Angel's Holiday* (20th, 1937), *Wild and Woolly* (20th, 1937), *Wife, Doctor and Nurse* (20th, 1937), *The Lady Escapes* (20th, 1937), *Love and Hisses* (20th, 1937), *One Mile From Heaven* (20th, 1937), *Second Honeymoon* (20th, 1937), *That I May Live* (20th, 1937), *City Girl* (20th, 1937), *Charlie Chan on Broadway* (20th, 1937), *Slave Ship* (20th, 1937), *Born Reckless* (20th, 1937), *Thin Ice* (20th, 1937), *Alexander's Ragtime Band* (20th, 1938), *Straight, Place and Show* (20th, 1938), *Walking Down Broadway* (20th, 1938), *Passport Husband* (20th, 1938), *Road Demon* (20th, 1938), *Submarine Patrol* (20th, 1938), *Mr. Moto's Gamble* (20th, 1938), *Speed to Burn* (20th, 1938), *Happy Landing* (20th, 1938), *Josette* (20th, 1938), *Jesse James* (20th, 1939), *Frontier Marshal* (20th, 1939), *Charlie Chan in City in Darkness* (20th,

1939), *Of Mice and Men* (UA, 1939), *Union Pacific* (Par., 1939), *One Million B.C.* (UA, 1940), *North West Mounted Police* (Par., 1940), *Riders of Death Valley* (Univ. serial, 1941), *Man-Made Monster* (Univ., 1941), *Billy the Kid* (MGM, 1941), *San Antonio Rose* (Univ., 1941), *Badlands of Dakota* (Univ., 1941), *Too Many Blondes* (Univ., 1941), *The Wolf Man* (Univ., 1941), *Overland Mail* (Univ. serial, 1942), *North to the Klondike* (Univ., 1942), *The Ghost of Frankenstein* (Univ., 1942), *The Mummy's Tomb* (Univ., 1942), *Frankenstein Meets the Wolf Man* (Univ., 1943), *Eyes of the Underworld* (Univ., 1943), *Frontier Badman* (Univ., 1943), *Son of Dracula* (Univ., 1943), *Crazy House* (Univ., 1943), *Calling Dr. Death* (Univ., 1943), *Follow the Boys* (Univ., 1944), *Ghost Catchers* (Univ., 1944), *Cobra Woman* (Univ., 1944), *The Mummy's Ghost* (Univ., 1944), *Weird Woman* (Univ., 1944), *Dead Man's Eyes* (Univ., 1944), *Here Come the Co-eds* (Univ., 1945), *House of Frankenstein* (Univ., 1945), *The Mummy's Curse* (Univ., 1945), *The Frozen Ghost* (Univ., 1945), *House of Dracula* (Univ., 1945), *The Daltons Ride Again* (Univ., 1945), *Pillow of Death* (Univ., 1945), *Strange Confession* (Univ., 1945), *My Favorite Brunette* (Par., 1947), *Albuquerque* (Par., 1948), *16 Fathoms Deep* (Mon. 1948), *Abbott and Costello Meet Frankenstein* (Univ., 1948), *The Counterfeiters* (20th, 1948), *There's a Girl in My Heart* (AA, 1949), *Captain China* (Par., 1949), *Once a Thief* (UA, 1950), *Inside Straight* (MGM, 1951), *Only the Valiant* (WB, 1951), *Behave Yourself* (RKO, 1951), *Flame of Araby* (Univ., 1951), *The Bushwhackers* (Realart, 1952), *High Noon* (UA, 1952), *Thief of Damascus* (Col., 1952), *Springfield Rifle* (WB, 1952), *The Black Castle* (Univ., 1952), *Raiders of the Seven Seas* (UA, 1953), *A Lion Is in the Streets* (WB, 1953), *Jivaro* (Par., 1954), *The Boy From Oklahoma* (WB, 1954), *Casanova's Big Night* (Par., 1954), *Passion* (RKO, 1954), *Silver Star* (Lip., 1955), *Big House, U.S.A.* (UA, 1955), *Not as a Stranger* (UA, 1955), *I Died a Thousand Times* (WB, 1955), *The Indian Fighter* (UA, 1955), *Manfish* (UA, 1956), *Pardners* (Par., 1956), *The Black Sleep* (UA, 1956), *The Indestructible Man* (AA, 1956), *Daniel Boone, Trail Blazer* (Rep., 1956), *Cyclops* (AA, 1957), *The Defiant Ones* (UA, 1958), *Money, Women and Guns* (Univ., 1958), *The Alligator People* (20th, 1959), *The Phantom* (American Releasing, 1961), *Rebellion in Cuba* (International, 1961), *The Haunted Palace* (AIP, 1963), *Law of the Lawless* (Par., 1964), *Stage to Thunder Rock* (Par., 1964), *Witchcraft* (20th, 1964), *Black Spurs* (Par., 1965), *Young Fury* (Par., 1965), *Town Tamer* (Par., 1965), *Apache Uprising* (Par., 1966), *Johnny Reno* (Par., 1966), *Welcome to Hard Times* (MGM, 1967), *Hillbillies in a Haunted House* (Woolner, 1967). *Dr. Terror's Gallery of Horrors* (Par., 1967), *The Frontiersman* (Par., 1968), *Buckskin* (Par., 1968).

Will Rogers, Jr., and Lon Chaney, Jr., in *The Boy From Oklahoma*.

CHARLES CHAPLIN (Charles Spencer Chaplin) Born April 16, 1889, London, England. Married Mildred Harris (1917); divorced 1920. Married Lita Grey (1924), children: Charles, Sydney; divorced 1927. Married Paulette Goddard (1936); divorced 1942. Married Oona O'Neill (1943), children: Geraldine, Michael, Josephine, Victoria, Jane, Annette, Eugene, Christopher.

Marlon Brando and Charles Chaplin in *A Countess From Hong Kong.*

Sound Feature Films: *The Great Dictator* (UA, 1940), *Monsieur Verdoux* (UA, 1947), *Limelight* (UA, 1952), *A King in New York* (UA, 1957), *A Countess From Hong Kong* (Univ., 1967).

CYD CHARISSE (Tula Ellice Finklea) Born March 8, 1921, Amarillo, Texas. Married Nico Charisse (1939), child: Nicky; divorced 1947. Married Tony Martin (1948), child: Tony.

Margaret O'Brien and Cyd Charisse in *The Unfinished Dance.*

Feature Films:
   As **Lily Norwood** *Mission to Moscow* (WB, 1943), *Something to Shout About* (Col., 1943).
   As **Cyd Charisse** *Ziegfeld Follies of 1946* (MGM, 1946), *The Harvey Girls* (MGM, 1946), *Three Wise Fools* (MGM, 1946), *Till the Clouds Roll By* (MGM, 1946), *Fiesta* (MGM, 1947), *The Unfinished Dance* (MGM, 1947), *On an Island With You* (MGM, 1948), *Words and Music* (MGM, 1948), *The Kissing Bandit* (MGM, 1949), *East Side, West Side* (MGM, 1949), *Tension* (MGM, 1949), *Mark of the Renegade* (Univ., 1951), *The Wild North* (MGM, 1952), *Singin' in the Rain* (MGM, 1952), *Sombrero* (MGM, 1953), *The Band Wagon* (MGM, 1953), *Easy to Love* (MGM, 1953),* *Brigadoon* (MGM, 1954), *Deep in My Heart* (MGM, 1954), *It's Always Fair Weather* (MGM, 1955), *Meet*

Me in Las Vegas (MGM, 1956), *Invitation to the Dance* (MGM, 1957), *Silk Stockings* (MGM, 1957), *Twilight for the Gods* (Univ., 1958), *Party Girl* (MGM, 1958), *Five Golden Hours* (Col., 1961), *Black Tights* (Magna, 1962), *Two Weeks in Another Town* (MGM, 1962), *The Silencers* (Col., 1966), *Maroc 7* (Univ., 1967), *Assassination in Rome* (Walter Manly, 1967).

*Unbilled guest appearance

RUTH CHATTERTON Born December 24, 1893, New York, New York. Married Ralph Forbes (1924); divorced 1932. Married George Brent (1932); divorced 1934. Married Barry Thomson (1942); widowed 1960. Died November 21, 1961.

Sound Feature Films: *The Doctor's Secret* (Par., 1929), *The Dummy* (Par., 1929), *Madame X* (MGM, 1929), *Charming Sinners* (Par., 1929), *The Laughing Lady* (Par., 1929), *Sarah and Son* (Par., 1930), *Paramount on Parade* (Par., 1930), *The Lady of Scandal* (MGM, 1930), *Anybody's Woman* (Par., 1930), *The Right to Love* (Par., 1930), *Unfaithful* (Par., 1931), *Magnificent Lie* (Par., 1931), *Once a Lady* (Par., 1931), *Tomorrow and Tomorrow* (Par., 1932), *The Rich Are Always With Us* (WB, 1932), *The Crash* (WB, 1932), *Frisco Jenny* (WB, 1933), *Lilly Turner* (WB, 1933), *Female* (WB, 1933), *Journal of a Crime* (WB, 1934), *Lady of Secrets* (Col., 1936), *Girls' Dormitory* (20th, 1936), *Dodsworth* (UA, 1936), *The Rat* (London Films, 1938), *The Royal Divorce* (Imperator, 1938).

Robert Allen and Ruth Chatterton in *Lady of Secrets.*

MAURICE CHEVALIER (Maurice Auguste Chevalier) Born September 12, 1888, Paris, France. Married Yvonne Vallee (1927); divorced 1935.

English-Language Sound Feature Films: *Innocents of Paris* (Par., 1929), *The Love Parade* (Par., 1929), *Paramount on Parade* (Par., 1930), *The Big Pond* (Par., 1930), *The Playboy of Paris* (Par., 1930), *The Smiling Lieutenant* (Par., 1931), *One Hour With You* (Par., 1932) *Make Me a Star* (Par., 1932),* *Love Me Tonight* (Par., 1932), *A Bedtime Story* (Par., 1933), *The Way to Love* (Par., 1933), *The Merry Widow* (MGM, 1934), *Folies Bergere* (UA, 1935), *The Beloved Vagabond* (Col., 1937), *Love in the Afternoon* (AA, 1957), *Gigi* (MGM, 1958), *Count Your Blessings* (MGM, 1959), *A Breath of Scandal* (Par., 1960), *Can-Can* (20th, 1960), *Pepe* (Col., 1960), *Fanny* (WB, 1961), *Jessica* (UA, 1962), *Black Tights* (Magna, 1962), *In Search of the Castaways* (BV, 1962), *A New Kind of Love* (Par., 1963), *Panic Button* (Gorton Associates, 1964), *I'd Rather Be Rich* (Univ., 1964), *Monkeys, Go Home* (BV, 1967).

*Unbilled guest appearance

Myrna Loy, Maurice Chevalier and Jeanette MacDonald in *Love Me Tonight.*

DANE CLARK (Bernard Zanville) Born February 18, 1915, New York, New York. Married Margo Yoder (1941).

Feature Films: *The Glass Key* (Par., 1942), *Sunday Punch* (MGM, 1942), *Pride of the Yankees* (RKO, 1942), *Wake Island* (Par., 1942), *Tennessee Johnson* (MGM, 1942), *Action in the North Atlantic* (WB, 1943), *Destination Tokyo* (WB, 1943), *The Very Thought of You* (WB, 1944), *Hollywood Canteen* (WB, 1944), *God Is My Co-Pilot* (WB, 1945), *Pride of the Marines* (WB, 1945), *Her Kind of Man* (WB, 1946), *A Stolen Life* (WB, 1946), *That Way With Women* (WB, 1947), *Deep Valley* (WB, 1947), *Moonrise* (Rep., 1948), *Embraceable You* (WB, 1948), *Whiplash* (WB, 1948), *Without Honor* (UA, 1949), *Barricade* (WB, 1950), *Backfire* (WB, 1950), *Time Running Out* (British, 1950), *Never Trust a Gambler* (Col., 1951), *Fort Defiance* (UA, 1951), *Highly Dangerous* (Lip., 1951), *Gambler and the Lady* (Lip., 1952), *Go, Man, Go!* (UA, 1954), *Paid to Kill* (Lip., 1954), *Blackout* (Lip., 1954), *Port of Hell* (AA, 1954), *Thunder Pass* (Lip., 1954), *Toughest Man Alive* (AA, 1955), *Massacre* (20th, 1956), *The Man Is Armed* (Rep., 1956), *Outlaw's Son* (UA, 1957), *Whistle* (MPO Videotronics-ASA Films, 1967).

Tony Martinez, Frank Marlowe, Dane Clark and Robert Douglas in *Barricade.*

FRED CLARK (Frederic Leonard Clark) Born March 9, 1914, Lincoln, California. Married Benay Venuta (1952); divorced 1963. Married Gloria Glaser (1966).

Feature Films: *The Unsuspected* (WB, 1947), *Ride the Pink Horse* (Univ., 1947), *Hazard* (Par., 1948), *Cry of the City* (20th, 1948), *Two Guys From Texas* (WB, 1948), *Alias Nick Beal* (Par., 1949), *Flamingo Road* (WB, 1949), *The Younger Brothers* (WB, 1949), *Task Force* (WB,

Ginger Rogers and Fred Clark in *Dream Boat.*

1949), *White Heat* (WB, 1949), *The Lady Takes a Sailor* (WB, 1949), *Sunset Boulevard* (Par., 1950), *The Eagle and the Hawk* (Par., 1950), *Return of the Frontiersman* (WB, 1950), *The Jackpot* (20th, 1950), *Mrs. O'Malley and Mr. Malone* (MGM, 1950), *The Lemon Drop Kid* (Par., 1951), *Hollywood Story* (Univ., 1951), *A Place in the Sun* (Par., 1951), *Meet Me After the Show* (20th, 1951), *Three for Bedroom C* (WB, 1952), *Dreamboat* (20th, 1952), *The Stars Are Singing* (Par., 1953), *The Caddy* (Par., 1953), *How to Marry a Millionaire* (20th, 1953), *Here Come the Girls* (Par., 1953), *Living It Up* (Par., 1954), *Abbott And Costello Meet the Keystone Kops* (Univ., 1955), *Daddy Long Legs* (20th, 1955), *How to Be Very, Very Popular* (20th, 1955), *The Court-Martial of Billy Mitchell* (WB, 1955), *Miracle in the Rain* (WB, 1956), *The Birds and the Bees* (Par., 1956), *The Solid Gold Cadillac* (Col., 1956), *Back From Eternity* (RKO, 1956), *Joe Butterfly* (Univ., 1957), *The Fuzzy Pink Nightgown* (UA, 1957), *Don't Go Near the Water* (MGM, 1957), *Mardi Gras* (20th, 1958), *Auntie Mame* (WB, 1958), *The Mating Game* (MGM, 1959), *It Started With a Kiss* (MGM, 1959), *Visit To a Small Planet* (Par., 1960), *Bells Are Ringing* (MGM, 1960), *Zotz!* (Col., 1962), *Boys' Night Out* (MGM, 1962), *Hemingway's Adventures of a Young Man* (20th, 1962), *Move Over, Darling* (20th, 1963), *John Goldfarb, Please Come Home* (20th, 1964), *The Curse of the Mummy's Tomb* (Col., 1965), *Sergeant Deadhead* (AIP, 1965), *Dr. Goldfoot and the Bikini Machine* (AIP, 1965), *When the Boys Meet the Girls* (MGM, 1965), *War Italian Style* (AIP, 1967), *Year of the Horse* (BV, 1968).

MAE CLARKE Born August 16, 1910, Philadelphia, Pennsylvania. Married Lew Brice (1928); divorced 1930. Married Stephen Bancroft (1937); divorced. Married Herbert Langdon; divorced.

Jack Holt and Mae Clarke in *Trouble in Morocco.*

Feature Films: *Big Time* (Fox, 1929), *Nix on Dames* (Fox, 1929), *Fall Guy* (WB, 1930), *Dancers* (Fox, 1930), *Front Page* (UA, 1931), *Men on Call* (Fox, 1931), *Public Enemy* (WB, 1931), *Good Bad Girl!* (Col., 1931), *Waterloo Bridge* (Univ., 1931), *Reckless Living* (Col., 1931), *Frankenstein* (Univ., 1931), *Final Edition* (Col., 1932), *Three Wise Girls* (Col., 1932), *Impatient Maiden* (Col., 1932), *Night World* (Univ., 1932), *Breach of Promise* (World Wide, 1932), *Penguin Pool Murder* (RKO, 1932), *Fast Workers* (MGM, 1933), *Parole Girl* (Col., 1933), *Made on Broadway* (MGM, 1933), *Turn Back the Clock* (MGM, 1933), *As the Devil Commands* (Col., 1933), *Penthouse* (MGM, 1933), *Lady Killer* (WB, 1933), *Flaming Gold* (RKO, 1934), *This Side of Heaven* (MGM, 1934), *Nana* (UA, 1934), *Let's Talk It Over* (Univ., 1934), *Operator 13* (MGM, 1934), *Man With Two Faces* (WB, 1934), *The Daring Young Man* (Fox, 1935), *Silk Hat Kid* (Fox, 1935), *Hitch Hike Lady* (Rep., 1935), *The House of a Thousand Candles* (Rep., 1936), *Hearts in Bondage* (Rep., 1936), *Wild Brian Kent* (20th, 1936), *Great Guy* (GN, 1936), *Hats Off* (GN, 1936), *Trouble in Morocco* (Col., 1937), *Outlaws of the Orient* (Col., 1937), *Women in War* (Rep., 1940), *Sailors on Leave* (Rep., 1941), *Flying Tigers* (Rep., 1942), *Lady From Chungking* (PRC, 1942), *Here Come the Waves* (Par., 1944), *And Now Tomorrow* (Par., 1944), *Kitty* (Par., 1945), *Daredevils of the Clouds* (Rep., 1948), *King of the Rocket Men* (Rep. serial, 1949), *Streets of San Francisco* (Rep., 1949), *Gun Runner* (Mon., 1949), *Annie Get Your Gun* (MGM, 1950), *The Yellow Cab Man* (MGM, 1950), *The Great Caruso* (MGM, 1951), *Mr. Imperium* (MGM, 1951), *The People Against O'Hara* (MGM, 1951), *Callaway Went Thataway* (MGM, 1951), *The Unknown Man* (MGM, 1951), *Because of You* (MGM, 1952), *Horizons West* (Univ., 1952), *Singin' in the Rain* (MGM, 1952), *Thunderbirds* (Rep., 1952), *Pat and Mike* (MGM, 1952), *Magnificent Obsession* (Univ., 1954), *Women's Prison* (Col., 1955), *Not as a Stranger* (UA, 1955), *Wichita* (AA, 1955), *I Died a Thousand Times* (WB, 1955), *Come Next Spring* (Rep., 1956), *Mohawk* (20th, 1956), *The Desperadoes Are in Town* (20th, 1956), *Ride the High Iron* (Col., 1956), *Voice in the Mirror* (Univ., 1958), *Ask Any Girl* (MGM, 1959), *Big Hand for the Little Lady* (WB, 1966), *Thoroughly Modern Millie* (Univ., 1967).

William Holden and Lee J. Cobb in *The Dark Past.*

Feature Films: *North of Rio Grande* (Par., 1937), *Ali Baba Goes to Town* (20th, 1937), *Rustler's Valley* (Par., 1937), *Danger on the Air,* (Univ., 1938), *The Phantom Creeps* (Univ. serial, 1939), *Golden Boy* (Col., 1939), *Men of Boys Town* (MGM, 1941), *This Thing Called Love* (Col., 1941), *Paris Calling* (Univ., 1941), *Tonight We Raid Calais* (20th, 1943), *Buckskin Frontier* (UA, 1943), *The Moon Is Down* (20th, 1943), *The Song of Bernadette* (20th, 1943), *Winged Victory* (20th, 1944), *Anna and the King of Siam* (20th, 1946), *Boomerang* (20th, 1947), *Johnny O'Clock* (Col., 1947), *Captain From Castile* (20th, 1947), *Call Northside 777* (20th, 1948), *The Miracle of the Bells* (RKO, 1948), *The Luck of the Irish* (20th, 1948), *The Dark Past* (Col., 1948), *Thieves' Highway* (20th, 1949), *The Man Who Cheated Himself* (20th, 1950), *Sirocco* (Col., 1951), *The Family Secret* (Col., 1951), *The Fighter* (UA, 1952), *The Tall Texan* (Lip., 1953), *Yankee Pasha* (Univ., 1954), *Gorilla at Large* (20th, 1954), *On the Waterfront* (Col., 1954), *Day of Triumph* (George J. Schaefer, 1954), *The Racers* (20th, 1955), *The Road to Denver* (Rep., 1955), *The Left Hand of God* (20th, 1955), *The Man in the Gray Flannel Suit* (20th, 1956), *Miami Exposé* (Col., 1956), *12 Angry Men* (UA, 1957), *The Garment Jungle* (Col., 1957), *The Three Faces of Eve* (20th, 1957), *The Brothers Karamazov* (MGM, 1958), *Man of the West* (UA, 1958), *Party Girl* (MGM, 1958), *The Trap* (Par., 1959), *Green Mansions* (MGM, 1959), *But Not for Me* (Par., 1959), *Exodus* (UA, 1960), *The Four Horsemen of the Apocalypse* (MGM, 1962), *How the West Was Won* (MGM, 1963), *Come Blow Your Horn* (Par., 1963), *Our Man Flint* (20th, 1966), *In Like Flint* (20th, 1967), *MacKenna's Gold* (Col., 1968), *Our Man From Las Vegas* (WB-7 Arts, 1968).

Charles Coburn and Spencer Tracy in *Edison the Man.*

Cornell Borchers and Montgomery Clift in *The Big Lift.*

MONTGOMERY CLIFT (Edward Montgomery Clift) Born October 17, 1920, Omaha, Nebraska. Died July 23, 1966.

Feature Films: *The Search* (MGM, 1948), *Red River* (UA, 1948), *The Heiress* (Par., 1949), *The Big Lift* (20th, 1950), *A Place in the Sun* (Par., 1951), *I Confess* (WB, 1953), *From Here to Eternity* (Col., 1953), *Indiscretion of an American Wife* (Col., 1954), *Raintree County* (MGM, 1957), *The Young Lions* (20th, 1958), *Lonelyhearts* (UA, 1959), *Suddenly, Last Summer* (Col., 1959), *Wild River* (20th, 1960), *The Misfits* (UA, 1961), *Judgment at Nuremberg* (UA, 1961), *Freud* (Univ., 1962), *The Defector* (7 Arts, 1966).

LEE J. COBB (Leo Jacob) Born December 8, 1911, New York, New York. Married Helen Beverly (1940), children: Vincent, Julie; divorced 1952. Married Mary Hirsch (1957), children: Tony, Jerry.

CHARLES COBURN (Charles Douville Coburn) Born June 19, 1877, Savannah, Georgia. Married Ivah Wills (1906); widowed 1937. Married Winifred Natzka (1959). Died August 30, 1961.

Feature Films: *The People's Enemy* (RKO, 1935), *Of Human Hearts* (MGM, 1938), *Vivacious Lady* (RKO, 1938), *Yellow Jack* (MGM, 1938), *Lord Jeff* (MGM, 1938), *Idiot's Delight* (MGM, 1939), *The Story of Alexander Graham Bell* (20th, 1939), *Made for Each Other* (UA, 1939), *Bachelor Mother* (RKO, 1939), *Stanley and Livingstone* (20th, 1939), *In Name Only* (RKO, 1939), *Road to Singapore* (Par., 1940), *Florian* (MGM, 1940), *Edison, The Man* (MGM, 1940), *Three Faces West* (Rep., 1940), *The Captain Is a Lady* (MGM, 1940), *The Lady Eve* (Par., 1941), *The Devil and Miss Jones* (RKO, 1941), *Our Wife* (Col., 1941), *Unexpected Uncle* (RKO, 1941), *H. M. Pulham, Esq.* (MGM, 1941), *Kings Row* (WB, 1941), *In This Our Life* (WB, 1942), *George Washington Slept Here* (WB, 1942), *The More the Merrier* (Col., 1943), *The Constant Nymph* (WB, 1943), *Heaven Can Wait* (20th, 1943), *Princess O'Rourke* (WB, 1943), *My Kingdom for a Cook* (Col., 1943), *Knickerbocker Holiday* (UA, 1944), *Wilson* (20th, 1944), *The Impatient Years* (Col., 1944), *A Royal Scandal* (20th, 1945), *Rhapsody in Blue* (WB, 1945), *Over 21* (Col., 1945), *Colonel Effingham's Raid* (20th, 1945), *Shady Lady* (Univ., 1945), *The Green Years* (MGM, 1946), *Lured* (UA, 1947), *B. F.'s Daughter* (MGM, 1948), *The Paradine Case* (Selznick, 1948), *Green Grass of Wyoming* (20th, 1948), *Impact* (UA, 1949), *Yes Sir, That's My Baby* (Univ., 1949), *Everybody Does It* (20th, 1949), *The Doctor and the Girl* (MGM, 1949), *The Gal Who Took the West* (Univ., 1949), *Louisa* (Univ., 1950), *Peggy* (Univ., 1950), *Mr. Music* (Par., 1950), *The Highwayman* (AA, 1951), *Monkey Business* (20th, 1952), *Has Anybody Seen My Gal* (Univ., 1952), *Gentlemen Prefer Blondes* (20th, 1953), *Trouble Along the Way* (WB, 1953), *The Long Wait* (UA, 1954), *The Rocket Man* (20th, 1954), *How To Be Very, Very Popular* (20th, 1955), *The Power and the Prize* (MGM, 1956), *Around the World in 80 Days* (UA, 1956), *Town on Trial* (Col., 1957), *The Story of Mankind* (WB, 1957), *How to Murder a Rich Uncle* (Col., 1957), *Stranger in My Arms* (Univ., 1959), *The Remarkable Mr. Pennypacker* (20th, 1959), *John Paul Jones* (WB, 1959), *Pepe* (Col., 1960).

JAMES COBURN Born August 31, 1928, Laurel, Nebraska. Married Beverly Kelly (1958), children: Lisa, James.

Anthony Quinn and James Coburn in A *High Wind in Jamaica.*

Feature Films: *Ride Lonesome* (Col., 1959), *Face of a Fugitive* (Col., 1959), *The Magnificent Seven* (UA, 1960), *Hell Is for Heroes* (Par., 1962), *The Great Escape* (UA, 1963), *Charade* (Univ., 1963), *The Man From Galveston* (WB, 1964), *The Americanization of Emily* (MGM, 1964), *Major Dundee* (Col., 1965), *A High Wind in Jamaica* (20th, 1965), *The Loved One* (MGM, 1965), *Our Man Flint* (20th, 1966), *Dead Heat on a Merry-Go-Round* (Col., 1966), *In Like Flint* (20th, 1967), *Waterhole No. 3* (Par., 1967), *The President's Analyst* (Par., 1967), *Duffy* (Col., 1968).

Gene Nelson, Steve Cochran, Paul Picerni (on stage) and Paul Bryar in *She's Back on Broadway.*

STEVE COCHRAN (Robert A. Cochran) Born May 25, 1917, Eureka, California. Married Florence Lockwood, child: Xandra; divorced 1946. Married Fay McKenzie (1946); divorced 1948. Married Jonna Jensen (1961); divorced. Died June 15, 1965.

English-Language Feature Films: *Wonder Man* (RKO, 1945), *Boston Blackie Booked on Suspicion* (Col., 1945), *The Gay Senorita* (Col., 1945), *The Best Years of Our Lives* (RKO, 1946), *The Chase* (UA, 1946), *Copacabana* (UA, 1947), *The Kid From Brooklyn* (RKO, 1947), *A Song Is Born* (RKO, 1948), *White Heat* (WB, 1949), *The Damned Don't Cry* (WB, 1950), *Dallas* (WB, 1950), *Highway 301* (WB, 1950), *Storm Warning* (WB, 1950), *Raton Pass* (WB, 1951), *Inside the Walls of Folsom Prison* (WB, 1951), *Jim Thorpe—All American* (WB, 1951), *Tomorrow Is Another Day* (WB, 1951), *The Tanks Are Coming* (WB, 1951), *The Lion and the Horse* (WB, 1952), *Operation Secret* (WB, 1952), *She's Back on Broadway* (WB, 1953), *The Desert Song* (WB, 1953), *Back to God's Country* (Univ., 1953), *Shark River* (UA, 1953), *Carnival Story* (RKO, 1954), *Private Hell 36* (Filmakers, 1954), *Come Next Spring* (Rep., 1956), *Slander* (MGM, 1956), *The Weapon* (Rep., 1957), *Quantrill's Raiders* (AA, 1958), *I, Mobster* (20th, 1958), *The Big Operator* (MGM, 1959), *The Beat Generation* (MGM, 1959), *The Deadly Companions* (Pathé-American, 1961), *Of Love and Desire* (20th, 1963), *Mozambique* (7 Arts, 1965), *Tell Me in the Sunlight* (Movie-Rama Color Corp., 1967).

CLAUDETTE COLBERT (Lily Chauchoin) Born September 13, 1905, Paris, France. Married Norman Foster (1928); divorced 1935. Married Joel Pressman (1935); widowed 1968.

John Barrymore and Claudette Colbert in *Midnight.*

English-Language Sound Feature Films: *The Hole in the Wall* (Par., 1929), *The Lady Lies* (Par., 1929), *Manslaughter* (Par., 1930), *The Big Pond* (Par., 1930), *Young Man of Manhattan* (Par., 1930), *The Smiling Lieutenant* (Par., 1931), *Honor Among Lovers* (Par., 1931), *Secrets of a Secretary* (Par., 1931), *His Woman* (Par., 1931), *The Wiser Sex* (Par., 1932), *Make Me a Star* (Par., 1932),* *Misleading Lady* (Par., 1932), *Man From Yesterday* (Par., 1932), *Phantom President* (Par., 1932), *The Sign of the Cross* (Par., 1932), *Tonight Is Ours* (Par., 1933), *I Cover the Waterfront* (UA, 1933), *Three-Cornered Moon* (Par., 1933), *Torch Singer* (Par., 1933), *Four Frightened People* (Par., 1934), *It Happened One Night* (Col., 1934), *Cleopatra* (Par., 1934), *Imitation of Life* (Univ., 1934), *The Gilded Lily* (Par., 1935), *Private Worlds* (Par., 1935), *She Married Her Boss* (Col., 1935), *The Bride Comes Home* (Par., 1935), *Under Two Flags* (20th, 1936), *Maid of Salem* (Par., 1937), *I Met Him in Paris* (Par., 1937), *Tovarich* (WB, 1937), *Bluebeard's Eighth Wife* (Par., 1938), *Zaza* (Par., 1939), *Midnight* (Par., 1939), *It's a Wonderful World* (MGM, 1939), *Drums Along the Mohawk* (20th, 1939), *Boom Town* (MGM, 1940), *Arise, My Love* (Par., 1940), *Skylark* (Par., 1941), *The Palm Beach Story* (Par., 1942), *Remember the Day* (20th, 1942), *No Time for Love* (Par., 1943), *So Proudly We Hail* (Par., 1943), *Since You Went Away* (UA, 1944), *Practically Yours* (Par., 1944), *Guest Wife* (UA, 1945), *Without Reservations* (RKO, 1946), *Tomorrow Is Forever* (RKO, 1946), *The Secret Heart* (MGM, 1946), *The Egg and I* (Univ., 1947), *Sleep, My Love* (UA, 1948), *Family Honeymoon* (Univ., 1949), *Bride for Sale* (RKO, 1949), *Three Came Home* (20th, 1950), *The Secret Fury* (RKO, 1950), *Thunder on the Hill* (Univ., 1951), *Let's Make It Legal* (20th, 1951), *Outpost in Malaya* (UA, 1952), *Texas Lady* (RKO, 1955), *Parrish* (WB, 1961).

*Unbilled guest appearance

JOAN COLLINS Born May 23, 1933, London, England. Married Maxwell Reed (1952); divorced 1957. Married Anthony Newley (1963), children: Tara, Anthony.

Dolores Gray, Leslie Nielsen, June Allyson, Joan Collins, Sam Levene and Jonathan Hale in *The Opposite Sex*.

Feature Films: *Lady Godiva Rides Again* (Carroll Pictures, 1951), *Cosh Boy* ("The Slasher"—British Lion, 1952), *I Believe in You* (Univ., 1953), *Turn the Key Softly* (Rank, 1953), *The Square Ring* (Rep., 1953), *Decameron Nights* (RKO, 1953), *The Woman's Angle* (Associated British, 1954), *The Good Die Young* (UA, 1954), *Our Girl Friday* ("The Adventures of Sadie"—Associated British, 1954), *Judgement Deferred* (Eros, 1955), *Land of the Pharaohs* (WB, 1955), *The Virgin Queen* (20th, 1955), *The Girl in the Red Velvet Swing* (20th, 1955), *The Opposite Sex* (MGM, 1956), *The Wayward Bus* (20th, 1957), *Island in the Sun* (20th, 1957), *Sea Wife* (20th, 1957), *Stopover Tokyo* (20th, 1957), *The Bravados* (20th, 1958), *Rally 'Round the Flag, Boys!* (20th, 1958), *Seven Thieves* (20th, 1959), *Esther and the King* (20th, 1960), *Road to Hong Kong* (UA, 1962), *Warning Shot* (Par., 1967).

Ronald Colman (dual role) and Halliwell Hobbes in *The Masquerader*.

RONALD COLMAN Born February 9, 1891, Richmond, Surrey, England. Married Thelma Raye (1919); divorced 1934. Married Benita Hume (1938), child: Juliet. Died May 19, 1958.

Sound Feature Films: *Bulldog Drummond* (UA, 1929), *Condemned* (UA, 1929), *Raffles* (UA, 1930), *The Devil to Pay* (UA, 1930), *The Unholy Garden* (UA, 1931), *Arrowsmith* (UA, 1931), *Cynara* (UA, 1932), *The Masquerader* (UA, 1933), *Bulldog Drummond Strikes Back* (UA, 1934), *Clive of India* (UA, 1935), *The Man Who Broke the Bank at Monte Carlo* (Fox, 1935), *A Tale of Two Cities* (MGM, 1935), *Under Two Flags* (20th, 1936), *Lost Horizon* (Col., 1937), *The Prisoner of Zenda* (UA, 1937), *If I Were King* (Par., 1938), *The Light That Failed* (Par., 1939), *Lucky Partners* (RKO, 1940), *My Life With Caroline* (RKO, 1941), *The Talk of the Town* (Col., 1942), *Random Harvest* (MGM, 1942), *Kismet* (MGM, 1944), *The Late George Apley* (20th, 1947), *A Double Life* (Univ., 1948), *Champagne For Caesar* (UA, 1950), *Around the World in 80 Days* (UA, 1956), *The Story of Mankind* (WB, 1957).

SEAN CONNERY (Thomas Connery) Born August 25, 1930, Edinburgh, Scotland. Married Diana Cilento (1962), children: Giovanna, Jason.

Lana Turner and Sean Connery in *Another Time, Another Place*.

Feature Films: *Action of the Tiger* (MGM, 1957), *No Road Back* (RKO, 1957), *Timelock* (DCA, 1957), *Hell Drivers* (Rank, 1957), *Another Time, Another Place* (Par., 1958), *Darby O'Gill and the Little People* (BV, 1959), *Tarzan's Greatest Adventure* (Par., 1959), *On The Fiddle* ("Operation Snafu"—Anglo Amalgamated, 1961), *The Frightened City* (AA, 1961), *The Longest Day* (20th, 1962), *Dr. No* (UA, 1963), *From Russia With Love* (UA, 1964), *Marnie* (Univ., 1964), *Woman of*

Straw (UA, 1964), *Goldfinger* (UA, 1964), *The Hill* (UA, 1965), *Thunderball* (UA, 1965), *A Fine Madness* (WB, 1966), *You Only Live Twice* (UA, 1967).

WALTER CONNOLLY Born April 8, 1887, Cincinnati, Ohio. Married Hedda Harrington (1923), child: Anne. Died May 28, 1940.

Walter Connolly and Verree Teasdale in *First Lady.*

Sound Feature Films: *No More Orchids* (Col., 1932), *Washington Merry-Go-Round* (Col., 1932), *Man Against Woman* (Col., 1932), *Lady For a Day* (Col., 1933), *East of Fifth Avenue* (Col., 1933), *The Bitter Tea of General Yen* (Col., 1933), *Paddy the Next Best Thing* (Col., 1933), *Master of Men* (Col., 1933), *Man's Castle* (Col., 1933), *It Happened One Night* (Col., 1934), *Once to Every Woman* (Col., 1934), *Eight Girls in a Boat* (Par., 1934), *Twentieth Century* (Col., 1934), *Whom the Gods Destroy* (Col., 1934), *Servant's Entrance* (Fox, 1934), *Lady by Choice* (Col., 1934), *Broadway Bill* (Col., 1934), *The Captain Hates the Sea* (Col., 1934), *White Lies* (Col., 1934), *Father Brown, Detective* (Par., 1935), *She Couldn't Take It* (Col., 1935), *So Red the Rose* (Par., 1935), *One Way Ticket* (Col., 1935), *The Music Goes 'Round* (Col., 1936), *Soak the Rich* (Par., 1936), *The King Steps Out* (WB, 1936), *Libeled Lady* (MGM, 1936), *The Good Earth* (MGM, 1937), *Nancy Steele Is Missing* (20th, 1937), *Let's Get Married* (Col., 1937), *The League Of Frightened Men* (Col., 1937), *First Lady* (WB, 1937), *Nothing Sacred* (UA, 1937), *Penitentiary* (Col., 1938), *Start Cheering* (Col., 1938), *Four's a Crowd* (WB, 1938), *Too Hot to Handle* (MGM, 1938), *The Girl Downstairs* (MGM, 1939), *Adventures of Huckleberry Finn* (MGM, 1939), *Bridal Suite* (MGM, 1939), *Good Girls Go to Paris* (Col., 1939), *Coast Guard* (Col., 1939), *Those High Gray Walls* (Col., 1939), *Fifth Avenue Girl* (RKO, 1939), *The Great Victor Herbert* (Par., 1939).

GARY COOPER (Frank James Cooper) Born May 7, 1901, Helena, Montana. Married Veronica Balfe (1933), child: Marie. Died May 13, 1961.

Sound Feature Films: *The Virginian* (Par., 1929), *Only the Brave* (Par., 1930), *Paramount on Parade* (Par., 1930), *The Texan* (Par., 1930), *Seven Days Leave* (Par., 1930), *A Man From Wyoming* (Par., 1930), *The Spoilers* (Par., 1930), *Morocco* (Par., 1930), *Fighting Caravans* (Par., 1931), *City Streets* (Par., 1931), *I Take This Woman* (Par., 1931), *His Woman* (Par., 1931), *The Devil and the Deep* (Par., 1932), *Make Me a Star* (Par., 1932), *If I Had a Million* (Par., 1932), *Farewell To Arms* (Par., 1932), *Today We Live* (MGM, 1933), *One Sunday Afternoon* (Par., 1933), *Design For Living* (Par., 1933), *Alice in Wonderland* (Par., 1933), *Operator 13* (MGM, 1934), *Now and Forever* (Par., 1934), *The Wedding Night* (UA, 1935), *Lives of a Bengal Lancer* (Par., 1935), *Peter Ibbetson* (Par., 1935), *Desire* (Par., 1936), *Mr. Deeds Goes to Town* (Col., 1936), *The General Died at Dawn* (Par., 1936), *Hollywood Boulevard* (Par., 1936), *The Plainsman* (Par., 1936), *Souls at Sea* (Par., 1937), *Adventures of Marco Polo* (UA, 1938), *Bluebeard's Eighth Wife* (Par., 1938), *The Cowboy and the Lady* (UA, 1938), *Beau*

Sigrid Gurie and Gary Cooper in *The Adventures of Marco Polo.*

Geste (Par., 1939), *The Real Glory* (UA, 1939), *The Westerner* (UA, 1940), *North West Mounted Police* (Par., 1940), *Meet John Doe* (WB, 1941), *Sergeant York* (WB, 1941), *Ball of Fire* (RKO, 1941), *The Pride of the Yankees* (RKO, 1942), *For Whom The Bell Tolls* (Par., 1943), *The Story Of Dr. Wassell* (Par., 1944), *Casanova Brown* (RKO, 1944), *Along Came Jones* (RKO, 1945), *Saratoga Trunk* (WB, 1945), *Cloak and Dagger* (WB, 1946), *Unconquered* (Par., 1947), *Variety Girl* (Par., 1947), *Good Sam* (RKO, 1948), *The Fountainhead* (WB, 1949), *It's a Great Feeling* (WB, 1949), *Task Force* (WB, 1949), *Bright Leaf* (WB, 1950), *Dallas* (WB, 1950), *You're in the Navy Now* (20th, 1951), *Starlift* (WB, 1951), *It's a Big Country* (MGM, 1951), *Distant Drums* (WB, 1951), *High Noon* (UA, 1952), *Springfield Rifle* (WB, 1952), *Return To Paradise* (UA, 1953), *Blowing Wild* (WB, 1953), *Garden of Evil* (20th, 1954), *Vera Cruz* (UA, 1954), *The Court-Martial Of Billy Mitchell* (WB, 1955), *Friendly Persuasion* (AA, 1956), *Love in the Afternoon* (AA, 1957), *Ten North Frederick* (20th, 1958), *Man of the West* (UA, 1958), *The Hanging Tree* (WB, 1959), *They Came to Cordura* (Col., 1959), *The Wreck of the Mary Deare* (MGM, 1959), *Alias Jesse James* (UA, 1959),* *The Naked Edge* (UA, 1961).

*Unbilled guest appearance

GLADYS COOPER Born December 18, 1888, Lewisham, England. Married Herbert Buckmaster (1908) children: Joan, John; divorced 1922. Married Sir Neville Pearson (1928), child: Sally; divorced 1936. Married Philip Merivale (1937); widowed 1946.

Gladys Cooper, Claude Rains and Ilka Chase in *Now, Voyager.*

Sound Feature Films: *The Iron Duke* (Gaumont-British, 1935), *Rebecca* (UA, 1940), *Kitty Foyle* (RKO, 1940), *That Hamilton Woman* (UA, 1941), *The Black Cat* (Univ., 1941), *The Gay Falcon* (RKO, 1941), *This Above All* (20th, 1942), *Eagle Squadron* (Univ., 1942), *Now, Voyager* (WB, 1942), *Forever and a Day* (RKO, 1943), *Mr. Lucky* (RKO, 1943), *Princess O'Rourke* (WB, 1943), *The Song of Bernadette* (20th, 1943), *The White Cliffs of Dover* (MGM, 1944), *Mrs. Parkington* (Par., 1944), *Valley of Decision* (MGM, 1945), *Love Letters* (Par., 1945), *The Green Years* (MGM, 1946), *The Cockeyed Miracle* (MGM, 1946), *Green Dolphin Street* (MGM, 1947), *The Bishop's Wife* (RKO, 1947), *Beware of Pity* (Two Cities, 1947), *Homecoming* (MGM, 1948), *The Pirate* (MGM, 1948), *The Secret Garden* (MGM, 1949), *Madame Bovary* (MGM, 1949), *Thunder on the Hill* (Univ., 1951), *At Sword's Point* (RKO, 1952), *The Man Who Loved Redheads* (UA, 1955), *Separate Tables* (UA, 1958), *The List of Adrian Messenger* (Univ., 1963), *My Fair Lady* (WB, 1964), *The Happiest Millionaire* (BV, 1967).

JACKIE COOPER (John Cooper, Jr) Born September 15, 1922, Los Angeles, California. Married June Horne (1944), child: John; divorced 1945. Married Hildy Parks (1949); divorced 1950. Married Barbara Kraus (1954), children: Russell, Julie, Christina.

Ralph Graves, Jackie Cooper and Charles "Chic" Sale in *When a Feller Needs a Friend.*

Sound Feature Films: *Sunny Side Up* (Fox, 1929), *Skippy* (Par., 1931), *Young Donovan's Kid* (RKO, 1931), *The Champ* (MGM, 1931), *Sooky* (Par., 1931), *When a Feller Needs a Friend* (MGM, 1932), *Divorce in the Family* (MGM, 1932), *Broadway to Hollywood* (MGM, 1933), *The Bowery* (UA, 1933), *Lone Cowboy* (Par., 1934), *Treasure Island* (MGM, 1934), *Peck's Bad Boy* (Fox, 1934), *Dinky* (WB, 1935), *O'Shaughnessy's Boy* (MGM, 1935), *Tough Guy* (MGM, 1936), *The Devil Is a Sissy* (MGM, 1936), *Boy of the Streets* (Mon., 1937), *White Banners* (WB, 1938), *Gangster's Boy* (Mon., 1938), *That Certain Age* (Univ., 1938), *Newsboys' Home* (Univ., 1939), *Scouts to the Rescue* (Univ. serial, 1939), *Spirit of Culver* (Univ., 1939), *Streets of New York* (Mon., 1939), *What a Life!* (Par., 1939), *Two Bright Boys* (Univ., 1939), *The Big Guy* (Univ., 1940), *Seventeen* (Par., 1940), *The Return of Frank James* (20th, 1940), *Gallant Sons* (MGM, 1940), *Life With Henry* (Par., 1941), *Ziegfeld Girl* (MGM, 1941), *Her First Beau* (Col., 1941), *Glamour Boys* (Par., 1941), *Syncopation* (RKO, 1942), *Men of Texas* (Univ., 1942), *The Navy Comes Thru* (RKO, 1942), *Where Are Your Children?* (Mon., 1943), *Stork Bites Man* (UA, 1947), *Kilroy Was Here* (Mon., 1947), *French Leave* (Mon., 1948).

ELLEN CORBY (Ellen Hansen) Born June 3, 1913, Racine, Wisconsin.

Feature Films: *The Dark Corner* (20th, 1946), *Cornered* (RKO, 1945), *From This Day Forward* (RKO, 1946), *It's a Wonderful Life* (RKO, 1946), *Till the End of Time* (RKO, 1946), *Cuban Pete* (Univ., 1946), *Crack-Up* (RKO, 1946), *The Spiral Staircase* (RKO, 1946), *Sister Kenny* (RKO, 1946), *Lover Come Back* (Univ., 1946), *The Truth About Murder*

Ellen Corby and Philip Tonge in *Macabre.*

(RKO, 1946), *Beat the Band* (RKO, 1947), *Born to Kill* (RKO, 1947), *Forever Amber* (20th, 1947), *They Won't Believe Me* (RKO, 1947), *Driftwood* (Rep., 1947), *Fighting Father Dunne* (RKO, 1948), *Strike It Rich* (AA, 1948), *I Remember Mama* (RKO, 1948), *The Noose Hangs High* (EL, 1948), *If You Knew Susie* (RKO, 1948), *Little Women* (MGM, 1949), *Mighty Joe Young* (RKO, 1949), *The Dark Past* (Col., 1949), *Rusty Saves a Life* (Col., 1949), *A Woman's Secret* (RKO, 1949), *Madame Bovary* (MGM, 1949), *Captain China* (Par., 1949), *The Gunfighter* (20th, 1950), *Caged* (WB, 1950), *Peggy* (Univ., 1950), *Edge of Doom* (RKO, 1950), *Harriet Craig* (Col., 1950), *Goodbye, My Fancy* (WB, 1951), *The Mating Season* (Par., 1951), *Angels in the Outfield* (MGM, 1951), *The Sea Hornet* (Rep., 1951), *The Barefoot Mailman* (Col., 1951), *On Moonlight Bay* (WB, 1951), *The Big Trees* (WB, 1952,) *Fearless Fagan* (MGM, 1952), *Monsoon* (UA, 1952), *Shane* (Par., 1953), *The Woman They Almost Lynched* (Rep., 1953), *The Vanquished* (Par., 1953), *A Lion Is in the Streets* (WB, 1953), *Untamed Heiress* (Rep., 1954), *About Mrs. Leslie* (Par., 1954), *The Bowery Boys Meet the Monster* (AA, 1954), *Sabrina* (Par., 1954), *Susan Slept Here* (RKO, 1954), *Illegal* (WB, 1955), *Slightly Scarlet* (RKO, 1956), *Stagecoach to Fury* (20th, 1956), *Night Passage* (Univ., 1957), *The Seventh Sin* (MGM, 1957), *God is My Partner* (20th, 1957), *Rockabilly Baby* (20th, 1957), *All Mine to Give* (Univ., 1957), *Macabre* (AA, 1958), *Vertigo* (Par., 1958), *Visit to a Small Planet* (Par., 1960), *A Pocketful of Miracles* (UA, 1961), *Saintly Sinners* (UA, 1962), *The Caretaker* (UA, 1963), *The Strangler* (AA, 1964), *Hush . . . Hush, Sweet Charlotte* (20th, 1965), *The Family Jewels* (Par., 1965), *The Night of the Grizzly* (Par., 1966), *The Gnome-Mobile* (BV, 1967), *A Quiet Couple* (CBS Theatrical Films, 1968).

WENDELL COREY Born March 20, 1914, Dracut, Massachusetts. Married Alice Wiley (1939), children: Robin, Jonathan, Jennifer, Ronald.

Feature Films: *Desert Fury* (Par., 1947), *I Walk Alone* (Par., 1947), *The Search* (MGM, 1948), *Man-Eater of Kumaon* (Univ., 1948), *Sorry, Wrong Number* (Par., 1948), *The Accused* (Par., 1948), *Any Number Can Play* (MGM, 1949), *File on Thelma Jordan* (Par., 1949), *Holiday Affair* (RKO, 1949), *No Sad Songs for Me* (Col., 1950), *The Furies* (Par., 1950), *Harriet Craig* (Col., 1950), *The Great Missouri Raid* (Par., 1950), *Rich, Young and Pretty* (MGM, 1951), *The Wild Blue Yonder* (Rep., 1951), *The Wild North* (MGM, 1952), *Carbine Williams*

Mary Astor and Wendell Corey in *Any Number Can Play.*

(MGM, 1952), *My Man and I* (MGM, 1952), *Jamaica Run* (Par., 1953), *Hell's Half Acre* (Rep., 1954), *Rear Window* (Par., 1954), *The Big Knife* (UA, 1955), *The Bold and the Brave* (RKO, 1956), *The Killer Is Loose* (UA, 1956), *The Rack* (MGM, 1956), *The Rainmaker* (Par., 1956), *Loving You* (Par., 1957), *The Light in the Forest* (BV, 1958), *Alias Jesse James* (UA, 1959), *Blood on the Arrow* (AA, 1964), *Agent for H.A.R.M.* (Univ., 1965), *Waco* (Par., 1966), *Women of the Prehistoric Planet* (Realart, 1966), *Picture Mommy Dead* (Embassy, 1966), *Red Tomahawk* (Par., 1967), *Cyborg 2087* (PRO, 1967), *The Astro Zombies* (ATV Mikels Productions, 1968), *Buckskin* (Par., 1968).

RICARDO CORTEZ (Jake Krantz) Born September 19, 1899, Brooklyn, New York. Married Alma Rubens (1926); widowed 1931.

William Boyd, Ricardo Cortez and Kay Francis in *The House on 56th Street.*

Sound Feature Films: *The Phantom in The House* (Continental, 1929), *Lost Zeppelin* (Tif., 1930), *Montana Moon* (MGM, 1930), *Her Man* (Pathé, 1930), *Big Business Girl* (WB, 1931), *Illicit* (WB, 1931), *Ten Cents a Dance* (Col., 1931), *Behind Office Doors* (RKO, 1931), *The Maltese Falcon* (WB, 1931), *White Shoulders* (RKO, 1931), *Transgression* (RKO, 1931), *Bad Company* (Pathé, 1931), *Reckless Living* (Univ., 1931), *No One Man* (Par., 1932), *Men of Chance* (RKO, 1932), *Symphony of Six Million* (RKO, 1932), *Is My Face Red?* (RKO, 1932), *Thirteen Women* (RKO, 1932), *Phantom of Crestwood* (RKO, 1932), *Flesh* (MGM, 1932), *Broadway Bad* (Fox., 1933), *Midnight Mary* (MGM, 1933), *Big Executive* (Par., 1933), *Torch Singer* (Par., 1933), *House on 56th Street* (WB, 1933), *Big Shakedown* (WB, 1934), *Wonder Bar* (WB, 1934), *Mandalay* (WB, 1934), *Man With Two Faces* (WB, 1934), *Hat, Coat and Glove* (WB, 1934), *A Lost Lady* (WB, 1934), *The Firebird* (WB, 1934), *I Am a Thief* (WB, 1935), *Shadow of Doubt* (MGM, 1935), *White Cockatoo* (WB, 1935), *Manhattan Moon* (Univ., 1935), *Special Agent* (WB, 1935), *Frisco Kid* (WB, 1935), *Man Hunt* (WB, 1936), *The Murder of Dr. Harrigan* (WB, 1936), *The Walking

Dead (WB, 1936), *Postal Inspector* (Univ., 1936), *The Case of the Black Cat* (WB, 1936), *Her Husband Lies* (Par., 1937), *Talk of the Devil* (Gaumont-British, 1937), *The Californian* (20th, 1937), *West of Shanghai* (WB, 1937), *City Girl* (20th, 1937), *Mr. Moto's Last Warning* (20th, 1939), *Charlie Chan in Reno* (20th, 1939), *Murder Over New York* (20th, 1940), *Romance of the Rio Grande* (20th, 1941), *A Shot in the Dark* (WB, 1941), *World Premiere* (Par., 1941), *I Killed That Man* (Mon., 1941), *Who Is Hope Schuyler?* (20th, 1942), *Rubber Racketeers* (Mon., 1942), *Tomorrow We Live* (PRC, 1942), *Make Your Own Bed* (WB, 1944), *The Inner Circle* (Rep., 1946), *The Locket* (RKO, 1946), *Blackmail* (Rep., 1947), *Mystery In Mexico* (RKO, 1948), *Bunco Squad* (RKO, 1950), *The Last Hurrah* (Col., 1958).

JOSEPH COTTEN (Joseph Chesire Cotten) Born May 15, 1905, Petersburg, Virginia. Married Lenore Kipp (1931); widowed 1960. Married Patricia Medina (1960).

Jennifer Jones and Joseph Cotten in *Portrait of Jennie.*

English-Language Feature Films: *Citizen Kane* (RKO, 1941), *Lydia* (UA, 1941), *The Magnificent Ambersons* (RKO, 1942), *Journey into Fear* (RKO, 1942), *Shadow of a Doubt* (Univ., 1943), *Hers to Hold* (Univ., 1943), *Gaslight* (MGM, 1944), *Since You Went Away* (UA, 1944), *I'll Be Seeing You* (UA, 1944), *Love Letters* (Par., 1945); *Duel in the Sun* (Selznick, 1946), *The Farmer's Daughter* (RKO, 1947), *Portrait of Jennie* (Selznick, 1948), *Under Capricorn* (WB, 1949), *Beyond the Forest* (WB, 1949), *The Third Man* (Selznick, 1950), *Walk Softly, Stranger* (RKO, 1950), *Two Flags West* (20th, 1950), *September Affair* (Par., 1950), *Half Angel* (20th, 1951), *Peking Express* (Par., 1951), *The Man With a Cloak* (MGM, 1951), *Untamed Frontier* (Univ., 1952), *The Steel Trap* (20th, 1952), *Niagara* (20th, 1953), *Blueprint for Murder* (20th, 1953), *Special Delivery* (Col., 1955), *The Bottom of the Bottle* (20th, 1956), *The Killer Is Loose* (UA, 1956), *The Halliday Brand* (UA, 1957), *Touch of Evil* (Univ., 1958),* *From the Earth to the Moon* (WB, 1958), *The Angel Wore Red* (MGM, 1960), *The Last Sunset* (Univ., 1961), *Hush . . . Hush, Sweet Charlotte* (20th, 1965), *The Great Sioux Massacre* (Col., 1965), *The Oscar* (Par., 1966), *The Tramplers* (Embassy, 1966), *The Money Trap* (MGM, 1966), *Brighty of the Grand Canyon* (Feature Film Corp. of America, 1967), *The Diamond Spy* (Embassy, 1967), *Jack of Diamonds* (MGM, 1967), *Some May Live* (RKO, 1967), *The Hellbenders* (Embassy, 1967), *Days of Fire* (Italian, 1968).

*Unbilled guest appearance

JEROME COWAN (Jerome Palmer Cowan) Born October 6, 1897, New York, New York. Married, child: William; divorced. Married Helen Dodge (1938), child: Suzanne.

Sound Feature Flims: *Beloved Enemy* (UA, 1936), *You Only Live Once* (UA, 1937), *Shall We Dance* (RKO, 1937), *New Faces of 1937* (RKO, 1937), *Vogues of 1938* (UA, 1937), *The Hurricane* (UA, 1937), *The Goldwyn Follies* (UA, 1938), *There's Always a Woman* (Col., 1938),

Marie McDonald, Barry Sullivan, Dennis O'Keefe and Jerome Cowan in *Getting Gertie's Garter.*

The Saint Strikes Back (RKO, 1939,) *St. Louis Blues* (Par., 1939), *Exile Express* (GN, 1939), *East Side of Heaven* (Univ., 1939), *The Gracie Allen Murder Case* (Par., 1939), *She Married a Cop* (Rep., 1939), *The Old Maid* (WB, 1939), *The Great Victor Herbert* (Par., 1939), *Wolf of New York* (Rep., 1940), *Castle on the Hudson* (WB 1940), *Ma, He's Making Eyes at Me* (Univ., 1940), *Torrid Zone* (WB, 1940), *Framed* (Univ., 1940). *Street of Memories* (20th, 1940), *City for Conquest* (WB, 1940), *The Quarterback* (Par., 1940), *Meet the Wildcat* (Univ., 1940), *Melody Ranch* (Rep., 1940), *Victory* (Par., 1940), *High Sierra* (WB, 1941), *The Roundup* (Par., 1941), *The Great Lie* (WB, 1941), *Affectionately Yours* (WB, 1941), *Out of the Fog* (WB, 1941), *Rags to Riches* (Rep., 1941), *Too Many Blondes* (Univ., 1941), *The Maltese Falcon* (WB, 1941), *One Foot in Heaven* (WB, 1941), *Mr. and Mrs. North* (MGM, 1941), *A Gentleman at Heart* (20th, 1942), *Moontide* (20th, 1942), *The Girl From Alaska* (Rep., 1942), *Thru Different Eyes* (20th, 1942), *Joan of Ozark* (Rep., 1942), *Street of Chance* (Par., 1942), *Who Done It?* (Univ., 1942), *Frisco Lil* (Univ., 1942), *Ladies' Day* (RKO, 1943), *Mission to Moscow* (WB, 1943), *Silver Spurs* (Rep., 1943,) *Hi'Ya, Sailor* (Univ., 1943), *Find the Blackmailer* (WB, 1943), *The Song of Bernadette* (20th, 1943), *No Place for a Lady* (Col., 1943), *Crime Doctor's Strangest Case* (Col., 1943), *Sing a Jingle* (Univ., 1944), *Mr. Skeffington* (WB, 1944), *South of Dixie* (Univ., 1944), *Minstrel Man* (PRC, 1944), *Crime by Night* (WB, 1944), *Guest in the House* (UA, 1944), *Fog Island* (PRC, 1945), *G. I. Honeymoon* (Mon., 1945), *The Crime Doctor's Courage* (Col., 1945), *Divorce* (Mon., 1945), *Blonde Ransom* (Univ., 1945), *Jungle Captive* (Univ., 1945), *Behind City Lights* (Rep., 1945), *Getting Gertie's Garter* (UA, 1945), *My Reputation* (WB, 1946), *One Way to Love* (Col., 1946), *Murder in the Music Hall* (Rep., 1946), *The Kid From Brooklyn* (RKO, 1946), *Deadline at Dawn* (RKO, 1946,) *A Night in Paradise* (Univ., 1946), *One Exciting Week* (Rep., 1946), *Mr. Ace* (UA, 1946), *Claudia and David* (20th, 1946), *Blondie Knows Best* (Col., 1946), *The Perfect Marriage* (Par., 1946), *Blondie's Holiday* (Col., 1947), *The Miracle on 34th Street* (20th, 1947), *Riffraff* (RKO, 1947), *Cry Wolf* (WB, 1947), *Blondie in the Dough* (Col., 1947), *Blondie's Big Moment* (Col., 1947), *Driftwood* (Rep., 1947), *Dangerous Years* (20th, 1947), *Blondie's Anniversary* (Col., 1947), *Arthur Takes Over* (20th, 1948), *So This Is New York* (UA, 1948), *Wallflower* (WB, 1948), *The Night Has a Thousand Eyes* (Par., 1948), *June Bride* (WB, 1948), *Blondie's Reward* (Col., 1948), *Blondie's Big Deal* (Col., 1949), *The Fountainhead* (WB, 1949), *The Girl From Jones Beach* (WB, 1949), *Scene of the Crime* (MGM, 1949), *Always Leave Them Laughing* (WB, 1949), *Blondie Hits the Jackpot* (Col., 1949), *Young Man With a Horn* (WB, 1950), *Joe Palooka Meets Humphrey* (Mon., 1950), *Peggy* (Univ., 1950), *When You're Smiling* (Col., 1950), *The Fuller Brush Girl* (Col., 1950), *Dallas* (WB, 1950), *The West Point Story* (WB, 1950), *The Fat Man* (Univ., 1951), *Criminal Lawyer* (Col., 1951), *Disc Jockey* (AA, 1951), *The System* (WB, 1953), *Have Rocket, Will Travel* (Col., 1959), *Visit to a Small Planet* (Par., 1960), *Private Property* (Citation, 1960), *All in a Night's Work* (Par., 1961), *Pocketful of Miracles* (UA, 1961), *Critic's Choice* (WB, 1963), *Black Zoo* (AA, 1963), *The Patsy* (Par., 1964), *John Goldfarb, Please Come Home* (20th, 1964), *Frankie and Johnny* (UA, 1965), *Penelope* (MGM, 1966), *The Gnome-mobile* (BV, 1967).

BUSTER LARRY CRABBE (Clarence Linden Crabbe) Born February 7, 1908, Oakland, California. Married Adah Held (1933), children: Caren, Susan, Cullen.

Feature Films: *Most Dangerous Game* (RKO, 1932), *That's My Boy* (Col., 1932), *Tarzan the Fearless* (Principal serial, 1933), *King of the Jungle* (Par., 1933), *Man of the Forest* (Par., 1933), *To the Last Man* (Par., 1933), *The Sweetheart of Sigma Chi* (Mon., 1933), *Thundering Herd* (Par., 1933), *Search for Beauty* (Par., 1934), *You're Telling Me* (Par., 1934), *Badge of Honor* (Mayfair, 1934), *We're Rich Again* (RKO, 1934), *The Oil Raider* (Mayfair, 1934), *She Had to Choose* (Majestic, 1934), *Hold 'Em Yale* (Par., 1935), *Nevada* (Par., 1935), *The Wanderer of the Wasteland* (Par., 1935), *Flash Gordon* (Univ. serial, 1936), *Drift Fence* (Par., 1936), *Desert Gold* (Par., 1936), *Arizona Raiders* (Par., 1936), *Lady Be Careful* (Par., 1936), *Rose Bowl* (Par., 1936), *Arizona Mahoney* (Par., 1937), *Murder Goes to College* (Par., 1937), *King of Gamblers* (Par., 1937), *Forlorn River* (Par., 1937), *Sophie Lang Goes West* (Par., 1937), *Daughter of Shanghai* (Par., 1937), *Thrill of a Lifetime* (Par., 1937), *Red Barry* (Univ. serial, 1938), *Flash Gordon's Trip to Mars* (Univ. serial, 1938), *Tip-Off Girls* (Par., 1938), *Hunted*

Monte Blue, Richard Carle, Raymond Hatton, Buster Crabbe and Sid Saylor in *Nevada.*

Men (Par., 1938), *Illegal Traffic* (Par., 1938), *Buck Rogers* (Univ. serial, 1939), *Unmarried* (Par., 1939), *Million Dollar Legs* (Par., 1939), *Colorado Sunset* (Rep., 1939), *Call a Messenger* (Univ., 1939), *Sailor's Lady* (20th, 1940), *Flash Gordon Conquers the Universe* (Univ. serial, 1940), *Billy the Kid Wanted* (PRC, 1941), *Jungle Man* (PRC, 1941), *Billy the Kid's Roundup* (PRC, 1941), *Billy the Kid Trapped* (PRC, 1942), *Smoking Guns* (PRC, 1942), *Jungle Siren* (PRC, 1942), *Wildcat* (Par., 1942), *Law and Order* (PRC, 1942), *Mysterious Rider* (PRC, 1942), *Sheriff of Sage Valley* (PRC, 1942), *Queen of Broadway* (PRC, 1942), *The Kid Rides Again* (PRC, 1943), *Fugitive of the Plains* (PRC, 1943), *Western Cyclone* (PRC, 1943), *The Renegade* (PRC, 1943), *Cattle Stampede* (PRC, 1943), *Blazing Frontier* (PRC, 1943), *Devil Riders* (PRC, 1943), *The Drifter* (PRC, 1944), *Nabonga* (PRC, 1944), *Frontier Outlaws* (PRC, 1944), *Thundering Gun Slingers* (PRC, 1944), *Valley of Vengeance* (PRC, 1944), *The Contender* (PRC, 1944), *Fuzzy Settles Down* (PRC, 1944), *Code of the Plains* (PRC, 1944), *Rustlers' Hideout* (PRC, 1944), *Wild Horse Phantom* (PRC, 1944), *Oath of Vengeance* (PRC, 1944), *His Brother's Ghost* (PRC, 1945), *Shadows of Death* (PRC, 1945), *Gangster's Den* (PRC, 1945), *Stagecoach Outlaws* (PRC, 1945), *Border Badmen* (PRC, 1945), *Fighting Bill Carson* (PRC, 1945), *Prairie Rustlers* (PRC, 1945), *Lightning Raiders* (PRC, 1945), *Ghost of Hidden Valley* (PRC, 1946), *Gentlemen With Guns* (PRC, 1946), *Terrors on Horseback* (PRC, 1946), *Overland Raiders* (PRC, 1946), *Outlaws of the Plains* (PRC, 1946), *Swamp Fire* (Par., 1946), *Prairie Badmen* (PRC, 1946), *Last of the Redmen* (Col., 1947), *The Sea Hound* (Col. serial, 1947), *Caged Fury* (Par., 1948), *Captive Girl* (Col., 1950), *Pirates of the High Seas* (Col. serial, 1950), *King of the Congo* (Col. serial, 1952), *Gun Brothers* (UA, 1956), *The Lawless Eighties* (Rep., 1957), *Badman's Country* (WB, 1958), *Gunfighters of Abilene* (UA, 1960), *The Bounty Killer* (Embassy, 1965), *Arizona Raiders* (Col., 1965).

JEANNE CRAIN Born May 25, 1925, Barstow, California. Married Paul Brinkman (1945), children: Paul, Michael, Timothy, Jeanine, Lisabette, Maria, Christopher.

Jeanne Crain and Lynn Bari in *Margie.*

English-Language Feature Films: *The Gang's All Here* (20th, 1943), *Home in Indiana* (20th, 1944), *In the Meantime, Darling* (20th, 1944), *Winged Victory* (20th, 1944), *State Fair* (20th, 1945), *Leave Her to Heaven* (20th, 1945), *Centennial Summer* (20th, 1946), *Margie* (20th, 1946), *Apartment for Peggy* (20th, 1948), *You Were Meant for Me* (20th, 1948), *A Letter to Three Wives* (20th, 1949), *The Fan* (20th, 1949), *Pinky* (20th, 1949), *Cheaper by the Dozen* (20th, 1950), *I'll Get By* (20th, 1950),* *Take Care of My Little Girl* (20th, 1951), *People Will Talk* (20th, 1951), *The Model and the Marriage Broker* (20th, 1952), *Belles on Their Toes* (20th, 1952), *O. Henry's Full House* (20th, 1952), *Dangerous Crossing* (20th, 1953), *City of Badmen* (20th, 1953), *Vicki* (20th, 1953), *Duel in the Jungle* (WB, 1954), *Man Without a Star* (Univ., 1955), *Gentlemen Marry Brunettes* (UA, 1955), *The Second Greatest Sex* (Univ., 1955), *The Fastest Gun Alive* (MGM, 1956), *The Tattered Dress* (Univ., 1957), *The Joker Is Wild* (Par., 1957), *Guns of the Timberland* (WB, 1960), *Twenty Plus Two* (AA, 1961), *Madison Avenue* (20th, 1962), *52 Miles to Terror* (MGM, 1964), *Hot Rods to Hell* (MGM, 1967).

*Unbilled guest appearance

Broderick Crawford, Randolph Scott, Kay Francis and Mary Gordon in *When the Daltons Rode.*

BRODERICK CRAWFORD (William Broderick Crawford) Born December 9, 1911, Philadelphia, Pennsylvania. Married Kay Griffith (1940), children: Kim, Kelly; divorced. Married Joan Tabor (1962); divorced 1967.

English-Language Feature Films: *Woman Chases Man* (UA, 1937), *Submarine D-1* (WB, 1937), *Start Cheering* (Col., 1938), *Sudden Money* (Par., 1939), *Ambush* (Par., 1939), *Undercover Doctor* (Par., 1939), *Beau Geste* (Par., 1939), *Eternally Yours* (UA, 1939), *Island of Lost Men* (Par., 1939), *The Real Glory* (UA, 1939), *Slightly Honorable* (UA,

1940), *I Can't Give You Anything But Love, Baby* (Univ., 1940), *When the Daltons Rode* (Univ., 1940), *Seven Sinners* (Univ., 1940), *Trail of the Vigilantes* (Univ., 1940), *Texas Rangers Ride Again* (Par., 1940), *The Black Cat* (Univ., 1941), *Tight Shoes* (Univ., 1941), *Badlands of Dakota* (Univ., 1941), *South of Tahiti* (Univ., 1941), *North of the Klondike* (Univ., 1942), *Larceny, Inc.* (WB, 1942), *Butch Minds the Baby* (Univ., 1942), *Broadway* (Univ., 1942), *Men of Texas* (Univ., 1942), *Sin Town* (Univ., 1942), *The Runaround* (Univ., 1946), *Black Angel* (Univ., 1946)), *Slave Girl* (Univ., 1947), *The Flame* (Rep., 1947), *The Time of Your Life* (UA, 1948), *Sealed Verdict* (Par., 1948), *Bad Men of Tombstone* (AA, 1948), *A Kiss in the Dark* (WB, 1949), *Night Unto Night* (WB, 1949), *Anna Lucasta* (Col., 1949), *All The King's Men* (Col., 1949), *Cargo to Capetown* (Col., 1950), *Convicted* (Col., 1950), *Born Yesterday* (Col., 1950), *The Mob* (Col., 1951), *Scandal Sheet* (Col., 1952), *Lone Star* (MGM, 1952), *Stop, You're Killing Me* (WB, 1952), *Last of the Comanches* (Col., 1952), *Night People* (20th, 1954), *Down Three Dark Streets* (UA, 1954), *Human Desire* (Col., 1954), *New York Confidential* (WB, 1955), *Big House, U.S.A.* (UA, 1955), *Not as a Stranger* (UA, 1955), *The Fastest Gun Alive* (MGM, 1956), *Between Heaven and Hell* (20th, 1956), *The Decks Ran Red* (MGM, 1958), *Convicts 4* (AA, 1962), *The Castilian* (WB, 1963), *Square of Violence* (MGM, 1963), *A House Is Not a Home* (Embassy, 1964), *Up From the Beach* (20th, 1965), *The Oscar* (Par, 1966), *Kid Rodelo* (Par., 1966), *The Texican* (Col., 1966), *Red Tomahawk* (Par., 1967), *The Vulture* (Par., 1967), *The Fakers* (East West International, 1968).

JOAN CRAWFORD (Lucille Le Sueur) Born March 23, 1904, San Antonio, Texas. Married Douglas Fairbanks, Jr. (1929); divorced 1933. Married Franchot Tone (1935); divorced 1939. Married Philip Terry (1942), child: Christopher; divorced 1946. Married Alfred Steele (1956); widowed 1959. Children adopted while Miss Crawford was unmarried: Christina, Cathy, Cindy.

Sound Feature Films: *Hollywood Revue of 1929* (MGM, 1929), *Untamed* (MGM, 1929), *Montana Moon* (MGM, 1930), *Our Blushing Brides* (MGM, 1930), *Paid* (MGM, 1930), *Dance, Fools, Dance* (MGM, 1931), *Laughing Sinners* (MGM, 1931), *This Modern Age* (MGM, 1931), *Possessed* (MGM, 1931), *Grand Hotel* (MGM, 1932), *Letty Lynton* (MGM, 1932), *Rain* (UA, 1932), *Today We Live* (MGM, 1933), *Dancing Lady* (MGM, 1933), *Sadie McKee* (MGM, 1934), *Chained* (MGM, 1934), *Forsaking All Others* (MGM, 1934), *No More Ladies* (MGM,

Clark Gable and Joan Crawford in *Dancing Lady.*

45

1935), *I Live My Life* (MGM, 1935), *The Gorgeous Hussy* (MGM, 1936), *Love on the Run* (MGM, 1936), *The Last of Mrs. Cheyney* (MGM, 1937), *The Bride Wore Red* (MGM, 1937), *Mannequin* (MGM, 1938), *The Shining Hour* (MGM, 1938), *Ice Follies of 1939* (MGM, 1939), *The Women* (MGM, 1939), *Strange Cargo* (MGM, 1940), *Susan and God* (MGM, 1940), *A Woman's Face* (MGM, 1941), *When Ladies Meet* (MGM, 1941), *They All Kissed the Bride* (Col., 1942), *Reunion in France* (MGM, 1942), *Above Suspicion* (MGM, 1943), *Hollywood Canteen* (WB, 1944), *Mildred Pierce* (WB, 1945), *Humoresque* (WB, 1946), *Possessed* (WB, 1947), *Daisy Kenyon* (20th, 1947), *Flamingo Road* (WB, 1949), *The Damned Don't Cry* (WB, 1950), *Harriet Craig* (Col., 1950), *Goodbye, My Fancy* (WB, 1951), *This Man Is Dangerous* (WB, 1952), *Sudden Fear* (RKO, 1952), *Torch Song* (MGM, 1953), *Johnny Guitar* (Rep., 1954), *Female on the Beach* (Univ., 1955), *Queen Bee* (Col., 1955), *Autumn Leaves* (Col., 1956), *The Best of Everything* (20th, 1959), *What Ever Happened to Baby Jane?* (WB, 1962), *The Caretakers* (UA, 1963), *Strait-Jacket* (Col., 1964), *I Saw What You Did* (Univ., 1965), *Berserk!* (Col., 1967).

LAIRD CREGAR (Samuel Laird Cregar) Born July 28, 1916, Philadelphia, Pennsylvania. Died December 9, 1944.

Monty Woolley, Laird Cregar and Gracie Fields in *Holy Matrimony*.

Feature Films: *Granny Get Your Gun* (WB, 1940), *Hudson's Bay* (20th, 1940), *Oh Johnny, How You Can Love* (Univ., 1940), *Blood and Sand* (20th, 1941), *Charley's Aunt* (20th, 1941), *I Wake Up Screaming* (20th, 1941), *Joan of Paris* (RKO, 1942), *Rings on Her Fingers* (20th, 1942), *This Gun for Hire* (Par., 1942), *Ten Gentlemen From West Point* (20th, 1942), *The Black Swan* (20th, 1942), *Hello, Frisco, Hello* (20th, 1943), *Heaven Can Wait* (20th, 1943), *Holy Matrimony* (20th, 1943), *The Lodger* (20th, 1944), *Hangover Square* (20th, 1945).

DONALD CRISP Born 1880, Aberfeddy, Scotland. Married Marie Stark; divorced 1919. Married Jane Murphin (1932); divorced 1944.

Sound Feature Films: *The Return of Sherlock Holmes* (Par., 1929), *Scotland Yard* (Fox, 1930), *Svengali* (WB, 1931), *Kick In* (Par., 1931), *Passport to Hell* (Fox, 1932), *Red Dust* (MGM, 1932), *Broadway Bad* (Fox, 1933), *Crime Doctor* (RKO, 1934), *Life of Vergie Winters* (RKO, 1934), *What Every Woman Knows* (MGM, 1934), *The Little Minister* (RKO, 1934), *Vanessa—Her Love Story* (MGM, 1935), *Laddie* (RKO, 1935), *Oil for the Lamps of China* (WB, 1935), *Mutiny on the Bounty* (MGM, 1935), *The White Angel* (WB, 1936), *Mary of Scotland* (RKO, 1936), *Charge of the Light Brigade* (WB, 1936), *A Woman Rebels* (RKO, 1936), *Beloved Enemy* (UA, 1936), *The Great O'Malley* (WB, 1937), *Parnell* (MGM, 1937), *That Certain Woman* (WB, 1937), *The Life of Emile Zola* (WB, 1937), *Confession* (WB, 1937), *Jezebel* (WB, 1938), *Sergeant Murphy* (WB, 1938), *Beloved Brat* (WB, 1938), *The Amazing Dr. Clitterhouse* (WB, 1938), *Valley of the Giants* (WB, 1938), *The Dawn Patrol* (WB, 1938), *Comet Over Broadway* (WB, 1938), *The Sisters* (WB, 1938), *Wuthering Heights* (UA, 1939), *The Oklahoma Kid* (WB, 1939), *Juarez* (WB, 1939), *Daughters Courageous* (WB, 1939),

James Stephenson, Donald Crisp and Vera Lewis in *Shining Victory*.

The Old Maid (WB, 1939), *The Private Lives of Elizabeth and Essex* (WB, 1939), *The Story of Dr. Ehrlich's Magic Bullet* (WB, 1940), *Brother Orchid* (WB, 1940), *The Sea Hawk* (WB, 1940), *City for Conquest* (WB, 1940), *Knute Rockne—All American* (WB, 1940), *Shining Victory* (WB, 1941), *Dr. Jekyll and Mr. Hyde* (WB, 1941), *How Green Was My Valley* (20th, 1941), *The Gay Sisters* (WB, 1942), *Forever and a Day* (RKO, 1943), *Lassie Come Home* (MGM, 1943), *The Uninvited* (Par., 1944), *The Adventures of Mark Twain* (WB, 1944), *National Velvet* (MGM, 1944), *Son of Lassie* (MGM, 1945), *Valley of Decision* (MGM, 1945), *Ramrod* (UA, 1947), *Hills of Home* (MGM, 1948), *Whispering Smith* (Par., 1948), *Bright Leaf* (WB, 1950), *Home Town Story* (MGM, 1951), *Prince Valiant* (20th, 1954), *The Long Gray Line* (Col., 1955), *The Man From Laramie* (Col., 1955), *Drango* (UA, 1957), *Saddle the Wind* (MGM, 1958), *The Last Hurrah* (Col., 1958), *A Dog of Flanders* (20th, 1959), *Pollyanna* (BV, 1960), *Greyfriar's Bobby* (BV, 1961), *Spencer's Mountain* (WB, 1963).

HUME CRONYN (Hume Blake) Born July 18, 1911, London, Ontario, Canada. Married Jessica Tandy (1942), children: Christopher, Tandy.

Hume Cronyn and John Carroll in *A Letter for Evie*.

Feature Films: *Shadow of a Doubt* (Univ., 1943), *Phantom of the Opera* (Univ., 1943), *The Cross of Lorraine* (MGM, 1943), *The Seventh Cross* (MGM, 1944), *Main Street After Dark* (MGM, 1944), *Lifeboat* (20th, 1944), *A Letter for Evie* (MGM, 1945), *The Sailor Takes a Wife* (MGM, 1945), *The Green Years* (MGM, 1946), *The Postman Always Rings Twice* (MGM, 1946), *The Ziegfeld Follies* (MGM, 1946), *The Secret Heart* (voice only; MGM, 1946), *The Beginning of the End* (MGM, 1947), *Brute Force* (Univ., 1947), *The Bride Goes Wild* (MGM, 1948), *Top o' the Morning* (Par., 1949), *People Will Talk* (20th, 1951), *Crowded Paradise* (Tudor, 1956), *Sunrise at Campobello* (WB, 1960), *Cleopatra* (20th, 1963), *Hamlet* (WB, 1964).

BING CROSBY (Harry Lillis Crosby) Born May 2, 1904, Tacoma, Washington. Married Dixie Lee (1930), children: Gary, Dennis, Philip, Lindsay; widowed 1952. Married Kathryn Grant (1957), children: Harry, Nathaniel, Mary.

Ned Sparks, Louise Campbell and Bing Crosby in *The Star Maker*.

Feature Films: *King of Jazz* (Univ., 1930), *The Big Broadcast* (Par., 1932), *College Humor* (Par., 1933), *Too Much Harmony* (Par., 1933), *Going Hollywood* (MGM, 1933), *We're Not Dressing* (Par., 1934), *She Loves Me Not* (Par., 1934), *Here Is My Heart* (Par., 1934), *Mississippi* (Par., 1935), *Two for Tonight* (Par., 1935), *Big Broadcast of 1936* (Par., 1935), *Anything Goes* (Par., 1936), *Rhythm on the Range* (Par., 1936), *Pennies From Heaven* (Par., 1936), *Waikiki Wedding* (Par., 1937), *Double or Nothing* (Par., 1937), *Dr. Rhythm* (Par., 1938), *Sing You Sinners* (Par., 1938), *Paris Honeymoon* (Par., 1939), *East Side of Heaven* (Univ., 1939), *The Star Maker* (Par., 1939), *Road to Singapore* (Par., 1940), *If I Had My Way* (Univ., 1940), *Rhythm on the River* (Par., 1940), *Road to Zanzibar* (Par., 1941), *Birth of the Blues* (Par., 1941), *My Favorite Blonde* (Par., 1942),* *Holiday Inn* (Par., 1942), *Road to Morocco* (Par., 1942), *Star Spangled Rhythm* (Par., 1942), *Dixie* (Par., 1943), *Going My Way* (Par., 1944), *The Princess and the Pirate* (RKO, 1944),* *Here Come the Waves* (Par., 1945), *Duffy's Tavern* (Par., 1945), *Road to Utopia* (Par., 1945), *Out of This World* (voice only; Par., 1945), *The Bells of St. Mary's* (RKO, 1945), *Blue Skies* (Par., 1946), *Variety Girl* (Par., 1947), *Welcome Stranger* (Par., 1947), *My Favorite Brunette* (Par., 1947),* *Road to Rio* (Par., 1947), *The Emperor Waltz* (Par., 1948), *A Connecticut Yankee In King Arthur's Court* (Par., 1949), *The Adventures of Ichabod and Mr. Toad* (voice only; RKO, 1949), *Top o' the Morning* (Par., 1949), *Riding High* (Par., 1950), *Mr. Music* (Par., 1950), *Here Comes the Groom* (Par., 1951), *The Greatest Show on Earth* (Par., 1952),* *Just for You* (Par., 1952), *Son of Paleface* (Par., 1952),* *Road to Bali* (Par., 1952), *Scared Stiff* (Par., 1953),* *Little Boy Lost* (Par., 1953), *White Christmas* (Par., 1954), *The Country Girl* (Par., 1954), *Anything Goes* (Par., 1956), *High Society* (MGM, 1956), *Man on Fire* (MGM, 1957), *Say One for Me* (20th, 1959), *Alias Jesse James* (UA, 1959),* *High Time* (20th, 1960), *Pepe* (Col., 1960), *Road to Hong Kong* (UA, 1962), *Robin and the 7 Hoods* (WB, 1964), *Bing Crosby's Cinerama Adventures* (Cinerama, 1966), *Stagecoach* (20th, 1966).

*Unbilled guest appearance

ROBERT CUMMINGS (Clarence Robert Orville Cummings) Born June 10, 1910, Joplin, Missouri. Married Vivian Janis (1933); divorced 1943. Married Mary Elliot (1945), children: Robert, Mary, Melinda, Sharon, Patricia, Laurel, Anthony.

Feature Films: *The Virginia Judge* (Par., 1935), *So Red the Rose* (Par., 1935), *Millions in the Air* (Par., 1935), *Forgotten Faces* (Par., 1936), *Desert Gold* (Par., 1936), *Arizona Mahoney* (Par., 1936), *Border Flight* (Par., 1936), *Three Cheers for Love* (Par., 1936), *Hollywood Boulevard* (Par., 1936), *The Accusing Finger* (Par., 1936), *Hideaway Girl*

Nina Koshetz, Alexis Minotis, Bob Cummings and Alex Montoya in *The Chase.*

(Par., 1937), *Last Train From Madrid* (Par., 1937), *Souls at Sea* (Par., 1937), *Wells Fargo* (Par., 1937), *College Swing* (Par., 1938), *You and Me* (Par., 1938), *The Texans* (Par., 1938), *Touchdown Army* (Par., 1938), *I Stand Accused* (Rep., 1938), *Three Smart Girls Grow Up* (Univ., 1939), *The Under-Pup* (Univ., 1939), *Rio* (Univ., 1939), *Everything Happens at Night* (20th, 1939), *Charlie McCarthy, Detective* (Univ., 1939), *And One Was Beautiful* (MGM, 1940), *Private Affairs* (Univ., 1940), *Spring Parade* (Univ., 1940), *One Night in the Tropics* (Univ., 1941), *Free and Easy* (MGM, 1941), *The Devil and Miss Jones* (RKO,, 1941), *Moon Over Miami* (20th, 1941), *It Started With Eve* (Univ., 1941), *Kings Row* (WB, 1941), *Saboteur* (Univ., 1942), *Between Us Girls* (Univ., 1942), *Forever and a Day* (RKO, 1943), *Princess O'Rourke* (WB, 1943), *Flesh and Fantasy* (Univ., 1943), *You Came Along* (Par., 1945), *The Bride Wore Boots* (Par., 1946), *The Chase* (UA, 1946), *Heaven Only Knows* (UA, 1947), *The Lost Moment* (Univ., 1947), *Sleep, My Love* (UA, 1948), *Let's Live a Little* (EL, 1948), *The Accused* (Par., 1948), *Free for All* (Univ., 1949), *Tell it to the Judge* (Col., 1949), *Paid in Full* (Par., 1950), *The Petty Girl* (Col., 1950), *For Heaven's Sake* (20th, 1950), *The Barefoot Mailman* (Col., 1951), *The First Time* (Col., 1952), *Marry Me Again* (RKO, 1953), *Lucky Me* (WB, 1954), *Dial M for Murder* (WB, 1954), *How to Be Very, Very Popular* (20th, 1955), *My Geisha* (Par., 1962), *Beach Party* (AIP, 1963), *What a Way to Go!* (20th, 1964), *The Carpetbaggers* (Par., 1964), *Promise Her Anything* (Par., 1966), *Stagecoach* (20th, 1966).

TONY CURTIS (Bernard Schwartz) Born June 3, 1925, Bronx, New York. Married Janet Leigh (1951), children: Kelly, Jamie; divorced 1962. Married Christine Kaufmann (1963), children: Alexandria, Allegra; divorced 1967.

Feature Films: *Criss Cross* (Univ., 1949), *City Across the River* (Univ., 1949), *The Lady Gambles* (Univ., 1949), *Johnny Stool Pigeon* (Univ., 1949), *Francis* (Univ., 1949), *I Was a Shoplifter* (Univ., 1950), *Winchester '73* (Univ., 1950), *The Prince Who Was a Thief* (Univ., 1951), *Flesh*

Tony Curtis in *The Great Imposter.*

47

and Fury (Univ., 1952), No Room for the Groom (Univ., 1952), Son of Ali Baba (Univ., 1952), Houdini (Par., 1953), The All American (Univ., 1953), Forbidden (Univ., 1953), Beachhead (UA, 1954), The Black Shield of Falworth (Univ., 1954), Johnny Dark (Univ., 1954), So This Is Paris (Univ., 1954), The Purple Mask (Univ., 1954), Six Bridges to Cross (Univ., 1955), The Square Jungle (Univ., 1955), Trapeze (UA, 1956), The Rawhide Years (Univ., 1956), Mister Cory (Univ., 1957), The Midnight Story (Univ., 1957), Sweet Smell of Success (UA, 1957), The Vikings (UA, 1958), Kings Go Forth (UA, 1958), The Defiant Ones (UA, 1958), The Perfect Furlough (Univ., 1958), Some Like It Hot (UA, 1959), Operation Petticoat (Univ., 1959), Pepe (Col., 1960),* Who Was That Lady? (Col., 1960), The Rat Race (Par., 1960), Spartacus (Univ., 1960), The Great Imposter (Univ., 1960), The Outsider (Univ., 1961), 40 Pounds of Trouble (Univ., 1962), Taras Bulba (UA, 1962), The List of Adrian Messenger (Univ., 1963), Captain Newman, M.D. (Univ., 1963), Paris When It Sizzles (Par., 1964), Wild and Wonderful (Univ., 1964), Goodbye Charlie (20th, 1964), Sex and the Single Girl (WB, 1964), The Great Race (WB, 1965), Boeing-Boeing (Par., 1965), Not With My Wife You Don't (WB, 1966), Chamber of Horrors (WB, 1966),* Arrivederci, Baby (Par., 1966), Don't Make Waves (MGM, 1967), The Chastity Belt (WB-7 Arts, 1968).

*Unbilled guest appearance

ARLENE DAHL (Arlene Carol Dahl) Born August 11, 1924, Minneapolis, Minnesota. Married Lex Barker (1951); divorced 1952. Married Fernando Lamas (1954), child: Lorenzo; divorced 1960. Married Christian Holmes (1960), child: Carol; divorced 1964. Married Alexi Lichine (1965); divorced 1967.

Tom Helmore, Van Johnson and Arlene Dahl in Scene of the Crime.

Feature Films: Life with Father (WB, 1947), My Wild Irish Rose (WB, 1947), The Bride Goes Wild (MGM, 1948), A Southern Yankee (MGM, 1948), Reign of Terror (EL, 1949), Scene of the Crime (MGM, 1949), Ambush (MGM, 1949), The Outriders (MGM, 1950), Three Little Words (MGM, 1950), Watch the Birdie (MGM, 1950), Inside Straight (MGM, 1951), No Questions Asked (MGM, 1951), Caribbean (Par., 1952), Jamaica Run (Par., 1953), Desert Legion (Univ., 1953), Sangaree (Par., 1953), The Diamond Queen (WB, 1953), Here Come the Girls (Par., 1953), Woman's World (20th, 1954), Bengal Brigade (Univ., 1954), Slightly Scarlet (RKO, 1956), Wicked as They Come (Col., 1957), She Played With Fire (Col., 1958), Journey to the Center of the Earth (20th, 1959), Kisses for My President (WB, 1964).

DAN DAILEY (Dan Dailey Jr.) Born December 14, 1917, New York, New York. Married Esther Rodier; divorced 1941. Married Elizabeth Hofert (1942), child: Dan; divorced 1951. Married Gwendolyn O'Connor (1955); divorced 1961.

Feature Films: The Mortal Storm (MGM, 1940), The Captain Is a Lady (MGM, 1940), Hullabaloo (MGM, 1940), Susan and God (MGM, 1940),

Dan Dailey and Lynn Bari in Moon Over Her Shoulder.

Ziegfeld Girl (MGM, 1941), Washington Melodrama (MGM, 1941), The Wild Man of Borneo (MGM, 1941), The Get-Away (MGM, 1941), Lady Be Good (MGM, 1941), Down in San Diego (MGM, 1941), Moon Over Her Shoulder (20th, 1941), Mokey (MGM, 1942), Sunday Punch (MGM, 1942), Panama Hattie (MGM, 1942), Timber (Univ., 1942), Give Out, Sister (Univ., 1942), Mother Wore Tights (20th, 1947), You Were Meant for Me (20th, 1948), Give My Regards to Broadway (20th, 1948), Chicken Every Sunday (20th, 1948), When My Baby Smiles at Me (20th, 1948), You're My Everything (20th, 1949), When Willie Comes Marching Home (20th, 1950), I'll Get By (20th, 1950), Ticket to Tomahawk (20th, 1950), My Blue Heaven (20th, 1950), I Can Get It for You Wholesale (20th, 1951), Call Me Mister (20th, 1951), The Pride of St. Louis (20th, 1952), What Price Glory (20th, 1952), Meet Me at the Fair (Univ., 1952), Taxi (20th, 1953), The Girl Next Door (20th, 1953), The Kid From Left Field (20th, 1953), There's No Business Like Show Business (20th, 1954), It's Always Fair Weather (MGM, 1955), The Best Things in Life Are Free (20th, 1956), The Wings of Eagles (MGM, 1957), Oh, Men! Oh, Women! (20th, 1957), The Wayward Bus (20th 1957), Underwater Warrior (MGM, 1958), Pepe (Col., 1960), Hemingway's Adventures of a Young Man (20th, 1962).

LINDA DARNELL (Monetta Eloyse Darnell) Born October 16, 1923, Dallas, Texas. Married Peverell Marley (1943), child: Charlotte; divorced 1952. Married Philip Leibman (1954); divorced 1955. Married Merle Robertson (1957); Divorced 1963. Died April 10, 1965.

English-Language Feature Films: Elsa Maxwell's Hotel for Women (20th, 1939), Daytime Wife (20th, 1939), Star Dust (20th, 1940), Brigham Young—Frontiersman (20th, 1940), The Mark of Zorro (20th, 1940), Chad Hanna (20th, 1940), Blood and Sand (20th, 1941), Rise and Shine (20th, 1941), Loves of Edgar Allan Poe (20th, 1942), City Without Men (Col., 1943), The Song of Bernadette (20th, 1943),* It Happened Tomorrow (UA, 1944), Buffalo Bill (20th, 1944), Summer Storm (UA, 1944), Sweet and Lowdown (20th, 1944), Hangover Square (20th, 1945), The Great John L. (UA, 1945), Fallen Angel (20th, 1945), Centennial Summer (20th, 1946), Anna and the King of Siam (20th,

George Murphy and Linda Darnell in Rise and Shine.

Jane Darwell and Sally Blane in *The Great Hospital Mystery.*

1946), *My Darling Clementine* (20th, 1946), *Forever Amber* (20th, 1947), *The Walls of Jericho* (20th, 1948), *Unfaithfully Yours* (20th, 1948), *A Letter to Three Wives* (20th, 1949), *Slattery's Hurricane* (20th, 1949), *Everybody Does It* (20th, 1949), *No Way Out* (20th, 1950), *Two Flags West* (20th, 1950), *The Thirteenth Letter* (20th, 1951), *The Guy Who Came Back* (20th, 1951), *The Lady Pays Off* (Univ., 1951), *Island of Desire* (UA, 1952), *Night Without Sleep* (20th, 1952), *Blackbeard the Pirate* (RKO, 1952), *Second Chance* (RKO, 1953), *This Is My Love* (RKO, 1954), *Dakota Incident* (Rep., 1956), *Zero Hour!* (Par., 1957), *Black Spurs* (Par., 1965).

*Unbilled guest appearance

JANE DARWELL (Patti Woodward) Born October 15, 1884, Palmyra, Missouri. Died August 14, 1967.

Feature Films: *Tom Sawyer* (Par., 1930), *Fighting Caravans* (Par., 1931), *Huckleberry Finn* (Par., 1931), *Ladies of the Big House* (Par., 1932), *Hot Saturday* (Par., 1932), *Back Street* (Par., 1932), *No One Man* (Par., 1932), *Murders in the Zoo* (Par., 1933), *Air Hostess* (Par., 1933), *Child of Manhattan* (Par., 1933), *Women Won't Tell* (Par., 1933), *Bondage* (Fox, 1933), *Design for Living* (Par., 1933), *Jennie Gerhardt* (Par., 1933), *One Sunday Afternoon* (Par., 1933), *Before Dawn* (RKO, 1933), *Emergency Call* (RKO, 1933), *Only Yesterday* (Univ., 1933), *Roman Scandals* (UA, 1933), *He Couldn't Take It* (Mon., 1933), *Once to Every Woman* (Col., 1934), *Happiness Ahead* (WB, 1934), *Wonder Bar* (WB, 1934), *Fashions of 1934* (WB, 1934), *Desirable* (WB, 1934), *Wake Up and Dream* (Univ., 1934), *The Firebird* (WB, 1934), *Let's Talk It Over* (Univ., 1934), *David Harum* (Fox, 1934), *Heat Lightning* (WB, 1934), *Change of Heart* (Fox, 1934), *Most Precious Thing in Life* (Col., 1934), *The Scarlet Empress* (Par., 1934), *Blind Date* (Col., 1934), *Embarrassing Moments* (Univ., 1934), *The White Parade* (Fox, 1934), *Gentlemen Are Born* (WB, 1934), *Journal of a Crime* (WB, 1934), *One More Spring* (Fox, 1935), *Million Dollar Ransom* (Univ., 1934), *One Night of Love* (Col., 1934), *Tomorrow's Youth* (Mon., 1935), *McFadden's Flats* (Par., 1935), *Life Begins at Forty* (Fox, 1935), *Curly Top* (Fox, 1935), *Metropolitan* (Fox, 1935), *Navy Wife* (Fox, 1935), *Paddy O'Day* (Fox, 1935), *Bright Eyes* (Fox, 1935), *We're Only Human* (RKO, 1936), *The Country Doctor* (20th, 1936), *Little Miss Nobody* (20th, 1936), *Captain January* (20th, 1936), *The First Baby* (20th, 1936), *Poor Little Rich Girl* (20th, 1936), *Private Number* (20th, 1936), *Star for a Night* (20th, 1936), *White Fang* (20th, 1936), *Ramona* (20th, 1936), *Craig's Wife* (Col., 1936), *Love Is News* (20th, 1937), *Laughing at Trouble* (20th, 1937), *Nancy Steele Is Missing* (20th, 1937), *Fifty Roads to Town* (20th, 1937), *Slave Ship* (20th, 1937), *The Great Hospital Mystery* (20th, 1937), *Wife, Doctor and Nurse* (20th, 1937), *The Singing Marine* (WB, 1937), *Dangerously Yours* (20th, 1937), *The Jury's Secret* (Univ., 1938), *Change of Heart* (20th, 1938), *Battle of Broadway* (20th, 1938), *Three Blind Mice* (20th, 1938), *Little Miss Broadway* (20th, 1938), *Time Out for Murder* (20th, 1938), *Five of a Kind* (20th, 1938), *Up the River* (20th, 1938), *Inside Story* (20th, 1938), *Jesse James* (20th, 1939), *Zero Hour* (Rep., 1939), *Grand Jury Secrets* (Par., 1939), *Unexpected Father* (Univ., 1939), *The Rains Came* (20th, 1939), *20,000 Men a Year* (20th, 1939), *Gone With the Wind* (MGM, 1939), *A Miracle on Main Street* (Col., 1940), *The Grapes of Wrath* (20th, 1940), *Untamed*

(Par., 1940), *Youth Will Be Served* (20th, 1940), *Chad Hanna* (20th, 1940), *Brigham Young—Frontiersman* (20th, 1940), *Private Nurse* (20th, 1941), *All That Money Can Buy* (RKO, 1941), *Small Town Deb* (20th, 1941), *All Through the Night* (WB, 1942), *On the Sunny Side* (20th, 1942), *Young America* (20th, 1942), *It Happened in Flatbush* (20th, 1942), *The Loves of Edgar Allan Poe* (20th, 1942), *Men of Texas* (Univ., 1942), *Highways by Night* (RKO, 1942), *The Great Gildersleeve* (RKO, 1942), *Gildersleeve's Bad Day* (RKO, 1943), *The Ox-Bow Incident* (20th, 1943), *Government Girl* (RKO, 1943), *Stage Door Canteen* (UA, 1943), *Tender Comrade* (RKO, 1943), *Music in Manhattan* (RKO, 1944), *Reckless Age* (Univ., 1944), *The Impatient Years* (Col., 1944), *She's a Sweetheart* (Col., 1944), *Sunday Dinner for a Soldier* (20th, 1944), *Captain Tugboat Annie* (Rep., 1945), *Three Wise Fools* (MGM, 1946), *My Darling Clementine* (20th, 1946), *The Dark Horse* (Univ., 1946), *The Red Stallion* (EL, 1947), *Keeper of the Bees* (Col., 1947), *Train to Alcatraz* (Rep., 1948), *Three Godfathers* (MGM, 1948), *Red Canyon* (Univ., 1949), *Wagonmaster* (RKO, 1950), *Caged* (WB, 1950), *The Daughter of Rosie O'Grady* (WB, 1950), *Redwood Forest Trail* (Rep., 1950), *Surrender* (Rep., 1950), *Three Husbands* (UA, 1950), *The Second Face* (EL, 1950), *Father's Wild Game* (Mon., 1950), *The Lemon Drop Kid* (Par., 1951), *Excuse My Dust* (MGM, 1951), *Journey into Light* (20th, 1951), *We're Not Married* (20th, 1952), *It Happens Every Spring* (Univ., 1953), *Affair With a Stranger* (RKO, 1953), *The Sun Shines Bright* (Rep., 1953), *There's Always Tomorrow* (Univ., 1956), *The Last Hurrah* (Col., 1958), *Hound-Dog Man* (20th, 1959), *Mary Poppins* (BV, 1964).

MARION DAVIES (Marion Cecilia Douras) Born January 3, 1900, New York, New York. Married Horace Brown (1951). Died September 22, 1961.

Robert Greig, Onslow Stevens and Marion Davies in *Peg o' My Heart.*

Sound Feature Films: *Marianne* (MGM, 1929), *Hollywood Revue of 1929* (MGM, 1929), *Not So Dumb* (MGM, 1930), *Floradora Girl* (MGM, 1930), *Bachelor Father* (MGM, 1931), *It's a Wise Child* (MGM 1931), *Five and Ten* (MGM, 1931), *Polly of the Circus* (MGM, 1932), *Blondie of the Follies* (MGM, 1932,) *Peg O' My Heart* (MGM, 1933), *Going Hollywood* (MGM, 1933), *Operator 13* (MGM, 1934), *Page Miss Glory* (WB, 1935), *Hearts Divided* (WB, 1936), *Cain and Mabel* (WB, 1936), *Ever Since Eve* (WB, 1937).

BETTE DAVIS (Ruth Elizabeth Davis) Born April 5, 1908, Lowell, Massachusetts. Married Harmon Nelson (1932); divorced 1938. Married Arthur Farnsworth (1940); widowed 1943. Married William Grant Sherry (1945), child: Barbara; divorced 1949. Married Gary Merrill (1950), children: Margo, Michael; divorced 1960.

Feature Films: *Bad Sister* (Univ., 1931), *Seed* (Univ., 1931), *Waterloo Bridge* (Univ., 1931), *Way Back Home* (RKO, 1932), *The Menace*

Bette Davis and Paul Muni in *Border Town*.

(Col., 1932), *Hell's House* (Capital Film Exchange, 1932), *Man Who Played God* (WB, 1932), *So Big* (WB, 1932), *The Rich Are Always With Us* (WB, 1932), *The Dark Horse* (WB, 1932), *Cabin in the Cotton* (WB, 1932), *Three on a Match* (WB, 1932), *20,000 Years in Sing Sing* (WB, 1933), *Parachute Jumper* (WB, 1933), *The Working Man* (WB, 1933), *Ex-Lady* (WB, 1933), *Bureau of Missing Persons* (WB, 1933), *Fashions of 1934* (WB, 1934), *The Big Shakedown* (WB, 1934), *Jimmy the Gent* (WB, 1934), *Fog Over Frisco* (WB, 1934), *Of Human Bondage* (RKO, 1934), *Housewife* (WB, 1934), *Bordertown* (WB, 1935), *The Girl From Tenth Avenue* (WB, 1935), *Front Page Woman* (WB, 1935), *Special Agent* (WB, 1935), *Dangerous* (WB, 1935), *The Petrified Forest* (WB, 1936), *The Golden Arrow* (WB, 1936), *Satan Met a Lady* (WB, 1936), *Marked Woman* (WB, 1937), *Kid Galahad* (WB, 1937), *That Certain Woman* (WB, 1937), *It's Love I'm After* (WB, 1937), *Jezebel* (WB, 1938), *The Sisters* (WB, 1938), *Dark Victory* (WB, 1939), *Juarez* (WB, 1939), *The Old Maid* (WB, 1939), *The Private Lives of Elizabeth and Essex* (WB, 1939), *All This, and Heaven Too* (WB, 1940), *The Letter* (WB, 1940), *The Bride Came C.O.D.* (WB, 1941), *The Little Foxes* (RKO, 1941), *The Man Who Came to Dinner* (WB, 1941), *In This Our Life* (WB, 1942), *Now, Voyager* (WB, 1942), *Watch on the Rhine* (WB, 1943), *Thank Your Lucky Stars* (WB, 1943), *Old Acquaintance* (WB, 1943), *Mr. Skeffington* (WB, 1944), *Hollywood Canteen* (WB, 1944), *The Corn Is Green* (WB, 1945), *A Stolen Life* (WB, 1946), *Deception* (WB, 1947), *Winter Meeting* (WB, 1948), *June Bride* (WB, 1948), *Beyond the Forest* (WB, 1949), *All About Eve* (20th, 1950), *Payment on Demand* (RKO, 1951), *Another Man's Poison* (UA, 1951), *Phone Call From a Stranger* (20th, 1952), *The Star* (20th, 1953), *The Virgin Queen* (20th, 1955), *Storm Center* (Col., 1956), *The Catered Affair* (MGM, 1956), *John Paul Jones* (WB, 1959), *The Scapegoat* (MGM, 1959), *A Pocketful of Miracles* (UA, 1961), *What Ever Happened to Baby Jane?* (WB, 1962), *Dead Ringer* (WB, 1964), *The Empty Canvas* (Embassy, 1964), *Where Love Has Gone* (Par., 1964), *Hush . . . Hush, Sweet Charlotte* (20th, 1965), *The Nanny* (20th, 1965), *The Anniversary* (20th, 1968).

JOAN DAVIS (Madonna Josephine Davis) Born June 29, 1907, St. Paul, Minnesota. Married Seranus Willis (1931), child: Beverly; divorced 1947. Died May 22, 1961.

Feature Films: *Millions in the Air* (Par., 1935), *The Holy Terror* (20th, 1937), *Time Out for Romance* (20th, 1937), *Nancy Steele Is Missing* (20th, 1937), *Wake Up and Live* (20th, 1937), *You Can't Have Everything* (20th, 1937), *Angel's Holiday* (20th, 1937), *The Great Hospital Mystery* (20th, 1937), *Thin Ice* (20th, 1937), *On the Avenue* (20th, 1937), *Life Begins in College* (20th, 1937), *Love and Hisses* (20th, 1937), *Sally, Irene and Mary* (20th, 1938), *Josette* (20th, 1938), *My Lucky Star* (20th, 1938), *Hold That Co-ed* (20th, 1938), *Just Around the Corner* (20th, 1938), *Tailspin* (20th, 1939), *Daytime Wife* (20th, 1939), *Too Busy to Work* (20th, 1939), *Free, Blonde and 21* (20th, 1940), *Manhattan Heartbeat* (20th, 1940), *Sailor's Lady* (20th, 1940), *For Beauty's Sake* (20th, 1941), *Sun Valley Serenade* (20th, 1941), *Hold That Ghost* (Univ., 1941), *Two Latins From Manhattan* (Col., 1941), *Yokel Boy*

(Rep., 1942), *Sweethearts of the Fleet* (Col., 1942), *He's My Guy* (Univ., 1943), *Two Senoritas From Chicago* (Col., 1943), *Around the World* (RKO, 1943), *Show Business* (RKO, 1944), *Beautiful But Broke* (Col., 1944), *Kansas City Kitty* (Col., 1944), *She Gets Her Man* (Univ., 1945), *George White's Scandals* (RKO, 1945), *She Wrote the Book* (Univ., 1946), *If You Knew Susie* (RKO, 1948), *Make Mine Laughs* (RKO, 1949), *Traveling Saleswoman* (Col., 1949), *Love That Brute* (20th, 1950), *The Groom Wore Spurs* (Univ., 1951), *Harem Girl* (Col., 1952).

Peggie Castle and Joan Davis in *Harem Girl*.

SAMMY DAVIS, JR. Born December 8, 1925, New York, New York. Married Loray White (1958); divorced 1959. Married May Britt (1960), children: Tracey, Mark, Jeff.

Feature Films: *Anna Lucasta* (UA, 1958), *Porgy and Bess* (Col., 1959), *Ocean's 11* (WB, 1960), *Pepe* (Col., 1960), *Sergeants 3* (UA, 1962), *Convicts 4* (AA, 1962), *Johnny Cool* (UA, 1963), *Robin and the 7 Hoods* (WB, 1964), *Nightmare in the Sun* (Zodiac, 1965), *A Man Called Adam* (Embassy, 1966), *Salt and Pepper* (UA, 1968), *Sweet Charity* (Univ., 1969).

Sammy Davis, Jr., in *Convicts Four*.

DORIS DAY (Doris von Kappelhoff) Born April 3, 1924, Cincinnati, Ohio. Married Al Jorden (1941), child: Terry; divorced 1943. Married George Weidler (1946); divorced 1949. Married Marty Melcher (1951).

Feature Films: *Romance on the High Seas* (WB, 1948), *My Dream Is Yours* (WB, 1949), *It's a Great Feeling* (WB, 1949), *Young Man With a Horn* (WB, 1950), *Tea for Two* (WB, 1950), *The West Point Story* (WB, 1950), *Storm Warning* (WB, 1950), *The Lullaby of Broadway* (WB, 1951), *On Moonlight Bay* (WB, 1951), *Starlift* (WB, 1951), *I'll See You in My Dreams* (WB, 1951), *April in Paris* (WB, 1952), *The Winning Team* (WB, 1952), *By the Light of the Silvery Moon* (WB, 1953), *Calamity Jane* (WB, 1953), *Lucky Me* (WB, 1954), *Young at*

Doris Day and Gordon MacRae in *By the Light of the Silvery Moon.*

Heart (WB, 1954), *Love Me or Leave Me* (MGM, 1955), *The Man Who Knew Too Much* (Par., 1956), *Julie* (MGM, 1956), *The Pajama Game* (WB, 1957), *Teacher's Pet* (Par., 1958), *The Tunnel of Love* (MGM, 1958), *It Happened to Jane* (Col., 1959), *Pillow Talk* (Univ., 1959), *Please Don't Eat the Daisies* (MGM, 1960), *Midnight Lace* (Univ., 1960), *Lover Come Back* (Univ., 1961), *That Touch of Mink* (Univ., 1962), *Billy Rose's Jumbo* (MGM, 1962), *The Thrill of It All* (Univ., 1963), *Move Over, Darling* (20th, 1963), *Send Me No Flowers* (Univ., 1964), *Do Not Disturb* (20th, 1965), *The Glass-Bottom Boat* (MGM, 1966), *Caprice* (20th, 1967), *The Ballad of Josie* (Univ., 1968), *Where Were You When the Lights Went Out?* (MGM, 1968).

LARAINE DAY (Loraine Johnson) Born October 13, 1919, Roosevelt, Utah. Married James Ray Hendricks (1942), children: Angela, Christopher, Melinda; divorced 1946. Married Leo Durocher (1947); divorced 1960. Married Michael Grilikhes (1961), children: Gigi, Dana.

Feature Films:

    as Laraine Johnson *Stella Dallas* (UA, 1937), *Border G-Men* (RKO, 1938), *Scandal Street* (Par., 1938), *Painted Desert* (RKO, 1938), *The Arizona Legion* (RKO, 1939), *Sergeant Madden* (MGM, 1939).

Laraine Day and Kirk Douglas in *My Dear Secretary.*

    as Laraine Day *Calling Dr. Kildare* (MGM, 1939), *Tarzan Finds a Son* (MGM, 1939), *Secret of Dr. Kildare* (MGM, 1939), *My Son, My Son* (UA, 1940), *I Take This Woman* (MGM, 1940), *And One Was Beautiful* (MGM, 1940), *Dr. Kildare's Strange Case* (MGM, 1940), *Foreign Correspondent* (UA, 1940), *Dr. Kildare Goes Home* (MGM, 1940), *Dr. Kildare's Crisis* (MGM, 1940), *The Bad Man* (MGM, 1941), *The Trial of Mary Dugan* (MGM, 1941), *The People vs. Dr. Kildare* (MGM, 1941), *Dr. Kildare's Wedding Day* (MGM, 1941), *Unholy Partners* (MGM, 1941), *Kathleen* (MGM, 1941), *Journey for Margaret* (MGM, 1942), *Fingers at the Window* (MGM, 1942), *A Yank on the Burma Road* (MGM, 1942), *Mr. Lucky* (RKO, 1943),

The Story of Dr. Wassell (Par., 1944), *Bride by Mistake* (RKO, 1944), *Those Endearing Young Charms* (RKO, 1945), *Keep Your Powder Dry* (MGM, 1945), *The Locket* (RKO, 1946), *Tycoon* (RKO, 1947), *My Dear Secretary* (UA, 1948), *I Married a Communist* ("The Woman On Pier 13—RKO, 1949), *Without Honor* (UA, 1949), *The High and the Mighty* (WB, 1954), *Toy Tiger* (Univ., 1956), *Three for Jamie Dawn* (AA, 1956), *The Third Voice* (20th, 1960).

JAMES DEAN (James Byron Dean) Born February 8, 1931, Marian, Nebraska. Died September 30, 1955.

Richard Davalos, James Dean and Jo Van Fleet in *East of Eden.*

Feature Films: *Sailor Beware* (Par., 1951), *Fixed Bayonets* (20th, 1951), *Has Anybody Seen My Gal* (Univ., 1952), *East of Eden* (WB, 1955), *Rebel Without a Cause* (WB, 1955), *Giant* (WB, 1956),

ROSEMARY DE CAMP Born November 14, 1914, Prescott, Arizona. Married John Shidler (1941) children: Margaret, Martha, Valerie, Nita.

Moroni Olsen, Dane Clark, Rosemary De Camp and John Garfield in *Pride of the Marines.*

Feature Films: *Cheers for Miss Bishop* (UA, 1941), *Hold Back the Dawn* (Par., 1941), *Jungle Book* (UA, 1942), *Yankee Doodle Dandy* (WB, 1942), *Eyes in the Night* (MGM, 1942), *Commandos Strike at Dawn* (Col., 1942), *Smith of Minnesota* (Col., 1942), *City Without Men* (Col., 1943), *This Is the Army* (WB, 1943), *The Merry Monahans* (Univ., 1944), *Bowery to Broadway* (Univ., 1944), *Blood on the Sun* (UA, 1945), *Practically Yours* (Par., 1945), *Weekend at the Waldorf* (MGM, 1945), *Rhapsody in Blue* (WB, 1945), *Pride of the Marines* (WB, 1945), *Danger Signal* (WB, 1945), *Too Young to Know* (WB, 1945), *From This Day*

Forward (RKO, 1946), *Two Guys From Milwaukee* (WB, 1946), *Nora Prentiss* (WB, 1947), *Night Unto Night* (WB, 1949), *The Life of Riley* (Univ., 1949), *Look for the Silver Lining* (WB, 1949), *The Story of Seabiscuit* (MGM, 1949), *The Big Hangover* (MGM, 1950), *Night into Morning* (MGM, 1951), *On Moonlight Bay* (WB, 1951), *Scandal Sheet* (Col., 1952), *The Treasure of Lost Canyon* (Univ., 1952), *By the Light of the Silvery Moon* (WB, 1953), *Main Street to Broadway* (MGM, 1953), *So This Is Love* (WB, 1953), *Strategic Air Command* (Par., 1955), *Many Rivers to Cross* (MGM, 1955), *13 Ghosts* (Col., 1960).

YVONNE DE CARLO (Peggy Yvonne Middleton) Born September 1, 1922, Vancouver, Canada. Married Robert Morgan (1955), children: Bruce, Michael.

English-Language Feature Films: *This Gun for Hire* (Par., 1942), *Har-*

Yvonne De Carlo and Alan Badel in *Magic Fire*.

vard, Here I Come (Col., 1942), *Road to Morocco* (Par., 1942), *Lucky Jordan* (Par., 1942), *Youth on Parade* (Col., 1942), *Let's Face It* (Par., 1943), *The Crystal Ball* (UA, 1943), *Salute for Three* (Par., 1943), *For Whom the Bell Tolls* (Par., 1943), *True to Life* (Par., 1943), *So Proudly We Hail!* (Par., 1943), *The Deerslayer* (Rep., 1943), *Practically Yours* (Par., 1944), *The Story of Dr. Wassell* (Par., 1944), *Standing Room Only* (Par., 1944), *Here Come the Waves* (Par., 1944), *Kismet* (MGM, 1944), *Salome, Where She Danced* (Univ., 1945), *Frontier Gal* (Univ., 1945), *Song of Scheherazade* (Univ., 1947), *Brute Force* (Univ., 1947), *Slave Girl* (Univ., 1947), *Black Bart* (Univ., 1948), *Casbah* (Univ., 1948), *River Lady* (Univ., 1948), *Criss Cross* (Univ., 1949), *Calamity Jane and Sam Bass* (Univ., 1949), *The Gal Who Took the West* (Univ., 1949), *Buccaneer's Girl* (Univ., 1950), *The Desert Hawk* (Univ., 1950), *Hotel Sahara* (UA, 1951), *Tomahawk* (Univ., 1951), *Silver City* (Par., 1951), *The San Francisco Story* (WB, 1952), *Scarlet Angel* (Univ., 1952), *Hurricane Smith* (Par., 1952), *Sombrero* (MGM, 1953), *Sea Devils* (RKO, 1953), *Fort Algiers* (UA, 1953), *The Captain's Paradise* (UA, 1953), *Border River* (Univ., 1954), *Passion* (RKO, 1954), *Tonight's the Night* (AA, 1954), *Shotgun* (AA, 1955), *Flame of the Islands* (Rep., 1955), *Magic Fire* (Rep., 1956), *Raw Edge* (Univ., 1956), *The Ten Commandments* (Par., 1956), *Death of a Scoundrel* (RKO, 1956), *Band of Angels* (WB, 1957), *Timbuctu* (UA, 1959), *McLintock* (UA, 1963), *A Global Affair* (MGM, 1964), *Law of the Lawless* (Par., 1964), *Munster, Go Home* (Univ., 1966), *Hostile Guns* (Par., 1967), *Arizona Bushwhackers* (Par., 1968), *The Power* (MGM, 1968).

SANDRA DEE (Alexandra Zuck) Born April 23, 1942, Bayonne, New Jersey. Married Bobby Darin (1960), child: Dodd; divorced 1967.

Feature Films: *Until They Sail* (MGM, 1957), *The Reluctant Debutante* (MGM, 1958), *The Restless Years* (Univ., 1958), *Stranger in My Arms* (Univ., 1959), *Imitation of Life* (Univ., 1959), *Snow Queen* (voice only, Univ., 1959), *The Wild and the Innocent* (Univ., 1959), *Gidget* (Col., 1959), *A Summer Place* (WB, 1959),

Teresa Wright and Sandra Dee in *The Restless Years*.

Portrait in Black (Univ., 1960), *Romanoff and Juliet* (Univ., 1961), *Tammy, Tell Me True* (Univ., 1961), *Come September* (Univ., 1961), *If a Man Answers* (Univ., 1962), *Tammy and the Doctor* (Univ., 1963), *Take Her, She's Mine* (20th, 1963), *I'd Rather Be Rich* (Univ., 1964), *That Funny Feeling* (Univ., 1965), *A Man Could Get Killed* (Univ., 1966), *Doctor, You've Got to Be Kidding!* (MGM, 1967), *Rosie!* (Univ., 1968).

GLORIA DE HAVEN (Gloria Mildred De Haven) Born July 23, 1924, Los Angeles, California. Married John Payne (1944), children: Kathleen, Thomas; divorced 1950. Married Martin Kimmel (1953); divorced 1954. Married Richard Fincher (1957), child: Harry; divorced 1963. Remarried 1964.

Feature Films: *The Great Dictator* (UA, 1940), *Susan and God* (MGM, 1940), *Keeping Company* (MGM, 1941), *Two-Faced Woman* (MGM, 1941), *The Penalty* (MGM, 1941), *Best Foot Forward* (MGM, 1943), *Thousands Cheer* (MGM, 1943), *Broadway Rhythm* (MGM, 1944), *Two Girls and a Sailor* (MGM, 1944), *Step Lively* (RKO, 1944), *The Thin Man Goes Home* (MGM, 1944), *Between Two Women* (MGM, 1945), *Summer Holiday* (MGM, 1948), *Scene of the Crime* (MGM, 1949), *The Doctor and the Girl* (MGM, 1949), *Yes Sir, That's My Baby* (Univ., 1949), *The Yellow Cab Man* (MGM, 1950), *Three Little Words* (MGM, 1950), *Summer Stock* (MGM, 1950), *I'll Get By* (20th, 1950), *Two Tickets to Broadway* (RKO, 1951), *Down Among the Sheltering Palms* (20th, 1953), *So This Is Paris* (Univ., 1955), *The Girl Rush* (Par., 1955).

William Lundigan, Gloria De Haven and Lyle Talbot in *Down Among the Sheltering Palms*.

OLIVIA DE HAVILLAND Born July 1, 1916, Tokyo, Japan. Married Marcus Goodrich (1946), child: Benjamin; divorced 1952. Married Pierre Paul Galante (1955), child: Giselle.

Gene Lockhart, Olivia De Havilland and Errol Flynn in *They Died With Their Boots On.*

Feature Films: *A Midsummer Night's Dream* (WB, 1935), *Alibi Ike* (WB, 1935), *The Irish in Us* (WB, 1935), *Captain Blood* (WB, 1935), *Anthony Adverse* (WB, 1936), *The Charge of the Light Brigade* (WB, 1936), *Call It a Day* (WB, 1937), *The Great Garrick* (WB, 1937), *It's Love I'm After* (WB, 1937), *Gold Is Where You Find It* (WB, 1938), *Hard to Get* (WB, 1938), *The Adventures of Robin Hood* (WB, 1938), *Four's a Crowd* (WB, 1938), *Wings of the Navy* (WB, 1939), *Dodge City* (WB, 1939), *The Private Lives of Elizabeth and Essex* (WB, 1939), *Gone With the Wind* (MGM, 1939), *Raffles* (UA, 1940), *My Love Came Back* (WB, 1940), *Santa Fe Trail* (WB, 1940), *Strawberry Blonde* (WB, 1941), *Hold Back the Dawn* (Par., 1941), *They Died With Their Boots On* (WB, 1941), *The Male Animal* (WB, 1942), *In This Our Life* (WB, 1942), *Thank Your Lucky Stars* (WB, 1943), *Princess O' Rourke* (WB, 1943), *Government Girl* (RKO, 1943), *Devotion* (WB, 1946), *The Well-Groomed Bride* (Par., 1946), *To Each His Own* (Par., 1946), *The Dark Mirror* (Univ., 1946), *The Snake Pit* (20th, 1948), *The Heiress* (Par., 1949), *My Cousin Rachel* (20th, 1953), *That Lady* (20th, 1955), *Not as a Stranger* (UA, 1955), *The Ambassador's Daughter* (UA, 1956), *Proud Rebel* (BV, 1958), *Libel* (MGM, 1959), *Light in the Piazza* (MGM, 1962), *Hush . . . Hush, Sweet Charlotte* (20th, 1964), *Lady in a Cage* (Par., 1964).

ALBERT DEKKER Born December 20, 1905, Brooklyn, New York. Married Esther Guerini (1929), children: Jan, John, Benjamin; divorced. Died May 5, 1968.

Feature Films: *The Great Garrick* (WB, 1937), *The Last Warning* (Univ., 1938), *She Married an Artist* (Col., 1938), *The Lone Wolf in Paris* (Col., 1938), *Extortion* (Col., 1938), *Marie Antoinette* (MGM, 1938), *Paris Honeymoon* (Par., 1939), *Never Say Die* (Par., 1939), *Hotel Imperial* (Par., 1939), *The Man in the Iron Mask* (UA, 1939), *The*

Albert Dekker, Porter Hall and Claire Trevor in *Woman of the Town.*

Great Commandment (20th, 1939), *Beau Geste* (Par., 1939), *Dr. Cyclops* (Par., 1940), *Strange Cargo* (MGM, 1940), *Rangers of Fortune* (Par., 1940), *Seven Sinners* (Univ., 1940), *You're the One* (Par., 1941), *Blonde Inspiration* (MGM, 1941), *Reaching for the Sun* (Par., 1941), *Buy Me That Town* (Par., 1941), *Among the Living* (Par., 1941), *Honky Tonk* (MGM, 1941), *The Lady Has Plans* (Par., 1942), *In Old California* (Rep., 1942), *Wake Island* (Par., 1942), *Night in New Orleans* (Par., 1942), *Yokel Boy* (Par., 1942), *Once Upon a Honeymoon* (RKO, 1942), *Star Spangled Rhythm* (Par., 1942), *Buckskin Frontier* (UA, 1943), *The Kansan* (UA, 1943), *In Old Oklahoma* (Rep., 1943), *The Woman of the Town* (UA, 1943), *The Hitler Gang* (narrator; Par., 1944), *Experiment Perilous* (RKO, 1944), *Salome, Where She Danced* (Univ., 1945), *Incendiary Blonde* (Par., 1945), *Hold That Blonde* (Par., 1945), *Suspense* (Mon., 1946), *The French Key* (Rep., 1946), *The Killers* (Univ., 1946), *Two Years Before the Mast* (Par., 1946), *California* (Par., 1946), *Wyoming* (Rep., 1947), *Slave Girl* (Univ., 1947), *The Pretender* (Rep., 1947), *The Fabulous Texan* (Rep., 1947), *Gentleman's Agreement* (20th, 1947), *Cass Timberlane* (MGM, 1947), *Fury at Furnace Creek* (20th, 1948), *Lulu Belle* (Col., 1948), *Bride of Vengeance* (Par., 1949), *Tarzan's Magic Fountain* (RKO, 1949), *Search for Danger* (Film Classics, 1949), *The Kid From Texas* (Univ., 1950), *Destination Murder* (RKO, 1950), *The Furies* (Par., 1950), *As Young As You Feel* (20th, 1951), *Wait Till the Sun Shines, Nellie* (20th, 1952), *The Silver Chalice* (WB, 1954), *Kiss Me Deadly* (UA, 1955), *Illegal* (WB, 1955), *East of Eden* (WB, 1955), *She Devil* (20th, 1957), *Machete* (UA, 1958), *These Thousand Hills* (20th, 1959), *The Sound and the Fury* (20th, 1959), *Middle of the Night* (Col., 1959), *The Wonderful Country* (UA, 1959), *Suddenly, Last Summer* (Col., 1959), *Come Spy With Me* (20th, 1967), *Gammera, the Invincible* (World Entertainment Corp., 1967).

DOLORES DEL RIO (Dolores Asunsolo) Born August 3, 1905, Durango, Mexico. Married Jaime Del Rio (1921); widowed 1928. Married Cedric Gibbons (1930); divorced 1941. Married Lewis Riley (1959).

James Leong, Dolores Del Rio, Dick Baldwin and June Lang in *International Settlement.*

English-language Feature Films: *Evangeline* (UA, 1929), *The Bad One* (UA, 1930), *Girl of the Rio* (RKO, 1932), *Bird of Paradise* (RKO, 1932), *Flying Down to Rio* (RKO, 1933), *Wonder Bar* (WB, 1934), *Madame Du Barry* (WB, 1934), *In Caliente* (WB, 1935), *I Live for Love* (WB, 1935), *Widow From Monte Carlo* (WB, 1935), *Accused* (UA, 1936), *Devil's Playground* (Col., 1937), *Lancer Spy* (20th, 1937), *International Settlement* (20th, 1938), *The Man From Dakota* (MGM, 1940), *Journey Into Fear* (RKO, 1942), *The Fugitive* (RKO, 1947), *Flaming Star* (20th, 1960), *Cheyenne Autumn* (WB, 1964), *More Than a Miracle* (MGM, 1967).

REGINALD DENNY (Reginald Leigh Dugmore Denny) Born November 20, 1891, Richmond, Surrey, England. Married Irene Haisman (1913), child: Barbara; divorced 1927. Married Isobel Steifeel (1928), children: Reginald, Joan. Died June 16, 1967.

Mary Nolan and Reginald Denny in *Good Morning Judge*.

James Cagney, Andy Devine and Ann Sheridan in *Torrid Zone*.

Sound Feature Films: *One Hysterical Night* (Univ., 1930), *What a Man!* (Sono Art-World Wide, 1930), *Embarrassing Moments* (Univ., 1930), *Those Three French Girls* (MGM, 1930), *A Lady's Morals* (MGM, 1930), *Madame Satan* (MGM, 1930), *Oh, For a Man!* (Fox, 1930), *Stepping Out* (MGM, 1931), *Kiki* (UA, 1931), *Parlor, Bedroom and Bath* (MGM, 1931), *Private Lives* (MGM, 1931), *Strange Justice* (RKO, 1932), *Iron Master* (Allied, 1933), *The Barbarian* (MGM, 1933), *Big Bluff* (Tower, 1933), *Only Yesterday* (Univ., 1933), *Fog* (Col., 1934), *Lost Patrol* (RKO, 1934), *We're Rich Again* (RKO, 1934), *The World Moves On* (Fox, 1934), *Dancing Man* (Pyramid, 1934), *Of Human Bondage* (RKO, 1934), *One More River* (Univ., 1934), *Richest Girl in the World* (RKO, 1934), *The Little Minister* (RKO, 1934), *Lottery Lover* (Fox, 1935), *Vagabond Lady* (MGM, 1935), *No More Ladies* (MGM, 1935), *Anna Karenina* (MGM, 1935), *Here's to Romance* (Fox, 1935), *Midnight Phantom* (Reliable, 1935), *Remember Last Night?* (Univ., 1935), *Lady in Scarlet* (Chesterfield, 1936), *Penthouse Party* (Liberty, 1936), *The Preview Murder Mystery* (Par., 1936), *Romeo and Juliet* (MGM, 1936), *It Couldn't Have Happened* (Invincible, 1936), *Two in a Crowd* (Univ., 1936), *More Than a Secretary* (Col., 1936), *Join the Marines* (Rep., 1937), *Women of Glamour* (Col., 1937), *Bulldog Drummond Escapes* (Par., 1937), *Let's Get Married* (Col., 1937), *The Great Gambini* (Par., 1937), *Bulldog Drummond Comes Back* (Par., 1937), *Beg, Borrow or Steal* (MGM, 1937), *Bulldog Drummond's Revenge* (Par., 1937), *Bulldog Drummond's Peril* (Par., 1938), *Four Men and a Prayer* (20th, 1938), *Blockade* (UA, 1938), *Bulldog Drummond in Africa* (Par., 1938), *Arrest Bulldog Drummond* (Par., 1939), *Bulldog Drummond's Secret Police* (Par., 1939), *Bulldog Drummond's Bride* (Par., 1939), *Rebecca* (UA, 1940), *Spring Parade* (Univ., 1940), *Seven Sinners* (Univ., 1940), *One Night in Lisbon* (Par., 1941), *International Squadron* (WB, 1941), *Appointment for Love* (Univ., 1941), *Sherlock Holmes and the Voice of Terror* (Univ., 1942), *Eyes in the Night* (MGM, 1942), *Thunder Birds* (20th, 1942), *Over My Dead Body* (20th, 1942), *Crime Doctor's Strangest Case* (Col., 1943), *Song of the Open Road* (UA, 1944), *Love Letters* (Par., 1945), *Tangier* (Univ., 1946), *The Locket* (RKO, 1946), *The Macomber Affair* (UA, 1947), *My Favorite Brunette* (Par., 1947), *The Secret Life of Walter Mitty* (RKO, 1947), *Escape Me Never* (WB, 1947), *Christmas Eve* (UA, 1947), *Mr. Blandings Builds His Dream House* (RKO, 1948), *The Iroquois Trail* (UA, 1950), *The Hindu* ("Sabaka"—Ferrin, 1953), *Abbott and Costello Meet Dr. Jekyll and Mr. Hyde* (Univ., 1953), *Fort Vengeance* (AA, 1953), *World for Ransom* (AA, 1954), *Escape to Burma* (RKO, 1955), *Around the World in 80 Days* (UA, 1956), *Cat Ballou* (Col., 1965), *Batman* (20th, 1966).

ANDY DEVINE Born October 7, 1905, Flagstaff, Arizona. Married Dorothy House (1933), children: Tad, Denny.

Sound Feature Films: *Spirit of Notre Dame* (Univ., 1931), *The Criminal Code* (Col., 1931), *Law and Order* (Univ., 1932), *Destry Rides Again* (Univ., 1932), *Three Wise Girls* (Col., 1932), *Impatient Maiden* (Univ., 1932), *Information Kid* (Univ., 1932), *Man Wanted* (WB, 1932), *Man From Yesterday* (Par., 1932), *Radio Patrol* (Univ., 1932), *Tom Brown of Culver* (Univ., 1932), *Fast Companions* (Univ., 1932), *All American* (Univ., 1932), *Cohens and Kellys in Trouble* (Univ., 1933), *Song of the Eagle* (Par., 1933), *The Big Cage* (Univ., 1933), *Midnight*

Mary (MGM, 1933), *Doctor Bull* (Fox, 1933), *Saturday's Millions* (Univ., 1933), *Chance at Heaven* (RKO, 1933), *Poor Rich* (Univ., 1934), *Stingaree* (RKO, 1934), *Let's Talk It Over* (Univ., 1934), *Upper World* (WB, 1934), *The Gift of Gab* (Univ., 1934), *Million Dollar Ransom* (Univ., 1934), *Wake Up and Dream* (Univ., 1934), *Hell in the Heavens* (Fox, 1934), *The President Vanishes* (Par., 1934), *Straight From the Heart* (Univ., 1935), *Hold 'Em Yale* (Par., 1935), *The Farmer Takes a Wife* (Fox., 1935), *Chinatown Squad* (Univ., 1935), *Fighting Youth* (Univ., 1935), *Way Down East* (Fox, 1935), *Coronado* (Par., 1935), *Small Town Girl* (MGM, 1936), *Romeo and Juliet* (MGM, 1936), *The Big Game* (RKO, 1936), *Yellowstone* (Univ., 1936), *Flying Hostess* (Univ., 1936), *Mysterious Crossing* (Univ., 1937), *A Star Is Born* (UA, 1937), *The Road Back* (Univ., 1937), *Double or Nothing* (Par., 1937), *You're a Sweetheart* (Univ., 1937), *In Old Chicago* (20th, 1938), *Dr. Rhythm* (Par., 1938), *Yellow Jack* (MGM, 1938), *The Storm* (Univ., 1938), *Personal Secretary* (Univ., 1938), *Men With Wings* (Par., 1938), *Strange Faces* (Univ., 1938), *Swing That Cheer* (Univ., 1938), *Stagecoach* (UA, 1939), *Never Say Die* (Par., 1939), *The Spirit of Culver* (Univ., 1939), *Geronimo* (Par., 1939), *Mutiny on the Blackhawk* (Univ., 1939), *Legion of Lost Flyers* (Par., 1939), *The Man From Montreal* (Univ., 1939), *Tropic Fury* (Univ., 1940), *Little Old New York* (20th, 1940), *Buck Benny Rides Again* (Par., 1940), *Danger on Wheels* (Univ., 1940), *Torrid Zone* (WB, 1940), *Hot Steel* (Univ., 1940), *When the Daltons Rode* (Univ., 1940), *The Leather Pushers* (Univ., 1940), *Black Diamonds* (Univ., 1940), *The Devil's Pipeline* (Univ., 1940), *Trail of the Vigilantes* (Univ., 1940), *A Dangerous Game* (Univ., 1941), *Lucky Devils* (Univ., 1941), *The Flame of New Orleans* (Univ., 1941), *Mutiny in the Arctic* (Univ., 1941), *Men of the Timberland* (Univ., 1941), *Badlands of Dakota* (Univ., 1941), *South of Tahiti* (Univ., 1941), *Road Agent* (Univ., 1941), *Raiders of the Desert* (Univ., 1941), *Unseen Enemy* (Univ., 1942), *North to the Klondike* (Univ., 1942), *Escape From Hong Kong* (Univ., 1942), *Danger in the Pacific* (Univ., 1942), *Between Us Girls* (Univ., 1942), *Sin Town* (Univ., 1942), *Top Sergeant* (Univ., 1942), *Rhythm of the Islands* (Univ., 1943), *Frontier Badmen* (Univ., 1943), *Corvette K-225* (Univ., 1943), *Crazy House* (Univ., 1943), *Ali Baba and the Forty Thieves* (Univ., 1944), *Follow the Boys* (Univ., 1944), *Ghost Catchers* (Univ., 1944), *Babes on Swing Street* (Univ., 1944), *Bowery to Broadway* (Univ., 1944), *Sudan* (Univ., 1945), *Frisco Sal* (Univ., 1945), *That's the Spirit* (Univ., 1945), *Frontier Gal* (Univ., 1945), *Canyon Passage* (Univ., 1946), *The Michigan Kid* (Univ., 1947), *Bells of San Angelo* (Rep., 1947), *Springtime in the Sierras* (Rep., 1947), *Slave Girl* (Univ., 1947), *The Marauders* (UA, 1947), *On the Old Spanish Trail* (Rep., 1947), *The Vigilantes Return* (Univ., 1947), *The Gay Ranchero* (Rep., 1948), *Old Los Angeles* (Rep., 1948), *Under California Skies* (Rep., 1948), *Eyes of Texas* (Rep., 1948), *Grand Canyon Trail* (Rep., 1948), *Nighttime in Nevada* (Rep., 1948), *The Far Frontier* (Rep., 1948), *The Last Bandit* (Rep., 1949), *Traveling Saleswoman* (Col., 1950), *Never a Dull Moment* (RKO 1950), *New Mexico* (UA, 1951), *The Red Badge of Courage* (MGM, 1951), *Slaughter Trail* (RKO, 1951), *Montana Belle* (RKO, 1952), *Island in the Sky* (WB, 1953), *Pete Kelly's Blues* (WB, 1955), *Around the World in 80 Days* (UA, 1956), *The Adventures of Huckleberry Finn* (MGM, 1960), *Two Rode Together* (Col., 1961), *The Man Who Shot Liberty Valance* (Par., 1962), *How the West Was Won* (MGM, 1963), *It's a Mad, Mad, Mad, Mad World* (UA, 1963), *Zebra in the Kitchen* (MGM, 1965), *The Ballad of Josie* (Univ., 1968).

Linda Evans, Brandon De Wilde and Walter Brennan in *Those Calloways*.

BRANDON DE WILDE (Andre Brandon de Wilde) Born April 9, 1942, Brooklyn, New York. Married Susan Maw (1963).

Feature Films: *The Member of the Wedding* (Col., 1952), *Shane* (Par., 1953), *Good-bye, My Lady* (WB, 1956), *Night Passage* (Univ., 1957). *The Missouri Traveler* (BV, 1958), *Blue Denim* (20th, 1959), *All Fall Down* (MGM, 1962), *Hud* (Par., 1963), *Those Calloways* (BV, 1964). *In Harm's Way* (Par., 1965).

BILLY DE WOLFE (William Andrew Jones) Born Wollaston, Massachusetts.

Billy De Wolfe, Gordon Jones, Edward Arnold, William Holden and Joan Caulfield in *Dear Wife*.

Feature Films: *Dixie* (Par., 1943), *Miss Susie Slagle's* (Par., 1945), *Our Hearts Were Growing Up* (Par., 1946), *Blue Skies* (Par., 1946), *Dear Ruth* (Par., 1947), *The Perils of Pauline* (Par., 1947), *Variety Girl* (Par., 1947), *Isn't It Romantic?* (Par., 1948), *Dear Wife* (Par., 1949), *Tea for Two* (WB, 1950), *Dear Brat* (Par., 1951), *Lullaby of Broadway* (WB, 1951), *Call Me Madam* (20th, 1953), *Billie* (UA, 1965).

ANGIE DICKINSON Born September 30, 1931, Kulm, North Dakota. Married Bert Bacharach (1965), child: Lea.

Angie Dickinson and Efram Zimbalist, Jr., in *A Fever in the Blood.*

Feature Films: *Lucky Me* (WB, 1954), *Man With the Gun* (UA, 1955), *Tennessee's Partner* (RKO, 1955), *The Return of Jack Slade* (AA, 1955), *Hidden Guns* (Rep., 1956), *Gun the Man Down* (UA, 1956), *Tension at Table Rock* (RKO, 1956), *The Black Whip* (20th, 1957), *Shoot-Out at Medicine Bend* (WB, 1957), *Calypso Joe* (AA, 1957), *China Gate* (20th, 1957), *Cry Terror* (MGM, 1958), *Rio Bravo* (WB, 1959), *The Bramble Bush* (WB, 1960), *Ocean's 11* (WB, 1960), *A Fever in the Blood* (WB, 1961), *The Sins of Rachel Cade* (WB, 1961), *Rome Adventure* (WB, 1962), *Jessica* (UA, 1962), *Captain Newman, M.D.* (Univ., 1963), *The Killers* (Univ., 1964), *The Art of Love* (Univ., 1965), *The Chase* (Col., 1966), *Cast a Giant Shadow* (UA, 1966), *Point Blank* (MGM, 1967), *The Last Challenge* (MGM, 1967).

MARLENE DIETRICH (Maria Magdalene von Lòsch) Born December 27, 1900, Schoenberg, Germany. Married Rudolf Sieber (1924), child: Maria.

Charles Boyer, Alan Marshall, Marlene Dietrich and Joseph Schildkraut in *The Garden of Allah.*

English-Language Feature Films: *The Blue Angel* (Par., 1930), *Morocco* (Par., 1930), *Dishonored* (Par., 1931), *Shanghai Express* (Par., 1932), *Blonde Venus* (Par., 1932), *The Song of Songs* (Par., 1933), *The Scarlet Empress* (Par., 1934), *The Devil Is a Woman* (Par., 1935), *Desire* (Par., 1936), *The Garden of Allah* (UA, 1936), *Knight Without Armour* (UA, 1937), *Angel* (Par., 1937), *Destry Rides Again* (Univ., 1939), *Seven Sinners* (Univ., 1940), *The Flame of New Orleans* (Univ., 1941), *Manpower* (WB, 1941), *The Lady Is Willing* (Col., 1942), *The Spoilers* (Univ., 1942), *Pittsburgh* (Univ., 1942), *Follow the Boys* (Univ., 1944), *Kismet* (MGM, 1944), *Golden Earrings* (Par., 1947), *A Foreign Affair* (Par., 1948), *Jigsaw* (UA, 1949),* *Stage Fright* (WB, 1950), *No Highway in the Sky* (20th, 1951), *Rancho Notorious* (RKO, 1952), *Around the World in 80 Days* (UA, 1956), *The Monte Carlo Story* (UA, 1957), *Witness for the Prosecution* (UA, 1957), *Touch of Evil* (Univ., 1958),* *Judgment at Nuremberg* (UA, 1961), *The Black Fox* (narrator; Capri 1963), *Paris When It Sizzles* (Par., 1964).*

*Unbilled guest appearance

RICHARD DIX (Ernest Carlton Brimmer) Born July 18, 1894, St. Paul, Minnesota. Married Winifred Coe (1931), child: Martha; divorced 1933. Married Virginia Webster (1934), children: Richard, Robert, Sara. Died September 20, 1949.

Sound Feature Films: *Nothing But the Truth* (Par., 1929), *The Wheel of Life* (Par., 1929), *The Love Doctor* (Par., 1929), *Seven Keys to Baldpate* (RKO, 1929), *Lovin' the Ladies* (RKO, 1930), *Shooting Straight* (RKO, 1930), *Cimarron* (RKO, 1931), *Young Donovan's Kid* (RKO, 1931), *Public Defender* (RKO, 1931), *Secret Service* (RKO, 1931), *The Lost Squadron* (RKO, 1932), *Roar of the Dragon* (RKO, 1932), *Hell's Highway* (RKO, 1932), *The Conquerors* (RKO, 1932), *The Great Jasper* (RKO, 1933), *No Marriage Ties* (RKO, 1933), *Day of Reckoning* (MGM, 1933), *The Ace of Aces* (RKO, 1933), *Stingaree* (RKO, 1934),

Boris Karloff, Richard Dix and Jackie Cooper in *Young Donovan's Kid*.

His Greatest Gamble (RKO, 1934), *West of the Pecos* (RKO, 1934), *The Arizonian* (RKO, 1935), *Trans-Atlantic Tunnel* (Gaumont-British, 1935), *Yellow Dust* (RKO, 1936), *Special Investigator* (RKO, 1936), *Devil's Squadron* (Col., 1936), *The Devil's Playground* (Col., 1937), *The Devil Is Driving* (Col., 1937), *It Happened in Hollywood* (Col., 1937), *Blind Alibi* (RKO, 1938), *Sky Giant* (RKO, 1938), *Twelve Crowded Hours* (RKO, 1939), *Man of Conquest* (Rep., 1939), *Here I Am a Stranger* (20th, 1939), *Reno* (RKO, 1939), *The Marines Fly High* (RKO, 1940), *Men Against the Sky* (RKO, 1940), *Cherokee Strip* (Par., 1940), *The Roundup* (Par., 1941), *Badlands of Dakota* (Univ., 1941), *Tombstone, the Town Too Tough to Die* (Par., 1942), *American Empire* (UA, 1942), *Eyes of the Underworld* (Univ., 1943), *Buckskin Frontier* (UA, 1943), *The Kansan* (UA, 1943), *Top Man* (Univ, 1943), *The Ghost Ship* (RKO, 1943), *The Whistler* (Col., 1944), *The Mark of the Whistler* (Col., 1944), *The Power of the Whistler* (Col., 1945), *The Voice of the Whistler* (Col., 1946), *The Mysterious Intruder* (Col., 1946), *The Secret of the Whistler* (Col., 1946), *The 13th Hour* (Col., 1947).

TROY DONAHUE (Merle Johnson, Jr.) Born January 27, 1937, New York, New York. Married Suzanne Pleshette (1964); divorced 1964. Married Valerie Allen (1966).

Feature Films: *Man Afraid* (Univ., 1957), *Tarnished Angels* (Univ., 1958), *This Happy Feeling* (Univ., 1958), *Voice in the Mirror* (Univ., 1958), *Summer Love* (Univ., 1958), *Live Fast, Die Young* (Univ., 1958), *Wild Heritage* (Univ., 1958), *Monster on the Campus* (Univ., 1958), *The Perfect Furlough* (Univ., 1959), *Imitation of Life* (Univ., 1959), *A Summer Place* (WB, 1959), *The Crowded Sky* (WB, 1960), *Parrish* (WB, 1961), *Susan Slade* (WB, 1961), *Rome Adventure* (WB, 1962), *Palm Springs Weekend* (WB, 1963), *A Distant Trumpet* (WB, 1964), *My Blood Runs Cold* (WB, 1965), *Come Spy With Me* (20th, 1967), *Blast-off* (AIP, 1967).

Troy Donahue (right) in *The Crowded Sky*.

Barbara Stanwyck and Brian Donlevy in *The Great Man's Lady*.

BRIAN DONLEVY Born February 9, 1903, Portadown County, Armagh, Eire. Married Marjorie Lane (1936), child: Judith; divorced 1947. Married Lillian Lugosi (1966).

Sound Feature Films: *Mother's Boy* (Pathé, 1929), *Gentlemen of the Press* (Par., 1929), *Barbary Coast* (UA, 1935), *Mary Burns, Fugitive* (Par., 1935), *Another Face* (RKO, 1935), *Strike Me Pink* (UA, 1936), *Human Cargo* (20th, 1936), *Half Angel* (20th, 1936), *High Tension* (20th, 1936), *36 Hours to Kill* (20th, 1936), *Crack-Up* (20th, 1936), *Midnight Taxi* (20th, 1937), *This Is My Affair* (20th, 1937), *Born Reckless* (20th, 1937), *In Old Chicago* (20th, 1938), *Battle of Broadway* (20th, 1938), *Sharpshooters* (20th, 1938), *Jesse James* (20th, 1939), *Union Pacific* (Par., 1939), *Allegheny Uprising* (RKO, 1939), *Behind Prison Gates* (Col., 1939), *Beau Geste* (Par., 1939), *Destry Rides Again* (Univ., 1939), *The Great McGinty* (Par., 1940), *When the Daltons Rode* (Univ., 1940), *Brigham Young—Frontiersman* (20th, 1940), *I Wanted Wings* (Par., 1941) *Hold Back the Dawn* (Par., 1941),* *Birth of the Blues* (Par., 1941), *South of Tahiti* (Univ., 1941), *Billy the Kid* (MGM, 1941), *The Great Man's Lady* (Par., 1942), *A Gentleman After Dark* (UA, 1942), *The Remarkable Andrew* (Par., 1942), *Two Yanks in Trinidad* (Col., 1942), *Wake Island* (Par., 1942), *The Glass Key* (Par., 1942), *Nightmare* (Univ., 1942), *Stand By for Action* (MGM, 1942), *Hangmen Also Die* (UA, 1943), *The Miracle of Morgan's Creek* (Par., 1944), *An American Romance* (MGM, 1944), *Duffy's Tavern* (Par., 1945), *The Virginian* (Par., 1946), *Our Hearts Were Growing Up* (Par., 1946), *Canyon Passage* (Univ., 1946), *Two Years Before the Mast* (Par., 1946), *Song of Scheherazade* (Univ., 1947), *The Beginning or the End* (MGM, 1947), *The Trouble With Women* (Par., 1947), *Kiss of Death* (20th, 1947), *Heaven Only Knows* (UA, 1947), *Killer McCoy* (MGM, 1947), *A Southern Yankee* (MGM, 1948), *Command Decision* (MGM, 1948), *Impact* (UA, 1949), *The Lucky Stiff* (UA, 1949), *Shakedown* (Univ., 1950), *Kansas Raiders* (Univ., 1950), *Fighting Coast Guards* (Rep., 1951), *Slaughter Trail* (RKO, 1951), *Hoodlum Empire* (Rep., 1952), *Ride the Man Down* (Rep., 1952), *The Woman They Almost Lynched* (Rep., 1953), *The Big Combo* (AA, 1955), *The Creeping Unknown* (UA, 1956), *A Cry in the Night* (WB, 1956), *Enemy From Space* (UA, 1957), *Escape From Red Rock* (20th, 1958), *Cowboy* (Col., 1958), *Juke Box Rhythm* (Col., 1959), *Never So Few* (MGM, 1959), *The Errand Boy* (Par., 1961), *The Pigeon That Took Rome* (Par., 1962), *The Curse of the Fly* (20th, 1965), *How to Stuff a Wild Bikini* (AIP, 1965), *The Fat Spy* (Magna, 1966), *Waco* (Par., 1966), *Gammera, the Invincible* (World Entertainment Corp., 1967), *Arizona Bushwhackers* (Par., 1968), *Hostile Guns* (Par., 1967), *Rogue's Gallery* (Par., 1968).

*Unbilled guest appearance

JEFF DONNELL (Jean Marie Donnell) Born July 10, 1921, South Windham, Maine. Married William Anderson (1940), children: Michael, Sally; divorced. Married Aldo Ray (1954); divorced 1956. Married John Bricker (1958).

John Gallaudet, Jeff Donnell and Roy Barcroft in *Outcasts of the Trail*.

Feature Films: *My Sister Eileen* (Col., 1942), *The Boogie Man Will Get You* (Col., 1942), *What's Buzzin' Cousin?* (Col., 1943), *A Night to Remember* (Col., 1943), *City Without Men* (Col., 1943), *She's a Soldier, Too* (Col., 1944), *Nine Girls* (Col., 1944), *Stars on Parade* (Col., 1944), *Three Is a Family* (UA, 1944), *Carolina Blues* (Col., 1944), *Mr. Winkle Goes to War* (Col., 1944), *Once Upon a Time* (Col., 1944), *Power of the Whistler* (Col., 1945), *Edie Was a Lady* (Col., 1945), *Dancing in Manhattan* (Col., 1945), *Over 21* (Col., 1945), *Tars and Spars* (Col., 1946), *Song of the Prairie* (Col., 1945), *Throw a Saddle on a Star* (Col., 1946), *The Phantom Thief* (Col., 1946), *Night Editor* (Col., 1946), *That Texas Jamboree* (Col., 1946), *The Unknown* (Col., 1946), *Singing on the Trail* (Col., 1946), *It's Great to Be Young* (Col., 1946), *Cowboy Blues* (Col., 1946), *Mr. District Attorney* (Col., 1947), *Roughshod* (RKO, 1949), *Stage Coach Kid* (RKO, 1949), *Easy Living* (RKO, 1949), *Post Office Investigator* (Rep., 1949), *Outcasts of the Trail* (Rep., 1949,) *In a Lonely Place* (Col., 1950), *Hoedown* (Col., 1950), *Walk Softly, Stranger* (RKO, 1950), *The Fuller Brush Girl* (Col., 1950), *Redwood Forest Trail* (Rep., 1950), *Tall Timber* (Mon., 1950), *Three Guys Named Mike* (MGM, 1951), *Skirts Ahoy* (MGM, 1952), *Thief of Damascus* (Col., 1952), *The First Time* (Col., 1952), *Because You're Mine* (MGM, 1952), *So This Is Love* (WB, 1953), *Flight Nurse* (Rep., 1953), *The Blue Gardenia* (WB, 1953), *Magnificent Roughnecks* (AA, 1956), *The Guns of Fort Petticoat* (Col., 1957), *Destination 60,000* (AA, 1957), *Sweet Smell of Success* (UA, 1957), *My Man Godfrey* (Univ., 1957), *Gidget Goes Hawaiian* (Col., 1961), *Gidget Goes to Rome* (Col., 1963), *The Swingin' Maiden* (Col., 1964).

RUTH DONNELLY Born May 17, 1896 Trenton, New Jersey. Married Basil de Guichard (1932); widowed 1958.

Feature Films: *Transatlantic* (Fox, 1931), *The Spider* (Fox, 1931), *Wicked* (Fox, 1931), *Rainbow Trail* (Fox, 1932), *Blessed Event* (WB, 1932), *Jewel Robbery* (WB, 1932), *Make Me a Star* (Par., 1932), *Hard to Handle* (WB, 1933), *Employees' Entrance* (WB, 1933), *The Ladies They Talk About* (WB, 1933), *Lilly Turner* (WB, 1933), *Goodbye*

Robert Allen, Ruth Donnelly and June Lang in *Meet the Girls*.

Again (WB, 1933), *Private Detective 62* (WB, 1933), *Sing Sinner Sing* (Majestic, 1933), *Bureau of Missing Persons* (WB, 1933), *Footlight Parade* (WB, 1933), *Ever in My Heart* (WB, 1933), *Female* (WB, 1933), *Havana Widows* (WB, 1933), *Convention City* (WB, 1933), *Wonder Bar* (WB, 1934), *Heat Lightning* (WB, 1934), *Mandalay* (WB, 1934), *Merry Wives of Reno* (WB, 1934), *Housewife* (WB, 1934), *Romance in the Rain* (Univ., 1934), *Happiness Ahead* (WB, 1934), *You Belong to Me* (Par., 1934), *The White Cockatoo* (WB, 1935), *Maybe It's Love* (WB, 1935), *Traveling Saleslady* (WB, 1935), *Alibi Ike* (WB, 1935), *Red Salute* (UA, 1935), *Metropolitan* (20th, 1935), *Personal Maid's Secret* (WB, 1935), *Hands Across the Table* (Par., 1935), *The Song and Dance Man* (20th, 1936), *13 Hours by Air* (Par., 1936), *Mr. Deeds Goes to Town* (Col., 1936), *Fatal Lady* (Par., 1936), *Cain and Mabel* (WB, 1936), *More Than a Secretary* (Col., 1936), *Roaring Timber* (Col., 1937), *Portia on Trial* (Rep., 1937), *A Slight Case of Murder* (WB, 1938), *Army Girl* (Rep., 1938), *Meet the Girls* (20th, 1938), *The Affairs of Annabel* (RKO, 1938), *Annabel Takes a Tour* (RKO, 1938), *Personal Secretary* (Univ., 1938), *The Family Next Door* (Univ., 1939), *The Amazing Mr. Williams* (Col., 1939), *Mr. Smith Goes to Washington* (Col., 1939), *My Little Chickadee* (Univ., 1940), *Scatterbrain* (Rep., 1940), *Meet the Missus* (Rep., 1940), *Model Wife* (Univ., 1941), *Petticoat Politics* (Rep., 1941), *The Roundup* (Par., 1941), *The Gay Vagabond* (Rep., 1941), *Sailors on Leave* (Rep., 1941), *Rise and Shine* (20th, 1941) *You Belong to Me* (Col., 1941), *Johnny Doughboy* (Rep., 1942), *This Is the Army* (WB, 1943), *Thank Your Lucky Stars* (WB, 1943), *Sleepy Lagoon* (Rep., 1943), *Pillow to Post* (WB, 1945), *The Bells of St. Mary's* (RKO, 1945), *Cinderella Jones* (WB, 1946), *In Old Sacramento* (Rep., 1946), *The Ghost Goes Wild* (Rep., 1947), *Little Miss Broadway* (Col., 1947), *The Fabulous Texan* (Rep., 1947), *Fighting Father Dunne* (RKO, 1948), *The Snake Pit* (20th, 1948), *Where the Sidewalk Ends* (20th, 1950), *I'd Climb the Highest Mountain* (20th, 1951), *The Secret of Convict Lake* (20th, 1951), *The Wild Blue Yonder* (Rep., 1951), *A Lawless Street* (Col., 1955), *The Spoilers* (Univ., 1955), *Autumn Leaves* (Col., 1956), *The Way to the Gold* (20th, 1957).

ANN DORAN Born July 28, 1913, Amarillo, Texas.

Beulah Bondi, Paulette Goddard and Ann Doran in *I Love a Soldier*.

Feature Films: *Charlie Chan in London* (Fox, 1934), *Servants' Entrance* (Fox, 1934), *One Exciting Adventure* (Univ., 1934), *Way Down East* (Fox, 1935), *Night Life of the Gods* (Univ., 1935), *Mary Burns, Fugitive* (Par., 1935), *Case of the Missing Man* (Col., 1935) *Dangerous Intrigue* (Col., 1936), *The Man Who Lived Twice* (Col., 1936), *Palm Springs* (Par., 1936), *Ring Around the Moon* (Chesterfield, 1936), *Let's Sing Again* (RKO, 1936), *The Little Red School House* (Chesterfield, 1936), *Missing Girls* (Chesterfield, 1936), *Devil's Playground* (Col., 1937), *The Shadow* (Col., 1937), *Paid to Dance* (Col., 1937), *Marry the Girl* (WB, 1937), *When You're in Love* (Col., 1937), *Red Lights Ahead* (Chesterfield, 1937), *City Streets* (Col., 1938), *Penitentiary* (Col., 1938), *Women in Prison* (Col., 1938), *Extortion* (Col., 1938), *Highway Patrol* (Col., 1938), *You Can't Take It With You* (Col., 1938), *The Lady*

Objects (Col., 1938), *Blondie* (Col., 1938), *The Spider's Web* (Col. serial, 1938), *Start Cheering* (Col., 1938), *The Main Event* (Col., 1938), *She Married an Artist* (Col., 1938), *Rio Grande* (Col., 1938), *The Green Hornet* (Univ. serial, 1939), *Smashing the Spy Ring* (Col., 1939), *Coast Guard* (Col, 1939), *Blind Alibi* (RKO, 1939), *The Man They Could Not Hang* (Col., 1939), *Mr. Smith Goes to Washington* (Col., 1939), *Flying G-Men* (Col. serial, 1939), *My Son Is a Criminal* (Col., 1939), *Romance of the Redwoods* (Col., 1939), *A Woman Is the Judge* (Col., 1939), *Manhattan Heartbeat* (20th, 1940), *Untamed* (Par., 1940), *Girls of the Road* (Col., 1940), *Five Little Peppers at Home* (Col., 1940), *Glamour For Sale* (Col., 1940), *Buy Me That Town* (Par., 1941), *Ellery Queen's Penthouse Mystery* (Col., 1941), *Dr. Kildare's Wedding Day* (MGM, 1941), *Penny Serenade* (Col., 1941), *The Kid From Kansas* (Univ., 1941), *Meet John Doe* (WB, 1941), *Blue, White and Perfect* (20th, 1941), *Sun Valley Serenade* (20th, 1941), *Murder Among Friends* (20th, 1941), *New York Town* (Par., 1941), *They All Kissed the Bride* (Col., 1942), *My Sister Eileen* (Col., 1942), *Mr. Wise Guy* (Mon., 1942), *Beyond the Blue Horizon* (Par., 1942), *The Hard Way* (WB, 1942), *Yankee Doodle Dandy* (WB, 1942), *Air Force* (WB, 1943), *So Proudly We Hail* (Par., 1943), *True to Life* (Par., 1943), *Old Acquaintance* (WB, 1943), *Gildersleeve on Broadway* (RKO, 1943), *The More the Merrier* (Col., 1943), *Slightly Dangerous* (MGM, 1943), *I Love a Soldier* (Par., 1944), *The Story of Dr. Wassell* (Par., 1944), *Henry Aldrich's Little Secret* (Par., 1944), *Mr. Skeffington* (WB, 1944), *Roughly Speaking* (WB, 1945), *Here Come the Waves* (Par., 1945), *Pride of the Marines* (WB, 1945), *The Strange Love of Martha Ivers* (Par., 1946), *Our Hearts Were Growing Up* (Par., 1946), *The Perfect Marriage* (Par., 1946), *Fear in the Night* (Par., 1947), *My Favorite Brunette* (Par., 1947), *Seven Were Saved* (Par., 1947), *The Crimson Key* (20th, 1947), *Second Chance* (20th, 1947), *Magic Town* (RKO, 1947) *Road to the Big House* (Screen Guild, 1947), *For the Love of Rusty* (Col., 1947), *The Son of Rusty* (Col., 1947), *Variety Girl* (Par., 1947), *The Babe Ruth Story* (AA, 1948), *My Dog Rusty* (Col., 1948), *The Return of the Whistler* (Col., 1948), *Pitfall* (UA, 1948), *No Minor Vices* (MGM, 1948), *The Snake Pit* (20th, 1948), *Rusty Leads the Way* (Col., 1948), *Sealed Verdict* (Par., 1948), *The Walls of Jericho* (20th, 1948), *Rusty Saves a Life* (Col., 1949), *The Clay Pigeon* (RKO, 1949), *Calamity Jane and Sam Bass* (Univ., 1949), *The Fountainhead* (WB, 1949), *One Last Fling* (WB, 1949), *The Kid From Cleveland* (Rep., 1949), *Beyond the Forest* (WB, 1949), *Air Hostess* (Col., 1949), *The Clay Pigeon* (Par., 1949), *Holiday in Havana* (Col., 1949), *Rusty's Birthday* (Col., 1949), *No Sad Songs for Me* (Col., 1950), *Lonely Hearts Bandits* (Rep., 1950), *Never a Dull Moment* (RKO, 1950), *Gambling House* (RKO, 1950), *Riding High* (Par., 1950), *Starlift* (WB, 1951), *Tomahawk* (Univ., 1951), *The Painted Hills* (MGM, 1951), *Her First Romance* (Col., 1952), *The People Against O'Hara* (MGM, 1951), *Rodeo* (Mon., 1951), *Here Come the Nelsons* (Univ., 1952), *Love Is Better Than Ever* (MGM, 1952), *The Rose Bowl Story* (Mon., 1952), *So This Is Love* (WB, 1953), *The Eddie Cantor Story* (WB, 1953), *The High and the Mighty* (WB, 1954), *The Bob Mathias Story* (AA, 1954), *Them* (WB, 1954), *The Desperate Hours* (Par., 1955), *Rebel Without a Cause* (WB, 1955), *The Man Who Turned to Stone* (Col., 1957), *Young and Dangerous* (20th, 1957), *Shoot-Out at Medicine Bend* (WB, 1957), *Step Down to Terror* (Univ., 1958), *The Badlanders* (MGM, 1958), *Day of the Bad Man* (Univ., 1958), *The Deep Six* (WB, 1958), *The Female Animal* (Univ., 1958), *Violent Road* (WB, 1958), *Voice in the Mirror* (Univ., 1958), *Life Begins at 17* (Col., 1958), *The Rawhide Trail* (AA, 1958), *It! The Terror From Beyond Space* (UA, 1958), *Joy Ride* (AA, 1958), *A Summer Place* (WB, 1959), *Riot in Juvenile Prison* (UA, 1959), *Cast a Long Shadow* (UA, 1959), *Warlock* (20th, 1959), *Captain Newman, M. D.* (Univ., 1963), *The Brass Bottle* (Univ., 1964), *Where Love Has Gone* (Par., 1964), *The Carpetbaggers* (Par., 1964), *Kitten With a Whip* (Univ., 1964), *Mirage* (Univ., 1965), *Not With My Wife You Don't* (WB, 1966), *The Hostage* (Heartland, 1966), *Rosie!* (Univ., 1968).

KIRK DOUGLAS (Issur Danielovitch) Born December 9, 1916, Amsterdam, New York. Married Diana Dill (1943), children: Michael, Joel; divorced 1951. Married Anne Buydens (1954), children: Peter, Vincent.

Beverly Washburn and Kirk Douglas in *The Juggler.*

Feature Films: *The Strange Love of Martha Ivers* (Par., 1946), *Mourning Becomes Electra* (RKO, 1947), *Out of the Past* (RKO, 1947), *I Walk Alone* (Par., 1947), *The Walls of Jericho* (20th, 1948), *My Dear Secretary* (UA, 1948), *A Letter to Three Wives* (20th, 1948), *Champion* (UA, 1949), *Young Man With a Horn* (WB, 1950), *The Glass Menagerie* (WB, 1950), *Along the Great Divide* (WB, 1951), *Ace in the Hole* ("The Big Carnival"—Par., 1951), *Detective Story* (Par., 1951), *The Big Trees* (WB, 1952), *The Big Sky* (RKO, 1952), *The Bad and the Beautiful* (MGM, 1952), *The Story of Three Loves* (MGM, 1953), *The Juggler* (Col., 1953), *Act of Love* (UA, 1953), *20,000 Leagues Under the Sea* (BV, 1954), *Man Without a Star* (Univ., 1955), *The Racers* (20th, 1955), *Ulysses* (Par., 1955), *The Indian Fighter* (UA, 1955), *Lust for Life* (MGM, 1956), *Top Secret Affair* (WB, 1957), *Gunfight at the O.K. Corral* (Par., 1957), *Paths of Glory* (UA, 1957), *The Vikings* (UA, 1958), *Last Train From Gun Hill* (Par., 1959), *The Devil's Disciple* (UA, 1959), *Strangers When We Meet* (Col., 1960), *Spartacus* (Univ., 1960), *The Last Sunset* (Univ., 1961), *Town Without Pity* (UA, 1961), *Lonely Are the Brave* (Univ., 1962), *Two Weeks in Another Town* (MGM, 1962), *The Hook* (MGM, 1963), *The List of Adrian Messenger* (Univ., 1963), *For Love or Money* (Univ., 1963), *Seven Days in May* (Par., 1964), *In Harm's Way* (Par., 1965), *The Heroes of Telemark* (Col., 1965), *Cast a Giant Shadow* (Par., 1966), *Is Paris Burning?* (Par., 1966), *The War Wagon* (Univ., 1967), *The Way West* (UA, 1967), *The Brotherhood* (Par., 1968), *A Lovely Way to Die* (Univ., 1968).

MELVYN DOUGLAS (Melvyn E. Hesselberg) Born April 5, 1901, Macon, Georgia. Married Helen Gahagan (1931), children: Gregory, Peter, Mary.

Feature Films: *Tonight or Never* (UA, 1931), *Prestige* (RKO, 1932), *The Wiser Sex* (Par., 1932), *Broken Wing* (Par., 1932), *As You Desire Me* (MGM, 1932), *The Old Dark House* (Univ., 1932), *Nagana* (Univ.,

Philip Friend, Melvyn Douglas and Phyllis Calvert in *My Own True Love.*

1933), *The Vampire Bat* (Majestic, 1933), *Counsellor-at-Law* (Univ., 1933), *Woman in the Dark* (RKO, 1934), *Dangerous Corner* (RKO, 1934), *People's Enemy* (RKO, 1935), *She Married Her Boss* (Col., 1935), *Mary Burns—Fugitive* (Par., 1935), *Annie Oakley* (RKO, 1935), *The Lone Wolf Returns* (Col., 1936), *And So They Were Married* (Col., 1936), *The Gorgeous Hussy* (MGM, 1936), *Theodora Goes Wild* (Col., 1936), *Women of Glamour* (Col., 1937), *Captains Courageous* (MGM, 1937), *I Met Him in Paris* (Par., 1937), *Angel* (Par., 1937), *I'll Take Romance* (Col., 1937), *There's Always a Woman* (Col., 1938), *Arsene Lupin Returns* (MGM, 1938), *The Toy Wife* (MGM, 1938), *Fast Company* (MGM, 1938), *That Certain Age* (Univ., 1938), *The Shining Hour* (MGM, 1938), *There's That Woman Again* (Col., 1938), *Tell No Tales* (MGM, 1939), *Good Girls Go to Paris* (Col., 1939), *The Amazing Mr. Williams* (Col., 1939), *Ninotchka* (MGM, 1939), *Too Many Husbands* (Col. 1940), *He Stayed for Breakfast* (Col., 1940), *Third Finger—Left Hand* (MGM, 1940), *This Thing Called Love* (Col., 1941), *That Uncertain Feeling* (Col., 1941), *A Woman's Face* (MGM, 1941), *Our Wife* (Col., 1941), *Two-Faced Woman* (MGM, 1941), *They All Kissed the Bride* (Col., 1942), *Three Hearts for Julia* (MGM, 1943), *The Sea of Grass* (MGM, 1947), *The Guilt of Janet Ames* (Col., 1947), *Mr. Blandings Builds His Dream House* (RKO, 1948), *My Own True Love* (Par., 1948), *A Woman's Secret* (RKO, 1949), *The Great Sinner* (MGM, 1949), *My Forbidden Past* (RKO, 1951), *On the Loose* (RKO, 1951), *Billy Budd* (AA, 1962), *Hud* (Par., 1963), *Advance to the Rear* (MGM, 1964), *The Americanization of Emily* (MGM, 1964), *Rapture* (International Classics, 1965), *Hotel* (WB, 1967).

PAUL DOUGLAS Born November 4, 1907, Philadelphia, Pennsylvania. Married Elizabeth Farnsworth; divorced. Married Sussie Welles; divorced. Married Geraldine Higgins; divorced. Married Virginia Field, child: Margaret; divorced 1946. Married Jan Sterling (1950), child: Adam. Died September 11, 1959.

Grace Kelly, Paul Douglas and Stewart Granger in *Green Fire.*

Feature Films: *A Letter to Three Wives* (20th, 1948), *It Happens Every Spring* (20th, 1949), *Everybody Does It* (20th, 1949), *The Big Lift* (20th, 1950), *Love That Brute* (20th, 1950), *Panic in the Streets* (20th, 1950), *14 Hours* (20th, 1951), *The Guy Who Came Back* (20th, 1951), *Rhubarb* (Par., 1951),* *When in Rome* (MGM, 1952), *Clash by Night* (RKO, 1952), *We're Not Married* (20th, 1952), *Never Wave at a WAC* (RKO, 1952), *Forever Female* (Par., 1953), *Executive Suite* (MGM, 1954), *The Maggie* ("High and Dry"—Univ., 1954), *Green Fire* (MGM, 1954), *Joe MacBeth* (Col. 1956), *The Leather Saint* (Par., 1956), *The Solid Gold Cadillac* (Col., 1956), *The Gamma People* (Col., 1956), *This Could Be the Night* (MGM, 1957), *Beau James* (Par., 1957), *The Mating Game* (MGM, 1959).

*Unbilled guest appearance

MARIE DRESSLER (Leila Von Koerber) Born November 9, 1869, Coburg, Canada. Died July 28, 1934.

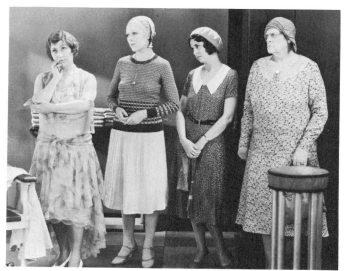

Polly Moran (left) and Marie Dressler (right) in *Reducing.*

Sound Feature Films: *Hollywood Revue of 1929* (MGM, 1929), *The Vagabond Lover* (RKO, 1929), *Chasing Rainbows* (MGM, 1930), *The Girl Said No* (MGM, 1930), *Anna Christie* (MGM, 1930), *One Romantic Night* (UA, 1930), *Caught Short* (MGM, 1930), *Let Us Be Gay* (MGM, 1930), *Min and Bill* (MGM, 1930), *Reducing* (MGM, 1931), *Politics* (MGM, 1931), *Emma* (MGM, 1932), *Prosperity* (MGM, 1932), *Dinner at Eight* (MGM, 1933), *Christopher Bean* (MGM, 1933), *Tugboat Annie* (MGM, 1933).

ELLEN DREW (Terry Ray) Born November 23, 1915, Kansas City, Missouri. Married Fred Wallace, (1935) child: David; divorced 1940. Married Sy Bartlett (1941); divorced 1950. Married William Walker (1951).

Feature Films:

as Terry Ray *College Holiday* (Par., 1936), *Yours for the Asking* (Par., 1936), *The Return of Sophie Lang* (Par., 1936), *My American Wife* (Par., 1936), *Rhythm on the Range* (Par., 1936), *Hollywood Boulevard* (Par., 1936), *Big Broadcast of 1937* (Par., 1936), *Murder With Pictures* (Par., 1936), *Wives Never Know* (Par., 1936), *Rose Bowl* (Par., 1936), *Lady Be Careful* (Par., 1936), *The Crime Nobody Saw* (Par., 1937), *Night of Mystery* (Par., 1937), *Internes Can't Take Money* (Par., 1937), *Make Way for Tomorrow* (Par., 1937), *Turn Off the Moon* (Par., 1937), *Hotel Haywire* (Par., 1937), *Mountain Music* (Par., 1937), *This Way Please* (Par., 1937), *Murder Goes to College* (Par., 1937), *Cocoanut Grove* (Par., 1938), *The Buccaneer* (Par., 1938), *Dangerous to Know* (Par., 1938), *Bluebeard's Eighth Wife* (Par., 1938), *You and Me* (Par., 1938).

as Ellen Drew *Sing You Sinners* (Par., 1938), *If I Were King* (Par., 1938), *The Lady's From Kentucky* (Par., 1939), *The Gracie Allen Murder Case* (Par., 1939), *Geronimo* (Par., 1939), *Women Without*

Vincent Price and Ellen Drew in *The Baron of Arizona.*

Names (Par., 1940), *Buck Benny Rides Again* (Par., 1940), *French Without Tears* (Par., 1940), *Christmas in July* (Par., 1940), *The Monster and the Girl* (Par., 1941), *Texas Rangers Ride Again* (Par., 1941), *The Mad Doctor* (Par., 1941), *Reaching for the Sun* (Par., 1941), *The Parson of Panamint* (Par., 1941), *The Night of January 16th* (Par., 1941), *Our Wife* (Col., 1941), *Star Spangled Rhythm* (Par., 1942), *The Remarkable Andrew* (Par., 1942), *My Favorite Spy* (RKO, 1942), *Ice-Capades Revue* (Rep., 1942), *Night Plane From Chungking* (Par., 1943), *The Impostor* (Univ., 1944), *Dark Mountain* (Par., 1944), *That's My Baby!* (Rep., 1944), *China Sky* (RKO, 1945), *Isle of the Dead* (RKO, 1945), *Man Alive* (RKO, 1945), *Sing While You Dance* (Col., 1946), *Crime Doctor's Man Hunt* (Col., 1946), *Johnny O'Clock* (Col., 1947), *The Swordsman* (Col., 1947), *The Man From Colorado* (Col., 1948), *The Crooked Way* (UA, 1949), *The Baron of Arizona* (Lip., 1950), *Cargo to Capetown* (Col., 1950), *Davy Crockett, Indian Scout* (UA, 1950), *Stars in My Crown* (MGM, 1950), *The Great Missouri Raid* (Par., 1950), *Man in the Saddle* (Col., 1951), *Outlaw's Son* (UA, 1957).

JOANNE DRU (Joanne Laycock) Born January 31, 1923, Logan, West Virginia. Married Dick Haymes (1941), children: Dick, Helen, Barbara; divorced 1949. Married John Ireland (1949), children: Peter, John; divorced 1956. Married George Pierose (1963).

Joanne Dru and Gilbert Roland in *The Wild and the Innocent.*

Feature Films: *Abie's Irish Rose* (UA, 1946), *Red River* (UA, 1948), *She Wore a Yellow Ribbon* (RKO, 1949), *All the King's Men* (Col., 1949), *Wagonmaster* (RKO, 1950), *711 Ocean Drive* (Col., 1950), *Vengeance Valley* (MGM, 1951), *Mr. Belvedere Rings the Bell* (20th, 1951), *Return of the Texan* (20th, 1952), *The Pride of St. Louis* (20th, 1952), *My Pal Gus* (20th, 1952), *Thunder Bay* (Univ., 1953), *Forbidden* (Univ., 1953), *Outlaw Territory* (Realart, 1953), *Duffy of San Quentin* (WB, 1954), *The Siege at Red River* (20th, 1954), *Southwest Passage* (UA, 1954), *Three Ring Circus* (Par., 1954), *Day of Triumph* (Geo. J. Schaefer, 1954), *The Warriors* (AA, 1955), *Sincerely Yours* (WB, 1955), *Hell on Frisco Bay* (WB, 1955), *Drango* (UA, 1957), *The Light in the Forest* (BV, 1958), *The Wild and the Innocent* (Univ., 1959), *September Storm* (20th, 1960), *Sylvia* (Par., 1965).

MARGARET DUMONT Born 1889. Married John Moller; widowed. Died March 6, 1965.

Feature Films: *The Cocoanuts* (Par., 1929), *Animal Crackers* (Par., 1930), *Girl Habit* (Par., 1931), *Duck Soup* (Par., 1933), *Kentucky Kernels* (RKO, 1934), *Fifteen Wives* (Invincible, 1934), *Gridiron Flash* (RKO, 1934), *A Night at the Opera* (MGM, 1935), *Orchids to You* (Fox, 1935), *Rendezvous* (MGM, 1935), *The Song and Dance Man* (20th, 1936), *Anything Goes* (Par., 1936), *A Day at the Races* (MGM, 1937), *The Life of the Party* (RKO, 1937), *Youth on Parole* (Rep., 1937), *High Flyers* (RKO, 1937), *Wise Girl* (RKO, 1937), *Dramatic School* (MGM, 1938), *At the Circus* (MGM, 1939), *The Big Store* (MGM, 1941), *For Beauty's Sake* (20th, 1941), *Never Give a Sucker an Even*

Margaret Dumont and Groucho Marx in *The Big Store.*

Break (Univ., 1941), *About Face* (UA, 1942), *Born to Sing* (MGM, 1942), *Sing Your Worries Away* (RKO, 1942), *Rhythm Parade* (Mon., 1942), *The Dancing Masters* (20th, 1943), *Seven Days Ashore* (RKO, 1944), *Up in Arms* (RKO, 1944), *Bathing Beauty* (MGM, 1944), *The Horn Blows at Midnight* (WB, 1945), *Diamond Horseshoe* (20th, 1945), *Sunset in Eldorado* (Rep., 1945), *Little Giant* (Univ., 1946), *Susie Steps Out* (UA, 1946), *Stop, You're Killing Me* (WB, 1951), *Three for Bedroom C* (WB, 1952), *Shake, Rattle and Rock* (AIP, 1956), *Auntie Mame* (WB, 1958), *Zotz!* (Col., 1962), *What a Way to Go!* (20th, 1964).

JAMES DUNN (James Howard Dunn) Born November 2, 1906, New York, New York. Married Edna D'Olier; divorced. Married Frances Gifford; divorced. Married Edna Rush. Died September 3, 1967.

Johnny Hines, James Dunn and Vince Barnett in *The Girl in 419.*

Feature Films: *Bad Girl* (Fox, 1931), *Sob Sister* (Fox, 1931), *Over the Hill* (Fox, 1931), *Dance Team* (Fox, 1932), *Society Girl* (Fox, 1932), *Walking Down Broadway* (Fox, 1932), *Handle With Care* (Fox, 1932), *Sailor's Luck* (Fox, 1933), *Hello Sister* (Fox, 1933), *Hold Me Tight* (Fox, 1933), *Girl in 419* (Par., 1933), *Arizona to Broadway* (Fox, 1933), *Take a Chance* (Par., 1933), *Jimmy and Sally* (Fox, 1933), *Hold That Girl* (Fox, 1934), *Stand Up and Cheer* (Fox, 1934), *Change of Heart* (Fox, 1934), *365 Nights in Hollywood* (Fox, 1934), *Bright Eyes* (Fox, 1934), *George White's Scandals of 1935* (Fox, 1935), *The Daring Young Man* (Fox, 1935), *The Pay-Off* (WB, 1935), *Welcome Home* (Fox, 1935), *Bad Boy* (Fox, 1935), *Don't Get Personal* (Univ., 1936), *Hearts in Bondage* (Rep., 1936), *Two-Fisted Gentleman* (Col., 1936), *Come Closer Folks* (Col., 1936), *Mysterious Crossing* (Univ., 1937), *We Have Our Moments* (Univ., 1937), *Venus Makes Trouble* (Col., 1937), *Living on Love* (RKO, 1937), *Shadows Over Shanghai* (GN, 1938), *Pride of the Navy* (Rep., 1939), *Son of the Navy* (Mon., 1940), *A Fugitive From Justice* (WB, 1940), *Mercy Plane* (PRC, 1940), *Hold That Woman* (PRC, 1940), *The Living Ghost* (Mon., 1942), *The Ghost and the Guest* (PRC, 1943), *Government Girl* (RKO, 1943), *Leave It to the Irish*

(Mon, 1944), *A Tree Grows in Brooklyn* (20th, 1945), *The Caribbean Mystery* (20th, 1945), *That Brennan Girl* (Rep., 1946), *Killer McCoy* (MGM, 1947), *The Golden Gloves Story* (EL, 1950), *A Wonderful Life* (Protestant Film Co., 1951), *The Bramble Bush* (WB, 1960), *Hemingway's Adventures of a Young Man* (20th, 1962), *The Oscar* (Par., 1966).

Irene Dunne and Melvyn Douglas in *Theodora Goes Wild.*

IRENE DUNNE Born December 20, 1904, Louisville, Kentucky. Married Francis Griffin (1928), child: Mary; widowed 1965.

Feature Films: *Leathernecking* (RKO, 1930), *Bachelor Apartment* (RKO, 1931), *Cimarron* (RKO, 1931), *Great Lover* (MGM, 1931), *Consolation Marriage* (RKO, 1931), *Symphony of Six Million* (RKO, 1932), *Thirteen Women* (RKO, 1932), *Back Street* (Univ., 1932), *Secret of Madame Blanche* (MGM, 1933), *No Other Woman* (RKO, 1933), *Silver Cord* (RKO, 1933), *Ann Vickers* (RKO, 1933), *If I Were Free* (RKO, 1933), *This Man Is Mine* (RKO, 1934), *Stingaree* (RKO, 1934), *Age of Innocence* (RKO, 1934), *Roberta* (RKO, 1935), *Sweet Adeline* (WB, 1935), *Magnificent Obsession* (Univ., 1935), *Showboat* (Univ., 1936), *Theodora Goes Wild* (Col., 1936), *High, Wide and Handsome* (Par., 1937), *The Awful Truth* (Col., 1937), *Joy of Living* (RKO, 1938), *Love Affair* (RKO, 1939), *Everything's on Ice* (RKO, 1939), *Invitation to Happiness* (Par., 1939), *When Tomorrow Comes* (Univ., 1939), *My Favorite Wife* (RKO, 1940), *Penny Serenade* (Col., 1941), *Unfinished Business* (Univ., 1941), *Lady in a Jam* (Univ., 1942), *A Guy Named Joe* (MGM, 1943), *The White Cliffs of Dover* (MGM, 1944), *Together Again* (Col., 1944), *Over 21* (Col., 1945), *Anna and the King of Siam* (20th, 1946), *Life With Father* (WB, 1947), *I Remember Mama* (RKO, 1948), *Never a Dull Moment* (RKO, 1950), *The Mudlark* (20th, 1950), *It Grows on Trees* (Univ., 1952).

MILDRED DUNNOCK (Mildred Dorothy Dunnock) Born January 25, 1906, Baltimore, Maryland. Married Keith Urmy (1933), children: Linda, Mary.

Danny Thomas, Mildred Dunnock and Peggy Lee in *The Jazz Singer.*

Feature Films: *The Corn Is Green* (WB, 1945), *Kiss of Death* (20th, 1947), *I Want You* (RKO, 1951), *Death of a Salesman* (Col., 1951), *The Girl in White* (MGM, 1952), *Viva Zapata!* (20th, 1952), *The Jazz Singer* (WB, 1953), *Bad for Each Other* (Col., 1953), *Hansel and Gretel* (voice only; RKO, 1954), *The Trouble With Harry* (Par., 1955), *Love Me Tender* (20th, 1956), *Baby Doll* (WB, 1956), *Peyton Place* (20th, 1957), *The Nun's Story* (WB, 1959), *The Story on Page One* (20th, 1959), *Butterfield 8* (MGM, 1960), *Something Wild* (UA, 1961), *Sweet Bird of Youth* (MGM, 1962), *Behold a Pale Horse* (Col., 1964), *Youngblood Hawke* (WB, 1964), *Seven Women* (MGM, 1965).

DEANNA DURBIN (Edna Mae Durbin) Born December 4, 1921, Winnipeg, Canada. Married Vaughn Paul (1941); divorced 1943. Married Felix Jackson (1945), child: Jessica; divorced 1948. Married Charles David (1950), child: Peter.

Herbert Marshall, Arthur Treacher and Deanna Durbin in *Mad About Music.*

Feature Films: *Three Smart Girls* (Univ., 1936), *100 Men and a Girl* (Univ., 1937), *Mad About Music* (Univ., 1938), *That Certain Age* (Univ., 1938), *Three Smart Girls Grow Up* (Univ., 1939), *First Love* (Univ., 1939), *It's a Date* (Univ., 1940), *Spring Parade* (Univ., 1940), *Nice Girl?* (Univ., 1941), *It Started With Eve* (Univ., 1941), *The Amazing Mrs. Holliday* (Univ., 1943), *Hers to Hold* (Univ., 1943), *His Butler's Sister* (Univ., 1944), *Christmas Holiday* (Univ., 1944), *Can't Help Singing* (Univ., 1944), *Lady on a Train* (Univ., 1945), *Because of Him* (Univ., 1946), *I'll Be Yours* (Univ., 1947), *Something in the Wind* (Univ., 1947), *Up in Central Park* (Univ., 1948), *For the Love of Mary* (Univ., 1948).

DAN DURYEA Born January 23, 1907, White Plains, New York. Married Helen Bryan (1931), children: Peter, Richard; widowed 1967.

Dan Duryea and Deanna Durbin in *Lady on a Train.*

English-Language Feature Films: *The Little Foxes* (RKO, 1941), *Ball of Fire* (RKO, 1941), *The Pride of the Yankees* (RKO, 1942), *That Other Woman* (20th, 1942), *Sahara* (Col., 1943), *None But the Lonely Heart* (RKO, 1944), *Mrs. Parkington* (MGM, 1944), *Ministry of Fear* (Par., 1944), *Woman in the Window* (RKO, 1944), *Valley of Decision* (MGM, 1945), *The Great Flamarion* (Rep., 1945), *Along Came Jones* (RKO, 1945), *Lady on a Train* (Univ., 1945), *Scarlet Street* (Univ., 1945), *Black Angel* (Univ., 1946), *White Tie and Tails* (Univ., 1946), *Black Bart* (Univ., 1948), *Another Part of the Forest* (Univ., 1948), *River Lady* (Univ., 1948), *Larceny* (Univ., 1948), *Criss Cross* (Univ., 1949), *Too Late for Tears* (UA, 1949), *Johnny Stool Pigeon* (Univ., 1949), *Manhandled* (Par., 1949), *One Way Street* (Univ., 1950), *Underworld Story* (UA, 1950), *Winchester '73* (Univ., 1950), *Al Jennings of Oklahoma* (Col., 1951), *Chicago Calling* (UA, 1951), *Thunder Bay* (Univ., 1953), *Sky Commando* (Col., 1953), *World for Ransom* (AA, 1954), *Ride Clear of Diablo* (Univ., 1954), *This Is My Love* (RKO, 1954), *Silver Lode* (RKO, 1954), *Rails into Laramie* (Univ., 1954), *The Marauders* (MGM, 1955), *Foxfire* (Univ., 1955), *Storm Fear* (UA, 1955), *Battle Hymn* (Univ., 1956), *The Burglar* (Col., 1957), *Night Passage* (Univ., 1957), *Slaughter on Tenth Avenue* (Univ., 1957), *Kathy O'* (Univ., 1958), *Platinum High School* (MGM, 1960), *Six Black Horses* (Univ., 1962), *He Rides Tall* (Univ., 1964), *Walk a Tightrope* (Par., 1964), *Taggart* (Univ., 1964), *The Bounty Killer* (Embassy, 1965), *The Flight of the Phoenix* (20th, 1965), *Incident at Phantom Hill* (Univ., 1966), *Operation Bluebook* (Jerry Fairbanks Productions, 1967), *A River of Dollars* (UA, 1967), *The Bamboo Saucer* (Jerry Fairbanks Productions, 1967).

ANN DVORAK (Ann McKim) Born August 2, 1912, New York, New York. Married Leslie Fenton (1932); divorced 1945. Married Igo Dega (1947); divorced 1950.

Ann Dvorak and Richard Barthelmess in *Massacre*.

Feature Films: *The Hollywood Revue of 1929* (MGM, 1929), *Way Out West* (MGM, 1930), *Free and Easy* (MGM, 1930), *The Guardsman* (MGM, 1931), *This Modern Age* (MGM, 1931), *Sky Devils* (UA, 1932), *The Crowd Roars* (WB, 1932), *Scarface* (UA, 1932), *The Strange Love of Molly Louvain* (WB, 1932), *Love Is a Racket* (WB, 1932), *Stranger in Town* (WB, 1932), *Crooner* (WB, 1932), *Three on a Match* (WB, 1932), *The Way to Love* (Par., 1933), *College Coach* (WB, 1933), *Massacre* (WB, 1934), *Heat Lightning* (WB, 1934), *Midnight Alibi* (WB, 1934), *Friends of Mr. Sweeney* (WB, 1934), *Housewife* (WB, 1934), *Side Streets* (WB, 1934), *Gentlemen Are Born* (WB, 1934), *I Sell Anything* (WB, 1934), *Murder in the Clouds* (WB, 1934), *Sweet Music* (WB, 1935), *G-Men* (WB, 1935), *Folies Bergere* (UA, 1935), *Bright Lights* (WB, 1935), *Dr. Socrates* (WB, 1935), *Thanks a Million* (Fox, 1935), *We Who Are About to Die* (RKO, 1936), *Racing Lady* (RKO, 1937), *Midnight Court* (WB, 1937), *She's No Lady* (Par., 1937), *The Case of the Stuttering Bishop* (WB, 1937), *Manhattan Merry-Go-Round*

(Rep., 1937), *Merrily We Live* (MGM, 1938), *Gangs of New York* (Rep., 1938), *Blind Alley* (Col., 1939), *Stronger Than Desire* (MGM, 1939), *Cafe Hostess* (Col., 1940), *Girls of the Road* (Col., 1940), *This Was Paris* (WB, 1942), *Squadron Leader X* (RKO, 1943), *Escape to Danger* (RKO, 1944), *Flame of Barbary Coast* (Rep., 1945), *Masquerade in Mexico* (Par., 1945), *The Bachelor's Daughters* (UA, 1946), *Abilene Town* (UA, 1946), *The Private Affairs of Bel Ami* (UA, 1947), *The Long Night* (RKO, 1947), *Out of the Blue* (EL, 1947), *The Walls of Jericho* (20th, 1948), *A Life of Her Own* (MGM, 1950), *Our Very Own* (RKO, 1950), *The Return of Jesse James* (Lip., 1950), *Mrs. O'Malley and Mr. Malone* (MGM, 1950), *I Was an American Spy* (AA, 1951), *The Secret of Convict Lake* (20th, 1951).

NELSON EDDY Born June 29, 1901, Providence, Rhode Island. Married Anne Franklin (1939). Died March 6, 1967.

Nelson Eddy, Illona Massey and Roland Varno in *Balalaika*.

Feature Films: *Broadway to Hollywood* (MGM, 1933), *Dancing Lady* (MGM, 1933), *Student Tour* (MGM, 1934), *Naughty Marietta* (MGM, 1935), *Rose Marie* (MGM, 1936), *Maytime* (MGM, 1937), *Rosalie* (MGM, 1937), *Girl of the Golden West* (MGM, 1938), *Sweethearts* (MGM, 1938), *Let Freedom Ring* (MGM, 1939), *Balalaika* (MGM, 1939), *New Moon* (MGM, 1940), *Bitter Sweet* (MGM, 1940), *The Chocolate Soldier* (MGM, 1941), *I Married an Angel* (MGM, 1942), *The Phantom of the Opera* (Univ., 1943), *Knickerbocker Holiday* (UA, 1944), *Make Mine Music* (voice only; RKO, 1946), *Northwest Outpost* (Rep., 1947).

SALLY EILERS (Dorothea Sally Eilers) Born December 11, 1908, New York, New York. Married Hoot Gibson (1930); divorced 1933. Married Harry Brown (1933), child: Harry; divorced. Married Howard Barney; divorced. Married John Hollingsworth Morse (1949).

Ward Bond, Sally Eilers and Robert Armstrong in *Without Orders*.

Sound Feature Films: *Cradle Snatchers* (WB, 1928), *Dry Martini* (Fox, 1928), *Broadway Daddies* (Col., 1928), *Good-Bye Kiss* (WB, 1928), *Broadway Babies* (WB, 1929), *Trial Marriage* (WB, 1929), *Show of Shows* (WB, 1929), *The Long, Long Trail* (Univ., 1929), *Sailor's Holiday* (Pathé, 1929), *She Couldn't Say No* (WB, 1930), *Let Us Be Gay* (MGM, 1930), *Roaring Ranch* (Univ., 1930), *Trigger Tricks* (Univ., 1930), *Dough Boys* (MGM, 1930), *Reducing* (MGM, 1931), *Quick Millions* (Fox, 1931), *Clearing the Range* (Capitol Film Exchange, 1931), *Black Camel* (Fox, 1931), *Bad Girl* (Fox, 1931), *Holy Terror* (Fox, 1931), *Over the Hill* (Fox, 1931), *Dance Team* (Fox, 1931), *Disorderly Conduct* (Fox, 1932), *Hat Check Girl* (Fox, 1932), *State Fair* (Fox, 1933), *Second Hand Wife* (Fox, 1933), *Sailor's Luck* (Fox, 1933), *Made on Broadway* (MGM, 1933), *I Spy* (BIP, 1933), *Central Airport* (WB, 1933), *Hold Me Tight* (Fox, 1933), *Walls of Gold* (Fox, 1933), *She Made Her Bed* (Par., 1934), *Three on a Honeymoon* (Fox, (1934), *Morning After* (Majestic, 1934), *Carnival* (Col., 1935), *Alias Mary Dow* (Univ., 1935), *Pursuit* (MGM, 1935), *Remember Last Night?* (Univ., 1935), *Don't Get Personal* (Univ., 1936), *Strike Me Pink* (UA, 1936), *Florida Special* (Par., 1936), *Without Orders* (RKO, 1936), *We Have Our Moments* (Univ., 1937), *Talk of the Devil* (Gaumont-British, 1937), *Danger Patrol* (RKO, 1937), *Lady Behave* (Rep., 1937), *Nurse From Brooklyn* (Univ., 1938), *Everybody's Doing It* (RKO, 1938), *Condemned Women* (RKO, 1938), *Tarnished Angel* (RKO, 1938), *They Made Her a Spy* (RKO, 1939), *Full Confession* (RKO, 1939), *I Was a Prisoner on Devil's Island* (Col., 1941), *A Wave, a Wac and a Marine* (Mon., 1944), *Strange Illusion* (PRC, 1945), *Coroner Creek* (Col., 1948), *Stage to Tucson* (Col., 1950).

LEON ERROL Born July 3, 1881, Sydney, New South Wales, Australia. Married Stella Chatelaine (1906); widowed 1946. Died October 12, 1951.

Leon Errol, ZaSu Pitts and Mitzi Green in *Finn and Hattie.*

Sound Feature Films: *Paramount on Parade* (Par., 1930), *Queen of Scandal* (UA, 1930), *Only Saps Work* (Par., 1930), *One Heavenly Night* (UA, 1930), *Finn and Hattie* (Par., 1931), *Her Majesty Love* (WB, 1931), *Alice in Wonderland* (Par., 1933), *We're Not Dressing* (Par., 1934), *The Notorious Sophie Lang* (Par., 1934), *The Captain Hates the Sea* (Col., 1934), *Princess O'Hara* (Univ., 1935), *Coronado* (Par., 1935), *Make a Wish* (RKO, 1937), *Girl From Mexico* (RKO, 1939), *Dancing Co-ed* (MGM, 1939), *Mexican Spitfire* (RKO, 1939), *Pop Always Pays* (RKO, 1940), *Mexican Spitfire Out West* (RKO, 1940), *The Golden Fleecing* (MGM, 1940), *Six Lessons From Madame La-Zonga* (Univ., 1941), *Where Did You Get That Girl?* (Univ., 1941), *Hurry, Charlie, Hurry* (RKO, 1941), *Mexican Spitfire's Baby* (RKO, 1941), *Moonlight in Hawaii* (Univ., 1941), *Never Give a Sucker an Even Break* (Univ., 1941), *Melody Lane* (Univ., 1941), *Mexican Spitfire at Sea* (RKO, 1942), *Mexican Spitfire Sees a Ghost* (RKO, 1942), *Mexican Spitfire's Elephant* (RKO, 1942), *Strictly in the Groove* (Univ., 1943), *Cowboy in Manhattan* (Univ., 1943), *Follow The Band* (Univ., 1943), *Mexican Spitfire's Blessed Event* (RKO, 1943), *Gals, Inc.* (Univ., 1943), *Higher and Higher* (RKO, 1943), *Hat Check Honey* (Univ., 1944), *Slightly Terrific* (Univ., 1944), *Invisible Man's Revenge* (Univ., 1944), *Twilight on the Prairie* (Univ., 1944), *Babes on Swing Street* (Univ., 1944), *She Gets Her Man* (Univ., 1945), *Under Western Skies* (Univ., 1945), *What a Blonde* (RKO, 1945), *Mama Loves Papa* (RKO, 1945), *Riverboat Rhythm* (RKO, 1946), *Joe Palooka, Champ* (Mon., 1946), *Gentleman Joe Palooka* (Mon., 1946), *Joe Palooka in the Knockout* (Mon., 1947), *Fighting Mad* (Mon., 1948), *The Noose Hangs High* (EL, 1948), *Variety Time* (RKO, 1948), *Joe Palooka in the Big Fight* (Mon., 1949), *Joe Palooka in the Counterpunch* (Mon., 1949), *Joe Palooka in Humphrey Takes a Chance* (Mon., 1950), *Footlight Varieties* (RKO, 1951).

STUART ERWIN Born February 14, 1903, Squaw Valley, California. Married June Collyer (1931), children: Stuart, Judy. Died December 21, 1967.

Helen Kane and Stuart Erwin in *Sweetie.*

Sound Feature Films: *The Trespasser* (UA, 1929), *The Sophomore* (Pathé, 1929), *Speakeasy* (Fox, 1929), *Thru Different Eyes* (Fox, 1929), *Cock-Eyed World* (Fox, 1929), *Dangerous Curves* (Par., 1929), *Sweetie* (Par., 1929), *This Thing Called Love* (Pathé, 1929), *Men Without Women* (Fox, 1930), *Paramount on Parade* (Par., 1930), *Young Eagles* (Par., 1930), *Dangerous Nan McGrew* (Par., 1930), *Love Among the Millionaires* (Par., 1930), *Playboy of Paris* (Par., 1930), *Only Saps Work* (Par., 1930), *Along Came Youth* (Par., 1930), *No Limit* (Par., 1930), *Dude Ranch* (Par., 1931), *Up Pops the Devil* (Par., 1931), *The Magnificent Lie* (Par., 1931), *Working Girls* (Par., 1931), *Two Kinds of Women* (Par., 1932), *Strangers in Love* (Par., 1932), *Misleading Lady* (Par., 1932), *Make Me a Star* (Par., 1932), *Big Broadcast* (Par., 1932), *Face in the Sky* (Fox., 1933), *Crime of the Century* (Par., 1933), *He Learned About Women* (Par., 1933), *Under the Tonto Rim* (Par., 1933), *The Stranger's Return* (Par., 1933), *Hold Your Man* (MGM, 1933), *International House* (Par., 1933), *Before Dawn* (RKO, 1933), *Day of Reckoning* (MGM, 1933), *Going Hollywood* (MGM, 1933), *Palooka* (UA, 1934), *Viva Villa!* (MGM, 1934), *The Party's Over* (Col., 1934), *Bachelor Bait* (RKO, 1934), *Chained* (MGM, 1934), *The Band Plays On* (MGM, 1934), *After Office Hours* (MGM, 1935), *Ceiling Zero* (WB, 1935), *Exclusive Story* (MGM, 1936), *Absolute Quiet* (MGM, 1936), *Women Are Trouble* (MGM, 1936), *All American Chump* (MGM, 1936), *Pigskin Parade* (20th, 1936), *Dance, Charlie, Dance* (WB, 1937), *Small Town Boy* (GN, 1937), *Slim* (WB, 1937), *Second Honeymoon* (20th, 1937), *Checkers* (20th, 1937), *I'll Take Romance* (Col., 1937), *Mr. Boggs Steps Out* (GN, 1938), *Passport Husband* (20th, 1938), *Three Blind Mice* (20th, 1938), *Back Door to Heaven* (Par., 1939), *It Could Happen to You* (20th, 1939), *Hollywood Cavalcade* (20th, 1939), *The Honeymoon's Over* (20th, 1939), *Our Town* (UA, 1940), *When the Daltons Rode* (Univ., 1940), *A Little Bit of Heaven* (Univ., 1940), *Sandy Gets Her Man* (Univ., 1940), *Cracked Nuts* (Univ., 1941), *The Bride Came C.O.D.* (WB, 1941), *The Adventures* of *Martin Eden* (Col., 1942), *Drums of the Congo* (Col., 1942), *Blondie for Victory* (Col., 1942), *He Hired the Boss* (20th, 1943), *Great Mike* (PRC, 1944), *Pillow to Post* (WB, 1945), *Killer Dill* (EL, 1947), *Heading for Heaven* (EL, 1947), *Strike It Rich* (AA, 1948), *Father Is a Bachelor* (Col., 1950), *Main Street to Broadway* (MGM, 1953), *For the Love of Mike* (20th, 1960), *Son of Flubber* (BV, 1964), *The Misadventures of Merlin Jones* (BV, 1964).

DALE EVANS (Frances Octavia Smith) Born October 31, 1912, Uvalde, Texas. Married Thomas Fox, (1928), child: Thomas; widowed 1929. Married Robert Dale Butts; divorced 1945. Married Roy Rogers (1947), children: Robin, John, Mary Little Doe, Marion, Deborah.

Roy Rogers, Forrest Taylor, Dale Evans, John Eldredge and Ken Carson in *Song of Nevada*.

Feature Films: *Orchestra Wives* (20th, 1942), *Girl Trouble* (20th, 1942), *The West Side Kid* (Rep., 1943), *Swing Your Partner* (Rep., 1943), *Hoosier Holiday* (Rep., 1943), *In Old Oklahoma* (Rep., 1943), *Here Comes Elmer* (Rep., 1943), *Casanova in Burlesque* (Rep., 1944), *The Cowboy and the Senorita* (Rep., 1944), *The Yellow Rose of Texas* (Rep., 1944), *Song of Nevada* (Rep., 1944), *San Fernando Valley* (Rep., 1944), *Lights of Old Santa Fe* (Rep., 1944), *Hitchhike to Happiness* (Rep., 1945), *Utah* (Rep., 1945), *The Big Show-Off* (Rep., 1945), *Bells of Rosarita* (Rep., 1945), *The Man From Oklahoma* (Rep., 1945), *Sunset in Eldorado* (Rep., 1945), *Don't Fence Me In* (Rep., 1945), *Along the Navajo Trail* (Rep., 1945), *Song of Arizona* (Rep., 1946), *Rainbow Over Texas* (Rep., 1946), *My Pal Trigger* (Rep., 1946), *Roll On, Texas Moon* (Rep., 1946), *Out California Way* (Rep., 1946), *Under Nevada Skies* (Rep., 1946), *Home in Oklahoma* (Rep., 1946), *Helldorado* (Rep., 1946), *Apache Rose* (Rep., 1947), *Bells of San Angelo* (Rep., 1947), *The Trespasser* (Rep., 1947), *Slippy McGee* (Rep., 1948), *Susanna Pass* (Rep., 1949), *Down Dakota Way* (Rep., 1949), *The Golden Stallion* (Rep., 1949), *Twilight in the Sierras* (Rep., 1950), *Bells of Coronado* (Rep., 1950), *Trigger, Jr.* (Rep., 1950), *South of Caliente* (Rep., 1951), *Pals of the Golden West* (Rep., 1951).

MADGE EVANS Born July 1, 1909, New York, New York. Married Sidney Kingsley (1939).

Sound Feature Films: *Sporting Blood* (MGM, 1931), *Son of India* (MGM, 1931), *Guilty Hands* (MGM, 1931), *Heartbreak* (Fox, 1931), *West of Broadway* (MGM, 1932), *Are You Listening?* (MGM, 1932), *Lovers Courageous* (MGM, 1932), *The Greeks Had a Word for Them* (UA, 1932), *Huddle* (MGM, 1932), *Fast Life* (MGM, 1932), *Hell Below* (MGM, 1933), *Hallelujah, I'm a Bum* (UA, 1933), *Made on Broadway* (MGM, 1933), *Dinner at Eight* (MGM, 1933), *The Nuisance* (MGM, 1933), *Mayor of Hell* (WB, 1933), *Broadway to Hollywood* (MGM, 1933), *Beauty for Sale* (MGM, 1933), *Day of Reckoning* (MGM, 1933), *Fugitive Lovers* (MGM, 1934), *The Show-Off* (MGM, 1934), *Stand Up and Cheer* (Fox, 1934), *Death on the Diamond* (MGM,

Spencer Tracy and Madge Evans in *The Show-off*.

1934), *Grand Canary* (Fox, 1934), *Paris Interlude* (MGM, 1934), *What Every Woman Knows* (MGM, 1934), *Helldorado* (Fox, 1935), *David Copperfield* (MGM, 1935), *Age of Indiscretion* (MGM, 1935), *Transatlantic Tunnel* (Gaumont-British, 1935), *Calm Yourself* (MGM, 1935), *Men Without Names* (Par., 1935), *Moonlight Murder* (MGM, 1936), *Exclusive Story* (MGM, 1936), *Piccadilly Jim* (MGM, 1936), *Pennies From Heaven* (Col., 1936), *Espionage* (MGM, 1937), *The Thirteenth Chair* (MGM, 1937), *Sinners in Paradise* (Univ., 1938), *Army Girl* (Rep., 1938).

DOUGLAS FAIRBANKS, JR. Born December 9, 1909. Married Joan Crawford (1928); divorced 1933. Married Mary Hartford (1939), children: Daphne, Victoria, Melissa.

English-Language Sound Feature Films: *The Forward Pass* (WB, 1929), *The Careless Age* (WB, 1929), *Fast Life* (WB, 1929), *Show of Shows* (WB, 1929), *Party Girl* (Tif., 1930), *Loose Ankles* (WB, 1930), *The Dawn Patrol* (WB, 1930), *Little Accident* (Univ., 1930), *The Way of All Men* (WB, 1930), *Outward Bound* (WB, 1930), *Little Caesar* (WB, 1930), *One Night at Susie's* (WB, 1930), *Chances* (WB, 1931), *I Like Your Nerve* (WB, 1931), *Union Depot* (WB, 1932), *It's Tough to Be Famous* (WB, 1932), *Love Is a Racket* (WB, 1932), *Parachute Jumper* (WB, 1933), *The Narrow Corner* (WB, 1933), *Morning Glory* (RKO, 1933), *Captured* (WB, 1933), *Catherine the Great* (UA, 1934), *Success at Any Price* (RKO, 1934), *Mimi* (Alliance, 1935), *The Amateur Gentleman* (UA, 1936), *Accused* (UA, 1936), *When Thief Meets Thief* (Univ., 1937), *The Prisoner of Zenda* (UA, 1937), *The Joy of Living* (RKO, 1938), *The Rage of Paris* (Univ., 1938), *Having Wonderful Time* (RKO, 1938), *The Young in Heart* (UA, 1938), *Gunga Din* (RKO, 1939), *The Sun Never Sets* (Par., 1939), *Rulers of the Sea* (Par., 1939), *Green Hell* (Univ., 1940), *Safari* (Par., 1940), *Angels Over Broadway* (Col., 1940), *The Corsican Brothers* (UA, 1941), *Sinbad the Sailor* (RKO, 1947), *The Exile* (Univ., 1947), *That Lady In Ermine* (20th, 1948), *The Fighting O'Flynn* (Univ., 1949), *State Secret* (Col., 1950), *Mr. Drake's Duck* (UA, 1951).

Douglas Fairbanks, Jr., Billy Gilbert and Lynne Overman in *Safari*.

Frances Farmer in *Ride a Crooked Mile*.

FRANCES FARMER Born September 19, 1910, Seattle, Washington. Married Leif Erikson (1934); divorced 1942. Married Alfred Lobley, 1954; divorced 1958. Married Leland Mikesell (1958).

Feature Films: *Too Many Parents* (Par., 1936), *Border Flight* (Par., 1936), *Rhythm on the Range* (Par., 1936), *Come and Get It* (UA, 1936), *The Toast of New York* (RKO, 1937), *Exclusive* (Par., 1937), *Ebb Tide* (Par., 1937), *Ride a Crooked Mile* (Par., 1938), *South of Pago Pago* (UA, 1940), *Flowing Gold* (WB, 1940), *World Premiere* (Par., 1941), *Badlands of Dakota* (Univ., 1941), *Among the Living* (Par., 1941), *Son of Fury* (20th, 1942), *The Party Crashers* (Par., 1958).

GLENDA FARRELL Born June 30, 1904, Enid, Oklahoma. Married Thomas Richards, child: Thomas; divorced. Married Henry Ross (1941).

Willard Robertson, Glenda Farrell and Barton MacLane in *Torchy Gets Her Man*.

Feature Films: *Lucky Boy* (Tif., 1929), *Little Caesar* (WB, 1930), *Scandal for Sale* (Univ., 1932), *Life Begins* (WB, 1932), *I Am a Fugitive From a Chain Gang* (WB, 1932), *Three on a Match* (WB, 1932), *The Match King* (WB, 1932), *Grand Slam* (WB, 1933), *Mystery of the Wax Museum* (WB, 1933), *Girl Missing* (WB, 1933), *The Keyhole* (WB, 1933), *Gambling Ship* (Par., 1933), *Lady for a Day* (Col., 1933), *Mary Stevens, M.D.* (WB, 1933), *Bureau of Missing Persons* (WB, 1933), *Havana Widows* (WB, 1933), *Man's Castle* (Col., 1933), *Big Shakedown* (WB, 1934), *I've Got Your Number* (WB, 1934), *Heat Lightning* (WB, 1934), *Hi Nellie* (WB, 1934), *Dark Hazard* (WB, 1934), *Merry Wives of Reno* (WB, 1934), *Personality Kid* (WB, 1934), *Kansas City Princess* (WB, 1934), *Gold Diggers of 1935* (WB, 1935), *The Secret Bride* (WB, 1935), *Traveling Saleslady* (WB, 1935), *Go into Your Dance* (WB, 1935), *In Caliente* (WB, 1935), *We're in the Money*

(WB, 1935), *Little Big Shot* (WB, 1935), *Miss Pacific Fleet* (WB, 1935), *Snowed Under* (WB, 1936), *The Law in Her Hands* (WB, 1936), *Nobody's Fool* (Univ., 1936), *High Tension* (20th, 1936), *Gold Diggers of 1937* (WB, 1936), *Smart Blonde* (WB, 1936), *Here Comes Carter!* (WB, 1936), *Fly-Away Baby* (WB, 1937), *Dance, Charlie, Dance* (WB, 1937), *You Live and Learn* (WB, 1937), *Breakfast for Two* (RKO, 1937), *The Adventurous Blonde* (WB, 1937), *Hollywood Hotel* (WB, 1937), *Blondes at Work* (WB, 1938), *Stolen Heaven* (Par., 1938), *The Road to Reno* (Univ., 1938), *Prison Break* (Univ., 1938), *Torchy Gets Her Man* (WB, 1938), *Exposed* (Univ., 1938), *Torchy Blane in Chinatown* (WB, 1939), *Torchy Runs for Mayor* (WB, 1939), *Johnny Eager* (MGM, 1941), *Twin Beds* (UA, 1942), *The Talk of the Town* (Col., 1942), *A Night for Crime* (PRC, 1942), *Klondike Kate* (Col., 1943), *City Without Men* (Col., 1943), *Ever Since Venus* (Col., 1944), *Heading for Heaven* (EL, 1947), *Mary-Lou* (Col., 1947), *I Love Trouble* (Col., 1947), *Lulu Belle* (Col., 1948), *Apache War Smoke* (MGM, 1952), *Girls in the Night* (Univ., 1953), *Secret of the Incas* (Par., 1954), *Susan Slept Here* (RKO, 1954), *The Girl in the Red Velvet Swing* (20th, 1955), *Middle of the Night* (Col., 1959), *Kissin' Cousins* (MGM, 1964), *The Disorderly Orderly* (Par., 1964).

ALICE FAYE (Alice Jeanne Leppert) Born May 5, 1912, New York, New York. Married Tony Martin (1937); divorced 1940. Married Phil Harris (1941), children: Alice, Phyllis.

Warner Baxter and Alice Faye in *Barricade*.

Feature Films: *George White's Scandals* (Fox, 1934), *Now I'll Tell* (Fox, 1934), *She Learned About Sailors* (Fox, 1934), *365 Nights in Hollywood* (Fox, 1934), *George White's Scandals of 1935* (Fox, 1935), *Every Night at Eight* (Par., 1935), *Music Is Magic* (Fox, 1935), *King of Burlesque* (20th, 1936), *Poor Little Rich Girl* (20th, 1936), *Sing, Baby, Sing* (20th, 1936), *Stowaway* (20th, 1936), *On the Avenue* (20th, 1937), *Wake Up and Live* (20th, 1937), *You Can't Have Everything* (20th, 1937), *You're a Sweetheart* (Univ., 1937), *Sally, Irene and Mary* (20th, 1938), *In Old Chicago* (20th, 1938), *Alexander's Ragtime Band* (20th, 1938), *Tail Spin* (20th, 1939), *Rose of Washington Square* (20th, 1939), *Hollywood Cavalcade* (20th, 1939), *Barricade* (20th, 1939), *Little Old New York* (20th, 1940), *Lillian Russell* (20th, 1940), *Tin Pan Alley* (20th, 1940), *That Night in Rio* (20th, 1941), *The Great American Broadcast* (20th, 1941), *Weekend in Havana* (20th, 1941), *Hello, Frisco, Hello* (20th, 1943), *The Gang's All Here* (20th, 1943), *Four Jills in a Jeep* (20th, 1944),* *Fallen Angel* (20th, 1945), *State Fair* (20th, 1962).

*Unbilled guest appearance

JOSÉ FERRER (José Vincente Ferrery Centron) Born January 8, 1909, Santurce, Puerto Rico. Married Uta Hagen (1938), child: Leticia; divorced 1948. Married Phyllis Hill (1948); divorced 1953. Married Rosemary Clooney (1953), children: Maria, Miguel, Gabriel, Monsita, Raphael.

Gene Tierney and José Ferrer in *Whirlpool*.

Bing Crosby and W. C. Fields in *Mississippi*.

English-Language Feature Films: *Joan of Arc* (RKO, 1948), *Whirlpool* (20th, 1949), *Crisis* (MGM, 1950), *Cyrano de Bergerac* (UA, 1950), *Anything Can Happen* (Par., 1952), *Moulin Rouge* (UA, 1952), *Miss Sadie Thompson* (Col., 1953), *The Caine Mutiny* (Col., 1954), *Deep in My Heart* (MGM, 1954), *The Shrike* (Univ., 1955), *The Cockleshell Heroes* (Col., 1956), *The Great Man* (Univ., 1956), *I Accuse!* (MGM, 1958), *The High Cost of Loving* (MGM, 1958), *Lawrence of Arabia* (Col., 1962), *Nine Hours to Rama* (20th, 1963), *Stop Train 349* (AA, 1964), *The Greatest Story Ever Told* (UA, 1965), *Ship of Fools* (Col., 1965), *Enter Laughing* (Col., 1967), *Cervantes* (AIP, 1968).

BETTY FIELD Born February 8, 1918, Boston, Massachusetts. Married Elmer Rice (1943), children: John, Judith, Paul; divorced 1956. Married Edward Lukas (1956).

Alan Ladd and Betty Field in *The Great Gatsby*.

Feature Films: *What a Life!* (Par., 1939), *Of Mice and Men* (UA, 1940), *Seventeen* (Par., 1940), *Victory* (Par., 1941), *The Shepherd of the Hills* (Par., 1941), *Blues in the Night* (WB, 1941), *Kings Row* (WB, 1942), *Are Husbands Necessary?* (Par., 1942), *Flesh and Fantasy* (Univ., 1943), *The Great Moment* (Par., 1944), *Tomorrow the World* (UA, 1944), *The Southerner* (UA, 1945), *The Great Gatsby* (Par., 1949), *Picnic* (Col., 1955), *Bus Stop* (20th, 1956), *Peyton Place* (20th, 1957), *Hound-Dog Man* (20th, 1959), *Butterfield 8* (MGM, 1960), *Bird Man of Alcatraz* (UA, 1962), *Seven Women* (MGM, 1965), *How to Save a Marriage—and Ruin Your Life* (Col., 1968).

W. C. FIELDS (William Claude Dukinfield) Born February 10, 1879, Philadelphia, Pennsylvania. Married Harriet Hughes (1900), child: William. Died December 25, 1946.

Sound Feature Films: *Her Majesty Love* (WB, 1931), *Million Dollar Legs* (Par., 1932), *If I Had a Million* (Par., 1932), *International House* (Par., 1933), *Tillie and Gus* (Par., 1933), *Alice in Wonderland* (Par., 1933), *Six of a Kind* (Par., 1934), *You're Telling Me* (Par., 1934), *Old-Fashioned Way* (Par., 1934), *Mrs. Wiggs of the Cabbage Patch* (Par., 1934), *It's a Gift* (Par., 1934), *David Copperfield* (MGM, 1935), *Mississippi* (Par., 1935), *The Man on the Flying Trapeze* (Par., 1935), *Poppy* (Par., 1936), *Big Broadcast of 1938* (Par., 1938), *You Can't Cheat an Honest Man* (Univ., 1939), *My Little Chickadee* (Univ., 1940), *The Bank Dick* (Univ., 1940), *Never Give A Sucker an Even Break* (Univ., 1941), *Follow the Boys* (Univ., 1944), *Song of the Open Road* (UA, 1944), *Sensations of 1945* (UA, 1944).

BARRY FITZGERALD (William Joseph Shields) Born March 10, 1888, Dublin, Ireland. Died January 4, 1961.

George Sanders, Barry Fitzgerald and William Henry in *Four Men and a Prayer*.

Feature Films: *Juno and the Paycock* (Bluebeard, 1930), *When Knights Were Bold* (Capital Films, 1936), *The Plough and the Stars* (RKO, 1936), *Ebb Tide* (Par., 1937), *Bringing Up Baby* (RKO, 1938), *Marie Antoinette* (MGM, 1938), *Four Men and a Prayer* (20th, 1938), *The Dawn Patrol* (WB, 1938), *The Saint Strikes Back* (RKO, 1939), *Pacific Liner* (RKO, 1939), *Full Confession* (RKO, 1939), *The Long Voyage Home* (UA, 1940), *San Francisco Docks* (Univ., 1941), *The Sea Wolf* (WB, 1941), *How Green Was My Valley* (20th, 1941), *Tarzan's Secret Treasure* (MGM, 1941), *The Amazing Mrs. Holliday* (Univ., 1943), *Two Tickets to London* (Univ., 1943), *Corvette K-225* (Univ., 1943), *Going My Way* (Par., 1944), *I Love a Soldier* (Par., 1944), *None But the Lonely Heart* (RKO, 1944), *Incendiary Blonde* (Par., 1945), *And Then There Were None* (20th, 1945), *Duffy's Tavern* (Par., 1945), *Stork Club* (Par., 1945), *Two Years Before the Mast* (Par., 1946), *California* (Par., 1946), *Easy Come, Easy Go* (Par., 1947), *Welcome Stranger* (Par., 1947), *Variety Girl*, (Par., 1947), *The Sainted Sisters* (Par., 1948), *The Naked City* (Univ., 1948), *Miss Tatlock's Millions* (Par., 1948), *Top o' the Morning* (Par., 1949), *The Story of Seabiscuit* (WB, 1949), *Union Station* (Par., 1950), *Silver City* (Par., 1951), *The Quiet Man* (Rep., 1952), *Tonight's the Night* (AA, 1954), *The Catered Affair* (MGM, 1956), *Rooney* (Rank, 1958), *Broth of a Boy* (Kingsley International, 1959).

Geraldine Fitzgerald and Jeffrey Lynn in *Flight From Destiny*.

GERALDINE FITZGERALD Born November 24, 1914, Dublin, Ireland. Married Edward Lindsay-Hogg (1936), child: Michael; divorced 1946. Married Stuart Scheftel (1946), child: Susan.

Feature Films: *The Turn of the Tide* (Gaumont-British, 1935), *Three Witnesses* (Universal-British, 1935), *Blind Justice* (British, 1935), *Radio Parade of 1935* (BIP, 1935), *Department Store* (RKO, 1935), *Mill on the Floss* (British Lion, 1936), *Wuthering Heights* (UA, 1939), *Dark Victory* (WB, 1939), *A Child Is Born* (WB, 1940), *Till We Meet Again* (WB, 1940), *Flight From Destiny* (WB, 1941), *Shining Victory* (WB, 1941), *The Gay Sisters* (WB, 1942), *Watch on the Rhine* (WB, 1943), *Ladies Courageous* (Univ., 1944), *Wilson* (20th, 1944), *The Strange Affair of Uncle Harry* (Univ., 1945), *Three Strangers* (WB, 1946), *O. S. S.* (Par., 1946), *Nobody Lives Forever* (WB, 1946), *So Evil, My Love* (Par., 1948), *The Late Edwina Black* ("The Obsessed"—UA, 1951), *10 North Frederick* (20th, 1958), *The Fiercest Heart* (20th, 1961), *The Pawnbroker* (Landau, 1965).

RHONDA FLEMING (Marilyn Louis) Born August 10, 1923, Los Angeles, California. Married Tom Lane (1940), child: Kent; divorced 1942. Married Lewis Morrill (1952); divorced 1958. Married Lang Jeffreys (1960); divorced 1962. Married Hall Bartlett (1966).

English-Language Feature Films: *In Old Oklahoma* (Rep., 1943), *Since You Went Away* (UA, 1944), *When Strangers Marry* ("Betrayed"—Mon., 1944), *Spellbound* (UA, 1945), *The Spiral Staircase* (RKO, 1945), *Abilene Town* (UA, 1946), *Adventure Island* (Par., 1947), *Out of the Past* (RKO, 1947), *A Connecticut Yankee in King Arthur's Court* (Par., 1949), *The Great Lover* (Par., 1949), *The Eagle and the Hawk* (Par., 1950), *The Redhead and the Cowboy* (Par., 1950), *Cry Danger* (RKO, 1951), *The Last Outpost* (Par., 1951), *Little Egypt* (Univ., 1951), *Crosswinds* (Par., 1951), *Hong Kong* (Par., 1951), *The Golden Hawk* (Col., 1953), *Tropic Zone* (Par., 1953), *Pony Express* (Par., 1953), *Serpent of the Nile* (Col., 1953), *Inferno* (20th, 1953), *Those Redheads From Seattle* (Par., 1953), *Jivaro* (Par., 1954), *Yankee Pasha* (Univ., 1954), *Tennessee's Partner* (RKO, 1955), *The Killer Is Loose* (UA, 1956), *Slightly Scarlet* (RKO, 1956), *While the City Sleeps* (RKO, 1956), *Odongo* (Col., 1956), *The Buster Keaton Story* (Par., 1957), *Gunfight at the O. K. Corral* (Par., 1957), *Gun Glory* (MGM, 1957), *Bullwhip* (AA, 1958), *Home Before Dark* (WB, 1958), *Alias Jesse*

James (UA, 1959), *The Big Circus* (AA, 1959), *The Crowded Sky* (WB, 1960), *The Patsy* (Par., 1964),* *Run for Your Wife* (AA, 1966), *An American Wife* (AA, 1967).

*Unbilled guest appearance

ERROL FLYNN (Erroll Leslie Flynn) Born June 20, 1909, Hobart, Tasmania. Married Lili Damita (1935), child: Sean; divorced 1943. Married Nora Eddington (1943), children: Deidre, Rory; divorced 1949. Married Patrice Wymore (1950). Died October 14, 1959.

Roman Bohnen, Errol Flynn and Ann Sheridan in *Edge of Darkness*.

Feature Films: *In the Wake of the Bounty* (Australian, 1933), *Murder in Monte Carlo* (WB, 1935), *The Case of the Curious Bride* (WB, 1935), *Don't Bet on Blondes* (WB, 1935), *Captain Blood* (WB, 1935), *I Found Stella Parish* (WB, 1935), *The Charge of the Light Brigade* (WB, 1936), *Green Light* (WB, 1937), *The Prince and the Pauper* (WB, 1937), *Another Dawn* (WB, 1937), *The Perfect Specimen* (WB, 1937), *The Adventures of Robin Hood* (WB, 1938), *Four's a Crowd* (WB, 1938), *The Sisters* (WB, 1938), *The Dawn Patrol* (WB, 1938), *Dodge City* (WB, 1939), *The Private Lives of Elizabeth and Essex* (WB, 1939), *Virginia City* (WB, 1940), *The Sea Hawk* (WB, 1940), *Santa Fe Trail* (WB, 1940), *Footsteps in the Dark* (WB, 1941), *Dive Bomber* (WB, 1941), *They Died With Their Boots On* (WB, 1941), *Desperate Journey* (WB, 1942), *Gentleman Jim* (WB, 1942), *Edge of Darkness* (WB, 1943), *Thank Your Lucky Stars* (WB, 1943), *Uncertain Glory* (WB, 1944), *Objective Burma* (WB, 1945), *San Antonio* (WB, 1945), *Never Say Goodbye* (WB, 1946), *Cry Wolf* (WB, 1947), *Escape Me Never* (WB, 1947), *Silver River* (1948), *The Adventures of Don Juan* (WB, 1948), *That Forsyte Woman* (MGM, 1949), *Hello God* (William Marshall, 1950), *Montana* (WB, 1950), *Rocky Mountain* (WB, 1950), *Kim* (MGM, 1950), *The Adventures of Captain Fabian* (Rep., 1951), *Mara Maru* (WB, 1952), *Against All Flags* (Univ., 1952), *The Master of Ballantrae* (WB, 1953), *Crossed Swords* (UA, 1953), *Lilacs in the Spring* (Rep., 1955), *The Warriors* (AA, 1955), *King's Rhapsody* (British Lion, 1955), *The Big Boodle* (UA, 1957), *Istanbul* (Univ., 1957), *The Sun Also Rises* (20th, 1957), *Too Much, Too Soon* (WB, 1958), *The Roots of Heaven* (20th, 1958), *Cuban Rebel Girls* (Joseph Brenner Associates, 1959).

NINA FOCH (Nina Consuelo Maud Fock) Born April 20, 1924, Leyden, Holland. Married James Lipton (1954); divorced 1958. Married Dennis Brite (1959); divorced 1963. Married Michael Dewell (1967).

Feature Films: *The Return of the Vampire* (Col., 1943), *Nine Girls* (Col., 1944), *Cry of the Werewolf* (Col., 1944), *She's a Soldier, Too* (Col., 1944), *Shadows in the Night* (Col., 1944), *She's a Sweetheart* (Col., 1944), *Strange Affair* (Col., 1944), *A Song to Remember* (Col., 1945), *I Love a Mystery* (Col., 1945), *Boston Blackie's Rendezvous* (Col., 1945), *My Name Is Julia Ross* (Col., 1945), *Prison Ship* (Col., 1945), *Johnny O'Clock* (Col., 1947), *The Guilt of Janet Ames* (Col., 1947), *The Dark Past* (Col., 1949), *The Undercover Man* (Col., 1949), *Johnny Allegro* (Col., 1949), *St. Benny the Dip* (UA, 1951), *An American*

Fernando Lamas, Rhonda Fleming and Brian Keith in *Jivaro*.

Otto Kruger and Nina Foch in *Escape in the Fog.*

in Paris (MGM 1951), *Scaramouche* (MGM, 1952), *Young Man With Ideas* (MGM, 1952), *Sombrero* (MGM, 1953), *Fast Company* (MGM, 1953), *Executive Suite* (MGM, 1954), *Four Guns to the Border* (Univ., 1954), *You're Never Too Young* (Par., 1955), *Illegal* (WB, 1955), *The Ten Commandments* (Par., 1956), *Three Brave Men* (20th, 1957), *Cash McCall* (WB, 1959), *Spartacus* (Univ., 1960).

HENRY FONDA (Henry Jaynes Fonda) Born May 16, 1905, Grand Island, Nebraska. Married Margaret Sullavan (1931); divorced 1933. Married Frances Brokaw (1936), children: Jane, Peter; widowed 1950. Married Susan Blanchard (1950), child: Amy; divorced 1956. Married Alfreda Franchetti (1957); divorced 1962. Married Shirlee Adams (1965).

Feature Films: *The Farmer Takes a Wife* (Fox, 1935), *Way Down East* (Fox, 1935), *I Dream Too Much* (RKO, 1935), *Trail of the Lonesome Pine* (Par., 1936), *The Moon's Our Home* (Par., 1936), *Spendthrift* (Par., 1936), *Wings of the Morning* (20th, 1937), *You Only Live Once* (UA, 1937), *Slim* (WB, 1937), *That Certain Woman* (WB, 1937), *I Met My Love Again* (UA, 1938), *Jezebel* (WB, 1938), *Blockade* (UA, 1938), *Spawn of the North* (Par., 1938), *The Mad Miss Manton* (RKO, 1938), *Jesse James* (20th, 1939), *Let Us Live* (Col., 1939), *Story of Alexander Graham Bell* (20th, 1939), *Young Mr. Lincoln* (20th, 1939), *Drums Along the Mohawk* (20th, 1939), *The Grapes of Wrath* (20th, 1940), *Lillian Russell* (20th, 1940), *The Return of Frank James* (20th, 1940), *Chad Hanna* (20th, 1940), *The Lady Eve* (Par., 1941), *Wild Geese Calling* (20th, 1941), *You Belong to Me* (Col., 1941), *The Male Animal* (WB, 1942), *Rings on Her Fingers* (20th, 1942), *The Magnificent Dope* (20th, 1942), *Tales of Manhattan* (20th, 1942), *The Big Street* (RKO, 1942), *The Immortal Sergeant* (20th, 1943), *The Ox-Bow Incident* (20th, 1943), *My Darling Clementine* (20th, 1946), *The Long Night* (RKO, 1947), *The Fugitive* (RKO, 1947), *Daisy Kenyon* (20th, 1947), *On Our Merry Way* (UA, 1948), *Fort Apache* (RKO, 1948),

Henry Fonda and Janet Gaynor in *The Farmer Takes a Wife.*

Jigsaw (UA, 1949), *Mister Roberts* (WB, 1955), *War and Peace* (Par., 1956), *The Wrong Man* (WB, 1957), *12 Angry Men* (UA, 1957), *The Tin Star* (Par., 1957), *Stage Struck* (BV, 1958), *Warlock* (20th., 1959), *The Man Who Understood Women* (20th, 1959), *Advise and Consent* (Col., 1962), *The Longest Day* (20th, 1962), *How the West Was Won* (MGM, 1963), *Spencer's Mountain* (WB, 1963), *The Best Man* (UA, 1964), *Fail Safe* (Col., 1964), *Sex and the Single Girl* (WB, 1964), *The Rounders* (MGM, 1965), *In Harm's Way* (Par., 1965), *The Battle of the Bulge* (WB, 1965), *The Dirty Game* (AIP, 1966), *A Big Hand for the Little Lady* (WB, 1966), *Welcome to Hard Times* (MGM, 1967), *Firecreek* (WB-7 Arts, 1968), *Madigan* (Univ., 1968), *Yours, Mine and Ours* (UA, 1968).

JANE FONDA (Jane Seymour Fonda) Born December 21, 1937, New York, New York. Married Roger Vadim (1965).

Ken Lynch, Jane Fonda, Capucine, Laurence Harvey and Barbara Stanwyck in *Walk on the Wild Side.*

English-Language Feature Films: *Tall Story* (WB, 1960), *Walk on the Wild Side* (Col., 1962), *The Chapman Report* (WB, 1962), *Period of Adjustment* (MGM, 1962), *In the Cool of the Day* (MGM, 1963), *Sunday in New York* (MGM, 1963), *Joy House* (MGM, 1964), *Cat Ballou* (Col., 1965), *The Chase* (Col., 1966), *Any Wednesday* (WB, 1966), *Hurry Sundown* (Par., 1967), *Barefoot in the Park* (Par., 1967), *Barbarella* (Par., 1968).

JOAN FONTAINE (Joan de Beauvoir de Havilland) Born October 22, 1917, Tokyo, Japan. Married Brian Aherne (1939); divorced 1945. Married William Dozier (1946), child: Deborah; divorced 1951. Married Collier Young (1952); divorced 1961. Married Alfred Wright (1964). Child adopted while Miss Fontaine was unmarried: Martita Pareja Calderon.

Feature Films: *No More Ladies* (MGM, 1935), *Quality Street* (RKO, 1937), *You Can't Beat Love* (RKO, 1937), *Music for Madame* (RKO, 1937), *A Damsel in Distress* (RKO, 1937), *A Million to One* (Puritan, 1938), *Maid's Night Out* (RKO, 1938), *Blonde Cheat* (RKO, 1938), *The Man Who Found Himself* (RKO, 1938), *Sky Giant* (RKO, 1938), *The Duke of West Point* (UA, 1938), *Gunga Din* (RKO, 1939), *Man of Conquest* (Rep., 1939), *The Women* (MGM, 1939), *Rebecca* (UA, 1940), *Suspicion* (RKO, 1941), *This Above All* (20th, 1942), *The Constant Nymph* (WB, 1943), *Jane Eyre* (20th, 1944), *Frenchman's Creek* (Par., 1945), *The Affairs of Susan* (Par., 1945), *From This Day Forward* (RKO, 1946), *Ivy* (Univ., 1947), *The Emperor Waltz* (Par., 1948), *Kiss the Blood Off My Hands* (Univ., 1948), *Letter From an Unknown Woman* (Univ., 1948), *You Gotta Stay Happy* (Univ., 1948), *Born to Be Bad* (RKO, 1950), *September Affair* (Par., 1950), *Darling, How Could You!* (Par., 1951), *Something to Live For* (Par., 1952), *Ivanhoe* (MGM, 1952), *Decameron Nights* (RKO, 1953), *Flight to Tangier*

Nino Martini, Joan Fontaine and Lee Patrick in *Music for Madame*.

(Par., 1953), *The Bigamist* (Filmakers, 1953), *Casanova's Big Night* (Par., 1954), *Othello* (UA, 1955),* *Serenade* (WB, 1956), *Beyond a Reasonable Doubt* (RKO, 1956), *Island in the Sun* (20th, 1957), *Until They Sail* (MGM, 1957), *A Certain Smile* (20th, 1958), *Voyage to the Bottom of the Sea* (20th, 1961), *Tender Is the Night* (20th, 1961), *The Devil's Own* (20th, 1967).

*Unbilled guest appearance

GLENN FORD (Gwyllyn Ford) Born May 1, 1916, Quebec, Canada. Married Eleanor Powell (1943), child: Peter; divorced 1959. Married Kathryn Hays (1966).

Feature Films: *Heaven With a Barbed Wire Fence* (20th, 1940), *My Son Is Guilty* (Col., 1940), *Convicted Woman* (Col., 1940), *Men Without Souls* (Col., 1940), *Babies for Sale* (Col., 1940), *Blondie Plays Cupid* (Col., 1940), *Lady in Question* (Col., 1940), *So Ends Our Night* (UA, 1941), *Texas* (Col., 1941), *Go West, Young Lady* (Col., 1941), *The Adventures of Martin Eden* (Col., 1942), *Flight Lieutenant* (Col., 1942), *The Desperadoes* (Col., 1943), *Destroyer* (Col., 1943), *Gilda* (Col., 1946), *A Stolen Life* (WB, 1946), *Framed* (Col., 1947), *The Mating of Millie* (Col., 1948), *The Loves of Carmen* (Col., 1948), *The Return of October* (Col., 1948), *The Man From Colorado* (Col., 1948), *The Undercover Man* (Col., 1949), *Mr. Soft Touch* (Col., 1949), *Lust for Gold* (Col., 1949), *The Doctor and the Girl* (MGM, 1949), *The White Tower* (RKO, 1950), *Convicted* (Col., 1950), *The Redhead and the Cowboy* (Par., 1950), *The Flying Missile* (Col., 1950), *Follow the Sun* (20th, 1951), *The Secret of Convict Lake* (20th, 1951), *The Green Glove* (UA, 1952), *Affair in Trinidad* (Col., 1952), *Young Man With Ideas* (MGM, 1952), *Terror on a Train* (MGM, 1953), *The Man From the Alamo* (Univ., 1953), *Plunder of the Sun* (WB, 1953), *The Big Heat* (Col., 1953), *Appointment in Honduras* (RKO, 1953), *Human Desire* (Col., 1954), *The Americano* (RKO, 1955), *The Violent Men* (Col., 1955), *The Blackboard Jungle* (MGM, 1955), *Interrupted Melody* (MGM, 1955), *Trial* (MGM,

1955), *Ransom* (MGM, 1956), *Jubal* (Col., 1956), *The Fastest Gun Alive* (MGM, 1956), *The Teahouse of the August Moon* (MGM, 1956), *3 : 10 to Yuma* (Col., 1957), *Don't Go Near the Water* (MGM, 1957), *Cowboy* (Col., 1958), *The Sheepman* (MGM, 1958), *Imitation General* (MGM, 1958), *Torpedo Run* (MGM, 1958), *It Started With a Kiss* (MGM, 1959), *The Gazebo* (MGM, 1959), *Cimarron* (MGM, 1960), *Cry for Happy* (Col., 1961), *Pocketful of Miracles* (UA, 1961), *The Four Horsemen of the Apocalypse* (MGM, 1962), *Experiment in Terror* (Col., 1962), *Love Is a Ball* (UA, 1963), *The Courtship of Eddie's Father* (MGM, 1963), *Advance to the Rear* (MGM, 1964), *Fate Is the Hunter* (20th, 1964), *Dear Heart* (WB, 1964), *The Rounders* (MGM, 1965), *The Money Trap* (MGM, 1966), *Is Paris Burning?* (Par., 1966), *The Rage* (Col., 1967), *The Last Challenge* (MGM, 1967), *A Time for Killing* (Col., 1968), *Evil Gun* (MGM, 1968).

WALLACE FORD (Samuel Jones) Born February 12, 1898, Batton, Lancashire, England. Married Martha Harworth (1922), child: Patricia; widowed 1966. Died 1966.

Feature Films: *Swellhead* (Tif., 1930), *Possessed* (MGM, 1931), *Hypnotized* (World Wide, 1932), *The Beast of the City* (MGM, 1932), *Freaks* (MGM, 1932), *Goodbye Again* (WB, 1933), *Headline Shooter* (RKO, 1933), *Night of Terror* (Col., 1933), *My Woman* (Col., 1933), *She Had to Say Yes* (WB, 1933), *East of Fifth Avenue* (Col., 1933), *Three-Cornered Moon* (Par., 1933), *The Lost Patrol* (RKO, 1934), *A Woman's Man* (Mon., 1934), *Money Means Nothing* (Mon., 1934), *Men in White* (MGM, 1934), *I Hate Women* (Goldsmith, 1934), *The Informer* (RKO, 1935), *The Nut Farm* (Mon., 1935), *The Whole Town's Talking* (Col., 1935), *In Spite of Danger* (Col., 1935), *Man of the Hour* (Col., 1935), *She Couldn't Take It* (Col., 1935), *The Mysterious Mr. Wong* (Mon., 1935), *The Man Who Reclaimed His Head* (Univ., 1935), *Sanders of the River* (UA, 1935), *Get That Man* (Empire, 1935), *Mary Burns—Fugitive* (Par., 1935), *Another Face* (RKO, 1935), *Absolute Quiet* (MGM, 1936), *Two in the Dark* (RKO, 1936), *A Son Comes Home* (Par., 1936), *The Rogues' Tavern* (Puritan, 1936), *Swing It Sailor* (GN, 1937), *Exiled to Shanghai* (Rep., 1937), *Dark Sands* (Record, 1938), *Two Girls on Broadway* (MGM, 1940), *Isle of Destiny* (RKO, 1940), *Scatterbrain* (Rep., 1940), *The Mummy's Hand* (Univ., 1940), *Love, Honor and Oh, Baby!* (Univ., 1940), *Give Us Wings* (Univ., 1940), *A Man Betrayed* (Rep., 1941), *The Roar of the Press* (Mon., 1941), *You're in the Army Now* (WB, 1941), *Blues in the Night* (WB, 1941), *X Marks the Spot* (Rep., 1942), *The Mummy's Tomb* (Univ., 1942), *Shadow of a Doubt* (Univ., 1943), *The Ape Man* (Mon., 1943), *The Marines Come Through* (Astor, 1943), *The Cross of Lorraine* (MGM, 1943), *Secret Command* (Col., 1944), *Machine Gun Mama* (PRC, 1944), *Spellbound* (UA, 1945), *They Were Expendable* (MGM, 1945), *Blood on the Sun* (UA, 1945), *A Guy Could Change* (Rep., 1946), *The Green Years* (MGM, 1946), *Lover Come Back* (Univ., 1946), *Crack-Up* (RKO, 1946), *Black Angel* (Univ., 1946), *Rendezvous With Annie* (Rep., 1946), *Magic Town* (RKO, 1947), *Dead Reckoning* (Col., 1947), *T-Men* (EL, 1947), *Shed No Tears* (EL, 1948), *Coroner Creek* (Col., 1948), *The Man From Texas* (EL, 1948), *Embraceable*

Peter Brocco, John Garfield, Wallace Ford, Guy Thomajan and William Campbell in *The Breaking Point*.

Harry Swoger and Glenn Ford in *Pocketful of Miracles*.

You (WB, 1948), *Belle Starr's Daughter* (20th, 1948), *Red Stallion in the Rockies* (EL, 1949), *The Set-Up* (RKO, 1949), *The Breaking Point* (WB, 1950), *The Furies* (Par., 1950), *Dakota Lil* (20th, 1950), *Harvey* (Univ., 1950), *Painting the Clouds With Sunshine* (WB, 1951), *Warpath* (Par., 1951), *He Ran All the Way* (UA, 1951), *Rodeo* (Mon., 1952), *Flesh and Fury* (Univ., 1952), *The Nebraskan* (Col., 1953), *Destry* (Univ., 1954), *Three Ring Circus* (Par., 1954), *The Man From Laramie* (Col., 1955), *Wichita* (AA, 1955), *The Spoilers* (Univ., 1955), *A Lawless Street* (Col., 1955), *Lucy Gallant* (Par., 1955), *The Rainmaker* (Par., 1956), *Twilight for the Gods* (Univ., 1958), *The Matchmaker* (Par., 1958), *The Last Hurrah* (Col., 1958), *Warlock* (20th, 1959), *Tess of the Storm Country* (20th, 1961), *A Patch of Blue* (MGM, 1965).

PRESTON FOSTER (Preston S. Foster) Born August 24, 1902, Ocean City, New Jersey. Married Gertrude Warren, child: Stephanie; divorced 1946. Married Sheila Darcy (1946).

George E. Stone and Preston Foster in *The Last Mile*.

Feature Films: *Heads Up* (Par., 1930), *Two Seconds* (WB, 1932), *The Last Mile* (World-Wide, 1932), *Life Begins* (WB, 1932), *Doctor X* (WB, 1932), *I Am a Fugitive From a Chain Gang* (WB, 1932), *You Said a Mouthful* (WB, 1932), *The All American* (Univ., 1932), *Ladies They Talk About* (WB, 1933), *Elmer the Great* (WB, 1933), *Corruption* (Imperial, 1933), *The Man Who Dared* (Fox, 1933), *Devil's Mate* (Mon., 1933), *Hoopla* (Fox, 1933), *Sensation Hunters* (Mon., 1933), *Wharf Angel* (Par., 1934), *Heat Lightning* (WB, 1934), *Sleepers East* (Fox, 1934), *The Band Plays On* (MGM, 1934), *Strangers All* (RKO, 1935), *People's Enemy* (RKO, 1935), *The Informer* (RKO, 1935), *The Arizonian* (RKO, 1935), *Last Days of Pompeii* (RKO, 1935), *Annie Oakley* (RKO, 1935), *We're Only Human* (RKO, 1936), *Muss 'Em Up* (RKO, 1936), *Love Before Breakfast* (Univ., 1936), *We Who Are About to Die* (RKO, 1936), *The Plough and the Stars* (RKO, 1936), *Sea Devils* (RKO, 1937), *Outcasts of Poker Flat* (RKO, 1937), *You Can't Beat Love* (RKO, 1937), *First Lady* (WB, 1937), *The Westland Case* (Univ., 1937), *Double Danger* (RKO, 1938), *Everybody's Doing It* (RKO, 1938), *Lady in the Morgue* (Univ., 1938), *Army Girl* (Rep., 1938), *The Last Warning* (Univ., 1938), *Up the River* (20th, 1938), *The Storm* (Univ., 1938), *Submarine Patrol* (20th, 1938), *Society Smugglers* (Univ., 1939), *Chasing Danger* (20th, 1939), *News Is Made at Night* (20th, 1939), *Geronimo* (Par., 1939), *Missing Evidence* (Univ., 1939), *20,000 Men a Year* (20th, 1939), *Cafe Hostess* (Col., 1940), *North West Mounted Police* (Par., 1940), *Moon Over Burma* (Par., 1940), *The Round-up* (Par., 1941), *Unfinished Business* (Univ., 1941), *A Gentleman After Dark* (UA, 1942), *Secret Agent of Japan* (20th, 1942), *Night in New Orleans* (Par., 1942), *Little Tokyo, USA* (20th, 1942), *Thunder Birds*

(20th, 1942), *American Empire* (UA, 1942), *My Friend Flicka* (20th, 1943), *Guadalcanal Diary* (20th, 1943), *Bermuda Mystery* (20th, 1944), *Roger Touhy, Gangster* (20th, 1944), *Thunderhead, Son of Flicka* (20th, 1945), *Abbott and Costello in Hollywood* (MGM, 1945), *Valley of Decision* (MGM, 1945), *Twice Blessed* (MGM, 1945), *Tangier* (Univ., 1946), *The Harvey Girls* (MGM, 1946), *Inside Job* (Univ., 1946), *Strange Triangle* (20th, 1946), *Blonde From Brooklyn* (Col., 1946), *Ramrod* (UA, 1947), *King of the Wild Horses* (Col., 1947), *I Shot Jesse James* (Screen Guild, 1949), *The Big Cat* (EL, 1949), *The Tougher They Come* (Col., 1950), *Tomahawk* (Univ., 1951), *3 Desperate Men* (Lip., 1951), *The Big Gusher* (Col., 1951), *The Big Night* (UA, 1951), *Montana Territory* (Col., 1952), *Kansas City Confidential* (UA, 1952), *Law and Order* (Univ., 1953), *I, The Jury* (UA, 1953), *Destination 60,000* (AA, 1957), *Advance to the Rear* (MGM, 1964), *The Man From Galveston* (WB, 1964), *The Time Travelers* (AIP, 1964), *Chubasco* (WB, 1967), *You've Got to Be Smart* (PRO, 1968).

SUSANNA FOSTER (Susanna DeLee Flanders Larson) Born December 6, 1924, Chicago, Illinois. Married Wilbur Evans (1948), children: Michael, Philip; divorced 1956.

Allan Jones, Lynne Overman and Susanna Foster in *Hard-boiled Canary*.

Feature Films: *The Great Victor Herbert* (Par., 1939), *The Hard-Boiled Canary* (Par., 1941), *Glamour Boy* (Par., 1941), *Star Spangled Rhythm* (Par., 1942), *Top Man* (Univ., 1943), *The Phantom of the Opera* (Univ., 1943), *Follow the Boys* (Univ., 1944), *This Is the Life* (Univ., 1944), *The Climax* (Univ., 1944), *Bowery to Broadway* (Univ., 1944), *Frisco Sal* (Univ., 1945), *That Night With You* (Univ., 1945).

ANNE FRANCIS Born September 16, 1930, Ossining, New York. Married Bamblet Price (1952); divorced 1955. Married Robert Abeloff (1960), child: Jane; divorced 1964.

Adeline de Walt Reynolds and Anne Francis in *Lydia Bailey*.

Feature Films: *Summer Holiday* (MGM, 1948), *Portrait of Jennie* (Selznick, 1948), *So Young, So Bad* (UA, 1950), *The Whistle at Eaton Falls* (Col., 1951), *Elopement* (20th, 1951), *Lydia Bailey* (20th, 1952), *Dreamboat* (20th, 1952), *A Lion Is in the Streets* (WB, 1953), *The Rocket Man* (20th, 1954), *Susan Slept Here* (RKO, 1954), *Rogue Cop* (MGM, 1954), *Bad Day at Black Rock* (MGM, 1954), *Battle Cry* (WB, 1955), *The Blackboard Jungle* (MGM, 1955), *The Scarlet Coat* (MGM, 1955), *Forbidden Planet* (MGM, 1956), *The Rack* (MGM, 1956), *The Great American Pastime* (MGM, 1956), *The Hired Gun* (MGM, 1957), *Don't Go Near the Water* (MGM, 1957), *Girl of the Night* (WB, 1960), *The Crowded Sky* (WB, 1960), *The Satan Bug* (UA, 1965), *Brainstorm* (WB, 1965), *Funny Girl* (Col., 1968), *Star* (20th, 1968).

KAY FRANCIS (Katherine Edwina Gibbs) Born January 13, 1903, Oklahoma City, Oklahoma. Married James Francis (1922); divorced 1925. Married William Gaston (1926); divorced 1928. Married Kenneth MacKenna (1931); divorced 1933.

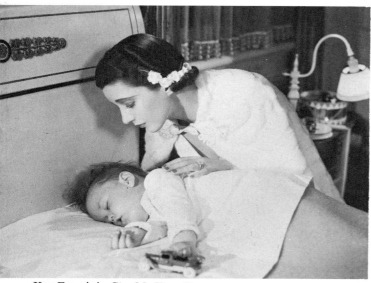

Kay Francis in *Give Me Your Heart*.

Feature Films: *Gentlemen of the Press* (Par., 1929), *The Cocoanuts* (Par., 1929), *Dangerous Curves* (Par., 1929), *Illusion* (Par., 1929), *The Marriage Playground* (Par., 1929), *Behind the Makeup* (Par., 1930), *The Street of Chance* (Par., 1930), *Paramount on Parade* (Par., 1930), *A Notorious Affair* (WB, 1930), *Raffles* (UA, 1930), *For the Defense* (Par., 1930), *Let's Go Native* (Par., 1930), *The Virtuous Sin* (Par., 1930), *Passion Flower* (MGM, 1930), *Scandal Sheet* (Par., 1931), *Ladies' Man* (Par., 1931), *The Vice Squad* (Par., 1931), *Transgression* (RKO, 1931), *Guilty Hands* (MGM, 1931), *24 Hours* (Par., 1931), *Girls About Town* (Par., 1931), *The False Madonna* (Par., 1932), *Strangers in Love* (Par., 1932), *Man Wanted* (WB, 1932), *Street of Women* (WB, 1932), *Jewel Robbery* (WB, 1932), *One Way Passage* (WB, 1932), *Trouble in Paradise* (Par., 1932), *Cynara* (UA, 1932), *The Keyhole* (WB, 1933), *Storm at Daybreak* (MGM, 1933), *Mary Stevens, M. D.* (WB, 1933), *I Loved a Woman* (WB, 1933), *House on 56th Street* (WB, 1933), *Mandalay* (WB, 1934), *Wonder Bar* (WB, 1934), *Doctor Monica* (WB, 1934), *British Agent* (WB, 1934), *Stranded* (WB, 1935), *The Goose and the Gander* (WB, 1935), *I Found Stella Parish* (WB, 1935), *The White Angel* (WB, 1936), *Give Me Your Heart* (WB, 1936), *Stolen Holiday* (WB, 1937), *Confession* (WB, 1937), *Another Dawn* (WB, 1937), *First Lady* (WB, 1937), *Women Are Like That* (WB, 1938), *My Bill* (WB, 1938), *Secrets of an Actress* (WB, 1938), *Comet Over Broadway* (WB, 1938), *King of the Underworld* (WB, 1939), *Women in the Wind* (WB, 1939), *In Name Only* (RKO, 1939), *It's a Date* (Univ., 1940), *Little Men* (RKO, 1940), *When the Daltons Rode* (Univ., 1940), *Play Girl* (RKO, 1940), *The Man Who Lost Himself* (Univ., 1941), *Charley's Aunt* (20th, 1941), *The Feminine Touch* (MGM, 1941), *Always in My Heart* (WB, 1942), *Between Us Girls* (Univ., 1942), *Four Jills in a Jeep* (20th, 1944), *Divorce* (Mon., 1945), *Allotment Wives* (Mon., 1945), *Wife Wanted* (Mon., 1946).

WILLIAM FRAWLEY Born February 26, 1887, Burlington, Iowa. Married 1914; divorced 1927. Died March 3, 1966.

Feature Films: *Moonlight and Pretzels* (Univ., 1933), *Hell and High Water* (Par., 1933), *Crime Doctor* (RKO, 1934), *Miss Fane's Baby Is Stolen* (Par., 1934), *Bolero* (Par., 1934), *The Witching Hour* (Par., 1934), *Shoot the Works* (Par., 1934), *The Lemon Drop Kid* (Par., 1934), *Here Is My Heart* (Par., 1934), *Car 99* (Par., 1935), *Hold 'Em Yale* (Par., 1935), *Alibi Ike* (WB, 1935), *College Scandal* (Par., 1935), *Welcome Home* (Fox, 1935), *Harmony Lane* (Mascot, 1935), *Ship Cafe* (Par., 1935), *Strike Me Pink* (UA, 1936), *F-Man* (Par., 1936), *Desire* (Par., 1936), *The Princess Comes Across* (Par., 1936), *Three Cheers for Love* (Par., 1936), *The General Died at Dawn* (Par., 1936), *Three Married Men* (Par., 1936), *Rose Bowl* (Par., 1936), *Something to Sing About* (GN, 1937), *Double or Nothing* (Par., 1937), *High, Wide and Handsome* (Par., 1937), *Blossoms on Broadway* (Par., 1937), *Mad About Music* (Univ., 1938), *Professor Beware* (Par., 1938), *Sons of the Legion* (Par., 1938), *Touchdown Army* (Par., 1938), *Ambush* (Par., 1939), *Adventures of Huckleberry Finn* (MGM, 1939), *St. Louis Blues* (Par., 1939), *Persons in Hiding* (Par., 1939), *Rose of Washington Square* (20th, 1939), *Ex-Champ* (Univ., 1939), *Grand Jury Secrets* (Par., 1939), *Stop, Look and Love* (20th, 1939), *Night Work* (Par., 1939), *The Farmer's Daughter* (Par., 1940), *Opened By Mistake* (Par., 1940), *Those Were the Days* (Par., 1940), *Untamed* (Par., 1940), *Golden Gloves* (Par., 1940), *Rhythm on the River* (Par., 1940), *The Quarterback* (Par., 1940), *One Night in the Tropics* (Univ., 1940), *Sandy Gets Her Man* (Univ., 1940), *Six Lessons From Madame La Zonga* (Univ., 1941), *Dancing on a Dime* (Par., 1941), *Footsteps in the Dark* (WB, 1941), *Cracked Nuts* (Univ., 1941), *The Bride Came C.O.D.* (WB, 1941), *Blondie in Society* (Col., 1941), *Public Enemies* (Rep., 1941), *Roxie Hart* (20th, 1942), *Treat 'Em Rough* (Univ., 1942), *It Happened in Flatbush* (20th, 1942), *Give Out, Sisters* (Univ., 1942), *Wildcat* (Par., 1942), *Gentleman Jim* (WB, 1942), *Moonlight in Havana* (Univ., 1942), *We've Never Been Licked* (Univ., 1943), *Whistling in Brooklyn* (MGM, 1943), *Larceny With Music* (Univ., 1943), *Fighting Seabees* (Rep., 1944), *Minstrel Man* (PRC, 1944), *Going My Way* (Par., 1944), *Lake Placid Serenade* (Rep., 1944), *Flame of Barbary Coast* (Rep., 1945), *Hitchhike to Happiness* (Rep., 1945), *Lady on a Train* (Univ., 1945), *The Ziegfeld Follies* (MGM, 1946), *The Virginian* (Par., 1946), *Rendezvous With Annie* (Rep., 1946), *The Inner Circle* (Rep., 1946), *The Crime Doctor's Manhunt* (Col., 1946), *Monsieur Verdoux* (UA, 1947), *The Miracle on 34th Street* (20th, 1947), *The Hit Parade of 1947* (Rep., 1947), *I Wonder Who's Kissing Her Now* (20th, 1947), *Mother Wore Tights* (20th, 1947), *Down to Earth* (Col., 1947), *Blondie's Anniversary* (Col., 1947), *My Wild Irish Rose* (WB, 1947), *The Babe Ruth Story* (AA, 1948), *Good Sam* (RKO, 1948), *Texas, Brooklyn and Heaven* (UA, 1948), *Joe Palooka in Winner Take All* (Mon., 1948), *Home in San Antone* (Col., 1949), *The Lady Takes a Sailor* (WB, 1949), *East Side, West Side* (MGM, 1949), *The Lone Wolf and His Lady* (Col., 1949), *Kill the Umpire!* (Col., 1950), *Pretty Baby* (WB, 1950), *Kiss Tomorrow Goodbye* (WB, 1950), *Blondie's Hero* (Col., 1950), *Abbott and Costello Meet the Invisible Man* (Univ., 1951), *The Lemon Drop Kid* (Par., 1951), *Rancho Notorious* (RKO, 1952), *Safe at Home!* (Col., 1962).

George Raft, Frances Drake and William Frawley in *Bolero.*

Scott Brady and Mona Freeman in *I Was a Shoplifter*.

MONA FREEMAN (Monica Freeman) Born June 9, 1926, Baltimore, Maryland. Married Patrick Nerney (1945), child: Mona; divorced 1952. Married Jack Ellis (1961).

Feature Films: *National Velvet* (MGM, 1944) *Our Hearts Were Young and Gay* (Par., 1944), *Till We Meet Again* (Par., 1944), *Here Come the Waves* (Par., 1944), *Together Again* (Col., 1944), *Roughly Speaking* (WB, 1945), *Junior Miss* (20th, 1945), *Danger Signal* (WB, 1945), *Black Beauty* (20th, 1946), *That Brennan Girl* (Rep., 1946), *Our Hearts Were Growing Up* (Par., 1946), *Variety Girl* (Par., 1947), *Dear Ruth* (Par., 1947), *Mother Wore Tights* (20th, 1947), *Isn't It Romantic?* (Par., 1948), *Streets of Laredo* (Par., 1949), *The Heiress* (Par., 1949), *Dear Wife* (Par., 1949), *Branded* (Par., 1950), *Copper Canyon* (Par., 1950), *I Was a Shoplifter* (Univ., 1950), *Dear Brat* (Par., 1951), *Darling, How Could You!* (Par., 1951), *The Lady From Texas* (Univ., 1951), *Flesh and Fury* (Univ., 1952), *Jumping Jacks* (Par., 1952), *The Greatest Show on Earth* (Par., 1952),* *Angel Face* (RKO, 1952), *Thunderbirds* (Rep., 1952), *Battle Cry* (WB, 1955), *The Road to Denver* (Rep., 1955), *The Way Out* (RKO, 1956), *Shadow of Fear* (UA, 1956), *Hold Back the Night* (AA, 1956), *Huk* (UA, 1956), *Dragoon Wells Massacre* (AA, 1957), *The World Was His Jury* (Col., 1958).

*Unbilled guest appearance

CLARK GABLE (William Clark Gable) Born Feb 1, 1901, Cadiz, Ohio. Married Josephine Dillon (1924); divorced 1930. Married Rhea Langham (1930); divorced 1939. Married Carole Lombard (1939); widowed 1942. Married Sylvia Hawkes (1949); divorced 1952. Married Kay Spreckels (1955), child: John. Died November 16, 1960.

Sound Feature Films: *The Painted Desert* (Pathé, 1931), *The Easiest Way* (MGM, 1931), *Dance Fools Dance* (MGM, 1931), *The Secret Six* (MGM, 1931), *Laughing Sinners* (MGM, 1931), *A Free Soul* (MGM, 1931), *Night Nurse* (WB, 1931), *Sporting Blood* (MGM, 1931),

Edgar Buchanan, Frank Morgan and Clark Gable in *Any Number Can Play*.

Susan Lennox—Her Fall and Rise (MGM, 1931), *Possessed* (MGM, 1931), *Hell Divers* (MGM, 1931), *Polly of the Circus* (MGM, 1932), *Strange Interlude* (MGM, 1932), *Red Dust* (MGM, 1932), *No Man of Her Own* (Par., 1932), *The White Sister* (MGM, 1933), *Hold Your Man* (MGM, 1933), *Night Flight* (MGM, 1933), *Dancing Lady* (MGM, 1933), *It Happened One Night* (Col., 1934), *Men in White* (MGM, 1934), *Manhattan Melodrama* (MGM, 1934), *Chained* (MGM, 1934), *Forsaking All Others* (MGM, 1934), *After Office Hours* (MGM, 1935), *Call of the Wild* (UA, 1935), *China Seas* (MGM, 1935), *Mutiny on the Bounty* (MGM, 1935), *Wife vs. Secretary* (MGM, 1936), *San Francisco* (MGM, 1936), *Cain and Mabel* (WB, 1936), *Love on the Run* (MGM, 1936), *Parnell* (MGM, 1937), *Saratoga* (MGM, 1937), *Test Pilot* (MGM, 1938), *Too Hot to Handle* (MGM, 1938), *Idiot's Delight* (MGM, 1939), *Gone With the Wind* (MGM, 1939), *Strange Cargo* (MGM, 1940), *Boom Town* (MGM, 1940), *Comrade X* (MGM, 1940), *They Met in Bombay* (MGM, 1941), *Honky Tonk* (MGM, 1941), *Somewhere I'll Find You* (MGM, 1942), *Adventure* (MGM, 1945), *The Hucksters* (MGM, 1947), *Homecoming* (MGM, 1948), *Command Decision* (MGM, 1948), *Any Number Can Play* (MGM, 1949), *Key to the City* (MGM, 1950), *To Please a Lady* (MGM, 1950), *Across the Wide Missouri* (MGM, 1951), *Callaway Went Thataway* (MGM, 1951), *Lone Star* (MGM, 1952), *Never Let Me Go* (MGM, 1953), *Mogambo* (MGM, 1953), *Betrayed* (MGM, 1954), *Soldier of Fortune* (20th, 1955), *The Tall Men* (20th, 1955), *The King and Four Queens* (UA, 1956), *Band of Angels* (WB, 1957), *Run Silent, Run Deep* (UA, 1958), *Teacher's Pet* (Par., 1958), *But Not for Me* (Par., 1959), *It Started in Naples* (Par., 1960), *The Misfits* (UA, 1961).

GRETA GARBO (Greta Lovisa Gustafsson) Born September 18, 1905, Stockholm, Sweden.

Clark Gable and Greta Garbo in *Susan Lennox, Her Rise and Fall*.

Sound Feature Films: *Anna Christie* (MGM, 1930), *Romance* (MGM, 1930), *Inspiration* (MGM, 1931), *Susan Lennox—Her Fall and Rise* (MGM, 1931), *Mata Hari* (MGM, 1931), *Grand Hotel* (MGM, 1932), *As You Desire Me* (MGM, 1932), *Queen Christina* (MGM, 1933), *The Painted Veil* (MGM, 1934), *Anna Karenina* (MGM, 1935), *Camille* (MGM, 1936), *Conquest* (MGM, 1937), *Ninotchka* (MGM, 1939), *Two-Faced Woman* (MGM, 1941).

REGINALD GARDINER (William Reginald Gardiner) Born February 27, 1903, Wimbelton, Surrey, England. Married Nayda Petrova (1942), children: Robert, Karen, Peter.

Feature Films: *Josser on the River* (British International, 1932), *The Lovelorn Lady* (British International, 1932), *Just Smith* (Gaumont-

Reginald Gardiner and Maureen O'Hara in *Do You Love Me?*

British, 1933), *Leave It to Smith* (Gaumont-British, 1933), *How's Chances?* (Fox, 1934), *Born to Dance* (MGM, 1936), *A Damsel in Distress* (RKO, 1937), *Everybody Sing* (MGM, 1938), *Marie Antoinette* (MGM, 1938), *Sweethearts* (MGM, 1938), *The Girl Downstairs* (MGM, 1939), *The Flying Deuces* (RKO, 1939), *The Night of Nights* (Par., 1939), *The Doctor Takes a Wife* (Col., 1940), *Dulcy* (MGM, 1940), *The Great Dictator* (UA, 1940), *My Life With Caroline* (RKO, 1941), *A Yank in the R.A.F.* (20th, 1941), *Sundown* (UA, 1941), *The Man Who Came to Dinner* (WB, 1941), *Captains of the Clouds* (WB, 1942), *The Immortal Sergeant* (20th, 1943), *Forever and a Day* (RKO, 1943), *Sweet Rosie O'Grady* (20th, 1943), *Claudia* (20th, 1943), *Molly and Me* (20th, 1945), *The Horn Blows at Midnight* (WB, 1945), *Christmas in Connecticut* (WB, 1945), *The Dolly Sisters* (20th, 1945), *Do You Love Me?* (20th, 1946), *Cluny Brown* (20th, 1946), *One More Tomorrow* (WB, 1946), *I Wonder Who's Kissing Her Now* (20th, 1947), *That Wonderful Urge* (20th, 1948), *Fury at Furnace Creek* (20th, 1948), *That Lady in Ermine* (20th, 1948), *Wabash Avenue* (20th, 1950), *Halls of Montezuma* (20th, 1950), *Elopement* (20th, 1951), *Androcles and the Lion* (RKO, 1952), *The Barefoot Contessa* (UA, 1954), *Black Widow* (20th, 1954), *Ain't Misbehavin'* (Univ., 1955), *Around the World in 80 Days* (UA, 1956), *The Birds and the Bees* (Par., 1956), *The Story of Mankind* (WB, 1957), *Rock-a-Bye Baby* (Par., 1958), *Back Street* (Univ., 1961), *Mr. Hobbs Takes a Vacation* (20th, 1962), *What a Way to Go!* (20th, 1964), *Do Not Disturb* (20th, 1965), *Sergeant Deadhead* (AIP, 1965).

AVA GARDNER (Ava Lavinia Gardner) Born December 24, 1922, Grabtown, North Carolina. Married Mickey Rooney (1942); divorced 1943. Married Artie Shaw (1945); divorced 1947. Married Frank Sinatra (1951); divorced 1957.

Feature Films: *We Were Dancing* (MGM, 1942), *Joe Smith, American* (MGM, 1942), *Sunday Punch* (MGM, 1942), *This Time for Keeps* (MGM, 1942), *Calling Dr. Gillespie* (MGM, 1942), *Kid Glove Killer* (MGM, 1942), *Pilot No. 5* (MGM, 1943), *Hitler's Madman* (MGM,

Gregory Peck and Ava Gardner in *The Great Sinner.*

1943), *Ghosts on the Loose* (Mon., 1943), *Reunion in France* (MGM, 1943), *Du Barry Was a Lady* (MGM, 1943), *Young Ideas* (MGM, 1943), *Lost Angel* (MGM, 1943), *Swing Fever* (MGM, 1944), *Music for Millions* (MGM, 1944), *Three Men in White* (MGM, 1944), *Blonde Fever* (MGM, 1944), *Maisie Goes to Reno* (MGM, 1944), *Two Girls and a Sailor* (MGM, 1944), *She Went to the Races* (MGM, 1945), *Whistle Stop* (UA, 1946), *The Killers* (Univ., 1946), *The Hucksters* (MGM, 1947), *Singapore* (Univ., 1947), *One Touch of Venus* (Univ., 1948), *The Great Sinner* (MGM, 1949), *East Side, West Side* (MGM, 1949), *The Bribe* (MGM, 1949), *My Forbidden Past* (RKO, 1951), *Show Boat* (MGM, 1951), *Pandora and the Flying Dutchman* (MGM, 1951), *Lone Star* (MGM, 1952), *The Snows of Kilimanjaro* (20th, 1952), *Ride Vaquero!* (MGM, 1953), *The Band Wagon* (MGM, 1953),* *Mogambo* (MGM, 1953), *Knights of the Round Table* (MGM, 1953), *The Barefoot Contessa* (UA, 1954), *Bhowani Junction* (MGM, 1956), *The Little Hut* (MGM, 1957), *The Sun Also Rises* (20th, 1957), *The Naked Maja* (UA, 1959), *On the Beach* (UA, 1959), *The Angel Wore Red* (MGM, 1960), *55 Days at Peking* (AA, 1963), *Seven Days in May* (Par., 1964), *The Night of the Iguana* (MGM, 1964), *The Bible* (20th, 1966), *Mayerling* (MGM, 1968).

*Unbilled guest appearance

JOHN GARFIELD (Julius Garfinkle) Born March 4, 1912, New York, New York. Married Roberta Mann (1933), children: David, Julie. Died May 20, 1952.

John Garfield and Claude Rains in *Daughters Courageous.*

Feature Films: *Footlight Parade* (WB, 1933), *Four Daughters* (WB, 1938), *They Made Me a Criminal* (WB, 1939), *Blackwell's Island* (WB, 1939), *Juarez* (WB, 1939), *Daughters Courageous* (WB, 1939), *Dust Be My Destiny* (WB, 1939), *Castle on the Hudson* (WB, 1940), *Saturday's Children* (WB, 1940), *Flowing Gold* (WB, 1940), *East of the River* (WB, 1940), *The Sea Wolf* (WB, 1941), *Out of the Fog* (WB, 1941), *Dangerously They Live* (WB, 1942), *Tortilla Flat* (MGM, 1942), *Air Force* (WB, 1943), *The Fallen Sparrow* (RKO, 1943), *Thank Your Lucky Stars* (WB, 1943), *Destination Tokyo* (WB, 1943), *Between Two Worlds* (WB, 1944), *Hollywood Canteen* (WB, 1944), *Pride of the Marines* (WB, 1945), *The Postman Always Rings Twice* (MGM, 1946), *Nobody Lives Forever* (WB, 1946), *Humoresque* (WB, 1946), *Body and Soul* (UA, 1947), *Gentleman's Agreement* (20th, 1947), *Force of Evil* (MGM, 1948), *We Were Strangers* (Col., 1949), *Jigsaw* (UA, 1949),* *Under My Skin* (20th, 1950), *The Breaking Point* (WB, 1950), *He Ran All the Way* (UA, 1951).

*Unbilled guest appearance

JUDY GARLAND (Frances Gumm) Born June 10, 1922, Grand Rapids, Minnesota. Married David Rose (1941); divorced 1943. Married Vincente Minnelli (1945), child: Liza; divorced 1950. Married

Gene Kelly and Judy Garland in *The Pirate*.

Sid Luft (1952), children: Lorna, Joseph; divorced 1965. Married Mark Herron (1965); divorced 1967.

Feature Films: *Pigskin Parade* (20th, 1936), *Broadway Melody of 1938* (MGM, 1937), *Thoroughbreds Don't Cry* (MGM, 1937), *Everybody Sing* (MGM, 1938), *Listen Darling* (MGM, 1938), *Love Finds Andy Hardy* (MGM, 1938), *The Wizard of Oz* (MGM, 1939), *Babes in Arms* (MGM, 1939), *Strike Up the Band* (MGM, 1940), *Little Nellie Kelly* (MGM, 1940), *Andy Hardy Meets Debutante* (MGM, 1940), *Ziegfeld Girl* (MGM, 1941), *Life Begins for Andy Hardy* (MGM, 1941), *Babes on Broadway* (MGM, 1941), *For Me and My Gal* (MGM, 1942), *Presenting Lily Mars* (MGM, 1943), *Girl Crazy* (MGM, 1943), *Thousands Cheer* (MGM, 1943), *Meet Me in St. Louis* (MGM, 1944), *The Clock* (MGM, 1945), *The Harvey Girls* (MGM, 1946), *Ziegfeld Follies* (MGM, 1946), *Till the Clouds Roll By* (MGM, 1946), *The Pirate* (MGM, 1948), *Easter Parade* (MGM, 1948), *Words and Music* (MGM, 1948), *In the Good Old Summertime* (MGM, 1949), *Summer Stock* (MGM, 1950), *A Star Is Born* (WB, 1954), *Pepe* (voice only; Col., 1960), *Judgment at Nuremberg* (UA, 1961), *Gay Purr-ee* (voice only; WB, 1962), *A Child Is Waiting* (UA, 1963), *I Could Go On Singing* (UA, 1963).

JAMES GARNER (James Baumgarner) Born April 7, 1928, Norman, Oklahoma. Married Lois Clarke (1956), children: Kimberly, Greta.

Andra Martin and James Garner in *Up Periscope*.

Feature Films: *Toward the Unknown* (WB, 1956), *The Girl He Left Behind* (WB, 1956), *Shoot-Out at Medicine Bend* (WB, 1957), *Sayonara* (WB, 1957), *Darby's Rangers* (WB, 1958), *Up Periscope* (WB, 1959),

Cash McCall (WB, 1959), *The Children's Hour* (UA, 1962), *Boys' Night Out* (MGM, 1962), *The Great Escape* (UA, 1963), *The Thrill of It All* (Univ., 1963), *The Wheeler Dealers* (MGM, 1963), *Move Over, Darling* (20th, 1963), *The Americanization of Emily* (MGM, 1964), *36 Hours* (MGM, 1964), *The Art of Love* (Univ., 1965), *Duel at Diablo* (UA, 1966), *A Man Could Get Killed* (Univ., 1966), *Mister Buddwing* (MGM, 1966), *Grand Prix* (MGM, 1966), *Hour of the Guns* (UA, 1967), *The Jolly Pink Jungle* (Univ., 1968), *How Sweet It Is* (National General, 1968).

PEGGY ANN GARNER Born February 3, 1931, Canton, Ohio. Married Richard Hayes (1951); divorced 1953. Married Albert Salmi (1956), child: Catherine; divorced 1963. Married Kenyon Brown (1964).

Peggy Ann Garner and Lon McCallister in *The Big Cat*.

Feature Films: *Little Miss Thoroughbred* (WB, 1938), *Blondie Brings Up Baby* (Col., 1939), *In Name Only* (RKO, 1939), *Abe Lincoln in Illinois* (RKO, 1940), *The Pied Piper* (20th, 1942), *Eagle Squadron* (Univ., 1942), *Jane Eyre* (20th, 1944), *A Tree Grows in Brooklyn* (20th, 1945), *Keys of the Kingdom* (20th, 1945), *Nob Hill* (20th, 1945), *Junior Miss* (20th, 1945), *Home Sweet Homicide* (20th, 1946), *Daisy Kenyon* (20th, 1947), *Thunder in the Valley* (20th, 1947), *The Sign of the Ram* (Col., 1948), *The Lovable Cheat* (Film Classics, 1949), *Bomba, the Jungle Boy* (Mon., 1949), *The Big Cat* (EL, 1949), *Teresa* (MGM, 1951), *Black Widow* (20th, 1954), *Eight Witnesses* (Vitapix, 1954), *The Black Forest* (Vitapix, 1954), *The Cat* (Embassy, 1967).

BETTY GARRETT Born May 23, 1919, St. Joseph, Missouri. Married Larry Parks (1944), children: Andrew, Gary.

Jack Lemmon and Betty Garrett in *My Sister Eileen*.

Feature Films: *Big City* (MGM, 1948), *Words and Music* (MGM, 1948), *Take Me Out to the Ball Game* (MGM, 1949), *Neptune's Daughter* (MGM, 1949), *On the Town* (MGM, 1949), *My Sister Eileen* (Col., 1955), *The Shadow on the Window* (Col., 1957).

GREER GARSON Born September 29, 1908, County Down, Ireland. Married Edwin Snelson (1933); divorced 1937. Married Richard Ney (1943); divorced 1947. Married Elijah (Buddy) Fogelson (1949).

Greer Garson and Richard Hart in *Desire Me*.

Feature Films: *Goodbye, Mr. Chips* (MGM, 1939), *Remember?* (MGM, 1939), *Pride and Prejudice* (MGM, 1940), *Blossoms in the Dust* (MGM, 1941), *When Ladies Meet* (MGM, 1941), *Mrs. Miniver* (MGM, 1942), *Random Harvest* (MGM, 1942), *The Youngest Profession* (MGM, 1943), *Madame Curie* (MGM, 1943), *Mrs. Parkington* (MGM, 1944), *Valley of Decision* (MGM, 1945), *Adventure* (MGM, 1945), *Desire Me* (MGM, 1947), *Julia Misbehaves* (MGM, 1948), *That Forsyte Woman* (MGM, 1949), *The Miniver Story* (MGM, 1950), *The Law and the Lady* (MGM, 1951), *Julius Caesar* (MGM, 1953), *Scandal at Scourie* (MGM, 1953), *Her Twelve Men* (MGM, 1954), *Strange Lady in Town* (WB, 1955), *Pepe* (Col., 1960), *Sunrise at Campobello* (WB, 1960), *The Singing Nun* (MGM, 1966), *The Happiest Millionaire* (BV, 1967).

JANET GAYNOR (Laura Gainor) Born October 6, 1906, Philadelphia, Pennsylvania. Married Lydell Peck (1929); divorced 1934. Married Gilbert Adrian (1939), child: Robin; widowed 1959. Married Paul Gregory (1964).

Henry Fonda and Janet Gaynor in *Way Down East*.

Sound Feature Films: *Sunny Side Up* (Fox, 1929), *Happy Days* (Fox, 1930), *High Society Blues* (Fox, 1930), *The Man Who Came Back* (Fox, 1930), *Daddy Long Legs* (Fox, 1931), *Merely Mary Ann* (Fox, 1931), *Delicious* (Fox, 1931), *The First Year* (Fox, 1932), *Tess of the Storm Country* (Fox, 1932), *State Fair* (Fox, 1933), *Adorable* (Fox, 1933), *Paddy The Next Best Thing* (Fox, 1933), *Carolina* (Fox, 1934), *Change of Heart* (Fox, 1934), *Servants' Entrance* (Fox, 1934), *One More Spring* (Fox, 1935), *The Farmer Takes a Wife* (Fox, 1935), *Small Town Girl* (MGM, 1936), *Ladies in Love* (20th, 1936), *A Star Is Born* (UA, 1937), *Three Loves Has Nancy* (MGM, 1938), *The Young in Heart* (UA, 1938), *Bernardine* (20th, 1957).

MITZI GAYNOR (Francesca Mitzi Gerber) Born September 4, 1930, Chicago, Illinois. Married Jack Bean (1954).

Mitzi Gaynor and Kirk Douglas in *For Love or Money*.

Feature Films: *My Blue Heaven* (20th, 1950), *Take Care of My Little Girl* (20th, 1951), *Golden Girl* (20th, 1951), *We're Not Married* (20th, 1952), *Bloodhounds of Broadway* (20th, 1952), *The I Don't Care Girl* (20th, 1953), *Down Among the Sheltering Palms* (20th, 1953), *Three Young Texans* (20th, 1954), *There's No Business Like Show Business* (20th, 1954), *Anything Goes* (Par., 1956), *The Birds and the Bees* (Par., 1956), *The Joker Is Wild* (Par., 1957), *Les Girls* (MGM, 1957), *South Pacific* (20th, 1958), *Happy Anniversary* (UA, 1959), *Surprise Package* (Col., 1960), *For Love or Money* (Univ., 1963).

GLADYS GEORGE (Gladys Anna Clare) Born September 13, 1900, Patten, Maine. Married Arthur Erway; divorced 1930. Married Edward Fowler (1933); divorced 1935. Married Leonard Penn (1935); divorced 1944. Married Kenneth Bradley (1946); divorced 1950. Died December 8, 1954.

Sound Feature Films: *Straight Is the Way* (MGM, 1934), *Valiant Is the*

Gladys George and Robert C. Fischer in *The Way of All Flesh*.

Word for Carrie (Par., 1936), *Madame X* (MGM, 1937), *They Gave Him a Gun* (MGM, 1937), *Love Is a Headache* (MGM, 1938), *Marie Antoinette* (MGM, 1938), *I'm From Missouri* (Par., 1939), *Here I Am a Stranger* (20th, 1939), *The Roaring Twenties* (WB, 1939), *A Child Is Born* (WB, 1940), *The House Across the Bay* (UA, 1940), *The Way of All Flesh* (Par., 1940), *Hit the Road* (Univ., 1941), *The Lady From Cheyenne* (Univ., 1941), *The Maltese Falcon* (WB, 1941), *The Hard Way* (WB, 1942), *Nobody's Darling* (Rep., 1943), *The Crystal Ball* (UA, 1943), *Christmas Holiday* (Univ., 1944), *Minstrel Man* (PRC, 1944), *Steppin' in Society* (Rep., 1945), *The Best Years of Our Lives* (RKO, 1946), *Millie's Daughter* (Col., 1947), *Alias a Gentleman* (MGM, 1948), *Flamingo Road* (WB, 1949), *Bright Leaf* (WB, 1950), *Undercover Girl* (Univ., 1950), *Lullaby of Broadway* (WB, 1951), *He Ran All the Way* (UA, 1951), *Silver City* (Par., 1951), *Detective Story* (Par., 1951), *It Happens Every Thursday* (Univ., 1953).

CONNIE GILCHRIST Born July 29, 1901, Brooklyn, New York. Married Edwin O'Hanlon (1928), child: Dorothy.

Connie Gilchrist and Leo Gorcey in *Sunday Punch*.

Feature Films: *Hullabaloo* (MGM, 1940), *Down in San Diego* (MGM, 1941), *Billy the Kid* (MGM, 1941), *Dr. Kildare's Wedding Day* (MGM, 1941), *The Wild Man of Borneo* (MGM, 1941), *A Woman's Face* (MGM, 1941), *H. M. Pulham, Esq.* (MGM, 1941), *Barnacle Bill* (MGM, 1941), *Johnny Eager* (MGM, 1941), *Whistling in the Dark* (MGM, 1941), *Two-Faced Woman* (MGM, 1941), *Married Bachelor* (MGM, 1941), *This Time for Keeps* (MGM, 1942), *Sunday Punch* (MGM, 1942), *Tortilla Flat* (MGM, 1942), *Grand Central Murder* (MGM, 1942), *Apache Trail* (MGM, 1942), *The War Against Mrs. Hadley* (MGM, 1942), *Thousands Cheer* (MGM, 1943), *Presenting Lily Mars* (MGM, 1943), *Swing Shift Maisie* (MGM, 1943), *Cry Havoc* (MGM, 1943), *The Heavenly Body* (MGM, 1943), *The Human Comedy* (MGM, 1943), *Rationing* (MGM, 1944), *See Here, Private Hargrove* (MGM, 1944), *Nothing But Trouble* (MGM, 1944), *Music for Millions* (MGM, 1944), *The Seventh Cross* (MGM, 1944), *The Thin Man Goes Home* (MGM, 1944), *Valley of Decision* (MGM, 1945), *Junior Miss* (20th, 1945), *Cloak and Dagger* (WB, 1946), *Bad Bascomb* (MGM, 1946), *Faithful in My Fashion* (MGM, 1946), *The Hucksters* (MGM, 1947), *Song of the Thin Man* (MGM, 1947), *Good News* (MGM, 1947), *Tenth Avenue Angel* (MGM, 1948), *The Big City* (MGM, 1948), *Luxury Liner* (MGM, 1948), *Act of Violence* (MGM, 1948), *A Letter to Three Wives* (20th, 1948), *Chicken Every Sunday* (20th, 1948), *Little Women* (MGM, 1949), *The Story of Molly X* (Univ., 1949), *Stars in My Crown* (MGM, 1950), *Buccaneer's Girl* (Univ., 1950), *A Ticket to Tomahawk* (20th, 1950), *Louisa* (Univ., 1950), *Peggy* (Univ., 1950), *Undercover Girl* (Univ., 1950), *Tripoli* (Par., 1950), *The Killer That Stalked New York* (Col., 1950), *Here Comes the Groom* (Par., 1951), *Thunder on the Hill* (Univ., 1951), *Chain of Circumstance* (Col., 1951), *One Big Affair* (UA, 1952), *The Half-Breed* (RKO, 1952), *Flesh and Fury* (Univ.,

1952), *Houdini* (Par., 1953), *The Great Diamond Robbery* (MGM, 1953), *It Should Happen to You* (Col., 1954), *Long John Silver* (DCA, 1955), *The Man in the Gray Flannel Suit* (20th, 1956), *Machine Gun Kelly* (AIP, 1958), *Auntie Mame* (WB, 1958), *Some Came Running* (MGM, 1958), *Say One for Me* (20th, 1959), *The Interns* (Col., 1962), *Swingin' Along* (20th, 1962), *A Tiger Walks* (BV, 1964), *The Misadventures of Merlin Jones* (BV, 1964), *A House Is Not a Home* (Embassy, 1964), *Two on a Guillotine* (WB, 1965), *Sylvia* (Par., 1965), *Fluffy* (Univ., 1965), *Tickle Me* (AA, 1965), *The Monkey's Uncle* (BV, 1965).

LILLIAN GISH (Lillian Diana Gish) Born October 14, 1896, Springfield, Ohio.

Lauren Bacall and Lillian Gish in *The Cobweb*.

Sound Feature Films: *One Romantic Night* (UA, 1930), *His Double Life* (Par., 1933), *The Commandos Strike at Dawn* (Col., 1942), *Top Man* (Univ., 1943), *Miss Susie Slagle's* (Par., 1945), *Duel in the Sun* (Selznick, 1946), *Portrait of Jennie* (Selznick, 1948), *The Cobweb* (MGM, 1955), *The Night of the Hunter* (UA, 1955), *Orders to Kill* (United Motion Picture Organization, 1958), *The Unforgiven* (UA, 1960), *Follow Me, Boys* (BV, 1966), *Warning Shot* (Par., 1967), *The Comedians* (MGM, 1967).

JAMES GLEASON Born May 23, 1886, New York, New York. Married Lucille Webster (1905), child: Russell; widowed 1947. Died April 12, 1959.

Feature Films: *The Shannons of Broadway* (Univ., 1929), *The Broadway Melody* (MGM, 1929), *Oh Yeah!* (Pathé, 1930), *Puttin' On the Ritz*

James Gleason, Gertrude Michael and Robert Armstrong in *Search for Beauty*.

(UA, 1930), *Swellhead* (Tif., 1930), *Dumbbells in Ermine* (WB, 1930), *Matrimonial Bed* (WB, 1930), *Her Man* (Pathé, 1930), *Big Money* (Pathé, 1930), *It's a Wise Child* (MGM, 1931), *Beyond Victory* (Pathé, 1931), *A Free Soul* (MGM, 1931), *Sweepstakes* (RKO, 1931), *Big Gamble* (Pathé, 1931), *Suicide Fleet* (Pathé, 1931), *Information Kid* (Univ., 1932), *Blondie of the Follies* (MGM, 1932), *Lady and Gent* (Par., 1932), *The Crooked Circle* (Sono Art-World Wide, 1932), *The Penguin Pool Murder* (RKO, 1932), *The All American* (Univ., 1932), *The Devil Is Driving* (Par., 1932), *Fast Companions* (Univ., 1932), *Orders Is Orders* (Gaumont-British, 1933), *Billion Dollar Scandal* (Par., 1933), *Clear All Wires* (MGM, 1933), *Hoopla* (Fox, 1933), *Search for Beauty* (Par., 1934), *Meanest Gal in Town* (RKO, 1934), *Murder on the Blackboard* (RKO, 1934), *West Point of the Air* (MGM, 1935), *Helldorado* (Fox, 1935), *Murder on a Honeymoon* (RKO, 1935), *Hot Tip* (RKO, 1935), *We're Only Human* (RKO, 1936), *The Ex-Mrs. Bradford* (RKO, 1936), *Murder on a Bridal Path* (RKO, 1936), *Yours for the Asking* (Par., 1936), *The Big Game* (RKO, 1936), *Don't Turn 'Em Loose* (RKO, 1936), *The Plot Thickens* (RKO, 1936), *Forty Naughty Girls* (RKO, 1937), *Manhattan Merry-Go-Round* (Rep., 1937), *Army Girl* (Rep., 1938), *The Higgins Family* (Rep., 1938), *My Wife's Relatives* (Rep., 1939), *On Your Toes* (WB, 1939), *Should Husbands Work?* (Rep., 1939), *The Covered Trailer* (Rep., 1939), *Money to Burn* (Rep., 1940), *Grandpa Goes to Town* (Rep., 1940), *Earl of Puddlestone* (Rep., 1940), *Meet John Doe* (WB, 1941), *Affectionately Yours* (WB, 1941), *Here Comes Mr. Jordan* (Col., 1941), *Tanks a Million* (UA, 1941), *Nine Lives Are Not Enough* (WB, 1941), *A Date With the Falcon* (RKO, 1941), *Babes on Broadway* (MGM, 1941), *Tramp, Tramp, Tramp* (Col., 1942), *Hay Foot* (UA, 1942), *My Gal Sal* (20th, 1942), *The Falcon Takes Over* (RKO, 1942), *Footlight Serenade* (20th, 1942), *Tales of Manhattan* (20th, 1942), *Manila Calling* (20th, 1942), *Crash Dive* (20th, 1943), *A Guy Named Joe* (MGM, 1943), *Once Upon a Time* (Col., 1944), *Arsenic and Old Lace* (WB, 1944), *A Tree Grows in Brooklyn* (20th, 1945), *This Man's Navy* (MGM, 1945), *Keys of the Kingdom* (20th, 1944), *The Clock* (MGM, 1945), *Captain Eddie* (20th, 1945), *The Hoodlum Saint* (MGM, 1946), *The Well-Groomed Bride* (Par., 1946), *Home Sweet Homicide* (20th, 1946), *Lady Luck* (RKO, 1946), *The Homestretch* (20th, 1947), *Down to Earth* (Col., 1947), *The Bishop's Wife* (RKO, 1947), *Tycoon* (RKO, 1947), *The Dude Goes West* (AA, 1948), *Smart Woman* (AA, 1948), *The Return of October* (Col., 1948), *When My Baby Smiles at Me* (20th, 1948), *The Life of Riley* (Univ., 1949), *Bad Boy* (AA, 1949), *Take One False Step* (Univ., 1949), *Miss Grant Takes Richmond* (Col., 1950), *Riding High* (Par., 1950), *Key to the City* (MGM, 1950), *The Jackpot* (20th, 1950), *Two Gals and a Guy* (UA, 1951), *Come Fill the Cup* (WB, 1951), *I'll See You in My Dreams* (WB, 1951), *Joe Palooka in Triple Cross* (Mon., 1951), *We're Not Married* (20th, 1952), *The Will Rogers Story* (WB, 1952), *What Price Glory* (20th, 1952), *Forever Female* (Par., 1953), *Suddenly* (UA, 1954), *The Night of the Hunter* (UA, 1955), *The Girl Rush* (Par., 1955), *Star in the Dust* (Univ., 1956), *Spring Reunion* (UA, 1957), *Loving You* (Par., 1957), *Man in the Shadow* (Univ., 1957), *The Female Animal* (Univ., 1958), *Man or Gun* (Rep., 1958), *Once Upon a Horse* (Univ., 1958), *Money, Women and Guns* (Univ., 1958), *Rock-a-Bye Baby* (Par., 1958), *The Last Hurrah* (Col., 1958).

PAULETTE GODDARD (Pauline Levy) Born June 3, 1911, Great Neck, New York. Married Edward James (1932); divorced 1932. Married Charles Chaplin (1936); divorced 1942. Married Burgess Meredith (1944); divorced (1950). Married Erich Maria Remarque (1958).

Feature Films: *The Girl Habit* (Par., 1931), *The Mouthpiece* (WB, 1932), *The Kid From Spain* (UA, 1932), *Modern Times* (UA, 1936), *The Young in Heart* (UA, 1938), *Dramatic School* (MGM, 1938), *The Women* (MGM, 1939), *The Cat and the Canary* (Par., 1939), *The Ghost Breakers* (Par., 1940), *The Great Dictator* (UA, 1940), *North West Mounted Police* (Par., 1940), *Second Chorus* (Par., 1940), *Pot o' Gold* (UA, 1941), *Nothing But the Truth* (Par., 1941), *Hold Back the Dawn* (Par., 1941), *The Lady Has Plans* (Par., 1942), *Reap the Wild Wind* (Par., 1942), *The Forest Rangers* (Par., 1942), *Star Spangled Rhythm* (Par., 1942), *The Crystal Ball* (UA, 1943), *So Proudly We Hail!* (Par., 1943), *Standing Room Only* (Par., 1944), *I Love a Soldier* (Par., 1944), *Duffy's Tavern* (Par., 1945), *Kitty* (Par., 1945), *The Diary of a*

Virginia Grey, Paulette Goddard, Lana Turner, Luise Rainer, Dorothy Granger and Ann Rutherford in *Dramatic School.*

Chambermaid (UA, 1946), *Suddenly It's Spring* (Par., 1947), *Variety Girl* (Par., 1947), *Unconquered* (Par., 1947), *An Ideal Husband* (20th, 1948), *On Our Merry Way* (UA, 1948), *Hazard* (Par., 1948), *Bride of Vengence* (Par., 1949), *Anna Lucasta* (Col., 1949), *The Torch* (EL, 1950), *Babes in Bagdad* (UA, 1952), *Vice Squad* (UA, 1953), *Paris Model* (Col., 1953), *Sins of Jezebel* (Lip., 1953), *Charge of the Lancers* (Col., 1954), *The Unholy Four* (Lip., 1954), *Time of Indifference* (Continental, 1966).

BETTY GRABLE (Elizabeth Grable) Born December 18, 1916, St. Louis, Missouri. Married Jackie Coogan (1937); divorced 1940. Married Harry James (1943), children: Victoria, Jessica; divorced 1965.

Betty Grable and Victor Mature in *Song of the Islands.*

Feature Films: *Let's Go Places* (Fox, 1930), *New Movietone Follies of 1930* (Fox, 1930), *Whoopee* (UA, 1930), *Kiki* (UA, 1931), *Palmy Days* (UA, 1931), *The Greeks Had a Word for Them* (UA, 1932), *The Kid From Spain* (UA, 1932), *Child of Manhattan* (Col., 1933), *Probation* (Chesterfield, 1932), *Hold 'Em Jail* (RKO, 1932), *Cavalcade* (Fox, 1933), *What Price Innocence* (Col., 1933), *Student Tour* (MGM, 1934), *The Gay Divorcee* (RKO, 1934), *The Nitwits* (RKO, 1935), *Old Man Rhythm* (RKO, 1935), *Collegiate* (Par., 1935), *Follow the Fleet* (RKO, 1936), *Pigskin Parade* (20th, 1936), *Don't Turn 'Em Loose* (RKO, 1936), *This Way Please* (Par., 1937), *Thrill of a Lifetime* (Par., 1937), *College Swing* (Par., 1938), *Give Me a Sailor* (Par., 1938), *Campus Confessions* (Par., 1938), *Man About Town* (Par., 1939), *Million Dollar*

Legs (Par., 1939), *The Day the Bookies Wept* (RKO, 1939), *Down Argentine Way* (20th, 1940), *Tin Pan Alley* (20th, 1940), *Moon Over Miami* (20th, 1941), *A Yank in the R.A.F.* (20th, 1941), *I Wake Up Screaming* (20th, 1941), *Footlight Serenade* (20th, 1942), *Song of the Islands* (20th, 1942), *Springtime in the Rockies* (20th, 1942), *Coney Island* (20th, 1943), *Sweet Rosie O'Grady* (20th, 1943), *Four Jills in a Jeep* (20th, 1944), *Pin-Up Girl* (20th, 1944), *Billy Rose's Diamond Horseshoe* (20th, 1945), *The Dolly Sisters* (20th, 1945), *Do You Love Me?* (20th, 1946),* *The Shocking Miss Pilgrim* (20th, 1947), *Mother Wore Tights* (20th, 1947), *That Lady in Ermine* (20th, 1948), *When My Baby Smiles at Me* (20th, 1948), *The Beautiful Blonde From Bashful Bend* (20th, 1949), *Wabash Avenue* (20th, 1950), *My Blue Heaven* (20th, 1950), *Call Me Mister* (20th, 1951), *Meet Me After the Show* (20th, 1951), *The Farmer Takes a Wife* (20th, 1953), *How To Marry a Millionaire* (20th, 1953), *Three for the Show* (Col., 1955), *How to Be Very, Very Popular* (20th, 1955).

*Unbilled guest appearance

GLORIA GRAHAME (Gloria Grahame Hallward) Born November 28, 1925, Los Angeles, California. Married Stanley Clements (1945); divorced 1948. Married Nicholas Ray (1948), child: Timothy; divorced 1952. Married Cy Howard (1954), child: Mariana; divorced 1957. Married Tony Ray (1961).

Humphrey Bogart and Gloria Grahame in *In a Lonely Place*.

Feature Films: *Blonde Fever* (MGM, 1944), *Without Love* (MGM, 1945), *It's a Wonderful Life* (RKO, 1946), *It Happened in Brooklyn* (MGM, 1947), *Merton of the Movies* (MGM, 1947), *Crossfire* (RKO, 1947), *Song of the Thin Man* (MGM, 1947), *A Woman's Secret* (RKO 1949), *Roughshod* (RKO, 1949), *In a Lonely Place* (Col., 1950), *Macao* (RKO, 1952), *The Greatest Show on Earth* (Par., 1952), *Sudden Fear* (RKO, 1952), *The Bad and the Beautiful* (MGM, 1952), *The Glass Wall* (Col., 1953), *Man on a Tightrope* (20th, 1953), *The Big Heat* (Col., 1953), *Prisoners of the Casbah* (Col., 1953), *Human Desire* (Col., 1954), *Naked Alibi* (Univ., 1954), *The Good Die Young* (UA, 1955), *Not as a Stranger* (UA, 1955), *The Cobweb* (MGM, 1955), *Oklahoma!* (Magna, 1955), *The Man Who Never Was* (20th, 1956), *Ride Out for Revenge* (UA, 1958), *Odds Against Tomorrow* (UA, 1959), *Ride Beyond Vengence* (Col., 1966).

FARLEY GRANGER (Farley Earle Granger) Born July 1, 1925, San Jose, California.

English-Language Feature Films: *The North Star* (RKO, 1943), *The Purple Heart* (20th, 1944), *They Live by Night* (RKO, 1948), *Rope* (WB, 1948), *Enchantment* (RKO, 1948), *Side Street* (MGM, 1949), *Edge of Doom* (RKO, 1950), *Our Very Own* (RKO, 1950), *Strangers on a Train* (WB, 1951), *I Want You* (RKO, 1951), *Behave Yourself* (RKO, 1951), *O. Henry's Full House* (20th, 1952), *Hans Christian Andersen*

Farley Granger and Evelyn Keyes in *Enchantment*.

(RKO, 1952), *The Story of Three Loves* (MGM, 1953), *Small Town Girl* (MGM, 1953), *The Naked Street* (UA, 1955), *The Girl in the Red Velvet Swing* (20th, 1955), *Rogue's Gallery* (Par., 1968).

STEWART GRANGER (James Stewart) Born May 6, 1913, London, England. Married Elspeth March, children: Jamie, Lindsay; divorced 1950. Married Jean Simmons (1950), child: Tracey; divorced 1960. Married Caroline Lecerf (1964).

Jean Simmons and Stewart Granger in *Young Bess*.

English-Language Feature Films: *So This Is London* (20th, 1940), *Convoy* (Ealing, 1940), *Secret Mission* (Hellman, 1941), *Thursday's Child* (Associated British, 1943), *The Lamp Still Burns* (Two Cities, 1943), *The Man in Grey* (Gainsborough, 1943) *Fanny by Gaslight* (Gainsborough, 1944), *Love Story* (Gainsborough, 1944), *Waterloo Road* (Gainsborough, 1945), *Madonna of the Seven Moons* (Rank, 1945), *Caesar and Cleopatra* (UA, 1946), *Caravan* (Gainsborough, 1946), *Magic Bow* (Gainsborough, 1946), *Captain Boycott* (Individual, 1947), *Blanche Fury* (Cineguild, 1947), *Precious Bane* (Soskind, 1947), *Saraband for Dead Lovers* (Ealing, 1948), *Woman Hater* (Rank, 1949), *Adam and Evalyn* (Two Cities, 1950), *King Solomon's Mines* (MGM, 1950), *Soldiers Three* (MGM, 1951), *The Light Touch* (MGM, 1951), *Wild North* (MGM, 1952), *Scaramouche* (MGM, 1952), *The Prisoner of Zenda* (MGM, 1952), *Salome* (Col., 1953), *Young Bess* (MGM, 1953), *All the Brothers Were Valiant* (MGM, 1953), *Beau Brummel* (MGM, 1954), *Green Fire* (MGM, 1954), *Moonfleet* (MGM, 1955), *Footsteps in the Fog* (Col., 1955), *Bhowani Junction* (MGM, 1956), *The Last Hunt* (MGM, 1956), *The Little Hut* (MGM, 1957), *Gun Glory* (MGM, 1957), *North to Alaska* (20th, 1960), *The Secret Partner*

(MGM,, 1961), *Swordsman of Siena* (MGM, 1963), *Sodom and Gomorrah* (20th, 1963), *The Secret Invasion* (UA, 1964), *Commando* (AIP, 1964), *Crooked Road* (7 Arts, 1965), *Mission to Hong Kong* (Woolner, 1967), *The Last Safari* (Par., 1967), *Red Dragon* (Woolner, 1967), *The Trygon Factor* (7 Arts, 1967), *The Flaming Frontier* (WB-7 Arts, 1968).

CARY GRANT (Alexander Archibald Leach) Born January 18, 1904, Bristol, England. Married Virginia Cherrill (1933); divorced 1935. Married Barbara Hutton (1942); divorced (1945). Married Betsy Drake (1949); divorced. Married Dyan Cannon (1965), child: Jennifer; divorced 1968.

Sig Rumann, Allyn Joslyn, Jean Arthur, Noah Beery, Jr., and Cary Grant in *Only Angels Have Wings*.

Feature Films: *This Is the Night* (Par., 1932), *Sinners in the Sun* (Par., 1932), *Merrily We Go to Hell* (Par., 1932), *Devil and the Deep* (Par., 1932), *Blonde Venus* (Par., 1932), *Hot Saturday* (Par., 1932), *Madame Butterfly* (Par., 1932), *She Done Him Wrong* (Par., 1933), *Woman Accused* (Par., 1933), *The Eagle and the Hawk* (Par., 1933), *Gambling Ship* (Par., 1933), *I'm No Angel* (Par., 1933), *Alice in Wonderland* (Par., 1933), *Thirty-Day Princess* (Par., 1934), *Born to Be Bad* (UA, 1934), *Kiss and Make Up* (Par., 1934), *Ladies Should Listen* (Par., 1934), *Enter Madame* (Par., 1934), *Wings in the Dark* (Par., 1935), *Last Outpost* (Par., 1935), *Sylvia Scarlett* (RKO, 1935), *Big Brown Eyes* (Par., 1936), *Suzy* (MGM, 1936), *Wedding Present* (Par., 1936), *Amazing Quest* (GN, 1936), *When You're in Love* (Col., 1937), *Toast of New York* (RKO, 1937), *Topper* (MGM, 1937), *The Awful Truth* (Col., 1937), *Bringing Up Baby* (RKO, 1938), *Holiday* (Col., 1938), *Gunga Din* (RKO, 1939), *Only Angels Have Wings* (Col., 1939), *In Name Only* (RKO, 1939), *His Girl Friday* (Col., 1940), *My Favorite Wife* (RKO, 1940), *The Howards of Virginia* (Col., 1940), *The Philadelphia Story* (MGM, 1940), *Penny Serenade* (Col., 1941), *Suspicion* (RKO, 1941), *Talk of the Town* (Col., 1942), *Once Upon a Honeymoon* (RKO, 1942), *Mr. Lucky* (RKO, 1943), *Destination Tokyo* (WB, 1943), *Once Upon a Time* (Col., 1944), *Arsenic and Old Lace* (WB, 1944) *None But the Lonely Heart* (RKO, 1944), *Night and Day* (WB, 1946), *Without Reservations* (RKO, 1946),* *Notorious* (RKO, 1946), *The Bachelor and the Bobby-Soxer* (RKO, 1947), *The Bishop's Wife* (RKO, 1947), *Mr. Blandings Builds His Dream House* (RKO, 1948), *Every Girl Should Be Married* (RKO, 1948), *I Was a Male War Bride* (20th, 1949), *Crisis* (MGM, 1950), *People Will Talk* (20th, 1951), *Room for One More* (WB, 1952), *Monkey Business* (20th, 1952), *Dream Wife* (MGM, 1953), *To Catch a Thief* (Par., 1955), *The Pride and the Passion* (UA, 1957), *An Affair to Remember* (20th, 1957), *Kiss Them for Me* (20th, 1957), *Indiscreet* (WB, 1958), *Houseboat* (Par., 1958), *North by Northwest* (MGM, 1959), *Operation Petticoat* (Univ., 1959), *The Grass Is Greener* (Univ., 1960), *That Touch of Mink* (Univ., 1962), *Charade* (Univ., 1963), *Father Goose* (Univ., 1964), *Walk, Don't Run* (Col., 1966).

*Unbilled guest appearance

Kay Johnson, Claude Rains and Bonita Granville in *White Banners*.

BONITA GRANVILLE Born February 2, 1923, New York, New York. Married Jack Wrather (1947), children: Molly, Jack, Linda, Christopher.

Feature Films: *Westward Passage* (RKO, 1932), *Silver Dollar* (WB, 1932), *Cavalcade* (Fox, 1933), *Cradle Song* (Par., 1933), *Life of Virgie Winters* (RKO, 1934), *A Wicked Woman* (MGM, 1934), *Ah, Wilderness* (MGM, 1935), *These Three* (UA, 1936), *Song of the Saddle* (WB, 1936), *The Plough and the Stars* (RKO, 1936), *The Garden of Allah* (UA, 1936), *Maid of Salem* (Par., 1937), *Call It a Day* (WB, 1937), *Quality Street* (RKO, 1937), *The Life of Emile Zola* (WB, 1937), *It's Love I'm After* (WB, 1937), *Merrily We Live* (MGM, 1938), *Beloved Brat* (WB, 1938), *White Banners* (WB, 1938), *My Bill* (WB, 1938), *Hard to Get* (WB, 1938), *Nancy Drew, Detective* (WB, 1938), *Angels Wash Their Faces* (WB, 1939), *Nancy Drew, Reporter* (WB, 1939), *Nancy Drew, Troubleshooter* (WB, 1939), *Nancy Drew and the Hidden Staircase* (WB, 1939), *Forty Little Mothers* (MGM, 1940), *Those Were the Days* (Par., 1940), *The Mortal Storm* (MGM, 1940), *Third Finger, Left Hand* (MGM, 1940), *Escape* (MGM, 1940), *Gallant Sons* (MGM, 1940), *The People vs. Dr. Kildare* (MGM, 1941), *Wild Man of Borneo* (MGM, 1941), *Down in San Diego* (MGM, 1941), *H. M. Pulham, Esq.* (MGM, 1941), *Syncopation* (RKO, 1942), *The Glass Key* (Par., 1942), *Now, Voyager* (WB, 1942), *Seven Miles From Alcatraz* (RKO, 1943), *Hitler's Children* (RKO, 1943), *Song of the Open Road* (UA, 1944), *Andy Hardy's Blonde Trouble* (MGM, 1944), *Youth Runs Wild* (RKO, 1944), *The Beautiful Cheat* (Univ., 1945), *Senorita From the West* (Univ., 1945), *The Truth About Murder* (RKO, 1946), *Breakfast in Hollywood* (UA, 1946), *Suspense* (Mon., 1946), *Love Laughs at Andy Hardy* (MGM, 1946), *The Guilty* (Mon., 1947), *Strike It Rich* (AA, 1948), *Guilty of Treason* (EL, 1950), *The Lone Ranger* (WB, 1956).

KATHRYN GRAYSON (Zelma Kathryn Hedrick) Born February 9, 1922, Winston Salem, North Carolina. Married John Shelton (1940); divorced 1946. Married Johnny Johnston (1947), child: Patricia; divorced 1951.

Kathryn Grayson and Theresa Harris in *Grounds for Marriage*.

79

Feature Films: *Andy Hardy's Private Secretary* (MGM, 1941), *The Vanishing Virginian* (MGM, 1941), *Rio Rita* (MGM, 1942), *Seven Sweethearts* (MGM, 1942), *Thousands Cheer* (MGM, 1943), *Anchors Aweigh* (MGM, 1945), *Two Sisters From Boston* (MGM, 1946), *Ziegfeld Follies of 1946* (MGM, 1946), *Till the Clouds Roll By* (MGM, 1946), *It Happened in Brooklyn* (MGM, 1947), *The Kissing Bandit* (MGM, 1948), *That Midnight Kiss* (MGM, 1949), *Toast of New Orleans* (MGM, 1950), *Grounds for Marriage* (MGM, 1950), *Show Boat* (MGM, 1951), *Lovely to Look At* (MGM, 1952), *The Desert Song* (WB, 1953), *So This Is Love* (WB, 1953), *Kiss Me, Kate!* (MGM, 1953), *The Vagabond King* (Par., 1956).

CHARLOTTE GREENWOOD (Frances Charlotte Greenwood) Born June 25, 1893, Philadelphia, Pennsylvania. Married Martin Broones (1924).

Harry Stubbs (with girl on back), Charlotte Greenwood, Reginald Denny and Leila Hyams in *Stepping Out*.

Sound Feature Films: *Baby Mine* (MGM, 1928), *So Long, Letty* (WB, 1929), *Parlor, Bedroom and Bath* (MGM, 1931), *Stepping Out* (MGM, 1931), *The Man in Possession* (MGM, 1931), *Palmy Days* (UA, 1931), *Flying High* (MGM, 1931), *Cheaters at Play* (Fox, 1932), *Orders Is Orders* (Gaumont-British, 1933), *Star Dust* (20th, 1940), *Young People* (20th, 1940), *Down Argentine Way* (20th, 1940), *Tall, Dark and Handsome* (20th, 1941), *Moon Over Miami* (20th, 1941), *The Perfect Snob* (20th, 1941), *Springtime in the Rockies* (20th, 1942), *Dixie Dugan* (20th, 1943), *The Gang's All Here* (20th, 1943), *Up in Mabel's Room* (UA, 1944), *Home in Indiana* (20th, 1944), *Wake Up and Dream* (20th, 1946), *Driftwood* (Rep., 1947), *The Great Dan Patch* (UA, 1949), *Oh, You Beautiful Doll* (20th, 1949), *Peggy* (Univ., 1950), *Dangerous When Wet* (MGM, 1953), *Oklahoma!* (Magna, 1955), *Glory* (RKO, 1956), *The Opposite Sex* (MGM, 1956).

JANE GREER (Bettyjane Greer) Born September 9, 1924, Washington, D.C. Married Rudy Vallee (1943); divorced 1945. Married Edward Lasker (1947), children: Albert, Lawrence, Stephen.

Feature Films:
    as Bettejane Greer *Pan Americana* (RKO, 1945), *Two O'Clock Courage* (RKO, 1945), *George White's Scandals* (RKO, 1945).
    as Jane Greer *Dick Tracy* (RKO, 1945), *The Falcon's Alibi* (RKO, 1946), *The Bamboo Blonde* (RKO, 1946), *Sunset Pass* (RKO, 1946), *Sinbad the Sailor* (RKO, 1947), *They Won't Believe Me* (RKO, 1947), *Out of the Past* (RKO, 1947), *Station West* (RKO, 1948), *The Big Steal* (RKO, 1949), *You're in the Navy Now* (20th, 1951), *The Company She Keeps* (RKO, 1951), *The Prisoner of Zenda* (MGM, 1952), *Desperate Search* (MGM, 1952), *You for Me* (MGM, 1952), *The Clown* (MGM, 1953), *Down Among the Sheltering Palms* (20th, 1953), *Run*

Jane Greer and Robert Young in *They Won't Believe Me.*

for the Sun (UA, 1956), *Man of a Thousand Faces* (Univ., 1957), *Where Love Has Gone* (Par., 1964), *Billie* (UA, 1965).

VIRGINIA GREY Born March 22, 1917, Los Angeles, California.

Sound Feature Films: *Misbehaving Ladies* (WB, 1931), *Secrets* (UA, 1933), *The St. Louis Kid* (WB, 1934), *Dames* (WB, 1934), *The Firebird* (WB, 1934), *She Gets Her Man* (Univ., 1935), *Gold Diggers of 1935* (WB, 1935), *Old Hutch* (MGM, 1936), *Secret Alley* (20th, 1936), *The Great Ziegfeld* (MGM, 1936), *Bad Guy* (MGM, 1937), *Rosalie* (MGM, 1937), *Test Pilot* (MGM, 1938), *Rich Man, Poor Girl* (MGM, 1938), *Ladies in Distress* (Rep., 1938), *Youth Takes a Fling* (Univ., 1938), *Dramatic School* (MGM, 1938), *Shopworn Angel* (MGM, 1938), *Idiot's Delight* (MGM, 1939), *Broadway Serenade* (MGM, 1939), *The Hardys Ride High* (MGM, 1939), *Thunder Afloat* (MGM, 1939), *Another Thin Man* (MGM, 1939), *The Women* (MGM, 1939), *Three Cheers for the Irish* (WB, 1940), *The Captain Is a Lady* (MGM, 1940), *Hullabaloo* (MGM, 1940), *The Golden Fleecing* (MGM, 1940), *Keeping Company* (MGM, 1941), *Blonde Inspiration* (MGM, 1941), *Washington Melodrama* (MGM, 1941), *The Big Store* (MGM, 1941), *Whistling in the Dark* (MGM, 1941), *Mr. and Mrs. North* (MGM, 1941), *Tarzan's New York Adventure* (MGM, 1942), *Grand Central Murder* (MGM, 1942), *Tish* (MGM, 1942), *Bells of Capistrano* (Rep., 1942), *Secrets of the Underground* (Rep., 1943), *Idaho* (Rep., 1943), *Stage Door Canteen* (UA, 1943), *Sweet Rosie O'Grady* (20th, 1943), *Strangers in the Night* (Rep., 1944), *Grissly's Millions* (Rep., 1945), *Flame of Barbary Coast*

Frank Morgan, Donald Meek, Dan Dailey and Virginia Grey in *Hullabaloo.*

(Rep., 1945), *Blonde Ransom* (Univ., 1945), *The Men in Her Diary* (Univ., 1945), *Smooth as Silk* (Univ., 1946), *Swamp Fire* (Par., 1946), *House of Horrors* (Univ., 1946), *Wyoming* (Rep., 1947), *Unconquered* (Par., 1947), *Who Killed "Doc" Robbin?* (UA, 1948), *Glamour Girl* (Col., 1948), *So This Is New York* (UA, 1948), *Unknown Island* (Film Classics, 1948), *Miraculous Journey* (Film Classics, 1948), *Mexican Hayride* (Univ., 1948), *When My Baby Smiles at Me* (20th, 1948), *Leather Gloves* (Col., 1948), *Jungle Jim* (Col., 1949), *The Threat* (RKO, 1949), *Highway 301* (WB, 1950), *The Bullfighter and the Lady* (Rep., 1951), *Three Desperate Men* (Lip., 1951), *Slaughter Trail* (RKO, 1951), *Desert Pursuit* (Mon., 1952), *The Fighting Lawman* (AA, 1953), *A Perilous Journey* (Rep., 1953), *Captain Scarface* (Astor, 1953), *Hurricane at Pilgrim Hill* (Howco, 1953), *The Forty-Niners* (AA, 1954), *Target Earth* (AA, 1954), *The Eternal Sea* (Rep., 1955), *The Last Command* (Rep., 1955), *All That Heaven Allows* (Univ., 1955), *The Rose Tattoo* (Par., 1955), *Accused of Murder* (Rep., 1956), *Crime of Passion* (UA, 1957), *Jeanne Eagles* (Col., 1957), *The Restless Years* (Univ., 1958), *No Name on the Bullet* (Univ., 1959), *Portrait in Black* (Univ., 1960), *Tammy, Tell Me True* (Univ., 1961), *Flower Drum Song* (Univ., 1961), *Back Street* (Univ., 1961), *Bachelor in Paradise* (MGM, 1961), *Black Zoo* (AA, 1963), *The Naked Kiss* (AA, 1964), *Love Has Many Faces* (Col., 1965), *Madame X* (Univ., 1966), *Rosie!* (Univ., 1968).

EDMUND GWENN Born September 26, 1875, Glamorgan, Wales. Married Minnie Terry (1901). Died September 6, 1959.

Patricia Neal and Edmund Gwenn in *Something for the Birds.*

English-Language Sound Feature Films: *How He Lied to Her Husband* (British International, 1931), *Money for Nothing* (British International, 1932), *Condemned to Death* (Timely, 1931), *Frail Women* (British, 1931), *Hindle Wakes* (Gaumont-British, 1931), *Tell Me Tonight* (Gaumont-UFA, 1932), *The Admiral's Secret* (British, 1932), *Love on Wheels* (Gaumont-British, 1932), *The Skin Game* (Powers, 1932), *The Good Companions* (Gaumont-British, 1933), *I Was a Spy* (Gaumont-British, 1933), *Early to Bed* (Gaumont-British, 1933), *Cash* (Par., 1933), *Friday the 13th* (Gaumont-British, 1933), *Marooned* (Fox, 1933), *Java Head* (Associated British, 1934), *Spring in the Air* (Pathé, 1934), *Channel Crossing* (Gaumont-British, 1934), *Passing Shadows* (Fox, 1934), *Waltzes From Vienna* ("Strauss' Great Waltz"—Arnold, 1934), *Father and Son* (British, 1934), *Warn London* (British Lion, 1934), *The Bishop Misbehaves* (MGM, 1935), *Sylvia Scarlett* (RKO, 1935), *The Walking Dead* (WB, 1936), *Anthony Adverse* (WB, 1936), *All American Chump* (MGM, 1936), *Mad Holiday* (MGM, 1936), *Laburnham Grove* (ATP, 1936), *Parnell* (MGM, 1937), *A Yank at Oxford* (MGM, 1938), *South Riding* (UA, 1938), *Penny Paradise* (Academy, 1938), *An Englishman's Home* (UA, 1939), *Cheer Boys Cheer* (Academy, 1940), *The Earl of Chicago* (MGM, 1940), *Mad Men of Europe* (Col., 1940), *The Doctor Takes a Wife* (Col, 1940), *Pride and Prejudice* (MGM, 1940), *Foreign Correspondent* (UA, 1940), *Scotland Yard* (20th, 1941), *Cheers for Miss Bishop* (UA, 1941), *The Devil and Miss Jones* (RKO, 1941), *Charley's Aunt* (20th, 1941), *One Night in Lisbon* (Par., 1941), *The Meanest Man in the World* (20th, 1943), *Forever and a Day* (RKO, 1943), *Lassie Come*

Home (MGM, 1943), *Between Two Worlds* (WB, 1944), *Keys of the Kingdom* (20th, 1945), *Bewitched* (MGM, 1945), *Dangerous Partners* (MGM, 1945), *She Went to the Races* (MGM, 1945), *Of Human Bondage* (WB, 1946), *Undercurrent* (MGM, 1946), *The Miracle on 34th Street* (20th, 1947), *Thunder in the Valley* (20th, 1947), *Life With Father* (WB, 1947), *Green Dolphin Street* (MGM, 1947), *Apartment for Peggy* (20th, 1948), *Hills of Home* (MGM, 1948), *Challenge to Lassie* (MGM, 1949), *A Woman of Distinction* (Col., 1950), *Louisa* (Univ., 1950), *Pretty Baby* (WB, 1950), *Mister 880* (20th, 1950), *For Heaven's Sake* (20th, 1950), *Peking Express* (Par., 1951), *Sally and Saint Anne* (Univ., 1952), *Bonzo Goes to College* (Univ., 1952), *Les Miserables* (20th, 1952), *Something for the Birds* (20th, 1952), *Mister Scoutmaster* (20th, 1953), *Them* (WB, 1954), *The Student Prince* (MGM, 1954), *The Trouble With Harry* (Par., 1955), *It's a Dog's Life* (MGM, 1955).

JEAN HAGEN (Jean Shirley Ver Hagen) Born Chicago, Illinois. Married Tom Seidel (1947), children: Christine, Aric.

Barry Sullivan and Jean Hagen in *No Questions Asked.*

Feature Films: *Side Street* (MGM, 1949), *Adam's Rib* (MGM, 1949), *Ambush* (MGM, 1950), *The Asphalt Jungle* (MGM, 1950), *A Life of Her Own* (MGM, 1950), *Night into Morning* (MGM, 1951), *No Questions Asked* (MGM, 1951), *Singin' in the Rain* (MGM, 1952), *Shadow in the Sky* (MGM, 1952), *Carbine Williams* (MGM, 1952), *Latin Lovers* (MGM, 1953), *Arena* (MGM, 1953), *Half a Hero* (MGM, 1953), *The Big Knife* (UA, 1955), *Spring Reunion* (UA, 1957), *The Shaggy Dog* (BV, 1959), *Sunrise at Campobello* (WB, 1960), *Panic in Year Zero* (AIP, 1962), *Dead Ringer* (WB, 1964).

ALAN HALE (Alan MacKahn) Born February 10, 1892, Washington, D.C. Married Gretchen Hartman (1914), children: Alan, Karen, Jeanne. Died January 22, 1950.

Alan Hale and Sonja Henie in *Thin Ice.*

Sound Feature Films: *The Leatherneck* (Pathé, 1929), *Sal of Singapore* (Pathé, 1929), *The Sap* (WB, 1929), *Red Hot Rhythm* (Pathé, 1929), *Sailor's Holiday* (Pathé, 1929), *She Got What She Wanted* (Tif., 1930), *Aloha* (Tif., 1931), *Night Angel* (Par., 1931), *Susan Lennox—Her Fall and Rise* (MGM, 1931), *The Sin of Madelon Claudet* (MGM, 1931), *Sea Ghost* (Peerless, 1931), *Union Depot* (WB, 1932), *So Big* (WB, 1932), *The Match King* (WB, 1932), *What Price Decency?* (Majestic, 1933), *Eleventh Commandment* (Allied Pictures, 1933), *Destination Unknown* (Univ., 1933), *Picture Brides* (Allied, 1933), *The Lost Patrol* (RKO, 1934), *It Happened One Night* (Col., 1934), *Miss Fane's Baby Is Stolen* (Par., 1934), *Fog Over Frisco* (WB, 1934), *Little Man, What Now?* (Univ., 1934), *Of Human Bondage* (RKO, 1934), *The Scarlet Letter* (Majestic, 1934), *There's Always Tomorrow* (Univ., 1934), *Imitation of Life* (Univ., 1934), *Babbitt* (WB, 1934), *Great Expectations* (Univ., 1934), *The Little Minister* (RKO, 1934), *The Good Fairy* (Univ., 1935), *Grand Old Girl* (RKO, 1935), *The Crusades* (Par., 1935), *Last Days of Pompeii* (RKO, 1935), *Another Face* (RKO, 1935), *Two in the Dark* (RKO, 1936), *The Country Beyond* (20th, 1936), *A Message to Garcia* (20th, 1936), *Parole!* (Univ., 1936), *Our Relations* (MGM, 1936), *Yellowstone* (Univ., 1936), *God's Country and the Woman* (WB, 1936), *The Prince and the Pauper* (WB, 1937), *Stella Dallas* (UA, 1937), *High, Wide and Handsome* (Par., 1937), *Thin Ice* (20th, 1937), *Music for Madame* (RKO, 1937), *The Adventures of Marco Polo* (UA, 1938), *Four Men and A Prayer* (20th, 1938), *The Adventures of Robin Hood* (WB, 1938), *Valley of the Giants* (WB, 1938), *Algiers* (UA, 1938), *Listen, Darling* (MGM, 1938), *The Sisters* (WB, 1938), *Pacific Liner* (RKO, 1939), *Dodge City* (WB, 1939), *The Man in the Iron Mask* (UA, 1939), *Dust Be My Destiny* (WB, 1939), *On Your Toes* (WB, 1939), *The Private Lives of Elizabeth and Essex* (WB, 1939), *Three Cheers for the Irish* (WB, 1940), *Green Hell* (Univ., 1940), *Virginia City* (WB, 1940), *The Fighting 69th* (WB, 1940), *They Drive by Night* (WB, 1940), *The Sea Hawk* (WB, 1940), *Tugboat Annie Sails Again* (WB, 1940), *Santa Fe Trail* (WB, 1940), *Strawberry Blonde* (WB, 1941), *Footsteps in the Dark* (WB, 1941), *Thieves Fall Out* (WB, 1941), *Manpower* (WB, 1941), *The Smiling Ghost* (WB, 1941), *The Great Mr. Nobody* (WB, 1941), *Captains of the Clouds* (WB, 1942), *Juke Girl* (WB, 1942), *Desperate Journey* (WB, 1942), *Gentleman Jim* (WB, 1942), *Action in the North Atlantic* (WB, 1943), *This is Your Army* (WB, 1943), *Thank Your Lucky Stars* (WB, 1943), *Destination Tokyo* (WB, 1943), *The Adventures of Mark Twain* (WB, 1944), *Make Your Own Bed* (WB, 1944), *Janie* (WB, 1944), *Hollywood Canteen* (WB, 1944), *Roughly Speaking* (WB, 1945), *God Is My Co-Pilot* (WB, 1945), *Hotel Berlin* (WB, 1945), *Escape in the Desert* (WB, 1945), *Perilous Holiday* (Col., 1946), *Night and Day* (WB, 1946), *The Time, the Place and the Girl* (WB, 1946), *The Man I Love* (WB, 1946), *That Way With Women* (WB, 1947), *Pursued* (WB, 1947), *Cheyenne* (WB, 1947), *My Wild Irish Rose* (WB, 1947), *My Girl Tisa* (WB, 1948), *Whiplash* (WB, 1948), *Adventures of Don Juan* (WB, 1948), *South of St. Louis* (WB, 1949), *The Younger Brothers* (WB, 1949), *The House Across the Street* (WB, 1949), *Always Leave Them Laughing* (WB, 1949), *The Inspector General* (WB, 1949), *Stars in My Crown* (MGM, 1950), *Colt. 45* (WB, 1950), *Rogues of Sherwood Forest* (Col., 1950).

BARBARA HALE Born April 18, 1922, DeKalb, Illinois. Married Bill Williams (1946), children: Barbara (Jody), William, Laura.

James Stewart and Barbara Hale in *The Jackpot.*

Feature Films: *Higher and Higher* (RKO, 1943), *Gildersleeve on Broadway* (RKO, 1943), *Government Girl* (RKO, 1943), *The Iron Major* (RKO, 1943), *Mexican Spitfire's Blessed Event* (RKO, 1943), *The Seventh Victim* (RKO, 1943), *Gildersleeve's Bad Day* (RKO, 1943), *The Falcon Out West* (RKO, 1944), *Belle of the Yukon* (RKO, 1944), *Heavenly Days* (RKO, 1944), *Goin' to Town* (RKO, 1944), *The Falcon in Hollywood* (RKO, 1944), *West of the Pecos* (RKO, 1945), *First Yank into Tokyo* (RKO, 1945), *Lady Luck* (RKO, 1946), *A Likely Story* (RKO, 1947), *The Boy With Green Hair* (RKO, 1948), *The Clay Pigeon* (RKO, 1949), *The Window* (RKO, 1949), *Jolson Sings Again* (Col., 1949), *And Baby Makes Three* (Col, 1950), *The Jackpot* (20th, 1950), *Emergency Wedding* (Col., 1950), *Lorna Doone* (Col., 1951), *The First Time* (Col., 1952), *Last of the Comanches* (Col., 1952), *Seminole* (Univ., 1953), *Lone Hand* (Univ., 1953), *A Lion Is in the Streets* (WB, 1953), *Unchained* (WB, 1955), *The Far Horizons* Par., 1955), *The Houston Story* (Col., 1956), *Seventh Cavalry* (Col., 1956), *The Oklahoman* (AA, 1957), *Slim Carter* (Univ., 1957), *Desert Hell* (20th, 1958), *Buckskin* (Par., 1968),, *The Frontiersman* (Par., 1968).

JON HALL (Charles Hall Locher) Born February 23, 1913, Fresno, California. Married Frances Langford (1938); divorced 1955. Married Racquel Ames (1959).

Douglass Dumbrille, Olympe Bradna, Jon Hall, Frances Farmer and Victor McLaglen in *South of Pago Pago.*

Feature Films:

as **Charles Locher** *Women Must Dress* (Mon., 1935), *Charlie Chan in Shanghai* (20th, 1935), *The Clutching Hand* (Stage and Screen serial, 1936), *The Lion Man* (Normandy Pictures, 1936), *The Mysterious Avenger* (Col., 1936).

as **Lloyd Crane** *Mind Your Own Business* (Par., 1936), *Girl From Scotland Yard* (Par., 1937).

as **Jon Hall** *The Hurricane* (UA, 1937), *Sailor's Lady* (20th, 1940), *Kit Carson* (UA, 1940), *Aloma of the South Seas* (Par., 1941), *Tuttles of Tahiti* (RKO, 1942), *Eagle Squadron* (Univ., 1942), *Invisible Agent* (Univ., 1942), *Arabian Nights* (Univ., 1942), *White Savage* (Univ., 1943), *Ali Baba and the Forty Thieves* (Univ., 1944), *Lady in the Dark* (Par., 1944), *Invisible Man's Revenge* (Univ., 1944), *Cobra Woman* (Univ., 1944), *Gypsy Wildcat* (Univ., 1944), *San Diego, I Love You* (Univ., 1944), *Sudan* (Univ., 1945), *Men in Her Diary* (Univ., 1945), *The Michigan Kid* (Univ., 1947), *Last of the Redmen* (Col., 1947), *The Vigilantes Return* (Univ., 1947), *The Prince of Thieves* (Col., 1948), *The Mutineers* (Col., 1949), *Zamba* (EL, 1949), *Deputy Marshal* (Screen Guild, 1949), *On the Isle of Samoa* (Col., 1950), *When the Redskins Rode* (Col., 1951), *China Corsair* (Col., 1951), *Hurricane Island* (Col., 1951), *Brave Warrior* (Col., 1952), *Last Train From Bombay* (Col., 1952), *Hell Ship Mutiny* (Rep., 1957), *Forbidden Island* (Col., 1959), *Beach Girls and the Monster* (United States Films, 1965).

GEORGE HAMILTON Born August 12, 1940, Memphis, Tennessee.

English-Language Feature Films: *Crime and Punishment, USA* (AA, 1959), *Home From the Hill* (MGM, 1960), *All the Fine Young Cannibals*

Mercedes McCambridge and George Hamilton in *Angel Baby*.

(MGM, 1960), *Where the Boys Are* (MGM, 1960), *Angel Baby* (AA, 1961), *By Love Possessed* (UA, 1961), *A Thunder of Drums* (MGM, 1961), *Light in the Piazza* (MGM, 1962), *Two Weeks in Another Town* (MGM, 1962), *The Victors* (Col., 1963), *Act One* (WB, 1963), *Looking for Love* (MGM, 1964),* *Your Cheatin' Heart* (MGM, 1964), *Doctor, You've Got to Be Kidding!* (MGM, 1967), *That Man George* (AA, 1967), *Jack of Diamonds* (MGM, 1967), *The Power* (MGM, 1968), *A Time for Killing* (Col., 1968).

    *Billed guest appearance

MARGARET HAMILTON (Margaret Brainard Hamilton) Born December 9, 1902, Cleveland, Ohio. Married Paul Meserve (1931), child: Hamilton; divorced 1938.

Feature Films: *Another Language* (MGM, 1933), *Hat, Coat and Glove* (RKO, 1934), *By Your Leave* (RKO, 1934), *Broadway Bill* (Col., 1934), *There's Always Tomorrow* (Univ., 1934), *The Farmer Takes a Wife* (Fox, 1935), *Way Down East* (Fox, 1935), *Chatterbox* (RKO, 1936), *The Trail of the Lonesome Pine* (Par., 1936), *These Three* (UA, 1936), *The Moon's Our Home* (Par., 1936), *The Witness Chair* (RKO, 1936), *Laughing at Trouble* (20th, 1937), *You Only Live Once* (UA, 1937), *When's Your Birthday?* (RKO, 1937), *Good Old Soak* (MGM, 1937), *Mountain Justice* (WB, 1937), *Nothing Sacred* (UA, 1937), *Saratoga* (MGM, 1937), *I'll Take Romance* (Col., 1937), *A Slight Case of Murder* (WB, 1938), *Adventures of Tom Sawyer* (UA, 1938), *Mother Carey's Chickens* (RKO, 1938), *Four's a Crowd* (WB, 1938), *Breaking the Ice* (RKO, 1938), *Stablemates* (MGM, 1938), *King of the Turf* (UA, 1939), *The Wizard of Oz* (MGM, 1939), *Angels Wash Their Faces* (WB, 1939), *Babes in Arms* (MGM, 1939), *Main Street Lawyer* (Rep., 1939), *My*

Margaret Hamilton and Harold Lloyd in *Mad Wednesday*.

Little Chickadee (Univ., 1940), *The Villain Still Pursued Her* (RKO, 1940), *I'm Nobody's Sweetheart Now* (Univ., 1940), *The Invisible Woman* (Univ., 1941), *Play Girl* (RKO, 1941), *The Gay Vagabond* (Rep., 1941), *The Shepherd of the Hills* (Par., 1941), *Twin Beds* (UA, 1942), *Meet the Stewarts* (Col., 1942), *The Affairs of Martha* (MGM, 1942), *City Without Men* (Col., 1943), *The Ox-Bow Incident* (20th, 1943), *Johnny Come Lately* (UA, 1943), *Guest in the House* (UA, 1944), *George White's Scandals* (RKO, 1945), *Janie Gets Married* (WB, 1946), *Faithful in My Fashion* (MGM, 1946), *Mad Wednesday* (UA, 1947), *Dishonored Lady* (UA, 1947), *Driftwood* (Rep., 1947), *State of the Union* (MGM, 1948), *Texas, Brooklyn and Heaven* (UA, 1948), *Bungalow 13* (20th, 1948), *The Sun Comes Up* (MGM, 1949), *The Red Pony* (Rep., 1949), *The Beautiful Blonde From Bashful Bend* (20th, 1949), *Riding High* (Par., 1950), *The Great Plane Robbery* (UA, 1950), *Wabash Avenue* (20th, 1950), *People Will Talk* (20th, 1951), *Comin' Round the Mountain* (Univ., 1951), *Thirteen Ghosts* (Col., 1960), *Paradise Alley* (Sutton, 1962), *The Daydreamer* (Voice only; Embassy, 1966), *Rosie!* (Univ., 1968).

NEIL HAMILTON (James Neil Hamilton) Born September 9, 1899, Lynn, Massachusetts. Married Elsa Whitner (1922).

Fay Wray, Gary Cooper, Neil Hamilton, Frances Fuller and Jack Clifford in *One Sunday Afternoon*.

Sound Feature Films: *Dangerous Woman* (Par., 1929), *Studio Murder Mystery* (Par., 1929), *Mysterious Dr. Fu Manchu* (Par., 1929), *Darkened Rooms* (Par., 1929), *Kibitzer* (Par., 1929), *Anybody's Woman* (Par., 1930), *Return of Dr. Fu Manchu* (Par., 1930), *Dawn Patrol* (WB, 1930), *Ladies Must Play* (Col., 1930), *The Cat Creeps* (Univ., 1930), *Widow From Chicago* (WB, 1930), *The Spy* (Fox, 1931), *Strangers May Kiss* (MGM, 1931), *Command Performance* (Tif., 1931), *Ex-Flame* (Tif., 1931), *This Modern Age* (MGM, 1931), *Laughing Sinners* (MGM, 1931), *Great Lover* (MGM, 1931), *The Sin of Madelon Claudet* (MGM, 1931), *Tarzan the Ape Man* (MGM, 1932), *Are You Listening?* (MGM, 1932), *Wet Parade* (MGM, 1932), *The Woman in Room 13* (Fox, 1932), *What Price Hollywood* (RKO, 1932), *Two Against the World* (WB, 1932), *Payment Deferred* (MGM, 1932), *The Animal Kingdom* (RKO, 1932), *Terror Aboard* (Par., 1933), *World Gone Mad* (Majestic, 1933), *Silk Express* (WB, 1933), *One Sunday Afternoon* (Par., 1933), *As the Devil Commands* (Col., 1933), *Tarzan and His Mate* (MGM, 1934), *Here Comes the Groom* (Par., 1934), *Blind Date* (Col., 1934), *Once to Every Bachelor* (Liberty, 1934), *One Exciting Adventure* (Univ., 1934), *By Your Leave* (RKO, 1934), *Fugitive Lady* (Col., 1934), *The Daring Young Man* (Fox, 1935), *Keeper of the Bees* (Mon., 1935), *Honeymoon Limited* (Mon., 1935), *Mutiny Ahead* (Majestic, 1936), *Southern Roses* (Grafton Films, 1936), *Everything in Life* (British, 1936), *Portia on Trial*

(Rep., 1937), *Lady Behave* (Rep., 1937), *Hollywood Stadium Mystery* (Rep., 1938), *Army Girl* (Rep., 1938), *The Saint Strikes Back* (RKO, 1939), *Queen of the Mob* (Par., 1940), *King of the Texas Rangers* (Rep., serial, 1941), *Federal Fugitives* (PRC, 1941), *Father Takes a Wife* (RKO, 1941), *Dangerous Lady* (PRC, 1941), *Look Who's Laughing* (RKO, 1941), *Too Many Women* (PRC, 1942), *X Marks the Spot* (Rep., 1942), *Secrets of the Underground* (Rep., 1943), *All by Myself* (Univ., 1943), *The Sky's the Limit* (RKO, 1943), *When Strangers Marry* (Mon., 1944), *Brewster's Millions* (UA, 1945), *The Devil's Hand* (Crown International, 1962), *The Little Shepherd of Kingdom Come* (20th, 1962), *The Patsy* (Par., 1964), *Good Neighbor Sam* (Col., 1964), *The Family Jewels* (Par., 1965), *Madame X* (Univ., 1966), *Batman* (20th, 1966).

ANN HARDING (Dorothy Walton Gatley) Born August 7, 1902, Fort Sam Houston, San Antonio, Texas. Married Harry Bannister (1926), child: Jane; divorced 1932. Married Werner Janssen (1937); divorced 1963.

Cedric Hardwicke, Joseph Calleia and Gene Kelly in *The Cross of Lorraine*.

Clive Brook and Ann Harding in *Gallant Lady*.

Feature Films: *Paris Bound* (Pathé, 1929), *Her Private Affair* (Pathé, 1929), *Condemned* (UA, 1929), *Holiday* (Pathé, 1930), *Girl of the Golden West* (WB, 1930), *East Lynne* (Fox, 1931), *Devotion* (RKO, 1931), *Prestige* (RKO, 1932), *Westward Passage* (RKO, 1932), *The Conquerors* (RKO, 1932), *The Animal Kingdom* (RKO, 1932), *When Ladies Meet* (MGM, 1933), *Double Harness* (RKO, 1933), *Right to Romance* (RKO, 1933), *Gallant Lady* (UA, 1933), *Life of Vergie Winters* (RKO, 1934), *The Fountain* (RKO, 1934), *Biography of a Bachelor Girl* (MGM, 1935), *Enchanted April* (RKO, 1935), *The Flame Within* (MGM, 1935), *Peter Ibbetson* (Par., 1935), *The Lady Consents* (RKO, 1936), *The Witness Chair* (RKO, 1936), *Love From a Stranger* (UA, 1937), *Eyes in the Night* (MGM, 1942), *Mission to Moscow* (WB, 1943), *The North Star* (RKO, 1943), *Janie* (WB, 1944), *Nine Girls* (Col., 1944), *Those Endearing Young Charms* (RKO, 1945), *Janie Gets Married* (WB, 1946), *It Happened on Fifth Avenue* (AA, 1947), *Christmas Eve* (UA, 1947), *The Magnificent Yankee* (MGM, 1950), *Two Weeks With Love* (MGM, 1950), *The Unknown Man* (MGM, 1951), *The Man in the Gray Flannel Suit* (20th, 1956), *I've Lived Before* (Univ., 1956), *Strange Intruder* (AA, 1956).

SIR CEDRIC HARDWICKE (Cedric Webster Hardwicke) Born February 19, 1893; Lye, England. Married Helena Pickard (1928), child: Edward; divorced 1948. Married Mary Scott (1950); divorced 1961. Died August 6, 1964.

Sound Feature Films: *Dreyfus* (Col., 1931), *Rome Express* (Gaumont-British, 1932), *Orders Is Orders* (Gaumont-British, 1933), *The Ghoul* (Gaumont-British, 1933), *Nell Gwynne* (British and Dominion Productions, 1934), *The Lady Is Willing* (Col., 1934), *Jew Süss* (Gaumont-British, 1934), *King of Paris* (British and Dominion Productions, 1934), *Bella Donna* (Twickenham, 1935), *Les Miserables* (UA, 1935), *Peg of*

Old Drury (British and Dominion Productions, 1935), *Becky Sharp* (Pioneer-RKO, 1935), *Things to Come* (Korda-UA, 1936), *Tudor Rose* (Gaumont-British, 1936), *Laburnham Grove* (ATP, 1936), *Green Light* (WB, 1937), *King Solomon's Mines* (Gaumont-British, 1937), *On Borrowed Time* (MGM, 1939), *Stanley and Livingstone* (20th, 1939), *The Hunchback of Notre Dame* (RKO, 1939), *The Invisible Man Returns* (Univ., 1940), *Tom Brown's School Days* (RKO, 1940), *The Howards of Virginia* (Col., 1940), *Victory* (Par., 1940), *Suspicion* (RKO, 1941), *Sundown* (UA, 1941), *The Ghost of Frankenstein* (Univ., 1942), *Valley of the Sun* (RKO, 1942), *Invisible Agent* (Univ., 1942), *Commandos Strike at Dawn* (Col., 1942), *Forever and a Day* (RKO, 1943), *The Moon Is Down* (20th, 1943), *The Cross of Lorraine* (MGM, 1943), *The Lodger* (20th, 1944), *Wing and a Prayer* (20th, 1944), *Wilson* (20th, 1944), *The Keys of the Kingdom* (20th, 1945), *The Picture of Dorian Gray* (narrator; MGM, 1945), *Sentimental Journey* (20th, 1946), *The Imperfect Lady* (Par., 1947), *Ivy* (Univ., 1947), *Lured* (UA, 1947), *Song of My Heart* (AA, 1947), *Beware of Pity* (Univ., 1947), *Nicholas Nickleby* (Univ., 1947), *Tycoon* (RKO, 1947), *I Remember Mama* (RKO, 1948), *Rope* (WB-Univ., 1948), *A Connecticut Yankee in King Arthur's Court* (Par., 1949), *Now Barabbas Was a Robber* (WB, 1949), *The Winslow Boy* (EL, 1950), *The White Tower* (RKO, 1950), *Mr. Imperium* (MGM, 1951), *The Desert Fox* (20th, 1951), *The Green Glove* (UA, 1952), *Caribbean* (Par., 1952), *Salome* (Col., 1953), *Botany Bay* (Par., 1953), *The War of the Worlds* (narrator; Par., 1953), *Bait* (Col., 1954), *Richard III* (Lopert, 1955), *Helen of Troy* (WB, 1955), *Diane* (MGM, 1956), *Gaby* (MGM, 1956), *The Vagabond King* (Par., 1956), *The Power and the Prize* (MGM, 1956), *The Ten Commandments* (Par., 1956), *Around the World in 80 Days* (UA, 1956), *The Story of Mankind* (WB, 1957), *Baby Face Nelson* (UA, 1957), *Five Weeks in a Balloon* (20th, 1962), *The Pumpkin Eater* (Col., 1964), *The Magic Fountain* (Davis Distributing, 1964).

JEAN HARLOW (Harlean Carpentier) Born March 3, 1911, Kansas City, Kansas. Married Charles McGrew (1927); divorced 1930. Married

Spencer Tracy, Warren Hymer and Jean Harlow in *Goldie*.

Paul Bern (1932); widowed 1932. Married Hal Rossen (1933); divorced 1935. Died June 7, 1937.

Sound Feature Films: *The Love Parade* (Par., 1929), *The Saturday Night Kid* (Par., 1929), *Hell's Angels* (UA, 1930), *The Secret Six* (MGM, 1931), *Iron Man* (Univ., 1931), *Public Enemy* (WB, 1931), *Goldie* (Fox, 1931), *Platinum Blonde* (Col., 1931), *Three Wise Girls* (Col., 1932), *The Beast of the City* (MGM, 1932), *Red-Headed Woman* (MGM, 1932), *Red Dust* (MGM, 1932), *Dinner at Eight* (MGM, 1933), *Hold Your Man* (MGM, 1933), *Bombshell* (MGM, 1933), *The Girl From Missouri* (MGM, 1934), *Reckless* (MGM, 1935), *China Seas* (MGM, 1935), *Riffraff* (MGM, 1935), *Wife vs. Secretary* (MGM, 1936), *Suzy* (MGM, 1936), *Libeled Lady* (MGM, 1936), *Personal Property* (MGM, 1937), *Saratoga* (MGM, 1937).

JULIE HARRIS (Julia Ann Harris) Born December 2, 1925, Grosse Pointe, Michigan. Married Jay Julien (1946); divorced 1954. Married Manning Gurian (1954), child: Peter.

Julie Harris and Claire Bloom in *The Haunting*.

Feature Films: *The Member of the Wedding* (Col., 1953), *East of Eden* (WB, 1955), *I Am a Camera* (DCA, 1955), *The Truth About Women* (Continental, 1958), *Sally's Irish Rogue* ("The Poacher's Daughter"—Show Corp., 1960), *Requiem for a Heavyweight* (Col., 1962), *The Haunting* (MGM, 1963), *Harper* (WB, 1966), *You're a Big Boy Now* (7 Arts, 1966), *Reflections in a Golden Eye* (WB-7 Arts, 1967).

REX HARRISON (Reginald Carey Harrison) Born March 5, 1908, Huyton, Lancashire, England. Married Marjorie Thomas (1934), child: Noel; divorced 1942. Married Lilli Palmer (1943), child: Carey; divorced 1957. Married Kay Kendall (1957); widowed 1959. Married Rachel Roberts (1962).

Feature Films: *Get Your Man* (British, 1929), *All at Sea* (British, 1935), *The Great Game* (Gaumont-British, 1930), *School For Scandal* (Albion Films, 1930), *Men are Not Gods* (London Films, 1936), *Storm in a Teacup* (London Films, 1937), *School for Husbands* (Richard Wainwright, 1937), *St. Martin's Lane* (Par., 1938), *The Citadel* (MGM, 1938), *Over the Moon* (London Films, 1939), *Ten Days in Paris* (Col., 1939), *The Silent Battle* (Mon., 1939), *Night Train to Munich* (Gaumont-British, 1940), *Major Barbara* (UA, 1941), *Journey Together* (English Films, Inc., 1944), *I Live In Grosvenor Square* ("A Yank In London" —Associated British, 1945), *Blithe Spirit* (Two Cities, 1945), *The Rake's Progress* (Individual Pictures, 1945), *Anna and the King of Siam* (20th, 1946), *The Ghost and Mrs. Muir* (20th, 1947), *The Foxes of Harrow* (20th, 1947), *Escape* (20th, 1948), *Unfaithfully Yours* (20th, 1948), *The Long Dark Hall* (UA, 1951), *The Fourposter* (Col., 1952), *Main Street to Broadway* (MGM, 1953), *King Richard and the Crusaders*

Rex Harrison in *Doctor Dolittle*.

(WB, 1954), *The Constant Husband* (London Films, 1955), *The Reluctant Debutante* (MGM, 1958), *Midnight Lace* (Univ., 1960), *The Happy Thieves* (UA, 1962), *Cleopatra* (20th, 1963), *My Fair Lady* (WB, 1964), *The Yellow Rolls-Royce* (MGM, 1965), *The Agony and the Ecstasy* (20th, 1965), *The Honey Pot* (UA, 1967), *Doctor Dolittle* (20th, 1967), *A Flea in Her Ear* (20th, 1968).

LAURENCE HARVEY (Lauruska Mischa Skikne) Born October 1, 1928, Yonishkis, Lithuania. Married Margaret Leighton (1957); divorced 1961.

Feature Films: *House of Darkness* (Associated British Pictures Corp., 1948), *Man on the Run* (Associated British Pictures Corp., 1948), *Man From Yesterday* (Associated British Pictures Corp., 1949), *Cairo Road* (Associated British Picture Corp., 1949), *The Scarlet Thread* (Buraders, 1949), *The Black Rose* (20th, 1950), *There's Another Sun* (Butchers, 1951), *A Killer Walks* (Associated British Pictures Corp., 1952), *Women of Twilight* (Romulus, 1952), *Landfall* (Stratford, 1953), *I Believe in You* (Univ., 1953), *Romeo and Juliet* (UA, 1954), *King Richard and the Crusaders* (WB, 1954), *The Good Die Young* (UA, 1955), *Innocents in Paris* (Tudor, 1955), *I Am a Camera* (DCA, 1955), *Storm Over the Nile* (Col., 1956), *The Silent Enemy* (Univ., 1958),

Shirley MacLaine and Laurence Harvey in *Two Loves*.

The Truth About Women (Continental, 1958), *Three Men in a Boat* (Valiant, 1959), *Room at the Top* (Continental, 1959), *Butterfield 8* (MGM, 1960), *Expresso Bongo* (Continental, 1960), *The Long and the Short and the Tall* (Continental, 1961), *Summer and Smoke* (Par., 1961), *Two Loves* (MGM, 1961), *The Wonderful World of the Brothers Grimm* (MGM, 1962), *Walk on the Wild Side* (Col., 1962), *The Manchurian Candidate* (UA, 1962), *A Girl Named Tamiko* (Par., 1962), *The Running Man* (Col., 1963), *The Ceremony* (UA, 1964), *The Outrage* (MGM, 1964), *Of Human Bondage* (MGM, 1964), *Darling* (Embassy, 1965), *Life at the Top* (Royal Films International, 1965), *The Spy With a Cold Nose* (Embassy, 1966), *The Winter's Tale* (7 Arts, 1967), *A Dandy in Aspic* (Col., 1968), *Charge of the Light Brigade* (UA, 1969).

SIGNE HASSO (Signe Eleonora Cecilia Larsson) Born August 15, 1915, Stockholm, Sweden. Married Henry Hasso (1936), child: Henry; divorced 1941.

Signe Hasso and Jean-Pierre Aumont in *Assignment in Brittany*.

English-Language Feature Films: *Assignment in Brittany* (MGM, 1943), *Heaven Can Wait* (20th, 1943), *The Story of Dr. Wassell* (Par., 1944), *The Seventh Cross* (MGM, 1944), *Dangerous Partners* (MGM, 1945), *Johnny Angel* (RKO, 1945), *The House on 92nd Street* (20th, 1945), *Strange Triangle* (20th, 1946), *A Scandal in Paris* (UA, 1946), *Where There's Life* (Par., 1947), *To the Ends of the Earth* (Col., 1948), *A Double Life* (Univ., 1948), *Outside the Wall* (Univ., 1950), *Crisis* (MGM, 1950), *The True and the False* (Helene Davis, 1955), *Picture Mommy Dead* (Embassy, 1966).

JUNE HAVER (June Stovenour) Born June 10, 1926, Rock Island, Illinois. Married Jimmy Zito (1947); divorced 1948. Married Fred MacMurray (1955), children: Kathryn, Laurie.

Randy Stuart, S.Z. Sakall, Walter Catlett and June Haver in *Look for the Silver Lining*.

Feature Films: *The Gang's All Here* (20th, 1943), *Home in Indiana* (20th, 1944), *Irish Eyes Are Smiling* (20th, 1944), *Where Do We Go From Here?* (20th, 1945), *The Dolly Sisters* (20th, 1945), *Three Little Girls in Blue* (20th, 1946), *Wake Up and Dream* (20th, 1946), *I Wonder Who's Kissing Her Now* (20th, 1947), *Scudda Hoo! Scudda Hay!* (20th, 1948), *Oh, You Beautiful Doll!* (20th, 1949), *Look for the Silver Lining* (WB, 1949), *The Daughter of Rosie O'Grady* (WB, 1950), *I'll Get By* (20th, 1950), *Love Nest* (20th, 1951), *The Girl Next Door* (20th, 1953).

STERLING HAYDEN (John Hamilton) Born March 26, 1916, Montclair, New Jersey. Married Madeleine Carroll (1937); divorced 1946. Married Betty DeNoon (1947), children: Christian, Dana, Gretchen, Matthew; divorced 1955, Married Catherine McConnell (1960).

Sterling Hayden, Howard Petrie and Chill Wills in *Timberjack*.

Feature Films: *Virginia* (Par., 1941), *Bahama Passage* (Par., 1941), *Variety Girl* (Par., 1947), *Blaze of Noon* (Par., 1947), *El Paso* (Par., 1949), *Manhandled* (Par., 1949), *The Asphalt Jungle* (MGM, 1950), *Journey into Light* (20th, 1951), *Flaming Feather* (Par., 1952), *The Denver and Rio Grande* (Par., 1952), *The Golden Hawk* (Col., 1952), *Flat Top* (AA, 1952), *The Star* (20th, 1953), *Take Me to Town* (Univ., 1953), *Kansas Pacific* (AA, 1953), *Fighter Attack* (AA, 1953), *So Big* (WB, 1953), *Crime Wave* (WB, 1954), *Arrow in the Dust* (AA, 1954) *Prince Valiant* (20th, 1954), *Johnny Guitar* (Rep., 1954), *Naked Alibi* (Univ., 1954), *Suddenly* (UA, 1954), *Timberjack* (Rep., 1955), *The Eternal Sea* (Rep., 1955), *Shotgun* (AA, 1955), *Battle Taxi* (UA, 1955), *The Last Command* (Rep., 1955), *Top Gun* (UA, 1955), *The Come-On* (AA, 1956), *The Killing* (UA, 1956), *Five Steps to Danger* (UA, 1957), *Crime of Passion* (UA, 1957), *The Iron Sheriff* (UA, 1957), *Valerie* (UA, 1957), *Zero Hour!* (Par., 1957), *Gun Battle at Monterey* (AA, 1957), *Terror in a Texas Town* (UA, 1958), *Ten Days to Tulara* (UA, 1958), *Dr. Strangelove* (Col., 1964).

GEORGE "GABBY" HAYES (George F. Hayes) Born May 7, 1885, Wellsville, New York. Married Olive Ireland (1914); widowed.

Sound Feature Films: *Big News* (Pathé, 1929), *Rainbow Man* (Par., 1929), *Smiling Irish Eyes* (WB, 1929), *For the Defense* (Par., 1930), *Rose of the Rio Grande* (1931), *Big Business Girl* (WB, 1931), *God's Country and the Man* (Syndicate, 1931), *Nevada Buckaroo* (Tif., 1931), *Cavalier of the West* (Artclass Pictures, 1931), *Dragnet Patrol* (Artclass Pictures, 1931), *Riders of the Desert* (Sono Art-World Wide, 1932), *Without Honor* (Artclass Pictures, 1932), *From Broadway to Cheyenne* (Mon., 1932), *Klondike* (Mon., 1932), *Love Me Tonight* (Par., 1932), *Texas Buddies* (Sono Art-World Wide, 1932), *The Boiling Point* (Allied Pictures, 1932), *The Fighting Champ* (Mon., 1932), *Wild Horse Mesa* (Par., 1933), *Self Defense* (Mon., 1933), *Phantom Broadcast* (Mon., 1933), *Trailing North* (Mon., 1933), *Breed of the Border* (Mon., 1933), *Return of Casey Jones* (Mon., 1933), *The Sphinx* (Mon., 1933), *Gallant Fool* (Mon., 1933), *Fighting Texans* (Mon., 1933), *Skyway* (Mon., 1933), *Devil's Mate* (Mon., 1933), *Rangers' Code*

Bob Livingston, Richard Arlen and George "Gabby" Hayes in *The Big Bonanza*.

(Mon., 1933), *The Fugitive* (Mon., 1933), *Galloping Romeo* (Mon., 1933), *Riders of Destiny* (Mon., 1933), *The Lost Jungle* (Mascot serial, 1934), *House of Mystery* (Mon., 1934), *Lucky Texan* (Mon., 1934), *West of the Divide* (Mon., 1934), *Beggars in Ermine* (Mon, 1934), *Mystery Liner* (Mon., 1934), *City Limits* (Mon., 1934), *Monte Carlo Nights* (Mon., 1934), *Blue Steel* (Mon., 1934), *Man From Utah* (Mon., 1934), *Randy Rides Alone* (Mon., 1934), *The Star Packer* (Mon., 1934), *Brand of Hate* (William Steiner, 1934), *In Old Santa Fe* (Mascot, 1934), *'Neath Arizona Skies* (Mon., 1934), *The Lost City* (Sherman Krellberg serial, 1935), *Lawless Frontier* (Mon., 1935), *Death Flies East* (Col., 1935), *Rainbow Valley* (Mon., 1935), *Hoosier Schoolmaster* (Mon., 1935), *Justice of the Range* (Col., 1935), *Honeymoon Limited* (Mon., 1935), *Hop-A-Long Cassidy* (Par., 1935), *Smoky Smith* (William Steiner, 1935), *Thunder Mountain* (Fox, 1935), *Tumbling Tumbleweeds* (Rep., 1935), *Eagle's Brood* (Par., 1935), *Bar 20 Rides Again* (Par., 1935), *$1,000 a Minute* (Rep., 1935), *The Throwback* (Univ., 1935), *Hitch-Hike Lady* (Rep., 1935), *Swifty* (First Division, 1935), *Welcome Home* (Fox, 1935), *The Outlaw Tamer* (Empire, 1935), *Valley of the Lawless* (Supreme, 1936), *Call of the Prairie* (Par., 1936), *I Married a Doctor* (WB, 1936), *Mr. Deeds Goes to Town* (Col., 1936), *The Lawless Nineties* (Rep., 1936), *Three on the Trail* (Par., 1936), *Hearts in Bondage* (Rep., 1936), *Texas Rangers* (Par., 1936), *Heart of the West* (Par., 1936), *Hopalong Cassidy Returns* (Par., 1936), *Valiant Is the Word for Carrie* (Par., 1936), *Trail Dust* (Par., 1936), *Borderland* (Par., 1937), *Hills of Old Wyoming* (Par., 1937), *North of Rio Grande* (Par., 1937), *Mountain Music* (Par., 1937), *Hopalong Rides Again* (Par., 1937), *Rustler's Valley* (Par., 1937), *Texas Trail* (Par., 1937), *Heart of Arizona* (Par., 1938), *Gold Is Where You Find It* (WB, 1938), *Bar 20 Justice* (Par., 1938), *In Old Mexico* (Par., 1938), *Sunset Trail* (Par., 1938), *The Frontiersman* (Par., 1938), *Silver on the Sage* (Par., 1939), *Fighting Thoroughbreds* (Rep., 1939), *Let Freedom Ring* (MGM, 1939), *Man of Conquest* (Rep., 1939), *In Old Caliente* (Rep., 1939), *Saga of Death Valley* (Rep., 1939), *In Old Monterey* (Rep., 1939), *Renegade Trail* (Par., 1939), *Wall Street Cowboy* (Rep., 1939), *The Arizona Kid* (Rep., 1939), *Days of Jesse James* (Rep., 1939), *Dark Command* (Rep., 1940), *Young Buffalo Bill* (Rep., 1940), *Wagons Westward* (Rep., 1940), *The Carson City Kid* (Rep., 1940), *The Ranger and the Lady* (Rep., 1940), *Colorado* (Rep., 1940), *Young Bill Hickok* (Rep., 1940), *The Border Legion* (Rep., 1940), *Melody Ranch* (Rep., 1940), *Robin Hood of the Pecos* (Rep., 1941), *In Old Cheyenne* (Rep., 1941), *Sheriff of Tombstone* (Rep., 1941), *Nevada City* (Rep., 1941), *Jesse James at Bay* (Rep., 1941), *Bad Man of Deadwood* (Rep., 1941), *Red River Valley* (Rep., 1941), *South of Santa Fe* (Rep., 1942), *Sunset on the Desert* (Rep., 1942), *Man of Cheyenne* (Rep., 1942), *Romance on the Range* (Rep., 1942), *Sons of the Pioneers* (Rep., 1942), *Sunset Serenade* (Rep., 1942), *Heart of the Golden West* (Rep., 1942), *Ridin' Down the Canyon* (Rep., 1942), *Calling Wild Bill Elliott* (Rep., 1943), *Bordertown Gun Fighters* (Rep., 1943), *Wagon Tracks West* (Rep., 1943), *Death Valley Manhunt* (Rep., 1943), *In Old Oklahoma* (Rep., 1943), *Tucson Raiders* (Rep., 1944), *Hidden Valley Outlaws* (Rep., 1944), *Marshal of Reno* (Rep., 1944), *Mojave Firebrand* (Rep., 1944), *Tall in the Saddle* (RKO, 1944), *Lights*

of Old Santa Fe (Rep., 1944), *Utah* (Rep., 1945), *The Big Bonanza* (Rep., 1945), *Bells of Rosarita* (Rep., 1945), *The Man From Oklahoma* (Rep,. 1945), *Sunset in Eldorado* (Rep., 1945), *Don't Fence Me In* (Rep., 1945), *Along the Navajo Trail* (Rep., 1945), *Song of Arizona* (Rep., 1946), *Badman's Territory* (RKO, 1946), *Rainbow Over Texas* (Rep., 1946), *My Pal Trigger* (Rep., 1946), *Roll on Texas Moon* (Rep., 1946), *Home in Oklahoma* (Rep., 1946), *Under Nevada Skies* (Rep., 1946), *Helldorado* (Rep., 1946), *Trail Street* (RKO, 1947), *Wyoming* (Rep., 1947), *Albuquerque* (Par., 1948), *The Untamed Breed* (Col., 1948), *El Paso* (Par., 1949), *The Cariboo Trail* (20th, 1950).

HELEN HAYES Born October 10, 1900, Washington, D.C. Married Charles MacArthur (1928), children: Mary, James; widowed 1956.

Brian Aherne and Helen Hayes in *What Every Woman Knows*.

Sound Feature Films: *The Sin of Madelon Claudet* (MGM, 1931), *Arrowsmith* (UA, 1931), *A Farewell to Arms* (Par., 1932), *The Son-Daughter* (MGM, 1933), *The White Sister* (MGM, 1933), *Another Language* (MGM, 1933), *Night Flight* (MGM, 1933), *What Every Woman Knows* (MGM, 1934), *Crime Without Passion* (Par.,.1934),* *Vanessa* (MGM, 1935), *Stage Door Canteen* (UA, 1943), *My Son John* (Par., 1952), *Main Street to Broadway* (MGM, 1953), *Anastasia* (20th, 1956), *Third Man on The Mountain* (BV, 1959).*

*Unbilled guest appearance

LOUIS HAYWARD Born March 19, 1909, Johannesburg, South Africa. Married Ida Lupino (1939); divorced 1945. Married Peggy Morrow (1946); divorced 1950. Married June Blanchard (1950).

Feature Films: *Self-Made Lady* (UA, 1932), *Chelsea Life* (Par., 1933), *Sorrell and Son* (UA, 1934), *The Flame Within* (MGM, 1935), *A Feather in Her Hat* (Col., 1935), *Absolute Quiet* (MGM, 1936), *Trouble for Two* (MGM, 1936), *Anthony Adverse* (WB, 1936), *The Luckiest Girl in the World* (Univ., 1936), *The Woman I Love* (RKO, 1937), *Condemned Women* (RKO, 1938), *Midnight Intruder* (Univ., 1938), *The Saint in New York* (RKO, 1938), *The Rage of Paris* (Univ., 1938), *The Duke of West Point* (UA, 1938), *The Man in the Iron Mask* (UA, 1939), *My Son, My Son* (UA, 1940), *Dance, Girl, Dance* (RKO, 1940), *The Son of Monte Cristo* (UA, 1940), *Ladies in Retirement* (Col., 1941), *The Magnificent Ambersons* (RKO, 1942),* *And Then There Were None* (20th, 1945), *Young Widow* (UA, 1946), *The Strange Woman* (UA, 1946), *The Return of Monte Cristo* (Col., 1946), *Repeat Performance* (EL, 1947), *Ruthless* (EL, 1948), *The Black Arrow* (Col., 1948), *Walk a Crooked Mile* (Col., 1948), *The Pirates of Capri* (Film Classics, 1949), *House by the River* (Rep., 1950), *Fortunes of Captain Blood* (Col.,

Louis Hayward and Joan Bennett in *The Man in the Iron Mask*.

1950), *The Lady and the Bandit* (Col., 1951), *The Son of Dr. Jekyll* (Col., 1951), *Lady in the Iron Mask* (20th, 1952), *Captain Pirate* (Col., 1952), *The Royal African Rifles* (AA, 1953), *The Saint's Girl Friday* (RKO, 1954), *Duffy of San Quentin* (WB, 1954), *The Search for Bridey Murphy* (Par., 1956), *Chuka* (Par., 1967), *The Christmas Kid* (PRO, 1967), *Electric Man* (PRO, 1967).

*His major scenes were cut from the final print, although he appears amid the crowd in the ballroom sequence.

SUSAN HAYWARD (Edythe Marrener) Born June 30, 1918, Brooklyn, New York. Married Jess Barker (1944), children: Timothy, Gregory; divorced 1953. Married Floyd Eaton Chalkley (1957); widowed 1966.

Feature Films: *Hollywood Hotel* (WB, 1937), *The Sisters* (WB, 1938), *Comet Over Broadway* (WB, 1938), *Girls on Probation* (WB, 1938), *Beau Geste* (Par., 1939), *Our Leading Citizen* (Par., 1939), *$1,000 a Touchdown* (Par., 1939), *Adam Had Four Sons* (Col., 1941), *Sis Hopkins* (Rep., 1941), *Among the Living* (Par., 1941), *Reap the Wild Wind*

Joseph Allen, Jr., and Susan Hayward in *Our Leading Citizen*.

(Par., 1942), *Forest Rangers* (Par., 1942), *I Married a Witch* (UA, 1942), *Star Spangled Rhythm* (Par., 1942), *Hit Parade of 1943* (Rep., 1943), *Young and Willing* (UA, 1943), *Jack London* (UA, 1943), *The Fighting Seabees* (Rep., 1944), *The Hairy Ape* (UA, 1944), *And Now Tomorrow* (Par., 1944), *Deadline at Dawn* (RKO, 1946), *Canyon Passage* (Univ., 1946), *Smash-Up, The Story of a Woman* (Univ., 1947), *The Lost Moment* (Univ., 1947), *They Won't Believe Me* (RKO, 1947), *Tap Roots* (Univ., 1948), *The Saxon Charm* (Univ., 1948), *Tulsa* (EL, 1949), *House of Strangers* (20th, 1949), *My Foolish Heart* (RKO, 1949), *I'd Climb the Highest Mountain* (20th, 1951), *Rawhide* (20th, 1951), *I Can Get It for You Wholesale* (20th, 1951), *David and Bathsheba* (20th, 1951), *With a Song in My Heart* (20th, 1952), *The Snows of Kilimanjaro* (20th, 1952), *The Lusty Men* (RKO, 1952), *The President's Lady* (20th, 1953), *White Witch Doctor* (20th, 1953), *Demetrius and the Gladiators* (20th, 1954) *Garden of Evil* (20th, 1954), *Untamed* (20th, 1955), *Soldier of Fortune* (20th, 1955), *I'll Cry Tomorrow* (MGM, 1955), *The Conqueror* (RKO, 1956), *Top Secret Affair* (WB, 1957), *I Want to Live* (UA, 1958), *Woman Obsessed* (20th, 1959), *Thunder in the Sun* (Par., 1959), *The Marriage-Go-Round* (20th, 1960), *Ada* (MGM, 1961), *Back Street* (Univ., 1961), *I Thank a Fool* (MGM, 1962), *Stolen Hours* (UA, 1963), *Where Love Has Gone* (Par., 1964), *The Honey Pot* (UA, 1967), *Valley of the Dolls* (20th, 1967).

RITA HAYWORTH (Margarita Carmen Cansino) Born October 17, 1918, Brooklyn, New York. Married Edward Judson (1937); divorced 1943. Married Orson Welles (1943), child: Rebecca; divorced 1947. Married Aly Kahn (1949), child: Yasmin; divorced 1951. Married Dick Haymes (1953); divorced 1955. Married James Hill (1958); divorced 1961.

Larry Parks and Rita Hayworth in *Down to Earth*.

Feature Films:
    as Rita Cansino *Dante's Inferno* (Fox, 1935), *Under the Pampas Moon* (Fox, 1935), *Charlie Chan in Egypt* (Fox, 1935), *Paddy O'Day* (Fox, 1935), *Human Cargo* (20th, 1936), *A Message to Garcia* (20th, 1936), *Meet Nero Wolfe* (Col., 1936), *Rebellion* (Crescent, 1936), *Old Louisiana* (Crescent, 1937), *Hit the Saddle* (Rep., 1937), *Trouble in Texas* (GN, 1937).
    as Rita Hayworth *Criminals of the Air* (Col., 1937), *Girls Can Play* (Col., 1937), *The Game That Kills* (Col., 1937), *Paid to Dance* (Col., 1937), *The Shadow* (Col., 1937), *Who Killed Gail Preston?* (Col., 1938), *There's Always a Woman* (Col., 1938), *Convicted* (Col., 1938), *Juvenile Court* (Col., 1938), *Homicide Bureau* (Col., 1939), *The Lone Wolf Spy Hunt* (Col., 1939), *Renegade Ranger* (RKO, 1939), *Only Angels Have Wings* (Col., 1939), *Special Inspector* (Syndicate, 1939), *Music in My Heart* (Col., 1940), *Blondie on a Budget* (Col., 1940), *Susan and God* (MGM, 1940), *The Lady in Question* (Col., 1940), *Angels Over Broadway* (Col., 1940), *Strawberry Blonde* (WB, 1941), *Affectionately Yours* (WB, 1941), *Blood and Sand* (20th, 1941), *You'll Never Get Rich* (Col., 1941), *My Gal Sal* (20th, 1942), *Tales of Manhattan* (20th, 1942), *You Were Never Lovelier* (Col., 1942), *Cover Girl* (Col., 1944), *Tonight and Every*

Night (Col., 1945), *Gilda* (Col., 1946), *Down to Earth* (Col., 1947), *The Lady From Shanghai* (Col., 1948), *The Loves of Carmen* (Col., 1948), *Affair in Trinidad* (Col., 1952), *Salome* (Col., 1953), *Miss Sadie Thompson* (Col., 1953), *Fire Down Below* (Col., 1957), *Pal Joey* (Col., 1957), *Separate Tables* (UA, 1958), *They Came to Cordura* (Col., 1959), *The Story on Page One* (20th, 1959), *The Happy Thieves* (UA, 1962), *Circus World* (Par., 1965), *The Money Trap* (MGM, 1966), *The Rover* (ABC, 1968).

VAN HEFLIN (Emmett Evan Heflin) Born December 13, 1910, Walters, Oklahoma. Married Frances Neal (1942), children: Vana, Cathlee, Tracy; divorced 1968.

Peggy Moran and Van Heflin in *Seven Sweethearts*.

Feature Films: *A Woman Rebels* (RKO, 1936), *Outcasts of Poker Flat* (RKO, 1937), *Flight From Glory* (RKO, 1937), *Saturday's Heroes* (RKO, 1937), *Annapolis Salute* (RKO, 1937), *Back Door to Heaven* (Par., 1939), *Santa Fe Trail* (WB, 1940), *The Feminine Touch* (MGM, 1941), *Johnny Eager* (MGM, 1941), *H. M. Pulham, Esq.* (MGM, 1941), *Kid Glove Killer* (MGM, 1942), *Seven Sweethearts* (MGM, 1942), *Grand Central Murder* (MGM, 1942), *Tennessee Johnson* (MGM, 1942), *Presenting Lily Mars* (MGM, 1943), *The Strange Love of Martha Ivers* (Par., 1946), *Till the Clouds Roll By* (MGM, 1946), *Possessed* (WB, 1947), *Green Dolphin Street* (MGM, 1947), *Tap Roots* (Univ., 1948), *B.F.'s Daughter* (MGM, 1948), *The Three Musketeers* (MGM, 1948), *Act of Violence* (MGM, 1948), *Madame Bovary* (MGM, 1948), *The Secret Land* (narrator; MGM, 1948), *An Act of Violence* (MGM, 1948), *East Side, West Side* (MGM, 1949), *Tomahawk* (Univ., 1951), *The Prowler* (UA,, 1951), *Week-End With Father* (Univ., 1951), *My Son, John* (Par. 1952), *Wings of the Hawk* (Univ., 1953), *Shane* (Par., 1953), *Tanganyika* (Univ., 1954), *The Golden Mask* (UA, 1954), *The Raid* (20th, 1954), *A Woman's World* (20th, 1954), *Black Widow* (20th, 1954), *Count Three and Pray* (Col., 1955), *Battle Cry* (WB, 1955), *Patterns* (UA, 1956), *3:10 to Yuma* (Col., 1957), *Gunman's Walk* (Col., 1958), *They Came to Cordura* (Col., 1959), *Tempest* (Par., 1959), *Five Branded Women* (Par., 1960), *Under Ten Flags* (Par., 1960), *Cry of Battle* (AA, 1963), *To Be a Man* ("The Wastrel"—Medallion, 1964), *The Greatest Story Ever Told* (UA, 1965), *Once a Thief* (MGM, 1965), *Stagecoach* (20th, 1966), *The Man Outside* (Trio Films, 1967), *Each Man for Himself* (PCM, 1968).

WANDA HENDRIX (Dixie Wanda Hendrix) Born November 3, 1928, Jacksonville, Florida. Married Audie Murphy (1949); divorced 1950. Married James Stack; divorced.

Feature Films: *Confidential Agent* (WB, 1945), *Nora Prentiss* (WB, 1947), *Welcome Stranger* (Par., 1947), *Variety Girl* (Par., 1947), *Ride the Pink Horse* (Univ., 1947), *Miss Tatlock's Millions* (Par., 1948), *My Own True Love* (Par., 1948), *Prince of Foxes* (20th, 1949), *Song of Surrender* (Par., 1949), *Sierra* (Univ., 1950), *Captain Carey, U.S.A.* (Par., 1950), *The Admiral Was a Lady* (UA, 1950), *Saddle Tramp*

Henry Hull, Ray Bennett, Clancy Cooper, Georgia Bakus, Wanda Hendrix in *Song of Surrender*.

(Univ., 1950), *My Outlaw Brother* (EL, 1951), *The Highwayman* (AA, 1951), *Montana Territory* (Col., 1952), *The Last Posse* (Col., 1953), *Sea of Lost Ships* (Rep., 1953), *The Golden Mask* (UA, 1954), *Highway Dragnet* (AA, 1954), *The Black Dakotas* (Col., 1954), *Boy Who Caught a Crook* (UA, 1961), *Johnny Cool* (UA, 1963), *Stage to Thunder Rock* (Par., 1964).

SONJA HENIE Born April 8, 1912, Oslo, Norway. Married Dan Topping (1940); divorced 1946. Married Winthrop Gardiner (1949); divorced 1955. Married Niels Onsted (1956).

Sonja Henie and John Payne in *Iceland*.

Feature Films: *One in a Million* (20th, 1936), *Thin Ice* (20th, 1937), *Happy Landing* (20th, 1938), *My Lucky Star* (20th, 1938), *Second Fiddle* (20th, 1939), *Everything Happens at Night* (20th, 1939), *Sun Valley Serenade* (20th, 1941), *Iceland* (20th, 1942), *Wintertime* (20th, 1943), *It's a Pleasure* (RKO, 1945), *The Countess of Monte Cristo* (Univ., 1948).

PAUL HENREID (Paul George Julius Von Henreid) Born January 10, 1908, Trieste, Italy. Married Elisabeth Gluck (1936), children: Monica, Mimi.

English-Language Feature Films:
  as Paul Von Henreid *Night Train* (Gaumont-British, 1939), *Goodbye, Mr. Chips* (MGM, 1939), *Under Your Hat* (British Lion, 1940).
  as Paul Henreid *Joan of Paris* (RKO, 1942), *Now, Voyager* (WB, 1942), *Casablanca* (WB, 1942), *In Our Time* (WB, 1944), *Between Two Worlds* (WB, 1944), *The Conspirators* (WB, 1944), *Hollywood Canteen* (WB, 1944), *The Spanish Main* (RKO, 1945), *Devotion* (WB, 1946), *Of Human Bondage* (WB, 1946), *Deception* (WB, 1946), *Song of Love*

Ida Lupino, Nazimova and Paul Henreid in *In Our Time*.

(MGM, 1947), *Hollow Triumph* (EL, 1948), *Rope of Sand* (Par., 1949), *So Young, So Bad* (UA, 1950), *Last of the Buccaneers* (Col., 1950), *Pardon My French* (UA, 1951), *For Men Only* (Lip., 1952), *Thief of Damascus* (Col., 1952), *Siren of Bagdad* (Col., 1953), *Man in Hiding* (UA, 1953), *Deep in My Heart* (MGM, 1954), *Pirates of Tripoli* (Col., 1955), *Meet Me in Las Vegas* (MGM, 1956), *A Woman's Devotion* (Rep., 1956), *Ten Thousand Bedrooms* (MGM, 1957), *Holiday for Lovers* (20th, 1959), *The Four Horsemen of the Apocalypse* (MGM, 1962), *Operation Crossbow* (MGM, 1965), *Peking Remembered* (narrator; Butler-Hall, 1967).

AUDREY HEPBURN (Audry Hepburn-Ruston) Born May 4, 1929, Brussels, Belgium. Married Mel Ferrer (1954), child: Sean.

Anthony Perkins and Audrey Hepburn in *Green Mansions*.

English-Language Feature Films: *One Wild Oat* (Eros Films, 1951), *Young Wives' Tale* (AA, 1951), *Laughter in Paradise* (Stratford, 1951), *The Lavender Hill Mob* (Univ., 1951), *Monte Carlo Baby* (Mon, 1952), *The Secret People* (Lip., 1952), *Roman Holiday* (Par., 1953), *Sabrina* (Par., 1954), *War and Peace* (Par., 1956), *Funny Face* (Par., 1957), *Love in the Afternoon* (AA, 1957), *The Nun's Story* (WB, 1959), *Green Mansions* (MGM, 1959), *The Unforgiven* (UA, 1960), *Breakfast at Tiffany's* (Par., 1961), *The Children's Hour* (UA, 1962), *Charade* (Univ., 1963), *Paris When It Sizzles* (Par., 1964), *My Fair Lady* (WB, 1964), *How to Steal a Million* (20th, 1966), *Two For the Road* (20th, 1967), *Wait Until Dark* (WB, 1967).

KATHARINE HEPBURN (Katharine Houghton Hepburn) Born November 9, 1909, Hartford, Connecticut. Married Ludlow Ogden Smith (1928); divorced 1934.

John Beal and Katharine Hepburn in *The Little Minister*.

Feature Films: *A Bill of Divorcement* (RKO, 1932), *Christopher Strong* (RKO, 1933), *Morning Glory* (RKO, 1933), *Little Women* (RKO, 1933), *Spitfire* (RKO, 1934), *Break of Hearts* (RKO, 1935), *The Little Minister* (RKO, 1934), *Alice Adams* (RKO, 1935), *Sylvia Scarlett* (RKO, 1935), *Mary of Scotland* (RKO, 1936), *A Woman Rebels* (RKO, 1936), *Quality Street* (RKO, 1937), *Stage Door* (RKO, 1937), *Bringing Up Baby* (RKO, 1938), *Holiday* (Col., 1938), *The Philadelphia Story* (MGM, 1940), *Woman of the Year* (MGM, 1942), *Keeper of the Flame* (MGM, 1942), *Stage Door Canteen* (UA, 1943), *Dragon Seed* (MGM, 1944), *Without Love* (MGM, 1945), *Undercurrent* (MGM, 1946), *The Sea of Grass* (MGM, 1947), *Song of Love* (MGM, 1947), *State of the Union* (MGM, 1948), *Adam's Rib* (MGM, 1949), *The African Queen* (UA, 1951), *Pat and Mike* (MGM, 1952), *Summertime* (UA, 1955), *The Rainmaker* (Par., 1956), *The Iron Petticoat* (MGM, 1956), *Desk Set* (20th, 1957), *Suddenly, Last Summer* (Col., 1959), *Long Day's Journey into Night* (Embassy, 1962), *Guess Who's Coming to Dinner* (Col., 1967), *The Lion in Winter* (Embassy, 1968), *The Madwoman of Chaillot* (WB-7 Arts, 1968).

JEAN HERSHOLT Born July 12, 1886, Copenhagen, Denmark. Married Via Andersen (1914), child: Allan. Died June 2, 1956.

Sound Feature Films: *Hell Harbor* (UA, 1930), *Climax* (Univ., 1930), *The Case of Sergeant Grischa* (RKO, 1930), *Mamba* (Tif., 1930), *Viennese*

Jean Hersholt in *Mask of Fu Manchu*.

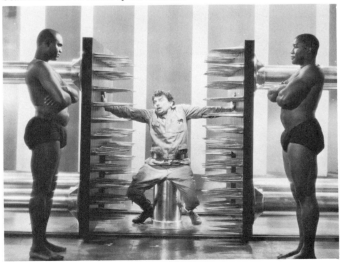

Nights (WB, 1930), *The Cat Creeps* (Univ., 1930), *East Is West* (Univ., 1930), *Third Alarm* (Tif., 1930), *Daybreak* (MGM, 1931), *Soldier's Plaything* (WB, 1931), *Susan Lennox—Her Fall and Rise* (MGM, 1931), *Phantom of Paris* (MGM, 1931), *Transatlantic* (Fox, 1931), *The Sin of Madelon Claudet* (MGM, 1931), *Private Lives* (MGM, 1931), *Beast of the City* (MGM, 1932), *Emma* (MGM, 1932), *Are You Listening?* (MGM, 1932), *Grand Hotel* (MGM, 1932), *Night Court* (MGM, 1932,) *New Morals for Old* (MGM, 1932), *Skyscraper Souls* (MGM, 1932), *Unashamed* (MGM, 1932), *Hearts of Humanity* (Majestic, 1932), *Flesh* (MGM, 1932), *The Mask of Fu Manchu* (MGM, 1932), *Crime of the Century* (Par., 1933), *Dinner at Eight* (MGM, 1933), *Song of the Eagle* (Par., 1933), *Christopher Bean* (MGM, 1933), *Cat and the Fiddle* (MGM, 1934), *Men in White* (MGM, 1934), *The Fountain* (RKO, 1934), *The Painted Veil* (MGM, 1934), *Mark of the Vampire* (MGM, 1935), *Murder in the Fleet* (MGM, 1935), *Break of Hearts* (RKO, 1935), *Tough Guy* (MGM, 1936), *The Country Doctor* (20th, 1936), *Sins of Man* (20th, 1936), *His Brother's Wife* (MGM, 1936), *Reunion* (20th, 1936), *One in a Million* (20th, 1936), *Seventh Heaven* (20th, 1937), *Heidi* (20th, 1937), *Happy Landing* (20th, 1938), *Alexander's Ragtime Band* (20th, 1938), *I'll Give a Million* (20th, 1938), *Five of a Kind* (20th, 1938), *Mr. Moto in Danger Island* (20th, 1939), *Meet Dr. Christian* (RKO, 1939), *Courageous Dr. Christian* (RKO, 1940), *Dr. Christian Meets the Women* (RKO, 1940), *Remedy for Riches* (RKO, 1940), *Melody for Three* (RKO, 1941), *Stage Door Canteen* (UA, 1943), *Dancing in the Dark* (20th, 1949), *Run for Cover* (Par., 1955).

CHARLTON HESTON Born October 4, 1924, Evanston, Illinois. Married Lydia Clark (1944), children: Fraser, Holly.

Lizabeth Scott and Charlton Heston in *Dark City.*

Feature Films: *Peer Gynt* (Brandon Films, 1942), *Julius Caesar* (Brandon Films, 1950), *Dark City* (Par., 1950), *The Greatest Show on Earth* (Par., 1952), *The Savage* (Par., 1952), *Ruby Gentry* (20th, 1952), *The President's Lady* (20th, 1953), *Pony Express* (Par., 1953), *Arrowhead* (Par., 1953), *Bad for Each Other* (Col., 1953), *The Naked Jungle* (Par., 1954), *Secret of the Incas* (Par., 1954), *The Far Horizons* (Par., 1955), *The Private War of Major Benson* (Univ., 1955), *Lucy Gallant* (Par., 1955), *The Ten Commandments* (Par., 1956), *Three Violent People* (Par., 1956), *Touch of Evil* (Univ., 1958), *The Big Country* (UA, 1958), *The Buccaneer* (Par., 1958), *The Wreck of the Mary Deare* (MGM, 1959), *Ben-Hur* (MGM, 1959), *El Cid* (UA, 1961), *The Pigeon That Took Rome* (Par., 1962), *Diamond Head* (Col., 1962), *55 Days at Peking* (AA, 1963), *The Greatest Story Ever Told* (UA, 1965), *Major Dundee* (Col., 1965), *The Agony and the Ecstasy* (20th, 1965), *The War Lord* (Univ., 1965), *Khartoum* (UA, 1966), *Counterpoint* (Univ., 1967), *Planet of the Apes* (20th, 1968), *Will Penny* (Par., 1968).

ROSE HOBART (Rose Kefer) Born May 1, 1906, New York, New York. Married Ben Webster (1924); divorced 1928. Married William Grosvenor (1932); divorced 1942. Married Barton Bosworth (1948).

Rose Hobart and Georges Renavent in *East of Borneo.*

Feature Films: *A Lady Surrenders* (Univ., 1930), *Liliom* (Fox, 1930), *Chances* (WB, 1931), *East of Borneo* (Univ., 1931), *Compromised* (British International, 1931), *Dr. Jekyll and Mr. Hyde* (Par., 1932), *Scandal for Sale* (Univ., 1932), *Shadow Laughs* (Invincible, 1933), *Convention Girl* (First Division, 1935), *The Tower of London* (Univ., 1939), *Wolf of New York* (Rep., 1940), *Susan and God* (MGM, 1940), *A Night at Earl Carroll's* (Par., 1940), *Ziegfeld Girl* (MGM, 1941), *Singapore Woman* (WB, 1941), *Lady Be Good* (MGM, 1941), *Nothing But the Truth* (Par., 1941), *I'll Sell My Life* (Select, 1941), *No Hands on the Clock* (Par., 1941), *Mr. and Mrs. North* (MGM, 1941), *Adventures of Smilin' Jack* (Univ. serial, 1942), *A Gentleman at Heart* (20th, 1942), *Who Is Hope Schuyler?* (20th, 1942), *Prison Girls* (PRC, 1942), *Dr. Gillespie's New Assistant* (MGM, 1942), *Salute to the Marines* (MGM, 1943), *Swing Shift Maisie* (MGM, 1943), *The Mad Ghoul* (Univ., 1943), *Crime Doctor's Strangest Case* (Col., 1943), *Song of the Open Road* (UA, 1944), *The Soul of a Monster* (Col., 1944), *Conflict* (WB, 1945), *The Brighton Strangler* (RKO, 1945), *The Cat Creeps* (Univ., 1946), *Canyon Passage* (Univ., 1946), *Claudia and David* (20th, 1946), *The Farmer's Daughter* (RKO, 1947), *The Trouble With Women* (Par., 1947), *Cass Timberlane* (MGM, 1947), *Mickey* (EL, 1948), *Bride of Vengeance* (Par., 1949).

JOHN HODIAK Born April 16, 1914, Pittsburgh, Pennsylvania. Married Anne Baxter (1946), child: Katrina; divorced 1953. Died October 19, 1955.

John Hodiak, Virginia Brissac and Lana Turner in *Marriage Is a Private Affair.*

Feature Films: *A Stranger in Town* (MGM, 1943), *Swing Shift Maisie* (MGM, 1943), *I Dood It* (MGM, 1943), *Song of Russia* (MGM, 1943), *Maisie Goes to Reno* (MGM, 1944) *Marriage Is a Private Affair* (MGM, 1944), *Lifeboat* (20th, 1944), *Sunday Dinner for a Soldier* (20th, 1944), *A Bell for Adano* (20th, 1945), *The Harvey Girls* (MGM,

1946), *Somewhere in the Night* (20th, 1946), *Two Smart People* (MGM, 1946), *The Arnelo Affair* (MGM, 1947), *Desert Fury* (Par., 1947), *Love From a Stranger* (EL, 1947), *Homecoming* (MGM, 1948), *Command Decision* (MGM, 1948), *The Bribe* (MGM, 1949), *Battleground* (MGM, 1949), *Malaya* (MGM, 1949), *Ambush* (MGM, 1949), *A Lady Without a Passport* (MGM, 1950), *The Miniver Story* (MGM, 1950), *Night into Morning* (MGM, 1951), *The People Against O'Hara* (MGM, 1951), *Across the Wide Missouri* (MGM, 1951), *The Sellout* (MGM, 1951), *Battle Zone* (AA, 1952), *Mission Over Korea* (Col., 1953), *Conquest of Cochise* (Col., 1953), *Ambush at Tomahawk Gap* (Col., 1953), *Dragonfly Squadron* (AA, 1954), *Trial* (MGM, 1955), *On the Threshold of Space* (20th, 1956).

WILLIAM HOLDEN (William Franklin Beedle) Born April 17, 1918, O'Fallon, Illinois. Married Brenda Marshall (1941), children: Virginia, Peter, Scott.

William Holden, Claire Trevor and Glenn Ford in *Texas*.

Feature Films: *Golden Boy* (Col., 1939), *Invisible Stripes* (WB, 1940), *Our Town* (UA, 1940), *Those Were the Days* (Par., 1940), *Arizona* (Col., 1940), *I Wanted Wings* (Par., 1941), *Texas* (Col., 1941), *The Fleet's In* (Par., 1942), *The Remarkable Andrew* (Par., 1942), *Meet the Stewarts* (Col., 1942), *Young and Willing* (UA, 1943), *Blaze of Noon* (Par., 1947), *Dear Ruth* (Par., 1947), *Variety Girl* (Par., 1947), *Rachel and the Stranger* (RKO, 1948), *Apartment for Peggy* (20th, 1948), *The Man From Colorado* (Col., 1948), *The Dark Past* (Col., 1949), *Streets of Laredo* (Par., 1949), *Miss Grant Takes Richmond* (Col., 1949), *Dear Wife* (Par., 1949), *Father Is a Bachelor* (Col., 1950), *Sunset Boulevard* (Par., 1950), *Union Station* (Par., 1950), *Born Yesterday* (Col., 1950), *Force of Arms* (WB, 1951), *Submarine Command* (Par., 1951), *Boots Malone* (Col., 1952), *The Turning Point* (Par., 1952), *Stalag 17* (Par., 1953), *The Moon Is Blue* (UA, 1953), *Forever Female* (Par., 1953), *Escape From Fort Bravo* (MGM, 1953), *Executive Suite* (MGM, 1954), *Sabrina* (Par., 1954), *The Country Girl* (Par., 1954), *The Bridges at Toko-Ri* (Par., 1954), *Love Is a Many-Splendored Thing* (20th, 1955), *Picnic* (Col., 1955), *The Proud and the Profane* (Par., 1956), *Toward the Unknown* (WB, 1956), *The Bridge on the River Kwai* (Col., 1957), *The Key* (Col., 1958), *The Horse Soldiers* (UA, 1959), *The World of Suzie Wong* (Par., 1960), *Satan Never Sleeps* (20th, 1962), *The Counterfeit Traitor* (Par., 1962), *The Lion* (20th, 1962), *Paris When It Sizzles* (Par., 1964), *The 7th Dawn* (UA, 1964), *Alvarez Kelly* (Col., 1966), *Casino Royale* (Col., 1967), *The Devil's Brigade* (UA, 1968).

JUDY HOLLIDAY (Judith Tuvim) Born June 21, 1922, New York, New York. Married David Oppenheim (1948), child: Jonathan; divorced 1958. Died June 7, 1965.

Judy Holliday in *Full of Life*.

Feature Films: *Greenwich Village* (20th, 1944), *Something for the Boys* (20th, 1944), *Winged Victory* (20th, 1944), *Adam's Rib* (MGM, 1949), *Born Yesterday* (Col., 1950), *The Marrying Kind* (Col., 1952), *It Should Happen to You* (Col., 1954), *Phffft* (Col., 1954), *The Solid Gold Cadillac* (Col., 1956), *Full of Life* (Col., 1956), *Bells Are Ringing* (MGM, 1960).

CELESTE HOLM Born April 29, 1919, New York, New York. Married Ralph Nelson, child: Theodore; divorced. Married Francis Davis (1940); divorced. Married Schuyler Dunning (1946), child: Daniel; divorced 1952.

Linda Darnell, Lucile Watson, Celeste Holm and Paul Douglas in *Everybody Does It*.

Feature Films: *Three Little Girls in Blue* (20th, 1946), *Carnival in Costa Rica* (20th, 1947), *Gentleman's Agreement* (20th, 1947), *Road House* (20th, 1948), *The Snake Pit* (20th, 1948), *Chicken Every Sunday* (20th 1948), *Come to the Stable* (20th, 1949), *Everybody Does It* (20th, 1949), *A Letter to Three Wives* (narrator; 20th, 1949), *All About Eve* (20th, 1950), *Champagne for Caesar* (UA, 1950), *The Tender Trap* (MGM, 1955), *High Society* (MGM, 1956), *Bachelor Flat* (20th, 1961), *Doctor, You've Got to Be Kidding!* (MGM, 1967).

BOB HOPE (Leslie Townes Hope) Born May 26, 1903, London, England. Married Dolores Reade (1933), children: Linda, Tony, Nora, Kelly.

Feature Films: *Big Broadcast of 1938* (Par., 1937), *College Swing* (Par., 1938), *Give Me a Sailor* (Par., 1938), *Thanks for the Memory* (Par., 1938), *Never Say Die* (Par., 1939), *Some Like It Hot* (Par., 1939), *The Cat and the Canary* (Par., 1939), *Road to Singapore* (Par., 1940), *The Ghost Breakers* (Par., 1940), *Road to Zanzibar* (Par., 1941), *Caught in the Draft* (Par., 1941), *Nothing But the Truth* (Par., 1941), *Louisiana Purchase* (Par., 1941), *My Favorite Blonde* (Par., 1942), *Road to Morocco* (RKO, 1942), *Star Spangled Rhythm* (Par., 1942), *They Got Me Cov-*

Jane Russell and Bob Hope in *Paleface*.

ered (Par., 1943), *Let's Face It* (Par., 1943), *The Princess and the Pirate* (Par., 1944), *Road to Utopia* (Par., 1945), *Monsieur Beaucaire* (Par., 1946), *My Favorite Brunette* (Par., 1947), *Where There's Life* (Par., 1947), *Variety Girl* (Par., 1947), *Road to Rio* (Par., 1948), *Paleface* (Par., 1948), *Sorrowful Jones* (Par., 1949), *The Great Lover* (Par., 1949), *Fancy Pants* (Par., 1950), *The Lemon Drop Kid* (Par., 1951), *My Favorite Spy* (Par., 1951), *The Greatest Show on Earth* (Par., 1952),* *Son of Paleface* (Par., 1952), *Road to Bali* (Par., 1952), *Off Limits* (Par., 1953), *Here Come the Girls* (Par., 1953), *Scared Stiff* (Par., 1953),* *Casanova's Big Night* (Par., 1954), *The Seven Little Foys* (Par., 1955), *That Certain Feeling* (Par., 1956), *The Iron Petticoat* (MGM, 1956), *Beau James* (Par., 1957), *Paris Holiday* (UA, 1958), *The Five Pennies* (Par., 1959),* *Alias Jesse James* (UA, 1959), *The Facts of Life* (UA, 1960), *Bachelor in Paradise* (MGM, 1961), *Road to Hong Kong* (UA, 1962), *Critic's Choice* (WB, 1963), *Call Me Bwana* (UA, 1963), *A Global Affair* (MGM, 1964), *I'll Take Sweden* (UA, 1965), *The Oscar* (Par., 1966),* *Boy, Did I Get a Wrong Number* (UA, 1966), *Eight on the Lam* (UA, 1967), *The Private Navy of Sgt. O'Farrell* (UA, 1968).

*Unbilled guest appearance

MIRIAM HOPKINS (Ellen Miriam Hopkins) Born October 18, 1902, Bainbridge, Georgia. Married Brandon Peters (1926); divorced 1931. Married Austin Parker (1931), child: Michael; divorced 1932. Married Anatole Litvak (1937); divorced 1939. Married Raymond Brock; divorced 1951.

Richard Ainley and Miriam Hopkins in *Lady With Red Hair*.

Feature Films: *Fast and Loose* (Par., 1930), *The Smiling Lieutenant* (Par., 1931), *24 Hours* (Par., 1931), *Dr. Jekyll and Mr. Hyde* (Par., 1932), *Two Kinds of Women* (Par., 1932), *Dancers in the Dark* (Par., 1932), *The World and the Flesh* (Par., 1932), *Trouble in Paradise* (Par., 1932), *The Story of Temple Drake* (Par., 1933), *Design for Living* (Par., 1933), *Stranger's Return* (MGM, 1933), *All of Me* (Par., 1934), *She Loves Me Not* (Par., 1934), *The Richest Girl in the World* (RKO, 1934), *Becky Sharp* (RKO, 1935), *Barbary Coast* (UA, 1935), *Splendor* (UA, 1935), *These Three* (UA, 1936), *Men Are Not Gods* (UA, 1937), *The Woman I Love* (RKO, 1937), *Woman Chases Man* (UA, 1937), *Wise Girl* (RKO, 1937), *The Old Maid* (WB, 1939), *Virginia City* (WB, 1940), *The Lady With Red Hair* (WB, 1940), *A Gentleman After Dark* (UA, 1942), *Old Acquaintance* (WB, 1943), *The Heiress* (Par., 1949), *The Mating Season* (Par., 1951), *Carrie* (Par., 1952), *Outcasts of Poker Flat* (20th, 1952), *The Children's Hour* (UA, 1962), *Fanny Hill: Memoirs of a Woman of Pleasure* (Favorite Films, 1965), *The Chase* (Col., 1966).

EDWARD EVERETT HORTON Born March 18, 1888, Brooklyn, New York.

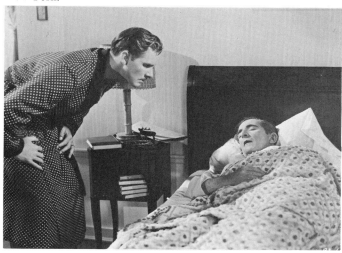

Errol Flynn and Edward Everett Horton in *The Perfect Specimen*.

Sound Feature Films: *The Hottentot* (WB, 1929), *Aviator* (WB, 1929), *Take the Heir* (Big Four, 1930), *Wide Open* (WB, 1930), *Holiday* (Pathé, 1930), *Once a Gentleman* (Sono Art-World Wide, 1930), *Kiss Me Again* (WB, 1931), *Reaching for the Moon* (UA, 1931), *Lonely Wives* (Pathé, 1931), *Front Page* (UA, 1931), *Six Cylinder Love* (Fox, 1931), *Smart Woman* (RKO, 1931), *Age for Love* (UA, 1931), *But the Flesh is Weak* (MGM, 1932), *Roar of the Dragon* (RKO, 1932), *Trouble in Paradise* (Par., 1932), *It's a Boy* (Gaumont-British, 1933), *A Bedtime Story* (Par., 1933), *The Way to Love* (Par., 1933), *Design for Living* (Par., 1933), *Alice in Wonderland* (Par., 1933), *A Woman in Command* (Gaumont-British, 1934), *Easy to Love* (WB, 1934), *Sing and Like It* (RKO, 1934), *Poor Rich* (Univ., 1934), *Smarty* (WB, 1934), *Success at Any Price* (RKO, 1934), *Uncertain Lady* (Univ., 1934), *Kiss and Make Up* (Par., 1934), *The Merry Widow* (MGM, 1934), *Ladies Should Listen* (Par., 1934), *The Gay Divorcee* (RKO, 1934), *The Private Secretary* (Twickenham-British, 1935,) *Biography of a Bachelor Girl* (MGM, 1935), *All the King's Horses* (Par., 1935), *The Night is Young* (MGM, 1935), *The Devil Is a Woman* (Par., 1935), *In Caliente* (WB, 1935), *$10 Raise* (Fox, 1935), *Going Highbrow* (WB, 1935), *Little Big Shot* (WB, 1935), *Top Hat* (RKO, 1935), *His Night Out* (Univ., 1935), *The Singing Kid* (WB, 1936), *Her Master's Voice* (Par., 1936), *Hearts Divided* (WB, 1936), *Nobody's Fool* (Univ., 1936), *The Man in the Mirror* (GN, 1937), *The King and the Chorus Girl* (WB, 1937), *Let's Make a Million* (Par., 1937), *Lost Horizon* (Col., 1937), *Shall We Dance* (RKO, 1937), *Oh Doctor!* (Univ., 1937), *Wild Money* (Par., 1937), *Angel* (Par., 1937), *The Perfect Specimen* (WB, 1937), *Danger—Love at Work* (20th, 1937), *The Great Garrick* (WB, 1937), *Hitting a New High* (RKO, 1937), *Bluebeard's Eighth Wife* (Par., 1938), *College Swing* (Par., 1938), *Holiday* (Col., 1938), *Little Tough Guys in Society* (Univ., 1938), *Paris Honeymoon* (Par., 1939), *That's Right—You're*

Wrong (RKO, 1939), *You're the One* (Par., 1941), *Ziegfeld Girl* (MGM, 1941), *Sunny* (RKO, 1941), *Bachelor Daddy* (Univ., 1941), *Here Comes Mr. Jordan* (Col., 1941), *Week-End for Three* (RKO, 1941), *Sandy Steps Out* (Univ., 1941), *I Married an Angel* (MGM, 1942), *The Magnificent Dope* (20th, 1942), *Springtime in the Rockies* (20th, 1942), *Forever and a Day* (RKO, 1943), *Thank Your Lucky Stars* (WB, 1943), *The Gang's All Here* (20th, 1943), *Summer Storm* (UA, 1944), *The Amazing Mr. Forrest* (PRC, 1944), *Her Primitive Man* (Univ., 1944), *San Diego, I Love You* (Univ., 1944), *Arsenic and Old Lace* (WB, 1944), *Brazil* (Rep., 1944), *The Town Went Wild* (PRC, 1944), *Steppin' in Society* (Rep., 1945), *Lady on a Train* (Univ., 1945), *Cinderella Jones* (WB, 1946), *Faithful in My Fashion* (MGM, 1946), *Earl Carroll's Sketchbook* (Rep., 1946), *The Ghost Goes Wild* (Rep., 1947), *Down to Earth* (Col., 1947), *Her Husband's Affair* (Col., 1947), *All My Sons* (Univ., 1948), *The Story of Mankind* (WB, 1957), *Pocketful of Miracles* (UA, 1961), *It's a Mad, Mad, Mad, Mad World* (UA, 1963), *Sex and the Single Girl* (WB, 1964), *The Perils of Pauline* (Univ., 1967).

LESLIE HOWARD (Leslie Howard Stainer) Born April 3, 1893; London, England. Married Ruth Martin (1916), children: Ronald, Leslie. Died June 1, 1943.

Kay Francis and Leslie Howard in *British Agent*.

Feature Films: *Outward Bound* (WB, 1930), *Never the Twain Shall Meet* (MGM, 1931), *A Free Soul* (MGM, 1931), *Five and Ten* (MGM, 1931), *Devotion* (RKO, 1931), *Reserved for Ladies* (Par., 1932), *Smilin' Through* (MGM, 1932), *The Animal Kingdom* (RKO, 1932), *Secrets* (UA, 1933), *Captured!* (WB, 1933), *Berkeley Square* (Fox, 1933), *The Lady Is Willing* (Col., 1934), *Of Human Bondage* (RKO, 1934), *British Agent* (WB, 1934), *The Scarlet Pimpernel* (UA, 1935), *The Petrified Forest* (WB, 1936), *Romeo and Juliet* (MGM, 1936), *It's Love I'm After* (WB, 1937), *Stand-In* (UA, 1937), *Pygmalion* (MGM, 1938), *Gone With the Wind* (MGM, 1939), *Intermezzo* (UA, 1939), *The First of the Few* ("Spitfire"—King, 1941), *Pimpernel Smith* (UA, 1942), *The Invaders* (Columbia, 1942).

ROCHELLE HUDSON Born March 6, 1914, Claremore, Oklahoma. Married Harold Thompson (1939); divorced 1947. Married Richard Hyland; divorced 1950.

Feature Films: *Are These Our Children?* (RKO, 1931), *Fanny Foley Herself* (RKO, 1931), *Beyond the Rockies* (RKO, 1932), *Hell's Highway* (RKO, 1932), *The Penguin Pool Murder* (RKO, 1932), *The Savage Girl* (Freuler, 1933), *She Done Him Wrong* (Par., 1933), *Love Is Dangerous* (Chesterfield, 1933), *Notorious But Nice* (Chesterfield, 1933), *Doctor Bull* (Fox, 1933), *Walls of Gold* (Fox, 1933), *Wild Boys of the Road* (WB, 1933), *Love Is Like That* (Chesterfield, 1933), *Mr. Skitch* (Fox, 1933), *Harold Teen* (WB, 1934), *Such Women Are Dangerous* (Fox,

Spring Byington, Rochelle Hudson, Margaret Hamilton and Slim Summerville in *Way Down East*.

1934), *Judge Priest* (Fox, 1934), *Bachelor Bait* (RKO, 1934), *Mighty Barnum* (UA, 1934), *Imitation of Life* (Univ., 1934), *I've Been Around* (Univ., 1935), *Life Begins at Forty* (Fox, 1935), *Les Miserables* (UA, 1935), *Way Down East* (Fox, 1935), *Curly Top* (Fox, 1935), *Show Them No Mercy* (20th, 1935), *The Music Goes Round* (Col., 1936), *Everybody's Old Man* (20th, 1936), *The Country Beyond* (20th, 1936), *Poppy* (Par., 1936), *Reunion* (20th, 1936), *Woman Wise* (20th, 1937), *That I May Live* (20th, 1937), *Born Reckless* (20th, 1937), *She Had to Eat* (20th, 1937), *Rascals* (20th, 1938), *Mr. Moto Takes a Chance* (20th, 1938), *Storm Over Bengal* (Rep., 1938), *Pride of the Navy* (Rep., 1939), *Missing Daughters* (Col., 1939), *A Woman Is the Judge* (Col., 1939), *Smuggled Cargo* (Rep., 1939), *Pirates of the Skies* (Univ., 1939), *Convicted Woman* (Col., 1940), *Konga, the Wild Stallion* (Col., 1940), *Men Without Souls* (Col., 1940), *Babies For Sale* (Col., 1940), *Island of Doomed Men* (Col., 1940), *Girls Under 21* (Col., 1940), *Meet Boston Blackie* (Col., 1941), *The Officer and the Lady* (Col., 1941), *The Stork Pays Off* (Col., 1941), *Rubber Racketeers* (Mon., 1942), *Queen of Broadway* (PRC, 1942), *Bush Pilot* (Screen Guild, 1947), *Devil's Cargo* (Film Classics, 1948), *Sky Liner* (Lip., 1949), *Rebel Without a Cause* (WB, 1955), *Strait-Jacket* (Col., 1964), *The Night Walker* (Univ., 1965), *Dr. Terror's Gallery of Horrors* (Par., 1967).

ROCK HUDSON (Roy Scherer, Jr.) Born November 17, 1927, Winnetka, Illinois. Married Phyllis Gates (1955); divorced 1958.

Doris Day and Rock Hudson in *Lover Come Back*.

Feature Films: *Fighter Squadron* (WB, 1948), *Undertow* (Univ., 1949), *I Was a Shoplifter* (Univ., 1950), *One Way Street* (Univ., 1950), *Winchester '73* (Univ., 1950), *Peggy* (Univ., 1950), *The Desert Hawk* (Univ., 1950), *The Fat Man* (Univ., 1951), *Air Cadet* (Univ., 1951), *Tomahawk* (Univ., 1951), *Iron Man* (Univ., 1951), *Bright Victory* (Univ., 1951), *Bend of the River* (Univ., 1952), *Here Come the Nelsons* (Univ., 1952)

94

Scarlet Angel (Univ., 1952), *Has Anybody Seen My Gal* (Univ., 1952), *Horizons West* (Univ., 1952), *The Lawless Breed* (Univ., 1952), *Seminole* (Univ., 1953), *Sea Devils* (RKO, 1953), *The Golden Blade* (Univ., 1953), *Back to God's Country* (Univ., 1953), *Taza, Son of Cochise* (Univ., 1954), *Magnificent Obsession* (Univ., 1954), *Bengal Brigade* (Univ., 1954), *Captain Lightfoot* (Univ., 1955), *One Desire* (Univ., 1955), *All That Heaven Allows* (Univ., 1955), *Never Say Goodbye* (Univ., 1956), *Giant* (WB, 1956), *Battle Hymn* (Univ., 1956), *Written on the Wind* (Univ., 1956), *Four Girls in Town* (Univ., 1956), *Some-thing of Value* (MGM, 1957), *The Tarnished Angels* (Univ., 1957), *A Farewell to Arms* (20th, 1957), *Twilight for the Gods* (Univ., 1958), *This Earth Is Mine* (Univ., 1959), *Pillow Talk* (Univ., 1959), *The Last Sunset* (Univ., 1961), *Come September* (Univ., 1961), *Lover, Come Back* (Univ., 1961), *The Spiral Road* (Univ., 1962), *A Gathering of Eagles* (Univ., 1963), *Man's Favorite Sport?* (Univ., 1964), *Send Me No Flowers* (Univ., 1964), *Strange Bedfellows* (Univ., 1964), *A Very Special Favor* (Univ., 1965), *Blindfold* (Univ., 1966), *Seconds* (Par., 1966), *Tobruk* (Univ., 1967), *Ice Station Zebra* (MGM, 1968), *The Quiet Couple* (CBS Films, 1968).

MARSHA HUNT (Marcia Virginia Hunt) Born October 17, 1917, Chicago, Illinois. Married Jerry Hopper (1938); divorced 1943. Married Robert Presnell (1946).

Walter Fenner, Keenan Wynn, Sara Haden, Alan Napier, Philip Merivale, Howard Freeman, Kathleen Lockhart, Elisabeth Risdon, Marsha Hunt and Donald Meek in *Lost Angel*.

Feature Films: *The Virginia Judge* (Par., 1935), *The Accusing Finger* (Par., 1936), *Gentle Julia* (20th, 1936), *Desert Gold* (Par., 1936), *Arizona Raiders* (Par., 1936), *Hollywood Boulevard* (Par., 1936), *Easy to Take* (Par., 1936), *College Holiday* (Par., 1936), *Murder Goes to College* (Par., 1937), *Easy Living* (Par., 1937), *Thunder Trail* (Par., 1937), *Annapolis Salute* (RKO, 1937), *The Long Shot* (GN, 1938), *Born to the West* (Par., 1938), *Come On, Leathernecks* (Rep., 1938), *The Hardys Ride High* (MGM, 1939), *The Star Reporter* (Mon., 1939), *These Glamour Girls* (MGM, 1939), *Joe and Ethel Turp Call on the President* (MGM, 1939), *Winter Carnival* (UA, 1939), *Pride and Pre-judice* (MGM, 1940), *Flight Command* (MGM, 1940), *Irene* (RKO, 1940), *Woman in Hiding* (Univ., 1940), *Ellery Queen, Master Detective* (Col., 1940), *Blossoms in the Dust* (MGM, 1941), *I'll Wait for You* (MGM, 1941), *The Trial of Mary Dugan* (MGM, 1941), *The Penalty* (MGM, 1941), *Cheers for Miss Bishop* (UA, 1941), *Unholy Partners* (MGM, 1941), *Kid Glove Killer* (MGM, 1942), *Joe Smith, American* (MGM, 1942), *The Affairs of Martha* (MGM, 1942), *Panama Hattie* (MGM, 1942), *Seven Sweethearts* (MGM, 1942), *Thousands Cheer* (MGM, 1943), *Pilot No. 5* (MGM, 1943), *The Human Comedy* (MGM, 1943), *Cry Havoc* (MGM, 1943), *Lost Angel* (MGM, 1943), *Bride by Mistake* (RKO, 1944), *None Shall Escape* (Col., 1944), *Music for Millions* (MGM, 1944), *Valley of Decision* (MGM, 1945), *A Letter for Evie* (MGM, 1945), *Smash-Up* (Univ., 1947), *Carnegie Hall* (UA,

1947), *The Inside Story* (Rep., 1948), *Raw Deal* (EL, 1948), *Jigsaw* (UA, 1949), *Take One False Step* (Univ., 1949), *Mary Ryan, Detective* (Col., 1950), *Actors and Sin* (UA, 1952), *The Happy Time* (Col., 1952), *Diplo-matic Passport* (Eros, 1954), *No Place to Hide* (AA, 1956), *Bombers B-52* (WB, 1957), *Back From the Dead* (20th, 1957), *Blue Denim* (20th, 1959), *The Plunderers* (AA, 1960).

JEFFREY HUNTER (Henry Herman McKinnies, Jr.) Born November 25, 1927, New Orleans, Louisiana. Married Barbara Rush (1950), child: Christopher; divorced 1955. Married Dusty Bartlett (1957), child: Toddy; divorced 1967.

Jeffrey Hunter, John Larch, Chill Wills and Dean Stockwell in *Gun for a Coward*.

English-Language Feature Films: *Julius Caesar* (Brandon Films, 1950), *Fourteen Hours* (20th, 1951), *Call Me Mister* (20th, 1951), *Take Care of My Little Girl* (20th, 1951), *The Frogmen* (20th, 1951), *Red Skies of Montana* (20th, 1952), *Belles on their Toes* (20th, 1952), *Dreamboat* (20th, 1952), *Lure of the Wilderness* (20th, 1952), *Sailor of the King* (20th, 1953), *Three Young Texans* (20th, 1954), *Princess of the Nile* (20th, 1954), *Seven Angry Men* (AA, 1955), *White Feather* (20th, 1955), *Seven Cities of Gold* (20th, 1955), *The Searchers* (WB, 1956), *The Great Locomotive Chase* (BV, 1956), *The Proud Ones* (20th, 1956), *A Kiss Before Dying* (UA, 1956), *Four Girls in Town* (Univ, 1956), *Gun for a Coward* (Univ., 1957), *The True Story of Jesse James* (20th, 1957), *No Down Payment* (20th, 1957), *Count Five and Die* (20th, 1958), *The Last Hurrah* (Col., 1958), *In Love and War* (20th, 1958), *Mardi Gras* (20th, 1958), *Sergeant Rutledge* (WB, 1960), *Hell to Eternity* (AA, 1960), *Key Witness* (MGM, 1960), *Man-Trap* (Par., 1961), *King of Kings* (MGM, 1961), *No Man is an Island* (Univ., 1962), *The Longest Day* (20th, 1962), *The Man From Galveston* (WB, 1964), *Brainstorm* (WB, 1965), *Murieta* (WB, 1965), *Dimension 5* (Feature Film Corp. of America, 1966), *Frozen Alive* (PRO, 1967), *Witch Without a Broom* (PRO, 1967), *Custer of the West* (Cinerama, 1967), *A Guide for the Married Man* (20th, 1967), *The Christmas Kid* (PRO, 1967), *The Private Navy of Sgt. O'Farrell* (UA, 1968).

KIM HUNTER (Janet Cole) Born November 12, 1922, Detroit, Michi-gan. Married William Baldwin (1944), child: Kathryn; divorced 1946. Married Robert Emmett (1951), child: Sean.

Humphrey Bogart and Kim Hunter in *Deadline, U.S.A.*

Feature Films: *The Seventh Victim* (RKO, 1943), *Tender Comrade* (RKO, 1943), *When Strangers Marry* (Mon., 1944), *You Came Along* (Par., 1945), *Stairway to Heaven* (Univ., 1947), *A Canterbury Tale* (EL, 1949), *A Streetcar Named Desire* (WB, 1951), *Deadline U.S.A.* (20th, 1952), *Anything Can Happen* (Par., 1952), *Storm Center* (Col., 1956), *The Young Stranger* (Univ., 1957), *Bermuda Affair* (DCA, 1957), *Money, Women and Guns* (Univ., 1958), *Lilith* (Col., 1964), *Planet of the Apes* (20th, 1968).

TAB HUNTER (Arthur Gelien) Born July 1, 1931, New York, New York.

Tab Hunter and William Bishop in *Gun Belt.*

Feature Films: *The Lawless* (Par., 1950), *Island of Desire* (UA, 1952), *Gun Belt* (UA, 1953), *The Steel Lady* (UA, 1953), *Return to Treasure Island* (UA, 1954), *Track of the Cat* (WB, 1954), *Battle Cry* (WB, 1955), *The Sea Chase* (WB, 1955), *The Burning Hills* (WB, 1956), *The Girl He Left Behind* (WB, 1956), *Lafayette Escadrille* (WB, 1958), *Gunman's Walk* (Col., 1958), *Damn Yankees* (WB, 1958), *That Kind of Woman* (Par., 1959), *They Came to Cordura* (Col., 1959), *The Pleasure of His Company* (Par., 1961), *Operation Bikini* (AIP, 1963), *The Golden Arrow* (MGM, 1964), *Ride the Wild Surf* (Col., 1964), *The Loved One* (MGM, 1965), *War Gods of the Deep* (AIP, 1965), *Birds Do It* (Col., 1966), *Fickle Finger of Fate* (PRO, 1967), *Hostile Guns* (Par., 1967), *Cup of St. Sebastian* (PRO, 1967).

RUTH HUSSEY (Ruth Carol O'Rourke) Born October 30, 1914, Providence, Rhode Island. Married Robert Longenecker (1942), children: George, John, Mary.

Feature Films: *Madame X* (MGM, 1937), *Judge Hardy's Children* (MGM, 1938), *Man-Proof* (MGM, 1938), *Marie Antoinette* (MGM,

Ruth Hussey and John Howard in *I, Jane Doe.*

1938), *Hold That Kiss* (MGM, 1938), *Rich Man—Poor Girl* (MGM, 1938), *Time Out for Murder* (20th, 1938), *Spring Madness* (MGM, 1938), *Honolulu* (MGM, 1939), *Within the Law* (MGM, 1939), *Maisie* (MGM, 1939), *The Women* (MGM, 1939), *Another Thin Man* (MGM, 1939), *Blackmail* (MGM, 1939), *Fast and Furious* (MGM, 1939), *Northwest Passage* (MGM, 1940), *Susan and God* (MGM, 1940), *The Philadelphia Story* (MGM, 1940), *Flight Command* (MGM, 1940), *Free and Easy* (MGM, 1941), *Our Wife* (Col., 1941), *Married Bachelor* (MGM, 1941), *H. M. Pulham, Esq.* (MGM, 1941), *Pierre of the Plains* (MGM, 1942), *Tennessee Johnson* (MGM, 1942), *Tender Comrade* (RKO, 1943), *The Uninvited* (Par., 1944), *Marine Raiders* (RKO, 1944), *Bedside Manner* (UA, 1945), *I, Jane Doe* (Rep., 1948), *The Great Gatsby* (Par., 1949), *Louisa* (Univ., 1950), *Mr. Music* (Par., 1950), *That's My Boy* (Par., 1951), *Woman of the North Country* (Rep., 1952), *Stars and Stripes Forever* (20th, 1952), *The Lady Wants Mink* (Rep., 1953), *The Facts of Life* (UA, 1960).

WALTER HUSTON (Walter Houghston) Born April 6, 1884, Toronto, Canada. Married Rhea Gore (1905), child: John; divorced 1913. Married Bayonne Whipple (1914); divorced. Married Nanette Sunderland (1931). Died April 7, 1950.

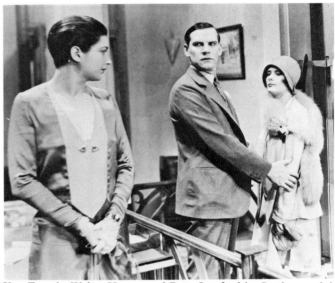

Kay Francis, Walter Huston and Betty Lawford in *Gentlemen of the Press.*

Feature Films: *Gentlemen of the Press* (Par., 1929), *The Lady Lies* (Par., 1929), *The Virginian* (Par., 1929), *The Bad Man* (WB, 1930), *The Virtuous Sin* (Par., 1930), *Abraham Lincoln* (UA, 1930), *The Criminal Code* (Col., 1931), *Star Witness* (WB, 1931), *The Ruling Voice* (WB, 1931), *A Woman From Monte Carlo* (WB, 1932), *A House Divided* (Univ., 1932), *Law and Order* (Univ., 1932), *The Beast of the City* (MGM, 1932), *The Wet Parade* (MGM, 1932), *Night Court* (MGM, 1932), *American Madness* (Col., 1932), *Kongo* (MGM, 1932), *Rain* (UA, 1932), *Hell Below* (MGM, 1933), *Gabriel Over the White House* (MGM, 1933), *The Prizefighter and the Lady* (MGM, 1933), *Storm at Daybreak* (MGM, 1933), *Ann Vickers* (RKO, 1933), *Keep 'Em Rolling!* (RKO, 1934), *Trans-Atlantic Tunnel* (Gaumont-British, 1935), *Rhodes of Africa* (Gaumont-British, 1936), *Dodsworth* (UA, 1936), *Of Human Hearts* (MGM, 1938), *The Light That Failed* (Par., 1940), *All That Money Can Buy* (RKO, 1941), *The Maltese Falcon* (WB, 1941),* *Swamp Water* (20th, 1941), *The Shanghai Gesture* (UA, 1941), *Always in My Heart* (WB, 1942), *In This Our Life* (WB, 1942),* *Yankee Doodle Dandy* (WB, 1942), *The Outlaw* (RKO, 1943), *Edge of Darkness* (WB, 1943), *Mission to Moscow* (WB, 1943), *The North Star* (RKO, 1943), *Dragon Seed* (MGM, 1944), *And Then There Were None* (20th, 1945), *Dragonwyck* (20th, 1946), *Duel in the Sun* (Selznick, 1946), *Treasure of the Sierra Madre* (WB, 1948), *Summer Holiday* (MGM, 1948), *The Great Sinner* (MGM, 1949), *The Furies* (Par., 1950).

*Unbilled guest appearance

BETTY HUTTON (Elizabeth June Thornburg) Born February 26, 1921, Battle Creek, Michigan. Married Ted Briskin (1945), children: Lindsay, Candice; divorced 1951. Married Charles O'Curran (1952); divorced 1955. Married Alan Livingston (1955); divorced 1958. Married Pete Candoli (1961), child: Carolyn; divorced 1966.

Diana Lynn, Dorothy Lamour, Raymond Walburn, Betty Hutton and Mimi Chandler in *And the Angels Sing*.

Feature Films: *The Fleet's In* (Par., 1942), *Star Spangled Rhythm* (Par., 1942), *Happy Go Lucky* (Par., 1943), *Let's Face It* (Par., 1943), *The Miracle of Morgan's Creek* (Par., 1944), *And the Angels Sing* (Par., 1944), *Here Come the Waves* (Par., 1944), *Incendiary Blonde* (Par., 1945), *Duffy's Tavern* (Par., 1945), *The Stork Club* (Par., 1945), *Cross My Heart* (Par., 1946), *The Perils of Pauline* (Par., 1947), *Dream Girl* (Par., 1948), *Red, Hot and Blue* (Par., 1949), *Annie Get Your Gun* (MGM, 1950), *Let's Dance* (Par., 1950), *Sailor Beware* (Par., 1951),* *Somebody Loves Me* (Par., 1952), *The Greatest Show on Earth* (Par., 1952), *Spring Reunion* (UA, 1957).

*Unbilled guest appearance

JIM HUTTON (James Hutton) Born Binghamton, New York. Married, children: Heidi, Timothy; divorced.

Lois Nettleton, Jim Hutton and Jane Fonda in *Period of Adjustment*.

Feature Films: *A Time to Love, and a Time to Die* (Univ., 1958), *Ten Seconds to Hell* (UA, 1959), *The Subterraneans* (MGM, 1960), *Where the Boys Are* (MGM, 1960), *The Honeymoon Machine* (MGM, 1961),

Bachelor in Paradise (MGM, 1961), *The Horizontal Lieutenant* (MGM, 1962), *Period of Adjustment* (MGM, 1962), *Looking for Love* (MGM, 1964),* *Major Dundee* (Col., 1965), *The Hallelujah Trail* (UA, 1965), *Never Too Late* (WB, 1965), *Walk, Don't Run* (Col., 1966), *The Trouble With Angels* (Col., 1966), *Who's Minding the Mint?* (Col., 1967), *The Green Berets* (WB-7 Arts, 1968).

*Unbilled guest appearance

MARTHA HYER Born August 10, 1924, Fort Worth, Texas. Married Ray Stahl (1951); divorced 1953. Married Hal Wallis (1966).

Martha Hyer, Van Johnson and Janet Leigh in *Wives and Lovers*.

English-Language Feature Films: *The Locket* (RKO, 1946), *Thunder Mountain* (RKO, 1947), *Born to Kill* (RKO, 1947), *Woman on the Beach* (RKO, 1947), *The Velvet Touch* (RKO, 1948), *Gun Smugglers* (RKO, 1948), *The Clay Pigeon* (RKO, 1949), *The Judge Steps Out* (RKO, 1949), *Roughshod* (RKO, 1949), *Rustlers* (RKO, 1949), *The Lawless* (Par., 1950), *Outcast of Black Mesa* (Col., 1950), *Salt Lake Raiders* (Rep., 1950), *Frisco Tornado* (Rep., 1950), *Wild Stallion* (Mon., 1952), *Yukon Gold* (Mon., 1952), *Geisha Girl* (Realart, 1952), *Abbott and Costello Go to Mars* (Univ., 1953), *So Big* (WB, 1953), *Riders to the Stars* (UA, 1954), *The Scarlet Spear* (UA, 1954), *Battle of Rogue River* (Col., 1954), *Lucky Me* (WB, 1954), *Down Three Dark Streets* (UA, 1954), *Sabrina* (Par., 1954), *Cry Vengeance* (AA, 1954), *Wyoming Renegades* (Col., 1955), *Francis in the Navy* (Univ., 1955), *Kiss of Fire* (Univ., 1955) *Paris Follies of 1956* (AA, 1955), *Red Sundown* (Univ., 1956), *Showdown at Abilene* (Univ., 1956), *Battle Hymn* (Univ., 1956), *Kelly and Me* (Univ., 1957), *Mister Cory* (Univ., 1957), *The Delicate Delinquent* (Par., 1957), *My Man Godfrey* (Univ., 1957), *Paris Holiday* (UA, 1958), *Once Upon a Horse* (Univ., 1958), *Houseboat* (Par., 1958), *Some Came Running* (MGM, 1958), *The Big Fisherman* (BV, 1959), *The Best of Everything* (20th, 1959), *Ice Palace* (WB, 1960), *Desire in the Dust* (20th, 1960), *The Right Approach* (20th, 1961), *The Last Time I Saw Archie* (UA, 1961), *A Girl Named Tamiko* (Par., 1962), *The Man From the Diners' Club* (Col., 1963), *Wives and Lovers* (Par., 1963), *The Carpetbaggers* (Par., 1964), *Pyro* (AIP, 1964), *Bikini Beach* (AIP, 1964), *First Men in the Moon* (Col., 1964), *Blood on the Arrow* (AA, 1964), *The Sons of Katie Elder* (Par., 1965), *The Chase* (Col., 1966), *The Night of the Grizzly* (Par., 1966), *Picture Mommy Dead* (Embassy, 1966), *The Happening* (Col., 1967), *Massacre at Fort Grant* (Butcher's, 1967), *Some May Live* (RKO, 1967), *War Italian Style* (AIP, 1967), *House of 1,000 Dolls* (AIP, 1968).

JOHN IRELAND (John Benjamin Ireland) Born January 30, 1914, Vancouver, British Columbia. Married Elaine Sheldon (1940); divorced 1948. Married Joanne Dru (1949), children: John, Peter; divorced 1956. Married Daphne Myrick (1962).

English-Language Feature Films: *A Walk in the Sun* (20th, 1945), *Behind Green Lights* (20th, 1946), *It Shouldn't Happen to a Dog* (20th,

97

John Ireland in *I Saw What You Did.*

1946), *My Darling Clementine* (20th, 1946), *Wake Up and Dream* (20th, 1946), *Railroaded* (EL, 1947), *The Gangster* (AA, 1947), *Open Secret* (EL, 1948), *Raw Deal* (EL, 1948), *I Love Trouble* (Col., 1948), *Red River* (UA, 1948), *A Southern Yankee* (MGM, 1948), *Joan of Arc* (RKO, 1948), *I Shot Jesse James* (Screen Guild, 1949), *Roughshod* (RKO, 1949), *The Walking Hills* (Col., 1949), *Anna Lucasta* (Col., 1949), *Mr. Soft Touch* (Col., 1949), *Doolins of Oklahoma* (Col., 1949), *All The King's Men* (Col., 1949), *Cargo to Capetown* (Col., 1950), *Return of Jesse James* (Lip., 1950), *The Scarf* (UA, 1951), *Little Big Horn* (Lip., 1951), *Vengeance Valley* (MGM, 1951), *The Basketball Fix* (Realart, 1951), *Red Mountain* (Par., 1951), *The Bushwhackers* (Realart, 1952), *Hurricane Smith* (Par., 1952), *Combat Squad* (Col., 1953), *The 49th Man* (Col., 1953), *Outlaw Territory* (Realart, 1953), *Security Risk* (AA, 1954), *Southwest Passage* (UA, 1954), *The Steel Cage* (UA, 1954), *The Fast and Furious* (American Releasing Corp., 1954), *Glass Tomb* (Lip., 1955), *The Good Die Young* (UA, 1955), *Queen Bee* (Col., 1955), *Hell's Horizon* (Col., 1955), *Gunfight at the O.K. Corral* (Par., 1957), *Stormy Crossing* ("Black Tide"—Eros, 1957), *Party Girl* (MGM, 1958), *No Place to Land* (Rep., 1958), *Spartacus* (Univ., 1960), *Return of a Stranger* (British, 1961), *Wild in the Country* (20th, 1961), *Brushfire!* (Par., 1962), *55 Days at Peking* (AA, 1963), *The Ceremony* (UA, 1963), *No Time to Kill* (Jerry Warren, 1963), *Faces in the Dark* (Pennington Eady, 1964), *The Fall of the Roman Empire* (Par., 1964), *I Saw What You Did* (Univ., 1965), *Day of the Nightmare* (Governor, 1966), *Fort Utah* (Par., 1967), *Flight of the Hawk* (C. B. Productions, 1967), *Arizona Bushwhackers* (Par., 1968).

DEAN JAGGER (Dean Jeffries) Born November 7, 1903, Lima, Ohio. Married Antoinette Lowrence (1935); divorced 1945. Married Gloria Ling (1947), child: Diane; divorced 1967.

Sound Feature Films: *Woman From Hell* (Fox, 1929), *Handcuffed* (Rayart 1929), *You Belong to Me* (Par., 1934), *College Rhythm* (Par., 1934), *Car 99* (Par., 1935), *Home on the Range* (Par., 1935), *Wings in*

Mary Astor and Dean Jagger in *Brigham Young, Frontiersman.*

the Dark (Par., 1935), *Behold My Wife* (Par., 1935), *People Will Talk* (Par., 1935), *Men Without Names* (Par., 1935), *Wanderer of the Wastelands* (Par., 1935), *Woman Trap* (Par., 1936), *13 Hours by Air* (Par., 1936), *Revolt of the Zombies* (Academy Pictures, 1936), *Pepper* (20th, 1936), *Star for a Night* (20th, 1936), *Dangerous Number* (MGM, 1937), *Under Cover of Night* (MGM, 1937), *Woman in Distress* (Col., 1937), *Escape by Night* (Rep., 1937), *Exiled to Shanghai* (Rep., 1937), *Brigham Young—Frontiersman* (20th, 1940), *Western Union* (Par., 1941), *The Men in Her Life* (Col., 1941), *Valley of the Sun* (RKO, 1942), *The Omaha Trail* (MGM, 1942), *I Escaped From the Gestapo* (Mon., 1943), *The North Star* (RKO, 1943), *When Strangers Marry* (Mon., 1944), *Alaska* (Mon., 1944), *I Live in Grosvenor Square* ("A Yank In London" —Associated British, 1945), *Sister Kenny* (RKO, 1946), *Pursued* (WB, 1947), *Driftwood* (Rep., 1947), *C-Man* (Film Classics, 1949), *Twelve O'Clock High* (20th, 1949), *Sierra* (Univ., 1950), *Dark City* (Par., 1950), *Rawhide* (20th, 1951), *Warpath* (Par., 1951), *The Denver and Rio Grande* (Par., 1952), *My Son, John* (Par., 1952), *It Grows on Trees* (Univ., 1952), *The Robe* (20th, 1953), *Executive Suite* (MGM, 1954), *Private Hell 36* (Filmakers, 1954) *White Christmas* (Par., 1954), *Bad Day at Black Rock* (MGM, 1954), *The Eternal Sea* (Rep., 1955), *It's a Dog's Life* (MGM, 1955), *On the Threshold of Space* (20th, 1956), *Red Sundown* (Univ., 1956), *The Great Man* (Univ., 1956), *Three Brave Men* (20th, 1957), *X The Unknown* (WB, 1957), *Bernardine* (20th, 1957), *Forty Guns* (20th, 1957), *The Proud Rebel* (BV, 1958), *King Creole* (Par., 1958), *The Nun's Story* (WB, 1959), *Cash McCall* (WB, 1959), *Elmer Gantry* (UA, 1960), *Parrish* (WB, 1961), *The Honeymoon Machine* (MGM, 1961), *Billy Rose's Jumbo* (MGM, 1962), *First to Fight* (WB, 1967), *Firecreek* (WB-7 Arts, 1968), *Evil Gun* (MGM, 1968).

GLORIA JEAN (Gloria Jean Schoonover) Born April 14, 1928, Buffalo, New York.

Bing Crosby, Gloria Jean and Moroni Olsen in *If I Had My Way.*

Feature Films: *The Under-Pup* (Univ., 1939), *If I Had My Way* (Par., 1940), *A Little Bit of Heaven* (Univ., 1940), *Never Give a Sucker an Even Break* (Univ., 1941), *What's Cooking?* (Univ., 1942), *Get Hep to Love* (Univ., 1942), *When Johnny Comes Marching Home* (Univ., 1943), *It Comes Up Love* (Univ., 1943), *Mister Big* (Univ., 1943), *Moonlight in Vermont* (Univ., 1943), *Follow the Boys* (Univ., 1944), *Pardon My Rhythm* (Univ., 1944), *Ghost Catchers* (Univ., 1944), *The Reckless Age* (Univ., 1944), *Destiny* (Univ., 1944), *I'll Remember April* (Univ., 1945), *Easy to Look at* (Univ., 1945), *River Gang* (Univ., 1945), *Copacabana* (UA, 1947), *An Old-Fashioned Girl* (EL, 1948), *I Surrender, Dear* (Col., 1948), *Manhattan Angel* (Col., 1949), *There's a Girl in My Heart* (AA, 1949), *Air Strike* (Lippert, 1955), *The Ladies' Man* (Par., 1961), *The Madcaps* (Boots and Saddles, 1963).

RITA JOHNSON Born August 13, 1913, Worcester, Massachusetts. Married L. Stanley Kahn (1940); divorced 1943. Died October 31, 1965.

Rita Johnson and John Carroll in *Congo Maisie*.

Feature Films: *London By Night* (MGM, 1937), *My Dear Miss Aldrich* (MGM, 1937), *Man-Proof* (MGM, 1938), *Rich Man—Poor Girl* (MGM, 1938), *Smashing the Rackets* (RKO, 1938), *Letter of Introduction* (Univ., 1938), *Honolulu* (MGM, 1939), *The Girl Downstairs* (MGM, 1939), *Broadway Serenade* (MGM, 1939), *Within the Law* (MGM, 1939), *6,000 Enemies* (MGM, 1939), *Stronger Than Desire* (MGM, 1939), *They All Come Out* (MGM, 1939), *Nick Carter, Master Detective* (MGM, 1939), *Congo Maisie* (MGM, 1940), *Forty Little Mothers* (MGM, 1940), *Edison the Man* (MGM, 1940), *The Golden Fleecing* (MGM, 1940), *Here Comes Mr. Jordan* (Col., 1941), *Appointment for Love* (Univ., 1941), *The Major and the Minor* (Par., 1942), *My Friend Flicka* (20th, 1943), *Thunderhead, Son of Flicka* (20th, 1945), *The Affairs of Susan* (Par., 1945), *The Naughty Nineties* (Univ., 1945), *Pardon My Past* (Col., 1946), *The Perfect Marriage* (Par., 1946), *The Michigan Kid* (Univ., 1947), *They Won't Believe Me* (RKO, 1947), *Sleep My Love* (UA, 1948), *The Big Clock* (Par., 1948), *An Innocent Affair* ("Don't Trust your Husband"—UA, 1948), *Family Honeymoon* (Univ., 1948), *The Second Face* (EL, 1950), *Susan Slept Here* (RKO, 1954), *Emergency Hospital* (UA, 1956), *All Mine to Give* (Univ., 1957).

VAN JOHNSON (Charles Van Johnson) Born August 25, 1916, Newport, Rhode Island. Married Eve Abbott (1947), child: Schuyler; divorced 1968.

Van Johnson, Lowell Gilmore, Noreen Corcoran, Dawn Addams and John Dehner in *Plymouth Adventure*.

Feature Films: *Too Many Girls* (RKO, 1940), *Somewhere I'll Find You* (MGM, 1942), *Murder in the Big House* (WB, 1942), *The War Against Mrs. Hadley* (MGM, 1942), *Dr. Gillespie's New Assistant* (MGM,

1942), *A Guy Named Joe* (MGM, 1943), *Dr. Gillespie's Criminal Case* (MGM, 1943), *The Human Comedy* (MGM, 1943), *Pilot No. 5* (MGM, 1943), *Madame Curie* (MGM, 1943), *White Cliffs of Dover* (MGM, 1944), *Three Men in White* (MGM, 1944), *Between Two Women* (MGM, 1944), *Thrill of a Romance* (MGM, 1945), *Ziegfeld Follies* (MGM, 1946), *Till the Clouds Roll By* (MGM, 1946), *No Leave, No Love* (MGM, 1946), *Easy to Wed* (MGM, 1946), *Command Decision* (MGM, 1948), *Battleground* (MGM, 1949), *Grounds for Marriage* (MGM, 1950), *Go for Broke* (MGM, 1951), *It's a Big Country* (MGM, 1951), *Three Guys Named Mike* (MGM, 1951), *Invitation* (MGM, 1952), *When in Rome* (MGM, 1952), *Washington Story* (MGM, 1952), *Plymouth Adventure* (MGM, 1952), *Confidentially Connie* (MGM, 1953), *Remains to Be Seen* (MGM, 1953), *Easy to Love* (MGM 1953), *The Caine Mutiny* (Col., 1954), *The Siege at Red River* (20th, 1954), *Men of the Fighting Lady* (MGM, 1954), *The Last Time I Saw Paris* (MGM, 1954), *Brigadoon* (MGM, 1954), *The End of the Affair* (Col., 1955), *Slander* (MGM, 1956), *Miracle in the Rain* (WB, 1956), *The Bottom of the Bottle* (20th, 1956), *23 Paces to Baker Street* (20th, 1956), *Kelly and Me* (Univ., 1957), *Action of the Tiger* (MGM, 1957), *The Last Blitzkrieg* (Col., 1958), *Web of Evidence* (AA, 1959), *Subway in the Sky* (UA, 1959), *Enemy General* (Col., 1960), *Wives and Lovers* (Par., 1963), *Divorce American Style* (Col., 1967), *Yours, Mine and Ours* (UA, 1968), *Where Angels Go...Trouble Follows* (Col., 1968).

AL JOLSON (Asa Yoelson) Born May 26, 1886, St. Petersburg, Russia. Married Henrietta Keller (1906); divorced 1919. Married Ethel Delmar (1922); divorced 1926. Married Ruby Keeler (1928), child; Al, Jr.; divorced 1939. Married Erle Galbraith (1945), child: Asa. Died October 23, 1950.

Beverly Roberts and Al Jolson in *The Singing Kid*.

Feature Films:* *The Jazz Singer* (WB, 1927), *Singing Fool* (WB, 1928), *Sonny Boy* (WB, 1929), *Say It With Songs* (WB, 1929), *Mammy* (WB, 1930), *Big Boy* (WB, 1930), *Hallelujah, I'm a Bum* (UA, 1933), *Wonder Bar* (WB, 1934), *Go Into Your Dance* (WB, 1935), *The Singing Kid* (WB, 1936), *Rose of Washington Square* (20th, 1939), *Hollywood Cavalcade* (20th, 1939), *Swanee River* (20th, 1939), *Rhapsody in Blue* (WB, 1945), *The Jolson Story* (voice only; Col., 1946), *Jolson Sings Again* (voice only; Col., 1949).
   *Part-talking films included

CAROLYN JONES (Carolyn Sue Jones) Born April 28, 1929, Amarillo, Texas. Married Aaron Spelling (1953); divorced 1964.

Feature Films: *The Turning Point* (Par., 1952), *Road to Bali* (Par., 1952), *Off Limits* (Par., 1953), *The War of the Worlds* (Par., 1953), *House of Wax* (WB, 1953), *Geraldine* (Rep., 1953), *The Big Heat* (Col., 1953), *Make Haste to Live* (Rep., 1954), *The Saracen Blade* (Col., 1954), *Shield for Murder* (UA, 1954), *Three Hours to Kill* (Col., 1954), *Desirée* (20th, 1954), *The Seven-Year Itch* (20th, 1955), *East of Eden* (WB, 1955), *The Tender Trap* (MGM, 1955), *Invasion of the Body Snatchers*, AA, 1956), *The Man Who Knew Too Much* (Par., 1956), *The Opposite Sex*

Carolyn Jones in *Johnny Trouble*.

(MGM, 1956), *The Bachelor Party* (UA, 1957), *Johnny Trouble* (WB, 1957), *Baby Face Nelson* (UA, 1957), *Marjorie Morningstar* (WB, 1958), *King Creole* (Par., 1958), *Last Train From Gun Hill* (Par., 1959), *A Hole in the Head* (UA, 1959), *The Man in the Net* (UA, 1959), *Career* (Par., 1959), *Ice Palace* (WB, 1960), *Sail a Crooked Ship* (Col., 1961), *How the West Was Won* (MGM, 1963), *A Ticklish Affair* (MGM, 1963).

JENNIFER JONES (Phyllis Isley) Born March 2, 1919, Tulsa, Oklahoma. Married Robert Walker (1939), children: Robert, Michael; divorced 1945. Married David O. Selznick (1949), child: Mary; widowed 1965.

Laurence Olivier, Eddie Albert and Jennifer Jones in *Carrie*.

Feature Films:
as Phyllis Isley *New Frontier* (Rep., 1939), *Dick Tracy's G-Men* (Rep. serial, 1939).
as Jennifer Jones *The Song of Bernadette* (20th, 1943), *Since You Went Away* (UA, 1944), *Love Letters* (Par., 1945), *Cluny Brown* (20th, 1946), *Duel in the Sun* (Selznick, 1946), *Portrait of Jennie* (Selznick, 1948), *We Were Strangers* (Col., 1949), *Madame Bovary* (MGM, 1949), *Carrie* (Par., 1952), *The Wild Heart* (RKO, 1952), *Ruby Gentry* (20th, 1952), *Indiscretion of an American Wife* (Col., 1954), *Beat the Devil* (UA, 1954), *Love Is a Many-Splendored Thing* (20th, 1955), *Good Morning, Miss Dove* (20th, 1955), *The Man in the Gray Flannel Suit* (20th, 1956), *The Barretts of Wimpole Street* (MGM, 1957), *A Farewell to Arms* (20th, 1957), *Tender Is the Night* (20th, 1961), *The Idol* (Embassy, 1966).

SHIRLEY JONES (Shirley Mae Jones) Born March 31, 1933, Smithton, Pennsylvania. Married Jack Cassidy (1956), children: Shaun, David, Patrick, Ryan.

Shirley Jones, Ronny Howard and Glenn Ford in *The Courtship of Eddie's Father*.

Feature Films: *Oklahoma!* (Magna, 1955), *Carousel* (20th, 1956), *April Love* (20th, 1957), *Never Steal Anything Small* (Univ., 1959), *Bobbikins* (20th, 1960), *Elmer Gantry* (UA, 1960), *Pepe* (Col., 1960), *Two Rode Together* (Col., 1961), *The Music Man* (WB, 1962), *The Courtship of Eddie's Father* (MGM, 1963), *A Ticklish Affair* (MGM, 1963), *Dark Purpose* (Univ., 1964), *Bedtime Story* (Univ., 1964), *Fluffy* (Univ., 1965), *The Secret of My Success* (MGM, 1965).

VICTOR JORY Born November 23, 1902, Dawson City, Alaska. Married Jean Inness (1928), children: Jon, Jean.

Victor Jory, William Phipps, Sonny Tufts and Marie Windsor in *Cat Women of the Moon*.

Feature Films: *The Pride of the Legion* (Mascot, 1932), *Sailor's Luck* (Fox, 1933), *Infernal Machine* (Fox, 1933), *State Fair* (Fox, 1933), *Broadway Bad* (Fox, 1933), *Second Hand Wife* (Fox, 1933), *Trick for Trick* (Fox, 1933), *I Loved You Wednesday* (Fox, 1933), *Devil's in Love* (Fox, 1933), *My Woman* (Fox, 1933), *Smoky* (Fox, 1933), *I Believed in You* (Fox, 1934), *Murder in Trinidad* (Fox, 1934), *He Was Her Man* (WB, 1934), *Madame Du Barry* (WB, 1934), *Pursued* (Fox, 1934), *White Lies* (Col., 1934), *Mills of the Gods* (Col., 1935), *Party*

Wire (Col., 1935), *Streamline Express* (Mascot, 1935), *A Midsummer Night's Dream* (WB, 1935), *Escape From Devil's Island* (Col., 1935), *Too Tough to Kill* (Col., 1935), *Hell-Ship Morgan* (Col., 1936), *The King Steps Out* (WB, 1936), *Meet Nero Wolfe* (Col., 1936), *Glamorous Night* (Associated British Pictures, 1937), *First Lady* (WB, 1937), *Bulldog Drummond at Bay* (Rep., 1937), *The Adventures of Tom Sawyer* (UA, 1938), *Blackwell's Island* (WB, 1939), *Dodge City* (WB, 1939), *Wings of the Navy* (WB, 1939), *Man of Conquest* (Rep., 1939), *Women in the Wind* (WB, 1939), *Susannah of the Mounties* (20th, 1939), *Men With Whips* (Hoffberg, 1939), *Each Dawn I Die* (WB, 1939), *I Stole a Million* (Univ., 1939), *Call a Messenger* (Univ., 1939), *Gone With the Wind* (MGM, 1939), *The Shadow* (Col. serial, 1940), *The Green Archer* (Col. serial, 1940), *Knights of the Range* (Par., 1940), *The Light of Western Stars* (Par., 1940), *The Lone Wolf Meets a Lady* (Col., 1940), *River's End* (WB, 1940), *Girl From Havana* (Rep., 1940), *Cherokee Strip* (Par., 1940), *Lady With Red Hair* (WB, 1940), *Give Us Wings* (Univ., 1940), *Border Vigilantes* (Par., 1941), *Wide Open Town* (Par., 1941), *Bad Men of Missouri* (WB, 1941), *Charlie Chan in Rio* (20th, 1941), *Secrets of the Lone Wolf* (Col., 1941), *Riders of the Timberline* (Par., 1941), *The Stork Pays Off* (Col., 1941), *Shut My Big Mouth* (Col., 1942), *Tombstone, The Town Too Tough to Die* (Par., 1942), *Hoppy Serves a Writ* (UA, 1943), *Buckskin Frontier* (UA, 1943), *The Leather Burners* (UA, 1943), *The Kansan* (UA, 1943), *Bar 20* (UA, 1943), *Colt Comrades* (UA, 1943), *The Unknown Guest* (Mon., 1943), *Power of the Press* (Col., 1943), *The Loves of Carmen* (Col., 1948), *The Gallant Blade* (Col., 1948), *A Woman's Secret* (RKO, 1949), *South of St. Louis* (WB, 1949), *Canadian Pacific* (20th, 1949), *Fighting Man of the Plains* (20th, 1949), *The Capture* (RKO, 1950), *The Cariboo Trail* (20th, 1950), *The Highwayman* (AA, 1951), *Cave of Outlaws* (Univ., 1951), *Flaming Feather* (Par., 1951), *Son of Ali Baba* (Univ., 1952), *Toughest Man in Arizona* (Rep., 1952), *Cat Women of the Moon* (Astor, 1953), *The Hindu* ("Sabaka"—Ferrin, 1953), *The Man From the Alamo* (Univ., 1953), *Valley of the Kings* (MGM, 1954), *Manfish* (UA, 1956), *Blackjack Ketchum, Desperado* (Col., 1956), *Death of a Scoundrel* (RKO, 1956), *The Man Who Turned to Stone* (Col., 1957), *Last Stagecoach West* (Rep., 1957), *The Fugitive Kind* (UA, 1960), *The Miracle Worker* (UA, 1962), *Cheyenne Autumn* (WB, 1964).

BORIS KARLOFF (William Henry Pratt) Born November 23, 1887, Dulwich, England. Married Helen Soule (1923); divorced 1928. Married Dorothy Stine (1929), child: Sara; divorced 1946. Married Evelyn Helmore (1946).

Bela Lugosi and Boris Karloff in *The Raven.*

English-Language Sound Feature Films: *King of the Kongo* (Mascot serial, 1929), *The Unholy Night* (MGM, 1929), *Behind That Curtain* (Fox, 1929), *The Bad One* (UA, 1930), *The Sea Bat* (MGM, 1930), *The Utah Kid* (Tif., 1930), *Mothers Cry* (WB, 1930), *King of the Wild* (Mascot serial, 1931), *The Criminal Code* (Col., 1931), *Cracked Nuts* (RKO, 1931), *Young Donovan's Kid* (RKO, 1931), *Smart Money* (WB, 1931),

The Public Defender (RKO, 1931), *I Like Your Nerve* (WB, 1931), *Five Star Final* (WB, 1931), *The Mad Genius* (WB, 1931), *Guilty Generation* (Col., 1931), *The Yellow Ticket* (Fox, 1931), *Graft* (Univ., 1931), *Frankenstein* (Univ., 1931), *Tonight or Never* (UA, 1931), *Business and Pleasure* (Fox, 1932), *Alias the Doctor* (WB, 1932), *Scarface* (UA, 1932), *Cohens and Kellys in Hollywood* (Univ., 1932), *The Miracle Man* (Par., 1932), *Behind the Mask* (Col., 1932), *The Mummy* (Univ., 1932), *The Old Dark House* (Univ., 1932), *Night World* (Univ., 1932), *The Mask of Fu Manchu* (MGM, 1932), *The Ghoul* (Gaumont-British, 1933), *The House of Rothschild* (UA, 1934), *The Lost Patrol* (RKO, 1934), *The Black Cat* (Univ., 1934), *Gift of Gab* (Univ., 1934) *Mysterious Mr. Wong* (Mon., 1935), *Bride of Frankenstein* (Univ., 1935), *The Raven* (Univ., 1935), *The Black Room* (Col., 1935), *The Invisible Ray* (Univ., 1936), *The Walking Dead* (WB, 1936), *Charlie Chan at the Opera* (20th, 1936), *The Man Who Changed His Mind* (Gaumont-British, 1936), *Juggernaut* (GN, 1936), *Night Key* (Univ., 1937), *West of Shanghai* (WB, 1937), *The Invisible Menace* (WB, 1938), *Mr. Wong, Detective* (Mon., 1938), *The Man They Could Not Hang* (Col., 1939), *Mr. Wong in Chinatown* (Mon., 1939), *Son of Frankenstein* (Univ., 1939), *Tower of London* (Univ., 1939), *The Fatal Hour* (Mon., 1940), *British Intelligence* (WB, 1940), *Black Friday* (Univ., 1940), *The Man With Nine Lives* (Col., 1940), *Devil's Island* (WB, 1940), *Doomed to Die* (Mon., 1940), *Before I Hang* (Col., 1940), *The Ape* (Mon., 1940), *You'll Find Out* (RKO, 1940), *The Devil Commands* (Col., 1941), *The Boogie Man Will Get You* (Col., 1942), *The Climax* (Univ., 1944), *The House of Frankenstein* (Univ., 1944), *The Body Snatcher* (RKO, 1945), *Isle of the Dead* (RKO, 1945), *Bedlam* (RKO, 1946), *Lured* (UA, 1947), *The Secret Life of Walter Mitty* (RKO, 1947), *Dick Tracy Meets Gruesome* (RKO, 1947), *Unconquered* (Par., 1947), *Tap Roots* (Univ., 1948), *Abbott and Costello Meet the Killer* (Univ., 1949), *The Strange Door* (Univ., 1951), *The Black Castle* (Univ., 1952), *The Hindu* ("Sabaka"—Ferrin, 1953), *Abbott and Costello Meet Dr. Jekyll and Mr. Hyde* (Univ., 1953), *Voodoo Island* (UA, 1957), *Frankenstein—1970* (AA, 1958), *Grip of the Strangler* ("Haunted Strangler"—MGM, 1958), *The Terror* (AIP, 1963), *Corridors of Blood* (MGM, 1963), *The Raven* (AIP, 1963), *A Comedy of Terrors* (AIP, 1963), *Bikini Beach* (AIP, 1964), *Die, Monster, Die* (AIP, 1965), *The Daydreamer* (voice only; Embassy, 1966), *Ghost in the Invisible Bikini* (AIP, 1966), *The Venetian Affair* (MGM, 1967), *Mad Monster Party* (voice only; Embassy, 1967), *Mondo Balordo* (narrator; AIP, 1967), *The Sorcerer* (Tenser Films, 1968).

ROSCOE KARNS September 7, 1893, San Bernardino, California. Married, child: Todd.

Gary Cooper, Jack Oakie and Roscoe Karns in *If I Had a Million.*

Sound Feature Films; *This Thing Called Love* (Pathé, 1929), *New York Nights* (UA, 1930), *Troopers Three* (Tif., 1930), *Safety in Numbers*

(Par., 1930), *Man Trouble* (Fox, 1930), *Little Accident* (Univ., 1930), *Costello Case* (Sono Art-World Wide, 1930), *Dirigible* (Col., 1931), *Laughing Sinners* (MGM, 1931), *Leftover Ladies* (Tif., 1931), *Roadhouse Murder* (RKO, 1932), *Week-End Marriage* (WB, 1932), *Two Against the World* (WB, 1932), *The Crooked Circle* (Sono Art-World Wide, 1932), *I Am a Fugitive From a Chain Gang* (WB, 1932), *One Way Passage* (WB, 1932), *Night After Night* (Par., 1932), *Under-Cover Man* (Par., 1932), *If I Had a Million* (Par., 1932), *Today We Live* (Par., 1933), *A Lady's Profession* (Par., 1933), *Gambling Ship* (Par., 1933), *One Sunday Afternoon* (Par., 1933), *Alice in Wonderland* (Par., 1933), *Come On Marines* (Par., 1934), *Search for Beauty* (Par., 1934), *It Happened One Night* (Col., 1934), *Twentieth Century* (Col., 1934), *Elmer and Elsie* (Par., 1934), *Shoot the Works* (Par., 1934), *I Sell Anything* (WB, 1934), *Red Hot Tires* (WB, 1935), *Wings in the Dark* (Par., 1935), *Four Hours to Kill* (Par., 1935), *Alibi Ike* (WB, 1935), *Front Page Woman* (WB, 1935), *Woman Trap* (Par., 1936), *Border Flight* (Par., 1936), *Three Cheers for Love* (Par., 1936), *Three Married Men* (Par., 1936), *Cain and Mabel* (WB, 1936), *Clarence* (Par., 1937), *Murder Goes to College* (Par., 1937), *On Such a Night* (Par, 1937), *Partners in Crime* (Par., 1937), *Night of Mystery* (Par., 1937), *Scandal Street* (Par., 1938), *Tip-Off Girls* (Par., 1938), *Dangerous to Know* (Par., 1938), *You and Me* (Par., 1938), *Thanks for the Memory* (Par., 1938), *King of Chinatown* (Par., 1939), *Everything's on Ice* (RKO, 1939), *That's Right—You're Wrong* (RKO, 1939), *Dancing Co-ed* (MGM, 1939), *Double Alibi* (Univ., 1940), *His Girl Friday* (Col., 1940), *Saturday's Children* (WB, 1940), *They Drive by Night* (WB, 1940), *Ladies Must Live* (WB, 1940), *Meet the Missus* (Rep., 1940), *Petticoat Politics* (Rep., 1941), *Footsteps in the Dark* (WB, 1941), *The Gay Vagabond* (Rep., 1941), *A Tragedy at Midnight* (Rep., 1942), *Woman of the Year* (MGM, 1942), *Road to Happiness* (Mon., 1942), *Yokel Boy* (Rep., 1942), *You Can't Escape Forever* (WB, 1942), *Stage Door Canteen* (UA, 1943), *My Son, the Hero* (PRC, 1943), *Old Acquaintance* (WB, 1943), *The Navy Way* (Par., 1944), *Hi, Good Lookin'* (Univ., 1944), *Minstrel Man* (PRC, 1944), *I Ring Doorbells* (PRC, 1946), *One Way to Love* (Col., 1946), *Avalanche* (PRC, 1946), *It's a Wonderful Life* (RKO, 1946), *Vigilantes of Boomtown* (Rep., 1947), *That's My Man* (Rep., 1947), *Devil's Cargo* (Film Classics, 1948), *The Inside Story* (Rep., 1948), *Texas, Brooklyn and Heaven* (UA, 1948), *Speed to Spare* (Par., 1948), *Onionhead* (WB, 1958), *Man's Favorite Sport?* (Univ., 1964).

DANNY KAYE (David Kuminsky) Born January 18, 1913, Brooklyn, New York. Married Sylvia Fine (1940), child: Dena.

Elsa Lanchester and Danny Kaye in *The Inspector General*.

Feature Films: *Up in Arms* (RKO, 1944), *Wonder Man* (RKO, 1945), *The Kid From Brooklyn* (RKO, 1946), *The Secret Life of Walter Mitty* (RKO, 1947), *A Song Is Born* (RKO, 1948), *The Inspector General* (WB, 1949), *It's a Great Feeling* (WB, 1949), *On the Riviera* (20th, 1951), *Hans Christian Andersen* (RKO, 1952), *Knock on Wood* (Par., 1954), *White Christmas* (Par., 1954), *The Court Jester* (Par., 1956), *Merry Andrew* (MGM, 1958), *Me and the Colonel* (Col., 1958), *The*

Five Pennies (Par., 1959), *On the Double* (Par., 1961), *The Man From the Diners' Club* (Col., 1963).

BUSTER KEATON (Joseph Frank Keaton) Born October 4, 1895, Piqua, Kansas. Married Natalie Talmadge (1921), children: Robert, James; divorced 1932. Married Mae Scribbens (1933); divorced 1935. Married Eleanor Norris (1940). Died February 1, 1966.

Buster Keaton and Jimmy Durante in *What! No Beer?*

Sound Feature Films: *Hollywood Revue of 1929* (MGM, 1929), *Free and Easy* (MGM, 1930), *Dough Boys* (MGM, 1930), *Parlor, Bedroom and Bath* (MGM, 1931), *Sidewalks of New York* (MGM, 1931), *Passionate Plumber* (MGM, 1932), *Speak Easily* (MGM, 1932), *What, No Beer?* (MGM, 1933), *An Old Spanish Custom* (M.F. Hoffberg, 1936), *Hollywood Cavalcade* (20th, 1939), *The Villain Still Pursued Her* (RKO, 1940), *L'il Abner* (RKO, 1940), *Forever and a Day* (RKO, 1943), *Bathing Beauty* (MGM, 1944), *San Diego, I Love You* (Univ., 1944), *That's the Spirit* (Univ., 1945), *That Night With You* (Univ., 1945), *The Lovable Cheat* (Film Classics, 1949), *In The Good Old Summertime* (MGM, 1949), *You're My Everything* (20th, 1949), *Sunset Boulevard* (Par., 1950), *Limelight* (UA, 1952), *Around the World in 80 Days* (UA, 1956), *The Adventures of Huckleberry Finn* (MGM, 1960), *It's a Mad, Mad, Mad, Mad World* (UA, 1963), *Pajama Party* (AIP, 1964), *Beach Blanket Bingo* (AIP, 1965), *How to Stuff a Wild Bikini* (AIP, 1965), *Sergeant Deadhead* (AIP, 1965), *A Funny Thing Happened on the Way to the Forum* (UA, 1966), *War Italian Style* (AIP, 1967).

HOWARD KEEL (Harold Clifford Keel) Born April 13, 1917, Gillespie, Illinois. Married Rosemary Randall; divorced 1948. Married Helen Anderson (1949), children: Kaija, Gunnar, Kristine.

Ava Gardner and Howard Keel in *Ride, Vaquero*.

Feature Films: *The Small Voice* (British Lion, 1948), *Annie Get Your Gun* (MGM, 1950), *Pagan Love Song* (MGM, 1950), *Three Guys Named Mike* (MGM, 1951), *Show Boat* (MGM, 1951), *Texas Carnival* (MGM, 1951), *Callaway Went Thataway* (MGM, 1951), *Lovely to Look At* (MGM, 1952), *Desperate Search* (MGM, 1952), *I Love Melvin* (MGM, 1953),* *Fast Company* (MGM, 1953), *Ride, Vaquero* (MGM, 1953), *Calamity Jane* (WB, 1953), *Kiss Me, Kate!* (MGM, 1953), *Rose Marie* (MGM, 1954), *Seven Brides for Seven Brothers* (MGM, 1954), *Deep in My Heart* (MGM, 1954), *Jupiter's Darling* (MGM, 1955), *Kismet* (MGM, 1955), *Floods of Fear* (Univ., 1959), *The Big Fisherman* (BV, 1959), *Armored Command* (AA, 1962), *The Day of the Triffids* (AA, 1963), *The Man From Button Willow* (voice only; United Screen Arts, 1965), *Waco* (Par., 1966), *Red Tomahawk* (Par., 1967), *The War Wagon* (Univ., 1967), *Arizona Bushwhackers* (Par., 1968).

*Unbilled guest appearance

RUBY KEELER Born August 25, 1909, Halifax, Nova Scotia, Canada. Married Al Jolson (1928), child: Al, Jr.; divorced 1939. Married John Lowe (1941), children: Kathleen, Christine, Theresa, John.

Ruby Keeler and Lee Dixon in *Ready, Willing and Able.*

Feature Films: *42nd Street* (WB, 1933), *Gold Diggers of 1933* (WB, 1933), *Footlight Parade* (WB, 1933), *Dames* (WB, 1934), *Flirtation Walk* (WB, 1934), *Go into Your Dance* (WB, 1935), *Shipmates Forever* (WB, 1935), *Colleen* (WB, 1936), *Ready, Willing and Able* (WB, 1937), *Mother Carey's Chickens* (RKO, 1938), *Sweetheart of the Campus* (Col., 1941).

CECIL KELLAWAY Born August 22, 1893, Capetown, South Africa. Married, children: Peter, Brian.

Feature Films: *It Isn't Done* (British Empire, 1937), *Double Danger* (RKO, 1938), *Everybody's Doing it* (RKO, 1938), *Night Spot* (RKO, 1938), *This Marriage Business* (RKO, 1938), *Maid's Night Out* (RKO, 1938), *Tarnished Angel* (RKO, 1938), *Wuthering Heights* (UA, 1939), *The Sun Never Sets* (Univ., 1939), *We Are Not Alone* (WB, 1939), *Intermezzo* (UA, 1939), *Mexican Spitfire* (RKO, 1939), *The Under-Pup* (Univ., 1939), *The Invisible Man Returns* (Univ., 1940), *The House of the Seven Gables* (Univ., 1940), *Brother Orchid* (WB, 1940), *Phantom Raiders* (MGM, 1940), *Mexican Spitfire Out West* (RKO, 1940), *The Mummy's Hand* (Univ., 1940), *Diamond Frontier* (Univ., 1940), *The Letter* (WB, 1940), *Lady With Red Hair* (WB, 1940), *South of Suez* (WB, 1940), *A Very Young Lady* (20th, 1941), *West Point Widow* (Par., 1941), *New York Town* (Par., 1941), *Night of January 16th* (Par., 1941), *Burma Convoy* (Par., 1941), *Small Town Deb* (MGM,

Cecil Kellaway, Tim Ryan and Tyrone Power in *The Luck of the Irish.*

1941), *Appointment for Love* (Univ., 1941), *Bahama Passage* (Par., 1941), *The Lady Has Plans* (Par., 1942), *Take a Letter, Darling* (Par., 1942), *Night in New Orleans* (Par., 1942), *Are Husbands Necessary?* (Par., 1942), *I Married a Witch* (UA, 1942), *My Heart Belongs to Daddy* (Par., 1942), *Star Spangled Rhythm* (Par., 1942), *Forever and a Day* (RKO, 1943), *It Ain't Hay* (Univ., 1943), *The Good Fellows* (Par., 1943), *The Crystal Ball* (UA, 1943), *Frenchman's Creek* (Par., 1944), *Mrs. Parkington* (MGM, 1944), *And Now Tomorrow* (Par., 1944), *Practically Yours* (Par., 1945), *Bring on the Girls* (Par., 1945), *Love Letters* (Par., 1945), *Kitty* (Par., 1945), *The Postman Always Rings Twice* (MGM, 1946), *Easy to Wed* (MGM, 1946), *Monsieur Beaucaire* (Par., 1946), *The Cockeyed Miracle* (MGM, 1946), *Unconquered* (Par., 1947), *Always Together* (WB, 1947), *Variety Girl* (Par., 1947), *The Luck of the Irish* (20th, 1948), *Joan of Arc* (RKO, 1948), *The Decision of Christopher Blake* (WB, 1948), *Portrait of Jennie* (Selznick, 1948), *Down to the Sea in Ships* (20th, 1949), *The Reformer and the Redhead* (MGM, 1950), *Harvey* (Univ., 1950), *Kim* (MGM, 1950), *Francis Goes to the Races* (Univ., 1951), *Katie Did It* (Univ., 1951), *Half Angel* (20th, 1951), *The Highwayman* (AA, 1951), *Just Across the Street* (Univ., 1952), *My Wife's Best Friend* (20th, 1952), *Young Bess* (MGM, 1953), *The Beast From 20,000 Fathoms* (WB, 1953), *Cruisin' Down the River* (Col., 1953), *Paris Model* (Col., 1953), *Hurricane at Pilgrim Hill* (Howco, 1953), *Interrupted Melody* (MGM, 1955), *The Prodigal* (MGM, 1955), *Female on the Beach* (Univ., 1955), *Toy Tiger* (Univ., 1956), *Johnny Trouble* (WB, 1957), *The Proud Rebel* (BV, 1958), *The Shaggy Dog* (BV, 1959), *The Private Lives of Adam and Eve* (Univ., 1960), *Tammy, Tell Me True* (Univ., 1961), *Francis of Assisi* (20th, 1961), *Zotz!* (Col., 1962), *The Cardinal* (Col., 1963), *Hush . . . Hush, Sweet Charlotte* (20th, 1965), *Spinout* (MGM, 1966), *The Adventures of Bullwhip Griffin* (BV, 1967), *Fitzwilly* (UA, 1967), *Guess Who's Coming to Dinner* (Col., 1967).

GENE KELLY (Eugene Curran Kelly) Born August 23, 1912, Pittsburgh, Pennsylvania. Married Betsy Blair (1940), child: Kerry; divorced 1957. Married Jeanne Covne (1960), child: Timothy.

George Murphy, Judy Garland and Gene Kelly in *For Me and My Gal.*

Feature Films: *For Me and My Gal* (MGM, 1942), *Pilot No. 5* (MGM, 1943), *Du Barry Was a Lady* (MGM, 1943), *Thousands Cheer* (MGM, 1943), *The Cross of Lorraine* (MGM, 1943), *Cover Girl* (Col., 1944), *Christmas Holiday* (Univ., 1944), *Anchors Aweigh* (MGM, 1945), *Ziegfeld Follies of 1946* (MGM, 1946), *Living in a Big Way* (MGM, 1947), *The Pirate* (MGM, 1948), *The Three Musketeers* (MGM, 1948), *Words and Music* (MGM, 1948), *Take Me Out to the Ball Game* (MGM, 1949), *On The Town* (MGM, 1949), *The Black Hand* (MGM, 1950), *Summer Stock* (MGM, 1950), *An American in Paris* (MGM, 1951), *It's a Big Country* (MGM, 1951), *Singin' in the Rain* (MGM, 1952), *The Devil Makes Three* (MGM, 1952), *Love Is Better Than Ever* (MGM, 1952), *Brigadoon* (MGM, 1954), *Crest of the Wave* (MGM, 1954), *Deep in My Heart* (MGM, 1954), *It's Always Fair Weather* (MGM, 1955), *Invitation to the Dance* (MGM, 1956), *The Happy Road* (MGM, 1957), *Les Girls* (MGM, 1957), *Marjorie Morningstar* (WB, 1958), *Inherit the Wind* (UA, 1960), *Let's Make Love* (20th, 1960), *What a Way to Go!* (20th, 1964), *The Young Girls of Rochefort* (WB-7 Arts, 1967).

GRACE KELLY Born November 12, 1928, Philadelphia, Pennsylvania. Married Prince Rainier (1956), children: Caroline, Albert, Stephanie.

Grace Kelly and Jessie Royce Landis in *The Swan*.

Feature Films: *Fourteen Hours* (20th, 1951), *High Noon* (UA, 1952), *Mogambo* (MGM, 1953), *Dial M for Murder* (WB, 1954), *Rear Window* (Par., 1954), *The Country Girl* (Par., 1954), *Green Fire* (MGM, 1954), *The Bridges at Toko-Ri* (Par., 1954), *To Catch a Thief* (Par., 1955), *The Swan* (MGM, 1956), *High Society* (MGM, 1956).

PATSY KELLY Born January 21, 1910, Brooklyn, New York.

Feature Films: *Going Hollywood* (MGM, 1933), *Countess of Monte Cristo* (Univ., 1934), *Party's Over* (Col., 1934), *The Girl From Missouri* (MGM, 1934), *Transatlantic Merry-Go-Round* (UA, 1934), *Go into Your Dance* (WB, 1935), *Every Night at Eight* (Par., 1935), *Page Miss Glory* (WB, 1935), *Thanks a Million* (20th, 1935), *Kelly the Second*

Ted Healy and Patsy Kelly in *Sing, Baby, Sing*.

(MGM, 1936), *Private Number* (20th, 1936), *Sing, Baby, Sing* (20th, 1936), *Pigskin Parade* (20th, 1936), *Nobody's Baby* (MGM, 1937), *Pick a Star* (MGM, 1937), *Wake Up and Live* (20th, 1937), *Ever Since Eve* (WB, 1937), *Merrily We Live* (MGM, 1938), *There Goes My Heart* (UA, 1938), *The Cowboy and the Lady* (UA, 1938), *The Gorilla* (20th, 1939), *The Hit Parade of 1941* (Rep., 1940), *Road Show* (UA, 1941), *Topper Returns* (UA, 1941), *Broadway Limited* (UA, 1941), *Playmates* (RKO, 1941), *Sing Your Worries Away* (RKO, 1942), *In Old California* (Rep., 1942), *My Son, the Hero* (PRC, 1943) *Ladies' Day* (RKO, 1943), *Danger! Women at Work* (PRC, 1943), *Please Don't Eat the Daisies* (MGM, 1960), *The Crowded Sky* (WB, 1960), *The Naked Kiss* (AA, 1964), *Ghost in the Invisible Bikini* (AIP, 1966), *C'mon, Let's Live a Little* (Par., 1967), *Rosemary's Baby* (Par., 1968).

PAUL KELLY (Paul Michael Kelly) Born August 9, 1899, Brooklyn, New York. Married Dorothy MacKaye (1931), children: Mimi, Mary; widowed 1940. Married Mardelle Zurcker (1941). Died November 6, 1956.

Paul Kelly and Chester Morris in *Public Hero Number One*.

Sound Feature Films: *Girl From Calgary* (Mon., 1932), *Broadway Through a Keyhole* (UA, 1933), *Love Captive* (Univ., 1934), *Side Streets* (WB, 1934), *Blind Date* (Col., 1934), *Death on the Diamond* (MGM, 1934), *School for Girls* (Liberty Productions, 1934), *The President Vanishes* (Par., 1934), *When a Man's a Man* (Fox, 1935), *Public Hero Number One* (MGM, 1935), *Star of Midnight* (RKO, 1935), *Silk Hat Kid* (Fox, 1935), *Speed Devils* (J.H. Hoffberg, 1935), *My Marriage* (20th, 1935), *It's a Great Life* (Par., 1936), *Here Comes Trouble* (20th,

1936), *The Song and Dance Man* (20th, 1936), *The Country Beyond* (20th, 1936), *Women Are Trouble* (MGM, 1936), *Murder With Pictures* (Par., 1936), *The Accusing Finger* (Par., 1936), *Parole Racket* (Col., 1937), *Join the Marines* (Rep., 1937), *It Happened Out West* (20th, 1937), *The Frame-up* (Col., 1937), *Fit for a King* (RKO, 1937), *Navy Blue and Gold* (MGM, 1937), *Nurse From Brooklyn* (Univ., 1938), *Torchy Blane in Panama* (WB, 1938), *Island in the Sky* (20th, 1938), *The Devil's Party* (Univ., 1938), *The Missing Guest* (Univ., 1938), *Juvenile Court* (Col., 1938), *Adventure in Sahara* (Col., 1938), *Forged Passport* (Rep., 1939), *The Flying Irishman* (RKO, 1939), *Within the Law* (MGM, 1939), *6,000 Enemies* (MGM, 1939), *The Roaring Twenties* (WB, 1939), *Invisible Stripes* (WB, 1940), *Queen of the Mob* (Par., 1940), *The Howards of Virginia* (Col., 1940), *Wyoming* (MGM, 1940), *Girls Under 21* (Col., 1940), *Flight Command* (MGM, 1940), *Ziegfeld Girl* (MGM, 1941), *I'll Wait for You* (MGM, 1941), *Parachute Battalion* (RKO, 1941), *Mystery Ship* (Col., 1941), *Mr. and Mrs. North* (MGM, 1941), *Gang Busters* (Univ. serial, 1942), *Call Out the Marines* (RKO, 1942), *Tarzan's New York Adventure* (RKO, 1942), *Tough as They Come* (Univ., 1942), *Flying Tigers* (Rep., 1942), *The Secret Code* (Col. serial, 1942), *The Man From Music Mountain* (Rep., 1943), *The Story of Dr. Wassell* (Par., 1944), *Dead Man's Eyes* (Univ., 1944), *Faces in the Fog* (Rep., 1944), *China's Little Devils* (Mon., 1945), *Grissly's Millions* (Rep., 1945), *Allotment Wives* (Mon., 1945), *San Antonio* (WB, 1945), *The Cat Creeps* (Univ., 1946), *The Glass Alibi* (Rep., 1946), *Deadline for Murder* (20th, 1946), *Strange Journey* (20th, 1946), *Fear in the Night* (Par., 1947), *Spoilers of the North* (Rep., 1947), *Crossfire* (RKO, 1947), *Adventure Island* (Par., 1947), *File on Thelma Jordan* (Par., 1949), *Side Street* (MGM, 1949), *Guilty of Treason* (EL, 1949), *The Secret Fury* (RKO, 1950), *Frenchie* (Univ., 1950), *The Painted Hills* (MGM, 1951), *Springfield Rifle* (WB, 1952), *Gunsmoke* (Univ., 1953), *Split Second* (RKO, 1953), *Duffy of San Quentin* (WB, 1954), *Johnny Dark* (Univ., 1954), *The High and the Mighty* (WB, 1954), *The Steel Cage* (UA, 1954), *The Square Jungle* (Univ., 1955), *Storm Center* (Col., 1956), *Bailout at 43,000* (UA, 1957).

ARTHUR KENNEDY (John Arthur Kennedy) Born February 17, 1914, Worcester, Massachusetts. Married Marie Cheffey (1938); children: Terence, Laurie.

Marlene Dietrich and Arthur Kennedy in *Rancho Notorious*.

English-Language Feature Films: *City for Conquest* (WB, 1940), *High Sierra* (WB, 1941), *Strange Alibi* (WB, 1941), *Knockout* (WB, 1941), *Highway West* (WB, 1941), *Bad Men of Missouri* (WB, 1941), *They Died With Their Boots On* (WB, 1941), *Desperate Journey* (WB, 1942), *Air Force* (WB, 1943), *Devotion* (WB, 1946), *Boomerang* (20th, 1947), *Cheyenne* (WB, 1947), *Too Late for Tears* (UA, 1949), *Champion* (UA, 1949), *The Window* (RKO, 1949), *The Walking Hills* (Col., 1949), *Chicago Deadline* (Rep., 1949), *The Glass Menagerie* (WB, 1950), *Bright Victory* (Univ., 1951), *Red Mountain* (Par., 1951), *Rancho Notorious* (RKO, 1952), *The Girl in White* (MGM, 1952), *Bend of the River* (Univ., 1952), *The Lusty Men* (RKO, 1952), *The Man From Lara-*

mie (Col., 1955), *Trial* (MGM, 1955), *The Naked Dawn* (Univ., 1955), *The Desperate Hours* (Par., 1955), *Crashout* (Filmakers, 1955), *The Rawhide Years* (Univ., 1956), *Peyton Place* (20th, 1957), *Twilight for the Gods* (Univ., 1958), *Some Came Running* (MGM, 1958), *A Summer Place* (WB, 1959), *Elmer Gantry* (UA, 1960), *Home Is the Hero* (Showcorporation of America, 1961), *Claudelle Inglish* (WB, 1961), *Murder, She Said* (MGM, 1962), *Hemingway's Adventures of a Young Man* (20th, 1962), *Barabbas* (Col., 1962), *Lawrence of Arabia* (Col., 1962), *Cheyenne Autumn* (WB, 1964), *Joy in the Morning* (MGM, 1965), *Murieta* (WB, 1965), *Nevada Smith* (Embassy, 1966), *Monday's Child* (DuRona Productions, 1968), *The Prodigal Gun* (Cinerama, 1968), *Anzio* (Col., 1968), *Evil Gun* (MGM, 1968).

EDGAR KENNEDY Born April 26, 1890, Monterey County, California. Married Patricia Allwyn (1924), Children: Larry, Colleen. Died November 9, 1948

Edgar Kennedy, Cliff Edwards and Tom Conway in *The Falcon Strikes Back*.

Sound Feature Films: *They Had to See Paris* (Fox, 1929), *Bad Company* (Pathé, 1931), *Carnival Boat* (RKO, 1932), *Hold 'Em Jail* (RKO, 1932), *The Penguin Pool Murder* (RKO, 1932), *Little Orphan Annie* (RKO, 1932), *Scarlet River* (RKO, 1933), *Professional Sweetheart* (RKO, 1933), *Son of the Border* (RKO, 1933), *Crossfire* (RKO, 1933), *Tillie and Gus* (Par., 1933), *Duck Soup* (Par., 1933), *All of Me* (Par., 1934), *Heat Lightning* (WB, 1934), *Money Means Nothing* (Mon., 1934), *Twentieth Century* (Col., 1934), *Murder on the Blackboard* (RKO, 1934), *We're Rich Again* (RKO, 1934), *King Kelly of the U.S.A.* (Mon., 1934), *Kid Millions* (UA, 1934), *Silver Streak* (RKO, 1934), *Flirting With Danger* (Mon., 1934), *Gridiron Flash* (RKO, 1934), *The Marines Are Coming* (Mascot, 1934), *Living on Velvet* (WB, 1935), *Rendezvous at Midnight* (Univ., 1935), *Cowboy Millionaire* (20th, 1935), *The Little Big Shot* (WB, 1935), *Woman Wanted* (MGM, 1935), *$1,000 a Minute* (Rep., 1935), *In Person* (RKO, 1935), *The Bride Comes Home* (Par., 1935), *The Return of Jimmy Valentine* (Rep., 1936), *Robin Hood of El Dorado* (MGM, 1936), *Small Town Girl* (MGM, 1936), *Fatal Lady* (Par., 1936), *Yours for the Asking* (Par., 1936), *Mad Holiday* (MGM, 1936), *Three Men on a Horse* (WB, 1936), *San Francisco* (MGM, 1936), *When's Your Birthday?* (RKO, 1937), *A Star Is Born* (UA, 1937), *Super Sleuth* (RKO, 1937), *Double Wedding* (MGM, 1937), *True Confession* (Par., 1937), *Hollywood Hotel* (WB, 1937), *The Black Doll* (Univ., 1938), *Scandal Street* (Par., 1938), *Peck's Bad Boy at the Circus* (RKO, 1938), *It's a Wonderful World* (MGM, 1939), *Little Accident* (Univ., 1939), *Everything's on Ice* (RKO, 1939), *Charlie McCarthy, Detective* (Univ., 1939), *Laugh It Off* (Univ., 1939), *Li'l Abner* (RKO, 1940), *Frolics On Ice* (RKO, 1940), *Sandy Is a Lady* (Univ., 1940), *Dr. Christian Meets the Women* (RKO, 1940), *Margie* (Univ., 1940), *The Quarterback* (Par., 1940), *Who Killed Aunt Maggie?* (Rep., 1940), *Remedy for Riches* (RKO, 1940), *Sandy Gets Her Man* (RKO, 1940), *The Bride Wore Crutches* (20th, 1941), *Public Enemies* (Rep., 1941), *Blondie in Society* (Col., 1941), *Snuffy Smith, Yard Bird* (Mon., 1942),

Pardon My Stripes (Rep., 1942), *In Old California* (Rep., 1942), *Hillbilly Blitzkrieg* (Mon., 1942), *The Falcon Strikes Back* (RKO, 1943), *Cosmo Jones—Crime Smasher* (Mon., 1943), *Air Raid Wardens* (MGM, 1943), *Hitler's Madman* (MGM, 1943), *The Girl From Monterey* (PRC, 1943), *Crazy House* (Univ., 1943), *The Great Alaskan Mystery* (Univ. serial, 1944), *It Happened Tomorrow* (UA, 1944), *Anchors Aweigh* (MGM, 1945), *Captain Tugboat Annie* (Rep., 1945), *Mad Wednesday* (UA, 1947), *Heaven Only Knows* (UA, 1947), *Variety Time* (RKO, 1948), *Unfaithfully Yours* (20th, 1948), *My Dream Is Yours* (WB, 1949).

DEBORAH KERR (Deborah Kerr-Trimmer) Born September 30, 1921, Helensburgh, Scotland. Married Anthony Bartley (1945), children: Francesca, Melanie; divorced 1959. Married Peter Viertel (1960).

Deborah Kerr and Spencer Tracy in *Edward, My Son.*

Feature Films: *Contraband* (British National, 1939), *Major Barbara* (Rank, 1940), *Love on the Dole* (British National, 1941), *Hatter's Castle* (Par., 1941), *The Courageous Mr. Penn* ("Penn of Pennsylvania" —British National, 1942), *The Avengers* ("The Day Will Dawn"— Denham, 1942), *Colonel Blimp* ("The Life and Death of Colonel Blimp"—Rank, 1943), *Vacation From Marriage* ("Perfect Strangers"— MGM, 1945), *The Adventuress* ("I See a Dark Stranger"—Rank, 1946), *Black Narcissus* (Rank, 1946), *The Hucksters* (MGM, 1947), *If Winter Comes* (MGM, 1947), *Edward, My Son* (MGM, 1949), *Please Believe Me* (MGM, 1950), *King Solomon's Mines* (MGM, 1950), *Quo Vadis* (MGM, 1951), *The Prisoner of Zenda* (MGM, 1952), *Thunder in the East* (Par., 1953), *Dream Wife* (MGM, 1953), *Young Bess* (MGM, 1953), *Julius Caesar* (MGM, 1953), *From Here to Eternity* (Col., 1953), *The End of the Affair* (Col., 1955), *The Proud and Profane* (Par., 1956), *The King and I* (20th, 1956), *Tea and Sympathy* (MGM, 1956), *Heaven Knows, Mr. Allison* (20th, 1957), *An Affair to Remember* (20th, 1957), *Bonjour Tristesse* (Col., 1958), *Separate Tables* (UA, 1958), *The Journey* (MGM, 1959), *Count Your Blessings* (MGM, 1959), *Beloved Infidel* (20th, 1959), *The Sundowners* (WB, 1960), *The Grass Is Greener* (Univ., 1960), *The Naked Edge* (UA, 1961), *The Innocents* (20th, 1961), *The Chalk Garden* (Univ., 1964), *The Night of the Iguana* (MGM, 1964), *Marriage on the Rocks* (WB, 1965), *Casino Royale* (Col.,1967), *Eye of the Devil* (MGM, 1967), *Prudence and the Pill* (20th, 1968).

EVELYN KEYES (Evelyn Louise Keyes) Born November 20, 1919, Port Arthur, Texas. Married Barton Bainbridge; widowed 1940. Married Charles Vidor; divorced 1945. Married John Huston (1946), child: Pablo; divorced 1950. Married Artie Shaw (1957).

Feature Films: *The Buccaneer* (Par., 1938), *Sons of the Legion* (Par., 1938), *Men With Wings* (Par., 1938), *Artists and Models Abroad* (Par., 1938). *Dangerous to Know* (Par., 1938), *Gone With the Wind* (MGM, 1939), *Union Pacific* (Par., 1939), *Paris Honeymoon* (Par., 1939), *Sudden Money* (Par., 1939), *Slightly Honorable* (UA, 1940),

Evelyn Keyes and Keenan Wynn in *The Thrill of Brazil.*

Before I Hang (Col., 1940), *Lady in Question* (Col., 1940), *The Face Behind the Mask* (Col., 1941), *Beyond the Sacramento* (Col., 1941), *Here Comes Mr. Jordan* (Col., 1941), *Ladies in Retirement* (Col., 1941), *The Adventures of Martin Eden* (Col., 1942), *Flight Lieutenant* (Col., 1942), *The Desperadoes* (Col., 1943), *Dangerous Blondes* (Col., 1943), *There's Something About a Soldier* (Col., 1943), *Nine Girls* (Col., 1944), *Strange Affair* (Col., 1944), *A Thousand and One Nights* (Col., 1945), *Renegades* (Col., 1946), *The Thrill of Brazil* (Col., 1946), *The Jolson Story* (Col., 1946), *Johnny O'Clock* (Col., 1947), *The Mating of Millie* (Col., 1948), *Enchantment* (RKO, 1948), *Mr. Soft Touch* (Col., 1949), *Mrs. Mike* (UA, 1949), *The Killer That Stalked New York* (Col., 1950), *Smuggler's Island* (Univ., 1951), *The Prowler* (UA, 1951), *The Iron Man* (Univ., 1951), *One Big Affair* (UA, 1952), *Shoot First* (UA, 1953), *99 River Street* (UA, 1953), *Hell's Half Acre* (Rep., 1954), *Top of the World* (UA, 1955), *The Seven-Year Itch* (20th, 1955), *Around the World in 80 Days* (UA, 1957).

GUY KIBBEE (Guy Bridges Kibbee) Born March 6, 1886, El Paso, Texas. Married Helen Shea (1918), children: John, Robert; divorced. Married Esther Reed (1928), children: John, Guy, Shirley. Died May 24, 1956.

Guy Kibbee, Clem Bevans, Walter Huston, Beulah Bondi, Gene Reynolds and Arthur Aylesworth in *Of Human Hearts.*

Sound Feature Films: *Stolen Heaven* (Par., 1931), *Man of the World* (Par., 1931), *City Streets* (Par., 1931), *Laughing Sinners* (MGM, 1931), *Side Show* (WB, 1931), *New Adventures of Get Rich Quick Wallingford*

(MGM, 1931), *Flying High* (MGM, 1931), *Blonde Crazy* (WB, 1931), *Taxi* (WB, 1932), *Fireman Save My Child* (WB, 1932), *High Pressure* (WB, 1932), *Union Depot* (WB, 1932), *Play Girl* (WB, 1932), *The Crowd Roars* (WB, 1932), *Two Seconds* (WB, 1932), *Man Wanted* (WB, 1932), *Strange Love of Molly Louvain* (WB, 1932), *So Big* (WB, 1932), *Winner Takes All* (WB, 1932), *Dark Horse* (WB, 1932), *Crooner* (WB, 1932), *Big City Blues* (WB, 1932), *Rain* (UA, 1932), *Scarlet Dawn* (WB, 1932), *The Conquerors* (RKO, 1932), *Central Park* (WB, 1932), *They Just Had to Get Married* (Univ., 1932), *42nd Street* (WB, 1933), *Girl Missing* (WB, 1933), *Gold Diggers Of 1933* (WB, 1933), *Lilly Turner* (WB, 1933), *Life of Jimmy Dolan* (WB, 1933), *Silk Express* (WB, 1933), *Lady for a Day* (Col., 1933), *Footlight Parade* (WB, 1933), *The World Changes* (WB, 1933), *Havana Widows* (WB, 1933), *Convention City* (WB, 1933), *Easy to Love* (WB, 1934), *Harold Teen* (WB, 1934), *Wonder Bar* (WB, 1934), *Merry Wives of Reno* (WB, 1934), *Dames* (WB, 1934), *The Merry Frinks* (WB, 1934), *Big-Hearted Herbert* (WB, 1934), *Babbitt* (WB, 1934), *While the Patient Slept* (WB, 1935), *Mary Jane's Pa* (WB, 1935), *Going Highbrow* (WB, 1935), *Don't Bet on Blondes* (WB, 1935), *I Live for Love* (WB, 1935), *Captain Blood* (WB, 1935), *Little Lord Fauntleroy* (UA, 1936), *Captain January* (20th, 1936), *The Big Noise* (WB, 1936), *I Married a Doctor* (WB, 1936), *Earthworm Tractors* (WB, 1936), *M'liss* (RKO, 1936), *Three Men on a Horse* (WB, 1936), *The Captain's Kid* (WB, 1936), *Don't Tell the Wife* (RKO, 1937), *Mama Steps Out* (MGM, 1937), *Mountain Justice* (WB, 1937), *Jim Hanvey, Detective* (Rep., 1937), *Riding on Air* (RKO, 1937), *The Big Shot* (RKO, 1937), *Of Human Hearts* (MGM, 1938), *Bad Man of Brimstone* (MGM, 1938), *Joy of Living* (RKO, 1938), *Three Comrades* (MGM, 1938), *Rich Man—Poor Girl* (MGM, 1938), *Let Freedom Ring* (MGM, 1939), *It's a Wonderful World* (MGM, 1939), *Mr. Smith Goes to Washington* (Col., 1939), *Babes in Arms* (MGM, 1939), *Bad Little Angels* (MGM, 1940), *Henry Goes Arizona* (MGM, 1940), *Our Town* (UA, 1940), *Street of Memories* (20th, 1940), *Scattergood Baines* (RKO, 1941), *Scattergood Pulls the Strings* (RKO, 1941), *Scattergood Meets Broadway* (RKO, 1941), *It Started With Eve* (Univ., 1941), *Design for Scandal* (MGM, 1941), *Scattergood Rides High* (RKO, 1942), *This Time for Keeps* (MGM, 1942), *Sunday Punch* (MGM, 1942), *Miss Annie Rooney* (UA, 1942), *Tish* (MGM, 1942), *Whistling in Dixie* (MGM, 1942), *Scattergood Survives a Murder* (RKO, 1942), *Cinderella Swings It* (RKO, 1943), *Girl Crazy* (MGM, 1943), *Dixie Jamboree* (PRC, 1944), *The Horn Blows at Midnight* (WB, 1945), *Gentleman Joe Palooka* (Mon., 1946), *Singing on the Trail* (Col., 1946), *Cowboy Blues* (Col., 1946), *Lone Star Moonlight* (Col., 1946), *Over the Santa Fe Trail* (Col., 1947), *The Red Stallion* (EL, 1947), *The Romance of Rosy Ridge* (MGM, 1947), *Fort Apache* (RKO, 1948).

OTTO KRUGER Born September 6, 1885, Toledo, Ohio. Married Sue MacManamy (1919), child: Ottilie.

Ralph Bellamy, Otto Kruger, Ronnie Crosby and Barbara Stanwyck in *Ever in My Heart*.

Sound Feature Films: *Turn Back the Clock* (MGM, 1933), *Beauty for Sale* (MGM, 1933), *The Prizefighter and the Lady* (MGM, 1933), *Ever in My Heart* (WB, 1933), *Gallant Lady* (UA, 1933), *The Women in His Life* (MGM, 1933), *Treasure Island* (MGM, 1934), *Chained* (MGM, 1934), *Paris Interlude* (MGM, 1934), *Men in White* (MGM, 1934), *The Crime Doctor* (RKO, 1934), *Springtime for Henry* (Fox, 1934), *Vanessa, Her Love Story* (MGM, 1935), *Two Sinners* (Rep., 1935), *Living Dangerously* (Gaumont-British, 1936), *Dracula's Daughter* (Univ., 1936), *Glamorous Night* (Associated British Pictures, 1937), *They Won't Forget* (WB, 1937), *Counsel for Crime* (Col., 1937), *The Barrier* (Par., 1937), *Thanks for the Memory* (Par., 1938), *I Am the Law* (Col., 1938), *Exposed* (Univ., 1938), *Disbarred* (Par., 1939), *Housemaster* (Alliance, 1939), *The Zero Hour* (Rep., 1939), *A Woman Is the Judge* (Col., 1939), *Dr. Ehrlich's Magic Bullet* (WB, 1940), *A Dispatch From Reuters* (WB, 1940), *Seventeen* (Par., 1940), *The Hidden Menace* (Alliance, 1940), *The Man I Married* (20th, 1940), *The Big Boss* (Col., 1941), *The Man in Her Life* (Col., 1941), *Mercy Island* (Rep., 1941), *Saboteur* (Univ., 1942), *Friendly Enemies* (UA, 1942), *Secrets of a Co-ed* (PRC, 1942), *Corregidor* (PRC, 1943), *Night Plane From Chungking* (Par., 1943), *Hitler's Children* (RKO, 1943), *The Gang's All Here* (PRC, 1944), *Knickerbocker Holiday* (UA, 1944), *Murder, My Sweet* (RKO, 1944), *Cover Girl* (Col., 1944) *They Live in Fear* (Col., 1944), *Escape in the Fog* (Col., 1945), *Earl Carroll's Vanities* (Rep., 1945), *Wonder Man* (RKO, 1945), *The Great John L* (UA, 1945), *The Woman Who Came Back* (Rep., 1945), *On Stage Everybody* (Univ., 1945), *Jungle Captive* (Univ., 1945), *The Chicago Kid* (Rep., 1945), *Allotment Wives* (Mon., 1945), *The Fabulous Suzanne* (Rep., 1946), *Love and Learn* (WB, 1947), *Smart Woman* (AA, 1948), *Lulu Belle* (Col., 1948), *711 Ocean Drive* (Col., 1950), *Payment on Demand* (RKO, 1951), *High Noon* (UA, 1952), *Magnificent Obsession* (Univ., 1954), *Black Widow* (20th, 1954), *The Last Command* (Rep., 1955), *The Young Philadelphians* (WB, 1959), *Cash McCall* (WB, 1959), *The Wonderful World of the Brothers Grimm* (MGM, 1962), *Sex and the Single Girl* (WB, 1964).

ALAN LADD Born September 3, 1913, Hot Springs, Arkansas. Married Sue Carol (1942), children: David, Alana. Died January 3, 1964.

Ralph Moody, Francis McDonald and Alan Ladd in *Red Mountain*.

English-Language Feature Films: *Once in a Lifetime* (Univ., 1932), *Pigskin Parade* (20th, 1936), *Last Train From Madrid* (Par., 1937), *Souls at Sea* (Par., 1937), *Hold 'Em Navy* (Par., 1937), *The Goldwyn Follies* (UA, 1938), *Come On Leathernecks* (Rep., 1938), *The Green Hornet* (Univ. serial, 1939), *Rulers of the Sea* (Par., 1939), *Beast of Berlin* (PRC, 1939), *Light of Western Stars* (Par., 1940), *Gangs of Chicago* (Rep., 1940), *In Old Missouri* (Rep., 1940), *The Howards of Virginia* (Col., 1940), *Those Were the Days* (Par., 1940), *Captain Caution* (UA, 1940), *Wildcat Bus* (RKO, 1940), *Meet the Missus* (Rep., 1940), *Great Guns* (20th, 1941), *Citizen Kane* (RKO, 1941), *Cadet Girl* (20th, 1941), *Petticoat Politics* (Rep., 1941), *The Black Cat* (Univ., 1941), *The Reluctant Dragon* (RKO, 1941), *Paper Bullets* (PRC, 1941), *Joan of Paris* (RKO, 1942), *This Gun for Hire* (Par., 1942), *The Glass Key* (Par., 1942), *Lucky Jordan* (Par., 1942), *Star Spangled Rhythm* (Par.,

1942), *China* (Par., 1943), *And Now Tomorrow* (Par., 1944), *Salty O' Rourke* (Par., 1945), *Duffy's Tavern* (Par., 1945), *The Blue Dahlia* (Par., 1946), *O.S.S.* (Par., 1946), *Two Years Before the Mast* (Par., 1946), *Calcutta* (Par., 1947), *Variety Girl* (Par., 1947), *Wild Harvest* (Par., 1947), *My Favorite Brunette* (Par., 1947),* *Saigon* (Par., 1948), *Beyond Glory* (Par., 1948), *Whispering Smith* (Par., 1948), *The Great Gatsby* (Par., 1949), *Chicago Deadline* (Par., 1949), *Captain Carey, U.S.A.* (Par., 1950), *Branded* (Par., 1951), *Appointment With Danger* (Par., 1951), *Red Mountain* (Par., 1952), *The Iron Mistress* (WB, 1952), *Thunder in the East* (Par., 1953), *Desert Legion* (Univ, 1953), *Shane* (Par,. 1953), *Botany Bay* (Par., 1953), *Paratrooper* (Col., 1954), *Saskatchewan* (Univ., 1954), *Hell Below Zero* (Col., 1954), *The Black Knight* (Col., 1954), *Drum Beat* (WB, 1954), *The McConnell Story* (WB, 1955), *Hell on Frisco Bay* (WB, 1955), *Santiago* (WB, 1956), *The Big Land* (WB, 1957), *Boy on a Dolphin* (20th, 1957), *The Deep Six* (WB, 1958), *The Proud Rebel* (BV, 1958), *The Badlanders* (MGM, 1958), *The Man in the Net* (UA, 1959), *Guns of the Timberland* (WB, 1960), *All the Young Men* (Col., 1960), *One Foot in Hell* (20th, 1960), *13 West Street* (Col., 1962), *The Carpetbaggers* (Par., 1964).

*Unbilled guest appearance

ARTHUR LAKE (Arthur Silverlake) Born April 17, 1905, Corbin, Kentucky. Married Patricia Van Cleve (1937), children: Arthur, Marion.

Arthur Lake, Penny Singleton, Larry Simms and Dorothy Moore in *Blondie*.

Sound Feature Films: *On With the Show!* (WB, 1929), *Dance Hall* (RKO, 1929), *Tanned Legs* (RKO, 1929), *Cheer Up and Smile* (Fox, 1930), *She's My Weakness* (RKO, 1930), *Indiscreet* (UA, 1931), *Midshipman Jack* (RKO, 1933), *Girl o' My Dreams* (Mon., 1934), *Silver Streak* (RKO, 1934), *Women Must Dress* (Mon.. 1935), *Orchids to You* (Fox., 1935), *I Cover Chinatown* (Steiner, 1936), *23½ Hours Leave* (GN, 1937), *Topper* (MGM, 1937), *Annapolis Salute* (RKO, 1937), *Exiled to Shanghai* (Rep., 1937), *True Confession* (Par., 1937), *Double Danger* (RKO, 1938), *Everybody's Doing It* (RKO, 1938), *Blondie* (Col., 1938), *There Goes My Heart* (UA, 1938), *Blondie Meets the Boss* (Col., 1939), *Blondie Takes a Vacation* (Col., 1939), *Blondie Brings Up Baby* (Col., 1939), *Blondie on a Budget* (Col., 1940), *Blondie Has Servant Trouble* (Col., 1940), *Blondie Plays Cupid* (Col., 1940), *Blondie Goes Latin* (Col., 1941), *Blondie in Society* (Col., 1941), *Blondie Goes to College* (Col., 1942), *The Daring Young Man* (Col., 1942),* *Footlight Glamour* (Col., 1943), *It's a Great Life* (Col., 1943), *Sailor's Holiday* (Col., 1944), *The Ghost That Walks Alone* (Col., 1944), *Three Is a Family* (UA, 1944), *The Big Show-Off* (Rep., 1945), *Leave It to Blondie* (Col., 1946), *Life With Blondie* (Col., 1946), *Blondie's Lucky Day* (Col., 1946), *Blondie Knows Best* (Col., 1946), *Blondie's Holiday* (Col., 1947), *Blondie's Big Moment* (Col., 1947), *Blondie's in the Dough* (Col., 1947), *Blondie's Anniversary* (Col., 1947),

16 Fathoms Deep (Mon., 1948), *Blondie's Reward* (Col., 1948), *Blondie's Big Deal* (Col., 1949), *Blondie Hits the Jackpot* (Col., 1949), *Beware of Blondie* (Col., 1950), *Blondie's Hero* (Col., 1950).

*Unbilled guest appearance

VERONICA LAKE (Constance Frances Marie Ockelman) Born November 14, 1919. Brooklyn, New York, New York. Married John Detlie, children: Anthony, Elaine; divorced 1943. Married Andre de Toth (1944), children: Michael, Diane; divorced 1952. Married Joseph McCarthy (1955); divorced 1959. Married Ron House (1962).

Veronica Lake and Joel McCrea in *Sullivan's Travels*.

Feature Films:
as **Constance Keane** *All Women Have Secrets* (Par., 1939), *Sorority House* (RKO, 1939), *Forty Little Mothers* (MGM, 1940).
as **Veronica Lake** *I Wanted Wings* (Par., 1941), *Sullivan's Travels* (Par., 1941), *Hold Back the Dawn* (Par., 1941),* *This Gun for Hire* (Par., 1942), *The Glass Key* (Par., 1942), *I Married a Witch* (UA, 1942), *Star Spangled Rhythm* (Par., 1942), *So Proudly We Hail* (Par., 1942), *The Hour Before the Dawn* (Par., 1944), *Bring On the Girls* (Par., 1945), *Out of This World* (Par., 1945), *Duffy's Tavern* (Par., 1945), *Hold That Blonde* (Par., 1945), *Miss Susie Slagle's* (Par., 1945), *The Blue Dahlia* (Par., 1946), *Ramrod* (UA, 1947), *Variety Girl* (Par., 1947), *The Sainted Sisters* (Par., 1948), *Saigon* (Par., 1948), *Isn't It Romantic?* (Par., 1948), *Slattery's Hurricane* (20th, 1949), *Stronghold* (Lip., 1952), *Footsteps in the Snow* (Evergreen Film, 1966).

*Unbilled guest appearance

HEDY LAMARR (Hedwig Eva Maria Kiesler) Born November 9, 1913, Vienna, Austria. Married Fritz Mandl (1933); divorced 1937. Married Gene Markey (1939); child: James; divorced 1940. Married John Loder (1943), children: Denise, Anthony; divorced 1947. Married Ernest Stauffer (1951); divorced 1952. Married W. Howard Lee (1953); divorced 1959. Married Lewis Bowles (1963); divorced 1965.

English-Language Feature Films: *Algiers* (UA, 1938), *Lady of the Tropics* (MGM, 1939), *I Take This Woman* (MGM, 1940), *Boom Town* (MGM, 1940), *Comrade X* (MGM, 1940), *Come Live With Me* (MGM, 1941), *Ziegfeld Girl* (MGM, 1941), *H. M. Pulham, Esq.* (MGM, 1941), *Tortilla Flat* (MGM, 1942), *Crossroads* (MGM, 1942), *White Cargo* (MGM, 1942), *The Heavenly Body* (MGM, 1943), *The Conspirators* (WB, 1944), *Experiment Perilous* (RKO, 1944), *Her Highness and the Bellboy* (MGM, 1945), *The Strange Woman* (UA, 1946), *Dishonored Lady* (UA, 1947), *Let's Live a Little* (EL, 1948), *Samson and Delilah* (Par., 1949), *A Lady Without Passport* (MGM, 1950), *Copper Canyon* (Par.,

Hedy Lamarr and Walter Pidgeon in *White Cargo*.

1950), *My Favorite Spy* (Par., 1951), *The Story of Mankind* (WB, 1957), *The Female Animal* (Univ., 1957).

DOROTHY LAMOUR (Dorothy Kaumeyer) Born December 10, 1914, New Orleans, Louisiana. Married Herbie Kaye (1935); divorced 1939. Married William Howard (1943), children: John, Richard.

Dorothy Lamour and Claire Trevor in *The Lucky Stiff*.

Feature Films: *The Jungle Princess* (Par., 1936), *Swing High, Swing Low* (Par., 1937), *Last Train From Madrid* (Par., 1937), *High, Wide and Handsome* (Par., 1937), *Thrill of a Lifetime* (Par., 1937), *The Hurricane* (UA, 1937), *Big Broadcast of 1938* (Par., 1938), *Her Jungle Love* (Par., 1938), *Spawn of the North* (Par., 1938), *Tropic Holiday* (Par., 1938), *St. Louis Blues* (Par., 1939), *Man About Town* (Par., 1939), *Disputed Passage* (Par., 1939), *Johnny Apollo* (20th, 1940), *Typhoon* (Par., 1940), *Road to Singapore* (Par., 1940), *Moon Over Burma* (Par., 1940), *Chad Hanna* (20th, 1940), *Road to Zanzibar* (Par., 1941), *Caught in the Draft* (Par., 1941), *Aloma of the South Seas* (Par., 1941), *The Fleet's In* (Par., 1942), *Beyond the Blue Horizon* (Par., 1942), *Road to Morocco* (Par., 1942), *Star Spangled Rhythm* (Par., 1942), *They Got Me Covered* (RKO, 1943), *Dixie* (Par., 1943), *Riding High* (Par., 1943), *And the Angels Sing* (Par., 1944), *Rainbow Island* (Par., 1944), *Road to Utopia* (Par., 1945), *A Medal for Benny* (Par., 1945), *Duffy's Tavern* (Par., 1945), *Masquerade in Mexico* (Par., 1945), *My Favorite Brunette* (Par., 1947), *Road to Rio* (Par., 1947), *Wild Harvest* (Par., 1947), *Variety Girl*

(Par., 1947), *On Our Merry Way* (UA, 1948), *Lulu Belle* (Col., 1948), *The Girl From Manhattan* (UA, 1948), *Slightly French* (Col., 1948), *Manhandled* (Par., 1948), *The Lucky Stiff* (UA, 1949), *Here Comes the Groom* (Par., 1951),* *The Greatest Show on Earth* (Par., 1952), *Road to Bali* (Par., 1952), *Road to Hong Kong* (UA, 1962), *Donovan's Reef* (Par., 1963), *Pajama Party* (AIP, 1964).

*Unbilled guest appearance

BURT LANCASTER (Burton Stephen Lancaster) Born November 2, 1913, New York, New York. Married Norma Anderson (1946), children: James, William, Susan, Joanne, Sighle.

Burt Lancaster and Barbara Stanwyck in *Sorry, Wrong Number*.

Feature Films: *The Killers* (Univ., 1946), *Variety Girl* (Par., 1947), *Brute Force* (Univ., 1947), *Desert Fury* (Par., 1947), *I Walk Alone* (Par., 1947), *All My Sons* (Univ., 1948), *Sorry, Wrong Number* (Par., 1948), *Kiss the Blood Off My Hands* (Univ., 1948), *Criss Cross* (Univ., 1949), *Rope of Sand* (Par., 1949), *The Flame and the Arrow* (WB, 1950), *Mister 880* (20th, 1950), *Vengeance Valley* (MGM, 1951), *Jim Thorpe —All American* (WB, 1951), *Ten Tall Men* (Col., 1951), *The Crimson Pirate* (WB, 1952), *Come Back, Little Sheba* (Par., 1952), *South Sea Woman* (WB, 1953), *From Here to Eternity* (Col., 1953), *His Majesty O'Keefe* (WB, 1953), *Three Sailors and a Girl* (WB, 1953),* *Apache* (UA, 1954), *Vera Cruz* (UA, 1954), *The Kentuckian* (UA, 1955), *The Rose Tattoo* (Par., 1955), *Trapeze* (UA, 1956), *The Rainmaker* (Par., 1956), *Gunfight at the O.K. Corral* (Par., 1957), *Sweet Smell of Success* (UA, 1957), *The Devil's Disciple* (UA, 1959), *The Unforgiven* (UA, 1960), *Elmer Gantry* (UA, 1960), *The Young Savages* (UA, 1961), *Judgment at Nuremberg* (UA, 1961), *Bird Man of Alcatraz* (UA, 1962), *A Child Is Waiting* (UA, 1963), *The List of Adrian Messenger* (Univ., 1963), *The Leopard* (20th, 1963), *Seven Days in May* (Par., 1964), *The Train* (UA, 1965), *The Hallelujah Trail* (UA, 1965), *The Professionals* (Col., 1966), *The Scalphunters* (UA, 1968), *Castle Keep* (Col., 1968), *The Swimmer* (Col., 1968).

*Unbilled guest appearance

ELSA LANCHESTER (Elizabeth Sullivan) Born October 28, 1902, Lewisham, England. Married Charles Laughton (1929); widowed 1962.

Sound Feature Films: *The Private Life of Henry VIII* (UA, 1933), *Bride of Frankenstein* (Univ., 1935), *Naughty Marietta* (MGM, 1935), *David Copperfield* (MGM, 1935), *Rembrandt* (UA, 1936), *The Ghost Goes West* (UA, 1936), *Ladies in Retirement* (Col., 1941), *Son of Fury* (20th, 1942), *Tales of Manhattan* (20th, 1942), *Forever and a Day* (RKO, 1943), *Thumbs Up* (Rep., 1943), *Lassie Come Home* (MGM, 1943), *Passport to Adventure* (RKO, 1944), *The Spiral Staircase* (RKO, 1946), *The Razor's Edge* (20th, 1946), *Northwest Outpost* (Rep., 1947),

Elsa Lanchester, Edith Barrett, Ida Lupino and Louis Hayward in *Ladies in Retirement*.

The Bishop's Wife (RKO, 1947), *The Big Clock* (Par., 1948), *The Secret Garden* (MGM, 1949), *Come to the Stable* (20th, 1949), *The Inspector General* (WB, 1949), *Buccaneer's Girl* (Univ., 1950), *Mystery Street* (MGM, 1950), *The Petty Girl* (Col., 1950), *Frenchie* (Univ., 1950), *Les Miserables* (20th, 1952), *Dreamboat* (20th, 1952), *Young Man With Ideas* (MGM, 1952), *Androcles and the Lion* (RKO, 1952), *The Girls of Pleasure Island* (Par., 1953), *Hell's Half Acre* (Rep., 1954), *Three Ring Circus* (Par., 1954), *The Glass Slipper* (MGM, 1955), *Witness for the Prosecution* (UA, 1957), *Bell, Book and Candle* (Col., 1958), *Honeymoon Hotel* (MGM, 1964), *Mary Poppins* (BV, 1964), *Pajama Party* (AIP, 1964), *That Darn Cat* (BV, 1965), *Easy Come, Easy Go* (Par., 1967), *Blackbeard's Ghost* (BV, 1968).

ELISSA LANDI (Elizabeth Marie Zanardi-Landi) Born December 6, 1904, Venice, Italy. Married John C. Lawrence (1928); divorced 1936. Married Curtiss Kinney (1943), child: Caroline. Died October 21, 1948.

Elissa Landi in *Enter Madame*.

English-Language Feature Films: *The Parisian* (Capitol Film Exchange, 1930), *Knowing Men* (Capitol Film Exchange, 1931), *The Price of Things* (Capitol Film Exchange, 1931), *The Inseparables* (Capitol Film Exchange, 1931), *Children of Chance* (British International, 1931), *Body and Soul* (Fox, 1931), *Always Goodbye* (Fox, 1931), *Wicked* (Fox, 1931), *The Yellow Ticket* (Fox, 1931), *The Devil's Lottery* (Fox, 1932), *Woman in Room 13* (Fox, 1932), *Passport to Hell* (Fox, 1932), *Sign of the Cross* (Par., 1932), *The Masquerader* (UA, 1933), *Warrior's Husband* (Fox, 1933), *I Loved You Wednesday* (Fox, 1933), *By Candlelight* (Univ., 1934), *Man of Two Worlds* (RKO, 1934), *Sisters Under the Skin* (Col., 1934), *Great Flirtation* (Par., 1934), *Count of Monte Cristo* (UA, 1934), *Enter Madame* (Par., 1935), *Without Regret* (Par., 1935), *The Amateur Gentleman* (UA, 1936), *Mad Holiday* (MGM,

1936), *After the Thin Man* (MGM, 1936), *The Thirteenth Chair* (MGM, 1937), *Corregidor* (PRC, 1943).

CAROLE LANDIS (Frances Lillian Mary Ridste) Born January 1, 1919, Fairchild, Wisconsin. Married Irving Wheeler (1934). divorced 1940. Married Willis Hunt (1940); divorced 1940. Married Thomas Wallace (1943); divorced 1945. Married W. Horace Schmidlapp (1945). Died July 5, 1948.

Phil Silvers, Kay Francis, Martha Raye, Carole Landis and Mitzi Mayfair in *Four Jills in a Jeep*.

Feature Films: *A Star Is Born* (UA, 1937), *A Day at the Races* (MGM, 1937), *Broadway Melody of 1938* (MGM, 1937), *The Emperor's Candlesticks* (MGM, 1937), *Varsity Show* (WB, 1937), *Adventurous Blonde* (WB, 1937), *Blondes at Work* (WB, 1937), *Hollywood Hotel* (WB, 1937), *Gold Diggers in Paris* (WB, 1938), *Boy Meets Girl* (WB, 1938), *Men Are Such Fools* (WB, 1938), *Over the Wall* (WB, 1938), *Four's a Crowd* (WB, 1938), *When Were You Born?* (WB, 1938), *Daredevils of the Red Circle* (Rep. serial, 1939), *Three Texas Steers* (Rep., 1939), *Cowboys From Texas* (Rep., 1939), *One Million B.C.* (UA, 1940), *Turnabout* (UA, 1940), *Mystery Sea Raider* (Par., 1940), *Road Show* (UA, 1941), *Topper Returns* (UA, 1941), *Dance Hall* (20th, 1941), *Moon Over Miami* (20th, 1941), *I Wake Up Screaming* (20th, 1941), *Cadet Girl* (20th, 1941), *A Gentleman at Heart* (20th, 1942), *It Happened in Flatbush* (20th, 1942), *My Gal Sal* (20th, 1942), *Orchestra Wives* (20th, 1942), *Manila Calling* (20th, 1942), *The Powers Girl* (UA, 1942), *Wintertime* (20th, 1943), *Secret Command* (Col., 1944), *Four Jills in a Jeep* (20th, 1944), *Having Wonderful Crime* (RKO, 1944), *Behind Green Lights* (20th, 1946), *It Shouldn't Happen to a Dog* (20th, 1946), *Scandal in Paris* (UA, 1946), *Out of the Blue* (EL, 1947), *The Brass Monkey* (UA, 1948), *The Silk Noose* (Mon., 1950).

JESSIE ROYCE LANDIS (Jessie Royse Medbury) Born November 25, 1904, Chicago, Illinois. Married Rex Smith (1937); divorced 1942. Married J.F.R. Seitz (1957).

Bob Hope, Jessie Royce Landis and Lucille Ball in *Critic's Choice*.

110

Feature Films: *Derelict* (Par., 1930), *Mr. Belvedere Goes to College* (20th, 1949), *It Happens Every Spring* (20th, 1949), *My Foolish Heart* (RKO, 1949), *Mother Didn't Tell Me* (20th, 1950), *Tonight at 8:30* (Continental, 1953), *To Catch a Thief* (Par., 1955), *The Swan* (MGM, 1956), *The Girl He Left Behind* (WB, 1956), *My Man Godfrey* (Univ., 1957), *I Married a Woman* (Univ., 1958), *North by Northwest* (MGM, 1959), *A Private Affair* (20th, 1959), *Goodbye Again* (UA, 1961), *Bon Voyage!* (BV, 1962), *Boys' Night Out* (MGM, 1962), *Critic's Choice* (WB, 1963), *Gidget Goes to Rome* (Col., 1963).

PRISCILLA LANE (Priscilla Mullican) Born June 12, 1917, Indianola, Iowa. Married Oren Haglund (1939); divorced 1940. Married Joseph Howard (1942), children: Larry, Hannah, Judith, James.

Priscilla Lane and May Robson in *Daughters Courageous*.

Feature Films: *Varsity Show* (WB, 1937), *Love, Honor and Behave* (WB, 1938), *Cowboy From Brooklyn* (WB, 1938), *Men Are Such Fools* (WB, 1938), *Four Daughters* (WB, 1938), *Brother Rat* (WB, 1938), *Yes, My Darling Daughter* (WB, 1939), *Daughters Courageous* (WB, 1939), *Dust Be My Destiny* (WB, 1939), *The Roaring Twenties* (WB, 1939), *Four Wives* (WB, 1939), *Three Cheers for the Irish* (WB, 1940), *Brother Rat and a Baby* (WB, 1940), *Ladies Must Live* (WB, 1940), *Four Mothers* (WB, 1941), *Million Dollar Baby* (WB, 1941), *Blues in the Night* (WB, 1941), *Saboteur* (Univ., 1942), *Silver Queen* (UA, 1942), *The Meanest Man in the World* (20th, 1943), *Arsenic and Old Lace* (WB, 1944), *Fun on a Weekend* (UA, 1947), *Bodyguard* (RKO, 1948).

HOPE LANGE Born November 28, 1935, Redding Ridge, Connecticut. Married Don Murray (1956), children: Christopher, Patricia; divorced 1961. Married Alan Pakula (1963).

Thomas Mitchell, Mickey Shaughnessy, Hope Lange, Glenn Ford and Peter Falk in *Pocketful of Miracles*.

Feature Films: *Bus Stop* (20th, 1956), *The True Story of Jesse James* (20th, 1957), *Peyton Place* (20th, 1957), *The Young Lions* (20th, 1958), *In Love and War* (20th, 1958), *The Best of Everything* (20th, 1959), *Wild in the Country* (20th, 1961), *Pocketful of Miracles* (UA, 1961), *Love Is a Ball* (UA, 1963).

ANGELA LANSBURY (Angela Brigid Lansbury) Born October 16, 1925, London, England. Married Richard Cromwell (1945); divorced 1946. Married Peter Shaw (1949), children: Anthony, Deirdre.

Angela Lansbury and Glenn Ford in *Dear Heart*.

Feature Films: *Gaslight* (MGM, 1944), *National Velvet* (MGM, 1944), *The Picture of Dorian Gray* (MGM, 1945), *The Harvey Girls* (MGM, 1946), *The Hoodlum Saint* (MGM, 1946), *Private Affairs of Bel Ami* (UA, 1947), *Till the Clouds Roll By* (MGM, 1946), *If Winter Comes* (MGM, 1947), *Tenth Avenue Angel* (MGM, 1948), *The Three Musketeers* (MGM, 1948), *State of the Union* (MGM, 1948), *The Red Danube* (MGM, 1949), *Samson and Delilah* (Par., 1949), *Kind Lady* (MGM, 1951), *Mutiny* (UA, 1952), *Remains to Be Seen* (MGM, 1953), *A Lawless Street* (Col., 1955), *The Purple Mask* (Univ., 1955), *Please Murder Me* (DCA, 1956), *The Court Jester* (Par., 1956), *The Reluctant Debutante* (MGM, 1958), *The Long Hot Summer* (20th, 1958), *The Dark at the Top of the Stairs* (WB, 1960), *A Breath of Scandal* (Par., 1960), *Blue Hawaii* (Par., 1961), *Season of Passion* (UA, 1961), *All Fall Down* (MGM, 1962), *The Four Horsemen of the Apocalypse* (voice only; MGM, 1962), *The Manchurian Candidate* (UA, 1962), *In the Cool of the Day* (MGM, 1963), *The World of Henry Orient* (UA, 1964), *Dear Heart* (WB, 1964), *The Greatest Story Ever Told* (UA, 1965), *Harlow* (Par., 1965), *The Amorous Adventures of Moll Flanders* (Par., 1965), *Mister Buddwing* (MGM, 1966).

MARIO LANZA (Alfred Arnold Cocozza) Born January 21, 1921, Philadelphia, Pennsylvania. Married Betty Hicks (1945), children: Colleen, Elisse, Damon. Died October 7, 1959.

Feature Films: *That Midnight Kiss* (MGM, 1949), *The Toast of New*

Mario Lanza and Johanna von Kocsian in *For the First Time*.

Orleans (MGM, 1950), *The Great Caruso* (MGM, 1951), *Because You're Mine* (MGM, 1952), *The Student Prince* (voice only; MGM, 1954), *Serenade* (WB, 1956), *The Seven Hills of Rome* (MGM, 1958), *For the First Time* (MGM, 1959).

CHARLES LAUGHTON Born July 1, 1899, Scarborough, England. Married Elsa Lanchester (1929). Died December 15, 1962.

Charles Laughton and Reginald Owen in *Captain Kidd.*

Sound Feature Films: *Piccadilly* (BIP, 1929), *Wolves* (British and Dominion Productions, 1930), *Down River* (Gaumont, 1931), *The Old Dark House* (Univ., 1932), *Devil and the Deep* (Par., 1932), *Payment Deferred* (MGM, 1932), *The Sign of the Cross* (Par., 1932), *If I Had a Million* (Par., 1932), *Island of Lost Souls* (Par., 1933), *The Private Life of Henry VIII* (UA, 1933), *White Woman* (Par., 1933), *The Barretts of Wimpole Street* (MGM, 1934), *Ruggles of Red Gap* (Par., 1935), *Les Miserables* (UA, 1935), *Mutiny on the Bounty* (MGM, 1935), *Rembrandt* (London Films, 1936), *Vessel of Wrath* (Par., 1938), *St. Martin's Lane* (Par., 1939), *Jamaica Inn* (Par., 1939), *The Hunchback of Notre Dame* (RKO, 1939), *They Knew What They Wanted* (RKO, 1940), *It Started With Eve* (Univ., 1941), *The Tuttles of Tahiti* (RKO, 1942), *Tales of Manhattan* (20th, 1942), *Stand by for Action* (MGM, 1942), *Forever and a Day* (RKO, 1943), *This Land Is Mine* (RKO, 1943), *The Man From Down Under* (MGM, 1943), *The Canterville Ghost* (MGM, 1944), *The Suspect* (Univ., 1944), *Captain Kidd* (UA, 1945), *Because of Him* (Univ., 1946), *The Paradine Case* (Selznick, 1948), *The Big Clock* (Par., 1948), *Arch of Triumph* (UA, 1948), *The Girl From Manhattan* (UA, 1948), *The Bribe* (MGM, 1949), *The Man on the Eiffel Tower* (RKO, 1949), *The Blue Veil* (RKO, 1951), *The Strange Door* (Univ., 1951), *O. Henry's Full House* (20th, 1952), *Abbott and Costello Meet Captain Kidd* (WB, 1952), *Salome* (Col., 1953), *Young Bess* (MGM, 1953), *Hobson's Choice* (UA, 1954), *Witness for the Prosecution* (UA, 1957), *Under Ten Flags* (Par., 1960), *Spartacus* (Univ., 1960), *Advise and Consent* (Col., 1962).

LAUREL AND HARDY

STAN LAUREL (Arthur Stanley Jefferson) Born June 16, 1895, Ulverson, England. Married Lois Neilson, child: Lois; divorced 1934. Married Virginia Ruth (1934); divorced 1936. Remarried (1938); divorced 1939. Married Ida Kitaeva (1946). Died February 23, 1965.

OLIVER HARDY (Oliver Norvell Hardy) Born January 18, 1892, Atlanta, Georgia. Married Myrtle Reeves (1921); divorced 1937. Married Lucille Jones (1940). Died August 7, 1957.

Sound Feature Films: *Hollywood Revue Of 1929* (MGM, 1929), *Rogue Song* (MGM, 1930), *Pardon Us* (MGM, 1931), *Pack Up Your Troubles* (MGM, 1932), *Devil's Brother* (MGM, 1933), *Sons of the Desert* (MGM, 1933), *Hollywood Party* (MGM, 1934), *Babes in Toyland* (MGM, 1934), *Bonnie Scotland* (MGM, 1935), *The Bohemian Girl* (MGM, 1936), *Our Relations* (MGM, 1936), *Way Out West* (MGM,

Oliver Hardy, Stan Laurel and Lupe Velez in *Hollywood Party.*

1936), *Swiss Miss* (MGM, 1938), *Blockheads* (MGM, 1938), *Zenobia* (UA, 1939),* *The Flying Deuces* (RKO, 1939), *A Chump at Oxford* (UA, 1940), *Saps at Sea* (UA, 1940), *Great Guns* (20th, 1941), *A-Haunting We Will Go* (20th, 1942), *Air Raid Wardens* (MGM, 1943), *Jitterbugs* (20th, 1943), *The Dancing Masters* (20th, 1943), *The Big Noise* (20th, 1944), *Nothing but Trouble* (MGM, 1944), *The Bull Fighters* (20th, 1945), *The Fighting Kentuckian* (Rep., 1949),* *Riding High* (Par., 1950),* *Atoll K* (Utopia-Fortezza Films, 1951).

*Hardy appeared without Laurel

PIPER LAURIE (Rosetta Jacobs) Born January 22, 1932, Detroit, Michigan. Married Joe Morgenstern (1962).

Piper Laurie, Joan Fontaine, Jean Simmons and Sandra Dee in *Until They Sail.*

Feature Films: *Louisa* (Univ., 1950), *The Milkman* (Univ., 1950), *The Prince Who Was a Thief* (Univ., 1951), *Francis Goes to the Races* (Univ., 1951), *No Room for the Groom* (Univ., 1952), *Has Anybody Seen My Gal?* (Univ., 1952), *Son of Ali Baba* (Univ., 1952), *Mississippi Gambler* (Univ., 1953), *The Golden Blade* (Univ., 1953), *Dangerous Mission* (RKO, 1954), *Johnny Dark* (Univ., 1954), *Dawn at Socorro* (Univ., 1954), *Smoke Signal* (Univ., 1955), *Ain't Misbehavin'* (Univ., 1955), *Kelly and Me* (Univ., 1957), *Until They Sail* (MGM, 1957), *The Hustler* (20th, 1961).

PETER LAWFORD Born September 7, 1923, London, England. Married Patricia Kennedy (1954), children: Christopher, Sydney, Victoria, Robin; divorced 1966.

Feature Films: *Old Bill* (British, 1930), *Lord Jeff* (MGM, 1938), *Mrs.*

Reginald Owen, Helen Walker, Peter Lawford, Jennifer Jones and Margaret Bannerman in *Cluny Brown*.

Glenn Ford and Janet Leigh in *The Doctor and the Girl*.

Miniver (MGM, 1942), *Eagle Squadron* (Univ., 1942), *Thunder Birds* (20th, 1942), *A Yank at Eton* (MGM, 1942), *London Blackout Murders* (Rep., 1942), *Random Harvest* (MGM, 1942), *Girl Crazy* (MGM, 1943), *The Purple V* (Rep., 1943), *The Immortal Sergeant* (20th, 1943), *Pilot No. 5* (MGM, 1943), *Above Suspicion* (MGM, 1943), *Someone to Remember* (Rep., 1943), *The Man From Down Under* (MGM, 1943), *Sherlock Holmes Faces Death* (Univ., 1943), *The Sky's the Limit* (RKO, 1943), *Paris After Dark* (20th, 1943), *Flesh and Fantasy* (Univ., 1943), *Assignment in Brittany* (MGM, 1943), *Sahara* (Col., 1943), *West Side Kid* (Rep., 1943), *Corvette K-225* (Univ., 1943), *The White Cliffs of Dover* (MGM, 1944), *The Canterville Ghost* (MGM, 1944), *Mrs. Parkington* (MGM, 1944), *Son of Lassie* (MGM, 1945), *The Picture of Dorian Gray* (MGM, 1945), *Two Sisters From Boston* (MGM, 1946), *Cluny Brown* (20th, 1946), *My Brother Talks to Horses* (MGM, 1946), *It Happened in Brooklyn* (MGM, 1947), *Good News* (MGM, 1947), *On an Island With You* (MGM, 1948), *Easter Parade* (MGM, 1948), *Julia Misbehaves* (MGM, 1948), *Little Women* (MGM, 1949), *The Red Danube* (MGM, 1949), *Please Believe Me* (MGM, 1950), *Just This Once* (MGM, 1952), *Kangaroo* (20th, 1952), *You for Me* (MGM, 1952), *The Hour of 13* (MGM, 1952), *Rogue's March* (MGM, 1952), *It Should Happen to You* (Col., 1954), *Never So Few* (MGM, 1959), *Ocean's 11* (WB, 1960), *Exodus* (UA, 1960), *Pepe* (Col., 1960), *Sergeants 3* (UA, 1962), *Advise and Consent* (Col., 1962), *The Longest Day* (20th, 1962), *Dead Ringer* (WB, 1964), *Sylvia* (Par., 1965), *Harlow* (Par., 1965), *The Oscar* (Par., 1966), *A Man Called Adam* (Embassy, 1966), *Salt and Pepper* (UA, 1968), *Buona Sera, Mrs. Campbell* (UA, 1968).

JANET LEIGH (Jeanette Helen Morrison) Born July 6, 1927, Merced, California. Married Kenneth Carlisle (1942); annulled 1942. Married Stanley Reames (1945); divorced 1948. Married Tony Curtis (1951); children: Kelly, Jamie; divorced 1962. Married Robert Brandt (1962).

Feature Films: *The Romance of Rosy Ridge* (MGM, 1947), *If Winter Comes* (MGM, 1947), *Hills of Home* (MGM, 1948), *Words and Music* (MGM, 1948), *Act of Violence* (MGM, 1948), *Little Women* (MGM, 1949), *That Forsyte Woman* (MGM, 1949), *The Doctor and the Girl* (MGM, 1949), *The Red Danube* (MGM, 1949), *Holiday Affair* (RKO, 1949), *Strictly Dishonorable* (MGM, 1951), *Angels in the Outfield* (MGM, 1951), *Two Tickets to Broadway* (RKO, 1951), *It's a Big Country* (MGM, 1951), *Just This Once* (MGM, 1952), *Scaramouche* (MGM, 1952), *Fearless Fagan* (MGM, 1952), *The Naked Spur* (MGM, 1953), *Confidentially Connie* (MGM, 1953), *Houdini* (Par., 1953), *Walking My Baby Back Home* (Univ., 1953), *Prince Valiant* (20th, 1954), *Living It Up* (Par., 1954), *The Black Shield of Falworth* (Univ., 1954), *Rogue Cop* (MGM, 1954), *Pete Kelly's Blues* (WB, 1955), *My Sister Eileen* (Col.,

1955), *Safari* (Col., 1956), *Jet Pilot* (Univ., 1957), *Touch of Evil* (Univ., 1958), *The Vikings* (UA, 1958), *The Perfect Furlough* (Univ., 1958), *Who Was That Lady?* (Col., 1960), *Psycho* (Par., 1960), *Pepe* (Col., 1960), *The Manchurian Candidate* (UA, 1962), *Bye Bye Birdie* (Col., 1963), *Wives and Lovers* (Par., 1963), *Three on a Couch* (Col., 1966), *Harper* (WB, 1966), *Kid Rodelo* (Par., 1966), *An American Dream* (WB, 1966), *Hello Down There* (Par., 1968), *Grand Slam* (Par., 1968).

VIVIEN LEIGH (Vivian Mary Hartley) Born November 5, 1913, Darjeeling, India. Married Herbert Holman (1932), child: Suzanne; divorced 1940. Married Laurence Olivier (1940); divorced 1960. Died July 8, 1967.

Robert Taylor and Vivien Leigh in *Waterloo Bridge*.

Feature Films: *Things Are Looking Up* (Gainsborough, 1934), *The Village Squire* (British and Dominions, 1935), *Gentleman's Agreement* (British and Dominions, 1935), *Look Up and Laugh* (Associated Talking Pictures, 1935), *Fire Over England* (UA, 1937), *Dark Journey* (UA, 1937), *Storm in a Teacup* (UA, 1937), *A Yank at Oxford* (MGM, 1938), *St. Martin's Lane* ("The Sidewalks of London"—Par., 1938), *Gone With the Wind* (MGM, 1939), *Waterloo Bridge* (MGM, 1940), *Twenty-one Days Together* (Col., 1940), *That Hamilton Woman* (UA, 1941), *Caesar and Cleopatra* (UA, 1946), *Anna Karenina* (20th, 1948), *A Streetcar Named Desire* (WB, 1951), *The Deep Blue Sea* (20th, 1955), *The Roman Spring of Mrs. Stone* (WB, 1961), *Ship of Fools* (Col., 1965).

Jack Lemmon and Judy Holliday in *It Should Happen to You*.

JACK LEMMON (John Uhler Lemmon III) Born February 8, 1925, Boston, Massachusetts. Married Cynthia Stone (1950), child: Christopher; divorced 1956. Married Felicia Farr (1962).

Feature Films: It Should Happen to You (Col., 1954), *Phffft* (Col., 1954), *Three for the Show* (Col., 1955), *My Sister Eileen* (Col., 1955), *Mister Roberts* (WB, 1955), *You Can't Run Away From It* (Col., 1956), *Operation Mad Ball* (Col., 1957), *Fire Down Below* (Col., 1957), *Cowboy* (Col., 1958), *Bell, Book and Candle* (Col., 1959), *It Happened to Jane* (Col., 1959), *Some Like it Hot* (UA, 1959), *The Apartment* (UA, 1960), *The Wackiest Ship in the Army* (Col., 1960), *Pepe* (Col., 1960), *The Notorious Landlady* (Col., 1962), *Days of Wine and Roses* (WB, 1962), *Irma La Douce* (UA, 1963), *Under the Yum Yum Tree* (Col., 1963), *Good Neighbor Sam* (Col., 1964), *How to Murder Your Wife* (UA, 1964), *The Great Race* (WB, 1965), *The Fortune Cookie* (UA, 1966), *Luv* (Col., 1967), *The Odd Couple* (Par., 1968).

JOAN LESLIE (Joan Agnes Theresa Sadie Brodel) Born January 26, 1925, Detroit, Michigan. Married William Caldwell (1950), children: Patrice, Ellen.

Fred Astaire and Joan Leslie in *The Sky's the Limit*.

Feature Films:
as **Joan Brodel** *Camille* (MGM, 1936), *Men With Wings* (Par., 1938), *Two Thoroughbreds* (RKO, 1939), *Nancy Drew, Reporter* (WB, 1939), *Winter Carnival* (UA, 1939), *Love Affair* (RKO, 1939), *Military Academy* (Col., 1940), *Star Dust* (20th, 1940), *Young as You Feel* (20th, 1940), *Susan and God* (MGM, 1940), *Laddie* (RKO, 1940), *Foreign Correspondent* (UA, 1940).
as **Joan Leslie** *High Sierra* (WB, 1941), *Thieves Fall Out* (WB,

1941), *The Wagons Roll at Night* (WB, 1941), *Great Mr. Nobody* (WB, 1941), *Sergeant York* (WB, 1941), *The Hard Way* (WB, 1942), *Yankee Doodle Dandy* (WB, 1942), *The Male Animal* (WB, 1942), *This Is the Army* (WB, 1943), *Thank Your Lucky Stars* (WB, 1943), *The Sky's the Limit* (RKO, 1943), *Hollywood Canteen* (WB, 1944), *Rhapsody in Blue* (WB, 1945), *Where Do We Go From Here?* (20th, 1945), *Too Young To Know* (WB, 1945), *Cinderella Jones* (WB, 1946), *Janie Gets Married* (WB, 1946), *Two Guys From Milwaukee* (WB, 1946), *Repeat Performance* (EL, 1947), *Northwest Stampede* (EL, 1948), *Born to Be Bad* (RKO, 1950), *The Skipper Surprised His Wife* (MGM, 1950), *Man in the Saddle* (Col., 1951), *Hellgate* (Lip., 1952), *Toughest Man in Arizona* (Rep., 1952), *The Woman They Almost Lynched* (Rep., 1953), *Flight Nurse* (Rep., 1953), *Jubilee Trail* (Rep., 1953), *Hell's Outpost* (Rep., 1954), *The Revolt of Mamie Stover* (20th, 1956).

JERRY LEWIS (Joseph Levitch) Born March 16, 1926, Newark, New Jersey. Married Patti Palmer (1944), children: Gary, Ronald, Scott, Christopher, Anthony, Joseph.

Thelma Ritter and Jerry Lewis in *Boeing-Boeing*.

Feature Films: *My Friend Irma* (Par., 1949), *My Friend Irma Goes West* (Par., 1950), *At War With the Army* (Par., 1951), *That's My Boy* (Par., 1951), *Sailor Beware* (Par., 1952), *Jumping Jacks* (Par., 1952), *Road to Bali* (Par., 1952),* *The Stooge* (Par., 1953), *Scared Stiff* (Par., 1953), *The Caddy* (Par., 1953), *Money From Home* (Par., 1954), *Living It Up* (Par., 1954), *Three Ring Circus* (Par., 1954), *You're Never Too Young* (Par., 1955), *Artists and Models* (Par., 1955), *Pardners* (Par., 1956), *Hollywood or Bust* (Par., 1956), *The Delicate Delinquent* (Par., 1957), *The Sad Sack* (Par., 1958), *Rock-a-Bye Baby* (Par., 1958), *The Geisha Boy* (Par., 1958), *Don't Give Up the Ship* (Par., 1959), *L'il Abner* (Par., 1959), *Visit to a Small Planet* (Par., 1960), *The Bellboy* (Par., 1960), *Cinderfella* (Par., 1960), *The Ladies' Man* (Par., 1961), *The Errand Boy* (Par., 1961), *It's Only Money* (Par., 1962), *It's a Mad, Mad, Mad, Mad World* (UA, 1963),* *The Nutty Professor* (Par., 1963), *Who's Minding the Store?* (Par., 1964), *The Patsy* (Par., 1964), *Disorderly Orderly* (Par., 1964), *Family Jewels* (Par., 1965), *Boeing-Boeing* (Par., 1965), *Three on a Couch* (Col., 1966), *Way, Way Out!* (20th, 1966), *The Big Mouth* (Col., 1967), *Don't Raise the Bridge, Lower the River* (Col., 1968).

*Unbilled guest appearance

VIVECA LINDFORS (Elsa Viveca Torstens-Dotter Lindfors) Born December 29, 1920, Uppsala, Sweden. Married Folke Rogard (1941), children: Jan, Lena; divorced 1949. Married Donald Siegel (1949), child: Christopher; divorced 1953. Married George Tabori (1954).

English-Language Feature Films: *To the Victor* (WB, 1948), *Adventures of Don Juan* (WB, 1948), *Night Unto Night* (WB, 1949), *Backfire* (WB, 1950), *No Sad Songs for Me* (Col., 1950), *This Side of the Law* (WB, 1950), *Dark City* (Par., 1950), *Four in a Jeep* (UA, 1951), *Gypsy Fury*

Viveca Lindfors and Ronald Reagan in *Night Unto Night*.

(Mon., 1951), *The Flying Missile* (Col., 1951), *Journey into Light* (20th, 1951), *The Raiders* (Univ., 1952), *No Time for Flowers* (RKO, 1952), *Run for Cover* (Par., 1955), *Moonfleet* (MGM, 1955), *The Halliday Brand* (UA, 1957), *I Accuse!* (MGM, 1958), *The Tempest* (Par., 1959), *The Story of Ruth* (20th, 1960), *Weddings and Babies* (Zenith, 1960), *King of Kings* (MGM, 1962), *No Exit* (Zenith, 1962), *These Are the Damned* (Col., 1962), *An Affair of the Skin* (Zenith, 1964), *Brainstorm* (WB, 1965), *Sylvia* (Par., 1965), *The Witnesses* (voice only; Altura Films International, 1967).

MARGARET LINDSAY (Margaret Kies) Born September 19, 1910, Dubuque, Iowa.

James Burke, Charley Grapewin, Margaret Lindsay, Charles Lane and Anna May Wong in *Ellery Queen's Penthouse Mystery*.

Feature Films: *The All American* (Univ., 1932), *Okay America* (Univ., 1932), *The Fourth Horseman* (Univ., 1932), *Cavalcade* (Fox, 1933), *West of Singapore* (Mon., 1933), *Private Detective 62* (WB, 1933), *Voltaire* (WB, 1933), *Baby Face* (WB, 1933), *Captured* (WB, 1933), *Paddy the Next Best Thing* (Fox, 1933), *The World Changes* (WB, 1933), *From Headquarters* (WB, 1933), *House on 56th Street* (WB, 1933), *Lady Killer* (WB, 1933), *Gentlemen Are Born* (WB, 1934), *Fog Over Frisco* (WB, 1934), *Merry Wives of Reno* (WB, 1934), *The Dragon Murder Case* (WB, 1934), *The Florentine Dagger* (WB, 1935), *Devil Dogs of the Air* (WB, 1935), *Bordertown* (WB, 1935), *The Case of the Curious Bride* (WB, 1935), *G-Men* (WB, 1935), *Personal Maid's Secret* (WB, 1935), *Frisco Kid* (WB, 1935), *Dangerous* (WB, 1935), *The Lady Consents* (RKO, 1936), *The Law in Her Hands* (WB, 1936), *Public Enemy's Wife* (WB, 1936), *Isle of Fury* (WB, 1936), *Sinner Take All* (MGM, 1936), *Green Light* (WB, 1937), *Song of the City* (MGM,

1937), *Slim* (WB, 1937), *Back in Circulation* (WB, 1937), *Jezebel* (WB, 1938), *Gold Is Where You Find It* (WB, 1938), *When Were You Born?* (WB, 1938), *There's That Woman Again* (Col., 1938), *Broadway Musketeers* (WB, 1938), *Garden of the Moon* (WB, 1938), *On Trial* (WB, 1939), *Hell's Kitchen* (WB, 1939), *The Under-Pup* (20th, 1939), *20,000 Men a Year* (20th, 1939), *British Intelligence* (WB, 1940), *Double Alibi* (Univ., 1940), *Honeymoon Deferred* (Univ., 1940), *The House of Seven Gables* (Univ., 1940), *Meet the Wildcat* (Univ., 1940), *Ellery Queen, Master Detective* (Col., 1940), *Ellery Queen's Penthouse Mystery* (Col., 1941), *There's Magic in Music* (Par., 1941), *Ellery Queen and the Perfect Crime* (Col., 1941), *Ellery Queen and the Murder Ring* (Col., 1941), *A Close Call for Ellery Queen* (Col., 1942), *A Tragedy at Midnight* (Rep., 1942), *The Spoilers* (Univ., 1942), *Enemy Agents Meet Ellery Queen* (Col., 1942), *A Desperate Chance for Ellery Queen* (Col., 1942), *Crime Doctor* (Col., 1943), *Let's Have Fun* (Col., 1943), *No Place for a Lady* (Col., 1943), *Alaska* (Mon., 1944), *The Adventures of Rusty* (Col., 1945), *Scarlet Street* (Univ., 1945), *Club Havana* (PRC, 1946), *Her Sister's Secret* (PRC, 1946), *Seven Keys to Baldpate* (RKO, 1947), *Louisiana* (Mon., 1947), *Cass Timberlane* (MGM, 1947), *The Vigilantes Return* (Univ., 1947), *B. F.'s Daughter* (MGM, 1948), *Emergency Hospital* (UA, 1956), *The Bottom of the Bottle* (20th, 1956), *The Restless Years* (Univ., 1958), *Please Don't Eat the Daisies* (MGM, 1960), *Jet Over the Atlantic* (Inter-Continent, 1960), *Tammy and the Doctor* (Univ., 1963).

GENE LOCKHART (Eugene Lockhart) Born July 18, 1891, London, Ontario, Canada. Married Kathleen Arthur (1924), child: June. Died March 31, 1957.

Kathleen Lockhart and Gene Lockhart in *A Christmas Carol*.

Sound Feature Films: *By Your Leave* (RKO, 1934), *I've Been Around* (Univ., 1935), *Star of Midnight* (RKO, 1935), *Captain Hurricane* (RKO, 1935), *Thunder in the Night* (Fox, 1935), *Storm Over the Andes* (Univ., 1935), *Crime and Punishment* (Col., 1935), *The Garden Murder Case* (MGM, 1936), *Brides Are Like That* (WB, 1936), *The First Baby* (20th, 1936), *Times Square Playboy* (WB, 1936), *Earthworm Tractors* (WB, 1936), *The Gorgeous Hussy* (MGM, 1936), *The Devil Is a Sissy*

(MGM, 1936), *Wedding Present* (Par., 1936), *Mind Your Own Business* (Par., 1936), *Career Woman* (20th, 1936), *Come Closer Folks* (Col., 1936), *Too Many Wives* (RKO, 1937), *Mama Steps Out* (MGM, 1937), *Something to Sing About* (GN, 1937), *The Sheik Steps Out* (Rep., 1937), *Of Human Hearts* (MGM, 1938), *Sinners in Paradise* (Univ., 1938), *Men Are Such Fools* (WB, 1938), *Algiers* (UA, 1938), *Penrod's Double Trouble* (WB, 1938), *Sweethearts* (MGM, 1938), *A Christmas Carol* (MGM, 1938), *Blondie* (Col., 1938), *Meet the Girls* (20th, 1938), *Listen Darling* (MGM, 1938), *The Story of Alexander Graham Bell* (20th, 1939), *I'm From Missouri* (Par., 1939), *Hotel Imperial* (Par., 1939), *Tell No Tales* (MGM, 1939), *Bridal Suite* (MGM, 1939), *Our Leading Citizen* (Par., 1939), *Blackmail* (MGM, 1939), *Geronimo* (Par., 1939), *His Girl Friday* (Col., 1940), *Edison the Man* (MGM, 1940), *We Who Are Young* (MGM, 1940), *A Dispatch From Reuters* (WB, 1940), *Dr. Kildare Goes Home* (MGM, 1940), *Meet John Doe* (WB, 1941), *The Sea Wolf* (WB, 1941), *Billy The Kid* (MGM, 1941), *All That Money Can Buy* (RKO, 1941), *International Lady* (UA, 1941), *One Foot in Heaven* (WB, 1941), *They Died With Their Boots On* (WB, 1941), *Steel Against the Sky* (WB, 1941), *Juke Girl* (WB, 1942), *The Gay Sisters* (WB, 1942), *You Can't Escape Forever* (WB, 1942), *Forever and a Day* (RKO, 1943), *Hangmen Also Die* (UA, 1943), *Find the Blackmailer* (WB, 1943), *Northern Pursuit* (WB, 1943), *The Desert Song* (WB, 1943), *Action in Arabia* (RKO, 1944), *Going My Way* (Par., 1944), *Man From Frisco* (Rep., 1944), *That's the Spirit* (Univ., 1945), *The House on 92nd Street* (20th, 1945), *Leave Her to Heaven* (20th, 1945), *Meet Me on Broadway* (Col., 1946), *A Scandal in Paris* (UA, 1946), *The Strange Woman* (UA, 1946), *The Shocking Miss Pilgrim* (20th, 1947), *Honeymoon* (RKO, 1947), *The Miracle on 34th Street* (20th, 1947), *Cynthia* (MGM, 1947), *Her Husband's Affair* (Col., 1947), *The Foxes of Harrow* (20th, 1947), *I, Jane Doe* (Rep., 1948), *The Inside Story* (Rep., 1948), *Apartment for Peggy* (20th, 1948), *Joan of Arc* (RKO, 1948), *That Wonderful Urge* (20th, 1948), *Down to the Sea in Ships* (20th, 1949), *Madame Bovary* (MGM, 1949), *Red Light* (UA, 1949), *The Inspector General* (WB, 1949), *The Big Hangover* (MGM, 1950), *I'd Climb the Highest Mountain* (20th, 1951), *Rhubarb* (Par., 1951), *The Lady From Texas* (Univ., 1951), *Seeds of Destruction* (Astor, 1951), *A Girl in Every Port* (RKO, 1952), *Hoodlum Empire* (Rep., 1952), *Bonzo Goes to College* (Univ., 1952), *Apache War Smoke* (MGM, 1952), *Androcles and the Lion* (RKO, 1952), *Face to Face* (RKO, 1952), *Confidentially Connie* (MGM, 1953), *The Lady Wants Mink* (Rep., 1953), *Down Among the Sheltering Palms* (20th, 1953), *Francis Covers the Big Town* (Univ., 1953), *World for Ransom* (AA, 1954), *The Vanishing American* (Rep., 1955), *Carousel* (20th, 1956), *The Man in the Gray Flannel Suit* (20th, 1956), *Jeanne Eagles* (Col., 1957).

GINA LOLLOBRIGIDA Born July 4, 1927, Sibriaco, Italy. Married Milko Skofic (1949), child: Milko; divorced 1968.

Rock Hudson and Gina Lollobrigida in *Strange Bedfellows*.

English-Language Feature Films: *Beat the Devil* (UA, 1954), *Crossed Swords* (UA, 1954), *Trapeze* (UA, 1956), *The Hunchback of Notre Dame* (AA, 1957), *Solomon and Sheba* (UA, 1959), *Never So Few* (MGM, 1959), *Go Naked in the World* (MGM, 1961), *Come September* (Univ., 1961), *Woman of Straw* (UA, 1964), *Strange Bedfellows* (Univ., 1964), *Hotel Paradiso* (MGM, 1966), *Cervantes* (Aip, 1968), *Buona Sera, Mrs. Campbell* (Univ., 1968), *The Private Navy of Sgt. O'Farrell* (UA, 1968).

CAROLE LOMBARD (Jane Alice Peters) Born October 6, 1908, Fort Wayne, Indiana. Married William Powell (1931); divorced 1933. Married Clark Gable (1939). Died January 16, 1942.

Ray Milland and Carole Lombard in *Bolero*.

Sound Feature Films: *Show Folks* (Pathé, 1928), *Ned McCobb's Daughter* (Pathé, 1929), *High Voltage* (Pathé, 1929), *Big News* (Pathé, 1929), *Dynamite* (Pathé, 1929), *The Racketeer* (Pathé, 1929), *Arizona Kid* (Fox, 1930), *Safety in Numbers* (Par., 1930), *Fast and Loose* (Par., 1930), *It Pays to Advertise* (Par., 1931), *Man of the World* (Par., 1931), *Ladies' Man* (Par., 1931), *Up Pops the Devil* (Par., 1931), *I Take This Woman* (Par., 1931), *No One Man* (Par., 1932), *Sinners in the Sun* (Par., 1932), *Virtue* (Col., 1932), *No More Orchids* (Col., 1932), *No Man of Her Own* (Par., 1932), *From Hell to Heaven* (Par., 1933), *Supernatural* (Par., 1933), *The Eagle and the Hawk* (Par., 1933), *Brief Moment* (Col., 1933), *White Woman* (Par., 1933), *Bolero* (Par., 1934), *We're Not Dressing* (Par., 1934), *Twentieth Century* (Col., 1934), *Now and Forever* (Par., 1934), *Lady by Choice* (Col., 1934), *The Gay Bride* (MGM, 1934), *Rumba* (Par., 1935), *Hands Across the Table* (Par., 1935), *Love Before Breakfast* (Univ., 1936), *My Man Godfrey* (Univ., 1936), *The Princess Comes Across* (Par., 1936), *Swing High, Swing Low* (Par., 1937), *True Confession* (Par., 1937), *Nothing Sacred* (UA, 1937), *Fools for Scandal* (WB, 1938), *Made for Each Other* (UA, 1939), *In Name Only* (RKO, 1939), *Vigil in the Night* (RKO, 1940), *They Knew What They Wanted* (RKO, 1940), *Mr. and Mrs. Smith* (RKO, 1941), *To Be or Not to Be* (UA, 1942).

SOPHIA LOREN (Sofia Villani Scicolone) Born September 20, 1932, Rome, Italy. Married Carlo Ponti (1957).

English-Language Feature Films: *Quo Vadis* (MGM, 1951), *Boy on a Dolphin* (20th, 1957), *The Pride and the Passion* (UA, 1957), *Legend of the Lost* (UA, 1957), *Desire Under the Elms* (Par., 1958), *The Key* (Col., 1958), *Houseboat* (Par., 1958), *That Kind of Woman* (Par., 1959), *Black Orchid* (Par., 1959), *Heller in Pink Tights* (Par., 1960), *It Started in Naples* (Par., 1960), *A Breath of Scandal* (Par., 1960), *The Millionaires* (20th, 1960), *El Cid* (AA, 1961), *The Condemned of Altona* (20th, 1963), *Five Miles to Midnight* (UA, 1963), *The Fall of the Roman Empire*

Sophia Loren and Tab Hunter in *That Kind of Woman*.

(Par., 1964), *Operation Crossbow* (MGM, 1965), *Judith* (Par., 1966), *Arabesque* (Univ., 1966), *Lady L* (MGM, 1966), *The Countess From Hong Kong* (Univ., 1967). *More than a Miracle* (MGM, 1967), *Ghost Italian Style* (MGM, 1968), *Best House in Naples* (MGM, 1968).

PETER LORRE Born June 26, 1904, Rosenberg, Hungary. Married Cecilia Lovovsky (1933); divorced 1945. Married Kaaren Verne (1945); divorced. Married Anna Brenning (1952), child: Kathryn. Died March 23, 1965.

Frances Drake and Peter Lorre in *Mad Love*.

English-Language Sound Feature Films: *The Man Who Knew Too Much* (Gaumont-British, 1934), *Mad Love* (MGM, 1935), *Crime and Punishment* (Col., 1935), *Secret Agent* (Gaumont-British, 1936), *Crack-Up* (20th, 1936), *Nancy Steele Is Missing* (20th, 1937), *Lancer Spy* (20th, 1937), *Think Fast, Mr. Moto* (20th, 1937), *Thank You, Mr. Moto* (20th, 1937), *Mr. Moto's Gamble* (20th, 1938), *Mr. Moto Takes a Chance* (20th, 1938), *I'll Give a Million* (20th, 1938), *Mysterious Mr. Moto* (20th, 1938), *Mr. Moto's Last Warning* (20th, 1939), *Mr. Moto Takes a Vacation* (20th, 1939), *Mr. Moto in Danger Island* (20th, 1939), *Strange Cargo* (MGM, 1940), *Island of Doomed Men* (Col. 1940), *I Was an Adventuress* (20th, 1940), *Stranger on the Third Floor* (RKO, 1940), *You'll Find Out* (RKO, 1940), *The Face Behind the Mask* (Col., 1941), *Mr. District Attorney* (Rep., 1941), *They Met in Bombay* (MGM,

1941), *The Maltese Falcon* (WB, 1941), *All Through the Night* (WB, 1942), *The Boogie Man Will Get You* (Col., 1942), *Invisible Agent* (Univ., 1942), *In This Our Life* (WB, 1942),* *Casablanca* (WB, 1942), *The Constant Nymph* (WB, 1943), *Background to Danger* (WB, 1943), *Cross of Lorraine* (MGM, 1943), *Arsenic and Old Lace* (WB, 1944), *Passage to Marseille* (WB, 1944), *Hollywood Canteen* (WB, 1944), *The Mask of Dimitrios* (WB, 1944), *Conspirators* (WB, 1944), *Confidential Agent* (WB, 1945), *Hotel Berlin* (WB, 1945), *Three Strangers* (WB, 1946), *The Verdict* (WB, 1946), *Black Angel* (Univ., 1946), *The Beast With Five Fingers* (WB, 1946), *The Chase* (UA, 1946), *My Favorite Brunette* (Par., 1947), *Casbah* (Univ., 1948), *Rope of Sand* (Par., 1949), *Quicksand* (UA, 1950), *Double Confession* (Associated British Pictures, 1951), *Beat the Devil* (UA, 1954), *20,000 Leagues Under the Sea* (BV, 1954), *Meet Me in Las Vegas* (MGM, 1956),* *Congo Crossing* (Univ., 1956), *Around the World in 80 Days* (UA, 1956), *The Buster Keaton Story* (Par., 1957), *The Story of Mankind* (WB, 1957), *The Sad Sack* (Par., 1957), *Silk Stockings* (MGM, 1957), *Hell Ship Mutiny* (Rep., 1958), *The Big Circus* (AA, 1959), *Scent of Mystery* (Mike Todd, Jr., 1960), *Voyage to the Bottom of the Sea* (20th, 1961), *Five Weeks in a Balloon* (20th, 1962), *Tales of Terror* (AIP, 1962), *The Raven* (AIP, 1963), *Comedy of Terrors* (AIP, 1963), *The Patsy* (Par., 1964), *Muscle Beach Party* (AIP, 1964).*

*Unbilled guest appearance

ANITA LOUISE (Anita Louise Fremault) Born January 29, 1915, New York, New York. Married Buddy Adler (1940); widowed 1960. Married Henry Bergers (1962).

Anita Louise, Ross Alexander and Joseph Cawthorn in *Brides Are Like That*.

Sound Feature Films: *Wonder of Women* (MGM, 1929), *Square Shoulders* (Pathé, 1929), *The Marriage Playground* (Par., 1929), *What a Man!* (World Wide, 1930), *The Floradora Girl* (MGM, 1930), *Just Like Heaven* (Tiff., 1930), *The Third Alarm* (Tiff., 1930), *Millie* (RKO, 1931), *The Great Meadow* (MGM, 1931), *Woman Between* (RKO, 1931), *Everything's Rosie* (RKO, 1931), *Heaven on Earth* (Univ., 1931), *The Phantom of Crestwood* (RKO, 1932), *Our Betters* (RKO, 1933), *Most Precious Thing in Life* (Col., 1934), *Are We Civilized?* (Raspin Productions, 1934), *I Give My Love* (Univ., 1934), *Cross Streets* (Chesterfield, 1934), *Madame Du Barry* (WB, 1934), *Judge Priest* (Fox, 1934), *The Firebird* (WB, 1934), *Bachelor of Arts* (Fox, 1934), *Lady Tubbs* (Univ., 1935), *Here's to Romance* (Fox, 1935), *A Midsummer Night's Dream* (WB, 1935), *Personal Maid's Secret* (WB, 1935), *The Story of Louis Pasteur* (WB, 1935), *Brides Are Like That* (WB, 1936), *Anthony Adverse* (WB, 1936), *Call It a Day* (WB, 1937), *Green Light* (WB, 1937), *The Go-Getter* (WB, 1937), *First Lady* (WB, 1937), *That Certain Woman* (WB, 1937), *Tovarich* (WB, 1937), *My Bill* (WB, 1938), *Marie Antoinette* (MGM, 1938), *Going Places* (WB, 1938), *The Sisters* (WB, 1938), *The Gorilla* (20th, 1939), *Hero for a Day* (Univ., 1939), *Reno* (RKO, 1939), *These Glamour Girls* (MGM, 1939), *Main Street Lawyer* (Rep.,

1939), *The Little Princess* (20th, 1939), *Wagons Westward* (Rep., 1940), *The Villain Still Pursued Her* (RKO, 1940), *Glamour for Sale* (Col., 1940), *The Phantom Submarine* (Col., 1941), *Two in a Taxi* (Col., 1941), *Harmon of Michigan* (Col., 1941), *Dangerous Blondes* (Col., 1943), *Nine Girls* (Col., 1944), *Casanova Brown* (RKO, 1944), *Love Letters* (Par., 1945), *The Fighting Guardsman* (Col., 1945), *Shadowed* (Col., 1946), *The Bandit of Sherwood Forest* (Col., 1946), *The Devil's Mask* (Col., 1946), *Personality Kid* (Col., 1946), *Blondie's Big Moment* (Col., 1947), *Bulldog Drummond at Bay* (Col., 1947), *Retreat, Hell!* (WB, 1952).

FRANK LOVEJOY Born March 28, 1914, Bronx, New York. Married Joan Banks (1940), children: Judith, Stephen. Died October 2, 1962.

John Agar, Suzanne Dalbert and Frank Lovejoy in *Breakthrough*.

Feature Films: *Black Bart* (Univ., 1948), *Home of the Brave* (UA, 1949), *South Sea Sinner* (Univ., 1950), *In a Lonely Place* (Col., 1950), *Three Secrets* (WB, 1950), *Breakthrough* (WB, 1950), *The Sound of Fury* (UA, 1950), *Goodbye, My Fancy* (WB, 1951), *I Was a Communist for the FBI* (WB, 1951), *Force of Arms* (WB, 1951), *Starlift* (WB, 1951), *I'll See You in My Dreams* (WB, 1951), *Retreat, Hell!* (WB, 1952), *The Winning Team* (WB, 1952), *The Hitch Hiker* (RKO, 1953), *She's Back on Broadway* (WB, 1953), *The System* (WB, 1953), *House of Wax* (WB, 1953), *The Charge at Feather River* (WB, 1953), *Men of the Fighting Lady* (MGM, 1954), *Beachhead* (UA, 1954), *Strategic Air Command* (Par., 1955), *Mad at the World* (Filmakers, 1955), *Top of the World* (UA, 1955), *The Americano* (RKO, 1955), *Finger Man* (AA, 1955), *The Crooked Web* (Col., 1955), *Shack-Out on 101* (AA, 1955), *Julie* (MGM, 1956), *Three Brave Men* (20th, 1957), *Cole Younger, Gunfighter* (AA, 1958).

MYRNA LOY (Myrna Williams) Born August 2, 1905, Raidersburg, Montana. Married Arthur Hornblow, Jr. (1936); divorced 1942. Married John Hertz, Jr. (1942); divorced 1944. Married Gene Markey (1946); divorced 1950. Married Howland Sargeant (1951); divorced 1960.

Sound Feature Films: *The Jazz Singer* (WB, 1927), *The Desert Song* (WB, 1929), *Black Watch* (Fox, 1929), *The Squall* (WB, 1929), *Hardboiled Rose* (WB, 1929), *Evidence* (WB, 1929), *Show of Shows* (WB, 1929), *The Great Divide* (WB, 1930), *The Jazz Cinderella* (Chesterfield, 1930), *Cameo Kirby* (Fox, 1930), *Isle of Escape* (WB, 1930), *Under a Texas Moon* (WB, 1930), *Cock o' the Walk* (Sono Art-World Wide, 1930), *Bride of the Regiment* (WB, 1930), *Last of the Duanes* (Fox, 1930), *The Truth About Youth* (WB, 1930), *Renegades* (Fox, 1930), *Rogue of the Rio Grande* (Sono Art-World Wide, 1930), *The Devil to Pay* (UA, 1930), *Naughty Flirt* (WB, 1931), *Body and Soul* (Fox, 1931), *A Connecticut Yankee* (Fox, 1931), *Hush Money* (Fox, 1931), *Transatlantic* (Fox, 1931), *Rebound* (RKO, 1931), *Skyline* (Fox, 1931), *Consolation Marriage* (RKO, 1931), *Arrowsmith* (UA, 1931), *Emma* (MGM, 1932), *The Wet Parade*

William Powell and Myrna Loy in *Double Wedding*.

(MGM, 1932), *Vanity Fair* (Hollywood Exchange, 1932), *The Woman in Room 13* (Fox, 1932), *New Morals for Old* (MGM, 1932), *Love Me Tonight* (Par., 1932), *Thirteen Women* (RKO, 1932), *The Mask of Fu Manchu* (MGM, 1932), *The Animal Kindgom* (RKO, 1932), *Topaze* (RKO, 1933), *The Barbarian* (MGM, 1933), *The Prizefighter and the Lady* (MGM, 1933), *When Ladies Meet* (MGM, 1933), *Penthouse* (MGM, 1933), *Night Flight* (MGM, 1933), *Men in White* (MGM, 1934), *Manhattan Melodrama* (MGM, 1934), *The Thin Man* (MGM, 1934), *Stamboul Quest* (MGM, 1934), *Evelyn Prentice* (MGM, 1934), *Broadway Bill* (Col., 1934), *Wings in the Dark* (Par., 1935), *Whipsaw* (MGM, 1935), *Wife vs. Secretary* (MGM, 1936), *Petticoat Fever* (MGM, 1936), *The Great Ziegfeld* (MGM, 1936), *To Mary—With Love* (20th, 1936), *Libeled Lady* (MGM, 1936), *After the Thin Man* (MGM, 1936), *Parnell* (MGM, 1937), *Double Wedding* (MGM, 1937), *Man-Proof* (MGM, 1938), *Test Pilot* (MGM, 1938), *Too Hot to Handle* (MGM, 1938), *Lucky Night* (MGM, 1939), *The Rains Came* (20th, 1939), *Another Thin Man* (MGM, 1939), *I Love You Again* (MGM, 1940), *Third Finger, Left Hand* (MGM, 1940), *Love Crazy* (MGM, 1941), *Shadow of the Thin Man* (MGM, 1941), *The Thin Man Goes Home* (MGM, 1944), *So Goes My Love* (Univ., 1946), *The Best Years of Our Lives* (RKO, 1946), *The Bachelor and the Bobby-Soxer* (RKO, 1947), *Song of the Thin Man* (MGM, 1947), *The Senator Was Indiscreet* (Univ., 1947),* *Mr. Blandings Builds His Dream House* (RKO, 1948), *The Red Pony* (Rep., 1949), *Cheaper by the Dozen* (20th, 1950), *This Be Sin* (UA, 1950), *Belles on Their Toes* (20th, 1952), *The Ambassador's Daughter* (UA, 1956), *Lonelyhearts* (UA, 1958), *From the Terrace* (20th, 1960), *Midnight Lace* (Univ., 1960).

*Unbilled guest appearance

BELA LUGOSI (Bela Blasko) Born October 20, 1882, Lugos, Hungary. Married Beatrice Weeks (1924); divorced. Married Lillian Arch (1933), child: Bela; divorced 1953. Married Hope Lininger (1955). Died August 16, 1956.

Bela Lugosi and Minerva Urecal in *The Ape Man*.

118

English-Language Sound Feature Films: *Renegades* (Fox, 1930), *Wild Company* (Fox, 1930), *Such Men Are Dangerous* (Fox, 1930), *Oh, for a Man!* (Fox, 1930), *Women of All Nations* (Fox, 1931), *Dracula* (Univ., 1931), *Fifty Million Frenchmen* (WB, 1931), *Broad-Minded* (WB, 1931), *Black Camel* (Fox, 1931), *Murders in the Rue Morgue* (Univ., 1932), *White Zombie* (UA, 1932), *Chandu the Magician* (Fox, 1932), *Whispering Shadow* (Mascot serial, 1933), *Island of Lost Souls* (Par., 1933), *Death Kiss* (World Wide, 1933), *International House* (Par., 1933), *Night of Terror* (Col., 1933), *Return of Chandu* (Principal serial, 1934), *The Black Cat* (Univ., 1934), *The Gift of Gab* (Univ., 1934), *Best Man Wins* (Col., 1935), *Mysterious Mr. Wong* (Mon., 1935), *Mystery of the Marie Celeste* ("The Phantom Ship"—Guaranteed Pictures, 1935), *Murder by Television* (Imperial Pictures, 1935), *Mark of the Vampire* (MGM, 1935), *The Raven* (Univ., 1935), *Shadow of Chinatown* (Victory serial, 1936), *The Invisible Ray* (Univ., 1936), *Dracula's Daughter* (Univ., 1936), *Postal Inspector* (Univ., 1936), *S.O.S. Coast Guard* (Rep. serial, 1937), *The Phantom Creeps* (Univ. serial, 1939), *Son of Frankenstein* (Univ., 1939), *Ninotchka* (MGM, 1939), *Dark Eyes of London* ("The Human Monster"—Mon., 1939), *Saint's Double Trouble* (RKO, 1940), *Black Friday* (Univ., 1940), *You'll Find Out* (RKO, 1940), *Devil Bat* (PRC, 1940), *The Wolf Man* (Univ., 1941), *The Black Cat* (Univ., 1941), *The Invisible Ghost* (Mon., 1941), *Spooks Run Wild* (Mon., 1941), *Black Dragons* (Mon., 1942), *The Corpse Vanishes* (Mon., 1942), *Night Monster* (Univ., 1942), *The Ghost of Frankenstein* (Univ., 1942), *Bowery at Midnight* (Mon., 1942), *The Ape Man* (Mon., 1943), *Ghosts on the Loose* (Mon., 1943), *Frankenstein Meets the Wolf Man* (Univ., 1943), *Return of the Vampire* (Col., 1943), *Voodoo Man* (Mon., 1944), *Return of the Ape Man* (Mon., 1944), *One Body Too Many* (Par., 1944), *Zombies on Broadway* (RKO, 1945), *The Body Snatcher* (RKO, 1945), *Genius at Work* (RKO, 1946), *Scared to Death* (Screen Guild, 1947), *Abbott and Costello Meet Frankenstein* (Univ., 1948), *Bela Lugosi Meets a Brooklyn Gorilla* (Realart, 1952), *Old Mother Riley Meets the Vampire* ("Vampire Over London"—Gordon Films, 1952), *Bride of the Monster* (Banner Films, 1956), *Plan 9 From Outer Space* ("Grave Robbers From Outer Space"—DCA, 1959).

PAUL LUKAS (Paul Lugacs) Born May 26, 1894, Budapest, Hungary. Married Gizella Benes (1927); widowed 1962. Married Anna Driesens (1963).

Errol Flynn, Jean Sullivan and Paul Lukas in *Uncertain Glory.*

English-Language Sound Feature Films: *Illusion* (Par., 1929), *Half Way to Heaven* (Par., 1929), *Slightly Scarlet* (Par., 1930), *Benson Murder Case* (Par., 1930), *Young Eagles* (Par., 1930), *Devil's Holiday* (Par., 1930), *Anybody's Woman* (Par., 1930), *Grumpy* (Par., 1930), *Right to Love* (Par., 1930), *Unfaithful* (Par., 1931), *City Streets* (Par., 1931), *Vice Squad* (Par., 1931), *Women Who Love* (Univ., 1931), *Beloved Bachelor* (Par., 1931), *Strictly Dishonorable* (Par., 1931), *Working Girls* (Par., 1931), *Tomorrow and Tomorrow* (Par., 1932), *No One*

Man (Par., 1932), *Thunder Below* (Par., 1932), *Passport to Hell* (Fox, 1932), *Downstairs* (MGM, 1932), *Rockabye* (RKO, 1932), *Grand Slam* (WB, 1933), *Kiss Before the Mirror* (Univ., 1933), *Sing Sinner Sing* (Majestic, 1933), *Captured* (WB, 1933), *Secret of the Blue Room* (Univ., 1933), *Little Women* (RKO, 1933), *By Candlelight* (Univ., 1934), *Countess of Monte Cristo* (Univ., 1934), *Glamour* (Univ., 1934), *I Give My Love* (Univ., 1934), *Affairs of a Gentleman* (Univ., 1934), *The Fountain* (RKO, 1934), *The Gift of Gab* (Univ., 1934), *Father Brown—Detective* (Par., 1935), *Casino Murder Case* (MGM, 1935), *Age of Indiscretion* (MGM, 1935), *The Three Musketeers* (RKO, 1935), *I Found Stella Parish* (WB, 1935), *Dodsworth* (UA, 1936), *Ladies in Love* (20th, 1936), *Espionage* (MGM, 1937), *Dinner at the Ritz* (20th, 1937), *The Mutiny on the Elsinore* (Associated British Pictures, 1938), *The Lady Vanishes* (Gaumont-British, 1938), *Dangerous Secrets* (GN, 1938), *Confessions of a Nazi Spy* (WB, 1939), *Lady in Distress* (Times, 1939), *Captain Fury* (UA, 1939), *Strange Cargo* (MGM, 1940), *The Ghost Breakers* (Par., 1940), *The Monster and the Girl* (Par., 1941), *They Dare Not Love* (Col., 1941), *Chinese Den* (Film Alliance of the United States, 1941), *Watch on the Rhine* (WB, 1943), *Hostages* (Par., 1943), *Uncertain Glory* (WB, 1944), *Address Unknown* (Col., 1944), *Experiment Perilous* (RKO, 1944), *Deadline at Dawn* (RKO, 1946), *Temptation* (Univ., 1946), *Whispering City* (EL, 1947), *Berlin Express* (RKO, 1948), *Kim* (MGM, 1950), *20,000 Leagues Under the Sea* (BV, 1954), *The Roots of Heaven* (20th, 1958), *Scent of Mystery* (Mike Todd, Jr., 1960), *Tender Is the Night* (20th, 1960), *The Four Horsemen of the Apocalypse* (MGM, 1962), *55 Days At Peking* (AA, 1963), *Fun in Acapulco* (Par., 1963), *Lord Jim* (Col., 1965), *Sol Madrid* (MGM, 1968).

IDA LUPINO Born February 4, 1918, London, England. Married Louis Hayward (1938); divorced 1945. Married Collier Young (1948); divorced 1950. Married Howard Duff (1951), child: Bridget.

Ida Lupino and Ronald Colman in *The Light That Failed.*

Feature Films: *Her First Affaire* (Sterling, 1933), *Money for Speed* (UA, 1933), *High Finance* (WB, 1933), *The Ghost Camera* (Radio, 1933), *I Lived With You* (Gaumont-British, 1934), *Prince of Arcadia* (Gaumont-British, 1934), *Search for Beauty* (Par., 1934), *Come On Marines* (Par., 1934), *Ready for Love* (Par., 1934), *Paris in Spring* (Par., 1935), *Smart Girl* (Par., 1935), *Peter Ibbetson* (Par., 1935), *Anything Goes* (Par., 1936), *One Rainy Afternoon* (UA, 1936), *Yours for the Asking* (Par., 1936), *The Gay Desperado* (UA, 1936), *Sea Devils* (RKO, 1937), *Let's Get Married* (Col., 1937), *Artists and Models* (Par., 1937), *Fight for Your Lady* (RKO, 1937), *The Lone Wolf Spy Hunt* (Col., 1939), *The Lady and the Mob* (Col., 1939), *The Adventures of Sherlock Holmes* (20th, 1939), *The Light That Failed* (Par., 1940), *They Drive by Night* (WB, 1940), *High Sierra* (WB, 1941), *The Sea Wolf* (WB, 1941), *Out of the Fog* (WB, 1941), *Ladies in Retirement* (Col., 1941), *Moontide* (20th, 1942), *The Hard Way* (WB, 1942),

Life Begins at 8:30 (20th, 1942), *Forever and a Day* (RKO, 1943), *Thank Your Lucky Stars* (WB, 1943), *In Our Time* (WB, 1944), *Hollywood Canteen* (WB, 1944), *Pillow to Post* (WB, 1945), *Devotion* (WB, 1946), *The Man I Love* (WB, 1947), *Deep Valley* (WB, 1947), *Escape Me Never* (WB, 1947), *Road House* (20th, 1948), *Lust for Gold* (Col., 1949), *Woman in Hiding* (Univ., 1950), *On Dangerous Ground* (RKO, 1951), *Beware My Lovely* (RKO, 1952), *Jennifer* (AA, 1953), *The Bigamist* (Filmakers, 1953), *Private Hell 36* (Filmakers, 1954), *Women's Prison* (Col., 1955), *The Big Knife* (UA, 1955), *While the City Sleeps* (RKO, 1956), *Strange Intruder* (AA, 1956).

DIANA LYNN (Dolores Loehr) Born October 7, 1926, Los Angeles, California. Married John Lindsay (1948); divorced 1954. Married Mortimer Hall (1956), children: Mathew, Dorothy, Mary.

Feature Films:

as **Dolly Loehr** *They Shall Have Music* (UA, 1939), *There's Magic in Music* (Par., 1941).

as **Diana Lynn** *Star Spangled Rhythm* (Par., 1942), *The Major and the Minor* (Par., 1942), *Henry Aldrich Gets Glamour* (Par., 1943), *The Miracle of Morgan's Creek* (Par., 1944), *And the Angels Sing* (Par., 1944), *Henry Aldrich Plays Cupid* (Par., 1944), *Our Hearts Were Young and Gay* (Par., 1944), *Out of This World* (Par., 1945), *Duffy's Tavern* (Par., 1945), *Our Hearts Were Growing Up* (Par., 1946), *The Bride Wore Boots* (Par., 1946), *Easy Come, Easy Go* (Par., 1947), *Variety Girl* (Par., 1947), *Ruthless* (EL, 1948), *Texas, Brooklyn and Heaven* (UA, 1948), *Every Girl Should Be Married* (RKO, 1948), *My Friend Irma* (Par., 1949), *Paid in Full* (Par., 1950), *My Friend Irma Goes West* (Par., 1950), *Rogues of Sherwood Forest* (Col., 1950), *Peggy* (Univ., 1950), *Bedtime for Bonzo* (Univ., 1951), *The People Against O'Hara* (MGM, 1951), *Meet Me at the Fair* (Univ., 1952), *Plunder*

Diana Lynn, Charles Drake, Charles Coburn and Charlotte Greenwood in *Peggy*.

of the Sun (WB, 1953), *Track of the Cat* (WB, 1954), *An Annapolis Story* (AA, 1955), *The Kentuckian* (UA, 1955), *You're Never Too Young* (Par., 1955).

JEANETTE MacDONALD Born June 18, 1901, Philadelphia, Pennsylvania. Married Gene Raymond (1937). Died January 14, 1965.

Feature Films: *The Love Parade* (Par., 1929), *The Vagabond King* (Par., 1930), *Monte Carlo* (Par., 1930), *Let's Go Native* (Par., 1930), *The Lottery Bride* (UA, 1930), *Oh, for a Man* (Fox, 1930), *Don't Bet on Women* (Fox, 1931), *Annabelle's Affairs* (Fox, 1931), *One Hour With You* (Par., 1932), *Love Me Tonight* (Par., 1932), *The Cat and the Fiddle* (MGM, 1934), *The Merry Widow* (MGM, 1934), *Naughty Marietta* (MGM, 1935), *Rose Marie* (MGM, 1936), *San Francisco* (MGM, 1936), *Maytime* (MGM, 1937), *The Firefly* (MGM, 1937), *The Girl of the Golden West* (MGM, 1938), *Sweethearts* (MGM, 1938), *Broadway Serenade* (MGM, 1939), *New Moon* (MGM, 1940), *Bitter Sweet* (MGM, 1940), *Smilin' Through* (MGM, 1941), *I Married*

Ramon Novarro, Charles Butterworth, Jeanette MacDonald and Frank Morgan in *Cat and the Fiddle*.

an Angel (MGM, 1942), *Cairo* (MGM, 1942), *Follow the Boys* (Univ., 1944), *Three Daring Daughters* (MGM, 1948), *The Sun Comes Up* (MGM, 1948).

SHIRLEY MacLAINE (Shirley MacLean Beaty) Born April 24, 1934, Richmond, Virginia. Married Steve Parker (1954), child: Stephanie.

Shirley MacLaine and Mickey Shaughnessy in *The Sheepman*.

Feature Films: *The Trouble With Harry* (Par., 1955), *Artists and Models* (Par., 1955), *Around the World in 80 Days* (UA, 1956), *The Sheepman* (MGM, 1958), *The Matchmaker* (Par., 1958), *Hot Spell* (Par., 1958), *Some Came Running* (MGM, 1958), *Ask Any Girl* (MGM, 1959), *Career* (Par., 1959), *Ocean's 11* (WB, 1960,* *Can-Can* (20th, 1960), *The Apartment* (UA, 1960), *All in a Night's Work* (Par., 1961), *Two Loves* (MGM, 1961), *The Children's Hour* (UA, 1962), *My Geisha* (Par., 1962), *Two for the Seesaw* (UA, 1962), *Irma La Douce* (UA, 1963), *What a Way to Go!* (20th, 1964), *John Goldfarb, Please Come Home* (20th, 1964), *The Yellow Rolls-Royce* (MGM, 1965), *Gambit* (Univ., 1966), *Woman Times Seven* (Embassy, 1967), *The Bliss of Mr. Blossom* (Par., 1968), *Sweet Charity* (Univ., 1968).

ALINE MacMAHON (Aline Laveen MacMahon) Born May 3, 1899, McKeesport, Pennsylvania. Married Clarence Stein (1928).

Feature Films: *Five Star Final* (WB, 1931), *Heart of New York* (WB,

Aline MacMahon and Guy Kibbee in *Babbitt*.

1932), *The Mouthpiece* (WB, 1932), *Weekend Marriage* (WB, 1932), *One Way Passage* (WB, 1932), *Life Begins* (WB, 1932), *Silver Dollar* (WB, 1932), *Once in a Lifetime* (Univ., 1932), *Gold Diggers of 1933* (WB, 1933), *The Life of Jimmy Dolan* (WB, 1933), *Heroes for Sale* (WB, 1933), *The World Changes* (WB, 1933), *Heat Lightning* (WB, 1934), *Side Streets* (WB, 1934), *Big-Hearted Herbert* (WB, 1934), *Babbitt* (WB, 1934), *The Merry Frinks* (WB, 1934), *While the Patient Slept* (WB, 1935), *Mary Jane's Pa* (WB, 1935), *I Live My Life* (MGM, 1935), *Kind Lady* (MGM, 1935), *Ah, Wilderness* (MGM, 1935), *When You're in Love* (Col., 1937), *Back Door to Heaven* (Par., 1939), *Out of the Fog* (WB, 1941), *The Lady Is Willing* (Col., 1942), *Tish* (MGM, 1942), *Stage Door Canteen* (UA, 1943), *Seeds of Freedom* (narrator; Potemkin Productions, 1943), *Dragon Seed* (MGM, 1944), *Guest in the House* (UA, 1944), *The Mighty McGurk* (MGM, 1946), *The Search* (MGM, 1948), *Roseanna McCoy* (RKO, 1949), *The Flame and the Arrow* (WB, 1950), *The Eddie Cantor Story* (WB, 1953), *The Man From Laramie* (Col., 1955), *Cimarron* (MGM, 1960), *The Young Doctors* (UA, 1961), *I Could Go On Singing* (UA, 1963), *Diamond Head* (Col., 1963), *All the Way Home* (Par., 1963).

FRED MacMURRAY Born August 30, 1908, Kankakee, Illinois. Married Lillian Lamont (1936), children: Susan, Robert; widowed 1953. Married June Haver (1954), children: Kathryn, Laurie.

Feature Films: *Friends of Mr. Sweeney* (WB, 1934), *Grand Old Girl* (RKO, 1935), *The Gilded Lily* (Par., 1935), *Car 99* (Par., 1935), *Men Without Names* (Par., 1935), *Alice Adams* (RKO, 1935), *Hands Across the Table* (Par., 1935), *The Bride Comes Home* (Par., 1935), *The Trail of the Lonesome Pine* (Par., 1936), *13 Hours by Air* (Par., 1936), *The Princess Comes Across* (Par., 1936), *The Texas Rangers* (Par., 1936), *Maid of Salem* (Par., 1937), *Champagne Waltz* (Par., 1937), *Swing High—Swing Low* (Par., 1937), *Exclusive* (Par., 1937), *True Confession* (Par., 1937), *Cocoanut Grove* (Par., 1938), *Sing You Sinners* (Par.,

Fred MacMurray, Madeleine Carroll and Charles "Buddy" Rogers in *Don't Trust Your Husband*.

1938), *Men With Wings* (Par., 1938), *Cafe Society* (Par., 1939), *Invitation to Happiness* (Par., 1939), *Honeymoon in Bali* (Par., 1939), *Little Old New York* (20th, 1940), *Remember the Night* (Par., 1940), *Too Many Husbands* (Par., 1940), *Rangers of Fortune* (Par., 1940), *Virginia* (Par., 1941), *One Night in Lisbon* (Par., 1941), *New York Town* (Par., 1941), *Dive Bomber* (WB, 1941), *The Lady Is Willing* (Par., 1942), *Take a Letter, Darling* (Par., 1942), *The Forest Rangers* (Par., 1942), *Star Spangled Rhythm* (Par., 1942), *Flight for Freedom* (RKO, 1943), *Above Suspicion* (MGM, 1943), *No Time for Love* (Par., 1943), *Standing Room Only* (Par., 1944), *And the Angels Sing* (Par., 1944), *Double Indemnity* (Par., 1944), *Murder, He Says* (Par., 1945), *Practically Yours* (Par., 1945), *Where Do We Go From Here?* (20th, 1945), *Captain Eddie* (20th, 1945), *Pardon My Past* (Col., 1946), *Smoky* (20th, 1946), *Suddenly It's Spring* (Par., 1947), *The Egg and I* (Univ., 1947), *Singapore* (Univ., 1947), *The Miracle of the Bells* (RKO, 1948), *On Our Merry Way* (UA, 1948), *Don't Trust Your Husband* (UA, 1948), *Family Honeymoon* (Univ., 1948), *Father Was a Fullback* (20th, 1949), *Borderline* (Univ., 1950), *Never a Dull Moment* (RKO, 1950), *A Millionaire for Christy* (20th, 1951), *Callaway Went Thataway* (MGM, 1951), *Fair Wind to Java* (Rep., 1953), *The Moonlighter* (WB, 1953), *The Caine Mutiny* (Col., 1954), *Pushover* (Col., 1954), *Woman's World* (20th, 1954), *The Far Horizons* (Par., 1955), *The Rains of Ranchipur* (20th, 1955), *At Gunpoint* (AA, 1955), *There's Always Tomorrow* (Univ., 1956), *Gun For a Coward* (Univ., 1957), *Quantez* (Univ., 1957), *Day of the Bad Man* (Univ., 1958), *Good Day for a Hanging* (Col., 1958), *The Shaggy Dog* (BV, 1959), *Face of a Fugitive* (Col., 1959), *The Oregon Trail* (20th, 1959), *The Apartment* (UA, 1960), *The Absent-Minded Professor* (BV, 1961), *Bon Voyage* (BV, 1962), *Son of Flubber* (BV, 1963), *Kisses for My President* (WB, 1964), *Follow Me, Boys* (BV, 1966), *The Happiest Millionaire* (BV, 1967).

GEORGE MacCREADY Born August 29, 1909, Providence, Rhode Island. Married, children: Michael, Marcia. Elizabeth; widowed.

George MacCready, Nina Foch and George Raft in *Johnny Allegro*.

Feature Films: *Commandos Strike at Dawn* (Col., 1942), *The Story of Dr. Wassell* (Par., 1944), *Follow the Boys* (Univ., 1944), *The Seventh Cross* (MGM, 1944), *Soul of a Monster* (Col., 1944), *Wilson* (20th, 1944), *The Conspirators* (WB, 1944), *A Song to Remember* (Col., 1945), *The Monster and the Ape* (Col. serial, 1945), *The Missing Juror* (Col., 1945), *I Love a Mystery* (Col., 1945), *Counter-Attack* (Col., 1945), *Don Juan Quilligan* (20th, 1945), *My Name Is Julia Ross* (Col., 1945), *The Fighting Guardsman* (Col., 1945), *Gilda* (Col., 1946), *The Man Who Dared* (Col., 1946), *The Bandit Of Sherwood Forest* (Col., 1946), *The Walls Came Tumbling Down* (Col., 1946), *The Return of Monte Cristo* (Col., 1946), *Down to Earth* (Col., 1947), *The Swordsman* (Col., 1947), *The Big Clock* (Par., 1948), *Beyond Glory* (Par., 1948), *The Black Arrow* (Col., 1948), *Coroner Creek* (Col., 1948), *The Gallant Blade* (Col., 1948), *Alias Nick Beal* (Par., 1949), *Knock on Any Door* (Col., 1949), *Johnny Allegro* (Col., 1949), *The Doolins of Oklahoma* (Col., 1949), *The Nevadan* (Col., 1950), *The Fortunes of Captain Blood*

(Col., 1950), *The Rogues of Sherwood Forest* (Col., 1950), *A Lady Without a Passport* (MGM, 1950), *The Desert Hawk* (Univ., 1950), *Tarzan's Peril* (RKO, 1951), *The Desert Fox* (20th, 1951), *The Golden Horde* (Univ., 1951), *Detective Story* (Par., 1951), *The Green Glove* (UA, 1952), *Julius Caesar* (MGM, 1953), *Duffy of San Quentin* (WB, 1954), *Vera Cruz* (UA, 1954), *A Kiss Before Dying* (UA, 1956), *Thunder Over Arizona* (Rep., 1956), *The Abductors* (20th, 1957), *Paths of Glory* (UA, 1957), *Gunfire Over Indian Gap* (Rep., 1957), *Jet Across the Atlantic* (Intercontinent Releasing, 1959), *Plunderers of Painted Flats* (Rep., 1959), *The Alligator People* (20th, 1959), *Two Weeks in Another Town* (MGM, 1962), *Taras Bulba* (UA, 1962), *Dead Ringer* (WB, 1964), *Seven Days in May* (Par., 1964), *Where Love Has Gone* (Par., 1964), *The Great Race* (WB, 1965), *The Human Duplicators* (AA, 1965).

MERCEDES McCAMBRIDGE (Carlotta Mercedes Agnes McCambridge) Born March 17, 1918, Joliet, Illinois. Married William Fifield (1940), child: Jon; divorced 1946. Married Fletcher Markle (1950); divorced 1962.

Henry Hull, Virginia Mayo and Joel McCrea in *Colorado Territory*.

Broderick Crawford and Mercedes McCambridge in *All the King's Men*.

Feature Films: *All the King's Men* (Col., 1949), *Lightning Strikes Twice* (WB, 1951), *The Scarf* (UA, 1951), *Inside Straight* (MGM, 1951), *Johnny Guitar* (Rep., 1954), *Giant* (WB, 1956), *A Farewell to Arms* (20th, 1957), *Touch of Evil* (Univ., 1958),* *Suddenly, Last Summer* (Col., 1959), *Cimarron* (MGM, 1960), *Angel Baby* (AA, 1961), *Run Home Slow* (Emerson Film Distributors, 1965).

*Unbilled guest appearance

JOEL McCREA Born November 5, 1905, Los Angeles, California. Married Frances Dee (1933), children: Jody, David.

Sound Feature Films: *So This Is College* (MGM, 1929), *Dynamite* (Par., 1929), *Lightnin'* (Fox, 1930), *Silver Horde* (RKO, 1930), *Once a Sinner* (Fox, 1931), *Kept Husbands* (RKO, 1931), *Born to Love* (RKO, 1931), *Girls About Town* (Par., 1931), *Business and Pleasure* (Fox, 1932), *Lost Squadron* (RKO, 1932), *Bird of Paradise* (RKO, 1932), *Most Dangerous Game* (RKO, 1932), *Rockabye* (RKO, 1932), *The Sport Parade* (RKO, 1932), *The Silver Cord* (RKO, 1933), *Bed of Roses* (RKO, 1933), *One Man's Journey* (RKO, 1933), *Chance at Heaven* (RKO, 1933), *Gambling Lady* (WB, 1934), *Half a Sinner* (Univ., 1934), *Richest Girl in the World* (RKO, 1934), *Private Worlds* (Par., 1935), *Our Little Girl* (Fox, 1935), *Woman Wanted* (MGM, 1935), *Barbary Coast* (UA, 1935), *Splendor* (UA, 1935), *These Three* (UA, 1936),

Two in a Crowd (Univ., 1936), *Adventure in Manhattan* (Col., 1936), *Come and Get It* (UA, 1936), *Banjo on My Knee* (20th, 1936), *Internes Can't Take Money* (Par., 1937), *Wells Fargo* (Par., 1937), *Woman Chases Man* (Par., 1937), *Dead End* (UA, 1937), *Three Blind Mice* (20th, 1938), *Youth Takes a Fling* (Univ., 1938), *Union Pacific* (Par., 1939), *They Shall Have Music* (UA, 1939), *Espionage Agent* (WB, 1939), *He Married His Wife* (20th, 1940), *Primrose Path* (RKO, 1940), *Foreign Correspondent* (UA, 1940), *Reaching for the Sun* (Par., 1941), *Sullivan's Travels* (Par., 1941), *The Great Man's Lady* (Par., 1942), *The Palm Beach Story* (Par., 1942), *The More the Merrier* (Col., 1943), *Buffalo Bill* (20th, 1944), *Great Moment* (Par., 1944), *The Unseen* (Par., 1945), *The Virginian* (Par., 1946), *Ramrod* (UA, 1947), *Four Faces West* (UA, 1948), *South of St. Louis* (WB, 1949), *Colorado Territory* (WB, 1949), *Stars in My Crown* (MGM, 1950), *The Outriders* (MGM, 1950), *Saddle Tramp* (Univ., 1950), *Frenchie* (Univ., 1950), *The Hollywood Story* (Univ., 1951),* *Cattle Drive* (Univ., 1951), *The San Francisco Story* (WB, 1952), *Lone Hand* (Univ., 1953), *Shoot First* (UA, 1953), *Border River* (Univ., 1954), *Stranger on Horseback* (UA, 1955), *Wichita* (AA, 1955), *The First Texan* (AA, 1956), *The Oklahoman* (AA, 1957), *Trooper Hook* (UA, 1957), *Gunsight Ridge* (UA, 1957), *The Tall Stranger* (AA, 1957), *Cattle Empire* (20th, 1958), *Fort Massacre* (UA, 1958), *The Gunfight at Dodge City* (UA, 1959), *Ride the High Country* (MGM, 1962).

*Unbilled guest appearance

HATTIE McDANIEL Born June 10, 1895, Wichita, Kansas. Married James Crawford; divorced. Married Larry Williams; divorced 1950. Died October 26, 1952.

Feature Films: *The Golden West* (Fox, 1932), *Blonde Venus* (Par., 1932), *Hypnotized* (World Wide, 1932), *Washington Masquerade* (MGM, 1932), *I'm No Angel* (Par., 1933), *The Story of Temple Drake* (Par., 1933), *Operator 13* (MGM, 1934), *Judge Priest* (Fox, 1934), *Lost in the Stratosphere* (Mon., 1934), *Babbitt* (WB, 1934), *Little Men* (RKO, 1934), *Imitation of Life* (Univ., 1934), *The Little Colonel* (Fox, 1935), *Alice Adams* (RKO, 1935), *Music Is Magic* (20th, 1935), *Another Face* (RKO, 1935), *Traveling Saleslady* (WB, 1935), *Next Time We Love* (Univ., 1936), *Libeled Lady* (MGM, 1936), *Gentle Julia* (20th, 1936), *The First Baby* (20th, 1936), *Show Boat* (Univ., 1936), *Hearts Divided* (WB, 1936), *High Treason* (20th, 1936), *Star for a Night* (20th, 1936), *The Postal Inspector* (Univ., 1936), *The Bride Walks Out* (RKO, 1936), *The Singing Kid* (WB, 1936), *Valiant Is the Word for Carrie* (Par., 1936), *Reunion* (20th, 1936), *Can This Be Dixie?* (20th, 1936), *Racing Lady* (RKO, 1937), *Don't Tell the Wife* (RKO, 1937), *The Crime Nobody Saw* (Par., 1937), *Saratoga* (MGM, 1937), *Merry-Go-Round of 1938* (Univ., 1937), *True Confession* (Par., 1937), *The Wildcatter* (Univ., 1937), *45 Fathers* (20th, 1937), *Over the Goal* (WB, 1937), *Nothing Sacred* (UA, 1937), *Battle of Broad-*

Ben Carter, Hattie McDaniel and John Payne in *Maryland*.

way (20th, 1938), *The Shopworn Angel* (MGM, 1938), *Carefree* (RKO, 1938), *The Shining Hour* (MGM, 1938), *The Mad Miss Manton* (RKO, 1938), *Everybody's Baby* (20th, 1939), *Zenobia* (UA, 1939), *Gone With the Wind* (MGM, 1939), *Maryland* (20th, 1940), *The Great Lie* (WB, 1941), *Affectionately Yours* (WB, 1941), *They Died With Their Boots On* (WB, 1941), *The Male Animal* (WB, 1942), *In This Our Life* (WB, 1942), *George Washington Slept Here* (WB, 1942), *Reap the Wild Wind* (Par., 1942), *Johnny Come Lately* (UA, 1943), *Thank Your Lucky Stars* (WB, 1943), *Janie* (WB, 1944), *Since You Went Away* (UA, 1944), *Three Is a Family* (UA, 1944), *Hi, Beautiful* (Univ., 1945), *Janie Gets Married* (WB, 1946), *Margie* (20th, 1946), *Song of the South* (RKO, 1946), *Never Say Goodbye* (WB, 1946), *The Flame* (Rep., 1947), *Mickey* (EL, 1948), *Mr. Blandings Builds His Dream House* (RKO, 1948), *Family Honeymoon* (Univ., 1948).

RODDY McDOWALL (Roderick Andrew McDowall) Born September 17, 1928, London, England.

Feature Films: *Scruffy* (Independent, 1937), *Murder in the Family* (20th, 1937), *I See Ice* (Balcon, 1937), *John Halifax, Gentleman* (MGM, 1938), *Convict 99* (Gainsborough, 1938), *Hey! Hey! U.S.A.* (Gainsborough, 1938), *Sarah Siddons* (RKO, 1938), *The Outsider* (RKO, 1938), *Poison Pen* (Associated British Producing, 1938), *Dead Men's Shoes* (Associated British Producing, 1938), *Just William* (Associated British Producing, 1939), *His Brother's Keeper* (WB, 1939), *Dirt* (Balcon, 1939), *Saloon Bar* (Balcon, 1939), *You Will Remember* (British Lion, 1940), *This England* (British National, 1940), *Man Hunt* (20th, 1941), *How Green Was My Valley* (20th, 1941), *Confirm or Deny* (20th, 1941), *Son of Fury* (20th, 1942), *On the Sunny Side* (20th, 1942), *The Pied Piper* (20th, 1942), *My Friend Flicka* (20th, 1943),

Roddy McDowall and Jane Powell in *Holiday in Mexico*.

Lassie Come Home (MGM, 1943), *The White Cliffs of Dover* (MGM, 1944), *The Keys of the Kingdom* (20th, 1944), *Thunderhead, Son of Flicka* (20th, 1945), *Molly and Me* (20th, 1945), *Holiday in Mexico* (MGM, 1946), *Macbeth* (Rep., 1948), *Rocky* (Mon., 1948), *Kidnapped* (Mon., 1948), *Tuna Clipper* (Mon., 1949), *Black Midnight* (Mon., 1949) *Killer Shark* (Mon., 1949), *Big Timber* (Mon., 1950), *The Steel Fist* (Mon., 1952), *The Subterraneans* (MGM, 1960), *Midnight Lace* (Univ., 1960), *Cleopatra* (20th, 1963), *Shock Treatment* (20th, 1964), *The Greatest Story Ever Told* (UA, 1965), *The Third Day* (WB, 1965), *That Darn Cat* (BV, 1965), *The Loved One* (MGM, 1965), *Lord Love a Duck* (UA, 1966), *Inside Daisy Clover* (WB, 1966), *The Defector* (7 Arts, 1966), *Is Paris Burning?* (Par., 1966), *The Adventures of Bullwhip Griffin* (BV, 1967), *The Cool Ones* (WB, 1967), *It* (WB-7 Arts, 1967), *Hello Down There* (Par., 1968), *Planet of the Apes* (20th, 1968).

DOROTHY McGUIRE (Dorothy Hackett McGuire) Born June 14, 1918, Omaha, Nebraska. Married John Swope (1943), children: Mary, Mark.

Randy Stuart and Dorothy McGuire in *Mother Didn't Tell Me*.

Feature Films: *Claudia* (20th, 1943), *A Tree Grows in Brooklyn* (20th, 1945), *The Enchanted Cottage* (RKO, 1945), *The Spiral Staircase* (RKO, 1946), *Claudia and David* (20th, 1946), *Till the End of Time* (RKO, 1946), *Gentleman's Agreement* (20th, 1947), *Mother Didn't Tell Me* (20th, 1950), *Mister 880* (20th, 1950), *Callaway Went Thataway* (MGM, 1951), *I Want You* (RKO, 1951), *Invitation* (MGM, 1952), *Make Haste to Live* (Rep., 1954), *Three Coins in the Fountain* (20th, 1954), *Trial* (MGM, 1955), *Friendly Persuasion* (AA, 1956), *Old Yeller* (BV, 1957), *The Remarkable Mr. Pennypacker* (20th, 1959), *This Earth Is Mine* (Univ., 1959), *A Summer Place* (WB, 1959), *The Dark at the Top of the Stairs* (WB, 1960), *Swiss Family Robinson* (BV, 1960), *Susan Slade* (WB, 1961), *Summer Magic* (BV, 1963), *The Greatest Story Ever Told* (UA, 1965).

FRANK McHUGH (Francis Curray McHugh) Born May 23, 1898, Homestead, Pennsylvania. Married Dorothy Spencer (1933), children: Peter, Susan.

Sound Feature Films: *Top Speed* (WB, 1930), *Dawn Patrol* (WB, 1930), *College Lovers* (WB, 1930), *Bright Lights* (WB, 1931), *Widow From Chicago* (WB, 1931), *Front Page* (UA, 1931), *Millie* (RKO, 1931), *Kiss Me Again* (WB, 1931), *Going Wild* (WB, 1931), *Traveling Husbands* (RKO, 1931), *Up for Murder* (Univ., 1931), *Men of the Sky* (WB, 1931), *Corsair* (UA, 1931), *Bad Company* (Pathé, 1931), *Union Depot* (WB, 1932), *High Pressure* (WB, 1932), *The Crowd Roars* (WB, 1932), *The Strange Love of Molly Louvain* (WB, 1932), *Dark Horse* (WB, 1932), *Blessed Event* (WB, 1932), *One Way Passage* (WB, 1932), *Life Begins* (WB, 1932), *Mystery of the Wax Museum* (WB, 1933), *Parachute Jumper* (WB, 1933), *Grand Slam* (WB, 1933), *Private Jones* (Univ., 1933), *Telegraph Trail* (WB, 1933),

Jean Ames, Frank McHugh and Humphrey Bogart in *All Through the Night*.

Ex-Lady (WB, 1933), *Elmer the Great* (WB, 1933), *Professional Sweetheart* (WB, 1933), *Hold Me Tight* (WB, 1933), *Lilly Turner* (WB, 1933), *Tomorrow at Seven* (RKO, 1933), *Footlight Parade* (WB, 1933), *Havana Widows* (WB, 1933), *Son of a Sailor* (WB, 1933), *The House on 56th Street* (WB, 1933), *Convention City* (WB, 1933), *Fashions of 1934* (WB, 1934), *Heat Lightning* (WB, 1934), *Smarty* (WB, 1934), *Let's Be Ritzy* (WB, 1934), *Merry Wives of Reno* (WB, 1934), *Return of the Terror* (WB, 1934), *Here Comes the Navy* (WB, 1934), *Six Day Bike Rider* (WB, 1934), *Happiness Ahead* (WB, 1934), *Maybe It's Love* (WB, 1935), *Gold Diggers of 1935* (WB, 1935), *Devil Dogs of the Air* (WB, 1935), *Page Miss Glory* (WB, 1935), *The Irish in Us* (WB, 1935), *A Midsummer Night's Dream* (WB, 1935), *Stars Over Broadway* (WB, 1935), *Moonlight Murder* (MGM, 1936), *Snowed Under* (WB, 1936), *Freshman Love* (WB, 1936), *Bullets or Ballots* (WB, 1936), *Stage Struck* (WB, 1936), *Three Men on a Horse* (WB, 1936), *Ever Since Eve* (WB, 1937), *Mr. Dodd Takes the Air* (WB, 1937), *Marry the Girl* (WB, 1937), *Submarine D-1* (WB, 1937), *Swing Your Lady* (WB, 1938), *He Couldn't Say No* (WB, 1938), *Little Miss Thoroughbred* (WB, 1938), *Boy Meets Girl* (WB, 1938), *Valley of the Giants* (WB, 1938), *Four Daughters* (WB, 1938), *Dodge City* (WB, 1939), *Wings of the Navy* (WB, 1939), *Daughters Courageous* (WB, 1939), *Dust Be My Destiny* (WB, 1939), *The Roaring Twenties* (WB, 1939), *On Your Toes* (WB, 1939), *Indianapolis Speedway* (WB, 1939), *Four Wives* (WB, 1939), *Virginia City* (WB, 1940), *The Fighting 69th* (WB, 1940), *Till We Meet Again* (WB, 1940), *I Love You Again* (MGM, 1940), *City for Conquest* (WB, 1940), *Back Street* (Univ., 1941), *Four Mothers* (WB, 1941), *Manpower* (WB, 1941), *Her Cardboard Lover* (MGM, 1942), *All Through the Night* (WB, 1942), *Going My Way* (Par., 1944), *Marine Raiders* (RKO, 1944), *Bowery to Broadway* (Univ., 1944), *A Medal for Benny* (Par., 1945), *State Fair* (20th, 1945), *The Hoodlum Saint* (MGM, 1946), *The Runaround* (Univ., 1946), *Little Miss Big* (Univ., 1946), *Easy Come, Easy Go* (Par., 1947), *Carnegie Hall* (UA, 1947), *The Velvet Touch* (RKO, 1948), *Mighty Joe Young* (RKO, 1949), *Miss Grant Takes Richmond* (Col., 1949), *Paid in Full* (Par., 1950), *The Tougher They Come* (Col., 1950), *My Son, John* (Par., 1952), *The Pace That Thrills* (RKO, 1952), *It Happens Every Thursday* (Univ., 1953), *A Lion Is in the Streets* (WB, 1953), *There's No Business Like Show Business* (20th, 1954), *The Last Hurrah* (Col., 1958), *Say One for Me* (20th, 1959), *Career* (Par., 1959), *A Tiger Walks* (BV, 1964), *Easy Come, Easy Go* (Par., 1967).

VICTOR McLAGLEN Born December 10, 1886, Tunbridge Wells, England. Married Enid Lamont (1918), children: Sheila, Andrew; widowed 1942. Married Suzanne Brueggsman (1943); divorced 1948. Married Margaret Humphrey (1948). Died November 7, 1959.

Sound Feature Films: *Black Watch* (Fox, 1929), *Cock-Eyed World* (Fox, 1929), *Hot for Paris* (Fox, 1929), *Happy Days* (Fox, 1930), *On the Level* (Fox, 1930), *Devil With Women* (Fox, 1930), *Dishonored* (Par., 1931), *Not Exactly Gentlemen* (Fox, 1931), *Annabelle's Affairs* (Fox, 1931), *Women of All Nations* (Fox, 1931), *Wicked* (Fox, 1931), *The Gay Caballero* (Fox, 1932), *Devil's Lottery* (Fox, 1932), *While Paris Sleeps* (Fox, 1932), *Guilty as Hell* (Par., 1932), *Rackety Rax*

Victor McLaglen and Mae West in *Klondike Annie*.

(Fox, 1932), *Dick Turpin* (Gaumont-British, 1933), *Hot Pepper* (Fox, 1933), *Laughing at Life* (Mascot, 1933), *No More Women* (Par., 1934), *The Lost Patrol* (RKO, 1934), *Wharf Angel* (Par., 1934), *Murder at the Vanities* (Par., 1934), *The Captain Hates the Sea* (Col., 1934), *Under Pressure* (Fox, 1935), *Great Hotel Murder* (Fox, 1935), *The Informer* (RKO, 1935), *Professional Soldier* (Fox, 1935), *Klondike Annie* (Par., 1936), *Under Two Flags* (20th, 1936), *Mary of Scotland* (RKO, 1936), *The Magnificent Brute* (Univ., 1936), *Sea Devils* (RKO, 1937), *Nancy Steele Is Missing* (20th, 1937), *This Is My Affair* (20th, 1937), *Wee Willie Winkie* (20th, 1937), *Battle of Broadway* (20th, 1938), *The Devil's Party* (Univ., 1938), *We're Going to Be Rich* (20th, 1938), *Pacific Liner* (RKO, 1939), *Let Freedom Ring* (MGM, 1939), *Captain Fury* (UA, 1939), *Ex-Champ* (Univ., 1939), *Full Confession* (RKO, 1939), *Rio* (Univ., 1939), *The Big Guy* (Univ., 1939), *Diamond Frontier* (Univ., 1940), *Broadway Limited* (UA, 1941), *Call Out the Marines* (RKO, 1942), *Powder Town* (RKO, 1942), *China Girl* (20th, 1942), *Forever and a Day* (RKO, 1943), *Tampico* (20th, 1944), *Roger Tuohy, Gangster* (20th, 1944), *The Princess and the Pirate* (RKO, 1944), *Rough, Tough and Ready* (Col., 1945), *Love, Honor and Goodbye* (Rep., 1945), *Whistle Stop* (UA, 1946), *Calendar Girl* (Rep., 1947), *The Michigan Kid* (Univ., 1947), *The Foxes of Harrow* (20th, 1947), *Fort Apache* (RKO, 1948), *She Wore a Yellow Ribbon* (RKO, 1949), *Rio Grande* (Rep., 1950), *The Quiet Man* (Rep., 1952), *Fair Wind to Java* (Rep., 1953), *Prince Valiant* (20th, 1954), *Trouble in the Glen* (Rep., 1954), *Many Rivers to Cross* (MGM, 1955), *City of Shadows* (Rep., 1955), *Bengazi* (RKO, 1955), *Lady Godiva* (Univ., 1955), *The Abductors* (20th, 1957).

STEVE McQUEEN Born March 24, 1930, Slater, Missouri. Married Neile Adams (1955), children: Terry, Chadwick.

Aneta Corseaut, Steve McQueen, Olin Howland and Stephen Chase in *The Blob*.

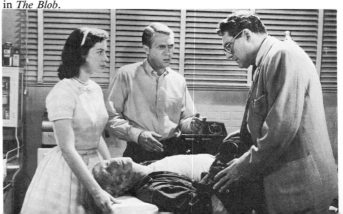

124

Feature Films: *Somebody Up There Likes Me* (MGM, 1956), *Never Love a Stranger* (AA, 1958), *The Blob* (Par., 1958), *Never So Few* (MGM, 1959), *The Great St. Louis Bank Robbery* (UA, 1959), *The Magnificent Seven* (UA, 1960), *The Honeymoon Machine* (MGM, 1961), *Hell Is for Heroes* (Par., 1961), *The War Lover* (Col., 1962), *The Great Escape* (UA, 1963), *Love With the Proper Stranger* (Par., 1963), *Soldier in the Rain* (AA, 1963), *Baby, the Rain Must Fall* (Col., 1965), *The Cincinnati Kid* (MGM, 1965), *Nevada Smith* (Par., 1966), *The Sand Pebbles* (20th, 1966), *Thomas Crown and Company* (UA, 1968).

MARJORIE MAIN (Mary Tomlinson) Born February 24, 1890, Acton, Indiana. Married Stanley Krebs (1921); widowed 1935.

Feature Films: *A House Divided* (Univ.; 1932), *Take a Chance* (Par., 1933), *Crime Without Passion* (Par., 1934), *Music in the Air* (Fox, 1934), *Naughty Marietta* (MGM, 1935), *Love in a Bungalow* (Univ., 1937), *Dead End* (UA, 1937), *Stella Dallas* (UA, 1937), *The Man Who Cried Wolf* (Univ., 1937), *The Wrong Road* (Rep., 1937), *The Shadow* (Col., 1937), *Boy of the Streets* (Mon., 1937), *Penitentiary* (Col., 1938), *King of the Newsboys* (Rep., 1938), *Test Pilot* (MGM, 1938), *Prison Farm* (Par., 1938), *Romance of the Limberlost* (Mon., 1938), *Little Tough Guy* (Univ., 1938), *Under the Big Top* (Mon., 1938), *Too Hot to Handle* (MGM, 1938), *Girls' School* (Col., 1938), *There Goes My Heart* (UA, 1938), *Three Comrades* (MGM, 1938), *City Girl* (20th, 1937), *Lucky Night* (MGM, 1939), *They Shall Have Music* (UA, 1939), *Angels Wash Their Faces* (WB, 1939), *The Women* (MGM, 1939), *Another Thin Man* (MGM, 1939), *Two Thoroughbreds* (RKO, 1939), *I Take This Woman* (MGM, 1940), *Women Without Names* (Par., 1940), *Dark Command* (Rep., 1940), *Turnabout* (UA, 1940), *Susan and God* (MGM, 1940), *The Captain Is a Lady* (MGM, 1940),

Marjorie Main and Wallace Beery in *Big Jack*.

Wyoming (MGM, 1940), *The Wild Man of Borneo* (MGM, 1941), *The Trial of Mary Dugan* (MGM, 1941), *A Woman's Face* (MGM, 1941), *Barnacle Bill* (MGM, 1941), *The Shepherd of the Hills* (Par., 1941), *Honky Tonk* (MGM, 1941), *The Bugle Sounds* (MGM, 1941), *We Were Dancing* (MGM, 1942), *The Affairs of Martha* (MGM, 1942), *Jackass Mail* (MGM, 1942), *Tish* (MGM, 1942), *Tennessee Johnson* (MGM, 1942), *Woman of the Town* (UA, 1943), *Heaven Can Wait* (20th, 1943), *Johnny Come Lately* (UA, 1943), *Rationing* (MGM, 1944), *Gentle Annie* (MGM, 1944), *Meet Me in St. Louis* (MGM, 1944), *Murder He Says* (Par., 1945), *The Harvey Girls* (MGM, 1946), *Bad Bascomb* (MGM, 1946), *Undercurrent* (MGM, 1946), *The Show-Off* (MGM, 1946), *The Egg and I* (Univ., 1947), *The Wistful Widow of Wagon Gap* (Univ., 1947), *Feudin', Fussin' and a-Fightin'* (Univ., 1948), *Ma and Pa Kettle* (Univ., 1949), *Big Jack* (MGM, 1949), *Ma and Pa Kettle Go to Town* (Univ., 1950), *Summer Stock* (MGM, 1950), *Mrs.*

O'Malley and Mr. Malone (MGM, 1950), *Ma and Pa Kettle Back on the Farm* (Univ., 1951), *The Law and the Lady* (MGM, 1951), *Mr. Imperium* (MGM, 1951), *It's a Big Country* (MGM, 1951), *The Belle of New York* (MGM, 1952), *Ma and Pa Kettle at the Fair* (Univ., 1952), *Ma and Pa Kettle on Vacation* (Univ., 1953), *Fast Company* (MGM, 1953), *The Long, Long Trailer* (MGM, 1954), *Rose Marie* (MGM, 1954), *Ma and Pa Kettle at Home* (Univ., 1954), *Ricochet Romance* (Univ., 1954), *Ma and Pa Kettle at Waikiki* (Univ., 1955), *The Kettles in the Ozarks* (Univ., 1956), *Friendly Persuasion* (AA, 1956), *The Kettles on Old MacDonald's Farm* (Univ., 1957).

KARL MALDEN (Malden Sukilovich) Born March 23, 1914, Gary, Indiana. Married Mona Graham (1938), children: Mila, Carla.

Karl Malden, Montgomery Clift and Brian Aherne in *I Confess*.

Feature Films: *They Knew What They Wanted* (RKO, 1940), *Winged Victory* (20th, 1944), *13 Rue Madeleine* (20th, 1946), *Boomerang* (20th, 1947), *The Gunfighter* (20th, 1950), *Where the Sidewalk Ends* (20th, 1950), *The Halls of Montezuma* (20th, 1950), *A Streetcar Named Desire* (WB, 1951), *Decision Before Dawn* (20th, 1952), *Diplomatic Courier* (20th, 1952), *Operation Secret* (WB, 1952), *Ruby Gentry* (20th, 1952), *I Confess* (WB, 1953), *Take the High Ground* (MGM, 1953), *Phantom of the Rue Morgue* (WB, 1954), *On the Waterfront* (Col., 1954), *Baby Doll* (WB, 1956), *Fear Strikes Out* (Par., 1957), *Bombers B-52* (WB, 1957), *The Hanging Tree* (WB, 1959), *Pollyanna* (BV, 1960), *The Great Imposter* (Univ., 1960), *Parrish* (WB, 1961), *One-Eyed Jacks* (Par., 1961), *Bird Man of Alcatraz* (UA, 1962), *Gypsy* (WB, 1962), *How the West Was Won* (MGM, 1963), *Come Fly With Me* (MGM, 1963), *Dead Ringer* (WB, 1964), *Cheyenne Autumn* (WB, 1964), *The Cincinnati Kid* (MGM, 1965), *Nevada Smith* (Par., 1966), *The Silencers* (Col., 1966), *Murderers' Row* (Col., 1966), *Hotel* (WB, 1967), *The Adventures of Bullwhip Griffin* (BV, 1967), *Billion Dollar Brain* (Par., 1967), *Blue* (Par., 1968).

DOROTHY MALONE (Dorothy Maloney) Born January 30, 1925, Chicago, Illinois. Married Jacques Bergerac (1959), children: Mimi, Diane; divorced 1964.

Dorothy Malone and Jack Carson in *Two Guys From Texas.*

Feature Films:

as Dorothy Maloney *Falcon and the Co-eds* (RKO, 1943), *One Mysterious Night* (Col., 1944), *Show Business* (RKO, 1944), *Seven Days Ashore* (RKO, 1944).

as Dorothy Malone *Hollywood Canteen* (WB, 1944), *Too Young to Know* (WB, 1945), *Janie Gets Married* (WB, 1946), *The Big Sleep* (WB, 1946), *Night and Day* (WB, 1946), *To the Victor* (WB, 1948), *Two Guys From Texas* (WB, 1948), *One Sunday Afternoon* (WB, 1948), *Flaxy Martin* (WB, 1949), *South of St. Louis* (WB, 1949), *Colorado Territory* (WB, 1949), *The Nevadan* (Col., 1950), *Convicted* (Col., 1950), *Mrs. O'Malley and Mr. Malone* (MGM, 1950), *The Killer That Stalked New York* (Col., 1950), *Saddle Legion* (RKO, 1951), *The Bushwhackers* (Realart, 1952), *Scared Stiff* (Par., 1953), *Torpedo Alley* (AA, 1953), *Law and Order* (Univ., 1953), *Jack Slade* (AA, 1953), *Loophole* (AA, 1954), *Pushover* (Col., 1954), *The Fast and Furious* (American Releasing Corp., 1954), *Security Risk* (AA, 1954), *Private Hell 36* (Filmakers, 1954), *Young at Heart* (WB, 1954), *The Lone Gun* (UA, 1954), *Five Guns West* (American Releasing Corp., 1955), *Battle Cry* (WB, 1955), *Tall Man Riding* (WB, 1955), *Sincerely Yours* (WB, 1955), *Artists and Models* (Par., 1955), *At Gunpoint* (AA, 1955), *Pillars of the Sky* (Univ., 1956), *Tension at Table Rock* (RKO, 1956), *Written on the Wind* (Univ., 1956), *Quantez* (Univ., 1957), *Man of a Thousand Faces* (Univ., 1957), *The Tarnished Angels* (Univ., 1957), *Tip on a Dead Jockey* (MGM, 1957), *Too Much, Too Soon* (WB, 1958), *Warlock* (20th, 1959), *The Last Voyage* (MGM, 1960), *The Last Sunset* (Univ., 1961), *Beach Party* (AIP, 1963), *Fate Is the Hunter* (20th, 1964).*

*Unbilled guest appearance

DAVID MANNERS (Rauff Acklon) Born April 30, 1902, Halifax, Nova Scotia.

David Manners and Jacqueline Wells (later Julie Bishop) in *The Black Cat.*

Feature Films: *Journey's End* (Tif., 1930), *He Knew Women* (RKO, 1930), *Sweet Mama* (WB, 1930), *Kismet* (WB, 1930), *Mother's Cry* (WB, 1930), *The Truth About Youth* (WB, 1930), *A Right to Love* (Par., 1930), *Dracula* (Univ., 1931), *The Millionaire* (WB, 1931), *The Miracle Woman* (Col., 1931), *Last Flight* (WB, 1931), *The Ruling Voice* (WB, 1931), *The Greeks Had a Word For Them* (UA, 1932), *Lady With a Past* (RKO, 1932), *Beauty and the Boss* (WB, 1932), *Man Wanted* (WB, 1932), *Stranger in Town* (WB, 1932), *Crooner* (WB, 1932), *A Bill of Divorcement* (RKO, 1932), *They Call It Sin* (WB, 1932), *The Mummy* (Univ., 1932), *The Death Kiss* (World Wide, 1933), *From Hell to Heaven* (Par., 1933), *The Warrior's Husband* (Fox, 1933), *The Girl in 419* (Par., 1933), *The Devil's in Love* (Fox, 1933), *Torch Singer* (Par., 1933), *Roman Scandals* (UA, 1933), *The Black Cat* (Univ., 1934), *The Great Flirtation* (Par., 1934), *The Moonstone* (Mon., 1934), *The Perfect Clue* (Majestic, 1935), *The Mystery of Edwin Drood* (Univ., 1935), *Jalna* (RKO, 1935), *Hearts in Bondage* (Rep., 1936), *A Woman Rebels* (RKO, 1936).

Leslie Brooks, Adolphe Menjou and Adele Mara in *You Were Never Lovelier.*

ADELE MARA (Adelaida Delgado) Born April 28, 1923, Highland Park, Michigan. Married Roy Huggins.

Feature Films: *Navy Blues* (WB, 1941), *Alias Boston Blackie* (Col., 1942), *Blondie Goes to College* (Col., 1942), *Shut My Big Mouth* (Col., 1942), *You Were Never Lovelier* (Col., 1942), *Vengeance of the West* (Col., 1942), *Lucky Legs* (Col., 1942), *Good Luck, Mr. Yates* (Col., 1943), *Redhead from Manhattan* (Col., 1943), *Reveille With Beverly* (Col., 1943), *Riders of the Northwest Mounted* (Col., 1943), *The Fighting Seabees* (Rep., 1944), *Atlantic City* (Rep., 1944), *Faces in the Fog* (Rep., 1944), *Thoroughbreds* (Rep., 1944), *The Vampire's Ghost* (Rep., 1945), *Grissly's Millions* (Rep., 1945), *Bells of Rosarita* (Rep., 1945), *Girls of the Big House* (Rep., 1945), *Song of Mexico* (Rep., 1945), *A Guy Could Change* (Rep., 1945), *The Tiger Woman* (Rep., 1945), *Passkey to Danger* (Rep., 1946), *The Catman of Paris* (Rep., 1946), *Flame of Barbary Coast* (Rep., 1945), *The Invisible Informer* (Rep., 1946), *The Last Crooked Mile* (Rep., 1946), *Night Train to Memphis* (Rep., 1946), *I've Always Loved You* (Rep., 1946), *The Inner Circle* (Rep., 1946), *The Magnificent Rogue* (Rep., 1946), *Traffic in Crime* (Rep., 1946), *Twilight on the Rio Grande* (Rep., 1947), *The Web of Danger* (Rep., 1947), *The Trespasser* (Rep., 1947), *Blackmail* (Rep., 1947), *Robin Hood of Texas* (Rep., 1947), *Exposed* (Rep., 1947), *The Gallant Legion* (Rep., 1948), *Campus Honeymoon* (Rep., 1948), *The Main Street Kid* (Rep., 1948), *Nighttime in Nevada* (Rep., 1948), *Wake of the Red Witch* (Rep., 1948), *Angel in Exile* (Rep., 1948), *I, Jane Doe* (Rep., 1948), *Sands of Iwo Jima* (Rep., 1949), *Rock Island Trail* (Rep., 1950), *The Avengers* (Rep., 1950), *California Passage* (Rep., 1950), *The Sea Hornet* (Rep., 1951), *Count the Hours* (RKO, 1953), *The Black Whip* (20th, 1956), *Back From Eternity* (RKO, 1956), *Curse of the Faceless Man* (UA, 1958), *The Big Circus* (AA, 1959).

FREDRIC MARCH (Ernest Frederick McIntyre Bickel) Born August 31, 1897, Racine, Wisconsin. Married Ellis Baker (1923); divorced. Married Florence Eldridge (1927), children: Penelope, Anthony.

Sound Feature Films: *The Dummy* (Par., 1929), *The Wild Party* (Par., 1929), *The Studio Murder Mystery* (Par., 1929), *Paris Bound* (Pathé, 1929), *Jealousy* (Par., 1929), *Footlights and Fools* (WB, 1929), *The Marriage Playground* (Par., 1929), *Sarah and Son* (Par., 1930), *Ladies Love Brutes* (Par., 1930), *Paramount on Parade* (Par., 1930), *True to the Navy* (Par., 1930), *Manslaughter* (Par., 1930), *Laughter* (Par., 1930), *The Royal Family of Broadway* (Par., 1930), *Honor Among Lovers* (Par., 1931), *The Night Angel* (Par., 1931), *My Sin* (Par., 1931), *Dr. Jekyll and Mr. Hyde* (Par., 1931), *Strangers in Love* (Par., 1932), *Merrily We Go to Hell* (Par., 1932), *Make Me a Star* (Par., 1932),* *Smilin' Through* (MGM, 1932), *The Sign of the Cross* (Par., 1932), *Tonight Is Ours* (Par., 1933), *The Eagle and the Hawk* (Par., 1933), *Design for Living* (Par., 1933), *All of Me* (Par., 1934), *Death Takes a Holiday* (Par., 1934), *Good Dame* (Par., 1934), *The Affairs of Cellini* (UA, 1934),

Miriam Hopkins, Fredric March and Gary Cooper in *Design for Living.*

The Barretts of Wimpole Street (MGM, 1934), *We Live Again* (UA, 1934), *Les Miserables* (UA, 1935), *Anna Karenina* (MGM, 1935), *The Dark Angel* (UA, 1935), *Anthony Adverse* (WB, 1936), *The Road to Glory* (20th, 1936), *Mary of Scotland* (RKO, 1936), *A Star Is Born* (UA, 1937), *Nothing Sacred* (UA, 1937), *The Buccaneer* (Par., 1938), *There Goes My Heart* (UA, 1938), *Trade Winds* (UA, 1938), *Susan and God* (MGM, 1940), *Victory* (Par., 1940), *So Ends Our Night* (UA, 1941), *One Foot in Heaven* (WB, 1941), *Bedtime Story* (Col., 1941), *I Married a Witch* (UA, 1942), *The Adventures of Mark Twain* (WB, 1944), *Tomorrow the World* (UA, 1944), *The Best Years of Our Lives* (RKO, 1946), *Another Part of the Forest* (Univ., 1948), *Live Today for Tomorrow* (Univ., 1948), *Christopher Columbus* (Rank, 1949), *It's a Big Country* (MGM, 1951), *Death of a Salesman* (Col., 1951), *Man on a Tightrope* (20th, 1953), *Executive Suite* (MGM, 1954), *The Bridges at Toko-Ri* (Par., 1954), *The Desperate Hours* (Par., 1955), *Alexander the Great* (UA, 1956), *The Man in the Gray Flannel Suit* (20th, 1956), *Albert Schweitzer* (narrator; DeRochemont, 1957), *Middle of the Night* (Col., 1959), *The Condemned of Altona* (20th, 1963), *Seven Days in May* (Par., 1964), *Hombre* (20th, 1967).

*Unbilled guest appearance

MARGO (Maria Margarita Guadalupe Bolado y Castilla) Born May 10, 1918, Mexico City, Mexico. Married Eddie Albert (1945), children: Edward, Marisa.

Margo and George Raft in *Rumba.*

Feature Films: *Crime Without Passion* (Par., 1934), *Rumba* (Par., 1935), *Robin Hood of El Dorado* (MGM, 1936), *Winterset* (RKO, 1936), *Lost Horizon* (Col., 1937), *A Miracle on Main Street* (Col., 1940), *The Leopard Man* (RKO, 1943), *Behind the Rising Sun* (RKO, 1943), *Gangway for Tomorrow* (RKO, 1943), *Viva Zapata!* (20th, 1952), *I'll Cry Tomorrow* (MGM, 1955), *From Hell to Texas* (20th, 1958), *Who's Got the Action?* (Par., 1962).

HERBERT MARSHALL Born May 23, 1890, London, England. Married Molly Maitland (1915); divorced 1928. Married Edna Best (1928), child: Sarah; divorced 1940. Married Lee Russell (1940), child: Anne; divorced 1946. Married Boots Mallory; widowed 1958. Married Dee Kahmann (1960). Died January 21, 1966.

Robert Montgomery, Herbert Marshall and Norma Shearer in *Riptide.*

Sound Feature Films: *The Letter* (Par., 1929), *Murder* (BIP, 1930), *Secrets of a Secretary* (Par., 1931), *Michael and Mary* (Univ., 1932), *Blonde Venus* (Par., 1932), *Trouble in Paradise* (Par., 1932), *Evenings for Sale* (Par., 1932), *Solitaire Man* (MGM, 1933), *Faithful Heart* (Helber Pictures, 1933), *I Was a Spy* (Fox, 1934), *Four Frightened People* (Par., 1934), *Riptide* (MGM, 1934), *Outcast Lady* (MGM, 1934), *The Painted Veil* (MGM, 1934), *The Good Fairy* (Univ., 1935), *The Flame Within* (MGM, 1935), *Accent on Youth* (Par., 1935), *The Dark Angel* (UA, 1935), *If You Could Only Cook* (Col., 1935), *The Lady Consents* (RKO, 1936), *Till We Meet Again* (Par., 1936), *Girls' Dormitory* (20th, 1936), *A Woman Rebels* (RKO, 1936), *Make Way for a Lady* (RKO, 1936), *Breakfast for Two* (RKO, 1937), *Angel* (Par., 1937), *Mad About Music* (Univ., 1938), *Always Goodbye* (20th, 1938), *Woman Against Woman* (MGM, 1938), *Zaza* (Par., 1939), *A Bill of Divorcement* (RKO, 1940), *Foreign Correspondent* (UA, 1940), *The Letter* (WB, 1940), *Adventure in Washington* (Col., 1941), *The Little Foxes* (RKO, 1941), *When Ladies Meet* (MGM, 1941), *Kathleen* (MGM, 1941), *The Moon and Sixpence* (UA, 1942), *Flight for Freedom* (RKO, 1943), *Forever and a Day* (RKO, 1943), *Young Ideas* (MGM, 1943), *Andy Hardy's Blonde Trouble* (MGM, 1944), *The Unseen* (Par., 1945), *The Enchanted Cottage* (RKO, 1945), *Crack-Up* (RKO, 1946), *The Razor's Edge* (20th, 1946), *Duel in the Sun* (Selznick, 1946), *Ivy* (Univ., 1947), *High Wall* (MGM, 1947), *The Secret Garden* (MGM, 1949), *The Underworld Story* (UA, 1950), *Anne of the Indies* (20th, 1951), *Angel Face* (RKO, 1952), *Captain Black Jack* (Classic, 1952), *Riders to the Stars* (UA, 1954), *Gog* (UA, 1954), *The Black Shield of Falworth* (Univ., 1954), *The Virgin Queen* (20th, 1955), *Wicked as They Come* (Col., 1957), *The Weapon* (Rep., 1957), *Stage Struck* (BV, 1958), *The Fly* (20th, 1958), *Midnight Lace* (Univ., 1960), *College Confidential* (Univ., 1960), *A Fever in the Blood* (WB, 1961), *Five Weeks in a Balloon* (20th, 1962), *The List of Adrian Messenger* (Univ., 1963), *The Caretaker* (UA, 1963), *The Third Day* (WB, 1965).

Martin Balsam, Dean Martin and Susan Hayward in *Ada*.

DEAN MARTIN (Dino Crocetti) Born June 17, 1917, Steubenville, Ohio. Married Betty McDonald (1940), children: Craig, Claudia, Gail, Dina; divorced 1949. Married Jean Bigger (1949), children: Dino, Ricci, Gina.

Feature Films: *My Friend Irma* (Par., 1949), *My Friend Irma Goes West* (Par., 1950), *At War With the Army* (Par., 1950), *That's My Boy* (Par., 1951), *Sailor Beware* (Par., 1951), *Jumping Jacks* (Par., 1952), *Road to Bali* (Par., 1952),* *The Stooge* (Par., 1952), *Scared Stiff* (Par., 1953), *The Caddy* (Par., 1953), *Money From Home* (Par., 1953), *Living it Up* (Par., 1954), *Three Ring Circus* (Par., 1954), *You're Never Too Young* (Par., 1955), *Artists and Models* (Par., 1955), *Pardners* (Par., 1956), *Hollywood or Bust* (Par., 1956), *Ten Thousand Bedrooms* (MGM, 1957), *The Young Lions* (20th, 1958), *Some Came Running* (MGM, 1958), *Rio Bravo* (WB, 1959), *Career* (Par., 1959), *Who Was That Lady?* (Col., 1960), *Bells Are Ringing* (MGM, 1960), *Ocean's 11* (WB, 1960), *Pepe* (Col., 1960),* *All in a Night's Work* (Par., 1961), *Ada* (MGM, 1961), *Sergeants 3* (UA, 1962), *Road to Hong Kong* (UA, 1962),* *Who's Got the Action?* (Par., 1962), *Come Blow Your Horn* (Par., 1963),* *Toys In The Attic* (UA, 1963), *Who's Been Sleeping in My Bed?* (Par., 1963), *4 for Texas* (WB, 1963), *What a Way to Go!* (20th, 1964), *Robin and the 7 Hoods* (WB, 1964), *Kiss Me, Stupid* (Lopert, 1964), *The Sons of Katie Elder* (Par., 1965), *The Silencers* (Col., 1966), *Texas Across the River* (Univ., 1966), *Murderers' Row* (Col., 1966), *Rough Night in Jericho* (Univ., 1967), *The Ambushers* (Col., 1967), *Bandolero* (20th, 1968), *How to Save a Marriage—And Ruin Your Life* (Col., 1968).

    *Unbilled guest appearance

LEE MARVIN Born February 19, 1924, New York, New York. Married Betty Edeling (1951), children: Christopher, Courtenay, Cynthia, Claudia; divorced 1967.

Feature Films: *You're in the Navy Now* (20th, 1951), *Diplomatic Courier* (20th, 1952), *We're Not Married* (20th, 1952), *The Duel at*

Randolph Scott, Lee Marvin and Donna Reed in *Hangman's Knot*.

Silver Creek (Univ., 1952), *Eight Iron Men* (Col., 1952), *Hangman's Knot* (Col., 1952), *Seminole* (Univ., 1953), *Down Among the Sheltering Palms* (20th, 1953), *The Glory Brigade* (20th, 1953), *The Stranger Wore a Gun* (Col., 1953), *The Big Heat* (Col., 1953), *Gun Fury* (Col., 1953), *The Wild One* (Col., 1954), *Gorilla at Large* (20th, 1954), *The Caine Mutiny* (Col., 1954), *The Raid* (20th, 1954), *Bad Day at Black Rock* (MGM, 1954), *A Life in the Balance* (20th, 1955), *Violent Saturday* (20th, 1955), *Not as a Stranger* (UA, 1955), *Pete Kelly's Blues* (WB, 1955), *I Died a Thousand Times* (WB, 1955), *Shack-Out on 101* (AA, 1955), *The Rack* (MGM, 1956), *Seven Men From Now* (WB, 1956), *Pillars of the Sky* (Univ., 1956), *Attack!* (UA, 1956), *Raintree County* (MGM, 1957), *The Missouri Traveler* (BV, 1958), *The Comancheros* (20th, 1961), *The Man Who Shot Liberty Valance* (Par., 1962), *Donovan's Reef* (Par., 1963), *The Killers* (Univ., 1964), *Ship of Fools* (Col., 1965), *Cat Ballou* (Col., 1965), *The Professionals* (Col., 1966), *The Dirty Dozen* (MGM, 1967), *Point Blank* (MGM, 1967), *Tonite Let's Make Love in London* (documentary; Lorrimer, 1967), *Sergeant Ryker* (Univ., 1968).

MARX BROTHERS, THE

    CHICO (Leonard Marx) Born March 22, 1891, New York, New York. Married Betty Carp, child: Maxine; divorced. Married Mary DiVithas (1958). Died October 11, 1961.

    HARPO (Adolph Arthur Marx) Born November 23, 1893, New York, New York. Married Susan Fleming (1936), children: William, Alexander, Minny, James. Died September 28, 1964.

    GROUCHO (Julius Henry Marx) Born October 2, 1895, New York, New York. Married Ruth Johnson (1920), children: Arthur, Miriam; divorced 1942. Married Catherine Gorcey (1945), child: Melinda; divorced 1951. Married Eden Hartford (1954).

    ZEPPO (Herbert Marx) Born February 25, 1901, New York, New York. Married Marion Benda (1927), child: Tim; divorced.

Chico, Zeppo, Groucho and Harpo Marx in *Duck Soup*.

Sound Feature Films:

    with Chico, Harpo, Groucho, Zeppo *The Cocoanuts* (Par., 1929), *Animal Crackers* (Par., 1930), *Monkey Business* (Par., 1931), *Horse Feathers* (Par., 1932), *Duck Soup* (Par., 1933).

    with Chico, Harpo, Groucho *A Night at the Opera* (MGM, 1935), *A Day at the Races* (MGM, 1937), *Room Service* (RKO, 1938), *At the Circus* (MGM, 1939), *Go West* (MGM, 1940), *The Big Store* (MGM, 1941), *A Night in Casablanca* (UA, 1946), *Love Happy* (UA, 1950), *The Story of Mankind* (WB, 1957).

    with Harpo *Stage Door Canteen* (UA, 1943).

    with Groucho *Copacabana* (UA, 1947), *Mr. Music* (Par., 1950), *Double Dynamite* (RKO, 1951), *A Girl in Every Port* (RKO, 1952), *Will Success Spoil Rock Hunter?* (20th, 1957).*

    *Unbilled guest appearance

Angie Dickinson, James Mason and Jack Klugman in *Cry Terror*.

Illona Massey in *Rosalie*.

JAMES MASON (James Neville Mason) Born May 15, 1909, Huddersfield, England. Married Pamela Kellino (1939), children: Portland, Morgan; divorced 1964.

Feature Films: *Late Extra* (Fox, 1935), *Troubled Waters* (Fox, 1935), *Twice Branded* (George Smith, 1936), *The Prison Breakers* (George Smith, 1936), *Blind Man's Bluff* (20th, 1936), *The Secret of Stamboul* (Wainwright, 1936), *The Mill on the Floss* (John Klein, 1936), *The High Command* (Fanfare, 1937), *Catch as Catch Can* (20th, 1937), *Fire Over England* (London Films, 1937), *The Return of the Scarlet Pimpernel* (UA, 1937), *Deadwater* (KMK, 1937), *I Met a Murderer* (Gamma Films, 1939), *Hatter's Castle* (Par., 1941), *The Patient Vanishes* (Associated British Pictures, 1941), *This Man Is Dangerous* (Pathé, 1941), *Secret Mission* (Hellman, 1942), *Thunder Rock* (Charter, 1942), *Alibi* (British Lion, 1943), *The Bells Go Down* (Ealing, 1943), *Candlelight in Algeria* (King, 1943), *The Man in Grey* (Gainsborough, 1943), *They Met in the Dark* (Hellman, 1943), *Fanny by Gaslight* (Gainsborough, 1944), *Hotel Reserve* (RKO, 1944), *A Place of One's Own* (Gainsborough, 1945), *They Were Sisters* (Gainsborough, 1945), *The Wicked Lady* (Gainsborough, 1945), *The Seventh Veil* (Ortus, 1945), *Odd Man Out* (Rank, 1947), *The Upturned Glass* (Rank, 1947), *A Place of One's Own* (Rank, 1949), *Madame Bovary* (MGM, 1949), *The Reckless Moment* (Col., 1949), *East Side, West Side* (MGM, 1949), *One Way Street* (Univ., 1950), *The Desert Fox* (20th, 1951), *Pandora and the Flying Dutchman* (MGM, 1951), *Five Fingers* (20th, 1952), *Lady Possessed* (Rep., 1952), *The Prisoner of Zenda* (MGM, 1952), *Face to Face* (RKO, 1952), *The Story of Three Loves* (MGM, 1953), *The Desert Rats* (20th, 1953), *Julius Caesar* (MGM, 1953), *Botany Bay* (Par., 1953), *The Man Between* (UA, 1953), *Prince Valiant* (20th, 1954), *A Star Is Born* (WB, 1954), *20,000 Leagues Under the Sea* (BV, 1954), *Forever Darling* (MGM, 1956), *Bigger Than Life* (20th, 1956), *Island in the Sun* (20th, 1957), *Cry Terror* (MGM, 1958), *The Decks Ran Red* (MGM, 1958), *North by Northwest* (MGM, 1959), *Journey to the Center of the Earth* (20th, 1959), *A Touch of Larceny* (Par., 1960), *The Green Carnation* (Warwick, 1960), *The Marriage-Go-Round* (20th, 1960), *Escape From Zahrain* (Par., 1962), *Lolita* (MGM, 1962), *Hero's Island* (UA, 1962), *Tiara Tahiti* (Zenith International, 1963), *Torpedo Bay* (AIP, 1964), *The Fall of the Roman Empire* (Par., 1964), *The Pumpkin Eater* (Royal Film International, 1964), *Lord Jim* (Col., 1965), *Genghis Khan* (Col., 1966), *Georgy Girl* (Col., 1966), *The Deadly Affair* (Col., 1967), *Cop Out* (Cinerama, 1968), *Duffy* (Col., 1968), *Mayerling* (MGM, 1969).

ILONA MASSEY (Ilona Hajmassy) Born 1910, Budapest, Hungary. Married Nicholas Szavozd; divorced. Married Alan Curtis (1941); divorced 1942. Married Charles Walker (1952); divorced 1955. Married Donald Dawson (1955).

Feature Films: *Rosalie* (MGM, 1937), *Balalaika* (MGM, 1949), *New Wine* (UA, 1941), *International Lady* (UA, 1941), *Invisible Agent* (Univ., 1942), *Frankenstein Meets the Wolf Man* (Univ., 1943), *Holiday in Mexico* (MGM, 1946), *The Gentleman Misbehaves* (Col., 1946), *Northwest Outpost* (Rep., 1947), *The Plunderers* (Rep., 1948), *Love Happy* (UA, 1949), *Jet Over the Atlantic* (Inter-Continent, 1959).

RAYMOND MASSEY (Raymond Hart Massey) Born August 30, 1896, Toronto, Canada. Married Peggy Fremantle (1923), child: Geoffrey; divorced 1929. Married Adrianne Allen (1929), children: Daniel, Anna; divorced 1939. Married Dorothy Whitney (1939).

Moroni Olsen, Christian Rub, Ilka Gruning, Nancy Coleman, John Garfield and Raymond Massey in *Dangerously They Live*.

Feature Films: *The Speckled Band* (First Division, 1931), *The Old Dark House* (Univ., 1932), *The Scarlet Pimpernel* (UA, 1934), *Things to Come* (UA, 1936), *Fire Over England* (Korda, 1937), *Under the Red Robe* (20th, 1937), *The Prisoner of Zenda* (UA, 1937), *The Hurricane* (UA, 1937), *Drums* (UA, 1938), *Black Limelight* (Alliance Films, 1939), *Abe Lincoln in Illinois* (RKO, 1940), *Santa Fe Trail* (WB, 1940), *Dangerously They Live* (WB, 1941), *The Invaders* (Col., 1942), *Desperate Journey* (WB, 1942), *Reap the Wild Wind* (Par., 1942), *Action in the North Atlantic* (WB, 1943), *Arsenic and Old Lace* (WB, 1944), *The Woman in the Window* (RKO, 1944), *God Is My Co-Pilot* (WB, 1945), *Hotel Berlin* (WB, 1945), *Stairway to Heaven* (Rank, 1946), *Mourning Becomes Electra* (RKO, 1947), *Possessed* (WB, 1947), *The Fountainhead* (WB, 1949), *Roseanna McCoy* (RKO, 1949), *Chain Lightning* (WB, 1949), *Barricade* (WB, 1950), *Dallas* (WB, 1950), *Sugarfoot* (WB, 1951), *Come Fill the Cup* (WB, 1951), *David and Bathsheba* (20th, 1951), *Carson City* (WB, 1952), *The Desert Song* (WB, 1953), *Battle Cry* (WB, 1955), *Seven Angry Men* (AA, 1955), *Prince of Players* (20th, 1955), *East of Eden* (WB, 1955), *Omar Khayyam* (Par., 1957), *The Naked and the Dead* (WB, 1958), *The Great Impostor* (Univ.,

1960), *The Fiercest Heart* (20th, 1961), *The Queen's Guard* (Michael Powell Productions, 1961), *How the West Was Won* (MGM, 1963), *MacKenna's Gold* (Col., 1968).

WALTER MATTHAU (Walter Matthow) Born October 1, 1920, New York, New York. Married Grace Johnson (1948); divorced 1958. Married Carol Marcus (1959).

Walter Matthau, Jack Lemmon and Ned Glass in *The Fortune Cookie.*

Feature Films: *The Kentuckian* (UA, 1955), *The Indian Fighter* (UA, 1955), *Bigger Than Life* (20th, 1956), *A Face in the Crowd* (WB, 1957), *Slaughter on Tenth Avenue* (Univ., 1957), *Voice in the Mirror* (Univ., 1958), *King Creole* (Par., 1958), *Ride a Crooked Trail* (Univ., 1958), *Onionhead* (WB, 1958), *The Gangster Story* (Jonathan Daniels, 1960), *Strangers When We Meet* (Col., 1960), *Lonely Are the Brave* (Univ., 1962), *Who's Got the Action?* (Par., 1962), *Island of Love* (WB, 1963), *Charade* (Univ., 1963), *Ensign Pulver* (WB, 1964), *Fail Safe* (Col., 1964), *Goodbye Charlie* (20th, 1964), *Mirage* (Univ., 1965), *The Fortune Cookie* (UA, 1966), *A Guide for the Married Man* (20th, 1967), *The Odd Couple* (Par., 1968), *Guide for the Married Woman* (20th, 1968), *Candy* (Cinerama, 1968).

VICTOR MATURE Born January 29, 1916, Louisville, Kentucky. Married Frances Charles; divorced 1940. Married Martha Kemp; divorced 1943. Married Dorothy Berry (1948); divorced 1955. Married Adrianne Urwich (1959).

Robert Barrat, Louise Platt and Victor Mature in *Captain Caution.*

English-Language Feature Films: *The Housekeeper's Daughter* (UA, 1939), *One Million B.C.* (UA, 1940), *Captain Caution* (UA, 1940),

No, No, Nanette (RKO, 1940), *I Wake Up Screaming* (20th, 1941), *The Shanghai Gesture* (UA, 1941), *Song of the Islands* (20th, 1942), *My Gal Sal* (20th, 1942), *Footlight Serenade* (20th, 1942), *Seven Days' Leave* (RKO, 1942), *My Darling Clementine* (20th, 1946), *Moss Rose* (20th, 1947), *Kiss of Death* (20th, 1947), *Fury at Furnace Creek* (20th, 1948), *Cry of the City* (20th, 1948), *Red Hot and Blue* (Par., 1949), *Easy Living* (RKO, 1949), *Samson and Delilah* (Par., 1949), *Wabash Avenue* (20th, 1950), *I'll Get By* (20th, 1950),* *Stella* (20th, 1950), *Gambling House* (RKO, 1950), *The Las Vegas Story* (RKO, 1952), *Androcles and the Lion* (RKO, 1952), *Something for the Birds* (20th, 1952), *Million Dollar Mermaid* (MGM, 1952), *The Glory Brigade* (20th, 1953), *Affair With a Stranger* (RKO, 1953), *The Robe* (20th, 1953), *Veils of Bagdad* (Univ., 1953), *Dangerous Mission* (RKO, 1954), *Demetrius and the Gladiators* (20th, 1954), *Betrayed* (MGM, 1954), *The Egyptian* (20th, 1954), *Chief Crazy Horse* (Univ., 1955), *Violent Saturday* (20th, 1955), *The Last Frontier* (Col., 1955), *Safari* (Col., 1956), *The Sharkfighters* (UA, 1956), *Zarak* (Col., 1957), *Pickup Alley* (Col., 1957), *The Long Haul* (Col., 1957), *China Doll* (UA, 1958), *Tank Force* (Col., 1958), *Escort West* (UA, 1959), *The Bandit of Zhobe* (Col., 1959), *The Big Circus* (AA, 1959), *Timbuktu* (UA, 1959), *Hannibal* (WB, 1960), *After the Fox* (UA, 1966).

*Unbilled guest appearance

MARILYN MAXWELL (Marvel Marilyn Maxwell) Born August 3, 1921, Clarinda, Iowa. Married John Conte (1941); divorced 1946. Married Anders McIntyre (1950); divorced 1951. Married Jerry Davis (1954), child: Matthew; divorced 1960.

Mickey Rooney and Marilyn Maxwell in *Summer Holiday.*

Feature Films: *Stand By for Action* (MGM, 1942), *Du Barry Was a Lady* (MGM, 1943), *Presenting Lily Mars* (MGM, 1943), *Thousands Cheer* (MGM, 1943), *Dr. Gillespie's Criminal Case* (MGM, 1943), *Salute to the Marines* (MGM, 1943), *Swing Fever* (MGM, 1943), *Pilot No. 5* (MGM, 1943), *Best Foot Forward* (MGM, 1943), *Three Men in White* (MGM, 1944), *Lost in a Harem* (MGM, 1944), *Between Two Women* (MGM, 1945), *The Show-Off* (MGM, 1946), *High Barbaree* (MGM, 1947), *Summer Holiday* (MGM, 1948), *Race Street* (RKO, 1948), *Champion* (UA, 1949), *Key to the City* (MGM, 1950), *Outside the Wall* (Univ., 1950), *The Lemon Drop Kid* (Par., 1951), *New Mexico* (UA, 1951), *Off Limits* (Par., 1953), *East of Sumatra* (Univ., 1953), *Paris Model* (Col., 1953), *New York Confidential* (WB, 1955), *Forever, Darling* (MGM, 1956), *Rock-a-Bye Baby* (Par., 1958), *Critic's Choice* (WB, 1963), *Stage to Thunder Rock* (Par., 1964), *The Lively Set* (Univ., 1964), *Arizona Bushwhackers* (Par., 1968).

VIRGINIA MAYO (Virginia Jones) Born November 30, 1920, St. Louis, Missouri. Married Michael O'Shea (1947), child: Mary.

English-Language Feature Films: *The Adventures of Jack London* (UA,

Andrew Duggan and Virginia Mayo in *Westbound.*

1943), *Up in Arms* (RKO, 1944), *Seven Days Ashore* (RKO, 1944), *The Princess and the Pirate* (RKO, 1944), *Wonder Man* (RKO, 1945), *The Best Years of Our Lives* (RKO, 1946), *The Kid From Brooklyn* (RKO, 1947), *Out of the Blue* (EL, 1947), *The Secret Life of Walter Mitty* (RKO, 1947), *A Song Is Born* (RKO, 1948), *Smart Girls Don't Talk* (WB, 1948), *Flaxy Martin* (WB, 1949), *Colorado Territory* (WB, 1949), *The Girl From Jones Beach* (WB, 1949), *White Heat* (WB, 1949), *Red Light* (UA, 1949), *Always Leave Them Laughing* (WB, 1949), *Backfire* (WB, 1950), *The Flame and the Arrow* (WB, 1950), *The West Point Story* (WB, 1950), *Along the Great Divide* (WB, 1951), *Painting the Clouds With Sunshine* (WB, 1951), *Captain Horatio Hornblower* (WB, 1951), *Starlift* (WB, 1951), *She's Working Her Way Through College* (WB, 1952), *The Iron Mistress* (WB, 1952), *She's Back on Broadway* (WB, 1953), *South Sea Woman* (WB, 1953), *Devil's Canyon* (RKO, 1953), *King Richard and the Crusaders* (WB, 1954), *The Silver Chalice* (WB, 1954), *Pearl of the South Pacific* (RKO, 1955), *Great Day in the Morning* (RKO, 1956), *The Proud Ones* (20th, 1956), *Congo Crossing* (Univ., 1956), *The Big Land* (WB, 1957), *The Story of Mankind* (WB, 1957), *The Tall Stranger* (AA, 1957), *Fort Dobbs* (WB, 1958), *Westbound* (WB, 1959), *Jet Over the Atlantic* (Inter-Continent, 1959), *Young Fury* (Par., 1965), *Castle of Evil* (Feature Film Corp. of USA, 1966), *Fort Utah* (Par., 1967).

PATRICIA MEDINA Born July 19, 1923, London, England. Married Richard Greene (1941); divorced 1952. Married Joseph Cotten (1960).

Alan Ladd and Patricia Medina in *Botany Bay.*

English-Language Feature Films: *The Day Will Dawn* (Soskin, 1942), *They Met in the Dark* (Hellman, 1942), *Hotel Reserve* (RKO, 1944), *Don't Take It to Heart* (Two Cities, 1944), *Kiss the Boys Goodbye* (Butchers, 1944), *Waltz Time* (British International, 1945), *The Secret Heart* (MGM, 1946), *Moss Rose* (20th, 1947), *The Foxes of Harrow* (20th, 1947), *The Three Musketeers* (MGM, 1948), *O.K. Agostina* (Toeplitz, 1949), *The Fighting O'Flynn* (Univ., 1949), *Francis* (Univ., 1949), *Fortunes of Captain Blood* (Col., 1950), *Abbott and Costello in the Foreign Legion* (Univ., 1950), *The Jackpot* (20th, 1950), *Valentino*

(Col., 1951), *The Lady and the Bandit* (Col., 1951), *The Magic Carpet* (Col., 1951), *Aladdin and His Lamp* (Mon., 1952), *Lady in the Iron Mask* (20th, 1952), *Captain Pirate* (Col., 1952), *Desperate Search* (MGM, 1952), *Siren of Bagdad* (Col., 1953), *Sangaree* (Par., 1953), *Plunder of the Sun* (WB, 1953), *Botany Bay* (Par., 1953), *Phantom of the Rue Morgue* (WB, 1954), *Drums of Tahiti* (Col., 1954), *The Black Knight* (Col., 1954), *Pirates of Tripoli* (Col., 1955), *Duel on the Mississippi* (Col., 1955), *Mr. Arkadin* (WB, 1955), *Uranium Boom* (Col., 1956), *Stranger at My Door* (Rep., 1956), *Miami Exposé* (Col., 1956), *The Beast of Hollow Mountain* (UA, 1956), *The Buckskin Lady* (UA, 1957), *Missiles from Hell* (British, 1959), *Count Your Blessings* (MGM, 1959), *Snow White and the Three Stooges* (20th, 1961).

DONALD MEEK Born July 14, 1880, Glasgow, Scotland. Married Belle Walken (1909). Died November 18, 1946.

Shirley Temple and Donald Meek in *Little Miss Broadway.*

Sound Feature Films: *Hole in the Wall* (Par., 1929), *Love Kiss* (Celebrity Pictures, 1930), *Girl Habit* (Par., 1931), *Personal Maid* (Par., 1931), *Love, Honor and Oh-Baby!* (Univ., 1933), *College Coach* (WB, 1933), *Hi Nellie* (WB, 1934), *Bedside* (WB, 1934), *Last Gentleman* (UA, 1934), *Murder at the Vanities* (Par., 1934), *The Defense Rests* (Col., 1934), *The Merry Widow* (MGM, 1934), *Mrs. Wiggs of the Cabbage Patch* (Par., 1934), *The Captain Hates the Sea* (Col., 1934), *The Whole Town's Talking* (Col., 1935), *The Gilded Lily* (Par., 1935), *Mark of the Vampire* (MGM, 1935), *Baby Face Harrington* (MGM, 1935), *Society Doctor* (MGM, 1935), *Biography of a Bachelor Girl* (RKO, 1935), *Village Tale* (RKO, 1935), *The Informer* (RKO, 1935), *China Seas* (MGM, 1935), *Accent on Youth* (Par., 1935), *Old Man Rhythm* (RKO, 1935), *Return of Peter Grimm* (RKO, 1935), *She Couldn't Take It* (Col., 1935), *Barbary Coast* (UA, 1935), *Kind Lady* (MGM, 1935), *The Bride Comes Home* (Par., 1935), *Peter Ibbetson* (Par., 1935), *Captain Blood* (WB, 1935), *Happiness C.O.D.* (Chesterfield, 1935), *Everybody's Old Man* (20th, 1936), *Three Wise Guys* (MGM, 1936), *And So They Were Married* (Col., 1936), *One Rainy Afternoon* (UA, 1936), *Three Married Men* (Par., 1936), *Two in a Crowd* (Univ., 1936), *Old Hutch* (MGM, 1936), *Pennies From Heaven* (Col., 1936), *Maid of Salem* (Par., 1937), *The Three Legionnaires* (General Films, 1937), *Parnell* (MGM, 1937), *Behind the Headlines* (RKO, 1937), *Artists and Models* (Par., 1937), *Double Wedding* (MGM, 1937), *The Toast of New York* (RKO, 1937), *Make a Wish* (RKO, 1937), *Breakfast for Two* (RKO, 1937), *You're a Sweetheart* (Univ., 1937), *The Adventures of Tom Sawyer* (UA, 1938), *Double Danger* (RKO, 1938), *Goodbye Broadway* (Univ., 1938), *Little Miss Broadway* (20th, 1938), *Having Wonderful Time* (RKO, 1938), *You Can't Take It With You* (Col., 1938), *Hold That Co-ed* (20th, 1938), *Jesse James* (20th, 1939), *Stagecoach* (UA, 1939), *Young Mr. Lincoln* (20th, 1939), *The Housekeeper's Daughter* (UA, 1939), *Blondie Takes a Vacation*

(Col., 1939), *Nick Carter—Master Detective* (MGM, 1939), *My Little Chickadee* (Univ., 1940), *Oh Johnny, How You Can Love* (Univ., 1940), *Dr. Ehrlich's Magic Bullet* (WB, 1940), *The Man From Dakota* (MGM, 1940), *Turnabout* (UA, 1940), *Star Dust* (20th, 1940), *Phantom Raiders* (MGM, 1940), *The Return of Frank James* (20th, 1940), *Third Finger, Left Hand* (MGM, 1940), *Hullabaloo* (MGM, 1940), *Sky Murder* (MGM, 1940), *The Ghost Comes Home* (MGM, 1940), *Blonde Inspiration* (MGM, 1941), *Come Live With Me* (MGM, 1941), *A Woman's Face* (MGM, 1941), *The Wild Man of Borneo* (MGM, 1941), *Barnacle Bill* (MGM, 1941), *The Feminine Touch* (MGM, 1941), *Rise and Shine* (20th, 1941), *Babes on Broadway* (MGM, 1941), *Tortilla Flat* (MGM, 1942), *Maisie Gets Her Man* (MGM, 1942), *Seven Sweethearts* (MGM, 1942), *The Omaha Trail* (MGM, 1942), *Keeper of the Flame* (MGM, 1942), *They Got Me Covered* (RKO, 1943), *Air Raid Wardens* (20th, 1943), *Du Barry Was a Lady* (MGM, 1943), *Lost Angel* (MGM, 1943), *Rationing* (MGM, 1944), *Two Girls and a Sailor* (MGM, 1944), *Bathing Beauty* (MGM, 1944), *Barbary Coast Gent* (MGM, 1944), *Maisie Goes to Reno* (MGM, 1944), *The Thin Man Goes Home* (MGM, 1944), *State Fair* (20th, 1945), *Colonel Effingham's Raid* (20th, 1945), *Because of Him* (Univ., 1946), *Janie Gets Married* (WB, 1946), *Affairs of Geraldine* (Rep., 1946), *Magic Town* (RKO, 1947), *The Hal Roach Comedy Carnival* (UA, 1947).

ADOLPHE MENJOU (Adolph Jean Menjou) Born February 18, 1890, Pittsburgh, Pennsylvania. Married Katherine Tinsley (1919); divorced 1927. Married Kathryn Carver (1927); divorced 1933. Married Verree Teasdale (1934), child: Peter. Died October 29, 1963.

Christian Rub and Adolphe Menjou in *Cafe Metropole*.

English-Language Sound Feature Films: *Fashions in Love* (Par., 1929), *Morocco* (Par., 1930), *New Moon* (MGM, 1930), *Men Call it Love* (MGM, 1931), *The Easiest Way* (MGM, 1931), *The Front Page* (UA, 1931), *The Great Lover* (MGM, 1931), *Friends and Lovers* (RKO, 1931), *Prestige* (RKO, 1932), *Forbidden* (Univ., 1932), *Two White Arms* (MGM, 1932), *The Man From Yesterday* (Par., 1932), *Bachelor's Affairs* (Fox, 1932), *Night Club Lady* (Col., 1932), *A Farewell to Arms* (Par., 1932), *Blame the Woman* (Principal, 1932), *Circus Queen Murder* (Col., 1933), *Morning Glory* (RKO, 1933), *Worst Woman in Paris?* (Fox, 1933), *Convention City* (WB, 1933), *Journal of a Crime* (WB, 1934), *Easy to Love* (WB, 1934), *The Trumpet Blows* (Par., 1934), *Little Miss Marker* (Par., 1934), *Great Flirtation* (Par., 1934), *The Human Side* (Univ., 1934), *The Mighty Barnum* (UA, 1934), *Gold Diggers of 1935* (WB, 1935), *Broadway Gondolier* (WB, 1935), *The Milky Way* (Par., 1936), *Sing Baby, Sing* (20th, 1936), *Wives Never Know* (Par., 1936), *One in a Million* (20th, 1936), *A Star Is Born* (UA, 1937), *Cafe Metropole* (20th, 1937), *100 Men and a Girl* (Univ., 1937), *Stage Door* (RKO, 1937), *Goldwyn Follies* (UA, 1938), *Letter of Introduction* (Univ., 1938), *Thanks for Everything* (20th, 1938), *King of the Turf* (UA, 1939), *That's Right—You're Wrong* (RKO, 1939), *Golden Boy* (Col., 1939), *The Housekeeper's Daughter* (UA, 1939), *A Bill of Divorcement* (RKO, 1940), *Turnabout* (UA, 1940), *Road Show* (UA, 1941),

Father Takes a Wife (RKO, 1941), *Roxie Hart* (20th, 1942), *Syncopation* (RKO, 1942), *You Were Never Lovelier* (Col., 1942), *Hi Diddle Diddle* (UA, 1943), *Sweet Rosie O'Grady* (20th, 1943), *Step Lively* (RKO, 1944), *Man Alive* (RKO, 1945), *Heartbeat* (RKO, 1946), *The Bachelor's Daughters* (UA, 1946), *I'll Be Yours* (Univ., 1947), *Mr. District Attorney* (Col., 1947), *The Hucksters* (MGM, 1947), *State of the Union* (MGM, 1948), *My Dream Is Yours* (WB, 1949), *Dancing in the Dark* (20th, 1949), *To Please a Lady* (MGM, 1950), *The Tall Target* (MGM, 1951), *Across the Wide Missouri* (MGM, 1951), *The Sniper* (Col., 1952), *Man on a Tightrope* (20th, 1953), *Timberjack* (Rep., 1955), *The Ambassador's Daughter* (UA, 1956), *Bundle of Joy* (RKO, 1956), *The Fuzzy Pink Nightgown* (UA, 1957), *Paths of Glory* (UA, 1957), *I Married a Woman* (Univ., 1958), *Pollyanna* (BV, 1960).

BURGESS MEREDITH (Burgess George) Born November 16, 1908, Cleveland, Ohio. Married Helen Derby (1932); divorced 1935. Married Margaret Perry (1936); divorced 1938. Married Paulette Goddard (1944); divorced 1949. Married Kava Sundsten (1950), children: Jonathan, Tala.

Burgess Meredith, Paulette Goddard and Fred Astaire in *Second Chorus*.

Feature Films: *Winterset* (RKO, 1936), *There Goes the Groom* (RKO, 1937), *Spring Madness* (MGM, 1938), *Idiot's Delight* (MGM, 1939), *Of Mice and Men* (UA, 1939), *Castle on the Hudson* (WB, 1940), *Second Chorus* (Par., 1940), *San Francisco Docks* (Univ., 1941), *That Uncertain Feeling* (UA, 1941), *Tom, Dick and Harry* (RKO, 1941), *Street of Chance* (Par., 1942), *The Story of G.I. Joe* (UA, 1945), *The Diary of a Chambermaid* (UA, 1946), *Magnificent Doll* (Univ., 1946), *On Our Merry Way* (UA, 1948), *Mine Own Executioner* (20th, 1948), *Jigsaw* (UA, 1949),* *The Man on the Eiffel Tower* (RKO, 1949), *The Gay Adventure* (UA, 1953), *Joe Butterfly* (Univ., 1957), *Advise and Consent* (Col., 1962), *The Cardinal* (Col., 1963), *The Kidnappers* ("Man on the Run"—Manson, 1964), *In Harm's Way* (Par., 1965), *Crazy Quilt* (narrator; Walter Reade, 1966), *A Big Hand for the Little Lady* (WB, 1966), *Madame X* (Univ., 1966), *Batman* (20th, 1966), *Hurry Sundown* (Par., 1967), *The Torture Garden* (Col., 1968), *MacKenna's Gold* (Col., 1968), *Stay Away Joe* (MGM, 1968).

    *Unbilled guest appearance

UNA MERKEL Born December 10, 1903, Covington, Kentucky. Married Ronald Burla (1932); divorced 1945.

Sound Feature Films: *Abraham Lincoln* (UA, 1930), *Eyes of the World* (UA, 1930), *The Bat Whispers* (UA, 1931), *Command Performance* (Tiff., 1931), *Don't Bet on Women* (Fox, 1931), *The Maltese Falcon* (WB, 1931), *Daddy Long Legs* (Fox, 1931), *Six Cylinder Love* (Fox, 1931), *The Bargain* (WB, 1931), *Secret Witness* ("Terror by Night"—Famous Attractions, 1931), *Private Lives* (MGM, 1931), *Secret Witness* (Col., 1931), *Huddle* (MGM, 1932), *She Wanted a Millionaire* (Fox,

Bob Burns and Una Merkel in *Comin' Round the Mountain*.

1932), *The Impatient Maiden* (Univ., 1932), *Man Wanted* (WB, 1932), *Red-Headed Woman* (MGM, 1932), *They Call It Sin* (WB, 1932), *42nd Street* (WB, 1933), *Clear All Wires* (MGM, 1933), *Secret of Madame Blanche* (MGM, 1933), *Whistling in the Dark* (MGM, 1933), *Men Are Such Fools* (RKO, 1933), *Reunion in Vienna* (MGM, 1933), *Midnight Mary* (MGM, 1933), *Broadway to Hollywood* (MGM, 1933), *Her First Mate* (Univ., 1933), *Beauty for Sale* (MGM, 1933), *Bombshell* (MGM, 1933), *Day of Reckoning* (MGM, 1933), *The Women in His Life* (MGM, 1933), *This Side of Heaven* (MGM, 1934), *Bulldog Drummond Strikes Back* (UA, 1934), *Have a Heart* (MGM, 1934), *The Cat's Paw* (Fox, 1934), *The Merry Widow* (MGM, 1934), *Paris Interlude* (MGM, 1934), *Murder in the Private Car* (MGM, 1934), *Biography of a Bachelor Girl* (MGM, 1934), *Evelyn Prentice* (MGM, 1934), *The Night Is Young* (MGM, 1934), *Baby Face Harrington* (MGM, 1935), *One New York Night* (MGM, 1935), *Murder in the Fleet* (MGM, 1935), *Broadway Melody of 1936* (MGM, 1935), *It's in the Air* (MGM, 1935), *Riffraff* (MGM, 1935), *Speed* (MGM, 1936), *Born to Dance* (MGM, 1936), *We Went to College* (MGM, 1936), *Don't Tell the Wife* (RKO, 1937), *Good Old Soak* (MGM, 1937), *Saratoga* (MGM, 1937), *True Confession* (Par., 1937), *Checkers* (20th, 1937), *Four Girls in White* (MGM, 1939), *Some Like It Hot* (Par., 1939), *On Borrowed Time* (MGM, 1939), *Destry Rides Again* (Univ., 1939), *Comin' 'Round the Mountain* (Par., 1940), *The Bank Dick* (Univ., 1940), *Sandy Gets Her Man* (Univ., 1940), *Road to Zanzibar* (Par., 1941), *Double Date* (Univ., 1941), *Cracked Nuts* (Univ., 1941), *Twin Beds* (UA, 1942), *The Mad Doctor of Market Street* (Univ., 1942), *The Silent Witness* (Mon., 1942), *This Is the Army* (WB, 1943), *Sweethearts of the U.S.A.* (Mon., 1944), *It's a Joke, Son* (EL, 1947), *The Bride Goes Wild* (MGM, 1948), *The Man From Texas* (EL, 1948), *Kill the Umpire* (Col., 1950), *My Blue Heaven* (20th, 1950), *Emergency Wedding* (Col., 1950), *Rich, Young and Pretty* (MGM, 1951), *A Millionaire for Christy* (20th, 1951), *Golden Girl* (20th, 1951), *With a Song in My Heart* (20th, 1952), *The Merry Widow* (MGM, 1952), *I Love Melvin* (MGM, 1953), *The Kentuckian* (UA, 1955), *The Kettles in the Ozarks* (Univ., 1956), *Bundle of Joy* (RKO, 1956), *The Fuzzy Pink Nightgown* (UA, 1957), *The Girl Most Likely* (Univ., 1957), *The Mating Game* (MGM, 1959), *The Parent Trap* (BV, 1961), *Summer and Smoke* (Par., 1961), *Summer Magic* (BV, 1963), *A Tiger Walks* (BV, 1964), *Spinout* (MGM, 1966).

ETHEL MERMAN (Ethel Zimmerman) Born January 16, 1909, Astoria, New York. Married William Smith (1940); divorced 1941. Married Robert Levitt (1941), children: Ethel, Robert; divorced 1952.

Bing Crosby and Ethel Merman in *Anything Goes*.

Married Robert Six (1953); divorced 1960. Married Ernest Borgnine (1964); divorced 1964.

Feature Films: *Follow the Leader* (Par., 1930), *We're Not Dressing* (Par., 1934), *Kid Millions* (UA, 1934), *Anything Goes* (Par., 1936), *Strike Me Pink* (UA, 1936), *Happy Landing* (20th, 1938), *Alexander's Ragtime Band* (20th, 1938), *Straight, Place and Show* (20th, 1938), *Stage Door Canteen* (UA, 1943), *Call Me Madam* (20th, 1953), *There's No Business Like Show Business* (20th, 1954), *Its a Mad, Mad, Mad, Mad World* (UA, 1963), *The Art of Love* (Univ., 1965).

GERTRUDE MICHAEL Born June 1, 1911, Talladega, Alabama. Died January 1, 1965.

Arthur Byron and Gertrude Michael in *The Notorious Sophie Lang*.

Feature Films: *Wayward* (Par., 1932), *Unashamed* (MGM, 1932), *Sailor Be Good* (RKO, 1933), *A Bedtime Story* (Par., 1933), *Night of Terror* (Col., 1933), *Ann Vickers* (RKO, 1933), *I'm No Angel* (Par., 1933), *Cradle Song* (Par., 1933), *Bolero* (Par., 1934), *I Believed in You* (Fox, 1934), *Search for Beauty* (Par., 1934), *Hold That Girl* (Fox, 1934), *Murder at the Vanities* (Par., 1934), *Murder on the Blackboard* (RKO, 1934), *Cleopatra* (Par., 1934), *Notorious Sophie Lang* (Par., 1934), *Menace* (Par., 1934), *George White's Scandals* (Fox, 1934), *The Witching Hour* (Par., 1934), *Father Brown, Detective* (Par., 1935), *It Happened in New York* (Univ., 1935), *Four Hours to Kill* (Par., 1935), *The Last Outpost* (Par., 1935), *Woman Trap* (Par., 1936), *Till We Meet Again* ("Forgotten Faces"—Par., 1936), *Return of Sophie Lang* (Par., 1936), *Second Wife* (RKO, 1936), *Make Way for a Lady* (RKO, 1936), *Mr. Dodd Takes the Air* (WB, 1937), *Sophie Lang Goes West* (Par., 1937), *Hidden Power* (Col., 1939), *Just Like a Woman* (Alliance, 1940), *The Hidden Menace* (Alliance, 1940), *The Farmer's Daughter* (Par., 1940), *Parole Fixer* (Par., 1940), *I Can't Give You Anything But Love, Baby* (Univ., 1940), *Slightly Tempted* (Univ., 1940), *Prisoner of Japan* (PRC, 1942), *Behind Prison Walls* (PRC, 1943), *Where Are Your Children?* (Mon., 1943), *Women in Bondage* (Mon., 1943), *Faces in the Fog* (Rep., 1944), *Three's a Crowd* (Rep., 1945), *Allotment Wives* (Mon., 1945), *Club Havana* (PRC, 1946), *Flamingo Road* (WB, 1949), *Caged* (WB, 1950), *Darling, How Could You!* (Par., 1951), *Bugles in the Afternoon* (WB, 1952), *No Escape* (UA, 1953), *Women's Prison* (Col., 1955), *The Outsider* (Univ., 1961), *Twist All Night* (AIP, 1962).

VERA MILES (Vera Ralston) Born August 23, 1930, Boise City, Idaho. Married Robert Miles (1948), children: Debra, Kelly; divorced 1954. Married Gordon Scott (1956), child: Michael; divorced. Married Keith Larsen (1960), child: Keith.

Feature Films: *Two Tickets to Broadway* (RKO, 1951), *For Men Only* (Lip., 1952), *The Rose Bowl Story* (Mon., 1952), *The Charge at Feather River* (WB, 1953), *So Big* (WB, 1953), *Pride of the Blue Grass* (AA, 1954), *Tarzan's Hidden Jungle* (RKO, 1955), *Wichita* (AA, 1955), *The Searchers* (WB, 1956), *Autumn Leaves* (Col., 1956), *23 Paces to*

Vera Miles and Van Johnson in *23 Paces to Baker Street*.

Baker Street (20th, 1956), *The Wrong Man* (WB, 1957), *Beau James* (Par., 1957), *The F.B.I. Story* (WB, 1959), *Web of Evidence* (AA, 1959), *A Touch of Larceny* (Par., 1960), *Five Branded Women* (Par., 1960), *Psycho* (Par., 1960), *Back Street* (Univ., 1961), *The Man Who Shot Liberty Valance* (Par., 1962), *A Tiger Walks* (BV, 1964), *Those Calloways* (BV, 1964), *Follow Me, Boys!* (BV, 1966), *The Spirit Is Willing* (Par., 1967), *Kona Coast* (WB-7 Arts, 1968), *Gentle Giant* (Par., 1967), *Sergeant Ryker* (WB, 1968).

RAY MILLAND (Reginald Truscott-Jones) Born January 3, 1907, Neath, Wales. Married Muriel Weber (1932), children: Daniel, Victoria.

Robert Preston, Gary Cooper and Ray Milland in *Beau Geste*.

Feature Films: *The Plaything* (British, 1930), *The Flying Scotsman* (British, 1930), *Bachelor Father* (WB, 1931), *Just a Gigolo* (MGM, 1931), *Bought* (WB, 1931), *Ambassador Bill* (Fox, 1931), *Blonde Crazy* (WB, 1931), *Polly of the Circus* (MGM, 1932), *The Man Who Played God* (WB, 1932), *Payment Deferred* (MGM, 1932), *This Is the Life* (British Lion, 1933), *Orders Is Orders* (Gaumont-British, 1933), *Bolero* (Par., 1934), *We're Not Dressing* (Par., 1934), *Many Happy Returns* (Par., 1934), *Menace* (Par., 1934), *Charlie Chan in London* (Fox, 1934), *The Gilded Lily* (Par., 1935), *One Hour Late* (Par., 1935), *Four Hours to Kill* (Par., 1935), *The Glass Key* (Par., 1935), *Alias Mary Dow* (Univ., 1935), *Next Time We Love* (Univ., 1936), *Return of Sophie Lang* (Par., 1936), *Big Broadcast of 1937* (Par., 1936), *The Jungle Prin-*

cess (Par., 1936), *Three Smart Girls* (Univ., 1937), *Wings Over Honolulu* (Univ., 1937), *Easy Living* (Par., 1937), *Ebb Tide* (Par., 1937), *Wise Girl* (RKO, 1937), *Bulldog Drummond Escapes* (Par., 1937), *Her Jungle Love* (Par., 1938), *Men With Wings* (Par., 1938), *Say it in French* (Par., 1938), *Hotel Imperial* (Par., 1939), *Beau Geste* (Par., 1939), *Everything Happens at Night* (20th, 1939), *French Without Tears* (Par., 1940), *Irene* (RKO, 1940), *The Doctor Takes a Wife* (Col., 1940), *Untamed* (Par., 1940), *Arise, My Love* (Par., 1941), *I Wanted Wings* (Par., 1941), *Skylark* (Par., 1941), *The Lady Has Plans* (Par., 1942), *Are Husbands Necessary?* (Par., 1942), *The Major and the Minor* (Par., 1942), *Reap the Wild Wind* (Par., 1942), *Star Spangled Rhythm* (Par., 1942), *Forever and a Day* (RKO, 1943), *The Crystal Ball* (UA, 1943), *The Uninvited* (Par., 1944), *Lady in the Dark* (Par., 1944), *Till We Meet Again* (Par., 1944), *Ministry of Fear* (Par., 1944), *The Lost Weekend* (Par., 1945), *Kitty* (Par., 1945), *The Well-Groomed Bride* (Par., 1946), *California* (Par., 1946), *The Imperfect Lady* (Par., 1947), *The Trouble With Women* (Par., 1947), *Golden Earrings* (Par., 1947), *Variety Girl* (Par., 1947), *The Big Clock* (Par., 1948), *So Evil My Love* (Par., 1948), *Sealed Verdict* (Par., 1948), *Alias Nick Beal* (Par., 1949), *It Happens Every Spring* (20th, 1949), *A Woman of Distinction* (Col., 1950), *A Life of Her Own* (MGM, 1950), *Copper Canyon* (Par., 1950), *Circle of Danger* (EL, 1951), *Night into Morning* (MGM, 1951), *Rhubarb* (Par., 1951), *Close to My Heart* (WB, 1951), *Bugles in the Afternoon* (WB, 1952), *Something to Live For* (Par., 1952), *The Thief* (UA, 1952), *Jamaica Run* (Par., 1953), *Let's Do it Again* (Col., 1953), *Dial M for Murder* (WB, 1954), *A Man Alone* (Rep., 1955), *The Girl in the Red Velvet Swing* (20th, 1955), *Lisbon* (Rep., 1956), *Three Brave Men* (20th, 1957), *The River's Edge* (20th, 1957), *The Safecracker* (MGM, 1958), *High Flight* (Col., 1958), *Premature Burial* (AIP, 1962), *Panic in Year Zero* (AIP, 1962), *"X" The Man with the X-Ray Eyes* (AIP, 1963).

ANN MILLER (Lucille Ann Collier) Born April 12, 1919, Chireno, Texas. Married Reese Milner (1946); divorced 1947. Married William Moss (1958); divorced 1961. Married Arthur Cameron (1961); annulled 1962.

John Hubbard, Ann Miller, Freddy Martin and his orchestra in *What's Buzzin' Cousin?*

Feature Films: *New Faces of 1937* (RKO, 1937), *Stage Door* (RKO, 1937), *Life of the Party* (RKO, 1937), *Radio City Revels* (RKO, 1938), *Room Service* (RKO, 1938), *You Can't Take It With You* (Col., 1938), *Tarnished Angel* (RKO, 1938), *Having Wonderful Time* (RKO, 1938), *Too Many Girls* (RKO, 1940), *The Hit Parade of 1941* (Rep., 1940), *Melody Ranch* (Rep., 1940), *Time Out for Rhythm* (Col., 1941), *Go West, Young Lady* (Col., 1941), *True to the Army* (Par., 1942), *Priorities on Parade* (Par., 1942), *Reveille With Beverly* (Col., 1943),

What's Buzzin', Cousin? (Col., 1943), *Jam Session* (Col., 1944), *Hey, Rookie* (Col., 1944), *Carolina Blues* (Col., 1944), *Eve Knew Her Apples* (Col., 1945), *Eadie Was a Lady* (Col., 1945), *Thrill of Brazil* (Col., 1946), *The Kissing Bandit* (MGM, 1948), *Easter Parade* (MGM, 1948), *On the Town* (MGM, 1949), *Watch the Birdie* (MGM, 1950), *Texas Carnival* (MGM, 1951), *Two Tickets to Broadway* (RKO, 1951), *Lovely To Look At* (MGM, 1952), *Kiss Me, Kate!* (MGM, 1953), *Small Town Girl* (MGM, 1953), *Deep in My Heart* (MGM, 1954), *Hit the Deck* (MGM, 1955), *The Opposite Sex* (MGM, 1956), *The Great American Pastime* (MGM, 1956).

HAYLEY MILLS (Hayley Catherine Rose Vivian Mills) Born April 18, 1946, London, England.

John Mills and Hayley Mills in *The Chalk Garden*.

Feature Films: *Tiger Bay* (Continental, 1959), *Pollyanna* (BV, 1960), *The Parent Trap* (BV, 1961), *Whistle Down the Wind* (Pathé-American, 1962), *In Search of the Castaways* (BV, 1962), *Summer Magic* (BV, 1963), *The Chalk Garden* (Univ., 1964), *The Moonspinners* (BV, 1964), *The Truth About Spring* (Univ., 1965), *That Darn Cat* (BV, 1965), *The Trouble With Angels* (Col., 1966), *The Daydreamer* (voice only; Embassy, 1966), *The Family Way* (WB, 1966), *Gypsy Girl* (Continental, 1967), *Pretty Polly* (Univ., 1968), *A Matter of Innocence* (Univ., 1968).

SAL MINEO (Salvadore Mineo) Born January 10, 1939, Bronx, New York.

Dolores Del Rio and Sal Mineo in *Cheyenne Autumn*.

Feature Films: *Six Bridges to Cross* (Univ., 1955), *The Private War of Major Benson* (Univ., 1955), *Rebel Without a Cause* (WB, 1955), *Crime in the Streets* (AA, 1956), *Somebody Up There Likes Me* (MGM,

1956), *Giant* (WB, 1956), *Rock, Pretty Baby* (Univ., 1956), *Dino* (AA, 1957), *The Young Don't Cry* (Col., 1957), *Tonka* (BV, 1958), *A Private's Affair* (20th, 1959), *The Gene Krupa Story* (Col., 1959), *Exodus* (UA, 1960), *Escape From Zahrain* (Par., 1962), *The Longest Day* (20th, 1962), *Cheyenne Autumn* (WB, 1964), *The Greatest Story Ever Told* (UA, 1965), *Who Killed Teddy Bear?* (Magna, 1966), *East of Java* (Cinerama, 1968).

CARMEN MIRANDA (Maria Do Carmo Miranda Da Cunha) Born February 9, 1914, Lisbon, Portugal. Married David Sebastian (1947). Died August 5, 1955.

John Payne and Carmen Miranda in *Week-End in Havana*.

English-Language Feature Films: *Down Argentine Way* (20th, 1940), *That Night in Rio* (20th, 1941), *Week-End in Havana* (20th, 1941), *Springtime in the Rockies* (20th, 1942), *The Gang's All Here* (20th, 1943), *Four Jills in a Jeep* (20th, 1944), *Greenwich Village* (20th, 1944), *Something for the Boys* (20th, 1944), *Doll Face* (20th, 1945), *If I'm Lucky* (20th, 1946), *Copacabana* (UA, 1947), *A Date With Judy* (MGM, 1948), *Nancy Goes to Rio* (MGM, 1950), *Scared Stiff* (Par., 1953).

THOMAS MITCHELL Born July 11, 1892, Elizabeth, New Jersey. Married, child: Anne. Died December 17, 1962.

Sound Feature Films: *Adventures in Manhattan* (Col., 1936), *Craig's Wife* (Col., 1936), *Theodora Goes Wild* (Col., 1936), *When You're in Love* (Col., 1937), *Man of the People* (MGM, 1937), *Lost Horizon* (Col., 1937), *I Promise to Pay* (Col., 1937), *Make Way For Tomorrow* (Par., 1937), *The Hurricane* (UA, 1937), *Love, Honor and Behave* (WB, 1938), *Trade Winds* (UA, 1938), *Stagecoach* (UA, 1939), *Only Angels Have Wings* (Col., 1939), *Mr. Smith Goes to Washington* (Col., 1939), *The Hunchback of Notre Dame* (RKO, 1939), *Gone With the Wind* (MGM, 1939), *Swiss Family Robinson* (RKO, 1940), *Three Cheers for the Irish* (WB, 1940), *Our Town* (UA, 1940), *The Long Voyage Home* (UA, 1940), *Angels Over Broadway* (Col., 1940), *Flight From Destiny* (WB, 1941), *Out of the Fog* (WB, 1941), *Joan of Paris* (RKO, 1942), *Song of the Islands* (20th, 1942), *Moontide* (20th, 1942), *This Above All* (20th, 1942), *Tales of Manhattan* (20th, 1942), *The Black Swan* (20th, 1942), *The Immortal Sergeant* (20th, 1943), *The Outlaw* (RKO, 1943), *Bataan* (MGM, 1943), *Flesh and Fantasy* (Univ., 1943), *The Sullivans* (20th, 1944), *Buffalo Bill* (20th, 1944), *Wilson* (20th, 1944), *Dark Waters* (UA, 1944), *Keys of the Kingdom* (20th, 1945), *Within These Walls* (20th, 1945), *Captain Eddie* (20th, 1945), *Adventure* (MGM, 1945), *Three Wise Fools* (MGM, 1946), *The Dark Mirror* (Univ., 1946), *High Barbaree* (MGM, 1947), *The Romance of Rosy Ridge* (MGM, 1947), *Silver River* (WB, 1948), *Alias Nick Beal* (Par., 1949), *The Big Wheel* (UA, 1949), *Journey into*

Roy Roberts and Thomas Mitchell in *Within These Walls*.

Light (20th, 1951), *High Noon* (UA, 1952), *Tumbleweed* (Univ., 1953), *Secret of the Incas* (Par., 1954), *Destry* (Univ., 1954), *While the City Sleeps* (RKO, 1956), *Handle With Care* (MGM, 1958), *Too Young to Love* (Go Pictures, 1961), *By Love Possessed* (UA, 1961), *Pocketful of Miracles* (UA, 1961).

ROBERT MITCHUM Born August 6, 1917, Bridgeport, Connecticut. Married Dorothy Spence (1940), children: James, Christopher, Petrine.

Robert Mitchum and Jane Greer in *Out of the Past*.

Feature Films: *Hoppy Serves a Writ* (UA, 1943), *The Leather Burners* (UA, 1943), *Border Patrol* (UA, 1943), *Follow the Band* (Univ., 1943), *Colt Comrades* (UA, 1943), *The Human Comedy* (MGM, 1943), *We've Never Been Licked* (Wanger-Univ., 1943), *Beyond the Last Frontier* (Rep., 1943), *Bar 20* (UA, 1943), *Doughboys in Ireland* (Col., 1943), *Corvette K-225* (Univ., 1943), *Aerial Gunner* (Par., 1943), *The Lone Star Trail* (Univ., 1943), *False Colors* (UA, 1943), *Dancing Masters* (20th, 1943), *Riders of the Deadline* (UA, 1943), *Cry Havoc* (MGM, 1943), *Gung Ho!* (Univ., 1943), *Johnny Doesn't Live Here Any More* (Mon., 1944), *When Strangers Marry* (Mon., 1944), *The Girl Rush* (RKO, 1944), *Thirty Seconds Over Tokyo* (MGM, 1944), *Nevada* (RKO, 1944), *West of the Pecos* (RKO, 1945), *The Story of G.I. Joe* (UA, 1945), *Till the End of Time* (RKO, 1946), *Undercurrent* (MGM, 1946), *The Locket* (RKO, 1946), *Pursued* (WB, 1947), *Crossfire* (RKO, 1947), *Desire Me* (MGM, 1947), *Out of the Past* (RKO,

1947), *Rachel and the Stranger* (RKO, 1948), *Blood on the Moon* (RKO, 1948), *The Red Pony* (Rep., 1949), *The Big Steal* (RKO, 1949), *Holiday Affair* (RKO, 1949), *Where Danger Lives* (RKO, 1950), *My Forbidden Past* (RKO, 1951), *His Kind of Woman* (RKO, 1951), *The Racket* (RKO, 1951), *Macao* (RKO, 1952), *One Minute to Zero* (RKO, 1952), *The Lusty Men* (RKO, 1952), *Angel Face* (RKO, 1952), *White Witch Doctor* (20th, 1953), *Second Chance* (RKO, 1953), *She Couldn't Say No* (RKO, 1954), *River of No Return* (20th, 1954), *Track of the Cat* (WB, 1954), *Not as a Stranger* (UA, 1955), *The Night of the Hunter* (UA, 1955), *Man With the Gun* (UA, 1955), *Foreign Intrigue* (UA, 1956), *Bandido* (UA, 1956), *Heaven Knows, Mr. Allison* (20th, 1957), *Fire Down Below* (Col., 1957), *The Enemy Below* (20th, 1957), *Thunder Road* (UA, 1958), *The Hunters* (20th, 1958), *The Angry Hills* (MGM, 1959), *The Wonderful Country* (UA, 1959), *Home From the Hill* (MGM, 1960), *The Night Fighters* (UA, 1960), *The Grass Is Greener* (Univ., 1960), *The Sundowners* (WB, 1960), *The Last Time I Saw Archie* (UA, 1961), *Cape Fear* (Univ., 1962), *The Longest Day* (20th, 1962), *Two for the Seesaw* (UA, 1962), *The List of Adrian Messenger* (Univ., 1963), *Rampage* (WB, 1963), *Man in the Middle* (20th, 1964), *What a Way To Go!* (20th, 1964), *Mr. Moses* (UA, 1965), *El Dorado* (Par., 1967), *Anzio* (Col., 1968), *Villa Rides* (Par., 1968).

MARILYN MONROE (Norma Jean Mortenson) Born June 1, 1926, Los Angeles, California. Married James Dougherty (1944); divorced 1946. Married Joe Di Maggio (1954); divorced 1954. Married Arthur Miller (1956); divorced 1961. Died August 5, 1962.

Yves Montand and Marilyn Monroe in *Let's Make Love*.

Feature Films: *Dangerous Years* (20th, 1947), *Ladies of the Chorus* (Col., 1948), *Love Happy* (UA, 1949), *A Ticket to Tomahawk* (20th, 1950), *The Asphalt Jungle* (MGM, 1950), *All About Eve* (20th, 1950), *Right Cross* (MGM, 1950), *The Fireball* (20th, 1950), *Hometown Story* (MGM, 1951), *As Young as You Feel* (20th, 1951), *Love Nest* (20th, 1951), *Let's Make It Legal* (20th, 1951), *Clash by Night* (RKO, 1952), *We're Not Married* (20th, 1952), *Don't Bother to Knock* (20th, 1952), *Monkey Business* (20th, 1952), *O. Henry's Full House* (20th, 1952), *Niagara* (20th, 1953), *Gentlemen Prefer Blondes* (20th, 1953), *How to Marry a Millionaire* (20th, 1953), *River of No Return* (20th, 1954), *There's No Business Like Show Business* (20th, 1954), *The Seven-Year Itch* (20th, 1955), *Bus Stop* (20th, 1956), *The Prince and the Showgirl* (WB, 1957), *Some Like It Hot* (UA, 1959), *Let's Make Love* (20th, 1960), *The Misfits* (UA, 1961).

RICARDO MONTALBAN Born November 25, 1920, Mexico City, Mexico. Married Georgiana Young (1944), children: Laura, Mark, Anita, Victor.

English-Language Feature Films: *Fiesta* (MGM, 1947), *On an Island With You* (MGM, 1948), *The Kissing Bandit* (MGM, 1948), *Neptune's Daughter* (MGM, 1949), *Border Incident* (MGM, 1949), *Battleground* (MGM, 1949), *Mystery Street* (MGM, 1950), *Right Cross* (MGM,

Cyd Charisse, Ricardo Montalban and Ann Miller in *The Kissing Bandit*.

1950), *Two Weeks With Love* (MGM, 1950), *Mark of the Renegade* (Univ., 1951), *Across the Wide Missouri* (MGM, 1951), *My Man and I* (MGM, 1952), *Sombrero* (MGM, 1953), *Latin Lovers* (MGM, 1953), *The Saracen Blade* (Col., 1954), *A Life in the Balance* (20th, 1955), *Three for Jamie Dawn* (AA, 1956), *Sayonara* (WB, 1957), *Let No Man Write My Epitaph* (Col., 1960), *Hemingway's Adventures of a Young Man* (20th, 1962), *The Reluctant Saint* (Davis-Royal Films International, 1962), *Love Is a Ball* (UA, 1963), *Cheyenne Autumn* (WB, 1964), *The Money Trap* (MGM, 1966), *Madame X* (Univ., 1966), *The Singing Nun* (MGM, 1966), *Sol Madrid* (MGM, 1968), *Blue* (Par., 1968).

MARIA MONTEZ (Maria Africa Vidal de Santo Silas) Born June 6, 1920, Barahona, Dominican Republic. Married Jean Pierre Aumont (1943), child: Maria Christina. Died September 7, 1951.

English-Language Feature Films: *Lucky Devils* (Univ., 1941), *The Invisible Woman* (Univ., 1941), *Boss of Bullion City* (Univ., 1941), *That Night in Rio* (20th, 1941), *Raiders of the Desert* (Univ., 1941), *Moonlight in Hawaii* (Univ., 1941), *South of Tahiti* (Univ., 1941), *Bombay*

Broderick Crawford, Maria Montez and Brian Donlevy in *South of Tahiti*.

Clipper (Univ., 1942), *Mystery of Marie Roget* (Univ., 1942), *Arabian Nights* (Univ., 1943), *Ali Baba and the Forty Thieves* (Univ., 1944), *Follow the Boys* (Univ., 1944), *Cobra Woman* (Univ., 1944), *Gypsy Wildcat* (Univ., 1944), *Bowery to Broadway* (Univ., 1944), *Sudan* (Univ., 1945), *Tangier* (Univ., 1946), *The Exile* (Univ., 1947), *Pirates of Monterey* (Univ., 1947), *Siren of Atlantis* (UA, 1948), *The Thief of Venice* (20th, 1952).

ROBERT MONTGOMERY (Henry Montgomery, Jr.) Born May 21, 1904, Beacon, New York. Married Elizabeth Allan (1928), children: Robert, Elizabeth; divorced 1950. Married Elizabeth Harkness (1950).

Robert Montgomery and Edward Arnold in *Earl of Chicago*.

Sound Feature Films: *So This Is College* (MGM, 1929), *Untamed* (MGM, 1929), *Three Live Ghosts* (MGM, 1929), *Single Standard* (MGM, 1929), *Their Own Desire* (MGM, 1930), *Free and Easy* (MGM, 1930), *The Divorcee* (MGM, 1930), *Big House* (MGM, 1930), *Our Blushing Brides* (MGM, 1930), *Sins of the Children* ("Richest Man in the World"—MGM, 1930), *Love in the Rough* (MGM, 1930), *War Nurse* (MGM, 1930), *The Easiest Way* (MGM, 1931), *Strangers May Kiss* (MGM, 1931), *Inspiration* (MGM, 1931), *Shipmates* (MGM, 1931), *Man in Possession* (MGM, 1931), *Private Lives* (MGM, 1931), *Lovers Courageous* (MGM, 1932), *But the Flesh Is Weak* (MGM, 1932), *Letty Lynton* (MGM, 1932), *Blondie of the Follies* (MGM, 1932), *Faithless* (MGM, 1932), *Hell Below* (MGM, 1933), *Made on Broadway* (MGM, 1933), *When Ladies Meet* (MGM, 1933), *Night Flight* (MGM, 1933), *Another Language* (MGM, 1933), *Fugitive Lovers* (MGM, 1934), *Riptide* (MGM, 1934), *Mystery of Mr. X* (MGM, 1934), *Hideout* (MGM, 1934), *Forsaking All Others* (MGM, 1935), *Vanessa, Her Love Story* (MGM, 1935), *Biography of a Bachelor Girl* (MGM, 1935), *No More Ladies* (MGM, 1935), *Petticoat Fever* (MGM, 1936), *Trouble for Two* (MGM, 1936), *Piccadilly Jim* (MGM, 1936), *The Last of Mrs. Cheyney* (MGM, 1937), *Night Must Fall* (MGM, 1937), *Ever Since Eve* (WB, 1937), *Live, Love and Learn* (MGM, 1937), *The First Hundred Years* (MGM, 1938), *Yellow Jack* (MGM, 1938), *Three Loves Has Nancy* (MGM, 1938), *Fast and Loose* (MGM, 1939), *The Earl of Chicago* (MGM, 1940), *Haunted Honeymoon* (MGM, 1940), *Rage in Heaven* (MGM, 1941), *Mr. and Mrs. Smith* (RKO, 1941), *Here Comes Mr. Jordan* (Col., 1941), *Unfinished Business* (Univ., 1941), *They Were Expendable* (MGM, 1945), *Lady in the Lake* (MGM, 1946), *Ride the Pink Horse* (Univ., 1947), *The Saxon Charm* (Univ., 1948), *The Secret Land* (narrator; MGM, 1948), *June Bride* (WB, 1948), *Once More, My Darling* (Univ., 1949), *Eye Witness* (EL, 1950).

IDA MOORE Born 1883, Altoona, Kansas.

Feature Films: *The Ghost That Walks Alone* (Col., 1944), *She's a Soldier, Too* (Col., 1944), *Riders of the Santa Fe* (Univ., 1944), *The Uninvited* (Par., 1944), *The Soul of a Monster* (Col., 1944), *Once Upon*

137

Barry Fitzgerald and Ida Moore in *Easy Come, Easy Go*.

a Time (Col., 1944), *Reckless Age* (Univ., 1944), *Rough, Tough and Ready* (Col., 1945), *Easy to Look At* (Univ., 1945), *Her Lucky Night* (Univ., 1945), *She Wouldn't Say Yes* (Col., 1945), *Girls of the Big House* (Rep., 1945), *From This Day Forward* (RKO, 1946), *To Each His Own* (Par., 1946), *The Bride Wore Boots* (Par., 1946), *The Dark Mirror* (Univ., 1946), *Cross My Heart* (Par., 1946), *The Show-Off* (MGM, 1946), *Talk About a Lady* (Col., 1946), *It's a Joke, Son* (EL, 1947), *Easy Come, Easy Go* (Par., 1947), *The Egg and I* (Univ., 1947), *Money Madness* (Film Classics, 1948), *Johnny Belinda* (WB, 1948), *Rusty Leads the Way* (Col., 1948), *Good Sam* (RKO, 1948), *Return of the Bad Men* (RKO, 1948), *Ma and Pa Kettle* (Univ., 1949), *Hold That Baby* (Mon., 1949), *Manhattan Angel* (Col., 1949), *Leave It to Henry* (Mon., 1949), *Dear Wife* (Par., 1949), *Roseanna McCoy* (RKO, 1949), *Rope of Sand* (Par., 1949), *The Sun Comes Up* (MGM, 1949), *Let's Dance* (Par., 1950), *Paid in Full* (Par., 1950), *Backfire* (WB, 1950), *Mr. Music* (Par., 1950), *Fancy Pants* (Par., 1950), *Harvey* (Univ., 1950), *Mother Didn't Tell Me* (20th, 1950), *Honeychile* (Rep., 1951), *Double Dynamite* (RKO, 1951), *The Lemon Drop Kid* (Par., 1951), *Comin' 'Round the Mountain* (Univ., 1951), *Leave It to the Marines* (Lip., 1951), *Showboat* (MGM, 1951), *Scandal Sheet* (Col., 1952), *The First Time* (Col., 1952), *Rainbow 'Round My Shoulder* (Col., 1952), *Carson City* (WB, 1952), *Just This Once* (MGM, 1952), *Something to Live For* (Par., 1952), *A Slight Case of Larceny* (MGM, 1953), *Scandal at Scourie* (MGM, 1953), *The Country Girl* (Par., 1954), *The Long, Long Trailer* (MGM, 1954), *Ma and Pa Kettle at Waikiki* (Univ., 1955), *Desk Set* (20th, 1957), *Rock-a-Bye Baby* (Par., 1958).

TERRY MOORE (Helen Koford) Born January 7, 1929, Los Angeles, California. Married Glenn Davis (1951); divorced 1952. Married Eugene McGrath (1956); divorced 1958. Married Stuart Cramer (1959), children: Stuart, Grant.

Feature Films:
    as Helen Koford *Maryland* (20th, 1940), *The Howards of Virginia* (Col., 1940), *On the Sunny Side* (20th, 1942), *Sweet and Lowdown* (20th,

Terry Moore, Mickey Rooney and Ned Glass in *He's a Cockeyed Wonder*.

1944), *Since You Went Away* (UA, 1944), *Son of Lassie* (MGM, 1945), *Shadowed* (Col., 1946), *Summer Holiday* (MGM, 1948).
    as Judy Ford *My Gal Sal* (20th, 1942), *True to Life* (Par., 1943), *Gaslight* (MGM, 1944).
    as Jan Ford *The Devil on Wheels* (PRC, 1947).
    as Terry Moore *The Return of October* (Col., 1948), *Mighty Joe Young* (RKO, 1949), *The Great Rupert* (EL, 1950), *He's a Cockeyed Wonder* (Col., 1950), *Gambling House* (RKO, 1950), *Two of a Kind* (Col., 1951), *On the Sunny Side of the Street* (Col., 1951), *The Barefoot Mailman* (Col., 1951), *Come Back, Little Sheba* (Par., 1952), *Man on a Tightrope* (20th, 1953), *Beneath the 12-Mile Reef* (20th, 1953), *King of the Khyber Rifles* (20th, 1953), *Daddy Long Legs* (20th, 1955), *Shack-Out on 101* (AA, 1955), *Postmark for Danger* (RKO, 1956), *Between Heaven and Hell* (20th, 1956), *Bernardine* (20th, 1957), *Peyton Place* (20th, 1957), *A Private Affair* (20th, 1959), *Cast a Long Shadow* (UA, 1959), *Platinum High School* (MGM, 1960), *Why Must I Die?* (AIP, 1960), *Black Spurs* (Par., 1965), *Town Tamer* (Par., 1965), *City of Fear* (AA, 1965), *Waco* (Par., 1966), *A Man Called Dagger* (MGM, 1968).

AGNES MOOREHEAD (Agnes Robertson Moorehead) Born December 6, 1906, Clinton, Massachusetts. Married John Lee (1930), child: Sean; divorced 1952. Married Robert Gist (1953); divorced 1958.

Eleanor Parker and Agnes Moorehead in *Caged*.

Feature Films: *Citizen Kane* (RKO, 1941), *The Magnificent Ambersons* (RKO, 1942), *Journey into Fear* (RKO, 1942), *The Big Street* (RKO, 1942), *The Youngest Profession* (MGM, 1943), *Government Girl* (RKO, 1943), *Jane Eyre* (20th, 1944), *Since You Went Away* (UA, 1944), *Dragon Seed* (MGM, 1944), *The Seventh Cross* (MGM, 1944), *Mrs. Parkington* (MGM, 1944), *Tomorrow the World* (UA, 1944), *Keep Your Powder Dry* (MGM, 1945), *Our Vines Have Tender Grapes* (MGM, 1945), *Her Highness and the Bellboy* (MGM, 1945), *The Beginning or the End* (MGM, 1947) (Her scenes were deleted from release print.), *Dark Passage* (WB, 1947), *The Lost Moment* (Univ., 1947), *Summer Holiday* (MGM, 1948), *The Woman in White* (WB, 1948), *Stations West* (RKO, 1948), *Johnny Belinda* (WB, 1948), *The Stratton Story* (MGM, 1949), *The Great Sinner* (MGM, 1949), *Without Honor* (UA, 1949), *Caged* (WB, 1950), *Fourteen Hours* (20th, 1951), *Show Boat* (MGM, 1951), *The Blue Veil* (RKO, 1951), *The Adventures of Captain Fabian* (Rep., 1951), *Captain Black Jack* (Classic, 1952), *The Blazing Forest* (Par., 1952), *The Story of Three Loves* (MGM, 1953), *Scandal at Scourie* (MGM, 1953), *Main Street to Broadway* (MGM, 1953), *Those Redheads From Seattle* (Par., 1953), *Magnificent Obsession* (Univ., 1954), *Untamed* (20th, 1955), *The Left Hand of God* (20th, 1955), *All That Heaven Allows* (Univ., 1956), *Meet Me in Las Vegas* (MGM, 1956), *The Conqueror* (RKO, 1956), *The Revolt of Mamie Stover* (20th, 1956), *The Swan* (MGM, 1956), *Pardners* (Par., 1956), *The Opposite Sex* (MGM, 1956), *Raintree County* (MGM, 1957), *The True Story of Jesse James* (20th, 1957), *Jeanne Eagels* (Col., 1957), *The Story of Mankind* (WB, 1957), *Night of the Quarter Moon* (MGM, 1959), *The Tempest* (Par., 1959), *The Bat* (AA, 1959), *Pollyanna* (BV, 1960), *Twenty Plus Two* (AA, 1961), *Bachelor in Paradise* (MGM,

1961), *Jessica* (UA, 1962), *How the West Was Won* (MGM, 1963), *Who's Minding the Store?* (Par., 1963), *Hush . . . Hush, Sweet Charlotte* (20th, 1964), *The Singing Nun* (MGM, 1966).

MANTAN MORELAND

Louis Armstrong, Rex Ingram and Mantan Moreland in *Cabin in the Sky*.

Feature Films: *Spirit of Youth* (GN, 1937), *Next Time I Marry* (RKO, 1938), *Frontier Scout* (GN, 1938), *There's That Woman Again* (Col., 1938) *Irish Luck* (Mon., 1939), *Tell No Tales* (MGM, 1939), *One Dark Night* (Sack Amusements, 1939), *Riders of the Frontier* (Mon., 1939), *Millionaire Playboy* (RKO, 1940), *Chasing Trouble* (Mon., 1940), *Pier 13* (20th, 1940), *The City of Chance* (20th, 1940), *The Man Who Wouldn't Talk* (20th, 1940), *Star Dust* (20th, 1940), *Maryland* (20th, 1940), *Viva Cisco Kid* (20th, 1940), *On the Spot* (Mon., 1940), *Laughing at Danger* (Mon., 1940), *Drums of the Desert* (Mon., 1940), *Ellery Queen's Penthouse Mystery* (Col., 1941), *Cracked Nuts* (Univ., 1941), *Up in the Air* (Mon., 1941), *King of the Zombies* (Mon., 1941), *The Gang's All Here* (Mon., 1941), *Hello Sucker* (Univ., 1941), *Dressed to Kill* (20th, 1941), *Four Jacks and a Jill* (RKO, 1941), *Footlight Fever* (RKO, 1941), *You're Out of Luck* (Mon., 1941), *Sign of the Wolf* (Mon., 1941), *Let's Go Collegiate* (Mon., 1941), *Sleepers West* (20th, 1941), *Marry the Boss's Daughter* (20th, 1941), *World Premiere* (Par., 1941), *Professor Creeps* (Dixie National, 1942), *Andy Hardy's Double Life* (MGM, 1942), *Strange Case of Dr. RX* (Univ., 1942), *Treat 'Em Rough* (Univ., 1942), *Mexican Spitfire Sees a Ghost* (RKO, 1942), *The Palm Beach Story* (Par., 1942), *Footlight Serenade* (20th, 1942), *Phantom Killer* (Mon., 1942), *Eyes in the Night* (MGM, 1942), *Girl Trouble* (20th, 1942), *Tarzan's New York Adventure* (MGM, 1942), *Hit the Ice* (Univ., 1943), *Cabin in the Sky* (MGM, 1943), *Cosmo Jones—Crime Smasher* (Mon., 1943), *Sarong Girl* (Mon., 1943), *Revenge of the Zombies* (Mon., 1943), *Melody Parade* (Mon., 1943), *She's for Me* (Univ., 1943), *My Kingdom for a Cook* (Col., 1943), *Slightly Dangerous* (MGM, 1943), *Swing Fever* (MGM, 1943), *You're a Lucky Fellow, Mr. Smith* (Univ., 1943), *We've Never Been Licked* (Univ., 1943), *This Is the Life* (Univ., 1944), *The Mystery of the River Boat* (Univ. serial, 1944), *The Chinese Cat* (Mon., 1944), *Moon Over Las Vegas* (Univ., 1944), *Chip off the Old Block* (Univ., 1944), *Pin-Up Girl* (20th, 1944), *South of Dixie* (Univ., 1944), *Black Magic* (Mon., 1944), *Bowery to Broadway* (Univ., 1944), *Charlie Chan in the Secret Service* (Mon., 1944), *See Here, Private Hargrove* (MGM, 1944), *She Wouldn't Say Yes* (Col., 1945), *The Scarlet Clue* (Mon., 1945), *The Jade Mask* (Mon., 1945), *The Shanghai Cobra* (Mon., 1945), *The Spider* (20th, 1945), *Captain Tugboat Annie* (Rep., 1945), *Mantan Messes Up* (Toddy Pictures, 1946), *Mantan Runs For Mayor* (Toddy Pictures, 1946), *Dark Alibi* (Mon., 1946), *Shadows Over Chinatown* (Mon., 1946), *The Trap* (Mon., 1947), *The Chinese Ring* (Mon., 1947), *Docks of New Orleans* (Mon., 1948), *The Mystery of the Golden Eye*

(Mon., 1948), *The Feathered Serpent* (Mon., 1948), *The Shanghai Chest* (Mon., 1948), *Best Man Wins* (Col., 1948), *Sky Dragon* (Mon., 1949), *Rockin' the Blues* (Fritz Pollard Assoc., 1956), *Rock 'n' Roll Revue* (Studio Films, 1956), *Rock 'n' Roll Jamboree* (Studio Films, 1957), *Enter Laughing* (Col., 1967).

RITA MORENO (Rosita Dolores Alverio) Born December 11, 1931, Humacao, Puerto Rico. Married Leonard Gordon (1965), child: Fernanda.

J. Carroll Naish, Mario Lanza and Rita Moreno in *Toast of New Orleans*.

Feature Films:
   as Rosita Moreno *So Young, So Bad* (UA, 1950).
   as Rita Moreno *Toast of New Orleans* (MGM, 1950), *Pagan Love Song* (MGM, 1950), *The Fabulous Señorita* (Rep., 1952), *Singin' in the Rain* (MGM, 1952), *The Ring* (UA, 1952), *Cattle Town* (WB, 1952), *Ma and Pa Kettle on Vacation* (Univ., 1953), *Latin Lovers* (MGM, 1953), *Fort Vengeance* (AA, 1953), *El Alamein* (Col., 1953), *Jivaro* (Par., 1954), *The Yellow Tomahawk* (UA, 1954), *Garden of Evil* (20th, 1954), *Untamed* (20th, 1955), *Seven Cities of Gold* (20th, 1955), *The Lieutenant Wore Skirts* (20th, 1956), *The King and I* (MGM, 1956), *The Vagabond King* (Par., 1956), *The Deerslayer* (20th, 1957), *This Rebel Breed* (WB, 1960), *Summer and Smoke* (Par., 1961), *West Side Story* (UA, 1961), *Samar* (WB, 1962), *Cry of Battle* (AA, 1963), *The Night of the Following Day* (Univ., 1968).

DENNIS MORGAN (Stanley Morner) Born December 30, 1910, Prentice, Wisconsin. Married Lillian Vedder (1933), children: Stanley, Kristine, James.

Alan Hale, Jr., Don De Fore, Dennis Morgan and Ben Blue in *One Sunday Afternoon*.

Feature Films:

as Stanley Morner *I Conquer the Sea* (Academy Pictures, 1936), *Suzy* (MGM, 1936), *The Great Ziegfeld* (MGM, 1936), *Piccadilly Jim* (MGM, 1936), *Down the Stretch* (WB, 1936), *Old Hutch* (MGM, 1936), *Song of the City* (MGM, 1937), *Mama Steps Out* (MGM, 1937), *Navy Blue and Gold* (MGM, 1937), *Persons in Hiding* (Par., 1938), *Men With Wings* (Par., 1938), *King of Alcatraz* (Par., 1938).

as Dennis Morgan *Waterfront* (WB, 1939), *Return of Dr. X* (WB, 1939), *No Place to Go* (WB, 1939), *Three Cheers for the Irish* (WB, 1940), *The Fighting 69th* (WB, 1940), *Tear Gas Squad* (WB, 1940), *Flight Angels* (WB, 1940), *River's End* (WB, 1940), *Kitty Foyle* (RKO, 1940), *Affectionately Yours* (WB, 1941), *Bad Men of Missouri* (WB, 1941), *Captains of the Clouds* (WB, 1942), *In This Our Life* (WB, 1942), *Wings for the Eagle* (WB, 1942), *The Hard Way* (WB, 1942), *Thank Your Lucky Stars* (WB, 1943), *The Desert Song* (WB, 1943), *The Very Thought of You* (WB, 1944), *Hollywood Canteen* (WB, 1944), *Shine on Harvest Moon* (WB, 1944), *God Is My Co-Pilot* (WB, 1945), *Christmas in Connecticut* (WB, 1945), *One More Tomorrow* (WB, 1946), *Two Guys From Milwaukee* (WB, 1946), *The Time, the Place and the Girl* (WB, 1946), *Cheyenne* (WB, 1947), *My Wild Irish Rose* (WB, 1947), *Always Together* (WB, 1947),* *To the Victor* (WB, 1948), *Two Guys From Texas* (WB, 1948), *One Sunday Afternoon* (WB, 1948), *It's a Great Feeling* (WB, 1949), *The Lady Takes a Sailor* (WB, 1949), *Perfect Strangers* (WB, 1950), *Pretty Baby* (WB, 1950), *Raton Pass* (WB, 1951), *Painting the Clouds With Sunshine* (WB, 1951), *This Woman Is Dangerous* (WB, 1952), *Cattle Town* (WB, 1952), *The Nebraskan* (Col., 1953), *Pearl of the South Pacific* (RKO, 1955), *The Gun That Won the West* (Col., 1955), *Uranium Boom* (Col., 1956), *Rogue's Gallery* (Par., 1968).

*Unbilled guest appearance

FRANK MORGAN (Francis Philip Wuppermann) Born June 1, 1890, New York, New York. Married Alma Muller (1914). Died September 18, 1949.

Billie Burke, Cora Witherspoon and Frank Morgan in *Piccadilly Jim*.

Sound Feature Films: *Queen High* (Par., 1930), *Dangerous Nan McGrew* (Par., 1930), *Fast and Loose* (Par., 1930), *Laughter* (Par., 1930), *Secrets of the French Police* (RKO, 1932), *The Half-Naked Truth* (RKO, 1932), *Hallelujah, I'm a Bum* (UA, 1933), *Luxury Liner* (Par., 1933), *Billion Dollar Scandal* (Par., 1933), *Sailor's Luck* (Fox, 1933), *Reunion in Vienna* (MGM, 1933), *When Ladies Meet* (MGM, 1933), *Kiss Before the Mirror* (Univ., 1933), *The Nuisance* (MGM, 1933), *Best of Enemies* (Fox, 1933), *Broadway to Hollywood* (MGM, 1933), *Bombshell* (MGM, 1933), *The Cat and the Fiddle* (MGM, 1933), *Sisters Under the Skin* (Col., 1934), *Affairs of Cellini* (UA, 1934), *Success at Any Price* (RKO, 1934), *A Lost Lady* (WB, 1934), *There's Always Tomorrow* (Univ., 1934), *Naughty Marietta* (MGM, 1935), *Good Fairy* (Univ., 1935), *Enchanted April* (RKO, 1935), *Escapade* (MGM, 1935), *The Perfect Gentleman* (MGM, 1935), *I Live My Life*

(MGM, 1935), *The Great Ziegfeld* (MGM, 1936), *The Dancing Pirate* (RKO, 1936), *Trouble for Two* (MGM, 1936), *Piccadilly Jim* (MGM, 1936), *Dimples* (20th, 1936), *The Last of Mrs. Cheyney* (MGM, 1937), *The Emperor's Candlesticks* (MGM, 1937), *Saratoga* (MGM, 1937), *Beg, Borrow or Steal* (MGM, 1937), *Rosalie* (MGM, 1937), *Paradise for Three* (MGM, 1938), *The Crowd Roars* (MGM, 1938), *Port of Seven Seas* (MGM, 1938), *Sweethearts* (MGM, 1938), *Broadway Serenade* (MGM, 1939), *The Wizard of Oz* (MGM, 1939), *Balalaika* (MGM, 1939), *The Shop Around the Corner* (MGM, 1940), *Broadway Melody of 1940* (MGM, 1940), *Henry Goes Arizona* (MGM, 1940), *The Mortal Storm* (MGM, 1940), *Boom Town* (MGM, 1940), *Hullabaloo* (MGM, 1940), *The Ghost Comes Home* (MGM, 1940), *Honky Tonk* (MGM, 1941), *The Vanishing Virginian* (MGM, 1941), *Washington Melodrama* (MGM, 1941), *Wild Man of Borneo* (MGM, 1941), *Tortilla Flat* (MGM, 1942), *White Cargo* (MGM, 1942), *A Stranger in Town* (MGM, 1943), *The Human Comedy* (MGM, 1943), *Thousands Cheer* (MGM, 1943), *The Miracle of Morgan's Creek* (Par., 1944), *The White Cliffs of Dover* (MGM, 1944), *Hail the Conquering Hero* (Par., 1944), *Casanova Brown* (RKO, 1944), *Yolanda and the Thief* (MGM, 1945), *Pardon My Past* (Col., 1946), *Courage of Lassie* (MGM, 1946), *Lady Luck* (RKO, 1946), *The Cockeyed Miracle* (MGM, 1946), *Green Dolphin Street* (MGM, 1947), *Summer Holiday* (MGM, 1948), *The Three Musketeers* (MGM, 1948), *The Stratton Story* (MGM, 1949), *Any Number Can Play* (MGM, 1949), *The Great Sinner* (MGM, 1949), *Key to the City* (MGM, 1950).

RALPH MORGAN (Raphael Kuhner Wuppermann) Born July 6, 1883, New York, New York. Married Grace Arnold, child: Claudia; widowed. Died June 11, 1956.

Patricia Morison, Alan Curtin and Ralph Morgan in *Hitler's Madman*.

Sound Feature Films: *Honor Among Lovers* (Par., 1931), *Cheaters at Play* (Fox, 1932), *Charlie Chan's Chance* (Fox, 1932), *Dance Team* (Fox, 1932), *Disorderly Conduct* (Fox, 1932), *Devil's Lottery* (Fox, 1932), *Strange Interlude* (MGM, 1932), *Rasputin and the Empress* (MGM, 1932), *The Son-Daughter* (MGM, 1932), *Humanity* (Fox, 1933), *Trick for Trick* (Fox, 1933), *Shanghai Madness* (Fox, 1933), *Power and the Glory* (Fox, 1933), *Doctor Bull* (Fox, 1933), *Walls of Gold* (Fox, 1933), *Kennel Murder Case* (WB, 1933), *Mad Game* (Fox, 1933), *Orient Express* (Fox, 1934), *No Greater Glory* (Col., 1934), *Stand Up and Cheer* (Fox, 1934), *She Was a Lady* (Fox, 1934), *Their Big Moment* (RKO, 1934), *Girl of the Limberlost* (Mon., 1934), *Hell in the Heavens* (Fox, 1934), *Transatlantic Merry-Go-Round* (UA, 1934), *Little Men* (Mascot, 1934), *I've Been Around* (Univ., 1935), *Unwelcome Stranger* (Col., 1935), *Star of Midnight* (RKO, 1935), *Calm Yourself* (MGM, 1935), *Condemned to Live* (Chesterfield, 1935), *The Magnificent Obsession* (Univ., 1935), *Muss 'Em Up* (RKO, 1936), *Little Miss Nobody* (20th, 1936), *Human Cargo* (20th, 1936), *The Ex-Mrs. Bradford* (RKO, 1936), *Anthony Adverse* (WB, 1936), *Speed* (MGM, 1936), *Yellowstone* (Univ., 1936), *General Spanky* (MGM, 1936), *Crack-Up* (20th, 1936), *The Man in Blue* (Univ., 1937), *The Life of Emile Zola* (WB, 1937), *Behind Prison*

Bars (Mon., 1937), *Mannequin* (MGM, 1937), *Wells Fargo* (Par., 1937), *Love Is a Headache* (MGM, 1938), *That's My Story* (Univ., 1938), *Wives Under Suspicion* (Univ., 1938), *Army Girl* (Rep., 1938), *Mother Carey's Chickens* (RKO, 1938), *Barefoot Boy* (Mon., 1938), *Shadows Over Shanghai* (GN, 1938), *Orphans of the Street* (Rep., 1938), *Out West With the Hardys* (MGM, 1938), *Trapped in the Sky* (Col., 1939), *Fast and Loose* (MGM, 1939), *The Lone Wolf Spy Hunt* (Col., 1939), *Man of Conquest* (Rep., 1939), *Smuggled Cargo* (Rep., 1939), *Way Down South* (RKO, 1939), *Geronimo* (Par., 1939), *Forty Little Mothers* (RKO, 1940), *I'm Still Alive* (RKO, 1940), *Dick Tracy vs. Crime Inc.*, (Rep. serial, 1941), *Adventure in Washington* (Col., 1941), *Gang Busters* (Univ. serial, 1942), *The Mad Doctor* (Par., 1941), *Klondike Fury* (Mon., 1942), *Night Monster* (Univ., 1942), *The Traitor Within* (Rep., 1942), *Stage Door Canteen* (UA, 1943), *Hitler's Madman* (MGM, 1943), *Jack London* (UA, 1943), *Great Alaskan Mystery* (Univ. serial, 1944), *Weird Woman* (Univ., 1944), *Trocadero* (Rep., 1944), *Enemy of Women* (Mon., 1944), *The Impostor* (Univ., 1944), *The Monster Maker* (PRC, 1944), *The Monster and the Ape* (Col. serial, 1945), *This Love of Ours* (Univ., 1945), *Black Market Babies* (Mon., 1945), *Hollywood and Vine* (PRC, 1945), *Mr. District Attorney* (Col., 1947), *Song of the Thin Man* (MGM, 1947), *The Last Round-Up* (Col., 1947), *Sleep, My Love* (UA, 1948), *Sword of the Avenger* (EL, 1948), *Heart of the Rockies* (Rep., 1951), *Gold Fever* (Mon., 1952).

CHESTER MORRIS (John Chester Brooks Morris) Born February 16, 1901, New York, New York. Married Suzanne Kilborn (1927), children: Brooks, Cynthia; divorced 1938. Married Lillian Barker (1940).

Claire Rochelle and Chester Morris (right) in *Double Exposure.*

Sound Feature Films: *Alibi* (Univ., 1929), *Fast Life* (WB, 1929), *Woman Trap* (Par., 1929), *Show of Shows* (WB, 1929), *She Couldn't Say No* (WB, 1930), *Second Choice* (WB, 1930), *The Case of Sergeant Grischa* (RKO, 1930), *Playing Around* (WB, 1930), *The Divorcee* (MGM, 1930), *Big House* (MGM, 1930), *Bat Whispers* (UA, 1931), *Corsair* (UA, 1931), *The Miracle Man* (Par., 1932), *Cock of the Air* (UA, 1932), *Sinners in the Sun* (Par., 1932), *Red-Headed Woman* (MGM, 1932), *Breach of Promise* (Sono Art-World Wide, 1932), *Infernal Machine* (Fox, 1933), *Blondie Johnson* (WB, 1933), *Tomorrow at Seven* (RKO, 1933), *Golden Harvest* (Par., 1933), *King for a Night* (Univ., 1933), *Let's Talk it Over* (Univ., 1934), *Embarrassing Moments* (Univ., 1934), *The Gift of Gab* (Univ., 1934), *Gay Bride* (MGM, 1934), *I've Been Around* (Univ., 1935), *Public Hero Number One* (MGM, 1935), *Frankie and Johnnie* (RKO, 1935), *Society Doctor* (MGM, 1935), *Pursuit* (MGM, 1935), *Moonlight Murder* (MGM, 1936), *The Three Godfathers* (MGM, 1936), *Counterfeit* (Col., 1936), *They Met in a Taxi* (Col., 1936), *Devil's Playground* (Col., 1937), *I Promise to Pay* (Col., 1937), *Flight From Glory* (RKO, 1937), *Law of the Underworld* (RKO, 1938), *Sky Giant* (RKO, 1938), *Smashing the Rackets* (RKO, 1938), *Pacific Liner* (RKO, 1939), *Blind Alibi* (Col., 1939), *Five Came Back* (RKO, 1939), *Thunder*

Afloat (MGM, 1939), *The Marines Fly High* (RKO, 1940), *Wagons Westward* (Rep., 1940), *Girl From God's Country* (Rep., 1940), *No Hands on the Clock* (Par., 1941), *Confessions of Boston Blackie* (Col., 1941), *Meet Boston Blackie* (Col., 1941), *I Live on Danger* (Par., 1942), *Wrecking Crew* (Par., 1942), *Tornado* (Par., 1943), *The Chance of a Lifetime* (Col., 1943), *Aerial Gunner* (Par., 1943), *After Midnight With Boston Blackie* (Col., 1943), *High Explosive* (Par., 1943), *Gambler's Choice* (Par., 1944), *Secret Command* (Col., 1944), *One Mysterious Night* (Col., 1944), *Double Exposure* (Par., 1944), *Rough, Tough and Ready* (Col., 1945), *Boston Blackie Booked on Suspicion* (Col., 1945), *Boston Blackie's Rendezvous* (Col., 1945), *One Way to Love* (Col., 1946), *A Close Call for Boston Blackie* (Col., 1946), *The Phantom Thief* (Col., 1946), *Boston Blackie and the Law* (Col., 1946), *Blind Spot* (Col., 1947), *Trapped By Boston Blackie* (Col., 1948), *Boston Blackie's Chinese Venture* (Col., 1949), *Unchained* (WB, 1955).

WAYNE MORRIS (Bert de Wayne Morris) Born February 17, 1914, Oakland, California. Married Leonora Schinasi (1939), children: Bert, Patricia, Melinda; divorced 1940. Married Patricia O'Rourke (1942). Died September 14, 1959.

Ed Brophy, May Robson, Pat O'Brien, Joan Blondell and Wayne Morris in *The Kid From Kokomo.*

Feature Films: *China Clipper* (WB, 1936), *Here Comes Carter!* (WB, 1936), *King of Hockey* (WB, 1936), *Polo Joe* (WB, 1936), *Smart Blonde* (WB, 1936), *Once a Doctor* (WB, 1937), *Kid Galahad* (WB, 1937), *Submarine D-1* (WB, 1937), *Love, Honor and Behave* (WB, 1938), *The Kid Comes Back* (WB, 1938), *Men Are Such Fools* (WB, 1938), *Valley of the Giants* (WB, 1938), *Brother Rat* (WB, 1938), *The Kid From Kokomo* (WB, 1939), *The Return of Dr. X* (WB, 1939), *Brother Rat and a Baby* (WB, 1940), *Double Alibi* (WB, 1940), *An Angel From Texas* (WB, 1940), *Flight Angels* (WB, 1940), *Ladies Must Live* (WB, 1940), *The Quarterback* (Par., 1940), *Gambling on the High Seas* (WB, 1940), *Three Sons o' Guns* (WB, 1941), *I Wanted Wings* (Par., 1941), *Bad Men of Missouri* (WB, 1941), *The Smiling Ghost* (WB, 1941), *Deep Valley* (WB, 1947), *The Voice of the Turtle* (WB, 1947), *The Big Punch* (WB, 1948), *The Time of Your Life* (UA, 1948), *A Kiss in the Dark* (WB, 1949), *The Younger Brothers* (WB, 1949), *John Loves Mary* (WB, 1949), *The House Across the Street* (WB, 1949), *Task Force* (WB, 1949), *Johnny One-Eye* (UA, 1950), *The Tougher They Come* (Col., 1950), *Stage to Tucson* (Col., 1950), *Sierra Passage* (Mon., 1951), *The Big Gusher* (Col., 1951), *Yellow Fin* (Mon., 1951), *The Bushwhackers* (Realart, 1952), *Desert Pursuit* (Mon., 1952), *Arctic Flight* (Mon., 1952), *The Fighting Lawman* (AA, 1953), *The Marksman* (AA, 1953), *The Star of Texas* (AA, 1953), *Master Plan* (Astor, 1954), *Riding Shotgun* (WB, 1954), *The Desperado* (AA, 1954), *Two Guns and a Badge* (AA, 1954), *Port of Hell* (AA, 1954), *Lord of the Jungle* (AA, 1955), *The Green Buddha* (Rep., 1955), *Cross Channel* (Rep., 1955), *Lonesome Trail* (Lip., 1955), *Dynamiters* (Astor, 1956), *Paths of Glory* (UA, 1957), *Plunder Road* (20th, 1957), *The Crooked Sky* (Rank, 1959).

Paul Muni and John Sutton in *Hudson's Bay.*

PAUL MUNI (Muni Weisenfreund) Born September 22, 1895, Lwow (Lemberg) Poland. Married Bella Finkel (1921). Died August 25, 1967.

Feature Films: *The Valiant* (Fox, 1929), *Seven Faces* (Fox, 1929), *Scarface* (UA, 1932), *I Am a Fugitive From a Chain Gang* (WB, 1932), *The World Changes* (WB, 1933), *Hi Nellie* (WB, 1934), *Bordertown* (WB, 1935), *Black Fury* (WB, 1935), *Dr. Socrates* (WB, 1935), *The Story of Louis Pasteur* (WB, 1935), *The Good Earth* (MGM, 1937), *The Woman I Love* (RKO, 1937), *The Life of Emile Zola* (WB, 1937), *Juarez* (WB, 1939), *We Are Not Alone* (WB, 1939), *Hudson's Bay* (20th, 1940), *Commandos Strike at Dawn* (Col., 1942), *Stage Door Canteen* (UA, 1943), *A Song to Remember* (Col., 1945), *Counter-Attack* (Col., 1945), *Angel on My Shoulder* (UA, 1946), *Stranger on the Prowl* (UA, 1953), *The Last Angry Man* (Col., 1959).

AUDIE MURPHY Born June 20, 1924, Kingston, Texas. Married Wanda Hendrix (1949); divorced 1950. Married Pamela Archer (1951), children: Terry, James.

Hugh Corcoran and Audie Murphy in *No Name on the Bullet.*

Feature Films: *Beyond Glory* (Par., 1948), *Texas, Brooklyn and Heaven* (UA, 1948), *Bad Boy* (AA, 1949), *Sierra* (Univ., 1950), *The Kid From Texas* (Univ., 1950), *Kansas Raiders* (Univ., 1950), *The Red Badge of Courage* (MGM, 1951), *The Cimarron Kid* (Univ., 1951), *The Duel at Silver Creek* (Univ., 1952), *Gunsmoke* (Univ., 1953), *Column South* (Univ., 1953), *Tumbleweed* (Univ., 1953), *Ride Clear of Diablo* (Univ., 1954), *Drums Across the River* (Univ., 1954), *Destry* (Univ., 1954), *To Hell and Back* (Univ., 1955), *World in My Corner* (Univ., 1956), *Walk the Proud Land* (Univ., 1956), *The Guns of Fort Petticoat* (Col., 1957), *Joe Butterfly* (Univ., 1957), *Night Passage* (Univ., 1957), *The Quiet American* (UA, 1958), *Ride a Crooked Trail* (Univ., 1958), *The Gun Runners* (UA, 1958), *No Name on the Bullet* (Univ., 1959),

The Wild and the Innocent (Univ., 1959), *Cast a Long Shadow* (UA, 1959), *Hell Bent for Leather* (Univ., 1960), *The Unforgiven* (UA, 1960), *Seven Ways From Sundown* (Univ., 1960), *Posse From Hell* (Univ., 1961), *Battle at Bloody Beach* (20th, 1961), *Six Black Horses* (Univ., 1962), *Showdown* (Univ., 1963), *Gunfight at Comanche Creek* (AA, 1963), *The Quick Gun* (Col., 1964), *Bullet for a Badman* (Univ., 1964), *Apache Rifles* (20th, 1964), *Arizona Raiders* (Col., 1965), *Gunpoint* (Univ., 1966), *Trunk to Cairo* (AIP, 1966), *The Texican* (Col., 1966), *40 Guns to Apache Pass* (Col., 1967).

GEORGE MURPHY (George Lloyd Murphy) Born July 4, 1902, New Haven, Connecticut. Married Julie Johnson (1926), children: Dennis, Melissa.

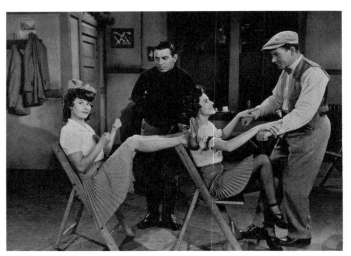

Joan Davis, Eddie Cantor, Constance and George Murphy in *Show Business.*

Feature Films: *Kid Millions* (UA, 1934), *Jealousy* (Col., 1934), *I'll Love You Always* (Col., 1935), *After the Dance* (Col., 1935), *Public Menace* (Col., 1935), *Woman Trap* (Par., 1936), *Top of the Town* (Univ., 1937), *Women Men Marry* (MGM, 1937), *London by Night* (MGM, 1937), *Broadway Melody of 1938* (MGM, 1937), *You're a Sweetheart* (Univ., 1937), *Little Miss Broadway* (20th, 1938), *Letter of Introduction* (Univ., 1938), *Hold That Co-ed* (Univ., 1938), *Risky Business* (Univ., 1939), *Broadway Melody of 1940* (MGM, 1940), *Two Girls on Broadway* (MGM, 1940), *Public Deb No. 1* (20th, 1940), *Little Nellie Kelly* (MGM, 1940), *A Girl, a Guy, and a Gob* (RKO, 1941), *Tom, Dick and Harry* (RKO, 1941), *Ringside Maisie* (MGM, 1941), *Rise and Shine* (20th, 1941), *The Mayor of 44th Street* (RKO, 1942), *For Me and My Gal* (MGM, 1942), *The Navy Comes Through* (RKO, 1942), *The Powers Girl* (UA, 1942), *Bataan* (MGM, 1943), *This Is the Army* (WB, 1943), *Broadway Rhythm* (MGM, 1944), *Show Business* (RKO, 1944), *Step Lively* (RKO, 1944), *Having Wonderful Crime* (RKO, 1945), *Up Goes Maisie* (MGM, 1946), *The Arnelo Affair* (MGM, 1947), *Cynthia* (MGM, 1947), *Tenth Avenue Angel* (MGM, 1948), *The Big City* (MGM, 1948), *Border Incident* (MGM, 1949), *Battleground* (MGM, 1949), *No Questions Asked* (MGM, 1951), *It's a Big Country* (MGM, 1951), *Walk East on Beacon* (Col., 1952), *Talk About a Stranger* (MGM, 1952).

DON MURRAY Born July 31, 1929, Hollywood, California. Married Hope Lange (1956), child: Christopher; divorced 1961. Married Betty Johnson (1962).

Feature Films: *Bus Stop* (20th, 1956), *The Bachelor Party* (UA, 1957), *A Hatful of Rain* (20th, 1957), *From Hell to Texas* (20th, 1958), *These Thousand Hills* (20th, 1959), *Shake Hands With the Devil* (UA, 1959), *One Foot in Hell* (20th, 1960), *The Hoodlum Priest* (UA, 1961), *Advise and Consent* (Col., 1962), *Escape From East Berlin* (MGM, 1962), *One Man's Way* (UA, 1964), *Baby, the Rain Must Fall* (Col., 1965), *Kid Rodelo* (Par., 1966), *The Plainsman* (Univ., 1966), *Sweet Love,*

Dr. Norman Vincent Peale and Don Murray in *One Man's Way.*

Bitter (Film 2 Associates, 1967), *The Viking Queen* (20th, 1967), *Tale of the Cock* (Sinners Co., 1967).

J. CARROLL NAISH (Joseph Patrick Carrol Naish) Born January 21, 1901, New York, New York. Married Gladys Hearney (1928), child: Elaine.

J. Carroll Naish and Leo Carrillo in *Moonlight Murder.*

Feature Films: *Good Intentions* (Fox, 1930), *Scotland Yard* (Fox, 1930), *Royal Bed* (RKO, 1931), *Gun Smoke* (Par., 1931), *Kick In* (Par., 1931), *Homicide Squad* (Univ., 1931), *Hatchet Man* (WB, 1932), *Beast of the City* (MGM, 1932), *Two Seconds* (WB, 1932), *It's Tough to Be Famous* (WB, 1932), *Famous Ferguson Case* (WB, 1932), *Crooner* (WB, 1932), *Tiger Shark* (WB, 1932), *No Living Witness* (Mayfair, 1932), *The Kid From Spain* (UA, 1932), *The Conquerors* (RKO, 1932), *Cabin in the Cotton* (WB, 1932), *Mystery Squadron* (Mascot serial, 1933), *No Other Woman* (RKO, 1933), *Frisco Jenny* (WB, 1933), *Infernal Machine* (Fox, 1933), *Central Airport* (WB, 1933), *World Gone Mad* (Majestic, 1933), *The Past of Mary Holmes* (RKO, 1933), *Elmer the Great* (WB, 1933), *The Avenger* (Mon., 1933), *Arizona to Broadway* (Fox, 1933), *The Devil's in Love* (Fox, 1933), *The Whirlwind* (Col., 1933), *Captured* (WB, 1933), *The Big Chance* (Arthur Greenblatt, 1933), *Notorious But Nice* (Chesterfield, 1933), *Last Trail* (Fox, 1933), *Mad Game* (Fox, 1933), *Silent Men* (Col., 1933), *Sleepers East* (Fox, 1934), *What's Your Racket?* (Mayfair-Shallenberger, 1934), *Murder in Trinidad* (Fox, 1934), *One Is Guilty* (Col., 1934), *Upper World* (WB, 1934), *Return of the Terror* (WB, 1934), *Hell Cat* (Col., 1934), *Girl in Danger* (Col., 1934), *The Defense Rests* (Col., 1934), *Hell in the Heavens* (Fox, 1934), *The President Vanishes* (Par., 1934), *Marie Galante* (Fox, 1934), *Lives of a Bengal Lancer* (Par., 1935), *Behind the Green Lights* (Mascot, 1935), *Black Fury* (WB, 1935), *Under the Pampas Moon* (Fox, 1935), *Little Big Shot* (WB, 1935), *Front Page Woman* (WB, 1935), *The Crusades* (Par., 1935), *Special Agent* (WB, 1935), *Confidential* (Mascot, 1935), *Captain Blood* (WB, 1935), *The Leather-*

necks Have Landed (Rep., 1936), *Moonlight Murder* (MGM, 1936), *The Return of Jimmy Valentine* (Rep., 1936), *Exclusive Story* (MGM, 1936), *Robin Hood of El Dorado* (MGM, 1936), *Two in the Dark* (RKO, 1936), *Absolute Quiet* (MGM, 1936), *Charlie Chan at the Circus* (20th, 1936), *Special Investigator* (RKO, 1936), *Anthony Adverse* (WB, 1936), *Ramona* (20th, 1936), *We Who Are About to Die* (RKO, 1936), *Charge of the Light Brigade* (WB, 1936), *Crack-Up* (20th, 1936), *Think Fast, Mr. Moto* (20th, 1937), *Song of the City* (MGM, 1937), *Border Cafe* (RKO, 1937), *Hideaway* (RKO, 1937), *Bulldog Drummond Comes Back* (Par., 1937), *Sea Racketeers* (Rep., 1937), *Thunder Trail* (Par., 1937), *Night Club Scandal* (Par., 1937), *Daughter of Shanghai* (Par., 1937), *Her Jungle Love* (Par., 1938), *Tip-Off Girls* (Par., 1938), *Hunted Men* (Par., 1938), *Prison Farm* (Par., 1938), *Bulldog Drummond in Africa* (Par., 1938), *Illegal Traffic* (Par., 1938), *King of Alcatraz* (Par., 1938), *Persons in Hiding* (Par., 1939), *Hotel Imperial* (Par., 1939), *Undercover Doctor* (Par., 1939), *Beau Geste* (Par., 1939), *Island of Lost Men* (Par., 1939), *Typhoon* (Par., 1940), *Queen of the Mob* (Par., 1940), *Golden Gloves* (Par., 1940), *Down Argentine Way* (20th, 1940), *A Night at Earl Carroll's* (Par., 1940), *Mr. Dynamite* (Univ., 1941), *That Night in Rio* (20th, 1941), *Blood and Sand* (20th, 1941), *Forced Landing* (Par., 1941), *Accent on Love* (20th, 1941), *Birth of the Blues* (Par., 1941), *The Corsican Brothers* (UA, 1941), *Sunday Punch* (MGM, 1942), *Dr. Broadway* (Par., 1942), *Jackass Mail* (MGM, 1942), *The Pied Piper* (20th, 1942), *Tales of Manhattan* (20th, 1942), *The Man in the Trunk* (20th, 1942), *Dr. Renault's Secret* (20th, 1942), *Batman* (Col. serial, 1943), *Harrigan's Kid* (MGM, 1943), *Good Morning, Judge* (Univ., 1943), *Behind the Rising Sun* (RKO, 1943), *Sahara* (Col., 1943), *Gung Ho!* (Univ., 1943), *Calling Dr. Death* (Univ., 1943), *Voice in the Wind* (UA, 1944), *The Monster Maker* (PRC, 1944), *Two-Man Submarine* (Col., 1944), *Waterfront* (PRC, 1944), *The Whistler* (Col., 1944), *Jungle Woman* (Univ., 1944), *Dragon Seed* (MGM, 1944), *Enter Arsene Lupin* (Univ., 1944), *A Medal for Benny* (Par., 1945), *The Southerner* (UA, 1945), *House of Frankenstein* (Univ., 1945), *Getting Gertie's Garter* (UA, 1945), *Strange Confession* (Univ., 1945), *Bad Bascomb* (MGM, 1946), *The Beast With Five Fingers* (WB, 1946), *Humoresque* (WB, 1946), *Carnival in Costa Rica* (20th, 1947), *The Fugitive* (RKO, 1947), *Joan of Arc* (RKO, 1948), *The Kissing Bandit* (MGM, 1948), *Canadian Pacific* (20th, 1949), *That Midnight Kiss* (MGM, 1949), *Black Hand* (MGM, 1950), *Please Believe Me* (MGM, 1950), *Annie Get Your Gun* (MGM, 1950), *The Toast of New Orleans* (MGM, 1950), *Rio Grande* (Rep., 1950), *Mark of the Renegade* (Univ., 1951), *Bannerline* (MGM, 1951), *Across the Wide Missouri* (MGM, 1951), *The Denver and Rio Grande* (Par., 1952), *Clash by Night* (RKO, 1952), *Woman of the North Country* (Rep., 1952), *Ride the Man Down* (Rep., 1952), *Beneath the 12-Mile Reef* (20th, 1953), *Fighter Attack* (AA, 1953), *Saskatchewan* (Univ., 1954), *Sitting Bull* (UA, 1954), *Hit the Deck* (MGM, 1955), *Rage at Dawn* (RKO, 1955), *Violent Saturday* (20th, 1955), *New York Confidential* (WB, 1955), *The Last Command* (Rep., 1955), *Desert Sands* (UA, 1955), *Rebel in Town* (UA, 1956), *Yaqui Drums* (AA, 1956), *This Could Be the Night* (MGM, 1957), *The Young Don't Cry* (Col., 1957).

MILDRED NATWICK Born June 19, 1908, Baltimore, Maryland.

Mildred Natwick and Shirley MacLaine in *The Trouble With Harry.*

Feature Films: *The Long Voyage Home* (UA, 1940), *The Enchanted Cottage* (RKO, 1945), *Yolanda and the Thief* (MGM, 1945), *The Late George Apley* (20th, 1947), *A Woman's Vengeance* (Univ., 1947), *Three Godfathers* (MGM, 1948), *The Kissing Bandit* (MGM, 1948), *She Wore a Yellow Ribbon* (RKO, 1949), *Cheaper by the Dozen* (20th, 1950), *The Quiet Man* (Rep., 1952), *Against All Flags* (Univ., 1952), *The Trouble With Harry* (Par., 1955), *The Court Jester* (Par., 1956), *Teenage Rebel* (20th, 1956), *Tammy and the Bachelor* (Univ., 1957), *Barefoot in the Park* (Par., 1967).

PATRICIA NEAL (Patricia Louise Neal) Born January 20, 1926, Packard, Kentucky. Married Roald Dahl (1953), children: Olivia, Tessa, Theo, Lucy, Ophelia.

Ruth Roman and Patricia Neal in *Three Secrets*.

English-Language Feature Films: *John Loves Mary* (WB, 1949), *The Fountainhead* (WB, 1949), *It's a Great Feeling* (WB, 1949), *The Hasty Heart* (WB, 1950), *Bright Leaf* (WB, 1950), *Three Secrets* (WB, 1950), *The Breaking Point* (WB, 1950), *Operation Pacific* (WB, 1951), *Raton Pass* (WB, 1951), *Diplomatic Courier* (20th, 1951), *The Day the Earth Stood Still* (20th, 1951), *Weekend With Father* (Univ., 1951), *Washington Story* (MGM, 1952), *Something for the Birds* (20th, 1952), *Stranger From Venus* ("Immediate Disaster"—Princess Pictures, 1954), *A Face in the Crowd* (WB, 1957), *Breakfast at Tiffany's* (Par., 1961), *Hud* (Par., 1963), *Psyche 59* (Col., 1964), *In Harm's Way* (Par., 1965), *The Subject Was Roses* (MGM, 1968).

PAUL NEWMAN Born January 26, 1925, Shaker Heights, Ohio. Married Jacqueline Witte (1947), children: Scott, Susan, Stephanie; divorced 1956. Married Joanne Woodward (1958), children: Eleanor, Tessa, Cleo.

Feature Films: *The Silver Chalice* (WB, 1954), *Somebody Up There*

Paul Newman, John Dierkes and Colin Keith-Johnston in *The Left-Handed Gun.*

Likes Me (MGM, 1956), *The Rack* (MGM, 1956), *Until They Sail* (MGM, 1957), *The Helen Morgan Story* (WB, 1957), *The Long, Hot Summer* (20th, 1958), *The Left-Handed Gun* (WB, 1958), *Rally Round the Flag, Boys!* (20th, 1958), *Cat on a Hot Tin Roof* (MGM, 1958), *The Young Philadelphians* (WB, 1959), *From the Terrace* (20th, 1960), *Exodus* (UA, 1960), *The Hustler* (20th, 1961), *Paris Blues* (UA, 1961), *Sweet Bird of Youth* (MGM, 1962), *Hemingway's Adventures of a Young Man* (20th, 1962), *Hud* (Par., 1963), *A New Kind of Love* (Par., 1963), *The Prize* (MGM, 1963), *What a Way to Go!* (20th, 1964), *The Outrage* (MGM, 1964), *Lady L* (MGM, 1965), *Torn Curtain* (Univ., 1966), *Harper* (WB, 1966), *Hombre* (20th, 1967), *Cool Hand Luke* (WB, 1967), *The Private War of Harry Frigg* (Univ., 1968).

DAVID NIVEN (James David Graham Niven) Born March 1, 1911, Kirriemuir, Scotland. Married Primula Rollo (1940), children: David, Jamie; widowed 1946. Married Hjordis Tersmedes (1948), children: Kristina, Fiona.

Arthur Treacher, Virginia Field and David Niven in *Thank You, Jeeves.*

English-Language Feature Films: *Without Regret* (Par., 1935), *A Feather in Her Hat* (Col., 1935), *Splendor* (UA, 1935), *Rose Marie* (MGM, 1936), *Thank You, Jeeves* (20th, 1936), *Palm Springs* (Par., 1936), *Charge of the Light Brigade* (WB, 1936), *Dodsworth* (UA, 1936), *Beloved Enemy* (UA, 1936), *We Have Our Moments* (Univ., 1937), *Dinner at the Ritz* (20th, 1937), *The Prisoner of Zenda* (UA, 1937), *Four Men and a Prayer* (20th, 1938), *Bluebeard's Eighth Wife* (Par., 1938), *Three Blind Mice* (20th, 1938), *The Dawn Patrol* (WB, 1938), *Wuthering Heights* (UA, 1939), *Bachelor Mother* (RKO, 1939), *The Real Glory* (UA, 1939), *Eternally Yours* (UA, 1939), *Raffles* (UA, 1940), *The First of the Few* ("Spitfire"—King, 1941), *The Way Ahead* ("Immortal Battalion"—Rank, 1944), *The Perfect Marriage* (Par., 1946), *The Magnificent Doll* (Univ., 1946), *A Matter of Life and Death* ("Stairway to Heaven"—Rank, 1946), *The Other Love* (UA, 1947), *The Bishop's Wife* (RKO, 1947), *Bonnie Prince Charlie* (Korda, 1947), *Enchantment* (RKO, 1948), *The Elusive Pimpernel* ("The Scarlet Pimpernel"—Carrol Pictures, 1948), *A Kiss in the Dark* (WB, 1949), *A Kiss for Corliss* (UA, 1949), *The Toast of New Orleans* (MGM, 1950), *Soldiers Three* (MGM, 1951), *Happy Go Lovely* (MGM, 1951), *The Lady Says No* (UA, 1951), *Island Rescue* (Univ., 1952), *The Moon is Blue* (UA, 1953), *Love Lottery* (Continental Distributing, 1954), *Tonight's the Night* (AA, 1954), *The King's Thief* (MGM, 1955), *Court-Martial* (Kingsley International, 1955), *The Birds and the Bees* (Par., 1956), *Around the World in 80 Days* (UA, 1956), *Oh, Men! Oh, Women!* (20th, 1957), *The Little Hut* (MGM, 1957), *My Man Godfrey* (Univ., 1957), *The Silken Affair* (DCA, 1957), *Bonjour Tristesse* (Col., 1958), *Separate Tables* (UA, 1958), *Ask Any Girl* (MGM, 1959), *Happy Anniversary* (UA, 1959), *Please Don't Eat the Daisies* (MGM, 1960), *The Guns of Navarone* (Col., 1961), *Guns of Darkness* (WB, 1962), *Road to Hong Kong* (UA, 1962),* *The Best of Enemies* (Col., 1962), *55 Days at Peking* (AA, 1963), *Pink Panther* (UA, 1964), *Bedtime Story* (Univ., 1964),

Where the Spies Are (MGM, 1965), *Lady L* (MGM, 1966), *Casino Royale* (Col., 1967), *Eye of the Devil* (MGM, 1967), *The Extraordinary Seaman* (MGM, 1968), *Prudence and the Pill* (20th, 1968), *The Impossible Years* (MGM, 1968).

*Unbilled guest appearance

LLOYD NOLAN Born August 11, 1903, San Francisco, California. Married Mel Efird (1933), children: Melinda, Jay.

Lloyd Nolan, Alexis Smith and Craig Stevens in *Steel Against the Sky*.

Feature Films: *Stolen Harmony* (Par., 1935), *G-Men* (WB, 1935), *Atlantic Adventure* (Col., 1935), *She Couldn't Take It* (Col., 1935), *One Way Ticket* (Col., 1935), *You May Be Next* (Col., 1936), *Lady of Secrets* (Col., 1936), *Big Brown Eyes* (Par., 1936), *Devil's Squadron* (Col., 1936), *Counterfeit* (Col., 1936), *The Texas Rangers* (Par., 1936), *15 Maiden Lane* (20th, 1936), *Internes Can't Take Money* (Par., 1937), *King of Gamblers* (Par., 1937), *Exclusive* (Par., 1937), *Ebb Tide* (Par., 1937), *Wells Fargo* (Par., 1937), *Every Day's a Holiday* (Par., 1937), *Dangerous to Know* (Par., 1938), *Tip-Off Girls* (Par., 1938), *Hunted Men* (Par., 1938), *Prison Farm* (Par., 1938), *King of Alcatraz* (Par., 1938), *St. Louis Blues* (Par., 1939), *Ambush* (Par., 1939), *Undercover Doctor* (Par., 1939), *The Magnificent Fraud* (Par., 1939), *The Man Who Wouldn't Talk* (20th, 1940), *The House Across the Bay* (UA, 1940), *Johnny Apollo* (20th, 1940), *Gangs of Chicago* (Rep., 1940), *The Man I Married* (20th, 1940), *Pier 13* (20th, 1940), *Golden Fleecing* (MGM, 1940), *Michael Shayne, Private Detective* (20th, 1940), *Charter Pilot* (20th, 1940), *Behind the News* (Rep., 1940), *Sleepers West* (20th, 1941), *Mr. Dynamite* (Univ., 1941), *Dressed to Kill* (20th, 1941), *Buy Me That Town* (Par., 1941), *Blues in the Night* (WB, 1941), *Steel Against the Sky* (WB, 1941), *Blue, White and Perfect* (20th, 1941), *It Happened in Flatbush* (20th, 1942), *Apache Trail* (MGM, 1942), *Just Off Broadway* (20th, 1942), *Manila Calling* (20th, 1942), *Time to Kill* (20th, 1942), *Bataan* (MGM, 1943), *Guadalcanal Diary* (20th, 1943), *A Tree Grows in Brooklyn* (20th, 1945), *Circumstantial Evidence* (20th, 1945), *Captain Eddie* (20th, 1945), *The House on 92nd Street* (20th, 1945), *Somewhere in the Night* (20th, 1946), *Two Smart People* (MGM, 1946), *Lady in the Lake* (MGM, 1946), *Green Grass of Wyoming* (20th, 1948), *The Street With No Name* (20th, 1948), *Bad Boy* (AA, 1949), *The Sun Comes Up* (MGM, 1949), *Easy Living* (RKO, 1949), *The Lemon Drop Kid* (Par., 1951), *Island in the Sky* (WB, 1953), *Crazylegs* (Rep., 1953), *The Last Hunt* (MGM, 1956), *Santiago* (WB, 1956), *Toward the Unknown* (WB, 1956), *Abandon Ship!* (Col., 1957), *A Hatful of Rain* (20th, 1957), *Peyton Place* (20th, 1957), *Portrait in Black* (Univ., 1960), *Girl of the Night* (WB, 1960), *Susan Slade* (WB, 1961), *We Joined the Navy* (Dial, 1962), *The Girl Hunters* (Colorama Features, 1963), *Circus World* (Par., 1964), *Never Too Late* (WB, 1965), *An American Dream* (WB, 1966), *Double Man* (WB, 1967), *Ice Station Zebra* (MGM, 1968).

Kim Novak and James Stewart in *Vertigo*.

KIM NOVAK (Marilyn Pauline Novak) Born February 13, 1933, Chicago, Illinois. Married Richard Johnson 1965; divorced 1966.

Feature Films: *The French Line* (RKO, 1953), *Pushover* (Col., 1954), *Phffft* (Col., 1954), *Five Against the House* (Col., 1955), *Son of Sinbad* (RKO, 1955), *Picnic* (Col., 1955), *The Man With the Golden Arm* (UA, 1955), *The Eddy Duchin Story* (Col., 1954), *Jeanne Eagles* (Col., 1957), *Pal Joey* (Col., 1957), *Vertigo* (Par., 1958), *Bell, Book and Candle* (Col., 1958), *Middle of the Night* (Col., 1959), *Strangers When We Meet* (Col., 1960), *Pepe* (Col., 1960), *Boys' Night Out* (MGM, 1962), *The Notorious Landlady* (Col., 1962), *Of Human Bondage* (MGM, 1964), *Kiss Me, Stupid* (Lopert, 1964), *The Amorous Adventures of Moll Flanders* (Par., 1965), *The Legend of Lylah Clare* (MGM, 1968).

JACK OAKIE (Lewis Delaney Offield) Born November 12, 1903, Sedalia, Missouri. Married Venita Varden; divorced.

Jack Oakie, Bradley Page, Ruth Donnelly and Lucille Ball in *Annabel Takes a Tour*.

Sound Feature Films: *Chinatown Nights* (Par., 1929), *The Dummy* (Par., 1929), *Wild Party* (Par., 1929), *Close Harmony* (Par., 1929), *The Man I Love* (Par., 1929), *Fast Company* (Par., 1929), *Street Girl* (RKO, 1929), *Hard to Get* (WB, 1929), *Sweetie* (Par., 1929), *Paramount on Parade* (Par., 1930), *Hit the Deck* (RKO, 1930), *Social Lion* (Par., 1930), *Let's Go Native* (Par., 1930), *The Sap From Syracuse* (Par., 1930), *Sea Legs* (Par., 1930), *Gang Busters* (Par., 1931), *June Moon* (Par., 1931), *Dude Ranch* (Par., 1931), *Touchdown* (Par., 1931), *Dancers in the Dark* (Par., 1932), *Sky Bride* (Par., 1932), *Make Me a Star* (Par., 1932), *Million Dollar Legs* (Par., 1932), *Madison Square Garden* (Par., 1932), *If I Had a Million* (Par., 1932), *Once in a Lifetime* (Univ., 1932), *Uptown New York* (Sono Art-World Wide, 1932), *From Hell to Heaven* (Par., 1933), *Sailor Be Good* (Par., 1933), *Eagle and the Hawk* (Par., 1933), *College Humor* (Par., 1933), *Too Much*

Harmony (Par., 1933), *Sitting Pretty* (Par., 1933), *Alice in Wonderland* (Par., 1933), *Looking for Trouble* (UA, 1934), *Murder at the Vanities* (Par., 1934), *Shoot the Works* (Par., 1934), *College Rhythm* (Par., 1934), *Call of the Wild* (UA, 1935), *Big Broadcast of 1936* (Par., 1935), *King of Burlesque* (Fox, 1935), *Collegiate* (Par., 1936), *Colleen* (WB, 1936), *Florida Special* (Par., 1936), *The Texas Rangers* (Par., 1936), *That Girl From Paris* (RKO, 1936), *Champagne Waltz* (RKO, 1937), *Super Sleuth* (RKO, 1937), *The Toast of New York* (RKO, 1937), *Fight for Your Lady* (RKO, 1937), *Hitting a New High* (RKO, 1937), *Radio City Revels* (RKO, 1938), *The Affairs of Annabel* (RKO, 1938), *Annabel Takes a Tour* (RKO, 1938), *Thanks for Everything* (20th, 1938), *Young People* (20th, 1940), *The Great Dictator* (UA, 1940), *Tin Pan Alley* (20th, 1940), *Little Men* (RKO, 1940), *Rise and Shine* (20th, 1941), *Great American Broadcast* (20th, 1941), *Hello, Frisco, Hello* (20th, 1943), *Wintertime* (20th, 1943), *Something to Shout About* (Col., 1943), *It Happened Tomorrow* (UA, 1944), *The Merry Monahans* (Univ., 1944), *Sweet and Low Down* (20th, 1944), *Bowery to Broadway* (Univ., 1944), *That's the Spirit* (Univ., 1945), *On Stage Everybody* (Univ., 1945), *She Wrote the Book* (Univ., 1946), *Northwest Stampede* (EL, 1948), *When My Baby Smiles at Me* (20th, 1948), *Thieves' Highway* (20th, 1949), *Last of the Buccaneers* (Col., 1950), *Tomahawk* (Univ., 1951), *Around the World in 80 Days* (UA, 1956), *The Wonderful Country* (UA, 1959), *The Rat Race* (Par., 1960), *Lover Come Back* (Univ., 1961).

MERLE OBERON (Estelle Merle O'Brien Thompson) Born February 19, 1911, Tasmania, Australia. Married Alexander Korda (1939); divorced 1945. Married Lucien Ballard (1945); divorced 1949. Married Bruno Pagliai (1957), children: Bruno, Francesca.

Merle Oberon and Geraldine Fitzgerald in *Till We Meet Again.*

Feature Films: *Service For Ladies* ("Reserved For Ladies"—Par., 1932), *Dance of Witches* (London Film Productions, 1932), *Wedding Rehearsal* (London Film Productions., 1932), *The Private Life of Henry VIII* (UA, 1933), *The Private Life of Don Juan* (UA, 1934), *Thunder in the East* ("The Battle"—Leon Garganoff, 1934), *Broken Melody* (Olympic Pictures, 1934), *Men of Tomorrow* (Mundus, 1935), *The Scarlet Pimpernel* (UA, 1935), *Folies Bergere* (UA, 1935), *The Dark Angel* (UA, 1935), *These Three* (UA, 1936), *Beloved Enemy* (UA, 1936), *The Divorce of Lady X* (UA, 1938), *The Cowboy and the Lady* (UA, 1938), *Wuthering Heights* (UA, 1939), *The Lion Has Wings* (UA, 1940), *Over the Moon* (UA, 1940), *Till We Meet Again* (WB, 1940), *Affectionately Yours* (WB, 1941), *Lydia* (UA, 1941), *That Uncertain Feeling* (UA, 1941), *Forever and a Day* (RKO, 1943), *Stage Door Canteen* (UA, 1943), *First Comes Courage* (Col., 1943), *The Lodger* (20th, 1944), *Dark Waters* (UA, 1944), *A Song to Remember* (Col., 1945), *This Love of Ours* (Univ., 1945), *A Night in Paradise* (Univ., 1946), *Temptation* (Univ., 1946), *Night Song* (RKO, 1947), *Berlin Express* (RKO, 1948), *Pardon My French* (UA, 1951), *Affair in Monte Carlo* (AA, 1953), *Desirée* (20th, 1954), *Deep in My Heart*

(MGM, 1954), *The Price of Fear* (Univ., 1956), *Of Love and Desire* (20th, 1963), *The Oscar* (Par., 1966), *Hotel* (WB, 1967).

EDMOND O'BRIEN Born September 10, 1915, New York, New York. Married Nancy Kelly (1941); divorced 1942. Married Olga San Juan (1948), children: Maria, Bridgette, Brenden.

Wendell Corey, Edmond O'Brien, Paul Newman, Anne Francis and Walter Pidgeon in *The Rack.*

Feature Films: *The Hunchback of Notre Dame* (RKO, 1939), *A Girl, a Guy and a Gob* (RKO, 1941), *Parachute Battalion* (RKO, 1941), *Obliging Young Lady* (RKO, 1941), *Powder Town* (RKO, 1942), *Amazing Mrs. Holliday* (Univ., 1943), *Winged Victory* (20th, 1944), *The Killers* (Univ., 1946), *The Web* (Univ., 1947), *Another Part of the Forest* (Univ., 1948), *A Double Life* (Univ., 1948), *An Act of Murder* (Univ., 1948), *For the Love of Mary* (Univ., 1948), *Fighter Squadron* (WB, 1948), *White Heat* (WB, 1949), *D.O.A.* (UA, 1949), *Backfire* (WB, 1950), *711 Ocean Drive* (Col., 1950), *The Admiral Was a Lady* (UA, 1950), *Between Midnight and Dawn* (Col., 1950), *The Redhead and the Cowboy* (Par., 1950), *Warpath* (Par., 1951), *Two of a Kind* (Col., 1951), *Silver City* (Par., 1951), *The Greatest Show on Earth* (Par., 1952),* *Denver and Rio Grande* (Par., 1952), *The Hitchhiker* (RKO, 1953), *Julius Caesar* (MGM, 1953), *Cow Country* (AA, 1953), *Man in the Dark* (Col., 1953), *China Venture* (Col., 1953), *The Bigamist* (Filmaker, 1953), *Shanghai Story* (Rep., 1954), *The Barefoot Contessa* (UA, 1954), *Shield for Murder* (UA, 1954), *Pete Kelly's Blues* (WB, 1955), *1984* (Col., 1956), *A Cry in the Night* (WB, 1956), *D-Day, the Sixth of June* (20th, 1956), *The Rack* (MGM, 1956), *The Girl Can't Help It* (20th, 1956), *The Big Land* (WB, 1957), *The World Was His Jury* (Col., 1958), *Sing Boy Sing* (20th, 1958), *Up Periscope* (WB, 1959), *The Last Voyage* (MGM, 1959), *The Third Voice* (20th, 1960), *The Great Impostor* (Univ., 1961), *Man Trap* (Par., 1961), *Bird Man of Alcatraz* (Col., 1962), *Moon Pilot* (BV, 1962), *The Man Who Shot Liberty Valance* (Par., 1962), *The Longest Day* (20th, 1962), *Seven Days in May* (20th, 1964), *The Climbers* (Robert Dorfman, 1964), *Rio Conchos* (20th, 1964), *Sylvia* (Par., 1965), *Synanon* (Col., 1965), *Fantastic Voyage* (20th, 1966), *The Viscount* (WB, 1967).

*Unbilled guest appearance

GEORGE O'BRIEN Born April 19, 1900, San Francisco, California. Married Marguerite Churchill (1933), children: Orin, Darcy; divorced 1948.

Sound Feature Films: *Salute* (Fox, 1929), *The Lone Star Ranger* (Fox, 1930), *Rough Romance* (Fox, 1930), *Last of the Duanes* (Fox, 1930), *Fair Warning* (Fox, 1931), *The Seas Beneath* (Fox, 1931), *A Holy Terror* (Fox, 1931), *Riders of the Purple Sage* (Fox, 1931), *The Rainbow*

Charles Middleton, Cecilia Parker, Noble Johnson, George O'Brien and Charlie Stevens in *Mystery Ranch*.

Trail (Fox, 1931), *The Gay Caballero* (Fox, 1932), *Mystery Ranch* (Fox, 1932), *The Golden West* (Fox, 1932), *Robber's Roost* (Fox, 1933), *Smoke Lightning* (Fox, 1933), *Life in the Raw* (Fox, 1933), *The Last Trail* (Fox, 1933), *Frontier Marshal* (Fox, 1934), *Ever Since Eve* (Fox, 1934), *The Dude Ranger* (Fox, 1934), *When a Man's a Man* (Fox, 1935), *The Cowboy Millionaire* (Fox, 1935), *Hard Rock Harrigan* (Fox, 1935), *Thunder Mountain* (20th, 1935), *Whispering Smith Speaks* (20th, 1935), *O'Malley of the Mounted* (20th, 1936), *The Border Patrolman* (20th, 1936), *Daniel Boone* (RKO, 1936), *Park Avenue Logger* (RKO, 1937), *Hollywood Cowboy* (RKO, 1937), *Windjammer* (RKO, 1937), *Gun Law* (RKO, 1938), *Border G-Man* (RKO, 1938), *Painted Desert* (RKO, 1938), *The Renegade Ranger* (RKO, 1938), *Lawless Valley* (RKO, 1938), *The Arizona Legion* (RKO, 1939), *Trouble in Sundown* (RKO, 1939), *Racketeers of the Range* (RKO, 1939), *Timber Stampede* (RKO, 1939), *The Fighting Gringo* (RKO, 1939), *The Marshal of Mesa City* (RKO, 1939), *Legion of the Lawless* (RKO, 1940), *Bullet Code* (RKO, 1940), *Prairie Law* (RKO, 1940), *Stage to Chino* (RKO, 1940), *Triple Justice* (RKO, 1940), *My Wild Irish Rose* (WB, 1947), *Fort Apache* (RKO, 1948), *She Wore a Yellow Ribbon* (RKO, 1949), *Gold Raiders* (UA, 1951), *Cheyenne Autumn* (WB, 1964).

MARGARET O'BRIEN (Angela Maxine O'Brien) Born January 15, 1937, Los Angeles, California. Married Harold Allen (1959).

Herbert Marshall, Brian Roper and Margaret O'Brien in *The Secret Garden*.

Feature Films: *Babes on Broadway* (MGM, 1941), *Journey for Margaret* (MGM, 1942), *Dr. Gillespie's Criminal Case* (MGM, 1943), *Thousands Cheer* (MGM, 1943), *Lost Angel* (MGM, 1943), *Madame Curie* (MGM, 1943), *Jane Eyre* (20th, 1944), *The Canterville Ghost* (MGM, 1944), *Meet Me in St. Louis* (MGM, 1944), *Music for Millions* (MGM, 1944),

Our Vines Have Tender Grapes (MGM, 1945), *Bad Bascomb* (MGM, 1946), *Three Wise Fools* (MGM, 1946), *The Unfinished Dance* (MGM, 1947), *Tenth Avenue Angel* (MGM, 1947), *Big City* (MGM, 1948), *Little Women* (MGM, 1949), *The Secret Garden* (MGM, 1949), *Her First Romance* (Col., 1951), *Glory* (RKO, 1956), *Heller in Pink Tights* (Par., 1960).

PAT O'BRIEN (William Joseph Patrick O'Brien) Born November 11, 1899, Milwaukee, Wisconsin. Married Eloise Taylor (1931), children: Mavourneen, Patrick, Terence, Kathleen.

Leon Ames and Pat O'Brien in *The Iron Major*.

Feature Films: *Front Page* (UA, 1931), *Honor Among Lovers* (Par., 1931), *Personal Maid* (Par., 1931), *Flying High* (MGM, 1931), *Consolation Marriage* (RKO, 1931), *Final Edition* (Col., 1932), *Hell's House* (Capitol Film Exchange, 1932), *Strange Case of Clara Deane* (Par., 1932), *Scandal for Sale* (Univ., 1932), *American Madness* (Col., 1932), *Hollywood Speaks* (Col., 1932), *Virtue* (Col., 1932), *Air Mail* (Univ., 1932), *Laughter in Hell* (Univ., 1932), *Destination Unknown* (Univ., 1933), *World Gone Mad* (Majestic, 1933), *Bureau of Missing Persons* (WB, 1933), *Bombshell* (MGM, 1933), *College Coach* (WB, 1933), *Flaming Gold* (RKO, 1934), *Gambling Lady* (WB, 1934), *I've Got Your Number* (WB, 1934), *20 Million Sweethearts* (WB, 1934), *Here Comes the Navy* (WB, 1934), *Personality Kid* (WB, 1934), *I Sell Anything* (WB, 1934), *Flirtation Walk* (WB, 1934), *Devil Dogs of the Air* (WB, 1935), *In Caliente* (WB, 1935), *Oil for the Lamps of China* (WB, 1935), *Page Miss Glory* (WB, 1935), *The Irish in Us* (WB, 1935), *Stars Over Broadway* (WB, 1935), *Ceiling Zero* (WB, 1935), *I Married a Doctor* (WB, 1936), *Public Enemy's Wife* (WB, 1936), *China Clipper* (WB, 1936), *The Great O'Malley* (WB, 1937), *Slim* (WB, 1937), *San Quentin* (WB, 1937), *Back in Circulation* (WB, 1937), *Submarine D-1* (WB, 1937), *Women Are Like That* (WB, 1938), *The Cowboy From Brooklyn* (WB, 1938), *Boy Meets Girl* (WB, 1938), *Garden of the Moon* (WB, 1938), *Angels With Dirty Faces* (WB, 1938), *Off the Record* (WB, 1939), *The Kid From Kokomo* (WB, 1939), *Indianapolis Speedway* (WB, 1939), *The Night of Nights* (Par., 1939), *The Fighting 69th* (WB, 1940), *Slightly Honorable* (UA, 1940), *Castle on the Hudson* (WB, 1940), *Till We Meet Again* (WB, 1940), *Torrid Zone* (WB, 1940), *Flowing Gold* (WB, 1940), *Knute Rockne—All American* (WB, 1940), *Submarine Zone* (Col., 1941), *Two Yanks in Trinidad* (Col., 1942), *Broadway* (Univ., 1942), *Flight Lieutenant* (Col., 1942), *The Navy Comes Through* (RKO, 1942), *Bombardier* (RKO, 1943), *The Iron Major* (RKO, 1943), *His Butler's Sister* (Univ., 1943), *Secret Command* (Col., 1944), *Marine Raiders* (RKO, 1944), *Having Wonderful Crime* (RKO, 1945), *Man Alive* (RKO, 1945), *Perilous Holiday* (Col., 1946), *Riffraff* (RKO, 1947), *Fighting Father Dunne* (RKO, 1948), *The Boy With Green Hair* (RKO, 1948), *A Dangerous Profession* (RKO, 1949), *Johnny One-Eye* (UA, 1950), *The Fireball* (20th, 1950), *The People Against O'Hara* (MGM, 1951), *Criminal Lawyer* (Col., 1951), *Okinawa* (Col., 1952), *Jubilee Trail* (Rep., 1954), *Ring of Fear* (WB, 1954), *Inside Detroit* (Col., 1955), *Kill Me Tomorrow* (Tudor Pictures, 1957), *The Last*

Hurrah (Col., 1958), *Some Like it Hot* (UA, 1959), *Town Tamer* (Par., 1965).

VIRGINIA O'BRIEN Born April 18, 1921, Los Angeles, California. Married Kirk Alyn (1942), child: Theresa; divorced 1955.

Bert Lahr and Virginia O'Brien (right) in *Meet the People.*

Feature Films: *Hullabaloo* (MGM, 1940), *Sky Murder* (MGM, 1940), *The Big Store* (MGM, 1941), *Ringside Maisie* (MGM, 1941), *Lady Be Good* (MGM, 1941), *Ship Ahoy* (MGM, 1942), *Panama Hattie* (MGM, 1942), *Du Barry Was a Lady* (MGM, 1943), *Thousands Cheer* (MGM, 1943), *Two Girls and a Sailor* (MGM, 1944), *Meet the People* (MGM, 1944), *Ziegfeld Follies* (MGM, 1946), *The Harvey Girls* (MGM, 1946), *The Show-Off* (MGM, 1946), *Till the Clouds Roll By* (MGM, 1946), *Merton of the Movies* (MGM, 1947), *Francis in the Navy* (Univ., 1955).

ARTHUR O'CONNELL Born March 29, 1908, New York, New York. Married Anne Hall (1962).

Arthur O'Connell and George Hamilton in *A Thunder of Drums.*

Feature Films: *Freshman Year* (Univ., 1938), *Dr. Kildare Goes Home* (MGM, 1940), *The Leather Pushers* (Univ., 1940), *And One Was Beautiful* (MGM, 1940), *Two Girls on Broadway* (MGM, 1940), *Citizen*

Kane (RKO, 1941), *Man From Headquarters* (Mon., 1942), *Canal Zone* (Col., 1942), *Fingers at the Window* (MGM, 1942), *Law of the Jungle* (Mon., 1942), *Shepherd of the Ozarks* (Rep., 1942), *Yokel Boy* (Rep., 1942), *It Happened Tomorrow* (UA, 1944), *One Touch of Venus* (Univ., 1948), *Open Secret* (EL, 1948), *State of the Union* (MGM, 1948), *Naked City* (Univ., 1948), *Homecoming* (MGM, 1948), *Countess of Monte Cristo* (Univ., 1948), *Force of Evil* (MGM, 1948), *Picnic* (Col., 1955), *The Solid Gold Cadillac* (Col., 1956), *The Man in the Gray Flannel Suit* (20th, 1956), *The Proud Ones* (20th, 1956), *Bus Stop* (20th, 1956), *The Monte Carlo Story* (UA, 1957), *Operation Mad Ball* (Col., 1957), *April Love* (20th, 1957), *The Violators* (Univ., 1957), *Voice in the Mirror* (Univ., 1958), *Man of the West* (UA, 1958), *Gidget* (Col., 1959), *Anatomy of a Murder* (Col., 1959), *Operation Petticoat* (Univ., 1959), *Hound-Dog Man* (20th, 1959), *The Great Impostor* (Univ., 1960), *Cimarron* (MGM, 1960), *Misty* (20th, 1961), *A Thunder of Drums* (MGM, 1961), *A Pocketful of Miracles* (UA, 1961), *Follow That Dream* (UA, 1962), *Seven Faces of Dr. Lao* (MGM, 1964), *Kissin' Cousins* (MGM, 1964), *The Third Secret* (20th, 1964), *Your Cheatin' Heart* (MGM, 1964), *Nightmare in the Sun* (Zodiac, 1965), *The Third Day* (WB, 1965), *The Monkey's Uncle* (BV, 1965), *Ride Beyond Vengeance* (Col., 1966), *The Silencers* (Col., 1966), *Fantastic Voyage* (20th, 1966), *A Covenant With Death* (WB, 1967), *The Reluctant Astronaut* (Univ., 1967), *The Power* (MGM, 1968).

DONALD O'CONNOR (Donald David Dixon Ronald O'Connor) Born August 30, 1925, Chicago, Illinois. Married Gwendolyn Carter (1944), child: Donna; divorced 1954. Married Gloria Noble (1957), child: Alicia.

Donald O'Connor, Mary Boland, Charlie Ruggles and Billy Lee in *Boy Trouble.*

Feature Films: *Sing You Sinners* (Par., 1938), *Sons of the Legion* (Par., 1938), *Men With Wings* (Par., 1938), *Tom Sawyer, Detective* (Par., 1938), *Unmarried* (Par., 1939), *Death of a Champion* (Par., 1939), *Million Dollar Legs* (Par., 1939), *Night Work* (Par., 1939), *On Your Toes* (WB, 1939), *Beau Geste* (Par., 1939), *Private Buckaroo* (Univ., 1942), *Give Out, Sisters* (Univ., 1942), *Get Hep to Love* (Univ., 1942), *When Johnny Comes Marching Home* (Univ., 1942), *Strictly in the Groove* (Univ., 1943), *It Comes Up Love* (Univ., 1943), *Mister Big* (Univ., 1943), *Top Man* (Univ., 1943), *Chip Off the Old Block* (Univ., 1944), *This Is the Life* (Univ., 1944), *Follow the Boys* (Univ., 1944), *The Merry Monahans* (Univ., 1944), *Bowery to Broadway* (Univ., 1944), *Patrick the Great* (Univ., 1945), *Something in the Wind* (Univ., 1947), *Are You With It?* (Univ., 1948), *Feudin', Fussin' and a-Fightin'* (Univ., 1948), *Yes Sir, That's My Baby* (Univ., 1949), *Francis* (Univ., 1949), *Curtain Call at Cactus Creek* (Univ., 1950), *The Milkman* (Univ., 1950), *Double Crossbones* (Univ., 1950), *Francis Goes to the Races* (Univ., 1951), *Singin' in the Rain* (MGM, 1952), *Francis Goes to West Point* (Univ., 1952), *Call Me Madam* (20th, 1953), *I Love Melvin* (MGM, 1953), *Francis Covers the Big Town* (Univ., 1953), *Walking My Baby Back Home* (Univ., 1953), *Francis Joins the WACs* (Univ., 1954), *There's No Business Like Show Business* (20th, 1954), *Francis in the Navy* (Univ., 1955), *Anything Goes* (Par., 1956), *The Buster Keaton*

Story (Par., 1957), *Cry for Happy* (Col., 1961), *The Wonders of Aladdin* (MGM, 1961), *That Funny Feeling* (Univ., 1965).

UNA O'CONNOR Born October 23, 1880, Belfast, Ireland. Died February 4, 1959.

Henry Stephenson and Una O'Connor in *The Perfect Gentleman*.

Feature Films: *Dark Red Roses* (British Sound Films, 1929), *Murder* (British International, 1930), *To Oblige a Lady* (British Lion, 1930), *Timbuctoo* (British Lion, 1930), *Cavalcade* (Fox, 1933), *Pleasure Cruise* (Fox, 1933), *Mary Stevens, M.D.* (WB, 1933), *The Invisible Man* (Univ., 1933), *Orient Express* (Fox, 1934), *The Poor Rich* (Univ., 1934), *All Men Are Enemies* (Fox, 1934), *Stingaree* (RKO, 1934), *The Barretts of Wimpole Street* (MGM, 1934), *Chained* (MGM, 1934), *David Copperfield* (MGM, 1935), *Father Brown, Detective* (Par., 1935), *Bride of Frankenstein* (Univ., 1935), *The Informer* (RKO, 1935), *Thunder in the Night* (Fox, 1935), *The Perfect Gentleman* (MGM, 1935), *Little Lord Fauntleroy* (UA, 1936), *Rose Marie* (MGM, 1936), *Suzy* (MGM, 1936), *Lloyds of London* (20th, 1936), *The Plough and the Stars* (RKO, 1936), *Personal Property* (MGM, 1937), *Call It a Day* (WB, 1937), *The Return of the Frog* (Imperator-British Lion, 1938), *The Adventures of Robin Hood* (WB, 1938), *We Are Not Alone* (WB, 1939), *All Women Have Secrets* (Par., 1939), *It All Came True* (WB, 1940), *Lillian Russell* (20th, 1940), *The Sea Hawk* (WB, 1940), *He Stayed for Breakfast* (Col., 1940), *Kisses for Breakfast* (WB, 1941), *Strawberry Blonde* (WB, 1941), *Her First Beau* (Col., 1941), *Three Girls About Town* (Col., 1941), *How Green Was My Valley* (20th, 1941), *Always in My Heart* (WB, 1942), *My Favorite Spy* (RKO, 1942), *Random Harvest* (MGM, 1942), *This Land Is Mine* (RKO, 1943), *Forever and a Day* (RKO, 1943), *Holy Matrimony* (20th, 1943), *Government Girl* (RKO, 1943), *The Canterville Ghost* (MGM, 1944), *My Pal Wolf* (RKO, 1944), *Christmas in Connecticut* (WB, 1945), *The Bells of St. Mary's* (RKO, 1945), *Cluny Brown* (20th, 1946), *Of Human Bondage* (WB, 1946), *Child of Divorce* (RKO, 1946), *Unexpected Guest* (UA, 1946), *The Return of Monte Cristo* (Col., 1946), *Lost Honeymoon* (EL, 1947), *Banjo* (RKO, 1947), *Ivy* (Univ., 1947), *The Corpse Came C.O.D.* (Col., 1947), *Fighting Father Dunne* (RKO, 1948), *Adventures of Don Juan* (WB, 1948), *Witness for the Prosecution* (UA, 1957).

MAUREEN O'HARA (Maureen FitzSimmons) Born August 17, 1920, Dublin, Ireland. Married George Brown (1938); annulled 1941. Married Will Price (1941), child: Bronwyn; divorced 1953. Married Charles Blair (1968).

Feature Films: *Jamaica Inn* (Par., 1939), *The Hunchback of Notre Dame* (RKO, 1939), *My Irish Molly* (Mon, 1939), *A Bill of Divorcement* (RKO, 1940), *Dance, Girl, Dance* (RKO, 1940), *They Met in Argentina* (RKO, 1941), *How Green Was My Valley* (20th, 1941), *To the Shores of Tripoli* (20th, 1942), *Ten Gentlemen From West Point* (20th, 1942), *The Black Swan* (20th, 1942), *The Immortal Sergeant* (20th, 1943), *This Land Is Mine* (RKO, 1943), *The Fallen Sparrow* (RKO, 1943), *Buffalo Bill* (20th, 1944), *The Spanish Main* (RKO,

Douglas Fairbanks, Jr., Anthony Quinn, Maureen O'Hara, John Dehner and Alan Napier in *Sinbad the Sailor*.

1945), *Sentimental Journey* (20th, 1946), *Do You Love Me?* (20th, 1946), *Sinbad the Sailor* (RKO, 1947), *The Homestretch* (20th, 1947), *The Miracle on 34th Street* (20th, 1947), *The Foxes of Harrow* (20th, 1947), *Sitting Pretty* (20th, 1948), *The Forbidden Street* (20th, 1949), *A Woman's Secret* (RKO, 1949), *Father Was a Fullback* (20th, 1949), *Bagdad* (Univ., 1949), *Comanche Territory* (Univ., 1950), *Tripoli* (Par., 1950), *Rio Grande* (Rep., 1950), *Flame of Araby* (Univ., 1951), *At Sword's Point* (RKO, 1952), *Kangaroo* (20th, 1952), *The Quiet Man* (Rep., 1952), *Against All Flags* (Univ., 1952), *The Redhead From Wyoming* (Univ., 1952), *War Arrow* (Univ., 1953), *Fire Over Africa* (Col., 1954), *The Long Gray Line* (Col., 1955), *The Magnificent Matador* (20th, 1955), *Lady Godiva* (Univ., 1955), *Lisbon* (Rep., 1956), *Everything But the Truth* (Univ., 1956), *The Wings of Eagles* (MGM, 1957), *Our Man in Havana* (Col., 1960), *The Parent Trap* (BV, 1961), *The Deadly Companions* (Pathé-American, 1961), *Mr. Hobbs Takes a Vacation* (20th, 1962), *Spencer's Mountain* (WB, 1963), *McLintock!* (UA, 1963), *The Battle of the Villa Fiorita* (WB, 1965), *The Rare Breed* (Univ., 1966).

DENNIS O'KEEFE (Edward James Flanagan) Born March 29, 1908, Fort Madison, Iowa. Married Louise Stanely; divorced. Married Steffi Duna (1940), child: Edward.

Wallace Ford and Dennis O'Keefe in *T-Men*.

Feature Films:
as Bud Flanagan *Reaching for the Moon* (UA, 1931), *Cimarron* (RKO, 1931), *Crooner* (WB, 1932), *Two Against the World* (WB, 1932), *Cabin in the Cotton* (WB, 1932), *I Am a Fugitive From a Chain Gang* (WB, 1932), *Night After Night* (Par., 1932), *Central Park* (WB, 1932), *Hello Everybody!* (Par., 1933), *Girl Missing* (WB, 1933), *From Hell to Heaven* (Par., 1933), *The Eagle and the Hawk* (Par., 1933), *Gold Diggers of 1933* (WB, 1933), *Too Much Harmony* (Par., 1933), *I'm No Angel* (Par., 1933), *Duck Soup* (Par., 1933), *The House on 56th*

Street (Par., 1933), *Lady Killer* (WB, 1933), *Torch Singer* (Par., 1933), *Upperworld* (WB, 1934), *Wonder Bar* (WB, 1934), *Jimmy the Gent* (WB, 1934), *Smarty* (WB, 1934), *Registered Nurse* (WB, 1934), *Fog Over Frisco* (WB, 1934), *Man With Two Faces* (WB, 1934), *Madame Du Barry* (WB, 1934), *Lady By Choice* (Col., 1934), *College Rhythm* (Par., 1934), *Transatlantic Merry-Go-Round* (UA, 1934), *Imitation of Life* (Univ., 1934), *Devil Dogs of the Air* (WB, 1935), *Rumba* (Par., 1935), *Gold Diggers of 1935* (WB, 1935), *Mississippi* (Par., 1935), *Let 'Em Have It* (UA, 1935), *Doubting Thomas* (Fox, 1935), *The Daring Young Man* (Fox, 1935), *Every Night at Eight* (Par., 1935), *Anna Karenina* (MGM, 1935), *Personal Maid's Secret* (WB, 1935), *It's in the Air* (MGM, 1935), *Shipmates Forever* (WB, 1935), *Broadway Hostess* (WB, 1935), *Anything Goes* (Par., 1936), *Hats Off* (GN, 1936), *Love Before Breakfast* (Univ., 1936), *Mr. Deeds Goes to Town* (Col., 1936), *13 Hours By Air* (Par., 1936), *And So They Were Married* (Col., 1936), *Nobody's Fool* (Univ., 1936), *Sworn Enemy* (MGM, 1936), *Rhythm on the Range* (Par., 1936), *Yours for the Asking* (Par., 1936), *Libeled Lady* (MGM, 1936), *Theodora Goes Wild* (Col., 1936), *The Accusing Finger* (Par., 1936), *Born to Dance* (MGM, 1936), *The Plainsman* (Par., 1936), *Burning Gold* (Rep., 1936), *Great Guy* (GN, 1936), *Married Before Breakfast* (MGM, 1937), *Top of the Town* (Univ., 1937), *When's Your Birthday?* (RKO, 1937), *Parole Racket* (Col., 1937), *Swing High, Swing Low* (Par., 1937), *Captains Courageous* (MGM, 1937), *A Star Is Born* (UA, 1937), *Riding on Air* (RKO, 1937), *Girl From Scotland Yard* (Par., 1937), *Easy Living* (Par., 1937), *Saratoga* (MGM, 1937), *The Firefly* (MGM, 1937), *Blazing Barriers* (Mon., 1937).

as Dennis O'Keefe *Bad Man of Brimstone* (MGM, 1938), *Hold That Kiss* (MGM, 1938), *The Chaser* (MGM, 1938), *Vacation From Love* (MGM, 1938), *Burn 'Em Up O'Connor* (MGM, 1939), *The Kid From Texas* (MGM, 1939), *Unexpected Father* (Univ., 1939), *That's Right—You're Wrong* (RKO, 1939), *La Conga Nights* (Univ., 1940), *Alias the Deacon* (Univ., 1940), *Pop Always Pays* (RKO, 1940), *I'm Nobody's Sweetheart Now* (Univ., 1940), *Girl From Havana* (Rep., 1940), *Arise, My Love* (Par., 1940), *You'll Find Out* (RKO, 1940), *Mr. District Attorney* (Rep., 1941), *Bowery Boy* (Rep., 1941), *Topper Returns* (UA, 1941), *Broadway Limited* (UA, 1941), *Lady Scarface* (RKO, 1941), *Week-End for Three* (RKO, 1941), *The Affairs of Jimmy Valentine* (Rep., 1942), *Moonlight Masquerade* (Rep., 1942), *Hangmen Also Die* (UA, 1943), *Tahiti Honey* (Rep., 1943), *Good Morning, Judge* (Univ., 1943), *The Leopard Man* (RKO, 1943), *Hi Diddle Diddle* (UA, 1943), *The Fighting Seabees* (Rep., 1944), *Up in Mabel's Room* (UA, 1944), *The Story of Dr. Wassell* (Par., 1944), *Sensations of 1945* (UA, 1944), *Abroad With Two Yanks* (UA, 1944), *Earl Carroll's Vanities* (Rep., 1945), *Brewster's Millions* (UA, 1945), *The Affairs of Susan* (Par., 1945), *Getting Gertie's Garter* (UA, 1945), *Doll Face* (20th, 1945), *Her Adventurous Night* (Univ., 1946), *Mr. District Attorney* (Col., 1947), *Dishonored Lady* (UA, 1947), *T-Men* (EL, 1947), *Raw Deal* (EL, 1948), *Walk a Crooked Mile* (Col., 1948), *Siren of Atlantis* (UA, 1948), *Cover Up* (UA, 1949), *The Great Dan Patch* (UA, 1949), *Abandoned* (Univ., 1949), *The Eagle and the Hawk* (Par., 1950), *Woman on the Run* (Univ., 1950), *The Company She Keeps* (RKO, 1950), *Follow the Sun* (20th, 1951), *Passage West* (Par., 1951), *One Big Affair* (UA, 1952), *Everything I Have Is Yours* (MGM, 1952), *The Lady Wants Mink* (Rep., 1953), *The Fake* (UA, 1953), *The Diamond Wizard* (UA, 1953), *Drums of Tahiti* (Col., 1954), *Angela* (20th, 1955), *Las Vegas Shakedown* (AA, 1955), *Chicago Syndicate* (Col., 1955), *Inside Detroit* (Col., 1955), *Dragoon Wells Massacre* (AA, 1957), *Sail into Danger* (Patria, 1957), *Lady of Vengeance* (UA, 1957), *All Hands on Deck* (20th, 1961).

WARNER OLAND Born October 3, 1880, Ulmea, Sweden. Married Edith Shearn (1908). Died August 6, 1938.

Sound Feature Films: *Chinatown Nights* (Par., 1929), *The Studio Murder Mystery* (Par., 1929), *The Mysterious Dr. Fu Manchu* (Par., 1929), *The Mighty* (Par., 1929), *The Vagabond King* (Par., 1930), *Dangerous Paradise* (Par., 1930), *Paramount on Parade* (Par., 1930), *The Return of Dr. Fu Manchu* (Par., 1930), *Drums of Jeopardy* (Tif. 1931), *Dishonored* (Par., 1931), *Charlie Chan Carries On* (Fox, 1931), *Black Camel* (Fox, 1931), *Daughter of the Dragon* (Par., 1931), *The Big Gamble* (Pathé, 1931), *Shanghai Express* (Par., 1932), *Charlie Chan's Chance*

Virginia Field and Warner Oland in *Charlie Chan in Monte Carlo.*

(Fox, 1932), *Passport to Hell* (Fox, 1932), *The Son-Daughter* (MGM, 1932), *Charlie Chan's Greatest Case* (Fox, 1933), *Before Dawn* (RKO, 1933), *As Husbands Go* (Fox, 1934), *Mandalay* (WB, 1934), *Bulldog Drummond Strikes Back* (UA, 1934), *Charlie Chan in London* (Fox, 1934), *Charlie Chan's Courage* (Fox, 1934), *The Painted Veil* (MGM, 1934), *Charlie Chan in Paris* (Fox, 1935), *Charlie Chan in Egypt* (Fox, 1935), *The Werewolf of London* (Univ., 1935), *Shanghai* (Par., 1935), *Charlie Chan in Shanghai* (Fox, 1935), *Charlie Chan's Secret* (20th, 1936), *Charlie Chan at the Circus* (20th, 1936), *Charlie Chan at the Race Track* (20th, 1936), *Charlie Chan at the Opera* (20th, 1936), *Charlie Chan at the Olympics* (20th, 1937), *Charlie Chan on Broadway* (20th, 1937), *Charlie Chan at Monte Carlo* (20th, 1937).

EDNA MAY OLIVER (Edna May Cox-Oliver) Born November 9, 1883, Malden, Massachusetts. Married David Pratt (1928); divorced 1931. Died November 9, 1942.

Edna May Oliver and Joan Crawford in *No More Ladies.*

Sound Feature Films: *The Saturday Night Kid* (Par., 1929), *Hook, Line and Sinker* (RKO, 1930), *Half Shot at Sunrise* (RKO, 1930), *Cimarron* (RKO, 1931), *Cracked Nuts* (RKO, 1931), *Laugh and Get Rich* (RKO, 1931), *Newly Rich* (Par., 1931), *Fanny Foley Herself* (RKO, 1931), *Ladies of the Jury* (RKO, 1932), *Hold 'Em Jail* (RKO, 1932), *The Conquerors* (RKO, 1932), *The Penguin Pool Murder* (RKO,

1932), *Meet the Baron* (MGM, 1933), *The Great Jasper* (RKO, 1933), *It's Great to Be Alive* (Fox, 1933), *Ann Vickers* (RKO, 1933), *Only Yesterday* (Univ., 1933), *Little Women* (RKO, 1933), *Alice in Wonderland* (Par., 1933), *The Poor Rich* (Univ., 1934), *The Last Gentleman* (UA, 1934), *Murder on the Blackboard* (RKO, 1934), *We're Rich Again* (RKO, 1934), *David Copperfield* (MGM, 1935), *Murder on a Honeymoon* (RKO, 1935), *No More Ladies* (MGM, 1935), *A Tale of Two Cities* (MGM, 1935), *Romeo and Juliet* (MGM, 1936), *Parnell* (MGM, 1937), *My Dear Miss Aldrich* (MGM, 1937), *Rosalie* (MGM, 1937), *Paradise for Three* (MGM, 1938), *Little Miss Broadway* (20th, 1938), *Second Fiddle* (20th, 1938), *Nurse Edith Cavell* (RKO, 1939), *The Story of Vernon and Irene Castle* (RKO, 1939), *Drums Along the Mohawk* (20th, 1939), *Pride and Prejudice* (MGM, 1940), *Lydia* (UA, 1941).

SIR LAURENCE OLIVIER Born May 22, 1907, Dorking, Surrey, England. Married Jill Esmond (1930), child: Simon; divorced 1940. Married Vivien Leigh (1940); divorced 1960. Married Joan Plowright (1961), children: Richard, Tamsin.

Gloria Swanson and Laurence Olivier in *Perfect Understanding*.

Feature Films: *The Temporary Widow* (UFA, 1930), *Too Many Crooks* (Fox, 1930), *The Yellow Ticket* (Fox, 1931), *Friends and Lovers* (RKO, 1931), *Potiphar's Wife* (Elvey, 1931), *Westward Passage* (RKO, 1932), *The Perfect Understanding* (UA, 1933), *No Funny Business* (Principal, 1934), *Moscow Nights* (Lenauer, 1935), *As You Like It* (20th, 1936), *Fire Over England* (UA, 1937), *The Divorce of Lady X* (UA, 1938), *Conquest of the Air* (Shaw, 1938), *Twenty-One Days* (London, 1938), *Wuthering Heights* (UA, 1939), *Q Planes* (Col., 1939), *Rebecca* (UA, 1940), *Pride and Prejudice* (MGM, 1940), *The Invaders* ("The 49th Parallel"—Ortus, 1941), *Lady Hamilton* (Korda, 1941), *The Demi-Paradise* (Two Cities, 1942), *Henry V* (UA, 1946), *Hamlet* (Rank, 1948), *Carrie* (Par., 1952), *The Magic Box* (Rank, 1952), *The Beggar's Opera* (WB, 1953), *Richard III* (Lopert, 1955), *The Prince and the Showgirl* (WB, 1957), *The Devil's Disciple* (UA, 1959), *Spartacus* (Univ., 1960), *The Entertainer* (Continental Distributing, 1960), *Term of Trial* (WB, 1963), *Bunny Lake Is Missing* (Col., 1965), *Othello* (WB, 1965), *Khartoum* (UA, 1966).

MAUREEN O'SULLIVAN (Maureen Paula O'Sullivan) Born May 17, 1911, County Roscommon, Ireland. Married John Farrow (1936), children: Joseph, Maria (Mia), John, Prudence, Stephanie, Theresa, Michael; widowed 1963.

Feature Films: *Song o' My Heart* (Fox, 1930), *So This Is London* (Fox, 1930), *Just Imagine* (Fox, 1930), *Princess and the Plumber* (Fox, 1930), *A Connecticut Yankee* (Fox, 1931), *Skyline* (Fox, 1931), *Tarzan the Ape Man* (MGM, 1932), *The Silver Lining* (Patrician, 1932), *Big Shot* (RKO, 1932), *Information Kid* (Univ., 1932), *Strange Interlude* (MGM, 1932), *Skyscraper Souls* (MGM, 1932), *Payment Deferred* (MGM, 1932), *Okay America!* (Univ., 1932), *Fast Companions* (Univ., 1932), *Robber's Roost* (Fox, 1933), *Cohens and Kellys in Trouble* (Univ.,

Maureen O'Sullivan and Henry Fonda in *Let Us Live*.

1933), *Tugboat Annie* (MGM, 1933), *Stage Mother* (MGM, 1933), *Tarzan and His Mate* (MGM, 1934), *The Thin Man* (MGM, 1934), *The Barretts of Wimpole Street* (MGM, 1934), *Hideout* (MGM, 1934), *West Point of the Air* (MGM, 1935), *David Copperfield* (MGM, 1935), *Cardinal Richelieu* (UA, 1935), *The Flame Within* (MGM, 1935), *Anna Karenina* (MGM, 1935), *Woman Wanted* (MGM, 1935), *The Bishop Misbehaves* (MGM, 1935), *Tarzan Escapes* (MGM, 1936), *The Voice of Bugle Ann* (MGM, 1936), *The Devil-Doll* (MGM, 1936), *A Day at the Races* (MGM, 1937), *Between Two Women* (MGM, 1937), *The Emperor's Candlesticks* (MGM, 1937), *My Dear Miss Aldrich* (MGM, 1937), *A Yank at Oxford* (MGM, 1938), *Hold That Kiss* (MGM, 1938), *The Crowd Roars* (MGM, 1938), *Port of Seven Seas* (MGM, 1938), *Spring Madness* (MGM, 1938), *Let Us Live* (Col., 1939), *Tarzan Finds a Son* (MGM, 1939), *Pride and Prejudice* (MGM, 1940), *Sporting Blood* (MGM, 1940), *Maisie Was a Lady* (MGM, 1941), *Tarzan's Secret Treasure* (MGM, 1941), *Tarzan's New York Adventure* (MGM, 1942), *The Big Clock* (Par., 1948), *Where Danger Lives* (RKO, 1950), *Bonzo Goes to College* (Univ., 1952), *All I Desire* (Univ., 1953), *Mission Over Korea* (Col., 1953), *Duffy of San Quentin* (WB, 1954), *The Steel Cage* (UA, 1954), *The Tall T* (Col., 1957), *Wild Heritage* (Univ., 1958), *Never Too Late* (WB, 1965).

PETER O'TOOLE (Peter Seamus O'Toole) Born August 2, 1933, Connemara, County Galway, Ireland. Married Sian Phillips, child: Kate.

Hugh Miller, Donald Wolfit, Claude Rains and Peter O'Toole in *Lawrence of Arabia*.

Feature Films: *Kidnapped* (BV, 1960), *The Day They Robbed the Bank of England* (MGM, 1960), *The Savage Innocents* (Par., 1960), *Lawrence of Arabia* (Col., 1962), *Becket* (Par., 1964), *Lord Jim* (Col., 1965), *What's New, Pussycat?* (UA, 1965), *How to Steal a Million* (20th, 1966),

The Bible (20th, 1966), *The Night of the Generals* (Col., 1967), *Casino Royale* (Col., 1967),* *The Great Catherine* (WB-7 Arts, 1968), *The Lion in Winter* (Embassy, 1968).

*Unbilled guest appearance

MARIA OUSPENSKAYA Born July 29, 1867, Tula, Russia. Died December 3, 1949.

Catherine McLeod and Maria Ouspenskaya in *I've Always Loved You.*

Feature Films: *Dodsworth* (UA, 1936), *Conquest* (MGM, 1937), *Love Affair* (RKO, 1939), *The Rains Came* (20th, 1939), *Judge Hardy and Son* (MGM, 1939), *Dr. Ehrlich's Magic Bullet* (WB, 1940), *Waterloo Bridge* (MGM, 1940), *The Mortal Storm* (MGM, 1940), *The Man I Married* (20th, 1940), *Dance, Girl, Dance* (RKO, 1940), *Beyond Tomorrow* (RKO, 1940), *The Wolf Man* (Univ., 1941), *The Shanghai Gesture* (UA, 1941), *Kings Row* (WB, 1941), *The Mystery of Marie Roget* (Univ., 1942), *Frankenstein Meets the Wolf Man* (Univ., 1942), *Tarzan and the Amazons* (RKO, 1945), *I've Always Loved You* (Rep., 1946), *Wyoming* (Rep., 1947), *A Kiss in the Dark* (WB, 1949).

REGINALD OWEN (John Reginald Owen) Born August 5, 1887, Wheathampstead, England. Married Lydia Bilbrooke (1908); divorced 1923. Married Mrs. Harold Austin; widowed 1956. Married Barbara Haveman (1956).

Reginald Owen, James Gleason, Lynne Overman and Edgar Kennedy in *Yours for the Asking.*

Feature Films: *The Letter* (Par., 1929), *Platinum Blonde* (Col., 1931), *The Man in Possession* (MGM, 1931), *Sherlock Holmes* (Fox, 1932),

A Study in Scarlet (World Wide, 1933), *Double Harness* (RKO, 1933), *The Narrow Corner* (WB, 1933), *Voltaire* (WB, 1933), *Queen Christina* (MGM, 1933), *Nana* (UA, 1934), *The House of Rothschild* (UA, 1934), *Of Human Bondage* (RKO, 1934), *The Human Side* (Univ., 1934), *Countess of Monte Cristo* (Univ., 1934), *Here Is My Heart* (Par., 1934), *Fashions of 1934* (WB, 1934), *Mandalay* (WB, 1934), *Madame Du Barry* (WB, 1934), *Where Sinners Meet* (RKO, 1934), *Music in the Air* (Fox, 1934), *Enchanted April* (RKO, 1935), *Anna Karenina* (MGM, 1935), *The Bishop Misbehaves* (MGM, 1935), *Escapade* (MGM, 1935), *A Tale of Two Cities* (MGM, 1935), *The Good Fairy* (Univ., 1935), *Call of the Wild* (UA, 1935), *Petticoat Fever* (MGM, 1936), *Rose Marie* (MGM, 1936), *Trouble for Two* (MGM, 1936), *The Great Ziegfeld* (MGM, 1936), *Conquest* (MGM, 1937), *Rosalie* (MGM, 1937), *Personal Property* (MGM, 1937), *Dangerous Number* (MGM, 1937), *A Christmas Carol* (MGM, 1938), *Everybody Sing* (MGM, 1938), *Paradise for Three* (MGM, 1938), *Three Loves Has Nancy* (MGM, 1938), *Vacation From Love* (MGM, 1938), *Pride and Prejudice* (MGM, 1940), *The Earl of Chicago* (MGM, 1940), *Florian* (MGM, 1940), *Free and Easy* (MGM, 1941), *Blonde Inspiration* (MGM, 1941), *Tarzan's Secret Treasure* (MGM, 1941), *Charley's Aunt* (20th, 1941), *Random Harvest* (MGM, 1942), *Woman of the Year* (MGM, 1942), *Mrs. Miniver* (MGM, 1942), *Assignment in Britanny* (MGM, 1943), *Madame Curie* (MGM, 1943), *The Valley of Decision* (MGM, 1945), *The Sailor Takes a Wife* (MGM, 1945), *Kitty* (Par., 1945), *Monsieur Beaucaire* (Par., 1946), *Cluny Brown* (20th, 1946), *Thunder in the Valley* (20th, 1947), *Green Dolphin Street* (MGM, 1947), *If Winter Comes* (MGM, 1947), *Piccadilly Incident* (MGM, 1948), *The Three Musketeers* (MGM, 1948), *The Secret Garden* (MGM, 1949), *Challenge to Lassie* (MGM, 1949), *Kim* (MGM, 1950), *Grounds for Marriage* (MGM, 1950), *The Miniver Story* (MGM, 1950), *The Great Diamond Robbery* (MGM, 1953), *Red Garters* (Par., 1954), *Five Weeks in a Balloon* (20th, 1962), *Tammy and the Doctor* (Univ., 1963), *The Thrill of it All* (Univ., 1963), *Voice of the Hurricane* (Selected Pictures, 1964), *Mary Poppins* (BV, 1964).

GERALDINE PAGE (Geraldine Sue Page) Born November 22, 1924, Kirksville, Missouri. Married Alexander Schneider; divorced. Married Rip Torn (1963), child: Angelica.

Geraldine Page and Glenn Ford in *Dear Heart.*

Feature Films: *Out of the Night* (Moody Bible Institute, 1947), *Taxi* (20th, 1953), *Hondo* (WB, 1953), *Summer and Smoke* (Par., 1961), *Sweet Bird of Youth* (MGM, 1962), *Toys in the Attic* (UA, 1963), *Dear Heart* (WB, 1964), *You're a Big Boy Now* (7 Arts, 1966), *The Happiest Millionaire* (BV, 1967), *Monday's Child* (DuRoda Productions, 1968).

JANIS PAIGE (Donna Mae Tjaden) Born September 16, 1922, Tacoma, Washington. Married Frank Martinelli (1947); divorced 1950. Married Arthur Stander (1956); divorced 1957. Married Ray Gilbert (1962).

Feature Films: *Bathing Beauty* (MGM, 1944), *Hollywood Canteen*

Dennis Morgan and Janis Paige in *One Sunday Afternoon*.

Jed Prouty, Adrienne Ames and Eugene Pallette in *Black Sheep*.

(WB, 1944), *Her Kind of Man* (WB, 1946), *Of Human Bondage* (WB, 1946), *Two Guys From Milwaukee* (WB, 1946), *The Time, the Place and the Girl* (WB, 1946), *Love and Learn* (WB, 1947), *Cheyenne* (WB, 1947), *Always Together* (WB, 1947),* *Winter Meeting* (WB, 1948), *Wallflower* (WB, 1948), *Romance on the High Seas* (WB, 1948), *One Sunday Afternoon* (WB, 1948), *The Younger Brothers* (WB, 1949), *The House Across the Street* (WB, 1949), *This Side of the Law* (WB, 1950), *Mr. Universe* (EL, 1951), *Fugitive Lady* (Rep., 1951), *Two Gals and a Guy* (UA, 1951), *Silk Stockings* (MGM, 1957), *Please Don't Eat the Daisies* (MGM, 1960), *Bachelor in Paradise* (MGM, 1961), *Follow the Boys* (MGM, 1963), *The Caretakers* (UA, 1963), *Welcome to Hard Times* (MGM, 1967).

*Unbilled guest appearance

JACK PALANCE (Walter Jack Palance) Born February 18, 1920, Lattimer, Pennsylvania. Married Virginia Baker (1949), children: Holly, Brook.

Constance Smith and Jack Palance in *Man in the Attic*.

English-Language Feature Films: *Panic in the Streets* (20th, 1950), *Halls of Montezuma* (20th, 1950), *Sudden Fear* (RKO, 1952), *Shane* (Par., 1953), *Second Chance* (RKO, 1953), *Arrowhead* (Par., 1953), *Flight to Tangier* (Par., 1953), *Man in the Attic* (20th, 1953), *Sign of the Pagan* (Univ., 1954), *The Silver Chalice* (WB, 1954), *Kiss of Fire* (Univ., 1955), *The Big Knife* (UA, 1955), *I Died a Thousand Times* (WB, 1955), *Attack!* (UA, 1956), *The Lonely Man* (Par., 1957), *House of Numbers* (MGM, 1957), *The Man Inside* (Col., 1958), *Ten Seconds to Hell* (UA, 1959), *Beyond All Limits* (Sutton Picture Corp., 1961), *Barabbas* (Col., 1962), *The Mongols* (Colorama, 1962), *Once a Thief* (MGM, 1965), *The Professionals* (Col., 1966), *Kill a Dragon* (UA, 1967), *Torture Garden* (Col., 1968), *The Scalphunters* (UA, 1968), *Our Man From Las Vegas* (WB-7 Arts, 1968).

EUGENE PALLETTE Born July 8, 1889, Winfield, Kansas. Died September 3, 1954.

Sound Feature Films: *Lights of New York* (WB, 1928), *The Canary Murder Case* (Par., 1929), *The Dummy* (Par., 1929), *The Greene Murder Case* (Par., 1929), *Studio Murder Mystery* (Par., 1929), *The Virginian* (Par., 1929), *Pointed Heels* (Par., 1929), *Love Parade* (Par., 1929), *Slightly Scarlet* (Par., 1930), *The Benson Murder Case* (Par., 1930), *Paramount on Parade* (Par., 1930), *Kibitzer* (Par., 1930), *Men Are Like That* (Par., 1930), *Border Legion* (Par., 1930), *Follow Through* (Par., 1930), *Let's Go Native* (Par., 1930), *Sea God* (Par., 1930), *Santa Fe Trail* (Par., 1930), *Playboy of Paris* (Par., 1930), *Sea Legs* (Par., 1930), *Fighting Caravans* (Par., 1931), *It Pays to Advertise* (Par., 1931), *Gun Smoke* (Par., 1931), *Dude Ranch* (Par., 1931), *Huckleberry Finn* (Par., 1931), *Girls About Town* (Par., 1931), *Dancers in the Dark* (Par., 1932), *Shanghai Express* (Par., 1932), *Thunder Below* (Par., 1932), *Strangers of the Evening* (Tif., 1932), *Night Mayor* (Col., 1932), *Wild Girl* (Fox, 1932), *Half-Naked Truth* (RKO, 1932), *Hell Below* (MGM, 1933), *Made on Broadway* (MGM, 1933), *Storm at Daybreak* (MGM, 1933), *Shanghai Madness* (Fox, 1933), *The Kennel Murder Case* (WB, 1933), *From Headquarters* (WB, 1933), *Mr. Skitch* (Fox, 1933), *I've Got Your Number* (WB, 1934), *Cross Country Cruise* (Univ., 1934), *Friends of Mr. Sweeney* (WB, 1934), *Strictly Dynamite* (RKO, 1934), *The Dragon Murder Case* (WB, 1934), *Caravan* (Fox, 1934), *One Exciting Adventure* (Univ., 1934), *Bordertown* (WB, 1935), *Baby Face Harrington* (MGM, 1935), *All the King's Horses* (Par., 1935), *Black Sheep* (Fox, 1935), *Steamboat 'Round the Bend* (Fox, 1935), *The Ghost Goes West* (UA, 1936), *The Golden Arrow* (WB, 1936), *My Man Godfrey* (Col., 1936), *Easy to Take* (Par., 1936), *Luckiest Girl in the World* (Univ., 1936), *Stowaway* (20th, 1936), *Clarence* (Par., 1937), *The Crime Nobody Saw* (Par., 1937), *She Had to Eat* (20th, 1937), *100 Men and a Girl* (Univ., 1937), *Topper* (MGM, 1937), *The Adventures of Robin Hood* (WB, 1938), *There Goes My Heart* (UA, 1938), *Wife, Husband and Friend* (20th, 1939), *First Love* (Univ., 1939), *Mr. Smith Goes to Washington* (Col., 1939), *Young Tom Edison* (MGM, 1940), *It's a Date* (Univ., 1940), *Sandy Is a Lady* (Col., 1940), *He Stayed for Breakfast* (Col., 1940), *A Little Bit of Heaven* (Univ., 1940), *The Mark of Zorro* (20th, 1940), *Ride Kelly, Ride* (20th, 1941), *The Lady Eve* (Par., 1941), *The Bride Came C.O.D.* (WB, 1941), *Unfinished Business* (Univ., 1941), *World Premiere* (Par., 1941), *Appointment for Love* (Univ., 1941), *The Male Animal* (WB, 1941), *Are Husbands Necessary?* (Par., 1942), *Lady in a Jam* (Univ., 1942), *Almost Married* (Univ., 1942), *Tales of Manhattan* (20th, 1942), *The Big Street* (RKO, 1942), *The Forest Rangers* (Par., 1942), *Silver Queen* (UA, 1942), *Slightly Dangerous* (MGM, 1943), *It Ain't Hay* (Univ., 1943), *The Kansan* (UA, 1943), *Heaven Can Wait* (20th, 1943), *The Gang's All Here* (20th, 1943), *Pin-Up Girl* (20th, 1944), *Sensations of 1945* (UA, 1944), *Step Lively* (RKO, 1944), *Heavenly Days* (RKO, 1944), *In the Meantime, Darling* (20th, 1944), *Lake Placid Serenade* (Rep., 1945), *The Cheaters* (Rep., 1945), *Suspense* (Mon., 1946), *In Old Sacramento* (Rep., 1946).

LILLI PALMER (Maria Lilli Peiser) Born May 24, 1914, Posen, Germany. Married Rex Harrison (1943), child: Carey; divorced 1958. Married Carlos Thompson (1958).

Lilli Palmer, Dana Andrews and Louis Jourdan in *No Minor Vices*.

English-Language Feature Films: *Crime Unlimited* (1934), *Bad Blood* (1935), *First Offense* (Gainsborough, 1935), *Secret Agent* (Gaumont-British, 1936), *Wolf's Clothing* (1936), *The Great Barrier* (Gaumont-British, 1937), *Sunset in Vienna* (Wilcox, 1937), *Good Morning, Boys* ("Where There's a Will"—Gaumont-British, 1937), *Command Performance* (Grosvenor, 1937), *Crackerjack* (Gaumont-British, 1938), *Man With a Hundred Faces* (Gaumont-British, 1938), *A Girl Must Live* (Gainsborough, 1938), *Blind Folly* (1940), *The Door With Seven Locks* ("Chamber of Horrors"—Argyle, 1941), *Thunder Rock* (Charter, 1942), *The Gentle Sex* (Two Cities, 1943), *English Without Tears* (Two Cities, 1943), *Beware of Pity* (Two Cities, 1945), *The Rake's Progress* ("Notorious Gentleman"—Univ., 1946), *Cloak and Dagger* (WB, 1946), *Body and Soul* (UA, 1947), *My Girl Tisa* (WB, 1948), *No Minor Vices* (MGM, 1948), *Her Man Gilbey* (Univ., 1949), *The Wicked City* (UA, 1951), *The Long Dark Hall* (EL, 1951), *The Fourposter* (Col., 1952), *Main Street to Broadway* (MGM, 1953), *But Not for Me* (Par., 1959), *Conspiracy of Hearts* (Par., 1960), *The Pleasure of His Company* (Par., 1961), *The Counterfeit Traitor* (Par., 1962), *The Miracle of the White Stallions* (BV, 1963), *Torpedo Bay* (AIP, 1964), *Operation Crossbow* (MGM, 1965), *The Amorous Adventures of Moll Flanders* (Par., 1965), *Jack of Diamonds* (MGM, 1967), *Sebastian* (Par., 1968), *Nobody Runs Forever* (Rank, 1968), *The High Commissioner* (American Broadcasting Co., 1968), *Oedipus* (Univ., 1968).

FRANKLIN PANGBORN Born January 23, 1893, Newark, New Jersey. Died July 20, 1958.

Sound Feature Films: *Not So Dumb* (MGM, 1930), *Cheer Up and Smile* (Fox, 1930), *Her Man* (Pathé, 1930), *A Lady Surrenders* (Univ., 1930), *Woman of Experience* (Pathé, 1931), *International House* (Par., 1933), *Professional Sweetheart* (RKO, 1933), *Important Witness* (Tower, 1933), *Headline Shooter* (RKO, 1933), *Only Yesterday* (Univ.,

Franklin Pangborn, Edna Murphy, Patsy Ruth Miller and Alan Hale in *The Sap*.

1933), *Design for Living* (Par., 1933), *Flying Down to Rio* (RKO, 1933), *Manhattan Love Song* (Mon., 1934), *Unknown Blonde* (Majestic, 1934), *Many Happy Returns* (Par., 1934), *Strictly Dynamite* (RKO, 1934), *Young and Beautiful* (Mascot, 1934), *Imitation of Life* (Univ., 1934), *King Kelly of the U.S.A.* (Mon., 1934), *That's Gratitude* (Col., 1934), *College Rhythm* (Par., 1934), *Tomorrow's Youth* (Mon., 1935), *Eight Bells* (Col., 1935), *Headline Woman* (Mon., 1935), *She Couldn't Take It* (Col., 1935), *$1,000 a Minute* (Rep., 1935), *Tango* (Invincible, 1936), *Don't Gamble With Love* (Col., 1936), *Mr. Deeds Goes to Town* (Col., 1936), *Doughnuts and Society* (Mascot, 1936), *To Mary—With Love* (20th, 1936), *The Mandarin Mystery* (Rep., 1936), *Hats Off* (GN, 1936), *The Luckiest Girl in the World* (Univ., 1936), *Dangerous Number* (MGM, 1937), *She's Dangerous* (Univ., 1937), *Swing High—Swing Low* (Par., 1937), *Step Lively, Jeeves!* (20th, 1937), *Turn Off the Moon* (Par., 1937), *A Star Is Born* (UA, 1937), *Danger, Love at Work* (20th, 1937), *Hotel Haywire* (Par., 1937), *Dangerous Holiday* (Rep., 1937), *She Had to Eat* (20th, 1937), *Stage Door* (RKO, 1937), *Life of the Party* (RKO, 1937), *Thrill of a Lifetime* (Par., 1937), *Living on Love* (RKO, 1937), *When Love Is Young* (Univ., 1937), *High Hat* (Imperial, 1937), *Bluebeard's Eighth Wife* (Par., 1938), *Love on Toast* (Par., 1938), *Mad About Music* (Univ., 1938), *Joy of Living* (RKO, 1938), *Rebecca of Sunnybrook Farm* (20th, 1938), *She Married an Artist* (Col., 1938), *Vivacious Lady* (RKO, 1938), *Dr. Rhythm* (Par., 1938), *Four's a Crowd* (WB, 1938), *Three Blind Mice* (20th, 1938), *Carefree* (RKO, 1938), *Just Around the Corner* (20th, 1938), *Meet the Mayor* (Times Pictures, 1938), *Topper Takes a Trip* (UA, 1939), *The Girl Downstairs* (MGM, 1939), *Broadway Serenade* (MGM, 1939), *Fifth Avenue Girl* (RKO, 1939), *Turnabout* (UA, 1940), *Christmas in July* (Par., 1940), *Spring Parade* (Univ., 1940), *Public Deb No. 1* (20th, 1940), *The Bank Dick* (Univ., 1940), *Where Did You Get That Girl?* (Univ., 1941), *The Hit Parade of 1941* (Rep., 1941), *A Girl, a Guy and a Gob* (RKO, 1941), *The Flame of New Orleans* (Univ., 1941), *Bachelor Daddy* (Univ., 1941), *Tillie the Toiler* (Col., 1941), *Never Give a Sucker an Even Break* (Univ., 1941), *Week-End for Three* (RKO, 1941), *Obliging Young Lady* (RKO, 1941), *Sullivan's Travels* (Par., 1941), *Mr. District Attorney in The Carter Case* (Rep., 1941), *Sandy Steps Out* (Univ., 1941), *What's Cooking?* (Univ., 1942), *Call out the Marines* (RKO, 1942), *Moonlight Masquerade* (Rep., 1942), *Now, Voyager* (WB, 1942), *George Washington Slept Here* (WB, 1942), *Palm Beach Story* (Par., 1942), *Strictly in the Groove* (Univ., 1943), *Two Weeks to Live* (RKO, 1943), *Honeymoon Lodge* (Univ., 1943), *Holy Matrimony* (20th, 1943), *Crazy House* (Univ., 1943), *His Butler's Sister* (Univ., 1943), *Stage Door Canteen* (UA, 1943), *Reveille With Beverly* (Col., 1943), *My Best Gal* (Rep., 1944), *The Great Moment* (Par., 1944), *Hail the Conquering Hero* (Par., 1944), *Reckless Age* (Univ., 1944), *The Horn Blows at Midnight* (WB, 1945), *You Came Along* (Par., 1945), *Tell It to a Star* (Rep., 1945), *Two Guys From Milwaukee* (WB, 1946), *I'll Be Yours* (Univ., 1947), *Calendar Girl* (Rep., 1947), *Mad Wednesday* (UA, 1947), *Romance on the High Seas* (WB, 1949), *My Dream Is Yours* (WB, 1949), *Down Memory Lane* (EL, 1949), *The Story of Mankind* (WB, 1957), *Oh, Men! Oh, Women!* (20th, 1957).

ELEANOR PARKER Born June 26, 1922, Cedarville, Ohio. Married Fred Losee (1943); divorced 1944. Married Bert Friedlob (1946), children: Susan, Sharon, Richard; divorced 1953. Married Paul Clemens (1954), child: Paul, Jr.; divorced 1964. Married Raymond Hirsch (1966).

Feature Films: *Busses Roar* (WB, 1942), *Mysterious Doctor* (WB, 1943), *Mission to Moscow* (WB, 1943), *Between Two Worlds* (WB, 1944), *Crime by Night* (WB, 1944), *The Last Ride* (WB, 1944), *The Very Thought of You* (WB, 1944), *Hollywood Canteen* (WB, 1944), *Pride of the Marines* (WB, 1945), *Of Human Bondage* (WB, 1946), *Never Say Goodbye* (WB, 1946), *Escape Me Never* (WB, 1947), *Always Together* (WB, 1947),* *The Voice of the Turtle* (WB, 1947), *The Woman in White* (WB, 1948), *It's a Great Feeling* (WB, 1949), *Chain Lightning* (WB, 1950), *Caged* (WB, 1950), *Three Secrets* (WB, 1950), *Valentino* (Col., 1951), *A Millionaire for Christy* (20th, 1951), *Detective Story* (Par., 1951), *Scaramouche* (MGM, 1952), *Above and Beyond* (MGM, 1952), *Escape From Fort Bravo* (MGM, 1953), *The Naked Jungle* (Par., 1954), *Valley of the Kings* (MGM, 1954), *Many Rivers to Cross*

Agnes Moorehead, Eleanor Parker and Sheila Stevens (MacRae) in *Caged.*

(MGM, 1955), *Interrupted Melody* (MGM, 1955), *The Man With the Golden Arm* (UA, 1955), *The King and Four Queens* (UA, 1956), *Lizzie* (MGM, 1957), *The Seventh Sin* (MGM, 1957), *A Hole in the Head* (UA, 1959), *Home From the Hill* (MGM, 1960), *Return to Peyton Place* (20th, 1961), *Madison Avenue* (20th, 1962), *Panic Button* (Gorton Associates, 1964), *The Sound of Music* (20th, 1965), *The Oscar* (Par., 1966), *An American Dream* (WB, 1966), *Warning Shot* (Par., 1967), *The Tiger and the Pussycat* (Embassy, 1967).

*Unbilled guest appearance

JEAN PARKER (Mae Green) Born August 11, 1912, Deer Lodge, Montana. Married George MacDonald (1936); divorced 1940. Married Douglas Dawson (1941); divorced. Married Curtis Grotter (1944); divorced 1949. Married Robert Lowery (1951); divorced 1957.

Jean Parker and Eric Linden in *Romance of the Limberlost.*

Feature Films: *Divorce in the Family* (MGM, 1932), *Rasputin and the Empress* (MGM, 1932), *Secret of Madame Blanche* (MGM, 1933), *Gabriel Over the White House* (MGM, 1933), *Made on Broadway* (MGM, 1933), *Storm at Daybreak* (MGM, 1933), *What Price Innocence* (Col., 1933), *Lady for a Day* (Col., 1933), *Little Women* (RKO, 1933), *Lazy River* (MGM, 1934), *You Can't Buy Everything* (MGM, 1934), *Two Alone* (RKO, 1934), *Operator 13* (MGM, 1934), *Caravan* (Fox, 1934), *Sequoia* (MGM, 1934), *A Wicked Woman* (MGM, 1934), *Limehouse Blues* (Par., 1934), *Have a Heart* (MGM, 1934), *Princess O'Hara* (Univ., 1935), *Murder in the Fleet* (MGM, 1935), *The Ghost Goes West* (UA, 1936), *The Farmer in the Dell* (RKO, 1936), *The Texas Rangers* (Par., 1936), *The Barrier* (Par., 1937), *Life Begins With Love* (Col., 1937), *Penitentiary* (Col., 1938), *Romance of the Limberlost* (Mon., 1938), *The Arkansas Traveler* (Par., 1938), *Zenobia* (UA, 1939), *Romance of the Redwoods* (Col., 1939), *She Married a Cop* (Rep., 1939), *Flight at Midnight* (Rep., 1939), *Parents on Trial* (Col., 1939).

The Flying Deuces (RKO, 1939), *Son of the Navy* (Mon., 1940), *Knights of the Range* (Par., 1940), *Beyond Tomorrow* (RKO, 1940), *The Roar of the Press* (Mon., 1941), *Power Dive* (Par., 1941), *Flying Blind* (Par., 1941), *The Pittsburgh Kid* (Rep., 1941), *No Hands on the Clock* (Par., 1941), *Torpedo Boat* (Par., 1942), *The Girl From Alaska* (Rep., 1942), *Hi, Neighbor* (Rep., 1942), *Hello, Annapolis* (Col., 1942), *I Live on Danger* (Par., 1942), *Tomorrow We Live* (PRC, 1942), *Wrecking Crew* (Par., 1942), *The Traitor Within* (Rep., 1942), *Alaska Highway* (Par., 1943), *Minesweeper* (Par., 1943), *The Deerslayer* (Rep., 1943), *High Explosive* (Par., 1943), *The Navy Way* (Par., 1944), *Detective Kitty O'Day* (Mon., 1944), *The Lady in the Death House* (PRC, 1944), *Oh, What a Night!* (Mon., 1944), *Dead Man's Eyes* (Univ., 1944), *Bluebeard* (PRC, 1944), *One Body Too Many* (Par., 1944), *The Adventures of Kitty O'Day* (Mon., 1945), *The Gunfighter* (20th, 1950), *Toughest Man in Arizona* (Rep., 1952), *Those Redheads From Seattle* (Par., 1953), *Black Tuesday* (UA, 1954), *A Lawless Street* (Col., 1955), *The Parson and the Outlaw* (Col., 1957), *Apache Uprising* (Par., 1966).

GAIL PATRICK (Margaret Fitzpatrick) Born June 20, 1916, Birmingham, Alabama. Married Robert Cobb (1936); divorced 1940. Married Arnold White (1944); divorced 1946. Married Cornwall Jackson (1947), children: Jennifer, Thomas.

Gail Patrick and Ricardo Cortez in *Her Husband Lies.*

Feature Films: *If I Had a Million* (Par., 1932), *Mysterious Rider* (Par., 1933), *Mama Loves Papa* (Par., 1933), *Pick-Up* (Par., 1933), *Murders in the Zoo* (Par., 1933), *Phantom Broadcast* (Mon., 1933), *To the Last Man* (Par., 1933), *Cradle Song* (Par., 1933), *Death Takes a Holiday* (Par., 1934), *Murder at the Vanities* (Par., 1934), *The Crime of Helen Stanley* (Col., 1934), *Wagon Wheels* (Par., 1934), *Take the Stand* (Liberty, 1934), *One Hour Late* (Par., 1935), *Rumba* (Par., 1935), *Mississippi* (Par., 1935), *Doubting Thomas* (Fox, 1935), *No More Ladies* (MGM, 1935), *Smart Girl* (Par., 1935), *The Big Broadcast of 1936* (Par., 1935), *Wanderer of the Wasteland* (Par., 1935), *Two in the Dark* (RKO, 1936), *The Lone Wolf Returns* (Col., 1936), *The Preview Murder Mystery* (Par., 1936), *Early to Bed* (Par., 1936), *My Man Godfrey* (Univ., 1936), *Murder With Pictures* (Par., 1936), *White Hunter* (20th, 1936), *John Meade's Woman* (Par., 1937), *Her Husband Lies* (Par., 1937), *Artists and Models* (Par., 1937), *Stage Door* (RKO, 1937), *Mad About Music* (Univ., 1938), *Dangerous to Know* (Par., 1938), *Wives Under Suspicion* (Univ., 1938), *King of Alcatraz* (Par., 1938), *Disbarred* (Par., 1939), *Man of Conquest* (Rep., 1939), *Grand Jury Secrets* (Par., 1939), *Reno* (RKO, 1939), *My Favorite Wife* (RKO, 1940), *The Doctor Takes a Wife* (Col., 1940), *Gallant Sons* (MGM, 1940), *Love Crazy* (MGM, 1941), *Kathleen* (MGM, 1941), *Tales of Manhattan* (20th, 1942), *Quiet Please—Murder* (20th, 1942), *We Were Dancing* (MGM, 1942), *The Hit Parade of 1943* (Rep., 1943), *Women in Bondage* (Mon., 1943), *Up in Mabel's Room* (UA, 1944), *Brewster's Millions* (UA, 1945), *Twice Blessed* (MGM, 1945), *The Madonna's Secret* (Rep., 1946), *Rendezvous With Annie*

(Rep., 1946), *Claudia and David* (20th, 1946), *The Plainsman and the Lady* (Rep., 1946), *Calendar Girl* (Rep., 1947), *King of the Wild Horses* (Col., 1947), *The Inside Story* (Rep., 1948).

LEE PATRICK (Lee Salome Patrick) Born November 22, 1911, New York, New York. Married Thomas Wood (1937).

Lee Patrick, Dale Belding and Nana Bryant in *Inner Sanctum.*

Feature Films: *Strange Cargo* (Pathé, 1929), *Border Cafe* (RKO, 1937), *Music for Madame* (RKO, 1937), *Danger Patrol* (RKO, 1937), *Crashing Hollywood* (RKO, 1938), *Night Spot* (RKO, 1938), *Condemned Women* (RKO, 1938), *Law of the Underworld* (RKO, 1938), *The Sisters* (WB, 1938), *Fisherman's Wharf* (RKO, 1939), *Invisible Stripes* (WB, 1940), *Saturday's Children* (WB, 1940), *City for Conquest* (WB, 1940), *Ladies Must Live* (WB, 1940), *Money and the Woman* (WB, 1940), *South of Suez* (WB, 1940), *Father Is a Prince* (WB, 1940), *Footsteps in the Dark* (WB, 1941), *Honeymoon for Three* (WB, 1941), *Million Dollar Baby* (WB, 1941), *The Nurse's Secret* (WB, 1941), *The Smiling Ghost* (WB, 1941), *The Maltese Falcon* (WB, 1941), *Dangerously They Live* (WB, 1941), *In This Our Life* (WB, 1942), *Now, Voyager* (WB, 1942), *Somewhere I'll Find You* (MGM, 1942), *George Washington Slept Here* (WB, 1942), *A Night to Remember* (Col., 1943), *Jitterbugs* (20th, 1943), *Nobody's Darling* (Rep., 1943), *Larceny With Music* (Univ., 1943), *Moon Over Las Vegas* (Univ., 1944), *Gambler's Choice* (Par., 1944), *Mrs. Parkington* (MGM, 1944), *Faces in the Fog* (Rep., 1944), *See My Lawyer* (Univ., 1945), *Keep Your Powder Dry* (MGM, 1945), *Over 21* (Col., 1945), *Mildred Pierce* (WB, 1945), *The Walls Came Tumbling Down* (Col., 1946), *Strange Journey* (20th, 1946), *Wake Up and Dream* (20th, 1946), *Mother Wore Tights* (20th, 1947), *Inner Sanctum* (Film Classics, 1948), *The Snake Pit* (20th, 1948), *Singin' Spurs* (Col., 1948), *The Doolins of Oklahoma* (Col., 1949), *The Lawless* (Par., 1950), *The Fuller Brush Girl* (Col., 1950), *Caged* (WB, 1950), *Tomorrow Is Another Day* (WB, 1951), *Take Me to Town* (Univ., 1953), *There's No Business Like Show Business* (20th, 1954), *Vertigo* (Par., 1958), *Auntie Mame* (WB, 1958), *Pillow Talk* (Univ., 1959), *Visit to a Small Planet* (Par., 1960), *Goodbye Again* (UA, 1961), *Summer and Smoke* (Par., 1961), *A Girl Named Tamiko* (Par., 1962), *Wives and Lovers* (Par., 1963), *7 Faces of Dr. Lao* (MGM, 1964), *The New Interns* (Col., 1964).

ELIZABETH PATTERSON (Mary Elizabeth Patterson) Born November 22, 1874, Savannah, Tennessee. Died January 31, 1966.

Sound Feature Films: *Timothy's Quest* (Gotham Productions, 1929), *Words and Music* (Fox, 1929), *South Sea Rose* (Fox, 1929), *Lone Star Ranger* (Fox, 1930), *Harmony at Home* (Fox, 1930), *The Big Party* (Fox, 1930), *The Cat Creeps* (Univ., 1930), *Penrod and Sam* (WB, 1931), *Tarnished Lady* (Par., 1931), *The Smiling Lieutenant* (Par., 1931), *Daddy Long Legs* (Fox, 1931), *Heaven on Earth* (Univ., 1931), *Two Against the World* (WB, 1932), *Husband's Holiday* (Par., 1932), *The Expert* (WB, 1932), *Play Girl* (WB, 1932), *So Big* (WB, 1932), *New Morals for Old* (MGM, 1932), *Miss Pinkerton* (WB, 1932), *Love Me Tonight* (Par., 1932), *Life Begins* (WB, 1932), *Guilty as Hell* (Par., 1932), *A Bill of Divorcement* (RKO, 1932), *They Call It Sin*

Cecilia Parker and Elizabeth Patterson in *Old Hutch.*

(WB, 1932), *Breach of Promise* (World Wide, 1932), *No Man of Her Own* (Par., 1932), *The Conquerors* (RKO, 1932), *They Just Had to Get Married* (Univ., 1933), *Infernal Machine* (Fox, 1933), *The Story of Temple Drake* (Par., 1933), *Dinner at Eight* (MGM, 1933), *Hold Your Man* (MGM, 1933), *Doctor Bull* (Fox, 1933), *Secret of the Blue Room* (Univ., 1933), *Hideout* (MGM, 1934), *Golden Harvest* (Par., 1933), *Chasing Yesterday* (RKO, 1935), *So Red the Rose* (Par., 1935), *Men Without Names* (Par., 1935), *Her Master's Voice* (Par., 1936), *Small Town Girl* (MGM, 1936), *Timothy's Quest* (Par., 1936), *Three Cheers for Love* (Par., 1936), *The Return of Sophie Lang* (Par., 1936), *Old Hutch* (MGM, 1936), *Go West, Young Man* (Par., 1936), *High, Wide and Handsome* (Par., 1937), *Hold 'Em Navy* (Par., 1937), *Night Club Scandal* (Par., 1937), *Night of Mystery* (Par., 1937), *Scandal Street* (Par., 1938), *Bluebeard's Eighth Wife* (Par., 1938), *Bulldog Drummond's Peril* (Par., 1938), *Sing You Sinners* (Par., 1938), *Sons of the Legion* (Par., 1938), *The Story of Alexander Graham Bell* (20th, 1939), *Bulldog Drummond's Secret Police* (Par., 1939), *Bulldog Drummond's Bride* (Par., 1939), *The Cat and the Canary* (Par., 1939), *Our Leading Citizen* (Par., 1939), *Remember the Night* (Par., 1940), *Bad Little Angel* (MGM, 1940), *Adventure in Diamonds* (Par., 1940), *Anne of Windy Poplars* (RKO, 1940), *Earthbound* (20th, 1940), *Who Killed Aunt Maggie?* (Rep., 1940), *Michael Shayne, Private Detective* (20th, 1940), *Tobacco Road* (20th, 1940), *Kiss the Boys Goodbye* (Par., 1940), *Belle Starr* (20th, 1941), *Lucky Legs* (Col., 1942), *Her Cardboard Lover* (MGM, 1942), *Almost Married* (Univ., 1942), *My Sister Eileen* (Col., 1942), *I Married a Witch* (UA, 1942), *Beyond the Blue Horizon* (Par., 1942), *Lucky Legs* (Col., 1942), *The Sky's the Limit* (RKO, 1943), *Follow the Boys* (Univ., 1944), *Hail the Conquering Hero* (Par., 1944), *Together Again* (Col., 1944), *Lady on a Train* (Univ., 1945), *Colonel Effingham's Raid* (20th, 1945), *I've Always Loved You* (Rep., 1946), *The Secret Heart* (MGM, 1946), *The Shocking Miss Pilgrim* (20th, 1947), *Welcome Stranger* (Par., 1947), *Out of the Blue* (EL, 1947), *Miss Tatlock's Millions* (Par., 1948), *Little Women* (MGM, 1949), *Song of Surrender* (Par., 1949), *Intruder in the Dust* (MGM, 1949), *Bright Leaf* (WB, 1950), *Katie Did It* (Univ., 1951), *Washington Story* (MGM, 1952), *Las Vegas Shakedown* (AA, 1955), *Pal Joey* (Col., 1957), *The Oregon Trail* (20th, 1959), *Tall Story* (WB, 1960).

KATINA PAXINOU (Katina Konstantopoulou) Born 1900, Piraeus, Greece. Married Ivannis Paxinou (1916); divorced. Married Alexis Minotis (1940), child: Iliana.

Walter Slezak and Katina Paxinou in *The Miracle.*

English-Language Feature Films: *For Whom the Bell Tolls* (Par., 1943), *Hostages* (Par., 1943), *Confidential Agent* (WB, 1945), *Mourning Becomes Electra* (RKO, 1947), *The Inheritance* (Fine Arts, 1947), *Prince of Foxes* (20th, 1949), *Mr. Arkadin* (WB, 1955), *The Miracle* (WB, 1959), *The Trial* (Gibraltar, 1962).

JOHN PAYNE Born May 23, 1912, Roanoke, Virginia. Married Anne Shirley (1937), child: Julie; divorced 1943. Married Gloria DeHaven (1944), children: Kathy, Thomas; divorced 1950. Married Alexandra Curtis (1953).

Glenn Miller, Sonja Henie and John Payne in *Sun Valley Serenade.*

Feature Films: *Dodsworth* (UA, 1936), *Hats Off* (GN, 1936), *Fair Warning* (20th, 1937), *Love on Toast* (Par., 1938), *College Swing* (Par., 1938), *Garden of the Moon* (WB, 1938), *Wings of the Navy* (WB, 1939), *Indianapolis Speedway* (WB, 1939), *Kid Nightingale* (WB, 1939), *Star Dust* (20th, 1940), *Maryland* (20th, 1940), *The Great Profile* (20th, 1940), *King of the Lumberjacks* (WB, 1940), *Tear Gas Squad* (WB, 1940), *The Great American Broadcast* (20th, 1941), *Week-End in Havana* (20th, 1941), *Remember the Day* (20th, 1941), *Sun Valley Serenade* (20th, 1941), *To the Shores of Tripoli* (20th, 1942), *Iceland* (20th, 1942), *Springtime in the Rockies* (20th, 1942), *Hello, Frisco, Hello* (20th, 1943), *The Dolly Sisters* (20th, 1945), *Sentimental Journey* (20th, 1946), *The Razor's Edge* (20th, 1946), *Wake Up and Dream* (20th, 1946), *The Miracle on 34th Street* (20th, 1947), *Larceny* (Univ., 1948), *The Saxon Charm* (Univ., 1948), *El Paso* (Par., 1949), *The Crooked Way* (UA, 1949), *Captain China* (Par., 1949), *The Eagle and the Hawk* (Par., 1950), *Tripoli* (Par., 1950), *Passage West* (Par., 1951), *Crosswinds* (Par., 1951), *Caribbean* (Par., 1952), *The Blazing Forest* (Par., 1952), *Kansas City Confidential* (UA, 1952), *Raiders of the Seven Seas* (UA, 1953), *The Vanquished* (Par., 1953), *99 River Street* (UA, 1953), *Rails into Laramie* (Univ., 1954), *Silver Lode* (RKO, 1954), *Santa Fe Passage* (Rep., 1955), *Hell's Island* (Par., 1955), *The Road to Denver* (Rep., 1955), *Tennessee's Partner* (RKO, 1955), *Slightly Scarlet* (RKO, 1956), *Rebel in Town* (UA, 1956), *Hold Back the Night* (AA, 1956), *The Boss* (UA, 1956), *Bailout at 43,000* (UA, 1957), *Hidden Fear* (UA, 1957), *Gift of the Nile* (PRO, 1968), *They Ran for Their Lives* (Color Vision, 1968).

GREGORY PECK (Eldred Gregory Peck) Born April 5, 1916, La Jolla, California. Married Greta Rice (1942), children: Jonathan, Stephen, Carey; divorced 1954. Married Veronique Passani (1955), children: Anthony, Cecelia.

Feature Films: *Days of Glory* (RKO, 1944), *The Keys of the Kingdom* (20th, 1944), *The Valley of Decision* (MGM, 1945), *Spellbound* (UA, 1945), *The Yearling* (MGM, 1946), *Duel in the Sun* (Selznick, 1946), *The Macomber Affair* (UA, 1947), *Gentleman's Agreement* (20th, 1947), *The Paradine Case* (Selznick, 1948), *Yellow Sky* (20th, 1948), *The Great Sinner* (MGM, 1949), *The Gun Fighter* (20th, 1949), *12 O'Clock High* (20th, 1949), *Captain Horatio Hornblower* (WB, 1951), *Only the Valiant*

Tamara Toumanova, Gregory Peck and Lowell Gilmore in *Days of Glory.*

(WB, 1951), *David and Bathsheba* (20th, 1951), *The Snows of Kilimanjaro* (20th, 1952), *Roman Holiday* (Par., 1953), *Night People* (20th, 1953), *Man With a Million* (UA, 1954), *The Purple Plain* (UA, 1955), *The Man in the Gray Flannel Suit* (20th, 1956), *Moby Dick* (WB, 1956), *Designing Woman* (MGM, 1957), *The Big Country* (UA, 1958), *The Bravados* (20th, 1958), *Pork Chop Hill* (UA, 1959), *Beloved Infidel* (20th, 1959), *On the Beach* (UA, 1959), *The Guns of Navarone* (Col., 1961), *Cape Fear* (Univ., 1962), *To Kill a Mockingbird* (Univ., 1962), *How the West Was Won* (MGM, 1963), *Behold a Pale Horse* (Col., 1964), *Captain Newman, M.D.* (Univ., 1964), *Mirage* (Univ., 1965), *Arabesque* (Univ., 1966), *MacKenna's Gold* (Col., 1968), *The Stalking Moon* (National *General*, 1968).

GEORGE PEPPARD Born October 1, 1933, Detroit, Michigan. Married Helen Davies (1954), children: Bradford, Julie; divorced 1965. Married Elizabeth Ashley (1966), child: Christopher.

Janice Rule and George Peppard in *The Subterraneans.*

Feature Films: *The Strange One* (Col., 1957), *Pork Chop Hill* (UA, 1959), *Home From the Hill* (MGM, 1960), *The Subterraneans* (MGM, 1960), *Breakfast at Tiffany's* (Par., 1961), *How the West Was Won* (MGM, 1963), *The Victors* (Col., 1963), *The Carpetbaggers* (Par., 1964), *Operation Crossbow* (MGM, 1965), *The Third Day* (WB, 1965), *The Blue Max* (20th, 1966), *Tobruk* (Univ., 1967), *Rough Night in Jericho* (Univ., 1967), *P.J.* (Univ., 1968), *What's So Bad About Feeling Good* (Univ., 1968), *House of Cards* (Univ., 1968).

TONY PERKINS (Anthony Perkins) Born April 4, 1932, New York, New York.

English-Language Feature Films: *The Actress* (MGM, 1953), *Friendly*

Tony Perkins and Sophia Loren in *Desire Under the Elms*.

Laraine Day, Susan Peters and Lana Turner in *Keep Your Powder Dry*.

Persuasion (AA, 1956), *The Lonely Man* (Par., 1957), *Fear Strikes Out* (Par., 1957), *The Tin Star* (Par., 1957), *This Angry Age* (Col., 1958), *The Matchmaker* (Par., 1958), *Green Mansions* (MGM, 1958), *On the Beach* (UA, 1959), *Tall Story* (WB, 1960), *Psycho* (Par., 1960), *Goodbye Again* (UA, 1961), *Phaedra* (Lopert, 1962), *Five Miles to Midnight* (UA, 1962), *The Trial* (Gibraltar, 1962), *Two Are Guilty* (MGM, 1964), *The Fool Killer* (Landau, 1965), *Is Paris Burning?* (Par., 1966), *The Champagne Murders* (Univ., 1968), *She Let Him Continue* (20th, 1968).

JEAN PETERS (Elizabeth Jean Peters) Born October 15, 1926, Canton, Ohio. Married Stuart Cramer (1954); divorced 1956. Married Howard Hughes (1957).

Joseph Cotten and Jean Peters in *A Blueprint for Murder*.

Feature Films: *Captain From Castile* (20th, 1947), *Deep Waters* (20th, 1948), *It Happens Every Spring* (20th, 1949), *Love That Brute* (20th, 1950), *Take Care of My Little Girl* (20th, 1951), *As Young as You Feel* (20th, 1951), *Anne of the Indies* (20th, 1951), *Viva Zapata!* (20th, 1952), *Wait Till the Sun Shines, Nellie* (20th, 1952), *Lure of the Wilderness* (20th, 1952), *O. Henry's Full House* (20th, 1952), *Niagara* (20th, 1953), *Pickup on South Street* (20th, 1953), *A Blueprint for Murder* (20th, 1953), *Vicki* (20th, 1953), *Three Coins in the Fountain* (20th, 1954), *Apache* (UA, 1954), *Broken Lance* (20th, 1954), *A Man Called Peter* (20th, 1955).

SUSAN PETERS (Suzanne Carnahan) Born July 3, 1921, Spokane, Washington. Married Richard Quine (1943), child: Timothy; divorced 1948. Died October 24, 1952.

Feature Films:
    as Suzanne Carnahan *Santa Fe Trail* (WB, 1940), *Money and the Woman* (WB, 1940), *The Man Who Talked Too Much* (WB, 1940), *Susan and God* (MGM, 1940), *Strawberry Blonde* (WB, 1941), *Meet John Doe* (WB, 1941), *Here Comes Happiness* (WB, 1941).
    as Susan Peters *Scattergood Pulls the Strings* (RKO, 1941), *Three Sons o' Guns* (WB, 1941), *Escape From Crime* (WB, 1942), *The Big Shot* (WB, 1942), *Tish* (MGM, 1942), *Random Harvest* (MGM, 1942), *Dr. Gillespie's New Assistant* (MGM, 1942), *Andy Hardy's Double Life* (MGM, 1942), *Assignment in Brittany* (MGM, 1943), *Young Ideas* (MGM, 1943), *Song of Russia* (MGM, 1943), *Keep Your Powder Dry* (MGM, 1945), *The Sign of the Ram* (Col., 1948).

WALTER PIDGEON Born September 23, 1897, East St. John, New Brunswick, Canada. Married Edna Pickles (1922), child: Edna; widowed 1924. Married Ruth Walker (1931).

Kay Francis, Eugene Pallette, Walter Pidgeon and Deanna Durbin in *It's a Date*.

Sound Feature Films: *Melody of Love* (Univ., 1928), *Her Private Life* (WB, 1929), *A Most Immoral Lady* (WB, 1929), *Bride of the Regiment* (WB, 1930), *Viennese Nights* (WB, 1930), *Sweet Kitty Bellaire* (WB, 1930), *Going Wild* (WB, 1931), *The Gorilla* (WB, 1931), *Kiss Me Again* (WB, 1931), *Hot Heiress* (WB, 1931), *Rockabye* (RKO, 1932), *The Kiss Before the Mirror* (Univ., 1933), *Journal of a Crime* (WB, 1934), *Fatal Lady* (Par., 1936), *Big Brown Eyes* (Par., 1936), *Girl Overboard* (Univ., 1937), *She's Dangerous* (Univ., 1937), *As Good as Married* (Univ., 1937), *Saratoga* (MGM, 1937), *My Dear Miss Aldrich* (MGM, 1937),

A Girl With Ideas (Univ., 1937), *Man-Proof* (MGM, 1938), *The Girl of the Golden West* (MGM, 1938), *The Shopworn Angel* (MGM, 1938), *Listen, Darling* (MGM, 1938), *Too Hot to Handle* (MGM, 1938), *Society Lawyer* (MGM, 1939), *6,000 Enemies* (MGM, 1939), *Stronger Than Desire* (MGM, 1939), *Nick Carter, Master Detective* (MGM, 1939), *It's a Date* (Univ., 1940), *Dark Command* (Rep., 1940), *The House Across the Bay* (UA, 1940), *Sky Murder* (MGM, 1940), *Flight Command* (MGM, 1940), *Man Hunt* (20th, 1941), *How Green Was My Valley* (20th, 1941), *Blossoms in the Dust* (MGM, 1941), *Design for Scandal* (MGM, 1941), *Mrs. Miniver* (MGM, 1942), *White Cargo* (MGM, 1942), *Madame Curie* (MGM, 1943), *The Youngest Profession* (MGM, 1943), *Mrs. Parkington* (MGM, 1944), *Weekend at the Waldorf* (MGM, 1945), *Holiday in Mexico* (MGM, 1946), *The Secret Heart* (MGM, 1946), *If Winter Comes* (MGM, 1947), *Cass Timberlane* (MGM, 1947)* *Julia Misbehaves* (MGM, 1948), *Command Decision* (MGM, 1948), *Red Danube* (MGM, 1949), *That Forsyte Woman* (MGM, 1949), *The Miniver Story* (MGM, 1950), *Soldiers Three* (MGM, 1951), *Calling Bulldog Drummond* (MGM, 1951), *The Unknown Man* (MGM, 1951), *The Sellout* (MGM, 1951), *Million Dollar Mermaid* (MGM, 1952), *The Bad and the Beautiful* (MGM, 1952), *Scandal at Scourie* (MGM, 1953), *Dream Wife* (MGM, 1953), *Executive Suite* (MGM, 1954), *Men of the Fighting Lady* (MGM, 1954), *The Last Time I Saw Paris* (MGM, 1954), *Deep in My Heart* (MGM, 1954), *Hit the Deck* (MGM, 1955), *Forbidden Planet* (MGM, 1956), *The Rack* (MGM, 1956), *Voyage to the Bottom of the Sea* (20th, 1961), *Big Red* (BV, 1962), *Advise and Consent* (Col., 1962), *Warning Shot* (Par., 1967), *Two Colonels* (Comet, 1967), *Funny Girl* (Col., 1968).

*Unbilled guest appearance

ZASU PITTS Born January 3, 1898, Parsons, Kansas. Married Tom Gallery (1921), child: Ann; divorced 1932. Married John Woodall (1934), child: Donald. Died June 7, 1963.

ZaSu Pitts, Helen Jerome Eddy and Marie Prevost in *War Nurse*.

Sound Feature Films: *The Dummy* (Par., 1929), *The Squall* (WB, 1929), *Twin Beds* (WB, 1929), *The Argyle Case* (WB, 1929), *This Thing Called Love* (Pathé, 1929), *Her Private Life* (WB, 1929), *The Locked Door* (UA, 1929), *Oh, Yeah!* (RKO, 1930), *No, No, Nanette* (WB, 1930), *Honey* (Par., 1930), *Devil's Holiday* (Par., 1930), *Monte Carlo* (Par., 1930), *Little Accident* (Univ., 1930), *Lottery Bride* (UA, 1930), *The Squealer* (Col., 1930), *Passion Flower* (MGM, 1930), *War Nurse* (MGM, 1930), *Sin Takes a Holiday* (RKO, 1930), *Finn and Hattie* (Par., 1931), *Bad Sister* (Univ., 1931), *River's End* (WB, 1931), *Beyond Victory* (RKO, 1931), *Seed* (Univ., 1931), *Woman of Experience* (RKO, 1931), *The Guardsman* (MGM, 1931), *Their Mad Moment* (Fox, 1931), *Big Gamble* (RKO, 1931), *Penrod and Sam* (WB, 1931), *Secret Witness* (Col., 1931), *Broken Lullaby* (Par., 1932), *Destry Rides Again* (Univ., 1932), *Unexpected Father* (Univ., 1932), *Steady Company* (Univ., 1932), *Shopworn* (Col., 1932), *The Trial of Vivienne Ware* (Fox, 1932), *Strangers of the Evening* (Tif., 1932), *Westward Passage* (RKO,

1932), *Is My Face Red?* (RKO, 1932), *Blondie of the Follies* (MGM, 1932), *Roar of the Dragon* (RKO, 1932), *Make Me a Star* (Par., 1932), *Vanishing Frontier* (Par., 1932), *The Crooked Circle* (Sono Art-World Wide, 1932), *Madison Square Garden* (Par., 1932), *Once in a Lifetime* (Univ., 1932), *Back Street* (Univ., 1932), *They Just Had to Get Married* (Univ., 1933), *Out All Night* (Univ., 1933), *Hello, Sister* (Fox, 1933), *Professional Sweetheart* (RKO, 1933), *Her First Mate* (Univ., 1933), *Aggie Appleby, Maker of Men* (RKO, 1933), *Meet the Baron* (MGM, 1933), *Love, Honor and Oh, Baby!* (Univ., 1933), *Mr. Skitch* (Par., 1933), *The Meanest Gal in Town* (RKO, 1934), *Sing and Like It* (RKO, 1934), *Two Alone* (RKO, 1934), *Love Birds* (Univ., 1934), *Three on a Honeymoon* (Fox, 1934), *Private Scandal* (Par., 1934), *Mrs. Wiggs of the Cabbage Patch* (Par., 1934), *The Gay Bride* (MGM, 1934), *Their Big Moment* (RKO, 1934), *Dames* (WB, 1934), *Ruggles of Red Gap* (Par., 1935), *Going Highbrow* (WB, 1935), *Hot Tip* (RKO, 1935), *She Gets Her Man* (Univ., 1935), *The Affairs of Susan* (Univ., 1935), *Spring Tonic* (Fox, 1935), *13 Hours By Air* (Par., 1936), *Mad Holiday* (MGM, 1936), *The Plot Thickens* (RKO, 1936), *Sing Me a Love Song* (WB, 1936), *Forty Naughty Girls* (RKO, 1937), *52nd Street* (UA, 1937), *Wanted* (British, 1937), *Merry Comes to Town* (Sound City, 1937), *The Lady's From Kentucky* (Par., 1939), *Mickey the Kid* (Rep., 1939), *Naughty but Nice* (WB, 1939), *Nurse Edith Cavell* (RKO, 1939), *Eternally Yours* (UA, 1939), *It All Came True* (WB, 1940), *No, No, Nanette* (RKO, 1940), *Broadway Limited* (UA, 1941), *Mexican Spitfire's Baby* (RKO, 1941), *Niagara Falls* (UA, 1941), *Weekend for Three* (RKO, 1941), *Miss Polly* (UA, 1941), *Mexican Spitfire at Sea* (RKO, 1942), *The Bashful Bachelor* (RKO, 1942), *Tish* (MGM, 1942), *Meet the Mob* (Mon., 1942), *So's Your Aunt Emma* (Mon., 1942), *Let's Face It* (Par., 1943), *Breakfast in Hollywood* (UA, 1946), *The Perfect Marriage* (Par., 1946), *Life With Father* (WB, 1947), *Francis* (Univ., 1949), *The Denver and Rio Grande* (Par., 1952), *Francis Joins the WACs* (Univ., 1954), *This Could Be the Night* (MGM, 1957), *The Gazebo* (MGM, 1959), *Teen-Age Millionaire* (UA, 1961), *The Thrill of It All* (Univ., 1963), *It's a Mad, Mad, Mad, Mad World* (UA, 1963).

SUZANNE PLESHETTE Born January 31, 1937, New York, New York. Married Troy Donahue (1964); divorced 1964.

Suzanne Pleshette and James Franciscus in *Youngblood Hawke*.

Feature Films: *The Geisha Boy* (Par., 1958), *Rome Adventure* (WB, 1962), *40 Pounds of Trouble* (Univ., 1962), *The Birds* (Univ., 1963), *Wall of Noise* (WB, 1963), *A Distant Trumpet* (WB, 1964), *Fate Is the Hunter* (20th, 1964), *Youngblood Hawke* (WB, 1964), *A Rage to Live* (UA, 1965), *The Ugly Dachshund* (BV, 1966), *Nevada Smith* (Par., 1966), *Mr. Buddwing* (MGM, 1966), *The Adventures of Bullwhip Griffin* (BV, 1967), *Blackbeard's Ghost* (BV, 1968), *What's in It for Harry?* (Palo-Alto-ABC, 1968).

SIDNEY POITIER Born February 20, 1927, Miami, Florida. Married Juanita Hardy, children: Beverly, Pamela, Sheri; divorced.

Feature Films: *From Whence Cometh Help* (U.S. Army, 1949), *No*

Elizabeth Hartman, Sidney Poitier and Shelley Winters in A *Patch of Blue.*

Way Out (20th, 1950), *Cry, the Beloved Country* (UA, 1952), *Red Ball Express* (Univ., 1952), *Go Man, Go!* (UA, 1954), *The Blackboard Jungle* (MGM, 1955), *Good-Bye, My Lady* (WB, 1956), *Edge of the City* (MGM, 1957), *Something of Value* (MGM, 1957), *Band of Angels* (WB, 1957), *The Mark of the Hawk* (Univ., 1958), *The Defiant Ones* (UA, 1958), *Porgy and Bess* (Col., 1959), *Virgin Island* (Films-Around-the-World, 1960), *All the Young Men* (Col, 1960), *A Raisin in the Sun* (Col., 1961), *Paris Blues* (UA, 1961), *Pressure Point* (UA, 1962), *Lilies of the Field* (UA, 1962), *The Long Ships* (Col., 1964), *The Greatest Story Ever Told* (UA, 1965), *The Bedford Incident* (Col., 1965), *A Patch of Blue* (MGM, 1965), *The Slender Thread* (Par., 1965), *Duel at Diablo* (UA, 1966), *In the Heat of the Night* (UA, 1967). *To Sir With Love* (Col., 1967), *Guess Who's Coming to Dinner* (Col., 1967), *For Love of Ivy* (Cinerama, 1968).

DICK POWELL (Richard E. Powell) Born November 14, 1904, Mountain View, Arkansas. Married Mildred Maund (1925); divorced 1932. Married Joan Blondell (1936), children: Norman, Ellen; divorced 1945. Married June Allyson (1945), children: Pamela, Richard. Died January 3, 1963.

Dick Powell and Anita Louise in *Going Places.*

Feature Films: *Blessed Event* (WB, 1932), *Too Busy to Work* (Fox,

1932), *The King's Vacation* (WB, 1933), *42nd Street* (WB, 1933), *Gold Diggers of 1933* (WB, 1933), *Footlight Parade* (WB, 1933), *College Coach* (WB, 1933), *Convention City* (WB, 1933), *Dames* (WB, 1934), *Wonder Bar* (WB, 1934), *Twenty Million Sweethearts* (WB, 1934), *Happiness Ahead* (WB, 1934), *Flirtation Walk* (WB, 1934), *Gold Diggers of 1935* (WB, 1935), *Page Miss Glory* (WB, 1935), *Broadway Gondolier* (WB, 1935), *A Midsummer Night's Dream* (WB, 1935), *Shipmates Forever* (WB, 1935), *Thanks a Million* (Fox, 1935), *Colleen* (WB, 1936), *Hearts Divided* (WB, 1936), *Stage Struck* (WB, 1936), *Gold Diggers of 1937* (WB, 1936), *On the Avenue* (20th, 1937), *The Singing Marine* (WB, 1937), *Varsity Show* (WB, 1937), *Hollywood Hotel* (WB, 1937), *Cowboy From Brooklyn* (WB, 1938), *Hard to Get* (WB, 1938), *Going Places* (WB, 1938), *Naughty but Nice* (WB, 1939), *Christmas in July* (Par., 1940), *I Want a Divorce* (Par., 1940), *Model Wife* (Univ., 1941), *In The Navy* (Univ., 1941), *Star Spangled Rhythm* (Par., 1942), *Happy Go Lucky* (Par., 1942), *True to Life* (Par., 1943), *Riding High* (Par., 1943), *It Happened Tomorrow* (UA, 1944), *Meet the People* (MGM, 1944), *Murder, My Sweet* (RKO, 1944), *Cornered* (RKO, 1945), *Johnny O'Clock* (Col., 1947), *To the Ends of the Earth* (Col., 1948), *Pitfall* (UA, 1948), *Station West* (RKO, 1948), *Rogue's Regiment* (Univ., 1948), *Mrs. Mike* (UA., 1949), *The Reformer and the Redhead* (MGM, 1950), *Right Cross* (MGM, 1950), *Callaway Went Thataway* (MGM, 1951), *Cry Danger* (RKO, 1951), *The Tall Target* (MGM, 1951), *You Never Can Tell* (Univ., 1951), *The Bad and the Beautiful* (MGM, 1952), *Susan Slept Here* (RKO, 1954).

ELEANOR POWELL (Eleanor Torrey Powell) Born November 21, 1912, Springfield, Massachusetts. Married Glenn Ford (1943), child: Peter; divorced 1959.

Eleanor Powell, Buddy Ebsen and George Murphy in *Broadway Melody of 1938.*

Feature Films: *George White's Scandals* (Fox, 1935), *Broadway Melody of 1936* (MGM, 1935), *Born to Dance* (MGM, 1936), *Broadway Melody of 1938* (MGM, 1937), *Rosalie* (MGM, 1937), *Honolulu* (MGM, 1939), *Broadway Melody of 1940* (MGM, 1940), *Lady Be Good* (MGM, 1941), *Ship Ahoy* (MGM, 1942), *I Dood It* (MGM, 1943), *Thousands Cheer* (MGM, 1943), *Sensations of 1945* (UA, 1944), *The Duchess of Idaho* (MGM, 1950).

JANE POWELL (Suzanne Burce) Born April 1, 1929, Portland, Oregon. Married Geary Steffen (1949), children: Geary, Suzanne; divorced 1953. Married Patrick Nerney (1954), child: Lindsey; divorced 1963. Married James Fitzgerald (1965).

Feature Films: *Song of the Open Road* (UA, 1944), *Delightfully Danger-*

Jane Powell in *The Girl Most Likely*.

ous (UA, 1945), *Holiday in Mexico* (MGM, 1946), *Three Daring Daughters* (MGM, 1948), *A Date With Judy* (MGM, 1948), *Luxury Liner* (MGM, 1948), *Nancy Goes to Rio* (MGM, 1950), *Two Weeks With Love* (MGM, 1950), *Royal Wedding* (MGM, 1951), *Rich, Young and Pretty* (MGM, 1951), *Small Town Girl* (MGM, 1953), *Three Sailors and a Girl* (WB, 1953), *Seven Brides for Seven Brothers* (MGM, 1954), *Athena* (MGM, 1954), *Deep in My Heart* (MGM, 1954), *Hit the Deck* (MGM, 1955), *The Girl Most Likely* (Univ., 1957), *The Female Animal* (Univ., 1958), *Enchanted Island* (WB, 1958).

WILLIAM POWELL (William Horatio Powell) Born July 29, 1892, Pittsburgh, Pennsylvania. Married Eileen Wilson, child: William; divorced 1931. Married Carole Lombard (1931); divorced 1933. Married Diana Lewis (1940).

William Powell, Ted Healy and Nat Pendleton in *Reckless*.

Sound Feature Films: *Interference* (Par., 1929), *The Canary Murder Case* (Par., 1929), *The Greene Murder Case* (Par., 1929), *Charming Sinners* (Par., 1929), *Four Feathers* (Par., 1929), *Pointed Heels* (Par., 1929), *The Benson Murder Case* (Par., 1930), *Paramount on Parade* (Par., 1930), *Shadow of the Law* (Par., 1930), *Behind the Makeup* (Par., 1930), *Street of Chance* (Par., 1930), *For the Defense* (Par., 1930), *Man of the World* (Par., 1931), *Ladies' Man* (Par., 1931), *Road to Singapore* (WB, 1931), *High Pressure* (WB, 1932), *Jewel Robbery* (WB, 1932), *One Way Passage* (WB, 1932), *Lawyer Man* (WB, 1932), *Double Harness* (RKO, 1933), *Private Detective 62* (WB, 1933), *The Kennel Murder Case* (WB, 1933), *Fashions of 1934* (WB, 1934), *The Key* (WB, 1934), *Manhattan Melodrama* (MGM, 1934), *The Thin Man* (MGM, 1934), *Evelyn Prentice* (MGM, 1934), *Reckless* (MGM, 1935), *Star of Midnight* (RKO, 1935), *Escapade* (MGM, 1935), *Rendezvous* (MGM, 1935), *The Great Ziegfeld* (MGM, 1936), *The Ex-Mrs. Bradford* (RKO,

1936), *My Man Godfrey* (Univ., 1936), *Libeled Lady* (MGM, 1936), *After the Thin Man* (MGM, 1936), *The Last of Mrs. Cheyney* (MGM, 1937), *The Emperor's Candlesticks* (MGM, 1937), *Double Wedding* (MGM, 1937), *The Baroness and the Butler* (20th, 1938), *Another Thin Man* (MGM, 1939), *I Love You Again* (MGM, 1940), *Love Crazy* (MGM, 1941), *Shadow of the Thin Man* (MGM, 1941), *Crossroads* (MGM, 1942), *The Youngest Profession* (MGM, 1943), *The Heavenly Body* (MGM, 1944), *The Thin Man Goes Home* (MGM, 1944), *Ziegfeld Follies* (MGM, 1946), *The Hoodlum Saint* (MGM, 1946), *Song of the Thin Man* (MGM, 1947), *Life With Father* (WB, 1947), *The Senator Was Indiscreet* (Univ., 1947), *Mr. Peabody and the Mermaid* (Univ., 1948), *Take One False Step* (Univ., 1949), *Dancing in the Dark* (20th, 1949), *The Treasure of Lost Canyon* (Univ., 1951), *It's a Big Country* (MGM, 1951), *The Girl Who Had Everything* (MGM, 1953), *How to Marry a Millionaire* (20th, 1953), *Mister Roberts* (WB, 1955).

TYRONE POWER (Tyrone Edmund Power) Born May 5, 1914, Cincinnati, Ohio. Married Annabella (1939); divorced 1948. Married Linda Christian (1949), children: Romina, Taryn; divorced 1955. Married Deborah Minardos (1958), child: Tyrone. Died November 15, 1958.

Tyrone Power and Joseph Schildkraut in *Suez*.

Feature Films: *Tom Brown of Culver* (Univ, 1932), *Flirtation Walk* (WB, 1934), *Girls' Dormitory* (20th, 1936), *Ladies in Love* (20th, 1936), *Lloyds of London* (20th, 1937), *Love Is News* (20th, 1937), *Cafe Metropole* (20th, 1937), *Thin Ice* (20th, 1937), *Second Honeymoon* (20th, 1937), *In Old Chicago* (20th, 1938), *Alexander's Ragtime Band* (20th, 1938), *Marie Antoinette* (MGM, 1938), *Suez* (20th, 1938), *Jesse James* (20th, 1939), *Rose of Washington Square* (20th, 1939), *Second Fiddle* (20th, 1939), *The Rains Came* (20th, 1939), *Daytime Wife* (20th, 1939), *Johnny Apollo* (20th, 1940), *Brigham Young—Frontiersman* (20th, 1940), *The Return of Frank James* (20th, 1940), *Mark of Zorro* (20th, 1940), *Blood and Sand* (20th, 1941), *A Yank in the R.A.F.* (20th, 1941), *Son of Fury* (20th, 1942), *This Above All* (20th, 1942), *The Black Swan* (20th, 1942), *Crash Dive* (20th, 1943), *The Razor's Edge* (20th, 1946), *Nightmare Alley* (20th, 1947), *Captain From Castile* (20th, 1947), *Luck of the Irish* (20th, 1948), *That Wonderful Urge* (20th, 1948), *Prince of Foxes* (20th, 1949), *The Black Rose* (20th, 1950), *An American Guerrilla in the Philippines* (20th, 1950), *Rawhide* (20th, 1951), *I'll Never Forget You* (20th, 1951), *Diplomatic Courier* (20th, 1952), *Pony Soldier* (20th, 1952), *Mississippi Gambler* (Univ., 1953), *King of the Khyber Rifles* (20th, 1953), *The Long Gray Line* (Col., 1955), *Untamed* (20th, 1955), *The Eddy Duchin Story* (Col., 1956), *Abandon Ship* (Col., 1957), *The Rising of the Moon* (WB, 1957), *The Sun Also Rises* (20th, 1957), *Witness for the Prosecution* (UA, 1957).

PAULA PRENTISS (Paula Ragusa) Born March 4, 1939, San Antonio, Texas. Married Richard Benjamin (1960).

Feature Films: *Where the Boys Are* (MGM, 1960), *The Honeymoon*

Steve McQueen, Brigid Bazlen, Paula Prentiss and Jim Hutton in *The Honeymoon Machine.*

Machine (MGM, 1961), *Bachelor in Paradise* (MGM, 1961), *The Horizontal Lieutenant* (MGM, 1962), *Follow the Boys* (MGM, 1963), *Man's Favorite Sport?* (Univ., 1964), *The World of Henry Orient* (UA, 1964), *Looking for Love* (MGM, 1964), *In Harm's Way* (Par., 1965), *What's New Pussycat?* (UA, 1965).

ELVIS PRESLEY Born January 8, 1935, Tupelo, Mississippi. Married Priscilla Beaulieu, (1967).

Dolores Del Rio and Elvis Presley in *Flaming Star.*

Feature Films: *Love Me Tender* (20th, 1956), *Loving You* (Par., 1957), *Jailhouse Rock* (MGM, 1957), *King Creole* (Par., 1958), *G.I. Blues* (Par., 1960), *Flaming Star* (20th, 1960), *Wild in the Country* (20th, 1961), *Blue Hawaii* (Par., 1961), *Kid Galahad* (UA, 1962), *Girls! Girls! Girls!* (Par., 1962), *Fun in Acapulco* (Par., 1963), *It Happened at the World's Fair* (MGM, 1963), *Kissin' Cousins* (MGM, 1964), *Viva Las Vegas* (MGM, 1964), *Roustabout* (Par., 1964), *Girl Happy* (MGM, 1965), *Tickle Me* (AA, 1965), *Harum Scarum* (MGM, 1965), *Frankie and Johnny* (UA, 1966), *Paradise—Hawaiian Style* (Par., 1966), *Spinout* (MGM, 1966), *Easy Come, Easy Go* (Par., 1967), *Double Trouble* (MGM, 1967), *Speedway* (MGM, 1968), *Stay Away, Joe* (MGM, 1968), *Clambake* (MGM, 1968).

ROBERT PRESTON (Robert Preston Meservey) Born June 8, 1918, Newton Highlands, Massachusetts. Married Catherine Craig (1940).

Feature Films: *King of Alcatraz* (Par., 1938), *Illegal Traffic* (Par., 1938), *Disbarred* (Par., 1939), *Union Pacific* (Par., 1939), *Beau Geste* (Par., 1939), *Typhoon* (Par., 1940), *North West Mounted Police* (Par., 1940), *Moon Over Burma* (Par., 1940), *The Lady From Cheyenne* (Univ., 1941), *Parachute Battalion* (RKO, 1941), *New York Town* (Par., 1941), *Night*

Robert Preston and Susan Hayward in *Tulsa.*

of January 16th (Par., 1941), *Star Spangled Rhythm* (Par., 1942), *Reap the Wild Wind* (Par., 1942), *This Gun for Hire* (Par., 1942), *Wake Island* (Par., 1942), *Pacific Blackout* (Par., 1942), *Night Plane From Chungking* (Par., 1943), *Wild Harvest* (Par., 1947), *The Macomber Affair* (UA, 1947), *Variety Girl* (Par., 1947), *Whispering Smith* (Par., 1948), *The Big City* (MGM, 1948), *Blood on the Moon* (RKO, 1948), *Tulsa* (EL, 1949), *The Lady Gambles* (Univ., 1949), *The Sundowners* (EL, 1950), *My Outlaw Brother* (EL, 1951), *When I Grow Up* (EL, 1951), *Best of the Bad Men* (RKO, 1951), *Cloudburst* (UA, 1952), *Face to Face* (RKO, 1952), *The Last Frontier* (Col., 1955), *The Dark at the Top of the Stairs* (WB, 1960), *The Music Man* (WB, 1962), *How the West Was Won* (MGM, 1962), *Island of Love* (WB, 1963), *All the Way Home* (Par., 1963).

VINCENT PRICE Born May 27, 1911, St. Louis, Missouri. Married Edith Barrett, child: Barrett; divorced 1948. Married Mary Grant (1949), child: Mary.

Lon Chaney, Jr., and Vincent Price in *The Haunted Palace.*

English-Language Feature Films: *Service DeLuxe* (Univ., 1938), *The Private Lives of Elizabeth and Essex* (WB, 1939), *Tower of London* (Univ., 1939), *Green Hell* (Univ., 1940), *The House of the Seven Gables* (Univ., 1940), *The Invisible Man Returns* (Univ., 1940), *Brigham Young —Frontiersman* (20th, 1940), *Hudson's Bay* (20th, 1940), *The Song of Bernadette* (20th, 1943), *The Eve of St. Mark* (20th, 1944), *Buffalo Bill* (20th, 1944), *Wilson* (20th, 1944), *Laura* (20th, 1944), *The Keys of the Kingdom* (20th, 1944), *Leave Her to Heaven* (20th, 1945), *A Royal Scandal* (20th, 1945), *Dragonwyck* (20th, 1946), *Shock* (20th, 1947), *The Long Night* (RKO, 1947), *Moss Rose* (20th, 1947), *The Web* (Univ., 1947), *Up in Central Park* (Univ., 1948), *Abbott and Costello Meet Frankenstein* (voice only; Univ., 1948), *The Three Musketeers* (MGM, 1948), *Rogue's Regiment* (Univ., 1948), *The Bribe* (MGM, 1949), *Bagdad* (Univ., 1949), *The Baron of Arizona* (Lip., 1950), *Champagne for*

Caesar (Univ., 1950), *Curtain Call at Cactus Creek* (Univ., 1950), *His Kind of Woman* (RKO, 1951), *Adventures of Captain Fabian* (Rep., 1951), *The Las Vegas Story* (RKO, 1952), *House of Wax* (WB, 1953), *Casanova's Big Night* (Par., 1954), *Dangerous Mission* (RKO, 1954), *The Mad Magician* (Col., 1954), *Son of Sinbad* (RKO, 1955), *Serenade* (WB, 1956), *While the City Sleeps* (RKO, 1956), *The Ten Commandments* (Par., 1956), *The Story of Mankind* (WB, 1957), *The Fly* (20th, 1958), *House on Haunted Hill* (AA, 1958), *The Return of the Fly* (20th, 1959), *The Bat* (AA, 1959), *The Big Circus* (AA, 1959), *The Tingler* (Col., 1959), *House of Usher* (AIP, 1960), *The Master of the World* (AIP, 1961), *The Pit and the Pendulum* (AIP, 1961), *Poe's Tales of Terror* (AIP, 1962), *Convicts 4* (AA, 1962), *Confessions of an Opium Eater* (AA, 1962), *Tower of London* (UA, 1962), *The Raven* (AIP, 1963), *The Haunted Palace* (AIP, 1963), *Twice Told Tales* (AIP, 1963), *Comedy of Terrors* (AIP, 1963), *Masque of the Red Death* (AIP, 1964), *Last Man on Earth* (AIP, 1964), *Tomb of Leigia* (AIP, 1965), *War Gods of the Deep* (AIP, 1965), *Taboos of the World* (narrator; AIP, 1965), *Dr. Goldfoot and the Bikini Machine* (AIP, 1965), *Dr. Goldfoot and the Girl Bombs* (AIP, 1966), *2165 A.D.—When the Sleeper Wakes* (AIP, 1967), *House of 1,000 Dolls* (AIP, 1968), *The Conquering Worm* (AIP, 1968), *Witchfinder General* (AIP, 1968).

ANTHONY QUINN Born April 21, 1915, Chihuahua, Mexico. Married Katherine DeMille (1937), children: Christina, Kathleen, Duncan Valentina; divorced. Married Yolanda Addolori (1966), child: Lawrence.

Barbara Stanwyck and Anthony Quinn in *Blowing Wild*.

English-Language Feature Films: *Parole!* (Univ., 1936), *Swing High— Swing Low* (Par., 1937), *Waikiki Wedding* (Par., 1937), *Last Train From Madrid* (Par., 1937), *Partners in Crime* (Par., 1937), *Daughter of Shanghai* (Par., 1937), *The Buccaneer* (Par., 1938), *Dangerous to Know* (Par., 1938), *Tip-Off Girls* (Par., 1938), *Hunted Men* (Par., 1938), *Bulldog Drummond In Africa* (Par., 1938), *King of Alcatraz* (Par., 1938), *King of Chinatown* (Par., 1939), *Union Pacific* (Par., 1939), *Island of Lost Men* (Par., 1939), *Television Spy* (Par., 1939), *Emergency Squad* (Par., 1940), *Road to Singapore* (Par., 1940), *Parole Fixer* (Par., 1940), *The Ghost Breakers* (Par., 1940), *City for Conquest* (WB, 1940), *Texas Rangers Ride Again* (Par., 1941), *Blood and Sand* (20th, 1941), *Thieves Fall Out* (WB, 1941), *Knockout* (WB, 1941), *Bullets for O'Hara* (WB, 1941), *Manpower* (WB, 1941), *The Perfect Snob* (20th, 1941), *They Died With Their Boots On* (WB, 1941), *Larceny, Inc.* (WB, 1942), *Road to Morocco* (Par., 1942), *The Black Swan* (20th, 1942), *The Ox-Bow Incident* (20th, 1943), *Guadalcanal Diary* (20th, 1943), *Buffalo Bill* (20th, 1944), *Ladies of Washington* (20th, 1944), *Roger Touhy, Gangster* (20th, 1944), *Irish Eyes Are Smiling* (20th, 1944), *China Skies* (RKO, 1945), *Where Do We Go From Here?* (20th, 1945), *Back to Bataan* (RKO, 1945), *California* (Par., 1946), *Sinbad the Sailor* (RKO, 1947), *The Imperfect Lady* (Par., 1947), *Black Gold* (AA, 1947), *Tycoon* (RKO, 1947), *The Brave Bulls* (Col., 1951), *Mask of the Avenger* (Col., 1951),

Viva Zapata! (20th, 1952), *The World in his Arms* (Univ., 1952), *The Brigand* (Col., 1952), *Against All Flags* (Univ., 1952), *Seminole* (Univ., 1953), *City Beneath the Sea* (Univ., 1953), *Ride, Vaquero!* (MGM, 1953), *Blowing Wild* (WB, 1953), *The Long Wait* (UA, 1954), *The Magnificent Matador* (20th, 1955), *Ulysses* (Par., 1955), *The Naked Street* (UA, 1955), *Seven Cities of Gold* (20th, 1955), *Lust for Life* (MGM, 1956), *Man From Del Rio* (UA, 1956), *The Wild Party* (UA, 1956), *The River's Edge* (20th, 1957), *The Ride Back* (UA, 1957), *The Hunchback of Notre Dame* (AA, 1957), *Wild Is the Wind* (Par., 1957), *Hot Spell* (Par., 1958), *Warlock* (20th, 1959), *Last Train From Gun Hill* (Par., 1959), *Heller in Pink Tights* (Par., 1960), *Portrait in Black* (Univ., 1960), *The Savage Innocents* (Par., 1960), *The Guns of Navarone* (Col., 1961), *Barabbas* (Col., 1962), *Requiem for a Heavyweight* (Col., 1962), *Lawrence of Arabia* (Col., 1962), *Behold a Pale Horse* (Col., 1964), *The Visit* (20th, 1964), *Zorba the Greek* (International Classics, 1964), *A High Wind in Jamaica* (20th, 1965), *The Lost Command* (Col., 1966), *Marco the Magnificent* (MGM, 1966), *The 25th Hour* (MGM, 1967), *The Happening* (Col., 1967), *The Rover* (Cinerama, 1968). *The God Game* (20th, 1968), *Shoes of the Fisherman* (MGM, 1968), *Guns for San Sebastian* (MGM, 1968).

LUISE RAINER Born January 12, 1910, Vienna, Austria. Married Clifford Odets (1937); divorced 1940. Married Robert Knittel (1944), child: Franceska.

Luise Rainer in *The Toy Wife*.

Feature Films: *Escapade* (MGM, 1935), *The Great Ziegfeld* (MGM, 1936), *The Good Earth* (MGM, 1937), *The Big City* (MGM, 1937), *The Emperor's Candlesticks* (MGM, 1937), *The Great Waltz* (MGM, 1938), *The Toy Wife* (MGM, 1938), *Dramatic School* (MGM, 1938), *Hostages* (Par., 1943).

ELLA RAINES (Ella Wallace Raubes) Born August 6, 1921, Snoqualmie Falls, Washington. Married Kenneth Trout (1942); divorced 1945. Married Robin Olds (1947), children: Christina, Susan.

Ella Raines, Anna May Wong and Charles Coburn in *Impact*.

Feature Films: *Corvette K-225* (Univ., 1943), *Cry Havoc* (MGM, 1943), *Phantom Lady* (Univ., 1944), *Hail the Conquering Hero* (Par., 1944), *Tall in the Saddle* (RKO, 1944), *Enter Arsene Lupin* (Univ., 1944), *The Suspect* (Univ., 1945), *The Strange Affair of Uncle Harry* (Univ., 1945), *The Runaround* (Univ., 1946), *Time Out of Mind* (Univ., 1947), *The Web* (Univ., 1947), *Brute Force* (Univ., 1947), *The Senator Was Indiscreet* (Univ., 1947), *The Walking Hills* (Col., 1949), *Impact* (UA, 1949), *A Dangerous Profession* (RKO, 1949), *The Second Face* (EL, 1950), *Singing Guns* (Rep., 1950), *The Fighting Coast Guard* (Rep., 1951), *Ride the Man Down* (Rep., 1952), *Man in the Road* (Rep., 1957).

CLAUDE RAINS (William Claude Rains) Born November 10, 1889, London, England. Married Isabel Jeans (1913); divorced. Married Marie Hemingway (1920); divorced 1920. Married Beatrix Thomson (1924); divorced 1935. Married Frances Propper (1935), child: Jennifer; divorced 1959. Married Agi Jambor (1960). Died May 30, 1967.

Warren Hymer, George E. Stone, Robert Cummings, George Raft, Roscoe Karns, Joe Gray and Jack Pennick in *You and Me.*

Claude Rains and Billy Mauch in *The Prince and the Pauper.*

Feature Films: *The Invisible Man* (Univ., 1933), *Crime Without Passion* (Par., 1934), *The Man Who Reclaimed His Head* (Univ., 1935), *The Clairvoyant* (Gaumont-British, 1935), *The Mystery of Edwin Drood* (Univ., 1935), *The Last Outpost* (Par., 1935), *Anthony Adverse* (WB, 1936), *Hearts Divided* (WB, 1936), *Stolen Holiday* (WB, 1936), *The Prince and the Pauper* (WB, 1937), *They Won't Forget* (WB, 1937), *Gold Is Where You Find It* (WB, 1938), *The Adventures of Robin Hood* (WB, 1938), *White Banners* (WB, 1938), *Four Daughters* (WB, 1938), *They Made Me a Criminal* (WB, 1939), *Juarez* (WB, 1939), *Daughters Courageous* (WB, 1939), *Mr. Smith Goes to Washington* (Col., 1939), *Four Wives* (WB, 1939), *Saturday's Children* (WB, 1940), *The Sea Hawk* (WB, 1940), *The Lady With Red Hair* (WB, 1940), *Four Mothers* (WB, 1941), *Here Comes Mr. Jordan* (Col., 1941), *The Wolf Man* (Univ., 1941), *Kings Row* (WB, 1941), *Moontide* (20th, 1942), *Now, Voyager* (WB, 1942), *Casablanca* (WB, 1942), *The Phantom of the Opera* (Univ., 1943), *Forever and a Day* (RKO, 1943), *Passage to Marseilles* (WB, 1944), *Mr. Skeffington* (WB, 1944), *This Love of Ours* (Univ., 1945), *Angel on My Shoulder* (UA, 1946), *Caesar and Cleopatra* (UA, 1946), *Strange Holiday* (PRC, 1946), *Notorious* (RKO, 1946), *Deception* (WB, 1946), *The Unsuspected* (WB, 1947), *One Woman's Story* (Univ. 1949), *Rope of Sand* (Par., 1949), *Song of Surrender* (Par., 1949), *The White Tower* (RKO, 1950), *Where Danger Lives* (RKO, 1950), *Sealed Cargo* (RKO, 1951), *The Paris Express* (George J. Schaeffer, 1953), *Lisbon* (Rep., 1956), *This Earth Is Mine* (Univ., 1959), *The Lost World* (20th, 1960), *Lawrence of Arabia* (Col., 1962), *Twilight of Honor* (MGM, 1963), *The Greatest Story Ever Told* (UA, 1965).

GEORGE RAFT (George Ranft) Born September 24, 1903, New York, New York. Married Grace Mulrooney (1925).

English-Language Feature Films: *Queen of the Night Clubs* (WB, 1929),

Quick Millions (Fox, 1931), *Hush Money* (Fox, 1931), *Palmy Days* (UA, 1931), *Taxi* (WB, 1932), *Scarface* (UA, 1932), *Dancers in the Dark* (Par., 1932), *Madame Racketeer* (Par., 1932), *Night After Night* (Par., 1932), *If I Had a Million* (Par., 1932), *Undercover Man* (Par., 1932), *Pick-Up* (Par., 1933), *The Midnight Club* (Par., 1933), *The Bowery* (UA, 1933), *Bolero* (Par., 1934), *All of Me* (Par., 1934), *The Trumpet Blows* (Par., 1934), *Limehouse Blues* (Par., 1934), *Rumba* (Par., 1935), *Stolen Harmony* (Par., 1935), *The Glass Key* (Par., 1935), *Every Night at Eight* (Par., 1935), *She Couldn't Take It* (Col., 1935), *It Had to Happen* (20th, 1936), *Souls at Sea* (Par., 1937), *You and Me* (Par., 1938), *The Lady's From Kentucky* (Par., 1939), *Each Dawn I Die* (WB, 1939), *I Stole a Million* (Univ., 1939), *They Drive by Night* (WB, 1940), *Invisible Stripes* (WB, 1940), *House Across the Bay* (UA, 1940), *Manpower* (WB, 1941), *Broadway* (Univ., 1942), *Stage Door Canteen* (UA, 1943), *Background to Danger* (WB, 1943), *Follow the Boys* (Univ., 1944), *Johnny Angel* (RKO, 1945), *Nocturne* (RKO, 1946), *Mr. Ace* (UA, 1946), *Whistle Stop* (UA, 1946), *Christmas Eve* (UA, 1947), *Intrigue* (UA, 1947), *Race Street* (RKO, 1948), *Johnny Allegro* (Col., 1949), *A Dangerous Profession* (RKO, 1949), *Outpost in Morocco* (UA, 1949), *Red Light* (UA, 1949), *Lucky Nick Cain* (20th, 1951), *Loan Shark* (Lip., 1952), *I'll Get You* (Lip., 1953), *Man From Cairo* (Lip., 1953), *Rogue Cop* (MGM, 1954), *Black Widow* (20th, 1954), *A Bullet for Joey* (UA, 1955), *Around the World in 80 Days* (UA, 1956), *Jet Across the Atlantic* (Intercontinent Releasing, 1959), *Some Like It Hot* (UA, 1959), *Ocean's 11* (WB, 1960),* *Ladies' Man* (Par., 1961), *For Those Who Think Young* (UA, 1964), *The Patsy* (Par., 1964),* *Casino Royale* (Col., 1967),* *The Silent Treatment* (Ralph Andrew, 1968).

*Unbilled guest appearance

VERA RALSTON (Vera Hruba) Born July 12, 1919, Prague, Czecho-slovakia. Married Herbert Yates (1952); widowed 1966.

Feature Films:
   as Vera Hruba *Ice-Capades* (Rep., 1941), *Ice-Capades Revue* (Rep., 1942).

John Carroll and Vera Ralston in *Belle Le Grand.*

as **Vera Hruba Ralston** *The Lady and the Monster* (Rep., 1944), *Storm Over Lisbon* (Rep., 1944), *Lake Placid Serenade* (Rep., 1944), *Dakota* (Rep., 1945), *Murder in the Music Hall* (Rep., 1946).

as **Vera Ralston** *The Plainsman and the Lady* (Rep., 1946), *The Flame* (Rep., 1947), *Wyoming* (Rep., 1947), *I, Jane Doe* (Rep., 1948), *Angel on the Amazon* (Rep., 1948), *The Fighting Kentuckian* (Rep., 1949), *Surrender* (Rep., 1950), *Belle Le Grand* (Rep., 1951), *The Wild Blue Yonder* (Rep., 1951), *Hoodlum Empire* (Rep., 1952), *Fair Wind to Java* (Rep., 1953), *A Perilous Journey* (Rep., 1953), *Jubilee Trail* (Rep., 1954), *Timberjack* (Rep., 1955), *Accused of Murder* (Rep., 1956), *Spoilers of the Forest* (Rep., 1957), *Gunfire at Indian Gap* (Rep., 1957), *The Notorious Mr. Monks* (Rep., 1958), *The Man Who Died Twice* (Rep., 1958).

MARJORIE RAMBEAU Born July 15, 1889, San Francisco, California. Married Willard Mack (1912), divorced 1917. Married Hugh Dillman (1919); divorced 1923. Married Francis Gudger (1931).

Elizabeth Patterson and Marjorie Rambeau in *Tobacco Road.*

Sound Feature Films: *Her Man* (Pathé, 1930), *Min and Bill* (MGM, 1930), *The Easiest Way* (MGM, 1931), *Inspiration* (MGM, 1931), *A Tailor-Made Man* (MGM, 1931), *Strangers May Kiss* (MGM, 1931), *Secret Six* (MGM, 1931), *Laughing Sinners* (MGM, 1931), *This Modern Age* (MGM, 1931), *Son of India* (MGM, 1931), *Silence* (Par., 1931), *Hell Divers* (MGM, 1931), *Left Over Ladies* (Tiff., 1931), *Strictly Personal* (Par., 1933), *Warrior's Husband* (Fox, 1933), *Man's Castle* (Col., 1933), *Palooka* (UA-Reliance, 1934), *A Modern Hero* (WB, 1934), *Grand Canary* (Fox, 1934), *Ready for Love* (Par., 1934), *Under Pressure* (Fox, 1935), *Dizzy Dames* (Liberty, 1935), *First Lady* (WB, 1937), *Merrily We Live* (MGM, 1938), *Woman Against Woman* (MGM, 1938), *The Rains Came* (20th, 1939), *Laugh It Off* (Univ., 1939), *Sudden Money* (Par., 1939), *Primrose Path* (RKO, 1940), *Heaven With a Barbed Wire Fence* (20th, 1940), *Santa Fe Marshal* (Par., 1940), *Twenty Mule Team* (MGM, 1940), *East of the River* (WB, 1940), *Tugboat Annie Sails Again* (WB, 1940), *Tobacco Road* (20th, 1941), *Three Sons o' Guns* (WB, 1941), *Broadway* (Univ., 1942), *In Old Oklahoma* (Rep., 1943), *Army Wives* (Mon., 1944), *Oh, What a Night!* (Mon., 1944), *Salome, Where She Danced* (Univ., 1945), *The Walls of Jericho* (20th, 1948), *Any Number Can Play* (MGM, 1949), *The Lucky Stiff* (UA, 1949), *Abandoned* (Univ., 1949), *Torch Song* (MGM, 1953), *Forever Female* (Par., 1953), *Bad for Each Other* (Col., 1953), *A Man Called Peter* (20th, 1955), *The View From Pompey's Head* (20th, 1955), *Slander* (MGM, 1956), *Man of a Thousand Faces* (Univ., 1957).

TONY RANDALL (Anthony L. Randall) Born February 26, 1920, Tulsa, Oklahoma. Married Florence Mitchell (1942).

Feature Films: *Oh, Men! Oh, Women!* (20th, 1957), *Will Success*

Robert Preston and Tony Randall in *Island of Love.*

Spoil Rock Hunter? (20th, 1957), *No Down Payment* (20th, 1957), *The Mating Game* (MGM, 1959), *Pillow Talk* (Univ., 1959), *Adventures of Huckleberry Finn* (MGM, 1960), *Let's Make Love* (20th, 1960), *Lover Come Back* (Univ., 1961), *Boys' Night Out* (MGM, 1962), *Island of Love* (WB, 1963), *The Brass Bottle* (Univ., 1964), *The Seven Faces of Dr. Lao* (MGM, 1964), *Send Me No Flowers* (Univ., 1964), *Fluffy* (Univ., 1965), *The Alphabet Murders* (MGM, 1966), *Bang, Bang, You're Dead* (AIP, 1966).

BASIL RATHBONE (Philip St. John Basil Rathbone) Born June 13, 1892, Johannesburg, South Africa. Married Ethel Forman (1914), child: Rodion; divorced. Married Ouida Fitzmaurice (1926), child: Barbara. Died July 21, 1967.

Irving Bacon and Basil Rathbone in *Rio.*

English-Language Sound Feature Films: *The Last of Mrs. Cheyney* (MGM, 1929), *Barnum Was Right* (Univ., 1929), *This Mad World* (MGM, 1930), *Flirting Widow* (WB, 1930), *A Notorious Affair* (WB, 1930), *A Lady Surrenders* (Univ., 1930), *Sin Takes a Holiday* (Pathé, 1930), *The Bishop Murder Case* (MGM, 1930), *The Lady of Scandal* (MGM, 1930), *A Woman Commands* (RKO, 1932), *After the Ball* (Fox, 1933), *Loyalties* (Auten, 1934), *Captain Blood* (WB, 1935), *David Copperfield* (MGM, 1935), *Anna Karenina* (MGM, 1935), *The Last Days* of Pompeii (RKO, 1935), *A Tale of Two Cities* (MGM, 1935), *Kind Lady* (MGM, 1935), *A Feather in Her Hat* (Col., 1935), *Romeo and Juliet* (MGM, 1936), *The Garden of Allah* (UA, 1936), *Private Number* (20th, 1936), *Tovarich* (WB, 1937), *Love From a Stranger* (UA, 1937), *Confession* (WB, 1937), *Make a Wish* (RKO, 1937), *The Adventures of Robin Hood* (WB, 1938), *The Adventures of Marco Polo* (UA, 1938), *If I Were King* (Par., 1938), *Dawn Patrol* (WB, 1938), *The Son of Frankenstein* (Univ., 1939), *Tower of London* (Univ., 1939), *The Sun Never Sets* (Univ., 1939), *Rio* (Univ., 1939), *The Hound of the Baskervilles* (20th, 1939), *Adventures of Sherlock Holmes* (20th, 1939), *Rhythm on the River* (Par., 1940), *The Mark of Zorro* (20th, 1940), *The Mad Doctor* (Par., 1941), *The Black Cat* (Univ., 1941), *Paris Calling* (Univ, 1941), *International Lady* (UA, 1941), *Fingers at the Window* (MGM, 1942), *Crossroads* (MGM, 1942), *Sherlock Holmes and the Voice of Terror* (Univ., 1942), *Sherlock Holmes and the Secret Weapon* (Univ., 1942), *Sherlock Holmes in Washington* (Univ., 1943), *Sherlock Holmes Faces Death* (Univ., 1943) *Crazy House* (Univ., 1943),* *Above Suspicion* (MGM, 1943), *Frenchman's Creek* (Par., 1944), *Bathing Beauty* (MGM, 1944), *Sherlock Holmes and the Spider Woman* (Univ., 1944), *The Scarlet Claw* (Univ., 1944), *The Pearl of Death* (Univ., 1944), *The House of Fear* (Univ., 1945), *Pursuit to Algiers* (Univ., 1945), *The Woman Is Green* (Univ., 1945), *Terror by Night* (Univ., 1946), *Dressed to Kill* (Univ., 1946), *Heartbeat* (RKO, 1946), *The Adventures of Ichabod and Mr. Toad* (voice only; RKO, 1949), *Casanova's Big Night* (Par., 1954), *We're No Angels* (Par., 1955), *The Black Sleep* (UA, 1956), *The Court Jester* (Par., 1956), *The Last Hurrah* (Col., 1958), *The Magic Sword* (UA, 1962), *Tales of Terror* (AIP, 1962), *Comedy of Terrors* (AIP, 1963), *Queen of Blood* (AIP, 1966), *Ghost in the Invisible Bikini* (AIP, 1966), *Dr. Rock and Mr. Roll* (Blue Sky Productions, 1967), *Gill Women* (AIP, 1967), *Hillbillies in a Haunted House* (Woolner Bros., 1968),

*Unbilled guest appearance

MARTHA RAYE (Margaret Theresa Yvonne Reed) Born August 27, 1908, Butte, Montana. Married Bud Westmore (1937); divorced 1938. Married David Rose (1938); divorced 1941. Married Neil Lang (1941); divorced 1941. Married Nick Condos (1942), child: Melodye; divorced 1953. Married Edward Begley (1954); divorced 1956. Married Robert O'Shea (1958); divorced 1962.

Andy Devine, Martha Raye and Bob Hope in *Never Say Die.*

Feature Films: *Rhythm on the Range* (Par., 1936), *The Big Broadcast of 1937* (Par., 1936), *College Holiday* (Par., 1936), *Hideaway Girl* (Par., 1937), *Waikiki Wedding* (Par., 1937), *Mountain Music* (Par., 1937), *Double or Nothing* (Par., 1937), *Artists and Models* (Par., 1937), *The Big Broadcast of 1938* (Par., 1938), *College Swing* (Par., 1938), *Give Me a Sailor* (Par., 1938), *Tropic Holiday* (Par., 1938), *Never Say Die* (Par., 1939), *$1,000 a Touchdown* (Par., 1939), *The Farmer's Daughter* (Par., 1940), *The Boys From Syracuse* (Univ., 1940), *Navy Blues* (WB, 1941), *Keep 'Em Flying* (Univ., 1941), *Hellzapoppin'* (Univ., 1941), *Four Jills*

in a Jeep (20th, 1944), *Pin-Up Girl* (20th, 1944), *Monsieur Verdoux* (UA, 1947), *Billy Rose's Jumbo* (MGM, 1962).

RONALD REAGAN (Ronald Wilson Reagan) Born February 6, 1912, Tampico, Illinois. Married Jane Wyman (1940), children: Michael, Maureen; divorced 1948. Married Nancy Davis (1952), children: Patricia, Ronald.

Ronald Reagan and Shirley Temple in *That Hagen Girl.*

Feature Films: *Love Is on the Air* (WB, 1937), *Submarine D-1* (WB, 1937),* *Hollywood Hotel* (WB, 1937), *Sergeant Murphy* (WB, 1938), *Accidents Will Happen* (WB, 1938), *Cowboy From Brooklyn* (WB, 1938), *Boy Meets Girl* (WB, 1938), *Brother Rat* (WB, 1938), *Going Places* (WB, 1938), *Girls on Probation* (WB, 1938), *Dark Victory* (WB, 1939), *Secret Service of the Air* (WB, 1939), *Code of the Secret Service* (WB, 1939), *Naughty but Nice* (WB, 1939), *Hell's Kitchen* (WB, 1939), *Angels Wash Their Faces* (WB, 1939), *Smashing the Money Ring* (WB, 1939), *Brother Rat and a Baby* (WB, 1940), *An Angel From Texas* (WB, 1940), *Murder in the Air* (WB, 1940), *Knute Rockne, All American* (WB, 1940), *Tugboat Annie Sails Again* (WB, 1940), *Santa Fe Trail* (WB, 1940), *The Bad Man* (WB, 1941), *Million Dollar Baby* (WB, 1941), *Nine Lives Are Not Enough* (WB, 1941), *International Squadron* (WB, 1941), *Kings Row* (WB, 1941), *Juke Girl* (WB, 1942) *Desperate Journey* (WB, 1942), *This Is the Army* (WB, 1943), *Stallion Road* (WB, 1947), *That Hagen Girl* (WB, 1947), *The Voice of the Turtle* ("One for the Books"—WB, 1947), *John Loves Mary* (WB, 1949), *Night Unto Night* (WB, 1949), *The Girl From Jones Beach* (WB, 1949), *It's a Great Feeling* (WB, 1949), *The Hasty Heart* (WB, 1949), *Louisa* (Univ., 1950), *Storm Warning* (WB, 1950), *The Last Outpost* (Par., 1951), *Bedtime for Bonzo* (Univ., 1951), *Hong Kong* (Par., 1951), *She's Working Her Way Through College* (WB, 1952), *The Winning Team* (WB, 1952), *Tropic Zone* (Par., 1953), *Law and Order* (Univ., 1953), *Prisoner of War* (MGM, 1954), *Cattle Queen of Montana* (RKO, 1954), *Tennessee's Partner* (RKO, 1955), *Hellcat of the Navy* (Col., 1957), *The Young Doctors* (narrator; UA, 1961), *The Killers* (Univ., 1964).

*Scenes deleted from the final print

DONNA REED (Donna Mullenger) Born January 27, 1921, Denison, Iowa. Married William Tuttle (1943); divorced 1945. Married Tony Owen (1945), children: Penny, Tony, Timothy, Mary.

Feature Films:

 as **Donna Adams** *Babes on Broadway* (MGM, 1941), *The Get-Away* (MGM, 1941).

 as **Donna Reed** *The Shadow of the Thin Man* (MGM, 1941), *The Bugle Sounds* (MGM, 1941), *Calling Dr. Gillespie* (MGM, 1942), *The Courtship of Andy Hardy* (MGM, 1942), *Mokey* (MGM, 1942), *Eyes in the Night* (MGM, 1942), *Apache Trail* (MGM, 1942), *The Human Comedy* (MGM, 1943), *Dr. Gillespie's Criminal Case* (MGM, 1943), *Thousands Cheer* (MGM, 1943), *The Man From Down Under* (MGM, 1943), *See Here, Private Hargrove* (MGM, 1944), *Mrs.*

Donna Reed, George Dolenz and Van Johnson is *The Last Time I Saw Paris.*

Claudette Colbert and Anne Revere in *Remember the Day.*

Parkington (MGM, 1944), *Gentle Annie* (MGM, 1944), *The Picture of Dorian Gray* (MGM, 1945), *They Were Expendable* (MGM, 1945), *Faithful in My Fashion* (MGM, 1946), *It's a Wonderful Life* (RKO, 1946), *Green Dolphin Street* (MGM, 1947), *Beyond Glory* (Par., 1948), *Chicago Deadline* (Par., 1949), *Saturday's Hero* (Col., 1951), *Scandal Sheet* (Col., 1952), *Hangman's Knot* (Col., 1952), *Trouble Along the Way* (WB, 1953), *Raiders of the Seven Seas* (UA, 1953), *The Caddy* (Par., 1953), *From Here to Eternity* (Col., 1953), *Gun Fury* (Col., 1953), *Three Hours to Kill* (Col., 1954), *They Rode West* (Col., 1954), *The Last Time I Saw Paris* (MGM, 1954), *The Far Horizons* (Par., 1955), *Ransom* (MGM, 1956), *The Benny Goodman Story* (Univ., 1956), *Backlash* (Univ., 1956), *Beyond Mombasa* (Col., 1957), *The Whole Truth* (Col., 1958), *Pepe* (Col., 1960).

LEE REMICK (Lee Ann Remick) Born December 14, 1935, Quincy, Massachusetts. Married Bill Colleran (1957), children: Katherine, Matthew; divorced 1968.

Bradford Dillman and Lee Remick in *Sanctuary.*

Feature Films: *A Face in the Crowd* (WB, 1957), *The Long, Hot Summer* (20th, 1958), *These Thousand Hills* (20th, 1959), *Anatomy of a Murder* (Col., 1959), *Wild River* (20th, 1960), *Sanctuary* (20th, 1961), *Experiment in Terror* (Col., 1962), *Days of Wine and Roses* (WB, 1962), *The Running Man* (Col., 1963), *The Wheeler Dealers* (MGM, 1963), *Baby, the Rain Must Fall* (Col., 1965), *The Hallelujah Trail* (UA, 1965), *No Way to Treat a Lady* (Par., 1968), *The Detective* (20th, 1968).

ANNE REVERE Born June 25, 1903, New York, New York. Married Samuel Rosen (1935).

Feature Films: *Double Door* (Par., 1934), *One Crowded Hour* (RKO, 1940), *The Howards of Virginia* (Col., 1940), *Men of Boys Town* (MGM, 1941), *The Devil Commands* (Col., 1941), *H. M. Pulham, Esq.* (MGM, 1941), *Remember the Day* (20th, 1941), *The Falcon Takes Over* (RKO, 1942), *Meet the Stewarts* (Col., 1942), *The Gay Sisters* (WB, 1942), *Star Spangled Rhythm* (Par., 1942), *Shantytown* (Rep., 1943), *The Meanest Man in the World* (20th, 1943), *Old Acquaintance* (WB, 1943), *The Song of Bernadette* (20th, 1943), *Standing Room Only* (Par., 1944), *Rainbow Island* (Par., 1944), *The Thin Man Goes Home* (MGM, 1944), *Sunday Dinner for a Soldier* (20th, 1944), *National Velvet* (MGM, 1944), *The Keys of the Kingdom* (20th, 1944), *Don Juan Quilligan* (20th, 1945), *Fallen Angel* (20th, 1945), *Dragonwyck* (20th, 1946), *The Shocking Miss Pilgrim* (20th, 1947), *Carnival in Costa Rica* (20th, 1947), *Body and Soul* (UA, 1947), *Forever Amber* (20th, 1947), *Gentleman's Agreement* (20th, 1947), *Secret Beyond the Door* (Univ., 1948), *Scudda Hoo! Scudda Hay!* (20th, 1948), *Deep Waters* (20th, 1948), *You're My Everything* (20th, 1949), *The Great Missouri Raid* (Par., 1950), *A Place in the Sun* (Par., 1951).

DEBBIE REYNOLDS (Mary Frances Reynolds) Born April 1, 1932, El Paso, Texas. Married Eddie Fisher (1955), children: Carrie, Todd; divorced 1959. Married Harry Karl (1960).

Feature Films: *June Bride* (WB, 1948), *The Daughter of Rosie O'Grady* (WB, 1950), *Three Little Words* (MGM, 1950), *Two Weeks With Love* (MGM, 1950), *Mr. Imperium* (MGM, 1951), *Singin' in the Rain* (MGM,

Debbie Reynolds, Donald O'Connor and Noreen Corcoran in *I Love Melvin.*

1952), *Skirts Ahoy* (MGM, 1952),* *I Love Melvin* (MGM, 1953), *The Affairs of Dobie Gillis* (MGM, 1953), *Give the Girl a Break* (MGM, 1953), *Susan Slept Here* (RKO, 1954), *Athena* (MGM, 1954), *Hit the Deck* (MGM, 1955), *The Tender Trap* (MGM, 1955), *The Catered Affair* (MGM, 1956), *Bundle of Joy* (RKO, 1956), *Meet Me in Las Vegas* (MGM, 1956),* *Tammy and the Bachelor* (Univ., 1957), *This Happy Feeling* (Univ., 1958), *The Mating Game* (MGM, 1959), *Say One for Me* (20th, 1959), *It Started With a Kiss* (MGM, 1959), *The Gazebo* (MGM, 1959), *The Rat Race* (Par., 1960), *Pepe* (Col., 1960), *The Pleasure of His Company* (Par., 1961), *The Second Time Around* (20th, 1961), *How the West Was Won* (MGM, 1963), *My Six Loves* (Par., 1963), *Mary, Mary* (WB, 1963), *The Unsinkable Molly Brown* (MGM, 1964), *Goodbye Charlie* (20th, 1964), *The Singing Nun* (MGM, 1966), *Divorce American Style* (Col., 1967), *How Sweet It Is* (National General Pictures, 1968).

*Unbilled guest appearance

MARJORIE REYNOLDS (Marjorie Goodspeed) Born August 12, 1921, Buhl, Idaho. Married Jack Reynolds (1936), child: Linda.

Grant Withers, Marjorie Reynolds, James Flavin and Boris Karloff in *Mr. Wong in Chinatown*.

Sound Feature Films:

as **Marjorie Moore** *Collegiate* (Par., 1935).

as **Marjorie Reynolds** *Murder in Greenwich Village* (Col., 1937), *Tex Rides With the Boy Scouts* (GN, 1937), *The Overland Express* (Col., 1938), *Six Shootin' Sheriff* (GN, 1938), *Man's Country* (Mon., 1938), *Black Bandit* (Univ., 1938), *Rebellious Daughters* (Progressive Pictures, 1938), *Tailspin Tommy* (Mon., 1939), *Mystery Plane* (Mon., 1939), *Streets of New York* (Mon., 1939), *The Phantom Stage* (Univ., 1939), *Racketeers of the Range* (RKO, 1939), *Stunt Pilot* (Mon., 1939), *Mr. Wong in Chinatown* (Mon., 1939), *Danger Flight* (Mon., 1939), *Sky Patrol* (Mon., 1939), *Timber Stampede* (RKO, 1939), *Chasing Trouble* (Mon., 1940), *The Fatal Hour* (Mon., 1940), *Midnight Limited* (Mon., 1940), *Enemy Agent* (Univ., 1940), *Doomed to Die* (Mon., 1940), *Robin Hood of the Pecos* (Rep., 1941), *Up in the Air* (Mon., 1941), *Secret Evidence* (PRC, 1941), *The Great Swindle* (Col., 1941), *Dude Cowboy* (RKO, 1941), *Tillie the Toiler* (Col., 1941), *Cyclone on Horseback* (RKO, 1941), *Top Sergeant Mulligan* (Mon., 1941), *Holiday Inn* (Par., 1942), *Star Spangled Rhythm* (Par., 1942), *Dixie* (Par., 1943), *Up in Mabel's Room* (UA, 1944), *Ministry of Fear* (Par., 1944), *Three Is a Family* (UA, 1944), *Bring On the Girls* (Par., 1945), *Duffy's Tavern* (Par., 1945), *Meet Me on Broadway* (Col., 1946), *Monsieur Beaucaire* (Par., 1946), *The Time of Their Lives* (Univ., 1946), *Heaven Only Knows* (UA, 1947), *Bad Men of Tombstone* (AA, 1948), *That Midnight Kiss* (MGM, 1949), *Customs Agent* (Col., 1950), *The Great Jewel Robbery* (WB, 1950), *Rookie Fireman* (Col., 1950), *Home Town Story* (MGM, 1951), *His Kind of Woman* (RKO, 1951), *Models, Inc.* (Mutual Productions, 1952), *No Holds Barred* (Mon., 1952), *Mobs, Inc.* (Onyx Pictures, 1955), *Juke Box Rhythm* (Col., 1959), *The Silent Witness* (Emerson, Film Enterprises, 1964).

Luis Van Rooten, Thelma Ritter and Sharon McManus in *City Across the River*.

THELMA RITTER (Thelma Adele Ritter) Born February 14, 1905 Brooklyn, New York. Married Joseph Moran (1927), children: Joseph, Monica.

Feature Films: *The Miracle on 34th Street* (20th, 1947), *Call Northside 777* (20th, 1948), *A Letter to Three Wives* (20th, 1949), *City Across the River* (Univ., 1949), *Father Was a Fullback* (20th, 1949), *Perfect Strangers* (WB, 1950), *All About Eve* (20th, 1950), *I'll Get By* (20th, 1950), *The Mating Season* (Par., 1951), *As Young as You Feel* (20th, 1951), *The Model and the Marriage Broker* (20th, 1951), *With a Song in My Heart* (20th, 1952), *Titanic* (20th, 1953), *The Farmer Takes a Wife* (20th, 1953), *Pickup on South Street* (20th, 1953), *Rear Window* (Par., 1954), *Daddy Long Legs* (20th, 1955), *Lucy Gallant* (Par., 1955), *The Proud and Profane* (Par., 1956), *A Hole in the Head* (UA, 1959), *Pillow Talk* (Univ., 1959), *The Misfits* (UA, 1961), *The Second Time Around* (20th, 1961), *Bird Man of Alcatraz* (UA, 1962), *How the West Was Won* (MGM, 1963), *For Love or Money* (Univ., 1963), *A New Kind of Love* (Par., 1963), *Move Over, Darling* (20th, 1963), *Boeing-Boeing* (Par., 1965), *The Incident* (20th, 1967).

JASON ROBARDS, JR. (Jason Nelson Robards, Jr.) Born July 26, 1922, Chicago, Illinois. Married Eleanor Pitman (1946), children: Jason, Sarah, David; divorced 1958. Married Lauren Bacall (1961), child: Sam.

George Hamilton and Jason Robards, Jr., in *Act One*.

Feature Films: *The Journey* (MGM, 1959), *By Love Possessed* (UA, 1961), *Tender Is the Night* (20th, 1962), *Long Day's Journey into Night* (Embassy, 1962), *Act One* (WB, 1963), *A Thousand Clowns* (UA, 1965), *A Big Hand for the Little Lady* (WB, 1966), *Any Wednesday* (WB, 1966), *Divorce American Style* (Col., 1967), *Hour of the Guns* (UA, 1967), *St. Valentine's Day Massacre* (20th, 1967).

Lyda Roberti in *College Rhythm*.

LYDA ROBERTI Born May 20, 1909, Warsaw, Poland. Married Hugh Ernst (1935). Died March 12, 1938.

Feature Films: *Dancers in the Dark* (Par., 1932), *Million Dollar Legs* (Par., 1932), *The Kid From Spain* (UA, 1932), *Three-Cornered Moon* (Par., 1933), *Torch Singer* (Par., 1933), *College Rhythm* (Par., 1934), *George White's Scandals* (Fox, 1935), *The Big Broadcast of 1936* (Par., 1935), *Nobody's Baby* (MGM, 1937), *Pick a Star* (MGM, 1937), *Wide Open Faces* (Col., 1938).

CLIFF ROBERTSON (Clifford Parker Robertson III) Born September 9, 1925, La Jolla, California. Married Cynthia Stone (1957), child: Stephanie; divorced. Married Dina Merrill (1966).

Cliff Robertson and Robert Culp in *PT-109*.

Feature Films: *Picnic* (Col., 1955), *Autumn Leaves* (Col., 1956), *The Girl Most Likely* (Univ., 1957), *The Naked and the Dead* (WB, 1958), *Gidget* (Col., 1959), *Battle of the Coral Sea* (Col., 1959), *As the Sea Rages.* (Col., 1960), *All in a Night's Work* (Par., 1961), *The Big Show* (20th, 1961), *Underworld, U.S.A.* (Col., 1962), *The Interns* (Col., 1962), *My Six Loves* (Par., 1963), *PT-109* (WB, 1963), *Sunday in New York* (MGM, 1963), *The Best Man* (UA, 1964), *633 Squadron* (UA, 1964), *Up From the Beach* (20th, 1965), *Love Has Many Faces* (Col., 1965), *Masquerade* (UA, 1965), *The Honey Pot* (UA, 1967), *Charly* (Selmur, 1968), *The Devil's Brigade* (UA, 1968).

EDWARD G. ROBINSON (Emmanuel Goldenberg) Born December 12, 1893, Bucharest, Romania. Married Gladys Lloyd (1927), child: Emmanuel; divorced 1956.

Sound Feature Films: *The Hole in the Wall* (Par., 1929), *Night Ride*

Ed Brophy, Edward G. Robinson and John Carradine in *The Last Gangster*.

(Univ., 1930), *A Lady to Love* (MGM, 1930), *Outside the Law* (Univ., 1930), *East Is West* (Univ., 1930), *The Widow From Chicago* (WB, 1930), *Little Caesar* (WB, 1930), *Smart Money* (WB, 1931), *Five Star Final* (WB, 1931), *The Hatchet Man* (WB, 1932), *Two Seconds* (WB, 1932), *Tiger Shark* (WB, 1932), *Silver Dollar* (WB, 1932), *Little Giant* (WB, 1933), *I Loved a Woman* (WB, 1933), *Dark Hazard* (WB, 1934), *The Man With Two Faces* (WB, 1934), *The Whole Town's Talking* (Col., 1935), *Barbary Coast* (UA, 1935), *Bullets or Ballots* (WB, 1936), *Thunder in the City* (Col., 1937), *Kid Galahad* (WB, 1937), *The Last Gangster* (MGM, 1937), *A Slight Case of Murder* (WB, 1938), *The Amazing Dr. Clitterhouse* (WB, 1938), *I Am the Law* (Col., 1938), *Confessions of a Nazi Spy* (WB, 1939), *Blackmail* (MGM, 1939), *Dr. Ehrlich's Magic Bullet* (WB, 1940), *Brother Orchid* (WB, 1940), *A Dispatch From Reuters* (WB, 1940), *The Sea Wolf* (WB, 1941), *Manpower* (WB, 1941), *Larceny, Inc.* (WB, 1942), *Tales of Manhattan* (20th, 1942), *Destroyer* (Col., 1943), *Flesh and Fantasy* (Univ., 1943), *Tampico* (20th, 1944), *Double Indemnity* (Par., 1944), *Mr. Winkle Goes to War* (Col., 1944), *The Woman in the Window* (RKO, 1944), *Our Vines Have Tender Grapes* (MGM, 1945), *Scarlet Street* (Univ., 1945), *The Stranger* (RKO, 1946), *The Red House* (UA, 1947), *All My Sons* (Univ., 1948), *Key Largo* (WB, 1948), *The Night Has a Thousand Eyes* (Par., 1948), *House of Strangers* (20th, 1949), *It's a Great Feeling* (WB, 1949), *My Daughter Joy* (Col., 1950), *Actors and Sin* (UA, 1952), *Vice Squad* (UA, 1953), *The Big Leaguer* (MGM, 1953), *The Glass Web* (Univ., 1953), *Black Tuesday* (UA, 1954), *The Violent Men* (Col., 1955), *Tight Spot* (Col., 1955), *A Bullet for Joey* (UA, 1955), *Illegal* (WB, 1955), *Hell on Frisco Bay* (WB, 1955), *Nightmare* (UA, 1956), *The Ten Commandments* (Par., 1956), *A Hole in the Head* (UA, 1959), *Seven Thieves* (20th, 1960), *Pepe* (Col., 1960), *My Geisha* (Par., 1962), *Two Weeks in Another Town* (MGM, 1962), *Sammy Going South* (Bryanston, 1963), *The Prize* (MGM, 1963), *Good Neighbor Sam* (Col., 1964), *Robin and the 7 Hoods* (WB, 1964), *Cheyenne Autumn* (WB, 1964), *The Outrage* (MGM, 1964), *The Cincinnati Kid* (MGM, 1965) *The Biggest Bundle of Them All* (MGM, 1968), *Grand Slam* (Par., 1968), *MacKenna's Gold* (Col., 1968), *Operation St. Peter's* (Ultra-Marianne, 1968).

MAY ROBSON (Mary Robison) Born April 19, 1864, Melbourne, Australia. Married Edward Gore (1880) child: Edward; widowed 1883. Married A. H. Brown (1889); widowed 1922. Died October 20, 1942.

Sound Feature Films: *Mother's Millions* (Univ., 1931), *Strange Interlude* (MGM, 1932), *Letty Lynton* (MGM, 1932), *Red-Headed Woman* (MGM, 1932), *If I Had a Million* (Par., 1932), *Little Orphan Annie* (RKO, 1932), *The White Sister* (MGM, 1933), *Men Must Fight* (MGM, 1933), *Reunion in Vienna* (MGM, 1933), *Dinner at Eight* (MGM, 1933), *Lady for a Day* (Col., 1933), *Broadway to Hollywood* (MGM, 1933), *One Man's Journey* (RKO, 1933), *Beauty for Sale* (MGM, 1933), *The Solitaire Man* (MGM, 1933), *Dancing Lady* (MGM, 1933), *Alice in Wonderland* (Par., 1933), *You Can't Buy Everything* (MGM, 1934), *Straight Is the Way* (MGM, 1934), *Lady by Choice* (Col., 1934), *Grand Old Girl* (RKO, 1935), *Reckless* (MGM, 1935), *Mills of the Gods* (Col., 1935), *Vanessa—Her Love Story* (MGM, 1935), *Strangers All* (Radio, 1935), *Age of Indiscretion* (MGM, 1935), *Anna Karenina*

Ian Hunter, Roland Young, May Robson, Genevieve Tobin and Fay Bainter in *Yes, My Darling Daughter*.

(MGM, 1935), *Three Kids and a Queen* (Univ., 1935), *Wife vs. Secretary* (MGM, 1936), *Rainbow on the River* (RKO, 1936), *Woman in Distress* (Col., 1937), *A Star Is Born* (UA, 1937), *The Captain's Kid* (WB, 1937), *The Perfect Specimen* (WB, 1937), *Bringing Up Baby* (RKO, 1938), *The Adventures of Tom Sawyer* (UA, 1938), *The Texans* (Par., 1938), *Four Daughters* (WB, 1938), *Yes, My Darling Daughter* (WB, 1939), *They Made Me a Criminal* (WB, 1939), *The Kid From Kokomo* (WB, 1939), *Daughters Courageous* (WB, 1939), *That's Right—You're Wrong* (RKO, 1939), *Nurse Edith Cavell* (RKO, 1939), *Four Wives* (WB, 1939), *Granny, Get Your Gun* (WB, 1940), *Irene* (RKO, 1940), *Texas Rangers Ride Again* (Par., 1941), *Four Mothers* (WB, 1941), *Million Dollar Baby* (WB, 1941), *Playmates* (RKO, 1941), *Joan of Paris* (RKO, 1942).

GINGER ROGERS (Virginia Katherine McMath) Born July 16, 1911, Independence, Missouri. Married Jack Edward Culpepper (1929), divorced 1931. Married Lew Ayres (1934); divorced 1941. Married Jack Briggs (1943); divorced 1949. Married Jacques Bergerac (1953); divorced 1957. Married William Marshall (1961).

Ginger Rogers and Marjorie Rambeau in *The Primrose Path*.

Feature Films: *Young Man of Manhattan* (Par., 1930), *Queen High* (Par., 1930), *The Sap From Syracuse* (Par., 1930), *Follow the Leader* (Par., 1930), *Honor Among Lovers* (Par., 1931), *The Tip-Off* (Pathé, 1931), *Suicide Fleet* (Pathé, 1931), *Carnival Boat* (RKO, 1932), *The Tenderfoot* (WB, 1932), *The Thirteenth Guest* (Mon., 1932), *Hat Check Girl* (Fox, 1932), *You Said a Mouthful* (WB, 1932), *42nd Street* (WB,

1933), *Broadway Bad* (Fox, 1933), *Gold Diggers of 1933* (WB, 1933), *Professional Sweetheart* (RKO, 1933), *Shriek in the Night* (Allied, 1933), *Don't Bet on Love* (Univ., 1933), *Sitting Pretty* (Par., 1933), *Flying Down to Rio* (RKO, 1933), *Chance at Heaven* (RKO, 1933), *Rafter Romance* (RKO, 1934), *Finishing School* (RKO, 1934), *20 Million Sweethearts* (WB, 1934), *Change of Heart* (Fox, 1934), *Upper World* (WB, 1934), *The Gay Divorcee* (RKO, 1934), *Romance in Manhattan* (RKO, 1934), *Roberta* (RKO, 1935), *Star of Midnight* (RKO, 1935), *Top Hat* (RKO, 1935), *In Person* (RKO, 1935), *Follow the Fleet* (RKO, 1936), *Swing Time* (RKO, 1936), *Shall We Dance* (RKO, 1937), *Stage Door* (RKO, 1937), *Having Wonderful Time* (RKO, 1938), *Vivacious Lady* (RKO, 1938), *Carefree* (RKO, 1938), *The Story of Vernon and Irene Castle* (RKO, 1939), *Bachelor Mother* (RKO, 1939), *Fifth Avenue Girl* (RKO, 1939), *Primrose Path* (RKO, 1940), *Lucky Partners* (RKO, 1940), *Kitty Foyle* (RKO, 1940), *Tom, Dick and Harry* (RKO, 1941), *Roxie Hart* (20th, 1942), *Tales of Manhattan* (20th, 1942), *The Major and the Minor* (Par., 1942), *Once Upon a Honeymoon* (RKO, 1942), *Tender Comrade* (RKO, 1943), *Lady in the Dark* (Par., 1944), *I'll Be Seeing You* (Selznick-UA, 1944), *Weekend at the Waldorf* (MGM, 1945), *Heartbeat* (RKO, 1946), *Magnificent Doll* (Univ., 1946), *It Had to Be You* (Col., 1947), *The Barkleys of Broadway* (MGM, 1949), *Perfect Strangers* (WB, 1950), *Storm Warning* (WB, 1950), *The Groom Wore Spurs* (Univ., 1951), *We're Not Married* (20th, 1952), *Monkey Business* (20th, 1952), *Dreamboat* (20th, 1952), *Forever Female* (Par., 1953), *Black Widow* (20th, 1954), *Twist of Fate* (UA, 1954), *Tight Spot* (Col., 1955), *The First Traveling Saleslady* (RKO, 1956), *Teenage Rebel* (20th, 1956), *Oh, Men! Oh, Women!* (20th, 1957), *The Confession* (Wm. Marshall Prod., 1964, unreleased), *Harlow* (Magna, 1965),

ROY ROGERS (Leonard Slye) Born November 5, 1912, Cincinnati, Ohio. Married Arlene Wilkins (1936), children: Cheryl, Darlene, Linda, Roy, Marion; widowed 1946. Married Dale Evans (1947), children: Robin, John, Mary Little Doe, Deborah.

Claire Trevor and Roy Rogers in *Dark Command*.

Feature Films: *The Old Homestead* (Liberty, 1935), *The Big Show* (Rep., 1936), *Gallant Defender* (Col., 1935), *The Mysterious Avenger* (Col., 1936), *Rhythm on the Range* (Par., 1936), *The Old Corral* (Rep., 1936), *The Old Wyoming Trail* (Col, 1937), *Wild Horse Rodeo* (Rep., 1937), *The Old Barn Dance* (Rep., 1938), *Under Western Stars* (Rep., 1938), *Billy the Kid Returns* (Rep., 1938), *Come On Rangers* (Rep., 1938), *Shine On Harvest Moon* (Rep., 1938), *Rough Riders' Round-Up* (Rep., 1939), *Frontier Pony Express* (Rep., 1939), *Southward, Ho!* (Rep., 1939), *In Old Caliente* (Rep., 1939), *Wall Street Cowboy* (Rep., 1939), *The Arizona Kid* (Rep., 1939), *Jeepers Creepers* (Rep., 1939), *Saga of Death Valley* (Rep., 1939), *Days of Jesse James* (Rep., 1939), *Young Buffalo Bill* (Rep., 1940), *Dark Command* (Rep., 1940), *The Carson City Kid* (Rep., 1940), *The Ranger and the Lady* (Rep., 1940), *Colorado* (Rep., 1940), *Young Bill Hickok* (Rep., 1940), *The Border Legion*

(Rep., 1940), *Robin Hood of the Pecos* (Rep., 1941), *Arkansas Judge* (Rep., 1941), *In Old Cheyenne* (Rep., 1941), *Sheriff of Tombstone* (Rep., 1941), *Nevada City* (Rep., 1941), *Bad Man of Deadwood* (Rep., 1941), *Jesse James at Bay* (Rep., 1941), *Red River Valley* (Rep., 1941), *The Man From Cheyenne* (Rep., 1942), *South of Santa Fe* (Rep., 1942), *Sunset on the Desert* (Rep., 1942), *Romance on the Range* (Rep., 1942), *Sons of the Pioneers* (Rep., 1942), *Sunset Serenade* (Rep., 1942), *Heart of the Golden West* (Rep., 1942), *Ridin' Down the Canyon* (Rep., 1942), *Idaho* (Rep., 1943), *King of the Cowboys* (Rep., 1943), *Song of Texas* (Rep., 1943), *Silver Spurs* (Rep., 1943), *The Man From Music Mountain* (Rep., 1943), *Hands Across the Border* (Rep., 1943), *The Cowboy and the Senorita* (Rep., 1944), *The Yellow Rose of Texas* (Rep., 1944), *Song of Nevada* (Rep., 1944), *San Fernando Valley* (Rep., 1944), *Lights of Old Santa Fe* (Rep., 1944), *Brazil* (Rep., 1944)*, *Lake Placid Serenade* (Rep., 1944), *Hollywood Canteen* (WB, 1944), *Utah* (Rep., 1945), *Bells of Rosarita* (Rep., 1945), *The Man From Oklahoma* (Rep., 1945), *Sunset in El Dorado* (Rep., 1945), *Don't Fence Me In* (Rep., 1945), *Along the Navajo Trail* (Rep., 1945), *Song of Arizona* (Rep., 1946), *Rainbow Over Texas* (Rep., 1946), *My Pal Trigger* (Rep., 1946), *Under Nevada Skies* (Rep., 1946), *Roll on Texas Moon* (Rep., 1946), *Home in Oklahoma* (Rep., 1946), *Out California Way* (Rep., 1946), *Helldorado* (Rep., 1946), *Apache Rose* (Rep., 1947) *Hit Parade of 1947* (Rep., 1947), *Bells of San Angelo* (Rep., 1947), *Springtime in the Sierras* (Rep., 1947), *On the Old Spanish Trail* (Rep., 1947), *The Gay Ranchero* (Rep., 1948), *Under California Stars* (Rep., 1948), *Eyes of Texas* (Rep., 1948), *Melody Time* (RKO, 1948), *Night Time in Nevada* (Rep., 1948), *Grand Canyon Trail* (Rep., 1948), *The Far Frontier* (Rep., 1948), *Susanna Pass* (Rep., 1949), *Down Dakota Way* (Rep., 1949), *The Golden Stallion* (Rep., 1949), *Bells of Coronado* (Rep., 1950), *Twilight in the Sierras* (Rep., 1950), *Trigger, Jr.* (Rep., 1950), *Sunset in the West* (Rep., 1950), *North of the Great Divide* (Rep., 1950), *Trail of Robin Hood* (Rep., 1950), *Spoilers of the Plains* (Rep., 1951), *Heart of the Rockies* (Rep., 1951), *In Old Amarillo* (Rep., 1951), *South of Caliente* (Rep., 1951), *Pals of the Golden West* (Rep., 1951), *Son of Paleface* (Par., 1952), *Alias Jesse James* (UA, 1959).*

*Unbilled guest appearance

WILL ROGERS (William Penn Adair Rogers) Born November 4, 1879, Cologah, Indian Territory (Oklahoma). Married Betty Balke (1908), children: Will, Mary, James. Died August 15, 1935.

Will Rogers and Sterling Holloway in *Doubting Thomas*.

Sound Feature Films: *They Had to See Paris* (Fox, 1929), *Happy Days* (Fox, 1930), *So This Is London* (Fox, 1930), *Lightnin'* (Fox, 1930), *A Connecticut Yankee* (Fox, 1931), *Young As You Feel* (Fox, 1931), *Ambassador Bill* (Fox, 1931), *Business and Pleasure* (Fox, 1932), *Down to Earth* (Fox, 1932), *Too Busy to Work* (Fox, 1932), *State Fair* (Fox, 1933), *Doctor Bull* (Fox, 1933), *Mr. Skitch* (Fox, 1933), *David Harum* (Fox, 1934), *Handy Andy* (Fox, 1934), *Judge Priest* (Fox, 1934), *County Chairman* (Fox, 1935), *Life Begins at 40* (Fox, 1935), *Doubting Thomas* (Fox, 1935), *In Old Kentucky* (Fox, 1935), *Steamboat 'Round the Bend* (Fox, 1935).

Bill Neff, Gilbert Roland and Chris-Pin Martin in *King of the Bandits*.

GILBERT ROLAND (Louis Antonio Damaso Alonso) Born December 11, 1905, Chihuahua, Mexico. Married Constance Bennett (1941), children: Lynda, Gyl; divorced 1946. Married Guillermina Cantu (1954).

English-Language Sound Feature Films: *New York Nights* (UA, 1930), *Men of the North* (MGM, 1930), *The Passionate Plumber* (MGM, 1932), *Life Begins* (WB, 1932), *No Living Witness* (Mayfair, 1932), *Parisian Romance* (Allied, 1932), *Call Her Savage* (Fox, 1932), *She Done Him Wrong* (Par., 1933), *Our Betters* (RKO, 1933), *Gigolettes of Paris* (Equitable, 1933), *After Tonight* (RKO, 1933), *Elinor Norton* (Fox, 1934), *Mystery Woman* (Fox, 1935), *Ladies Love Danger* (Fox, 1935), *Midnight Taxi* (20th, 1937), *Last Train From Madrid* (Par, 1937), *Thunder Trail* (Par., 1937), *Gateway* (20th, 1938), *Juarez* (WB, 1939), *Isle of Destiny* (RKO, 1940), *The Sea Hawk* (WB, 1940), *Rangers of Fortune* (Par., 1940), *Gambling on the High Seas* (WB, 1940), *Angels With Broken Wings* (Rep., 1941), *My Life With Caroline* (RKO, 1941), *Isle of Missing Men* (Mon., 1942), *Enemy Agents Meet Ellery Queen* (Col., 1942), *The Desert Hawk* (Col. serial, 1944), *Captain Kidd* (UA, 1945), *The Gay Cavalier* (Mon., 1946), *Pirates of Monterey* (Univ., 1947), *King of the Bandits* (Mon., 1947), *Robin Hood of Monterey* (Mon., 1947), *Riding the California Trail* (Mon., 1947), *High Conquest* (Mon., 1947), *The Other Woman* (UA, 1947), *The Dude Goes West* (AA, 1948), *We Were Strangers* (Col., 1949), *Malaya* (MGM, 1949), *The Torch* (EL, 1950), *Crisis* (MGM, 1950), *The Furies* (Par., 1950), *Mark of the Renegade* (Univ., 1951), *Ten Tall Men* (Col., 1951), *The Bullfighter and the Lady* (Rep., 1951), *My Six Convicts* (Col., 1952), *Glory Alley* (MGM, 1952), *The Miracle of Our Lady of Fatima* (WB, 1952), *Apache War Smoke* (MGM, 1952), *The Bad and the Beautiful* (MGM, 1952), *Beneath the 12-Mile Reef* (20th, 1953), *The Diamond Queen* (WB, 1953), *Thunder Bay* (Univ., 1953), *The French Line* (RKO, 1954), *Underwater* (RKO, 1955), *The Racers* (20th, 1955), *That Lady* (20th, 1955), *The Treasure of Pancho Villa* (RKO, 1955), *Bandido* (UA, 1956), *Around the World in 80 Days* (UA, 1956), *Three Violent People* (Par., 1956), *The Midnight Story* (Univ., 1957), *The Last of the Fast Guns* (Univ., 1958), *The Wild and The Innocent* (Univ., 1959), *The Big Circus* (AA, 1959), *Guns of the Timberland* (WB, 1960), *Samar* (WB, 1962), *Cheyenne Autumn* (WB, 1964), *The Reward* (20th, 1965), *Each Man for Himself* (PCM, 1968).

RUTH ROMAN Born December 22, 1924, Boston, Massachusetts. Married Jack Flaxman (1940); divorced 1941. Married Mortimer Hall (1950), child: Richard; divorced 1955. Married Buddy Moss (1956).

Feature Films: *Stage Door Canteen* (UA, 1943), *Ladies Courageous* (Univ., 1944), *Since You Went Away* (UA, 1944), *Storm Over Lisbon* (Rep., 1944), *Jungle Queen* (Univ. serial, 1945), *The Affairs of Susan* (Par., 1945), *See My Lawyer* (Univ., 1945), *You Came Along* (Par., 1945), *Incendiary Blonde* (Par., 1945), *A Night in Casablanca* (UA, 1946), *White Stallion* (Astor, 1947), *The Big Clock* (Par., 1948), *The Night Has a Thousand Eyes* (Par., 1948), *Good Sam* (RKO, 1948), *Belle Starr's Daughter* (20th, 1948), *The Window* (RKO, 1949), *Champion* (UA, 1949), *Beyond the Forest* (WB, 1949), *Always Leave Them Laughing* (WB, 1949), *Barricade* (WB, 1950), *Colt .45* (WB, 1950),

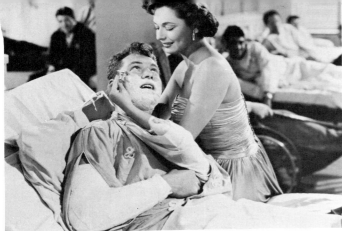

Ruth Roman in *Starlift.*

Three Secrets (WB, 1950), *Dallas* (WB, 1950), *Lightning Strikes Twice* (WB, 1951), *Strangers on a Train* (WB, 1951), *Starlift* (WB, 1951), *Tomorrow Is Another Day* (WB, 1951), *Invitation* (MGM, 1952), *Mara Maru* (WB, 1952), *Young Man With Ideas* (MGM, 1952), *Blowing Wild* (WB, 1953), *Tanganyika* (Univ., 1954), *Down Three Dark Streets* (UA, 1954), *The Shanghai Story* (Rep., 1954), *The Far Country* (Univ., 1955), *The Bottom of the Bottle* (20th, 1956), *Joe MacBeth* (Col., 1956), *Great Day in the Morning* (RKO, 1956), *Rebel in Town* (UA, 1956), *Five Steps to Danger* (UA, 1957), *Bitter Victory* (Col., 1958), *Desert Desperadoes* (RKO, 1959), *Look in Any Window* (AA 1961), *Love Has Many Faces* (Col., 1965).

CESAR ROMERO Born February 15, 1907, New York, New York.

Cesar Romero, George Montgomery and Jackie Gleason in *Orchestra Wives.*

Feature Films: *The Shadow Laughs* (Invincible, 1933), *The Thin Man* (MGM, 1934), *Cheating Cheaters* (Univ., 1934), *British Agent* (WB, 1934), *The Good Fairy* (Univ., 1935), *Strange Wives* (Univ., 1935), *Clive of India* (UA, 1935), *Cardinal Richelieu* (UA, 1935), *Hold 'Em Yale* (Par., 1935), *The Devil Is a Woman* (Par., 1935), *Diamond Jim* (Univ., 1935), *Metropolitan* (Fox, 1935), *Rendezvous* (MGM, 1935), *Show Them No Mercy* (Fox, 1935), *Love Before Breakfast* (Univ., 1936), *Nobody's Fool* (Univ., 1936), *Public Enemy's Wife* (WB, 1936), *15 Maiden Lane* (20th, 1936), *She's Dangerous* (Univ., 1937), *Armored Car* (Univ., 1937), *Wee Willie Winkie* (20th, 1937), *Dangerously Yours* (20th, 1937), *Happy Landing* (20th, 1938), *Always Goodbye* (20th, 1938), *My Lucky Star* (20th, 1938), *Five of a Kind* (20th, 1938), *Wife, Husband and Friend* (20th, 1939), *The Little Princess* (20th, 1939), *Return of the Cisco Kid* (20th, 1939), *Charlie Chan at Treasure Island* (20th, 1939), *Frontier Marshal* (20th, 1939), *Viva Cisco Kid* (20th, 1940), *He Married His Wife* (20th, 1940), *The Cisco Kid and the Lady* (20th, 1940), *The Gay Caballero* (20th, 1940), *Tall, Dark and Handsome*

(20th, 1941), *Romance of the Rio Grande* (20th, 1941), *Ride on, Vaquero* (20th, 1941), *The Great American Broadcast* (20th, 1941), *Dance Hall* (20th, 1941), *Week-End in Havana* (20th, 1941), *A Gentleman at Heart* (20th, 1942), *Tales of Manhattan* (20th, 1942), *Orchestra Wives* (20th, 1942), *Springtime in the Rockies* (20th, 1942), *Coney Island* (20th, 1943), *Wintertime* (20th, 1943), *Captain From Castile* (20th, 1947), *Carnival in Costa Rica* (20th, 1947), *Deep Waters* (20th, 1948), *That Lady in Ermine* (20th, 1948), *Julia Misbehaves* (MGM, 1948), *The Beautiful Blonde From Bashful Bend* (20th, 1949), *Love That Brute* (20th, 1950), *Once a Thief* (UA, 1950), *Happy Go Lovely* (RKO, 1951), *FBI Girl* (Lip., 1951), *The Lost Continent* (Lip., 1951), *Scotland Yard Inspector* (Lip., 1952), *The Jungle* (Lip., 1952), *Prisoners of the Casbah* (Col., 1953), *Shadow Man* (Lip., 1953), *Vera Cruz* (UA, 1954), *The Americano* (RKO, 1955), *The Racers* (20th, 1955), *Around the World in 80 Days* (UA, 1956), *The Sword of Granada* (Manson Dist. Co., 1956), *The Leather Saint* (Par., 1956), *The Story of Mankind* (WB, 1957), *Villa!* (20th, 1958), *Ocean's 11* (WB, 1960), *Pepe* (Col., 1960), *7 Women From Hell* (20th, 1961), *If a Man Answers* (Univ., 1962), *We Shall Return* (United International, 1963), *Donovan's Reef* (Par., 1963), *The Castilian* (WB, 1963), *A House Is Not a Home* (Embassy, 1964), *Two on a Guillotine* (WB, 1965), *Sergeant Deadhead* (AIP, 1965), *Marriage on the Rocks* (WB, 1965), *Batman* (20th, 1966).

MICKEY ROONEY (Joe Yule, Jr.) Born September 23, 1920, Brooklyn, New York. Married Ava Gardner (1942); divorced 1943. Married Betty Rase (1944), children: Mickey, Timothy; divorced 1947. Married Martha Vickers (1949), child: Ted; divorced 1951. Married Elaine Mahnken (1952); divorced 1959. Married Barbara Thomason (1959), children: Kelly, Kerry, Kimmy; widowed 1966. Married Margaret Lane (1966); divorced 1967.

Jeanne Cagney and Mickey Rooney in *Quicksand.*

Sound Feature Films: *Information Kid* (Univ., 1932), *Fast Companions* (Univ., 1932), *My Pal the King* (Univ., 1932), *Beast of the City* (MGM, 1932), *The Big Cage* (Univ., 1933), *The Life of Jimmy Dolan* (WB, 1933), *Broadway to Hollywood* (MGM, 1933), *The Big Chance* (Arthur Greenblatt, 1933), *The Chief* (MGM, 1933), *Lost Jungle* (Mascot serial, 1933), *Beloved* (Univ., 1934), *I Like It That Way* (Univ., 1934), *Love Birds* (Univ., 1934), *Manhattan Melodrama* (MGM, 1934), *Chained* (MGM, 1934), *Hide-Out* (MGM, 1934), *Upper World* (WB, 1934), *Half a Sinner* (Univ., 1934), *Blind Date* (Col., 1934), *Death on the Diamond* (MGM, 1934), *County Chairman* (Fox, 1935), *The Healer* (Mon., 1935), *A Midsummer Night's Dream* (WB, 1935), *Reckless* (MGM, 1935), *Ah, Wilderness* (MGM, 1935), *Riffraff* (MGM, 1935), *Little Lord Fauntleroy* (UA, 1936), *The Devil Is a Sissy* (MGM, 1936), *Down the Stretch* (WB, 1936), *Captains Courageous* (MGM, 1937), *A Family Affair* (MGM, 1937), *The Hoosier Schoolboy* (Mon., 1937), *Slave Ship* (20th, 1937), *Thoroughbreds Don't Cry* (MGM, 1937), *Live, Love and Learn* (MGM, 1937), *Love Is a Headache* (MGM, 1938), *Judge Hardy's Children* (MGM, 1938), *You're Only Young Once* (MGM,

1938), *Hold That Kiss* (MGM, 1938), *Lord Jeff* (MGM, 1938), *Love Finds Andy Hardy* (MGM, 1938), *Boys Town* (MGM, 1938), *Out West With the Hardys* (MGM, 1938), *Stablemates* (MGM, 1938), *Adventures of Huckleberry Finn* (MGM, 1939), *The Hardys Ride High* (MGM, 1939), *Andy Hardy Gets Spring Fever* (MGM, 1939), *Babes in Arms* (MGM, 1939), *Judge Hardy and Son* (MGM, 1939), *Young Tom Edison* (MGM, 1940), *Andy Hardy Meets Debutante* (MGM, 1940), *Strike Up the Band* (MGM, 1940), *Andy Hardy's Private Secretary* (MGM, 1941), *Men of Boys Town* (MGM, 1941), *Life Begins For Andy Hardy* (MGM, 1941), *Babes on Broadway* (MGM, 1941), *The Courtship of Andy Hardy* (MGM, 1942), *A Yank at Eton* (MGM, 1942), *Andy Hardy's Double Life* (MGM, 1942), *Andy Hardy Steps Out* (MGM, 1942), *The Human Comedy* (MGM, 1943), *Girl Crazy* (MGM, 1943), *Thousands Cheer* (MGM, 1943), *Andy Hardy's Blonde Trouble* (MGM, 1944), *National Velvet* (MGM, 1944), *Love Laughs at Andy Hardy* (MGM, 1946), *Killer McCoy* (MGM, 1947), *Summer Holiday* (MGM, 1948), *Words and Music* (MGM, 1948), *The Big Wheel* (UA, 1949), *Quicksand* (UA, 1950), *The Fireball* (20th, 1950), *He's a Cockeyed Wonder* (Col., 1950), *My Outlaw Brother*, (EL, 1951), *The Strip* (MGM, 1951), *Sound Off* (Col., 1952), *Off Limits* (Par., 1953), *A Slight Case of Larceny* (MGM, 1953), *Drive a Crooked Road* (Col., 1954), *The Atomic Kid* (Rep., 1954), *The Bridges at Toko-Ri* (Par., 1954), *The Twinkle in God's Eye* (Rep., 1955), *The Bold and the Brave* (RKO, 1956), *Francis in the Haunted House* (Univ., 1956), *Magnificent Roughnecks* (AA, 1956), *Operation Mad Ball* (Col., 1957), *Baby Face Nelson* (UA, 1957), *Andy Hardy Comes Home* (MGM, 1958), *A Nice Little Bank That Should Be Robbed* (20th, 1958), *The Last Mile* (UA, 1959), *The Big Operator* (MGM, 1959), *Platinum High School* (MGM, 1960), *The Private Lives of Adam And Eve* (Univ., 1960), *King of the Roaring 20's—The Story of Arnold Rothstein* (AA, 1961), *Breakfast at Tiffany's* (Par., 1961), *Everything's Ducky* (Col., 1961), *Requiem for a Heavyweight* (Col., 1962), *It's a Mad, Mad, Mad, Mad World* (UA, 1963), *The Secret Invasion* (UA, 1964), *How to Stuff a Wild Bikini* (AIP, 1965), *24 Hours to Kill* (7 Arts, 1965), *Ambush Bay* (UA, 1966), *The Extraordinary Seaman* (MGM, 1968), *The Devil in Love* (WB-7 Arts, 1968).

SHIRLEY ROSS (Bernice Gaunt) Born January 7, 1915, Omaha, Nebraska. Married Ken Dolan (1938), children: John, Ross; widowed 1951. Married Edward Blum, child: Victoria.

Edward Arnold and Shirley Ross in *Blossoms on Broadway*.

Feature Films: *Bombshell* (MGM, 1933), *Hollywood Party* (MGM, 1934), *Manhattan Melodrama* (MGM, 1934), *The Girl From Missouri* (MGM, 1934), *The Merry Widow* (MGM, 1934), *Age of Indiscretion* (MGM, 1935), *Calm Yourself* (MGM, 1935), *San Francisco* (MGM, 1936), *Devil's Squadron* (Col., 1936), *The Big Broadcast of 1937* (Par., 1936), *Hideaway Girl* (Par., 1937), *Waikiki Wedding* (Par., 1937), *Blossoms on Broadway* (Par., 1937), *Prison Farm* (Par., 1938), *Thanks for the Memory* (Par., 1938), *Paris Honeymoon* (Par., 1939), *Cafe Society* (Par., 1939), *Some Like It Hot* (Par., 1939), *Unexpected Father*

(Univ., 1939), *Sailors on Leave* (Rep., 1941), *Kisses for Breakfast* (WB, 1941), *A Song for Miss Julie* (Rep., 1945).

CHARLES RUGGLES (Charles Sherman Ruggles) Born February 8, 1892, Los Angeles, California. Married Adele Rowland (1914); divorced. Married Marion LaBarbe.

Fred MacMurray and Charles Ruggles in *Invitation to Happiness*.

Sound Feature Films: *Gentlemen of the Press* (Par., 1929), *The Lady Lies* (Par., 1929), *Battle of Paris* (Par., 1929), *Roadhouse Nights* (Par., 1930), *Young Man of Manhattan* (Par., 1930), *Queen High* (Par., 1930), *Her Wedding Night* (Par., 1930), *Charley's Aunt* (Col., 1930), *Honor Among Lovers* (Par., 1931), *The Smiling Lieutenant* (Par., 1931), *Girl Habit* (Par., 1931), *Beloved Bachelor* (Par., 1931), *Husband's Holiday* (Par., 1932), *This Reckless Age* (Par., 1932), *Make Me a Star* (Par., 1932), *Night of June 13* (Par., 1932), *One Hour With You* (Par., 1932), *This Is the Night* (Par., 1932), *70,000 Witnesses* (Par., 1932), *Trouble in Paradise* (Par., 1932), *Evenings for Sale* (Par., 1932), *If I Had a Million* (Par., 1932), *Madame Butterfly* (Par., 1932), *Love Me Tonight* (Par., 1932), *Murders in the Zoo* (Par., 1933), *Terror Aboard* (Par., 1933), *Mama Loves Papa* (Par., 1933), *Girl Without a Room* (Par., 1933), *Alice in Wonderland* (Par., 1933), *Goodbye Love* (RKO, 1933), *Melody Cruise* (RKO, 1933), *Melody in Spring* (Par., 1934), *Murder in the Private Car* (MGM, 1934), *Friends of Mr. Sweeney* (WB, 1934), *Six of a Kind* (Par., 1934), *Pursuit of Happiness* (Par., 1934), *Ruggles of Red Gap* (Par., 1935), *People Will Talk* (Par., 1935), *Big Broadcast of 1936* (Par., 1935), *No More Ladies* (MGM, 1935), *Anything Goes* (Par., 1936), *Early to Bed* (Par., 1936), *Wives Never Know* (Par., 1936), *Hearts Divided* (WB, 1936), *The Preview Murder Mystery* (Par., 1936), *Mind Your Own Business* (Par., 1936), *Turn Off the Moon* (Par., 1937), *Exclusive* (Par., 1937), *Bringing Up Baby* (RKO, 1938), *Breaking the Ice* (RKO, 1938), *Service DeLuxe* (Univ., 1938), *His Exciting Night* (Univ, 1938), *Yes, My Darling Daughter* (WB, 1939), *Boy Trouble* (Par., 1939), *Sudden Money* (Par., 1939), *Invitation to Happiness* (Par., 1939), *Night Work* (Par., 1939), *Balalaika* (MGM, 1939), *The Farmer's Daughter* (Par., 1940), *Opened by Mistake* (Par., 1940), *Maryland* (20th, 1940), *Public Deb No. 1* (20th, 1940), *No Time for Comedy* (WB, 1940), *The Invisible Woman* (Univ., 1941), *Go West, Young Lady* (Col., 1941), *Model Wife* (Univ., 1941), *The Perfect Snob* (20th, 1941), *The Parson of Panamint* (Par., 1941), *Friendly Enemies* (UA, 1942), *Dixie Dugan* (20th, 1943), *Our Hearts Were Young and Gay* (Par., 1944), *The Doughgirls* (WB, 1944), *Three Is a Family* (UA, 1944), *Incendiary Blonde* (Par., 1945), *Bedside Manner* (UA, 1945), *The Perfect Marriage* (Par., 1946), *Gallant Journey* (Col., 1946), *A Stolen Life* (WB, 1946), *My Brother Talks to Horses* (MGM, 1946), *It Happened on 5th Avenue* (AA, 1947), *Ramrod* (UA, 1947), *Give My Regards to Broadway* (20th, 1948), *Look for the Silver Lining* (WB, 1949), *The Lovable Cheat* (Film Classics, 1949), *All in a Night's Work* (Par., 1961), *The Pleasure of His Company* (Par., 1961), *The Parent Trap* (BV, 1961), *Son of Flubber* (BV, 1963), *Papa's Delicate Condition* (Par., 1963), *I'd Rather Be Rich* (Univ., 1964), *The Ugly Dachshund* (BV, 1965), *Follow Me, Boys* (BV, 1967).

Gale Sondergaard and Sig Rumann in *Seventh Heaven*.

Rhodes Reason, Barbara Rush and Rory Calhoun in *Flight to Hong Kong*.

SIG RUMANN (Siegfried Albon Ruman) Born c. 1890, Hamburg, Germany. Died February 14, 1967.

Feature Films: *The World Moves On* (Fox, 1934), *Servants' Entrance* (Fox, 1934), *Marie Galante* (Fox, 1934), *Under Pressure* (Fox, 1935), *The Wedding Night* (UA, 1935), *The Farmer Takes a Wife* (Fox, 1935), *A Night at the Opera* (MGM, 1935), *East of Java* (Univ., 1935), *The Princess Comes Across* (Par., 1936), *The Bold Caballero* (Rep., 1936), *On the Avenue* (20th, 1937), *Maytime* (MGM, 1937), *Midnight Taxi* (20th, 1937), *Think Fast, Mr. Moto* (20th, 1937), *This Is My Affair* (20th, 1937), *A Day at the Races* (MGM, 1937), *The Great Hospital Mystery* (20th, 1937), *Thin Ice* (20th, 1937), *Love Under Fire* (20th, 1937), *Lancer Spy* (20th, 1937), *Heidi* (20th, 1937), *Nothing Sacred* (UA, 1937), *Thank You, Mr. Moto* (20th, 1937), *Paradise for Three* (MGM, 1938), *The Saint in New York* (RKO, 1938), *I'll Give a Million* (20th, 1938), *Suez* (20th, 1938), *Girls on Probation* (WB, 1938), *The Great Waltz* (MGM, 1938), *Honolulu* (MGM, 1939), *Never Say Die* (Par., 1939), *Confessions of a Nazi Spy* (WB, 1939), *Only Angels Have Wings* (Col., 1939), *Ninotchka* (MGM, 1939), *Remember?* (MGM, 1939), *Dr. Ehrlich's Magic Bullet* (WB, 1940), *Outside the 3-Mile Limit* (Col., 1940), *I Was an Adventuress* (20th, 1940), *Four Sons* (20th, 1940), *Bitter Sweet* (MGM, 1940), *Comrade X* (MGM, 1940), *Victory* (Par., 1940), *So Ends Our Night* (UA, 1941), *That Uncertain Feeling* (UA, 1941), *The Man Who Lost Himself* (Univ., 1941), *The Wagons Roll at Night* (WB, 1941), *Love Crazy* (MGM, 1941), *Shining Victory* (WB, 1941), *World Premiere* (20th, 1941), *To Be or Not to Be* (UA, 1942), *Remember Pearl Harbor* (Rep., 1942), *Crossroads* (MGM, 1942), *Enemy Agents Meet Ellery Queen* (Col., 1942), *Desperate Journey* (WB, 1942), *Berlin Correspondent* (20th, 1942), *Tarzan Triumphs* (RKO, 1943), *They Came to Blow Up America* (20th, 1943), *Sweet Rosie O'Grady* (20th, 1943), *Government Girl* (RKO, 1943), *The Song of Bernadette* (20th, 1943), *It Happened Tomorrow* (UA, 1944), *The Hitler Gang* (Par., 1944), *Summer Storm* (UA, 1944), *House of Frankenstein* (Univ., 1944), *The Dolly Sisters* (20th, 1945), *A Royal Scandal* (20th, 1945), *The Men in Her Diary* (Univ., 1945), *She Went to the Races* (MGM, 1945), *A Night in Casablanca* (UA, 1946), *Faithful in My Fashion* (MGM, 1946), *Night and Day* (WB, 1946), *Mother Wore Tights* (20th, 1947), *If You Knew Susie* (RKO, 1948), *The Emperor Waltz* (Par., 1948), *Give My Regards to Broadway* (20th, 1948), *On The Riviera* (20th, 1951), *The World in His Arms* (Univ., 1952), *Ma and Pa Kettle on Vacation* (Univ., 1953), *Stalag 17* (Par., 1953), *Houdini* (Par., 1953), *The Glenn Miller Story* (Univ., 1954), *Living It Up* (Par., 1954), *Three Ring Circus* (Par., 1954), *Carolina Cannonball* (Rep., 1955), *Many Rivers to Cross* (MGM, 1955), *Spy Chasers* (AA, 1955), *The Wings of Eagles* (MGM, 1957), *The Errand Boy* (Par., 1961), *Robin and the 7 Hoods* (WB, 1964), *36 Hours* (MGM, 1964), *Last of the Secret Agents* (Par., 1966), *The Fortune Cookie* (UA, 1966).

BARBARA RUSH Born January 4, 1927, Denver, Colorado. Married Jeffrey Hunter (1950), child: Christopher; divorced 1955. Married Warren Cowan (1959), child: Claudia.

Feature Films: *The First Legion* (UA, 1951), *Molly* (Par., 1951), *Quebec* (Par., 1951), *Flaming Feather* (Par., 1951), *When Worlds Collide* (Par.,

1951), *It Came From Outer Space* (Univ., 1953), *Prince of Pirates* (Col., 1953), *Taza, Son of Cochise* (Univ., 1954), *Magnificent Obsession* (Univ., 1954), *The Black Shield of Falworth* (Univ., 1954), *Captain Lightfoot* (Univ., 1955), *Kiss of Fire* (Univ., 1955), *World in My Corner* (Univ., 1956), *Bigger Than Life* (20th, 1956), *Flight to Hong Kong* (UA, 1956), *Oh, Men! Oh, Women!* (20th, 1957), *No Down Payment* (20th, 1957), *The Young Lions* (20th, 1958), *Harry Black and the Tiger* (20th, 1958), *The Young Philadelphians* (WB, 1959), *The Bramble Bush* (WB, 1960), *Strangers When We Meet* (Col., 1960), *Come Blow Your Horn* (Par., 1963), *Robin and the 7 Hoods* (WB, 1964), *Hombre* (20th, 1967).

GAIL RUSSELL Born September 23, 1924, Chicago, Illinois. Married Guy Madison (1949); divorced 1954. Died August 26, 1961.

Gail Russell and Turhan Bey in *Song of India*.

Feature Films: *Henry Aldrich Gets Glamour* (Par., 1943), *Lady in the Dark* (Par., 1944), *The Uninvited* (Par., 1944), *Our Hearts Were Young and Gay* (Par., 1944), *Salty O'Rourke* (Par., 1945), *The Unseen* (Par., 1945), *Duffy's Tavern* (Par., 1945), *Our Hearts Were Growing Up* (Par., 1946), *The Bachelor's Daughters* (UA, 1946), *Calcutta* (Par., 1947), *Angel and the Badman* (Rep., 1947), *Variety Girl* (Par., 1947), *The Night Has a Thousand Eyes* (Par., 1948), *Moonrise* (Rep., 1948), *Wake of the Red Witch* (Rep., 1948), *El Paso* (Par., 1949), *Song of India* (Col., 1949), *The Great Dan Patch* (UA, 1949), *Captain China* (Par., 1949), *The Lawless* (Par., 1950), *Air Cadet* (Univ., 1951), *Seven Men From Now* (WB, 1956), *The Tattered Dress* (Univ., 1957), *No Place to Land* (Rep., 1958), *The Silent Call* (20th, 1961).

JANE RUSSELL (Ernestine Jane Geraldine Russell) Born June 21, 1921, Bemidji, Minnesota. Married Bob Waterfield (1943), children: Tracy, Thomas, Robert.

Feature Films: *The Outlaw* (RKO, 1943), *Young Widow* (UA, 1946), *The Paleface* (Par., 1948), *His Kind of Woman* (RKO, 1951), *Double*

Agnes Moorehead and Jane Russell in *The Revolt of Mamie Stover.*

Dynamite (RKO, 1951), *Las Vegas Story* (RKO, 1951), *Macao* (RKO, 1952), *Montana Belle* (RKO, 1952), *Son of Paleface* (Par., 1952), *Road to Bali* (Par., 1952)* *Gentlemen Prefer Blondes* (20th, 1953), *The French Line* (RKO, 1953), *Underwater* (RKO, 1955), *Foxfire* (Univ., 1955), *The Tall Men* (20th, 1955), *Gentlemen Marry Brunettes* (UA, 1955), *Hot Blood* (Col., 1956), *The Revolt of Mamie Stover* (20th, 1956), *The Fuzzy Pink Nightgown* (UA, 1957), *Fate Is the Hunter* (20th, 1964), *Johnny Reno* (Par., 1966), *Waco* (Par., 1966), *Born Losers* (AIP, 1967).

*Unbilled guest appearance

ROSALIND RUSSELL Born June 4, 1907, Waterbury, Connecticut. Married Fred Brisson (1941), child: Lance.

Ernest Truex, Roscoe Karns, Rosalind Russell and Frank Jenks in *His Girl Friday.*

Feature Films: *Evelyn Prentice* (MGM, 1934), *The President Vanishes* (Par., 1934), *West Point of the Air* (MGM, 1935), *Casino Murder Case* (MGM, 1935), *Reckless* (MGM, 1935), *China Seas* (MGM, 1935), *Rendezvous* (MGM, 1935), *Forsaking All Others* (MGM, 1935), *The Night Is Young* (MGM, 1935), *It Had to Happen* (20th, 1936), *Under Two Flags* (20th, 1936), *Trouble for Two* (MGM, 1936), *Craig's Wife* (Col., 1936), *Night Must Fall* (MGM, 1937), *Live, Love and Learn* (MGM, 1937), *Man-Proof* (MGM, 1938), *The Citadel* (MGM, 1938), *Four's a Crowd* (WB, 1938), *Fast and Loose* (MGM, 1939), *The Women* (MGM, 1939), *His Girl Friday* (Col., 1940), *No*

Time for Comedy (WB, 1940), *Hired Wife* (Univ., 1940), *This Thing Called Love* (Col., 1941), *They Met in Bombay* (MGM, 1941), *The Feminine Touch* (MGM, 1941), *Design For Scandal* (MGM, 1941), *Take a Letter, Darling* (Par., 1942), *My Sister Eileen* (Col., 1942), *Flight for Freedom* (RKO, 1943), *What a Woman* (Col., 1943), *Roughly Speaking* (WB, 1945), *She Wouldn't Say Yes* (Col., 1945), *Sister Kenny* (RKO, 1946), *The Guilt of Janet Ames* (Col., 1947), *Mourning Becomes Electra* (RKO, 1947), *The Velvet Touch* (RKO, 1948), *Tell It to the Judge* (Col., 1949), *A Woman of Distinction* (Col., 1950), *Never Wave at a WAC* (RKO, 1952), *The Girl Rush* (Par., 1955), *Picnic* (Col., 1955), *Auntie Mame* (WB, 1958), *A Majority of One* (WB, 1961), *Five Finger Exercise* (Col., 1962), *Gypsy* (WB, 1962), *The Trouble With Angels* (Col., 1966), *Oh Dad, Poor Dad, Mama's Hung You in the Closet and I'm Feeling So Sad* (Par., 1967), *Where Angels Go ... Trouble Follows*, (Col., 1968), *Rosie!* (Univ., 1968).

ANN RUTHERFORD Born November 2, 1917, Toronto, Canada. Married David May (1942), child: Gloria; divorced 1953. Married William Dozier (1953).

Snowflake, Ann Rutherford, John Wayne and Rodney Hildebrand in *The Lonely Trail.*

Feature Films: *Waterfront Lady* (Mascot, 1935), *The Fighting Marines* (Mascot serial, 1935), *Melody Trail* (Rep., 1935), *The Singing Vagabond* (Rep., 1935), *The Lawless Nineties* (Rep., 1936), *Doughnuts and Society* (Mascot, 1936), *The Harvester* (Rep., 1936), *Comin' Round the Mountain* (Rep., 1936), *Down to the Sea* (Rep., 1936), *The Oregon Trail* (Rep., 1936), *The Lonely Trail* (Rep., 1936), *The Devil Is Driving* (Col., 1937), *The Bride Wore Red* (MGM, 1937), *Public Cowboy No. One* (Rep., 1937), *Espionage* (MGM, 1937), *Live, Love and Learn* (MGM, 1937), *Of Human Hearts* (MGM, 1938), *Judge Hardy's Children* (MGM, 1938), *You're Only Young Once* (MGM, 1938), *Love Finds Andy Hardy* (MGM, 1938), *A Christmas Carol* (MGM, 1938), *Dramatic School* (MGM, 1938), *Out West With the Hardys* (MGM, 1938), *Four Girls in White* (MGM, 1939), *The Hardys Ride High* (MGM, 1939), *Andy Hardy Gets Spring Fever* (MGM, 1939), *These Glamour Girls* (MGM, 1939), *Dancing Co-ed* (MGM, 1939), *Judge Hardy and Son* (MGM, 1939), *Gone With the Wind* (MGM, 1939), *Pride and Prejudice* (MGM, 1940), *Andy Hardy Meets Debutante* (MGM, 1940), *Wyoming* (MGM, 1940), *The Ghost Comes Home* (MGM, 1940), *Keeping Company* (MGM, 1941), *Andy Hardy's Private Secretary* (MGM, 1941), *Washington Melodrama* (MGM, 1941), *Whistling in the Dark* (MGM, 1941), *Life Begins for Andy Hardy* (MGM, 1941), *Badlands of Dakota* (Univ., 1941), *The Courtship of Andy Hardy* (MGM, 1942), *This Time for Keeps* (MGM, 1942), *Orchestra Wives* (20th, 1942), *Whistling in Dixie* (MGM, 1942), *Andy Hardy's Double Life* (MGM, 1942), *Whistling in Brooklyn* (MGM, 1943), *Happy Land* (20th, 1943), *Bermuda Mystery* (20th, 1944), *Two O'Clock Courage* (RKO, 1945), *Bedside Manner* (UA, 1945), *Murder in the Music Hall* (Rep., 1946), *The Madonna's Secret* (Rep., 1946), *Inside Job* (Univ., 1946), *The Secret Life of Walter Mitty* (RKO, 1947), *The Adventures of Don Juan* (WB, 1948), *Operation Haylift* (Lip., 1950).

Trudy Marshall, Tim Ryan and Peggy Ryan in *Shamrock Hill*.

PEGGY RYAN (Margaret Orene Ryan) Born August 28, 1924, Long Beach, California. Married James Cross (1947), child: James; divorced 1952. Married Ray McDonald, child: Kerry; divorced. Married Edward Sherman (1958).

Feature Films: *Top of the Town* (Univ., 1937), *The Women Men Marry* (MGM, 1937), *The Flying Irishman* (RKO, 1939), *She Married a Cop* (Rep., 1939), *The Grapes of Wrath* (20th, 1940), *Sailor's Lady* (20th, 1940), *Girls' Town* (PRC, 1942), *Miss Annie Rooney* (UA, 1942), *Private Buckaroo* (Univ., 1942), *Give Out, Sisters* (Univ., 1942), *Get Hep to Love* (Univ., 1942), *Mister Big* (Univ., 1943), *Top Man* (Univ., 1944), *When Johnny Comes Marching Home* (Univ., 1944), *Chip Off the Old Block* (Univ., 1944), *Follow the Boys* (Univ., 1944), *This Is the Life* (Univ., 1944), *The Merry Monahans* (Univ., 1944), *Babes on Swing Street* (Univ., 1944), *Bowery to Broadway* (Univ., 1944), *Patrick the Great* (Univ., 1945), *Here Come the Co-eds* (Univ., 1945), *That's the Spirit* (Univ., 1945), *On Stage Everybody* (Univ., 1945), *Men in Her Diary* (Univ., 1945), *Shamrock Hill* (EL, 1949), *There's a Girl in My Heart* (AA, 1949), *All Ashore* (Col., 1953).

ROBERT RYAN Born November 11, 1909, Chicago, Illinois. Married Jessica Cadwalader (1939), children: Timothy, Cheney, Lisa.

Feature Films: *Golden Gloves* (Par., 1940), *Queen of the Mob* (Par., 1940), *North West Mounted Police* (Par., 1940), *Bombardier* (RKO, 1943), *The Sky's the Limit* (RKO, 1943), *Behind the Rising Sun* (RKO, 1943), *Gangway for Tomorrow* (RKO, 1943), *The Iron Major* (RKO, 1943), *Tender Comrade* (RKO, 1943), *Marine Raiders* (RKO, 1944), *Trail Street* (RKO, 1947), *The Woman on the Beach* (RKO, 1947), *Crossfire* (RKO, 1947), *Berlin Express* (RKO, 1948), *Return of the Bad Men* (RKO, 1948), *Act of Violence* (MGM, 1948), *The Boy With Green Hair* (RKO, 1948), *Caught* (MGM, 1949), *The Set-Up* (RKO, 1949), *I Married a Communist* (RKO, 1949), *The Secret Fury* (RKO, 1950), *Born to Be Bad* (RKO, 1950), *Best of the Bad Men* (RKO, 1951), *Flying Leathernecks* (RKO, 1951), *The Racket* (RKO, 1951), *On Dangerous Ground* (RKO, 1951), *Clash by Night* (RKO, 1952), *Beware My Lovely* (RKO, 1952), *Horizons West* (Univ., 1952), *City Beneath the Sea* (Univ., 1953), *The Naked Spur* (MGM, 1953), *Inferno* (20th,

1953), *Alaska Seas* (Par., 1954), *About Mrs. Leslie* (Par., 1954), *Her 12 Men* (MGM, 1954), *Bad Day at Black Rock* (MGM, 1954), *Escape to Burma* (RKO, 1955), *House of Bamboo* (20th, 1955), *The Tall Men* (20th, 1955), *The Proud Ones* (20th, 1956), *Back From Eternity* (RKO, 1956), *Men in War* (UA, 1957), *God's Little Acre* (UA, 1958), *Lonelyhearts* (UA, 1958), *Day of the Outlaw* (UA, 1959), *Odds Against Tomorrow* (UA, 1959), *Ice Palace* (WB, 1960), *The Canadians* (20th, 1961), *King of Kings* (MGM, 1961), *Billy Budd* (AA, 1962), *The Longest Day* (20th, 1962), *The Inheritance* (narrator; Shochiku Films of America, 1964), *Battle of the Bulge* (WB, 1965), *Crooked Road* (7 Arts, 1965), *The Dirty Game* (AIP, 1965), *The Professionals* (Col., 1966), *The Busybody* (Par., 1967), *Custer of the West* (Cinerama, 1967), *Hour of the Guns* (UA, 1967), *The Prodigal Gun* (Cinerama, 1968), *Anzio* (Col., 1968).

SABU (Sabu Dastagir) Born March 15, 1924, Karapur, Mysore, India. Married Marilyn Cooper (1948), children: Paul, Jasmine. Died December 2, 1963.

Wendell Corey and Sabu in *Man-Eater of Kumaon*.

Feature Films: *Elephant Boy* (UA, 1937), *Drums* (UA, 1938), *The Thief of Bagdad* (UA, 1940), *The Jungle Book* (UA, 1942), *Arabian Nights* (Univ., 1942), *White Savage* (Univ., 1943), *Cobra Woman* (Univ., 1943), *Tangier* (Univ., 1946), *Black Narcissus* (Rank, 1947), *The End of the River* (Univ., 1948), *Man-Eater of Kumaon* (Univ., 1948), *Song of India* (Col., 1949), *Savage Drums* (Lip., 1951), *The Black Panther* (1955), *Jungle Hell* (Howco, 1956), *Jaguar* (Rep., 1956), *Sabu and the Magic Ring* (AA, 1957), *Rampage* (WB, 1963), *A Tiger Walks* (BV, 1964).

EVA MARIE SAINT Born September 4, 1924, Newark, New Jersey. Married Jeffrey Hayden (1951), children: Darrell, Laurette.

Feature Films: *On the Waterfront* (Col., 1954), *That Certain Feeling*

Robert Ryan and Ginger Rogers in *Tender Comrade*.

Angela Lansbury, Karl Malden, Eva Marie Saint and Brandon de Wilde in *All Fall Down*.

(Par., 1956), *A Hatful of Rain* (20th, 1957), *Raintree County* (MGM, 1957), *North by Northwest* (MGM, 1959), *Exodus* (UA, 1960), *All Fall Down* (MGM, 1962), *36 Hours* (MGM, 1964), *The Sandpiper* (MGM, 1965), *The Russians Are Coming, The Russians Are Coming* (UA, 1966), *Grand Prix* (MGM, 1966), *The Stalking Moon* (National General, 1968).

S. Z. "CUDDLES" SAKALL (Szoke Szakall) Born February 2, 1890, Budapest, Hungary. Died February 12, 1955.

Kathryn Grayson, S.Z. Sakall and Van Heflin in *Seven Sweethearts*.

English-Language Feature Films: *The Lilac Domino* (Select Attractions, Ltd., 1940), *It's a Date* (Univ., 1940), *Florian* (MGM, 1940), *My Love Came Back* (WB, 1940), *Spring Parade* (Univ., 1940), *The Man Who Lost Himself* (Univ., 1941), *That Night in Rio* (20th, 1941), *The Devil and Miss Jones* (RKO, 1941), *Ball of Fire* (RKO, 1941), *Broadway* (Univ., 1942), *Yankee Doodle Dandy* (WB, 1942), *Seven Sweethearts* (MGM, 1942), *Casablanca* (WB, 1942), *Thank Your Lucky Stars* (WB, 1943), *The Human Comedy* (MGM, 1943), *Wintertime* (20th, 1943), *Shine On, Harvest Moon* (WB, 1944), *Hollywood Canteen* (WB, 1944), *Wonder Man* (RKO, 1945), *Christmas in Connecticut* (WB, 1945), *The Dolly Sisters* (20th, 1945), *San Antonio* (WB, 1945), *Cinderella Jones* (WB, 1946), *Two Guys From Milwaukee* (WB, 1946), *Never Say Goodbye* (WB, 1946), *The Time, the Place and the Girl* (WB, 1946), *Cynthia* (MGM, 1947), *April Showers* (WB, 1948), *Romance on the High Seas* (WB, 1948), *Embraceable You* (WB, 1948), *Whiplash* (WB, 1948), *My Dream Is Yours* (WB, 1949), *In the Good Old Summertime* (MGM, 1949), *It's a Great Feeling* (WB, 1949), *Look for the Silver Lining* (WB, 1949), *Oh, You Beautiful Doll!* (20th, 1949), *Montana* (WB, 1950), *The Daughter of Rosie O'Grady* (WB, 1950), *Tea for Two* (WB, 1950), *The Lullaby of Broadway* (WB, 1951), *Sugarfoot* (WB, 1951), *Painting the Clouds With Sunshine* (WB, 1951), *It's a Big Country* (MGM, 1951), *Small Town Girl* (MGM, 1953), *The Student Prince* (MGM, 1954).

GEORGE SANDERS Born July 3, 1906, St. Petersburg, Russia. Married Susan Larsen (1940); divorced 1947. Married Zsa Zsa Gabor (1949); divorced 1957. Married Benita Hume (1958); widowed 1967.

Feature Films: *Strange Cargo* (British, 1936), *The Man Who Could Work Miracles* (UA, 1936), *Things to Come* (UA, 1936), *Lloyds of London* (20th, 1936), *Love Is News* (20th, 1937), *Slave Ship* (20th, 1937), *The Lady Escapes* (20th, 1937), *Lancer Spy* (20th, 1937), *International Settlement* (20th, 1938), *Four Men and a Prayer* (20th, 1938), *Mr. Moto's Last Warning* (20th, 1939), *The Saint Strikes Back* (RKO, 1939), *Confessions of a Nazi Spy* (WB, 1939), *The Saint in London* (RKO, 1939), *Allegheny Uprising* (RKO, 1939), *Nurse Edith Cavell* (RKO, 1939), *The Outsider* (Alliance, 1939), *Green Hell* (Univ., 1940), *Rebecca* (UA, 1940), *The Saint's Double Trouble* (RKO, 1940), *The House of Seven Gables* (Univ., 1940), *The Saint Takes Over* (RKO, 1940), *Foreign Correspondent* (UA, 1940), *Bitter Sweet* (MGM, 1940), *The Son of Monte Cristo* (UA, 1940), *Rage in Heaven* (MGM, 1941),

George Sanders and Norma Shearer in *Her Cardboard Lover*.

The Saint in Palm Springs (RKO, 1941), *Man Hunt* (20th, 1941), *The Gay Falcon* (RKO, 1941), *A Date With the Falcon* (RKO, 1941), *Sundown* (UA, 1941), *Son of Fury* (20th, 1942), *The Falcon Takes Over* (RKO, 1942), *Her Cardboard Lover* (MGM, 1942), *Tales of Manhattan* (20th, 1942), *The Moon and Sixpence* (UA, 1942), *The Falcon's Brother* (RKO, 1942), *The Black Swan* (20th, 1942), *Quiet Please— Murder* (20th, 1942), *This Land Is Mine* (RKO, 1943), *They Came to Blow Up America* (20th, 1943), *Appointment in Berlin* (Col., 1943), *Paris After Dark* (20th, 1943), *Action in Arabia* (RKO, 1944), *The Lodger* (20th, 1944), *Summer Storm* (UA, 1944), *The Picture of Dorian Gray* (MGM, 1945), *Hangover Square* (20th, 1945), *The Strange Affair of Uncle Harry* (Univ., 1945), *A Scandal in Paris* (UA, 1946), *The Strange Woman* (UA, 1946), *The Private Affairs of Bel Ami* (UA, 1947), *The Ghost and Mrs. Muir* (20th, 1947), *Lured* (UA, 1947), *Forever Amber* (20th, 1947), *The Fan* (20th, 1949), *Samson and Delilah* (Par., 1949), *All About Eve* (20th, 1950), *I Can Get It for You Wholesale* (20th, 1951), *The Light Touch* (MGM, 1951), *Ivanhoe* (MGM, 1952), *Captain Blackjack* (Classic, 1952), *Assignment Paris* (Col., 1952), *Call Me Madam* (20th, 1953), *Witness to Murder* (UA, 1954), *King Richard and the Crusaders* (WB, 1954), *Moonfleet* (MGM, 1955), *The Scarlet Coat* (MGM, 1955), *The King's Thief* (MGM, 1955), *Night Freight* (AA, 1955), *Never Say Goodbye* (Univ., 1956), *While the City Sleeps* (RKO, 1956), *That Certain Feeling* (Par., 1956), *Death of a Scoundrel* (RKO, 1956), *The Seventh Sin* (MGM, 1957), *The Whole Truth* (Col., 1958), *From the Earth to the Moon* (WB, 1958), *That Kind of Woman* (Par., 1959), *Solomon and Sheba* (UA, 1959), *A Touch of Larceny* (Par., 1960), *The Last Voyage* (MGM, 1960), *Bluebeard's Ten Honeymoons* (AA, 1960), *The Village of the Damned* (MGM, 1960), *Call Me Genius* (Continental Distributing, 1961), *Five Golden Hours* (Col., 1961), *Trouble in the Sky* (Univ., 1961), *Operation Snatch* (Continental Distributing, 1962), *In Search of the Castaways* (BV, 1962), *The Cracksman* (Associated British Pathé, 1963), *Cairo* (MGM, 1963), *Dark Purpose* (Univ., 1964), *A Shot in the Dark* (UA, 1964), *The Amorous Adventures of Moll Flanders* (Par., 1965), *Ecco* (narrator; Cresa Roma, 1965), *Trunk to Cairo* (AIP, 1966), *The Quiller Memorandum* (20th, 1966), *Warning Shot* (Par., 1967), *Good Times* (Par., 1967), *The Jungle Book* (voice only; BV, 1967), *King of Africa* (NTA, 1968).

LIZABETH SCOTT (Emma Matzo) Born September 29, 1922, Scranton, Pennsylvania.

Feature Films: *You Came Along* (Par., 1945), *The Strange Love of*

Lizabeth Scott, Wendell Corey and John Hodiak in *Desert Fury*.

Margaret Perry, Randolph Scott, Alice Brady and Elizabeth Patterson in *Go West, Young Man*.

Martha Ivers (Par., 1946), *Dead Reckoning* (Col., 1947), *Desert Fury* (Par., 1947), *I Walk Alone* (Par., 1947), *Variety Girl* (Par., 1947), *Pitfall* (UA, 1948), *Too Late for Tears* (UA, 1949), *Easy Living* (RKO, 1949), *Paid in Full* (Par., 1950), *Dark City* (Par., 1950), *The Racket* (RKO, 1951), *The Company She Keeps* (RKO, 1951), *Two of a Kind* (Col., 1951), *Red Mountain* (Par., 1951), *Stolen Face* (Lip., 1952), *Scared Stiff* (Par., 1953), *Bad for Each Other* (Col., 1954), *Silver Lode* (RKO, 1954), *Loving You* (Par., 1957), *The Weapon* (Rep., 1957).

MARTHA SCOTT (Martha Ellen Scott) Born September 22, 1914, Jamesport, Missouri. Married Carleton Alsop (1940), child: Carleton, divorced 1946. Married Mel Powell (1946), children: Mary, Scott.

Cary Grant, Martha Scott and Sir Cedric Hardwicke in *The Howards of Virginia*.

Feature Films: *Our Town* (UA, 1940), *The Howards of Virginia* (Col., 1940), *Cheers for Miss Bishop* (UA, 1941), *They Dare Not Love* (Col., 1941), *One Foot in Heaven* (WB, 1941), *Hi Diddle Diddle* (UA, 1943), *Stage Door Canteen* (UA, 1943), *In Old Oklahoma* (Rep., 1943), *So Well Remembered* (RKO, 1947), *Strange Bargain* (RKO, 1949), *When I Grow Up* (EL, 1951), *The Desperate Hours* (Par., 1955), *The Ten Commandments* (Par., 1956), *Sayonara* (WB, 1957), *Eighteen and Anxious* (Rep., 1957), *Ben-Hur* (MGM, 1959).

RANDOLPH SCOTT (Randolph Crane) Born January 23, 1903, Orange County, Virginia. Married Marion Somerville; divorced. Married Pat Stillman (1944).

Sound Feature Films: *The Women Men Marry* (Headline Pictures, 1931), *Sky Bride* (Par., 1932), *Hot Saturday* (Par., 1932), *Wild Horse Mesa* (Par., 1933), *Hello, Everybody!* (Par., 1933), *Murders in the Zoo*

(Par., 1933), *Heritage of the Desert* (Par., 1933), *Supernatural* (Par., 1933), *Sunset Pass* (Par., 1933), *Cocktail Hour* (Col., 1933), *Man of the Forest* (Par., 1933), *To the Last Man* (Par., 1933), *Broken Dreams* (Mon., 1933), *The Thundering Herd* (Par., 1933), *Last Round-Up* (Par., 1934), *The Lone Cowboy* (Par., 1934), *Wagon Wheels* (Par., 1934), *Rocky Mountain Mystery* (Par., 1935), *Roberta* (Par., 1935), *Home on the Range* (Par., 1935), *Village Tale* (RKO, 1935), *She* (RKO, 1935), *So Red the Rose* (Par., 1935), *Follow the Fleet* (RKO, 1936), *And Sudden Death* (Par., 1936), *The Last of the Mohicans* (UA, 1936), *Go West Young Man* (Par., 1936), *High, Wide and Handsome* (Par., 1937), *Rebecca of Sunnybrook Farm* (20th, 1938), *Road to Reno* (Univ., 1938), *The Texans* (Par., 1938), *Jesse James* (20th, 1939), *Susannah of the Mounties* (20th, 1939), *Coast Guard* (Col., 1939), *Frontier Marshal* (20th, 1939), *20,000 Men a Year* (20th, 1939), *Virginia City* (WB, 1940), *My Favorite Wife* (RKO, 1940), *When the Daltons Rode* (Univ., 1940), *Western Union* (20th, 1941), *Belle Starr* (20th, 1941), *Paris Calling* (Univ., 1941), *To the Shores of Tripoli* (20th, 1942), *The Spoilers* (Univ., 1942), *Pittsburgh* (Univ., 1942), *The Desperadoes* (Col., 1943), *Bombardier* (RKO, 1943), *Corvette K-225* (Univ., 1943), *Gung Ho!* (Univ., 1943), *Belle of the Yukon* (RKO, 1944), *Follow the Boys* (Univ., 1944), *China Sky* (RKO, 1945), *Captain Kidd* (UA, 1945), *Abilene Town* (UA, 1946), *Badman's Territory* (RKO, 1946), *Home Sweet Homicide* (20th, 1946), *Trail Street* (RKO, 1947), *Gunfighters* (Col., 1947), *Christmas Eve* (UA, 1947), *Albuquerque* (Par., 1948), *Return of the Bad Men* (RKO, 1948), *Coroner Creek* (Col., 1948), *Canadian Pacific* (20th, 1949), *The Walking Hills* (Col., 1949), *The Doolins of Oklahoma* (Col., 1949), *Fighting Man of the Plains* (20th, 1949), *The Nevadan* (Col., 1950), *Colt .45* (WB, 1950), *The Cariboo Trail* (20th, 1950), *Sugarfoot* (WB, 1951), *Starlift* (WB, 1951), *Santa Fe* (Col., 1951), *Fort Worth* (WB, 1951), *Man in the Saddle* (Col., 1951), *Carson City* (WB, 1952), *Hangman's Knot* (Col., 1952), *The Man Behind the Gun* (WB, 1952), *The Stranger Wore a Gun* (Col., 1953), *Thunder Over the Plains* (WB, 1953), *Riding Shotgun* (WB, 1954), *The Bounty Hunter* (WB, 1954), *Rage at Dawn* (RKO, 1955), *Ten Wanted Men* (Col., 1955), *Tall Man Riding* (WB, 1955), *A Lawless Street* (Col., 1955), *Seven Men From Now* (WB, 1956), *Seventh Cavalry* (Col., 1956), *The Tall T* (Col., 1957), *Shoot-Out at Medicine Bend* (WB, 1957), *Decision At Sundown* (Col., 1957), *Buchanan Rides Alone* (Col., 1958), *Ride Lonesome* (Col., 1959), *Westbound* (WB, 1959), *Comanche Station* (Col., 1960), *Ride the High Country* (MGM, 1962).

ZACHARY SCOTT (Zachary Thomson Scott) Born February 24, 1914, Austin, Texas. Married Elaine Anderson (1935), child: Waverly; divorced 1950. Married Ruth Ford (1952), child: Shelley. Died October 3, 1965.

Feature Films: *Mask of Dimitrios* (WB, 1944), *Hollywood Canteen* (WB, 1944), *The Southerner* (UA, 1945), *Mildred Pierce* (WB, 1945), *Danger Signal* (WB, 1945), *Her Kind of Man* (WB, 1946), *Stallion Road* (WB, 1947), *The Unfaithful* (WB, 1947), *Cass Timberlane* (MGM, 1947), *Ruthless* (EL, 1948), *Whiplash* (WB, 1948), *Flaxy Martin* (WB, 1949), *Colt .45* (WB, 1949), *South of St. Louis* (WB, 1949), *One Last Fling* (WB, 1949), *Guilty Bystander* (Film Classics, 1950),

Alexis Smith and Zachary Scott in *One Last Fling*.

Shadow on the Wall (MGM, 1950), *Pretty Baby* (WB, 1950), *Born to Be Bad* (RKO, 1950), *Lightning Strikes Twice* (WB, 1951), *The Secret of Convict Lake* (20th, 1951), *Let's Make It Legal* (20th, 1951), *Wings of Danger* (Lip., 1952), *Stronghold* (Lip., 1952), *Appointment in Honduras* (RKO, 1953), *Treasure of Ruby Hills* (AA, 1955), *Shotgun* (AA, 1955), *Flame of the Islands* (Rep., 1955), *Bandido* (UA, 1956), *The Counterfeit Plan* (WB, 1957), *Man in the Shadow* ("Violent Stranger" —Anglo Amalgamated, 1957), *Flight into Danger* (Anglo Amalgamated, 1957), *Natchez Trace* (Panorama, 1960), *The Young One* (Vitalite, 1961), *It's Only Money* (Par., 1962).

ANNE SEYMOUR (Anne Seymour Eckert) Born September 11, 1909, New York, New York.

Anne Seymour and Arthur O'Connell in *Misty*.

Feature Films: *All the King's Men* (Col., 1949), *The Whistle at Eaton Falls* (Col., 1951), *Four Boys and a Gun* (UA, 1957), *Man on Fire* (MGM, 1957), *The Gift of Love* (20th, 1958), *Desire Under the Elms* (Par., 1958), *Handle With Care* (MGM, 1958), *Home from the Hill* (MGM, 1960), *Pollyanna* (BV, 1960), *The Subterraneans* (MGM, 1960), *All the Fine Young Cannibals* (MGM, 1960), *Misty* (20th, 1961), *Stage to Thunder Rock* (Par., 1964), *Good Neighbor Sam* (Col., 1964), *Where Love Has Gone* (Par., 1964), *Mirage* (Univ., 1965), *Blindfold* (Univ., 1966), *Waco* (Par., 1966), *How to Succeed in Business Without Really Trying* (UA, 1967), *Fitzwilly* (UA, 1967), *Stay Away, Joe* (MGM, 1968).

WINIFRED "WINI" SHAW (Winifred Lei Momi) Born February 25, 1910, San Francisco, California. Married Leo Cummins (1925), children: Elizabeth, James, John; widowed 1929. Married William O'Malley (1955).

Wini Shaw, Patricia Ellis and James Melton in *Melody for Two*.

Feature Films:
as Wini Shaw *Wild Gold* (Fox, 1934), *Three on a Honeymoon* (Fox, 1934), *The Gift of Gab* (Univ., 1934), *Million Dollar Ransom* (Univ., 1934), *Wake Up and Dream* (Univ., 1934).
as Winifred Shaw *Sweet Adeline* (WB, 1934), *Front Page Woman* (WB, 1935), *The Case of the Curious Bride* (WB, 1935), *Gold Diggers of 1935* (WB, 1935), *In Caliente* (WB, 1935), *Broadway Hostess* (WB, 1935), *The Singing Kid* (WB, 1936), *Sons o' Guns* (WB, 1936), *The Case of the Velvet Claws* (WB, 1936), *Satan Met a Lady* (WB, 1936), *Smart Blonde* (WB, 1936), *Fugitive in the Sky* (WB, 1937), *Ready, Willing and Able* (WB, 1937), *Melody for Two* (WB, 1937).

NORMA SHEARER (Edith Norma Shearer) Born August 10, 1900, Montreal, Canada. Married Irving Thalberg (1927), children: Irving, Katherine; widowed 1936. Married Martin Arrouge (1942).

Conrad Veidt and Norma Shearer in *Escape*.

Sound Feature Films: *The Trial of Mary Dugan* (MGM, 1929), *The Last of Mrs. Cheyney* (MGM, 1929), *The Hollywood Revue* (MGM, 1929), *Their Own Desire* (MGM, 1930), *The Divorcee* (MGM, 1930), *Let Us Be Gay* (MGM, 1930), *Strangers May Kiss* (MGM, 1931), *A Free Soul* (MGM, 1931), *Private Lives* (MGM, 1931), *Strange Interlude* (MGM, 1932), *Smilin' Through* (MGM, 1932), *Riptide* (MGM, 1934), *The Barretts of Wimpole Street* (MGM, 1934), *Romeo and Juliet* (MGM, 1936), *Marie Antoinette* (MGM, 1938), *Idiot's Delight* (MGM, 1939), *The Women* (MGM, 1939), *Escape* (MGM, 1940), *We Were Dancing* (MGM, 1942), *Her Cardboard Lover* (MGM, 1942).

James Cagney, Joyce Compton, Frank McHugh, Anthony Quinn, Ann Sheridan and George Tobias in *City for Conquest*.

ANN SHERIDAN (Clara Lou Sheridan) Born February 21, 1915, Denton, Texas. Married Edward Norris (1936); divorced 1939. Married George Brent (1932); divorced 1943. Married Scott McKay (1966). Died January 21, 1967.

Feature Films:

as **Clara Lou Sheridan** *Search for Beauty* (Par., 1934), *Bolero* (Par., 1934), *Come On, Marines!* (Par., 1934), *Murder at the Vanities* (Par., 1934), *Kiss and Make Up* (Par., 1934), *Shoot the Works* (Par., 1934), *Notorious Sophie Lang* (Par., 1934), *Ladies Should Listen* (Par., 1934), *Wagon Wheels* (Par., 1934), *Mrs. Wiggs of the Cabbage Patch* (Par., 1934), *College Rhythm* (Par., 1934), *You Belong to Me* (Par., 1934), *Limehouse Blues* (Par., 1934), *Enter Madame* (Par., 1935), *Home on the Range* (Par., 1935), *Rumba* (Par., 1935).

as **Ann Sheridan** *Behold My Wife* (Par., 1935), *Car 99* (Par., 1935), *Rocky Mountain Mystery* (Par., 1935), *Mississippi* (Par., 1935), *The Glass Key* (Par., 1935), *The Crusades* (Par., 1935), *Red Blood of Courage* (Ambassador, 1935), *Fighting Youth* (Univ., 1935), *Sing Me a Love Song* (WB, 1936), *Black Legion* (WB, 1936), *The Great O'Malley* (WB, 1937), *San Quentin* (WB, 1937), *Wine, Women and Horses* (WB, 1937), *The Footloose Heiress* (WB, 1937), *Alcatraz Island* (WB, 1938), *She Loved a Fireman* (WB, 1938), *The Patient in Room 18* (WB, 1938), *Mystery House* (WB, 1938), *Cowboy From Brooklyn* (WB, 1938), *Little Miss Thoroughbred* (WB, 1938), *Letter of Introduction* (Univ., 1938), *Broadway Musketeers* (WB, 1938), *Angels With Dirty Faces* (WB, 1938), *They Made Me a Criminal* (WB, 1939), *Dodge City* (WB, 1939), *Naughty but Nice* (WB, 1939), *Winter Carnival* (UA, 1939), *Indianapolis Speedway* (WB, 1939), *Angels Wash Their Faces* (WB, 1939), *Castle on the Hudson* (WB, 1940), *It All Came True* (WB, 1940), *Torrid Zone* (WB, 1940), *They Drive by Night* (WB, 1940), *City for Conquest* (WB, 1940), *Honeymoon for Three* (WB, 1941), *Navy Blues* (WB, 1941), *Kings Row* (WB, 1941), *The Man Who Came to Dinner* (WB, 1941), *Juke Girl* (WB, 1942), *Wings for the Eagle* (WB, 1942), *George Washington Slept Here* (WB, 1942), *Edge of Darkness* (WB, 1943), *Thank Your Lucky Stars* (WB, 1943), *Shine On, Harvest Moon* (WB, 1944), *The Doughgirls* (WB, 1944), *One More Tomorrow* (WB, 1946), *Nora Prentiss* (WB, 1947), *The Unfaithful* (WB, 1947), *Treasure of the Sierra Madre* (WB, 1948),* *Silver River* (WB, 1948), *Good Sam* (RKO, 1948), *I Was a Male War Bride* (20th, 1949), *Stella* (20th, 1950), *Woman on the Run* (Univ., 1950), *Steel Town* (Univ., 1952), *Just Across the Street* (Univ., 1952), *Take Me to Town* (Univ., 1953), *Appointment in Honduras* (RKO, 1953), *Come Next Spring* (Rep., 1956), *The Opposite Sex* (MGM, 1956), *Woman and the Hunter* (Gross-Krasne-Phoenix, 1957).

*Unbilled guest appearance

ANNE SHIRLEY (Dawn Evelyeen Paris) Born April 17, 1918, New York, New York. Married John Payne (1937), child: Julie; divorced 1943. Married Adrian Scott (1945); divorced 1949. Married Charles Lederer (1949).

Barbara Stanwyck and Anne Shirley in *Stella Dallas*.

Feature Films:

as **Dawn O'Day** *Mother Knows Best* (Fox, 1928), *Four Devils* (Fox, 1929), *City Girl* (Fox, 1930), *Rich Man's Folly* (Par., 1931), *Young America* (Fox, 1932), *So Big* (WB, 1932), *The Purchase Price* (WB, 1932), *Three on a Match* (WB, 1932), *Rasputin and the Empress* (MGM, 1932), *Life of Jimmy Dolan* (WB, 1933), *Finishing School* (RKO, 1934), *This Side of Heaven* (MGM, 1934), *The Key* (WB, 1934), *School for Girls* (Liberty, 1934).

as **Anne Shirley** *Anne of Green Gables* (RKO, 1934), *Steamboat 'Round the Bend* (Fox, 1935), *Chasing Yesterday* (RKO, 1935), *Chatterbox* (RKO, 1936), *M'Liss* (RKO, 1936), *Make Way for a Lady* (RKO, 1936), *Too Many Wives* (RKO, 1937), *Meet the Missus* (RKO, 1937), *Stella Dallas* (UA, 1937), *Condemned Women* (RKO, 1938), *Law of the Underworld* (RKO, 1938), *Mother Carey's Chickens* (RKO, 1938), *A Man to Remember* (RKO, 1938), *Girls' School* (Col., 1938), *Boy Slaves* (RKO, 1939), *Sorority House* (RKO, 1939), *Career* (RKO, 1939), *Vigil in the Night* (RKO, 1940), *Saturday's Children* (WB, 1940), *Anne of Windy Poplars* (RKO, 1940), *West Point Widow* (Par., 1941), *Unexpected Uncle* (RKO, 1941), *Four Jacks and a Jill* (RKO, 1941), *All That Money Can Buy* (RKO, 1941), *The Mayor of 44th Street* (RKO, 1942), *The Powers Girl* (UA, 1942), *Lady Bodyguard* (Par., 1943), *Bombardier* (RKO, 1943), *Government Girl* (RKO, 1943), *Man From Frisco* (Rep., 1944), *Music in Manhattan* (RKO, 1944), *Murder, My Sweet* (RKO, 1944).

SYLVIA SIDNEY (Sophia Kosow) Born August 8, 1910, New York, New York. Married Bennett Cerf (1935); divorced 1936. Married Luther Adler (1938); child: Jody; divorced 1947. Married Carlton Alsop (1947); divorced 1950.

Feature Films: *Through Different Eyes* (Fox, 1929), *City Streets* (Par., 1931), *Confessions of a Co-ed* (Par., 1931), *An American Tragedy* (Par., 1931), *Street Scene* (UA, 1931), *Ladies of the Big House* (Par., 1932), *The Miracle Man* (Par., 1932), *Merrily We Go to Hell* (Par., 1932), *Make Me a Star* (Par., 1932),* *Madame Butterfly* (Par., 1932), *Pick-Up* (Par., 1933), *Jennie Gerhardt* (Par., 1933), *Good Dame* (Par., 1934), *Thirty Day Princess* (Par., 1934), *Behold My Wife* (Par., 1934), *Accent on Youth* (Par., 1935), *Mary Burns, Fugitive* (Par., 1935), *Trail of the Lonesome Pine* (Par., 1936), *Fury* (MGM, 1936), *A Woman Alone* (1936), *You Only Live Once* (UA, 1937), *Dead End* (UA, 1937), *You and Me* (Par., 1938), *. . . One Third of a Nation* (Par., 1939), *The Wagons Roll at Night* (WB, 1941), *Blood on the Sun* (UA, 1945), *The Searching Wind* (Par., 1946), *Mr. Ace* (UA, 1946), *Love From a*

Fred MacMurray, Sylvia Sidney and Henry Fonda in *The Trail of the Lonesome Pine.*

Stranger (EL, 1947), *Les Miserables* (20th, 1952), *Violent Saturday* (20th, 1955), *Behind the High Wall* (Univ., 1956).

*Unbilled guest appearance

JEAN SIMMONS (Jean Marilyn Simmons) Born January 31, 1929, London, England. Married Stewart Granger (1950), child: Tracy; divorced 1960. Married Richard Brooks (1960), child: Kate.

J. Carroll Naish and Jean Simmons in *This Could Be the Night.*

Feature Films: *Give Us the Moon* (Gainsborough, 1943), *Johnny in the Clouds* ("The Way to the Stars"—Anatol De Grunwold Productions, 1945), *Sports Day* (Two Cities, 1944), *Mr. Emmanuel* (Two Cities, 1945), *Meet Sexton Blake* (British National, 1945), *Kiss the Bride Goodbye* (Butchers PSI, 1945), *Caesar and Cleopatra* (Rank, 1946), *Great Expectations* (Rank, 1946), *Hungry Hill* (Two Cities, 1947), *Black Narcissus* (Rank, 1946), *The Inheritance* ("Uncle Silas"—Rank-Fine Arts, 1947), *The Woman in the Hall* (Wessex, 1947), *Hamlet* (Rank, 1948), *The Blue Lagoon* (Rank, 1949), *Adam and Evelyn* (Rank, 1949), *So Long at the Fair* (Rank, 1950), *Trio* (Par., 1950), *The Clouded Yellow* (Rank, 1950), *Cage of Gold* (Ealing, 1951), *Androcles and the Lion* (RKO, 1952), *Angel Face* (RKO, 1952), *Young Bess* (MGM, 1953), *Affair With a Stranger* (RKO, 1953), *The Robe* (20th, 1953), *The Actress* (MGM, 1953), *She Couldn't Say No* (RKO, 1954), *The Egyptian* (20th, 1954), *A Bullet Is Waiting* (Col., 1954), *Desirée* (20th, 1954), *Footsteps in the Fog* (Col., 1955), *Guys and Dolls* (MGM, 1955), *Hilda Crane* (20th, 1956), *This Could Be the Night* (MGM, 1957), *Until They Sail* (MGM, 1957), *The Big Country* (UA, 1958), *Home Before Dark* (WB, 1958), *This Earth Is Mine* (Univ., 1959), *Elmer Gantry* (UA,

1960), *Spartacus* (Univ., 1960), *The Grass Is Greener* (Univ., 1961), *All the Way Home* (Par., 1963), *Life at the Top* (Col., 1965), *Mr. Buddwing* (MGM, 1966), *Rough Night in Jericho* (Univ., 1967), *Divorce American Style* (Col., 1967).

FRANK SINATRA Born December 12, 1915, Hoboken, New Jersey. Married Nancy Barbato (1939), children: Nancy, Frank, Christina; divorced 1951. Married Ava Gardner (1951); divorced 1957. Married Mia Farrow (1966); divorced 1968.

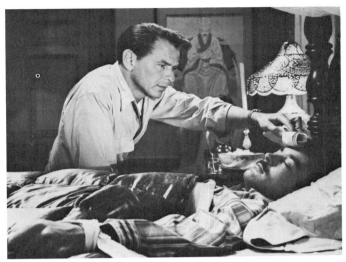

Frank Sinatra and Richard Johnson in *Never So Few.*

Feature Films: *Las Vegas Nights* (Par., 1941), *Ship Ahoy* (MGM, 1942), *Higher and Higher* (RKO, 1943), *Step Lively* (RKO, 1944), *Anchors Aweigh* (MGM, 1945), *Till the Clouds Roll By* (MGM, 1946), *It Happened in Brooklyn* (MGM, 1947), *Miracle of the Bells* (RKO, 1948), *The Kissing Bandit* (MGM, 1948), *Take Me Out to the Ball Game* (MGM, 1949), *On the Town* (MGM, 1949), *Double Dynamite* (RKO, 1951), *Meet Danny Wilson* (Univ., 1952), *From Here to Eternity* (Col., 1953), *Suddenly* (UA, 1954), *Young at Heart* (WB, 1954), *Not as a Stranger* (UA, 1955), *The Tender Trap* (MGM, 1955), *Guys and Dolls* (MGM, 1955), *The Man With the Golden Arm* (UA, 1955), *Meet Me in Las Vegas* (MGM, 1956),* *Johnny Concho* (UA, 1956), *Around the World in 80 Days* (UA, 1956), *High Society* (MGM, 1956), *The Pride and the Passion* (UA, 1957), *The Joker Is Wild* (Par., 1957), *Pal Joey* (Col., 1957), *Kings Go Forth* (UA, 1958), *Some Came Running* (MGM, 1958), *A Hole in the Head* (UA, 1959), *Never So Few* (MGM, 1959), *Can-Can* (20th, 1960), *Ocean's 11* (WB, 1960), *Pepe* (Col., 1960), *The Devil at 4 O'Clock* (Col., 1961), *Sergeants 3* (UA, 1962), *Road to Hong Kong* (UA, 1962),* *The Manchurian Candidate* (UA, 1962), *Come Blow Your Horn* (Par., 1963), *The List of Adrian Messenger* (Univ., 1963), *4 For Texas* (WB, 1963), *Robin and the 7 Hoods* (WB, 1964), *None But the Brave* (WB, 1965), *Von Ryan's Express* (20th, 1965), *Marriage on the Rocks* (WB, 1965), *The Oscar* (Par., 1966),* *Assault on a Queen* (Par., 1966), *Cast a Giant Shadow* (UA, 1966), *The Naked Runner* (WB, 1967), *Tony Rome* (20th, 1967), *The Detective* (20th, 1968).

*Unbilled guest appearance

PENNY SINGLETON (Mary Ann Dorothy McNulty) Born September 15, 1909, Philadelphia, Pennsylania. Married Lawrence Singleton (1937), child: Dorothy; divorced 1939. Married Robert Sparks (1941), child: Robin; widowed 1963.

Feature Films:
    as Dorothy McNulty *Good News* (MGM, 1930), *Love in the Rough* (MGM, 1930), *After the Thin Man* (MGM, 1936), *Vogues of 1938* (UA, 1937), *Sea Racketeers* (Rep., 1937).
    as Penny Singleton *Outside of Paradise* (Rep., 1938), *Swing Your Lady* (WB, 1938), *Men Are Such Fools* (WB, 1938), *Boy Meets Girl* (WB, 1938), *Mr. Chump* (WB, 1938), *The Mad Miss Manton* (RKO, 1938), *Garden of the Moon* (WB, 1938), *Secrets of an Actress* (WB,

Penny Singleton and Dick Wessel in *Blondie Hits the Jackpot*.

1938), *Hard to Get* (WB, 1938), *Blondie* (Col., 1938), *Racket Busters* (WB, 1938), *Blondie Meets the Boss* (Col., 1939), *Blondie Takes a Vacation* (Col., 1939), *Blondie Brings Up Baby* (Col., 1939), *Blondie on a Budget* (Col., 1940), *Blondie Has Servant Trouble* (Col., 1940), *Blondie Plays Cupid* (Col., 1940), *Blondie Goes Latin* (Col., 1941), *Blondie in Society* (Col., 1941), *Go West, Young Lady* (Col., 1941), *Blondie Goes to College* (Col., 1942), *Blondie's Blessed Event* (Col., 1942), *Blondie for Victory* (Col., 1942), *It's a Great Life* (Col., 1943), *Footlight Glamour* (Col., 1943), *Leave It to Blondie* (Col., 1945), *Life With Blondie* (Col., 1946), *Young Widow* (UA, 1946), *Blondie's Lucky Day* (Col., 1946), *Blondie Knows Best* (Col., 1946), *Blondie's Holiday* (Col., 1947), *Blondie's Big Moment* (Col., 1947), *Blondie in the Dough* (Col., 1947), *Blondie's Anniversary* (Col., 1947), *Blondie's Reward* (Col., 1948), *Blondie's Secret* (Col., 1948), *Blondie Hits the Jackpot* (Col., 1949), *Blondie's Big Deal* (Col., 1949), *Blondie's Hero* (Col., 1950), *Beware of Blondie* (Col., 1950), *The Best Man* (UA, 1964).

RED SKELTON (Richard Bernard Skelton) Born July 18, 1913, Vincennes, Indiana. Married Edna Stilwell (1938); divorced 1943. Married Georgia Morris (1945), children: Valentina, Richard.

Ann Codee (left) and Red Skelton in *Bathing Beauty*.

Feature Films: *Having a Wonderful Time* (RKO, 1938), *Flight Command* (MGM, 1940), *The People vs. Dr. Kildare* (MGM, 1941), *Lady Be Good* (MGM, 1941), *Whistling in the Dark* (MGM, 1941), *Dr. Kildare's Wedding Day* (MGM, 1941), *Ship Ahoy* (MGM, 1942), *Maisie Gets Her Man* (MGM, 1942), *Panama Hattie* (MGM, 1942), *Whistling in Dixie* (MGM, 1942), *Du Barry Was a Lady* (MGM, 1943), *I Dood It* (MGM, 1943), *Whistling in Brooklyn* (MGM, 1943), *Thousands Cheer* (MGM, 1943), *Bathing Beauty* (MGM, 1944), *Ziegfeld Follies of 1946* (MGM, 1946), *The Show-Off* (MGM, 1946), *Merton of the Movies* (MGM, 1947), *The Fuller Brush Man* (Col., 1948), *A*

Southern Yankee (MGM, 1948), *Neptune's Daughter* (MGM, 1949), *The Yellow Cab Man* (MGM, 1950), *Three Little Words* (MGM, 1950), *Watch the Birdie* (MGM, 1950), *Excuse My Dust* (MGM, 1951), *Texas Carnival* (MGM, 1951), *Lovely to Look At* (MGM, 1952), *The Clown* (MGM, 1953), *Half a Hero* (MGM, 1953), *The Great Diamond Robbery* (MGM, 1953), *Susan Slept Here* (RKO, 1954),* *Around the World in 80 Days* (UA, 1956), *Public Pigeon No. 1* (Univ., 1957), *Ocean's 11* (WB, 1960),* *Those Magnificent Men in Their Flying Machines* (20th, 1965).

*Unbilled guest appearance

ALISON SKIPWORTH (Alison Groom) Born July 25, 1883, London, England. Married Frank Markham Skipworth. Died July 5, 1952.

Dorothy Dell, Alison Skipworth and Victor McLaglen in *Wharf Angel*.

Sound Feature Films: *Strictly Unconventional* (MGM, 1930), *Raffles* (UA, 1930), *Oh, for a Man!* (Fox, 1930), *Outward Bound* (WB, 1930), *Du Barry* (UA, 1930), *Virtuous Husbands* (Univ., 1931), *Night Angel* (Par., 1931), *Road to Singapore* (WB, 1931), *Devotion* (Pathé, 1931), *Tonight or Never* (UA, 1931), *High Pressure* (WB, 1932), *Unexpected Father* (Univ., 1932), *Sinners in the Sun* (Par., 1932), *Madame Racketeer* (Par., 1932), *Night After Night* (Par., 1932), *If I Had a Million* (Par., 1932), *Tonight Is Ours* (Par., 1933), *A Lady's Profession* (Par., 1933), *He Learned About Women* (Par., 1933), *Midnight Club* (Par., 1933), *Song of Songs* (Par., 1933), *Tillie and Gus* (Par., 1933), *Alice in Wonderland* (Par., 1933), *Coming Out Party* (Fox, 1934), *Six of a Kind* (Par., 1934), *Wharf Angel* (Par., 1934), *Shoot the Works* (Par., 1934), *Notorious Sophie Lang* (Par., 1934), *Here Is My Heart* (Par., 1934), *The Captain Hates the Sea* (Col., 1934), *The Casino Murder Case* (MGM, 1935), *Doubting Thomas* (Fox, 1935), *The Devil Is a Woman* (Par., 1935), *Becky Sharp* (RKO, 1935), *The Girl From Tenth Avenue* (WB, 1935), *Shanghai* (Par., 1935), *Dangerous* (WB, 1935), *Hitch-Hike Lady* (Rep., 1935), *Stolen Holiday* (WB, 1936), *The Princess Comes Across* (Par., 1936), *Satan Met a Lady* (WB, 1936), *Two in a Crowd* (Univ., 1936), *The Gorgeous Hussy* (MGM, 1936), *White Hunter* (20th, 1936), *Two Wise Maids* (Rep., 1937), *King of the Newsboys* (Rep., 1938), *Wide Open Faces* (Col., 1938), *Ladies in Distress* (Rep., 1938).

WALTER SLEZAK Born May 3, 1902, Vienna, Austria. Married Johanna Van Ryn (1943), children: Erica, Ingrid, Leo.

English-Language Sound Feature Films: *Once Upon a Honeymoon* (RKO, 1942), *This Land Is Mine* (RKO, 1943), *The Fallen Sparrow* (RKO, 1943), *Lifeboat* (20th, 1944), *Till We Meet Again* (Par., 1944), *Step Lively* (RKO, 1944), *And Now Tomorrow* (Par., 1944), *The Princess and the Pirate* (RKO, 1944), *Salome, Where She Danced* (Univ., 1945),

Walter Slezak and Janet Leigh in *Confidentially Connie.*

Alexis Smith and Philo McCullough (right) in *Whiplash.*

The Spanish Main (RKO, 1945), *Cornered* (RKO, 1945), *Sinbad the Sailor* (RKO, 1947), *Born to Kill* (RKO, 1947), *Riffraff* (RKO, 1947), *The Pirate* (MGM, 1948), *The Inspector General* (WB, 1949), *The Yellow Cab Man* (MGM, 1950), *Spy Hunt* (Univ., 1950), *Abbott and Costello in the Foreign Legion* (Univ., 1951), *Bedtime for Bonzo* (Univ., 1951), *People Will Talk* (20th, 1951), *Call Me Madam* (20th, 1953), *Confidentially Connie* (MGM, 1953), *White Witch Doctor* (20th, 1953), *The Steel Cage* (UA, 1954), *Ten Thousand Bedrooms* (MGM, 1957), *Deadlier Than the Male* (Continental, 1957), *The Miracle* (WB, 1959), *Come September* (Univ., 1961), *The Wonderful World of the Brothers Grimm* (MGM, 1962), *Emil and the Detectives* (BV, 1964), *Wonderful Life* ("Swingers' Paradise"—Elstree, 1964), *A Very Special Favor* (Univ., 1965), *24 Hours to Kill* (7 Arts, 1965), *The Caper of the Golden Bulls* (Embassy, 1967), *Coppelia* (BHE, 1968).

EVERETT SLOANE Born October 1, 1909, New York, New York. Married Luba Herman (1933), children: Nathaniel, Erika. Died August 6, 1965.

Everett Sloane and Van Heflin in *Patterns.*

Feature Films: *Citizen Kane* (RKO, 1941), *Journey into Fear* (RKO, 1942), *The Lady From Shanghai* (Col., 1948), *Prince of Foxes* (20th, 1949), *The Men* (UA, 1950), *Bird of Paradise* (20th, 1951), *The Enforcer* (WB, 1951), *Sirocco* (Col., 1951), *The Prince Who Was a Thief* (Univ., 1951), *The Blue Veil* (RKO, 1951), *The Desert Fox* (20th, 1951), *The Sellout* (MGM, 1951), *Way of a Gaucho* (20th, 1952), *The Big Knife* (UA, 1955), *Patterns* (UA, 1956), *Somebody Up There Likes Me* (MGM, 1956), *Lust for Life* (MGM, 1956), *Marjorie Morningstar* (WB, 1958), *The Gun Runners* (UA, 1958), *Home From the Hill* (MGM, 1960), *By Love Possessed* (UA, 1961), *Brushfire!* (Par., 1962), *The Man From the Diners' Club* (Col., 1963), *The Patsy* (Par., 1964), *Ready for the People* (WB, 1964), *The Disorderly Orderly* (Par., 1964).

ALEXIS SMITH (Gladys Smith) Born June 8, 1921, Penticton, Canada. Married Craig Stevens (1944).

Feature Films: *Lady With Red Hair* (WB, 1940), *Affectionately Yours* (WB, 1941), *Singapore Woman* (WB, 1941), *Three Sons o' Guns* (WB, 1941), *She Couldn't Say No* (WB, 1941), *Passage From Hong Kong* (WB, 1941), *Flight From Destiny* (WB, 1941), *Steel Against the Sky* (WB, 1941), *The Smiling Ghost* (WB, 1941), *Dive Bomber* (WB, 1941), *Gentleman Jim* (WB, 1942), *Thank Your Lucky Stars* (WB, 1943), *The Constant Nymph* (WB, 1943), *Hollywood Canteen* (WB, 1944), *The Adventures of Mark Twain* (WB, 1944), *The Doughgirls* (WB, 1944), *Rhapsody in Blue* (WB, 1945), *Conflict* (WB, 1945), *San Antonio* (WB, 1945), *The Horn Blows at Midnight* (WB, 1945), *Night and Day* (WB, 1946), *One More Tomorrow* (WB, 1946), *Of Human Bondage* (WB, 1946), *The Two Mrs. Carrolls* (WB, 1947), *Stallion Road* (WB, 1947), *Always Together* (WB, 1947),* *Woman in White* (WB, 1948), *The Decision of Christopher Blake* (WB, 1948), *Whiplash* (WB, 1948), *South of St. Louis* (WB, 1949), *Any Number Can Play* (MGM, 1949), *One Last Fling* (WB, 1949), *Montana* (WB, 1950), *Wyoming Mail* (Univ., 1950), *Undercover Girl* (Univ., 1950), *Here Comes the Groom* (Par., 1951), *Cave of Outlaws* (Univ., 1951), *The Turning Point* (Par., 1952), *Split Second* (RKO, 1953), *The Sleeping Tiger* (Astor, 1954), *The Eternal Sea* (Rep., 1955), *Beau James* (Par., 1957), *This Happy Feeling* (Univ., 1958), *The Young Philadelphians* (WB, 1959).

*Unbilled guest appearance

SIR C. AUBREY SMITH (Charles Aubrey Smith) Born July 21, 1863, Brighton, England. Married Isabel Wood (1896), child: Honor. Died December 20, 1948.

Billie Burke, C. Aubrey Smith, Broderick Crawford and Loretta Young in *Eternally Yours.*

Sound Feature Films: *Trader Horn* (MGM, 1931), *Never the Twain Shall Meet* (MGM, 1931), *Bachelor Father* (MGM, 1931), *Daybreak*

183

(MGM, 1931), *Just a Gigolo* (MGM, 1931), *Son of India* (MGM, 1931), *Man in Possession* (MGM, 1931), *Phantom of Paris* (MGM, 1931), *Guilty Hands* (MGM, 1931), *Surrender* (Fox, 1931), *Polly of the Circus* (MGM, 1932), *Tarzan the Ape Man* (MGM, 1932), *But the Flesh Is Weak* (MGM, 1932), *Love Me Tonight* (Par., 1932), *Trouble in Paradise* (Par., 1932), *No More Orchids* (Col., 1932), *They Just Had to Get Married* (Univ., 1932), *Luxury Liner* (Par., 1933), *Secrets* (UA, 1933), *The Barbarian* (MGM, 1933), *Adorable* (Fox, 1933), *Monkey's Paw* (RKO, 1933), *Morning Glory* (RKO, 1933), *Bombshell* (MGM, 1933), *Queen Christina* (MGM, 1933), *House of Rothschild* (UA, 1934), *Gambling Lady* (WB, 1934), *Curtain at Eight* (Majestic, 1934), *Bulldog Drummond Strikes Back* (UA, 1934), *Cleopatra* (Par., 1934), *Madame Du Barry* (WB, 1934), *One More River* (Univ., 1934), *Caravan* (Fox, 1934), *The Firebird* (WB, 1934), *The Right to Live* (WB, 1935), *Lives of a Bengal Lancer* (Par., 1935), *Florentine Dagger* (WB, 1935), *The Gilded Lily* (Par., 1935), *Clive of India* (UA, 1935), *China Seas* (MGM, 1935), *Jalna* (RKO, 1935), *The Crusades* (Par., 1935), *Little Lord Fauntleroy* (UA, 1936), *Romeo and Juliet* (MGM, 1936), *The Garden of Allah* (UA, 1936), *Lloyds of London* (20th, 1936), *Wee Willie Winkie* (20th, 1937), *The Prisoner of Zenda* (UA, 1937), *Thoroughbreds Don't Cry* (MGM, 1937), *The Hurricane* (UA, 1937), *Four Men and a Prayer* (20th, 1938), *Kidnapped* (20th, 1938), *Sixty Glorious Years* (RKO, 1938), *East Side of Heaven* (Univ., 1939), *Five Came Back* (RKO, 1939), *The Sun Never Sets* (Univ., 1939), *Eternally Yours* (UA, 1939), *Another Thin Man* (MGM, 1939), *The Under-Pup* (Univ., 1939), *Balalaika* (MGM, 1939), *Rebecca* (UA, 1940), *City of Chance* (20th, 1940), *A Bill of Divorcement* (RKO, 1940), *Waterloo Bridge* (MGM, 1940), *Beyond Tomorrow* (RKO, 1940), *A Little Bit of Heaven* (Univ., 1940), *Free and Easy* (MGM, 1941), *Maisie Was a Lady* (MGM, 1941), *Dr. Jekyll and Mr. Hyde* (MGM, 1941), *Forever and a Day* (RKO, 1943), *Two Tickets to London* (Univ., 1943), *Flesh and Fantasy* (Univ., 1943), *Madame Curie* (MGM, 1943), *The White Cliffs of Dover* (MGM, 1944), *The Adventures of Mark Twain* (WB, 1944), *Secrets of Scotland Yard* (Rep., 1944), *Sensations of 1945* (UA, 1944), *They Shall Have Faith* (Mon., 1945), *And Then There Were None* (20th, 1945), *Scotland Yard Investigator* (Rep., 1945), *Cluny Brown* (20th, 1946), *Rendezvous With Annie* (Rep., 1946), *High Conquest* (Mon., 1947), *Unconquered* (Par., 1947), *Little Women* (MGM, 1949).

KENT SMITH (Frank Kent Smith) Born March 19, 1907, New York, New York. Married Elizabeth Gillette (1937), child: Elizabeth; divorced 1954. Married Edith Atwater (1962).

Dorothy McGuire, Troy Donahue, Kent Smith, Connie Stevens, Brian Aherne, Bert Convoy and Natalie Schafer in *Susan Slade.*

Feature Films: *Cat People* (RKO, 1942), *Forever and a Day* (RKO, 1943), *Hitler's Children* (RKO, 1943), *This Land Is Mine* (RKO, 1943), *Three Russian Girls* (UA, 1943), *The Curse of the Cat People* (RKO, 1944), *Youth Runs Wild* (RKO, 1944), *The Spiral Staircase* (RKO, 1946), *Magic Town* (RKO, 1947), *Nora Prentiss* (WB, 1947), *The Voice of the Turtle* (WB, 1947), *Design for Death* (narrator; RKO, 1948), *The Decision of Christopher Blake*, (WB, 1948), *The Fountain-*

head (WB, 1949), *My Foolish Heart* (RKO, 1949), *The Damned Don't Cry* (WB, 1950), *This Side of the Law* (WB, 1950), *Paula* (Col., 1952), *Comanche* (UA, 1956), *Sayonara* (WB, 1957), *The Imitation General* (MGM, 1958), *The Badlanders* (MGM, 1958), *The Mugger* (UA, 1958), *Party Girl* (MGM, 1958), *This Earth Is Mine* (Univ., 1959), *Strangers When We Meet* (Col., 1960), *Susan Slade* (WB, 1961), *Moon Pilot* (BV, 1962), *The Balcony* (Continental Distributing, 1963), *A Distant Trumpet* (WB, 1964), *The Young Lovers* (MGM, 1964), *Youngblood Hawke* (WB, 1964), *Trouble With Angels* (Col., 1966), *A Covenant With Death* (WB, 1967), *Assignment to Kill* (WB, 1968), *Games* (Univ., 1967).

GALE SONDERGAARD (Edith Holm Sondergaard) Born February 15, 1900, Litchfield, Minnesota. Married Neill O'Malley (1922); divorced 1930. Married Herbert Biberman (1930), children: Daniel, Joan.

Rondo Hatton and Gale Sondergaard in *The Spider Woman Strikes Back.*

Feature Films: *Anthony Adverse* (WB, 1936), *Maid of Salem* (Par., 1937), *Seventh Heaven* (20th, 1937), *The Life of Emile Zola* (WB, 1937), *Lord Jeff* (MGM, 1938), *Dramatic School* (MGM, 1938), *Never Say Die* (Par., 1939), *Juarez* (WB, 1939), *The Cat and the Canary* (Par., 1939), *The Llano Kid* (Par., 1940), *The Blue Bird* (20th, 1940), *The Mark of Zorro* (20th, 1940), *The Letter* (WB, 1940), *The Black Cat* (Univ., 1941), *Paris Calling* (Univ., 1941), *My Favorite Blonde* (Par., 1942), *Enemy Agent Meets Ellery Queen* (Col., 1942), *A Night to Remember* (Col., 1943), *Appointment in Berlin* (Col., 1943), *Isle of Forgotten Sins* (PRC, 1943), *The Strange Death of Adolf Hitler* (Univ., 1943), *The Spider Woman* (Univ., 1944), *Follow the Boys* (Univ., 1944), *Christmas Holiday* (Univ., 1944), *Invisible Man's Revenge* (Univ., 1944), *Gypsy Wildcat* (Univ., 1944), *The Climax* (Univ., 1944), *Enter Arsene Lupin* (Univ., 1944), *The Spider Woman Strikes Back* (Univ., 1946), *A Night in Paradise* (Univ., 1946), *Anna and the King of Siam* (20th, 1946), *The Time of Their Lives* (Univ., 1946), *Road to Rio* (Par., 1947), *The Pirates of Monterey* (Univ., 1947), *East Side, West Side* (MGM, 1949).

ANN SOTHERN (Harriette Lake) Born January 22, 1909, Valley City, North Dakota. Married Roger Pryor (1936); divorced 1942. Married Robert Sterling (1943), child: Patricia; divorced 1949.

Feature Films:
     as Harriet Lake *Show of Shows* (WB, 1929), *Dough Boys* (MGM, 1930).

     as Ann Sothern *Let's Fall in Love* (Col., 1934), *Melody in Spring* (Par., 1934), *Party's Over* (Col., 1934), *Hell Cat* (Col., 1934), *Blind Date* (Col., 1934), *Kid Millions* (UA, 1934), *Folies Bergere* (UA, 1935),

Virginia Weidler, Ann Sothern and Mary Nash in *Gold Rush Maisie*.

Eight Bells (Col., 1935), *Hooray for Love* (RKO, 1935), *The Girl Friend* (Col., 1935), *Grand Exit* (Col., 1935), *You May Be Next* (Col., 1936), *Hellship Morgan* (Col., 1936), *Don't Gamble With Love* (Col., 1936), *Walking on Air* (RKO, 1936), *My American Wife* (Par., 1936), *The Smartest Girl in Town* (RKO, 1936), *Dangerous Number* (MGM, 1937), *50 Roads to Town* (20th, 1937), *There Goes My Girl* (RKO, 1937), *Super Sleuth* (RKO, 1937), *Danger—Love At Work* (20th, 1937), *There Goes the Groom* (RKO, 1937), *She's Got Everything* (RKO, 1938), *Trade Winds* (UA, 1938), *Maisie* (MGM, 1939), *Fast and Furious* (MGM, 1939), *Elsa Maxwell's Hotel for Women* (20th, 1939), *Joe and Ethel Turp Call on the President* (MGM, 1939), *Congo Maisie* (MGM, 1940), *Brother Orchid* (WB, 1940), *Gold Rush Maisie* (MGM, 1940), *Dulcy* (MGM, 1940), *Maisie Was a Lady* (MGM, 1941), *Ringside Maisie* (MGM, 1941), *Lady Be Good* (MGM, 1941), *Maisie Gets Her Man* (MGM, 1942), *Panama Hattie* (MGM, 1942), *Three Hearts for Julia* (MGM, 1943), *Swing Shift Maisie* (MGM, 1943), *Thousands Cheer* (MGM, 1943), *Cry Havoc* (MGM, 1943), *Maisie Goes to Reno* (MGM, 1944), *Up Goes Maisie* (MGM, 1946), *Undercover Maisie* (MGM, 1947), *April Showers* (WB, 1948), *Words and Music* (MGM, 1948), *A Letter to Three Wives* (20th, 1948), *The Judge Steps Out* (RKO, 1949), *Nancy Goes to Rio* (MGM, 1950), *Shadow on the Wall* (MGM, 1950), *The Blue Gardenia* (WB, 1953), *Lady in a Cage* (Par., 1964), *The Best Man* (UA, 1964), *Sylvia* (Par., 1965), *Chubasco* (WB-7 Arts, 1968).

ROBERT STACK Born January 13, 1919, Los Angeles, California. Married Rosemarie Bowe (1956), children: Elizabeth, Charles.

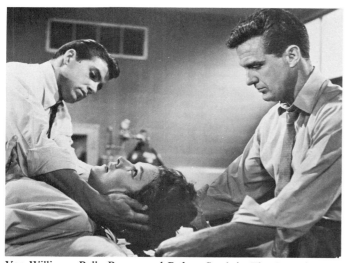

Van Williams, Polly Bergen and Robert Stack in *The Caretakers*.

Feature Films: *First Love* (Univ., 1939), *The Mortal Storm* (MGM, 1940), *A Little Bit of Heaven* (Univ., 1940), *Nice Girl?* (Univ., 1941), *Badlands of Dakota* (Univ., 1941), *To Be or Not to Be* (UA, 1942), *Eagle Squadron* (Univ., 1942), *Men of Texas* (Univ., 1942), *A Date With Judy* (MGM, 1948), *Miss Tatlock's Millions* (Par., 1948), *Fighter*

Squadron (WB, 1948), *Mr. Music* (Par., 1950), *My Outlaw Brother* (EL, 1951), *Bwana Devil* (UA, 1952), *War Paint* (UA, 1953), *Conquest of Cochise* (Col., 1953), *Sabre Jet* (UA, 1953), *The High and the Mighty* (WB, 1954), *The Iron Glove* (Col., 1954), *House of Bamboo* (20th, 1955), *Good Morning, Miss Dove* (20th, 1955), *Great Day in the Morning* (RKO, 1956), *Written on the Wind* (Univ., 1956), *The Tarnished Angels* (Univ., 1957), *The Gift of Love* (20th, 1958), *John Paul Jones* (WB, 1959), *The Last Voyage* (MGM, 1960), *The Caretakers* (UA, 1963), *Is Paris Burning?* (Par., 1966), *The Corrupt Ones* (WB-7 Arts, 1967), *Action Man* (Les Films Copernic, 1968).

BARBARA STANWYCK (Ruby Stevens) Born July 16, 1907, Brooklyn, New York. Married Frank Fay (1928), child: Dion; divorced 1935. Married Robert Taylor (1939); divorced 1952.

Gilbert Roland and Barbara Stanwyck in *The Other Love*.

Sound Feature Films: *Mexicali Rose* (Col., 1929), *Ladies of Leisure* (Col., 1930), *Ten Cents a Dance* (Col., 1931), *Illicit* (WB, 1931), *Miracle Woman* (Col., 1931), *Night Nurse* (WB, 1931), *Forbidden* (Col., 1932), *Shopworn* (Col., 1932), *So Big* (WB, 1932), *The Purchase Price* (WB, 1932), *The Bitter Tea of General Yen* (Col., 1933), *Ladies They Talk About* (WB, 1933), *Baby Face* (WB, 1933), *Ever in My Heart* (WB, 1933), *A Lost Lady* (WB, 1934), *Gambling Lady* (WB, 1934), *The Secret Bride* (WB, 1935), *The Woman in Red* (WB, 1935), *Red Salute* (UA, 1935), *Annie Oakley* (RKO, 1935), *A Message to Garcia* (20th, 1936), *The Bride Walks Out* (RKO, 1936), *His Brother's Wife* (MGM, 1936), *Banjo on My Knee* (20th, 1936), *The Plough and the Stars* (RKO, 1936), *Internes Can't Take Money* (Par., 1937), *This Is My Affair* (20th, 1937), *Stella Dallas* (UA, 1937), *Breakfast for Two* (RKO, 1937), *The Mad Miss Manton* (RKO, 1938), *Always Goodbye* (20th, 1938), *Union Pacific* (Par., 1939), *Golden Boy* (Col., 1939), *Remember the Night* (Par., 1940), *The Lady Eve* (Par., 1941), *Meet John Doe* (WB, 1941), *You Belong to Me* (Col., 1941), *Ball of Fire* (RKO, 1941), *The Great Man's Lady* (Par., 1942), *The Gay Sisters* (WB, 1942), *Lady of Burlesque* (UA, 1943), *Flesh and Fantasy* (Univ., 1943), *Double Indemnity* (Par., 1944), *Hollywood Canteen* (WB, 1944), *Christmas in Connecticut* (WB, 1945), *My Reputation* (WB, 1946), *The Bride Wore Boots* (Par., 1946), *The Strange Love of Martha Ivers* (Par., 1946), *California* (Par., 1946), *Variety Girl* (Par., 1947), *The Other Love* (UA, 1947), *The Two Mrs. Carrolls* (WB, 1947), *Cry Wolf* (WB, 1947), *B. F.'s Daughter* (MGM, 1948), *Sorry, Wrong Number* (Par., 1948), *The Lady Gambles* (Univ., 1949), *East Side, West Side* (MGM, 1949), *Thelma Jordan* (Par., 1949), *No Man of Her Own* (Par., 1950), *The Furies* (Par., 1950), *To Please a Lady* (MGM, 1950), *The Man With a Cloak* (MGM, 1951), *Clash by Night* (RKO, 1952), *Jeopardy* (MGM, 1953), *Titanic* (20th, 1953), *All I Desire* (Univ., 1953), *The Moonlighter* (WB, 1953), *Blowing Wild* (WB, 1953), *Executive Suite* (MGM, 1954), *Witness to Murder* (UA, 1954), *Cattle Queen of Montana* (RKO, 1954), *The Violent Men* (Col.,

1955), *Escape to Burma* (RKO, 1955), *There's Always Tomorrow* (Univ., 1956), *The Maverick Queen* (Rep., 1956), *These Wilder Years* (MGM, 1956), *Crime of Passion* (UA, 1957), *Trooper Hook* (UA, 1957), *Forty Guns* (20th, 1957), *Walk on the Wild Side* (Col., 1962), *Roustabout* (Par., 1964), *The Night Walker* (Univ., 1965).

ROD STEIGER (Rodney Stephen Steiger) Born April 14, 1925, Westhampton, Long Island, New York. Married Sally Gracie (1952); divorced 1954. Married Claire Bloom (1959), child: Anna.

Rod Steiger and Ayllene Gibbons in *The Loved One*.

Feature Films: *On the Waterfront* (Col., 1954), *Oklahoma!* (Magna, 1955), *The Big Knife* (UA, 1955), *The Court-Martial of Billy Mitchell* (WB, 1955), *The Harder They Fall* (Col., 1956), *Jubal* (Col., 1956), *Back From Eternity* (RKO, 1956), *Run of the Arrow* (Univ., 1957), *Across the Bridge* (Rank, 1957), *The Unholy Wife* (Univ., 1957), *Cry Terror* (MGM, 1958), *Al Capone* (AA, 1959), *Seven Thieves* (20th, 1960), *The Mark* (Continental Distributing, 1961), *On Friday at Eleven* ("World in My Pocket"—British Lion, 1961), *13 West Street* (Col., 1962), *Convicts 4* (AA, 1962), *The Longest Day* (20th, 1962), *The Pawnbroker* (Landau, 1965), *The Loved One* (MGM, 1965), *Doctor Zhivago* (MGM, 1965), *Time of Indifference* (Continental, 1966), *In the Heat of the Night* (UA, 1967), *The Girl and the General* (MGM, 1967) *The Sergeant* (WB-7 Arts, 1968), *No Way to Treat a Lady* (Par., 1968).

ANNA STEN (Anjuschka Stenski) Born December 3, 1910, Kiev, Russia. Married Eugene Frenke.

English-Language Feature Films: *Nana* (UA, 1934), *We Live Again* (UA, 1934), *The Wedding Night* (UA, 1935), *Two Who Dared* ("A Woman Alone"—GN, 1937), *Exile Express* (GN, 1939), *The Man I*

Lionel Atwill and Anna Sten in *Nana*.

Married (20th, 1940), *So Ends Our Night* (UA, 1941), *Chetniks* (20th, 1943), *They Came to Blow Up America* (20th, 1943), *Three Russian Girls* (UA, 1943), *Let's Live a Little* (EL, 1948), *Soldier of Fortune* (20th, 1955), *The Nun and the Sergeant* (UA, 1962).

JAN STERLING (Jane Sterling Adriance) Born April 3, 1923, New York, New York. Married Jack Merivale (1941); divorced 1948. Married Paul Douglas (1950), child: Adam; widowed 1959.

Jan Sterling and Carleton Carpenter in *Sky Full of Moon*.

Feature Films: *Johnny Belinda* (WB, 1948), *The Skipper Surprised His Wife* (MGM, 1950), *Mystery Street* (MGM, 1950), *Caged* (WB, 1950), *Union Station* (Par., 1950), *Appointment With Danger* (Par., 1951), *The Mating Season* (Par., 1951), *The Big Carnival* (Par., 1951), *Rhubarb* (Par., 1951), *Flesh and Fury* (Univ., 1952), *Sky Full of Moon* (MGM, 1952), *Split Second* (RKO, 1953), *The Vanquished* (Par., 1953), *Pony Express* (Par., 1953), *Alaska Seas* (Par., 1954), *The High and the Mighty* (WB, 1954), *Return From the Sea* (AA, 1954), *The Human Jungle* (AA, 1954), *Women's Prison* (Col., 1955), *Female on the Beach* (Univ., 1955), *Man With the Gun* (UA, 1955), *The Harder They Fall* (Col., 1956), *1984* (Col., 1956), *Slaughter on Tenth Avenue* (Univ., 1957), *The Female Animal* (Univ., 1958), *Kathy O'* (Univ., 1958), *High School Confidential* (MGM, 1958), *Love in a Goldfish Bowl* (Par., 1961), *The Incident* (20th, 1967).

JAMES STEWART (James Maitland Stewart) Born May 20, 1908, Indiana, Pennsylvania. Married Gloria McLean (1949), children: Judy, Kelly.

Feature Films: *Murder Man* (MGM, 1935), *Rose Marie* (MGM, 1936), *Next Time We Love* (Univ., 1936), *Wife vs. Secretary* (MGM, 1936), *Small Town Girl* (MGM, 1936), *Speed* (MGM, 1936), *The Gorgeous Hussy* (MGM, 1936), *Born to Dance* (MGM, 1936), *After the Thin Man*

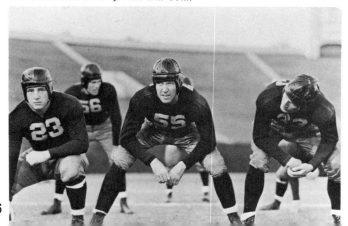

James Stewart in *Navy Blue and Gold*.

186

(MGM, 1936), *Seventh Heaven* (20th, 1937), *The Last Gangster* (MGM, 1937), *Navy Blue and Gold* (MGM, 1937), *Of Human Hearts* (MGM, 1938), *Vivacious Lady* (RKO, 1938), *Shopworn Angel* (MGM, 1938), *You Can't Take It With You* (Col., 1938), *Made for Each Other* (UA, 1939), *Ice Follies of 1939* (MGM, 1939), *It's a Wonderful World* (MGM, 1939), *Mr. Smith Goes to Washington* (Col., 1939), *Destry Rides Again* (Univ., 1939), *The Shop Around the Corner* (MGM, 1940), *The Mortal Storm* (MGM, 1940), *No Time for Comedy* (WB, 1940), *The Philadelphia Story* (MGM, 1940), *Come Live With Me* (MGM, 1941), *Pot o' Gold* (UA, 1941), *Ziegfeld Girl* (MGM, 1941), *It's a Wonderful Life* (RKO, 1946), *Magic Town* (RKO, 1947), *Call Northside 777* (20th, 1948), *On Our Merry Way* (UA, 1948), *Rope* (WB, 1948), *You Gotta Stay Happy* (Univ., 1948), *The Stratton Story* (MGM, 1949), *Malaya* (MGM, 1949), *Winchester '73* (Univ., 1950), *Broken Arrow* (20th, 1950), *The Jackpot* (20th, 1950), *Harvey* (Univ., 1950), *No Highway in the Sky* (20th, 1951), *The Greatest Show on Earth* (Par., 1952), *Bend of the River* (Univ., 1952), *Carbine Williams* (MGM, 1952), *The Naked Spur* (MGM, 1953), *Thunder Bay* (Univ., 1953), *The Glenn Miller Story* (Univ., 1954), *Rear Window* (Par., 1954), *The Far Country* (Univ., 1955), *Strategic Air Command* (Par., 1955), *The Man From Laramie* (Col., 1955), *The Man Who Knew Too Much* (Par., 1956), *The Spirit of St. Louis* (WB, 1957), *Night Passage* (Univ., 1957), *Vertigo* (Par., 1958), *Bell, Book and Candle* (Col., 1958), *Anatomy of a Murder* (Col., 1959), *The FBI Story* (WB, 1959), *The Mountain Road* (Col., 1960), *Two Rode Together* (Col., 1961), *X-15* (narrator; UA, 1961), *The Man Who Shot Liberty Valance* (Par., 1962), *Mr. Hobbs Takes a Vacation* (20th, 1962), *How the West Was Won* (MGM, 1963), *Take Her, She's Mine* (20th, 1963), *Cheyenne Autumn* (WB, 1964), *Dear Brigitte* (20th, 1965), *Shenandoah* (Univ., 1965), *Flight of the Phoenix* (20th, 1966), *The Rare Breed* (Univ., 1966), *Firecreek* (WB- Arts, 1968), *Bandolero* (20th, 1968).

DEAN STOCKWELL Born March 5, 1936, Los Angeles, California. Married Millie Perkins (1960); divorced 1964.

Richard Widmark (left) and Dean Stockwell (center) in *Down to the Sea in Ships.*

Feature Films: *Valley of Decision* (MGM, 1945), *Anchors Aweigh* (MGM, 1945), *Bud Abbott and Lou Costello in Hollywood* (MGM, 1945), *The Green Years* (MGM, 1946), *Home Sweet Homicide* (20th, 1946), *The Mighty McGurk* (MGM, 1947), *The Arnelo Affair* (MGM, 1947), *Song of the Thin Man* (MGM, 1947), *The Romance of Rosy Ridge* (MGM, 1947), *Gentleman's Agreement* (20th, 1947), *The Boy With Green Hair* (RKO, 1948), *Deep Waters* (20th, 1948), *Down to the Sea in Ships* (20th, 1949), *The Secret Garden* (MGM, 1949), *Stars in My Crown* (MGM, 1950), *The Happy Years* (MGM, 1950), *Kim* (MGM, 1950), *Cattle Drive* (Univ., 1951), *Gun for a Coward* (Univ., 1957), *The Careless Years* (UA, 1957), *Compulsion* (20th, 1959), *Sons and Lovers* (20th, 1960), *Long Day's Journey into Night* (Embassy, 1962), *Rapture* (International Classics, 1965), *Psych-Out* (AIP, 1968).

Lewis Stone and Jackie Cooper in *Treasure Island.*

LEWIS STONE Born November 15, 1879, Worcester, Massachusetts. Married Margaret Langham, widowed. Married Florence Oakley, children: Virginia, Barbara; divorced. Married Hazel Wolf (1930). Died September 12, 1953.

Sound Feature Films: *Trial of Mary Dugan* (MGM, 1929), *Madame X* (MGM, 1929), *Their Own Desire* (MGM, 1930), *Strictly Unconventional* (MGM, 1930), *Big House* (MGM, 1930), *Romance* (MGM, 1930), *Father's Son* (WB, 1930), *Office Wife* (WB, 1930), *Passion Flower* (MGM, 1930), *My Past* (WB, 1931), *Inspiration* (MGM, 1931), *Secret Six* (MGM, 1931), *Always Goodbye* (Fox, 1931), *Phantom of Paris* (MGM, 1931), *The Bargain* (WB, 1931), *The Sin of Madelon Claudet* (MGM, 1931), *Mata Hari* (MGM, 1931), *Grand Hotel* (MGM, 1932), *Wet Parade* (MGM, 1932), *Night Court* (MGM, 1932), *Letty Lynton* (MGM, 1932), *New Morals for Old* (MGM, 1932), *Unashamed* (MGM, 1932), *Divorce in the Family* (MGM, 1932), *Red-Headed Woman* (MGM, 1932), *Mask of Fu Manchu* (MGM, 1932), *The Son-Daughter* (MGM, 1932), *The White Sister* (MGM, 1933), *Men Must Fight* (MGM, 1933), *Looking Forward* (MGM, 1933), *Bureau of Missing Persons* (WB, 1933), *Queen Christina* (MGM, 1933), *You Can't Buy Everything* (MGM, 1934), *Mystery of Mr. X* (MGM, 1934), *Treasure Island* (MGM, 1934), *Girl From Missouri* (MGM, 1934), *Vanessa—Her Love Story* (MGM, 1935), *West Point of the Air* (MGM, 1935), *David Copperfield* (MGM, 1935), *Public Hero Number One* (MGM, 1935), *China Seas* (MGM, 1935), *Woman Wanted* (MGM, 1935), *Shipmates Forever* (WB, 1935), *Small Town Girl* (MGM, 1936), *The Three Godfathers* (MGM, 1936), *The Unguarded Hour* (MGM, 1936), *Sworn Enemy* (MGM, 1936), *Suzy* (MGM, 1936), *Don't Turn 'Em Loose* (RKO, 1936), *Outcast* (Par., 1937), *The Thirteenth Chair* (MGM, 1937), *The Man Who Cried Wolf* (Univ., 1937), *You're Only Young Once* (MGM, 1937), *Bad Man of Brimstone* (MGM, 1938), *Judge Hardy's Children* (MGM, 1938), *Stolen Heaven* (Par., 1938), *Yellow Jack* (MGM, 1938), *The Chaser* (MGM, 1938), *Love Finds Andy Hardy* (MGM, 1938), *Out West With the Hardys* (MGM, 1938), *Ice Follies of 1939* (MGM, 1939), *The Hardys Ride High* (MGM, 1939), *Andy Hardy Gets Spring Fever* (MGM, 1939), *Judge Hardy and Son* (MGM, 1939), *Joe and Ethel Turp Call on the President* (MGM, 1939), *Andy Hardy Meets Debutante* (MGM, 1940), *Sporting Blood* (MGM, 1940), *Andy Hardy's Private Secretary* (MGM, 1941), *Life Begins for Andy Hardy* (MGM, 1941), *The Bugle Sounds* (MGM, 1941), *The Courtship of Andy Hardy* (MGM, 1942), *Andy Hardy's Double Life* (MGM, 1942), *Andy Hardy's Blonde Trouble* (MGM, 1944), *The Hoodlum Saint* (MGM, 1946), *Three Wise Fools* (MGM, 1946), *Love Laughs at Andy Hardy* (MGM, 1946), *State of the Union* (MGM, 1948), *The Sun Comes Up* (MGM, 1949), *Any Number Can Play* (MGM, 1949), *Stars in My Crown* (MGM, 1950), *Key to the City* (MGM, 1950), *Grounds for Marriage* (MGM, 1950), *Night into Morning* (MGM, 1951), *Angels in the Outfield* (MGM, 1951), *Bannerline* (MGM, 1951), *It's a Big Country* (MGM, 1951), *The Unknown Man* (MGM, 1951), *Just This Once* (MGM, 1952), *Scaramouche* (MGM, 1952), *Talk About a Stranger* (MGM, 1952), *The Prisoner of Zenda* (MGM, 1952), *All the Brothers Were Valiant* (MGM, 1953).

Margaret Sullavan and James Stewart in *The Shop Around the Corner*.

MARGARET SULLAVAN (Margaret Brooke Sullavan) Born May 16, 1911, Norfolk, Virginia. Married Henry Fonda (1931); divorced 1932. Married William Wyler (1934); divorced 1936. Married Leland Hayward (1936), children: Brooke, Bridget, William; divorced 1947. Married Kenneth Wagg (1950). Died January 1, 1960.

Feature Films: *Only Yesterday* (Univ., 1933), *Little Man, What Now?* (Univ., 1934), *The Good Fairy* (Univ., 1935), *So Red the Rose* (Par., 1935), *Next Time We Love* (Univ., 1936), *The Moon's Our Home* (Par., 1936), *Three Comrades* (MGM, 1938), *The Shopworn Angel* (MGM, 1938), *The Shining Hour* (MGM, 1938), *The Shop Around the Corner* (MGM, 1940), *The Mortal Storm* (MGM, 1940), *So Ends Our Night* (UA, 1941), *Back Street* (Univ., 1941), *Appointment for Love* (Univ., 1941), *Cry Havoc* (MGM, 1943), *No Sad Songs for Me* (Col., 1950).

GLORIA SWANSON (Gloria Josephine May Swanson) Born March 27, 1898, Chicago, Illinois. Married Wallace Beery (1916); divorced 1919. Married Herbert Somborn (1919), child: Gloria; divorced 1923. Married Henri de la Falaise (1925); divorced 1930). Married Michael Farmer (1931), child: Michelle; divorced 1934. Married William Davey (1945); divorced 1946. Child adopted while Miss Swanson was unmarried: Joseph Swanson.

Gloria Swanson (center) in *What a Widow!*

English-Language Sound Feature Films: *The Trespasser* (UA, 1929),

What a Widow! (UA, 1930), *Indiscreet* (UA, 1931), *Tonight or Never* (UA, 1931), *Perfect Understanding* (UA, 1933), *Music in the Air* (Fox, 1934), *Father Takes a Wife* (RKO, 1941), *Sunset Boulevard* (Par., 1950), *Three for Bedroom C* (WB, 1952).

AKIM TAMIROFF Born October 29, 1899, Tiflis, Russia. Married Tamara Shayne.

Arthur Hoyt, Akim Tamiroff, Brian Donlevy and William Demarest in *The Great McGinty*.

English-Language Feature Films: *Gabriel Over the White House* (MGM, 1933), *Storm at Daybreak* (MGM, 1933), *Queen Christina* (MGM, 1933), *Fugitive Lovers* (MGM, 1934), *Sadie McKee* (MGM, 1934), *Great Flirtation* (Par., 1934), *Chained* (MGM, 1934), *Scarlet Empress* (Par., 1934), *Now and Forever* (Par., 1934), *The Merry Widow* (MGM, 1934), *Whom the Gods Destroy* (Col., 1934), *The Captain Hates the Sea* (Col., 1934), *Here Is My Heart* (Par., 1934), *Murder in the Private Car* (MGM, 1934), *Naughty Marietta* (MGM, 1935), *The Winning Ticket* (MGM, 1935), *Rumba* (Par., 1935), *Lives of a Bengal Lancer* (Par., 1935), *Go into Your Dance* (WB, 1935), *Two Fisted* (Par., 1935), *Black Fury* (WB, 1935), *Paris in Spring* (Par., 1935), *China Seas* (MGM, 1935), *Big Broadcast of 1936* (Par., 1935), *The Last Outpost* (Par., 1935), *The Story of Louis Pasteur* (WB, 1935), *Gay Deception* (Fox, 1935), *Woman Trap* (Par., 1936), *Desire* (Par., 1936), *Anthony Adverse* (WB, 1936), *The General Died at Dawn* (Par., 1936), *The Jungle Princess* (Par., 1936), *Her Husband Lies* (Par., 1937), *The Soldier and the Lady* (RKO, 1937), *King of Gamblers* (Par., 1937), *High, Wide and Handsome* (Par., 1937), *The Buccaneer* (Par., 1938), *Dangerous to Know* (Par., 1938), *Spawn of the North* (Par., 1938), *Ride a Crooked Mile* (Par., 1938), *King of Chinatown* (Par., 1939), *Paris Honeymoon* (Par., 1939), *Union Pacific* (Par., 1939), *The Magnificent Fraud* (Par., 1939), *Disputed Passage* (Par., 1939), *Honeymoon in Bali* (Par., 1939), *The Way of All Flesh* (Par., 1940), *Untamed* (Par., 1940), *The Great McGinty* (Par., 1940), *North West Mounted Police* (Par., 1940), *Texas Rangers Ride Again* (Par., 1941), *New York Town* (Par., 1941), *The Corsican Brothers* (UA, 1941), *Tortilla Flat* (MGM, 1942), *Five Graves to Cairo* (Par., 1943), *For Whom the Bell Tolls* (Par., 1943), *His Butler's Sister* (Univ., 1943), *The Miracle of Morgan's Creek* (Par., 1944), *Dragon Seed* (MGM, 1944), *The Bridge of San Luis Rey* (UA, 1944), *Can't Help Singing* (Univ., 1944), *Pardon My Past* (Col., 1946), *A Scandal in Paris* (UA, 1946), *Fiesta* (MGM, 1947), *The Gangster* (AA, 1947), *My Girl Tisa* (WB, 1948), *Relentless* (Col., 1948), *Outpost in Morocco* (UA, 1949), *Black Magic* (UA, 1949), *Desert Legion* (Univ., 1953), *You Know What Sailors Are* (UA, 1954), *They Who Dare* (British Lion, 1954), *Mr. Arkadin* (WB, 1955), *The Black Sleep* (UA, 1956), *Anastasia* (20th, 1956), *Battle Hell* (DCA, 1957), *Cartouche* (RKO, 1957), *Touch of Evil* (Univ., 1958), *Me and the Colonel* (Col., 1958), *Desert Desperadoes* (RKO, 1959), *Ocean's 11* (WB, 1960), *Romanoff And Juliet* (Univ., 1961), *The Reluctant Saint* (Davis Royal, 1962), *The Trial* (Gibraltar, 1962), *Panic Button* (Gorton

Associates, 1964), *Topkapi* (UA, 1964), *Lord Jim* (Col., 1965), *Chimes at Midnight* (Counor, 1965), *Lt. Robinson Crusoe, USN* (BV, 1966), *Marco the Magnificent* (MGM, 1966), *Hotel Paradiso* (MGM, 1966), *After the Fox* (UA, 1966), *The Liquidator* (MGM, 1966), *The Happening* (Col., 1967), *The Vulture* (Par., 1967), *Catherine the Great* (WB-7 Arts, 1968.).

ELIZABETH TAYLOR (Elizabeth Rosemond Taylor) Born February 27, 1932, Hampstead Heath, England. Married Nicky Hilton (1949); divorced 1951. Married Michael Wilding (1952), children: Michael, Christopher; divorced 1957. Married Michael Todd (1957), child: Elizabeth; widowed 1958. Married Eddie Fisher (1959), child: Maria; divorced 1964. Married Richard Burton (1964).

Elizabeth Taylor and Honor Blackman in *Conspirator.*

Feature Films: *There's One Born Every Minute* (Univ., 1942), *Lassie Come Home* (MGM, 1943), *Jane Eyre* (20th, 1944), *The White Cliffs of Dover* (MGM, 1944), *National Velvet* (MGM, 1944), *Courage of Lassie* (MGM, 1946), *Cynthia* (MGM, 1947), *Life With Father* (WB, 1947), *A Date With Judy* (MGM, 1948), *Julia Misbehaves* (MGM, 1948), *Little Women* (MGM, 1949), *Conspirator* (MGM, 1950), *The Big Hangover* (MGM, 1950), *Father of the Bride* (MGM, 1950), *Father's Little Dividend* (MGM, 1951), *A Place in the Sun* (Par., 1951), *Quo Vadis* (MGM, 1951),* *Ivanhoe* (MGM, 1952), *The Girl Who Had Everything* (MGM, 1953), *Rhapsody* (MGM, 1954), *Elephant Walk* (Par., 1954), *Beau Brummel* (MGM, 1954), *The Last Time I Saw Paris* (MGM, 1954), *Giant* (WB, 1956), *Raintree County* (MGM, 1957), *Cat on a Hot Tin Roof* (MGM, 1958), *Suddenly, Last Summer* (Col., 1959), *Scent of Mystery* (Michael Todd, Jr., 1960),* *Butterfield 8* (MGM, 1960), *Cleopatra* (20th, 1963), *The V.I.P.'s* (MGM, 1963), *The Sandpiper* (MGM, 1965), *Who's Afraid of Virginia Woolf?* (WB, 1966), *The Taming of the Shrew* (Col., 1967), *Reflections in a Golden Eye* (WB-7 Arts, 1967), *The Comedians* (MGM, 1967), *Dr. Faustus* (Col., 1968), *Boom* (Univ., 1968).

*Unbilled guest appearance

ROBERT TAYLOR (Spangler Arlington Brough) Born August 5, 1911, Finley, Nebraska. Married Barbara Stanwyck (1939); divorced 1952. Married Ursula Thiess (1954), children: Terence, Tessa.

Feature Films: *Handy Andy* (Fox, 1934), *There's Always Tomorrow* (Univ., 1934), *Wicked Woman* (MGM, 1934), *Society Doctor* (MGM, 1935), *West Point of the Air* (MGM, 1935), *Times Square Lady* (MGM, 1935), *Murder in the Fleet* (MGM, 1935), *Broadway Melody of 1936* (MGM, 1935), *Magnificent Obsession* (Univ., 1935), *Small Town Girl* (MGM, 1936), *Private Number* (20th, 1936), *His Brother's Wife* (MGM, 1936), *The Gorgeous Hussy* (MGM, 1936), *Camille* (MGM, 1936), *Personal Property* (MGM, 1937), *This Is My Affair* (20th, 1937), *Broadway Melody of 1938* (MGM, 1937), *A Yank at Oxford* (MGM, 1938), *Three Comrades* (MGM, 1938), *The Crowd*

Robert Taylor, Nat Pendleton and Ted Healy in *Murder in the Fleet.*

Roars (MGM, 1938), *Stand Up and Fight* (MGM, 1939), *Lucky Night* (MGM, 1939), *Lady of the Tropics* (MGM, 1939), *Remember?* (MGM, 1939), *Waterloo Bridge* (MGM, 1940), *Escape* (MGM, 1940), *Flight Command* (MGM, 1940), *Billy the Kid* (MGM, 1941), *When Ladies Meet* (MGM, 1941), *Johnny Eager* (MGM, 1942), *Her Cardboard Lover* (MGM, 1942), *Stand by for Action* (MGM, 1943), *The Youngest Profession* (MGM, 1943),* *Bataan* (MGM, 1943), *Song of Russia* (MGM, 1944), *Undercurrent* (MGM, 1946), *The High Wall* (MGM, 1947), *The Secret Land* (narrator; MGM, 1948), *The Bribe* (MGM, 1949), *Ambush* (MGM, 1949), *Devil's Doorway* (MGM, 1950), *Conspirator* (MGM, 1950), *Quo Vadis* (MGM, 1951), *Westward the Women* (MGM, 1951), *Ivanhoe* (MGM, 1952), *Above and Beyond* (MGM, 1952), *I Love Melvin* (MGM, 1953),* *Ride, Vaquero!* (MGM, 1953), *All the Brothers Were Valiant* (MGM, 1953), *Knights of the Round Table* (MGM, 1953), *Valley of the Kings* (MGM, 1954), *Rogue Cop* (MGM, 1954), *Many Rivers to Cross* (MGM, 1955), *Quentin Durward* (MGM, 1955), *The Last Hunt* (MGM, 1956), *D-Day, the Sixth of June* (20th, 1956), *The Power and the Prize* (MGM, 1956), *Tip on a Dead Jockey* (MGM, 1957), *Saddle the Wind* (MGM, 1958), *The Law and Jake Wade* (MGM, 1958), *Party Girl* (MGM, 1958), *The Hangman* (Par., 1959), *The House of the Seven Hawks* (MGM, 1959), *Killers of Kilimanjaro* (Col., 1960), *The Miracle of the White Stallions* (BV, 1963), *Cattle King* (MGM, 1963), *A House Is Not a Home* (Embassy, 1964), *The Night Walker* (Univ., 1965), *Savage Pampas* (Daca, 1966), *Johnny Tiger* (Univ., 1966), *Where Angels Go...Trouble Follows* (Col., 1968), *The Day the Hot Line Got Hot* (AIP, 1968), *Devil May Care* (Feature Film Corp. of America, 1968), *The Glass Sphinx* (AIP, 1968).

*Unbilled guest appearance

ROD TAYLOR (Rodney Taylor) Born June 11, 1930, Sydney, Australia. Married Mary Hilem (1954), child: Felicia.

English-Language Feature Films: *Long John Silver* (DCA, 1955), *The Virgin Queen* (20th, 1955), *Top Gun* (UA, 1955), *Hell on Frisco Bay* (WB, 1955), *World Without End* (AA, 1956), *The Rack* (MGM,

Richard Anderson, Rock Hudson, Rod Taylor and Henry Silva in *A Gathering of Eagles.*

1956), *The Catered Affair* (MGM, 1956), *King of the Coral Sea* (AA, 1956), *Giant* (WB, 1956), *Raintree County* (MGM, 1957), *Step Down to Terror* (Univ., 1958), *Separate Tables* (UA, 1958), *Ask Any Girl* (MGM, 1959), *The Time Machine* (MGM, 1960), *One Hundred and One Dalmatians* (voice only; BV, 1961), *Seven Seas to Calais* (MGM, 1963), *The Birds* (Univ., 1963), *A Gathering of Eagles* (Univ., 1963), *The V.I.P.'s* (MGM, 1963), *Sunday in New York* (MGM, 1963), *Fate Is the Hunter* (20th, 1964), *36 Hours* (MGM, 1964), *Young Cassidy* (MGM, 1965), *Do Not Disturb* (20th, 1965), *The Glass-Bottom Boat* (MGM, 1966), *The Liquidator* (MGM, 1966), *Hotel* (WB, 1967), *Chuka* (Par., 1967), *Dark of the Sun* (MGM, 1968), *A Time for Heroes* (Univ., 1968), *The High Commissioner* (Selmur, 1968), *Nobody Runs Forever* (Rank, 1968).

SHIRLEY TEMPLE (Shirley Jane Temple) Born April 23, 1928, Santa Monica, California. Married John Agar (1945), child: Linda Susan; divorced 1949. Married Charles Black (1950), child: Lori.

Claire Trevor and Shirley Temple in *Baby Take a Bow*.

Feature Films: *The Red-Haired Alibi* (Capitol Film Exchange, 1932), *To the Last Man* (Par., 1933), *Out All Night* (Univ., 1933), *Carolina* (Fox, 1934), *Mandalay* (WB, 1934), *Stand Up and Cheer* (Fox, 1934), *Now I'll Tell* (Fox, 1934), *Change of Heart* (Fox, 1934), *Little Miss Marker* (Par., 1934), *Baby Take a Bow* (Fox, 1934), *Now and Forever* (Par., 1934), *Bright Eyes* (Fox, 1934), *The Little Colonel* (Fox, 1935), *Our Little Girl* (Fox, 1935), *Curly Top* (Fox, 1935), *The Littlest Rebel* (Fox, 1935), *Captain January* (20th, 1936), *Poor Little Rich Girl* (20th, 1936), *Dimples* (20th, 1936), *Stowaway* (20th, 1936), *Wee Willie Winkie* (20th, 1937), *Heidi* (20th, 1937), *Rebecca of Sunnybrook Farm* (20th, 1938), *Little Miss Broadway* (20th, 1938), *Just Around the Corner* (20th, 1938), *The Little Princess* (20th, 1939), *Susannah of the Mounties* (20th, 1939), *The Blue Bird* (20th, 1940), *Young People* (20th, 1940), *Kathleen* (MGM, 1941), *Miss Annie Rooney* (UA, 1942), *Since You Went Away* (UA, 1944), *I'll Be Seeing You* (UA, 1944), *Kiss and Tell* (Col., 1945), *Honeymoon* (RKO, 1947), *The Bachelor and the Bobby-Soxer* (RKO, 1947), *That Hagen Girl* (WB, 1947), *Fort Apache* (RKO, 1948), *Mr. Belvedere Goes to College* (20th, 1949), *Adventure in Baltimore* (RKO, 1949), *Story of Seabiscuit* (WB, 1949), *A Kiss for Corliss* (UA, 1949).

PHYLLIS THAXTER (Phyllis St. Felix Thaxter) Born November 20, 1920, Portland, Maine. Married James Aubrey (1944), children: Susan, James; divorced 1962. Married Gilbert Lea (1962).

Hank Daniels, Phyllis Thaxter and Sharon McManus in *Bewitched*.

Feature Films: *Thirty Seconds Over Tokyo* (MGM, 1944), *Bewitched* (MGM, 1945), *Weekend at the Waldorf* (MGM, 1945), *The Sea of Grass* (MGM, 1947), *Living in a Big Way* (MGM, 1947), *The Sign of the Ram* (Col., 1948), *Tenth Avenue Angel* (MGM, 1948), *Blood on the Moon* (RKO, 1948), *Act of Violence* (MGM, 1948), *No Man of Her Own* (Par., 1950), *The Breaking Point* (WB, 1950), *Fort Worth* (WB, 1951), *Jim Thorpe—All American* (WB, 1951), *Come Fill the Cup* (WB, 1951), *She's Working Her Way Through College* (WB, 1952), *Springfield Rifle* (WB, 1952), *Operation Secret* (WB, 1952), *Women's Prison* (Col., 1955), *Man Afraid* (Univ., 1957), *The World of Henry Orient* (UA, 1964).

GENE TIERNEY (Gene Eliza Taylor Tierney) Born November 20, 1920, Brooklyn, New York. Married Oleg Cassini (1941), children: Daria, Christina; divorced 1952. Married W. Howard Lee (1960).

Gene Tierney, Tyrone Power and Isabel Randolph in *That Wonderful Urge*.

Feature Films: *Return of Frank James* (20th, 1940), *Hudson's Bay* (20th, 1940), *Tobacco Road* (20th, 1941), *Belle Starr* (20th, 1941), *Sundown* (UA, 1941), *The Shanghai Gesture* (UA, 1941), *Son of Fury* (20th, 1942), *Rings on Her Fingers* (20th, 1942), *Thunder Birds* (20th, 1942), *China Girl* (20th, 1942), *Heaven Can Wait* (20th, 1943), *Laura* (20th, 1944), *A Bell for Adano* (20th, 1945), *Leave Her to Heaven* (20th, 1945), *Dragonwyck* (20th, 1946), *The Razor's Edge* (20th, 1946), *The Ghost and Mrs. Muir* (20th, 1947), *The Iron Curtain* (20th, 1948), *That Wonderful Urge* (20th, 1948), *Whirlpool* (20th, 1949), *Night and the City* (20th, 1950), *Where the Sidewalk Ends* (20th, 1950), *The Mating Season* (Par., 1951), *On The Riviera* (20th, 1951), *The Secret of Convict Lake* (20th, 1951), *Close to My Heart* (WB, 1951), *Way of a Gaucho* (20th, 1952), *Plymouth Adventure* (MGM, 1952), *Never Let Me Go* (MGM, 1953), *Personal Affair* (UA, 1954), *Black Widow* (20th, 1954),

The Egyptian (20th, 1954), *The Left Hand of God* (20th, 1955), *Advise and Consent* (Col., 1962), *Toys in the Attic* (UA, 1963), *The Pleasure Seekers* (20th, 1964).

GENEVIEVE TOBIN Born November 29, 1904, New York, New York. Married William Keighley (1938).

Adolphe Menjou, Genevieve Tobin and Mary Astor in *Easy to Love*.

Feature Films: *A Lady Surrenders* (Univ., 1930), *Free Love* (Univ., 1930), *Seed* (Univ., 1931), *Up for Murder* (Univ., 1931), *Woman Pursued* (RKO, 1931), *The Gay Diplomat* (RKO, 1931), *One Hour With You* (Par., 1932), *Hollywood Speaks* (Col., 1932), *Cohens and Kellys in Hollywood* (Univ., 1932), *Infernal Machine* (Fox, 1933), *Perfect Understanding* (UA, 1933), *Pleasure Cruise* (Fox, 1933), *The Wrecker* (Col., 1933), *Goodbye Again* (WB, 1933), *I Loved a Woman* (WB, 1933), *Golden Harvest* (Par., 1933), *The Ninth Guest* (Col., 1934), *Easy to Love* (WB, 1934), *Dark Hazard* (WB, 1934), *Uncertain Lady* (Univ., 1934), *Success at Any Price* (RKO, 1934), *Kiss and Make Up* (Par., 1934), *By Your Leave* (RKO, 1934), *The Woman in Red* (WB, 1935), *The Goose and the Gander* (WB, 1935), *The Case of the Lucky Legs* (WB, 1935), *Here's to Romance* (Fox, 1935), *Broadway Hostess* (WB, 1935), *The Petrified Forest* (WB, 1936), *Snowed Under* (WB, 1936), *The Great Gambini* (Par., 1937), *The Duke Comes Back* (Rep., 1937), *The Man in the Mirror* (Twickenham, 1937), *Kate Plus Ten* (Wainwright-GFD, 1938), *Dramatic School* (MGM, 1938), *Zaza* (Par., 1939), *Yes, My Darling Daughter* (WB, 1939), *Our Neighbors the Carters* (Par., 1939), *No Time for Comedy* (WB, 1940).

THELMA TODD Born July 29, 1905, Lawrence, Massachusetts. Married Pasquale Di Cicco (1932); divorced 1934. Died December 16, 1935.

Sound Feature Films: *The Haunted House* (WB, 1928), *Naughty Baby* (WB, 1929), *Seven Footprints to Satan* (WB, 1929), *Bachelor Girl* (Col., 1929), *Careers* (WB, 1929), *House of Horror* (WB, 1929), *Her Private Life* (WB, 1929), *Follow Through* (Par., 1930), *Her Man* (Pathé, 1930), *Command Performance* (Tif., 1930), *Aloha* (Tif., 1930), *Swanee River* (World Wide, 1930), *No Limit* (Par., 1930), *The Hot Heiress* (WB, 1931), *Corsair* (UA, 1931),* *Broad-Minded* (WB, 1931), *Monkey Business* (Par., 1931), *The Maltese Falcon* (WB, 1931), *Beyond Victory* (Pathé, 1931), *This Is the Night* (Par., 1932), *Speak Easily* (MGM, 1932), *Horse Feathers* (Par., 1932), *Klondike* (Mon., 1932), *Big Timer* (Col., 1932), *Call Her Savage* (Fox, 1932), *Air Hostess* (Col., 1933), *Deception* (Col., 1933), *Devil's Brother* (MGM, 1933), *Cheating Blondes* (Capitol Film Exchange, 1933), *Mary Stevens, M.D.* (WB, 1933), *Counsellor at Law* (Univ., 1933), *Sitting Pretty* (Par., 1933), *Son of a Sailor* (WB, 1933), *Palooka* (UA, 1934), *Hips, Hips, Hooray* (RKO, 1934),

Thelma Todd, Chico and Groucho Marx in *Horse Feathers*.

Bottoms Up (Fox, 1934), *The Poor Rich* (Univ., 1934), *Cockeyed Cavaliers* (RKO, 1934), *Take the Stand* (Liberty, 1934), *Lightning Strikes Twice* (RKO, 1935), *After the Dance* (Col., 1935), *Two for Tonight* (Par., 1935), *The Bohemian Girl* (MGM, 1936).

*Billed as Alison Lloyd

SIDNEY TOLER Born April 28, 1874, Warrenburg, Missouri. Married Viva Tattersal. Died February 12, 1947.

Feature Films: *Madame X* (MGM, 1929), *White Shoulders* (RKO, 1931), *Strictly Dishonorable* (Univ., 1931), *Strangers in Love* (Par., 1932), *Is My Face Red?* (RKO, 1932), *Radio Patrol* (Univ., 1932), *Speak Easily* (MGM, 1932), *Blondie of the Follies* (MGM, 1932), *Blonde Venus* (Par., 1932), *Phantom President* (Par., 1932), *Tom Brown of Culver* (Univ., 1932), *Billion Dollar Scandal* (Par., 1933), *King of the Jungle* (Par., 1933), *He Learned About Women* (Par., 1933), *The Narrow Corner* (WB, 1933), *Way to Love* (Par., 1933), *Dark Hazard* (WB, 1934), *Massacre* (WB, 1934), *Spitfire* (RKO, 1934), *The Trumpet Blows* (Par., 1934), *Here Comes the Groom* (Par., 1934), *Operator 13* (MGM, 1934), *Registered Nurse* (WB, 1934), *Upper World* (WB, 1934), *The Daring Young Man* (Fox, 1935), *Call of the Wild* (UA, 1935), *Orchids to You* (Fox, 1935), *Champagne for Breakfast* (Col., 1935), *This Is the Life* (Fox, 1935), *The Three Godfathers* (MGM, 1936), *Give Us This Night* (Par., 1936), *The Longest Night* (MGM, 1936), *The Gorgeous Hussy* (MGM, 1936), *Our Relations* (MGM, 1936), *That Certain Woman* (WB, 1937), *Double Wedding* (MGM, 1937), *Gold Is Where You Find It* (WB, 1938), *Wide Open Faces* (Col., 1938), *One Wild Night* (20th, 1938), *Charlie Chan in Honolulu* (20th, 1938), *Up the River* (20th, 1938), *Mysterious Rider* (Par., 1938), *If I Were King* (Par., 1938), *King of Chinatown* (Par., 1939), *Disbarred* (Par., 1939), *Heritage of the Desert* (Par., 1939), *The Kid From Kokomo* (WB, 1939), *Charlie Chan in Reno* (20th, 1939), *Charlie Chan at Treasure Island* (20th, 1939), *Law of the Pampas* (Par., 1939), *Charlie Chan in City in Darkness*

Sidney Toler, Joseph Crehan and Gloria Warren in *Dangerous Money*.

Franchot Tone, Joan Crawford and Robert Young in *Today We Live*.

(20th, 1939), *Charlie Chan in Panama* (20th, 1940), *Charlie Chan's Murder Cruise* (20th, 1940), *Charlie Chan at the Wax Museum* (20th, 1940), *Murder Over New York* (20th, 1940), *Dead Men Tell* (20th, 1941), *Charlie Chan in Rio* (20th, 1941), *Castle in the Desert* (20th, 1942), *A Night to Remember* (Col., 1943), *White Savage* (Univ., 1943), *Isle of Forgotten Sins* (PRC, 1943), *Charlie Chan in the Secret Service* (Mon., 1944), *The Chinese Cat* (Mon., 1944), *Black Magic* (Mon., 1944), *The Scarlet Clue* (Mon., 1945), *It's in the Bag* (UA, 1945), *The Jade Mask* (Mon., 1945), *The Shanghai Cobra* (Mon., 1945), *The Red Dragon* (Mon., 1945), *Dark Alibi* (Mon., 1946), *The Trap* (Mon., 1947).

FRANCHOT TONE (Stanislas Pascal Franchot Tone) Born February 27, 1905, Niagara Falls, New York. Married Joan Crawford (1935); divorced 1939. Married Jean Wallace (1941); divorced 1948. Married Barbara Payton (1951); divorced 1952. Married Dolores Dorn-Heft (1956); divorced 1959.

Feature Films: *The Wiser Sex* (Par., 1932), *Gabriel Over the White House* (MGM, 1933), *Dancing Lady* (MGM, 1933), *Today We Live* (MGM, 1933), *Stage Mother* (MGM, 1933), *Bombshell* (MGM, 1933), *The Stranger's Return* (MGM, 1933), *Midnight Mary* (MGM, 1933), *Moulin Rouge* (UA, 1934), *The World Moves On* (Fox, 1934), *Straight Is the Way* (MGM, 1934), *Gentlemen Are Born* (WB, 1934), *The Girl From Missouri* (MGM, 1934), *Sadie McKee* (MGM, 1934), *Lives of a Bengal Lancer* (Par., 1935), *Mutiny on the Bounty* (MGM, 1935), *Reckless* (MGM, 1935), *No More Ladies* (MGM, 1935), *Dangerous* (WB, 1935), *One New York Night* (MGM, 1935), *Exclusive Story* (MGM, 1936), *The King Steps Out* (Col., 1936), *The Unguarded Hour* (MGM, 1936), *The Gorgeous Hussy* (MGM, 1936), *Between Two Women* (MGM, 1937), *The Bride Wore Red* (MGM, 1937), *They Gave Him a Gun* (MGM, 1937), *Quality Street* (RKO, 1937), *Three Comrades* (MGM, 1938), *Love Is a Headache* (MGM, 1938), *Man-Proof* (MGM, 1938), *Three Loves Has Nancy* (MGM, 1938), *Thunder Afloat* (MGM, 1939), *Fast and Furious* (MGM, 1939), *Trail of the Vigilantes* (Univ., 1940), *Nice Girl?* (Univ., 1941), *Highly Irregular* (Col., 1941), *She Knew All the Answers* (Col., 1941), *Virginia* (Par., 1941), *Star Spangled Rhythm* (Par., 1942), *His Butler's Sister* (Univ., 1943), *This Woman Is Mine* (Univ., 1943), *Five Graves to Cairo* (Par., 1943), *The Hour Before Dawn* (Par., 1944), *Phantom Lady* (Univ., 1944), *Dark Waters* (UA, 1944), *Her Husband's Affair* (Col., 1947), *Every Girl Should Be Married* (RKO, 1948), *I Love Trouble* (Col., 1948), *Jigsaw* (UA, 1949), *The Man on the Eiffel Tower* (RKO, 1949), *Without Honor* (UA, 1949), *Here Comes the Groom* (Par., 1951), *Uncle Vanya* (Continental Distributing, 1958), *Advise and Consent* (Col., 1962), *In Harm's Way* (Par., 1965), *Mickey One* (Col., 1965).

AUDREY TOTTER Born December 20, 1918, Joliet, Illinois. Married Leo Fred (1952), child: Mea.

Feature Films: *Main Street After Dark* (MGM, 1944), *Dangerous*

Brian Donlevy and Audrey Totter in *The Beginning or the End.*

Partners (MGM, 1945), *Her Highness and the Bellboy* (MGM, 1945), *The Sailor Takes a Wife* (MGM, 1945), *Adventure* (MGM, 1945), *The Hidden Eye* (MGM, 1945), *The Secret Heart* MGM, 1946), *The Postman Always Rings Twice* (MGM, 1946), *The Cockeyed Miracle* (MGM, 1946), *Lady in the Lake* (MGM, 1946), *The Beginning or the End* (MGM, 1947), *The Unsuspected* (WB, 1947), *High Wall* (MGM, 1947), *Tenth Avenue Angel* (MGM, 1948), *The Saxon Charm* (Univ., 1948), *The Set-Up* (RKO, 1949), *Alias Nick Beal* (Par., 1949), *Any Number Can Play* (MGM, 1949), *Tension* (MGM, 1949), *Under the Gun* (Univ., 1950), *The Blue Veil* (RKO, 1951), *FBI Girl* (Lip., 1951), *The Sellout* (MGM, 1951), *Assignment—Paris* (Col., 1952), *My Pal Gus* (20th, 1952), *The Woman They Almost Lynched* (Rep., 1953), *Man in the Dark* (Col., 1953), *Cruisin' Down the River* (Col., 1953), *Mission Over Korea* (Col., 1953), *Champ for a Day* (Rep., 1953), *Massacre Canyon* (Col., 1954), *A Bullet for Joey* (UA, 1955), *Women's Prison* (Col., 1955), *The Vanishing American* (Rep., 1955), *Ghost Diver* (20th, 1957), *Jet Attack* (AIP, 1958), *Man or Gun* (Rep., 1958), *The Carpetbaggers* (Par., 1964), *Harlow* (Magna, 1965), *Chubasco* (WB-7 Arts, 1968).).

LEE TRACY Born April 14, 1898, Atlanta, Georgia. Married Helen Thomas (1938).

Feature Films: *Big Time* (Fox, 1929), *Born Reckless* (Fox, 1930), *Liliom* (Fox, 1930), *She Got What She Wanted* (Tif. 1930), *The Strange Love of Molly Louvain* (WB, 1932), *Love Is a Racket* (WB, 1932), *Doctor X* (WB, 1932), *Blessed Event* (WB, 1932), *Washington Merry-Go-Round* (Col., 1932), *Night Mayor* (Col., 1932), *Half-Naked Truth* (RKO, 1932), *Clear All Wires* (MGM, 1933), *Private Jones* (Univ., 1933), *The Nuisance* (MGM, 1933), *Dinner at Eight* (MGM, 1933), *Turn Back the Clock* (MGM, 1933), *Bombshell* (MGM, 1933), *Advice to the Lovelorn* (UA, 1933), *I'll Tell the World* (Univ., 1934), *You Belong to Me* (Par., 1934), *Lemon Drop Kid* (Par., 1934), *Carnival* (Col., 1935), *Two Fisted* (Par., 1935), *Sutter's Gold* (Univ., 1936), *Wanted—Jane Turner* (RKO, 1936), *Criminal Lawyer* (RKO, 1937), *Behind the Headlines* (RKO, 1937), *Crashing Hollywood* (RKO, 1938), *Fixer Dugan* (RKO, 1939), *Spellbinder* (RKO, 1939), *Millionaires in*

Benita Hume and Lee Tracy in *Clear All Wires.*

Spencer Tracy and Gladys George in *They Gave Him a Gun*.

Prison (RKO, 1940), *The Payoff* (PRC, 1942), *Power of the Press* (Col., 1943), *Betrayal from the East* (RKO, 1945), *I'll Tell the World* (Univ., 1945), *High Tide* (Mon., 1947), *The Best Man* (UA, 1964).

SPENCER TRACY Born April 5, 1900, Milwaukee, Wisconsin. Married Louise Treadwell (1928), children: John, Susan. Died June 10, 1967.

Feature Films: *Up the River* (Fox, 1930), *Quick Millions* (Fox, 1931), *Six Cylinder Love* (Fox, 1931), *Goldie* (Fox, 1931), *She Wanted a Millionaire* (Fox, 1932), *Sky Devils* (UA, 1932), *Disorderly Conduct* (Fox, 1932), *Young America* (Fox, 1932), *Society Girl* (Fox, 1932), *Painted Woman* (Fox, 1932), *Me and My Gal* (Fox, 1932), *20,000 Years in Sing Sing* (WB, 1933), *Face in the Sky* (Fox, 1933), *The Power and the Glory* (Fox, 1933), *Shanghai Madness* (Fox, 1933), *The Mad Game* (Fox, 1933), *Man's Castle* (Col., 1933), *Looking for Trouble* (UA, 1934), *The Show-Off* (MGM, 1934), *Bottoms Up* (Fox, 1934), *Now I'll Tell* (Fox, 1934), *Marie Galante* (Fox, 1934), *It's a Small World* (Fox, 1935), *Murder Man* (MGM, 1935), *Dante's Inferno* (Fox, 1935), *Whipsaw* (MGM, 1935), *Riffraff* (MGM, 1936), *Fury* (MGM, 1936), *San Francisco* (MGM, 1936), *Libeled Lady* (MGM, 1936), *Captains Courageous* (MGM, 1937), *They Gave Him a Gun* (MGM, 1937), *The Big City* (MGM, 1937), *Mannequin* (MGM, 1938), *Test Pilot* (MGM, 1938), *Boys Town* (MGM, 1938), *Stanley and Livingstone* (20th, 1939), *I Take This Woman* (MGM, 1940), *Northwest Passage* (MGM, 1940), *Edison the Man* (MGM, 1940), *Boom Town* (MGM, 1940), *Men of Boys Town* (MGM, 1941), *Dr. Jekyll and Mr. Hyde* (MGM, 1941), *Woman of the Year* (MGM, 1942), *Tortilla Flat* (MGM, 1942), *Keeper of the Flame* (MGM, 1942), *A Guy Named Joe* (MGM, 1943), *The Seventh Cross* (MGM, 1944), *Thirty Seconds Over Tokyo* (MGM, 1944), *Without Love* (MGM, 1945), *The Sea of Grass* (MGM, 1947), *Cass Timberlane* (MGM, 1947), *State of the Union* (MGM, 1948), *Edward, My Son* (MGM, 1949), *Adam's Rib* (MGM, 1949), *Malaya* (MGM, 1949), *Father of the Bride* (MGM, 1950), *Father's Little Dividend* (MGM, 1951), *The People Against O'Hara* (MGM, 1951), *Pat and Mike* (MGM, 1952), *Plymouth Adventure* (MGM, 1952), *The Actress* (MGM, 1954), *Broken Lance* (20th, 1954), *Bad Day at Black Rock* (MGM, 1955), *The Mountain* (Par., 1956), *The Desk Set* (20th, 1957), *The Old Man and the Sea* (WB, 1958), *The Last Hurrah* (Col., 1958), *Inherit the Wind* (UA, 1960), *The Devil at 4 O'Clock* (Col., 1961), *Judgment at Nuremberg* (UA, 1961), *How the West Was Won* (MGM, 1963), *It's a Mad, Mad, Mad, Mad World* (UA, 1963), *Guess Who's Coming to Dinner* (Col., 1967).

ARTHUR TREACHER (Arthur Veary) Born July 23, 1894, Brighton, England. Married Virginia Taylor (1940).

Feature Films: *Battle of Paris* (Par., 1929), *Alice in Wonderland* (Par., 1933), *Fashions of 1934* (WB, 1934), *Desirable* (WB, 1934), *Viva Villa!* (MGM, 1934), *Madame Du Barry* (WB, 1934), *The Captain Hates the Sea* (Col., 1934), *Here Comes the Groom* (Par., 1934), *Holly-*

Eugene Pallette and Arthur Treacher in *She Had to Eat*.

wood Party (MGM, 1934), *Forsaking All Others* (MGM, 1934), *Bordertown* (WB, 1935), *No More Ladies* (MGM, 1935), *David Copperfield* (MGM, 1935), *Cardinal Richelieu* (UA, 1935), *I Live My Life* (MGM, 1935), *Personal Maid's Secret* (WB, 1935), *Bright Lights* (WB, 1935), *Curly Top* (Fox, 1935), *Remember Last Night?* (Univ., 1935), *Let's Live Tonight* (Col., 1935), *The Daring Young Man* (Fox, 1935), *Splendor* (UA, 1935), *Hitch-Hike Lady* (Rep., 1935), *A Midsummer Night's Dream* (WB, 1935), *Go Into Your Dance* (WB, 1935), *The Winning Ticket* (MGM, 1935), *Stowaway* (20th, 1936), *Anything Goes* (Par., 1936), *Thank You, Jeeves* (20th, 1936), *Heidi* (20th, 1937), *Mad About Music* (Univ., 1938), *The Little Princess* (20th, 1939), *Brother Rat and a Baby* (WB, 1940), *Star Spangled Rhythm* (Par., 1942), *The Amazing Mrs. Holliday* (Univ., 1943), *Forever and a Day* (RKO, 1943), *Chip Off the Old Block* (Univ., 1944), *National Velvet* (MGM, 1944), *Delightfully Dangerous* (UA, 1945), *The Countess of Monte Cristo* (Univ., 1948), *That Midnight Kiss* (MGM, 1949), *Mary Poppins* (BV, 1964).

CLAIRE TREVOR (Claire Wemlinger) Born March 8, 1912, Bensonhurst, New York. Married Clark Andrews (1938); divorced 1942. Married Cylos Dunsmoore (1943), child: Charles; divorced 1947. Married Milton Bren (1948).

Feature Films: *Life in the Raw* (Fox, 1933), *The Last Trail* (Fox, 1933), *The Mad Game* (Fox, 1933), *Jimmy and Sally* (Fox, 1933), *Hold That Girl* (Fox, 1934), *Wild Gold* (Fox, 1934), *Baby Take a Bow* (Fox, 1934), *Elinor Norton* (Fox, 1934), *Spring Tonic* (Fox, 1935), *Black Sheep* (Fox, 1935), *Dante's Inferno* (Fox, 1935), *Navy Wife* (Fox, 1935), *My Marriage* (20th, 1936), *The Song and Dance Man* (20th, 1936), *Human Cargo* (20th, 1936), *To Mary—With Love* (20th, 1936), *Star for a Night* (20th, 1936), *15 Maiden Lane* (20th, 1936), *Career Woman* (20th, 1936), *Time Out for Romance* (20th, 1937), *King of Gamblers* (Par., 1937), *One Mile From Heaven* (20th, 1937), *Dead End* (UA, 1937), *Second Honeymoon* (20th, 1937), *Big Town Girl* (20th, 1937), *Walking Down Broadway* (20th, 1938), *Two of a Kind* (20th, 1938), *The Amazing Dr. Clitterhouse* (WB, 1938), *Valley of the Giants* (WB, 1938), *Stagecoach* (UA, 1939), *I Stole a Million* (Univ., 1939), *Alle-*

Claire Trevor and Fred MacMurray in *Borderline*.

gheny Uprising (RKO, 1939), *Dark Command* (Rep., 1940), *Texas* (Col., 1941), *Honky Tonk* (MGM, 1941), *The Adventures of Martin Eden* (Col., 1942), *Crossroads* (MGM, 1942), *Street of Chance* (Par., 1942), *The Desperadoes* (Col., 1943), *Good Luck, Mr. Yates* (Col., 1943), *Woman of the Town* (UA, 1943), *Murder, My Sweet* (RKO, 1944), *Johnny Angel* (RKO, 1945), *Crack-Up* (RKO, 1946), *The Bachelor's Daughters* (UA, 1946), *Born to Kill* (RKO, 1947), *Raw Deal* (EL, 1948), *Key Largo* (WB, 1948), *The Velvet Touch* (RKO, 1948), *The Babe Ruth Story* (AA, 1948), *The Lucky Stiff* (UA, 1949), *Borderline* (Univ., 1950), *Best of the Badmen* (RKO, 1951), *Hard, Fast and Beautiful* (RKO, 1951), *Hoodlum Empire* (Rep., 1952), *My Man and I* (MGM, 1952), *Stop, You're Killing Me* (WB, 1952), *The Stranger Wore a Gun* (Col., 1953), *The High and the Mighty* (WB, 1954), *Man Without a Star* (Univ., 1955), *Lucy Gallant* (Par., 1955), *The Mountain* (Par., 1956), *Marjorie Morningstar* (WB, 1958), *Two Weeks in Another Town* (MGM, 1962), *The Stripper* (20th, 1963), *How to Murder Your Wife* (UA, 1965).

SONNY TUFTS (Bowen Charleston Tufts III) Born July 16, 1912, Boston, Massachusetts. Married Barbara Dare (1937); divorced.

Olivia De Havilland and Sonny Tufts in *Government Girl*.

Feature Films: *So Proudly We Hail!* (Par., 1943), *Government Girl* (RKO, 1943), *I Love a Soldier* (Par., 1944), *In the Meantime, Darling* (20th, 1944), *Here Come the Waves* (Par., 1944), *Bring on the Girls* (Par., 1945), *Duffy's Tavern* (Par., 1945), *Miss Susie Slagle's* (Par., 1945), *The Well-Groomed Bride* (Par., 1946), *The Virginian* (Par., 1946), *Cross My Heart* (Par., 1946), *Swell Guy* (Univ., 1946), *Easy Come, Easy Go* (Par., 1947), *Blaze of Noon* (Par., 1947), *Variety Girl* (Par., 1947), *The Untamed Breed* (Col., 1948), *The Crooked Way* (UA, 1949), *Easy Living* (RKO, 1949), *The Gift Horse* ("Glory at Sea"—Compton Bennett, 1952), *Run for the Hills* (Jack Broder, 1953), *No Escape* (UA, 1953), *Cat Women of the Moon* (Astor, 1953), *Serpent Island* (Astor, 1954), *The Seven Year Itch* (20th, 1955), *Come Next Spring* (Rep., 1956), *The Parson and the Outlaw* (Col., 1957), *Town Tamer* (Par., 1965), *Cottonpickin' Chickenpickers* (Southeastern Pictures, 1967).

LANA TURNER (Julia Jean Mildred Frances Turner) Born February 8, 1920, Wallace, Idaho. Married Artie Shaw (1940); divorced 1941. Married Stephen Crane (1942), child: Cheryl; divorced 1944. Married Bob Topping (1948); divorced 1952. Married Lex Barker (1953); divorced 1957. Married Fred May (1960); divorced 1962. Married Robert Eaton (1965).

Feature Films: *A Star Is Born* (UA, 1937), *They Won't Forget* (WB, 1937), *The Great Garrick* (WB, 1937), *The Adventures of Marco Polo* (UA, 1938), *Four's a Crowd* (WB, 1938), *Love Finds Andy Hardy* (MGM, 1938), *Rich Man, Poor Girl* (MGM, 1938), *Dramatic School* (MGM, 1938), *Calling Dr. Kildare* (MGM, 1939), *These Glamour*

Richard Carlson, Lana Turner and Monty Woolley in *Dancing Co-Ed*.

Girls (MGM, 1939), *Dancing Co-ed* (MGM, 1939), *Two Girls on Broadway* (MGM, 1940), *We Who Are Young* (MGM, 1940), *Ziegfeld Girl* (MGM, 1941), *Dr. Jekyll and Mr. Hyde* (MGM, 1941), *Honky Tonk* (MGM, 1941), *Johnny Eager* (MGM, 1941), *Somewhere I'll Find You* (MGM, 1942), *The Youngest Profession* (MGM, 1943), *Slightly Dangerous* (MGM, 1943), *Du Barry Was a Lady* (MGM, 1943),* *Marriage Is a Private Affair* (MGM, 1944), *Keep Your Powder Dry* (MGM, 1945), *Weekend at the Waldorf* (MGM, 1945), *The Postman Always Ring Twice* (MGM, 1946), *Green Dolphin Street* (MGM, 1947), *Cass Timberlane* (MGM, 1947), *Homecoming* (MGM, 1948), *The Three Musketeers* (MGM, 1948), *A Life of Her Own* (MGM, 1950), *Mr. Imperium* (MGM, 1951), *The Merry Widow* (MGM, 1952), *The Bad and the Beautiful* (MGM, 1952), *Latin Lovers* (MGM, 1953), *Flame and the Flesh* (MGM, 1954), *Betrayed* (MGM, 1954), *The Prodigal* (MGM, 1955), *The Sea Chase* (WB, 1955), *The Rains of Ranchipur* (20th, 1955), *Diane* (MGM, 1955), *Peyton Place* (20th, 1957), *The Lady Takes a Flyer* (Univ., 1958), *Another Time, Another Place* (Par., 1958), *Imitation of Life* (Univ., 1959), *Portrait in Black* (Univ., 1960), *By Love Possessed* (UA, 1961), *Bachelor in Paradise* (MGM, 1961), *Who's Got the Action?* (Par., 1962), *Love Has Many Faces* (Col., 1965), *Madame X* (Univ., 1966).

*Unbilled guest appearance

JO VAN FLEET Born December 30, 1919, Oakland, California. Married William Bales (1946), child: Michael.

James Dean and Jo Van Fleet in *East of Eden*.

Feature Films: *East of Eden* (WB, 1955), *The Rose Tattoo* (Par., 1955), *I'll Cry Tomorrow* (MGM, 1955), *The King and Four Queens* (UA, 1956), *Gunfight at the O.K. Corral* (Par., 1957), *This Angry Age* (Col., 1958), *Wild River* (20th, 1960), *Cool Hand Luke* (WB-7 Arts), *I Love You, Alice B. Toklas* (WB-7 Arts, 1968).

LUPE VELEZ (Guadeloupe Velez de Villalobos) Born July 18, 1908, San Luis de Potosí, Mexico. Married Johnny Weissmuller (1933); divorced 1938. Died December 14, 1944.

Lupe Velez and Leon Errol in *The Girl From Mexico*.

Sound Feature Films: *Lady of the Pavements* (UA, 1929), *Tiger Rose* (WB, 1929), *Wolf Song* (Par., 1929), *Where East Is East* (MGM, 1929), *The Storm* (Univ., 1930), *Hell Harbor* (UA, 1930), *East Is West* (Univ., 1930), *Resurrection* (Univ., 1931), *The Squaw Man* (MGM, 1931), *Cuban Love Song* (MGM, 1931), *The Broken Wing* (Par., 1932), *Kongo* (MGM, 1932), *The Half-Naked Truth* (RKO, 1932), *Hot Pepper* (Fox, 1933), *Mr. Broadway* (Broadway-Hollywood Productions, 1933), *Laughing Boy* (MGM, 1934), *Palooka* (UA, 1934), *Hollywood Party* (MGM, 1934), *Strictly Dynamite* (RKO, 1934), *The Morals of Marcus* (Twickenham, 1936), *Gypsy Melody* (Associated British Pathé, 1936), *High Flyers* (RKO, 1937), *Mad About Money* ("He Loved an Actress" —British Lion, 1938), *Girl From Mexico* (RKO, 1939), *Mexican Spitfire* (RKO, 1939), *Mexican Spitfire Out West* (RKO, 1940), *Six Lessons From Madame La Zonga* (Univ., 1941), *Mexican Spitfire's Baby* (RKO, 1941), *Playmates* (RKO, 1941), *Honolulu Lu* (Col., 1941), *Mexican Spitfire at Sea* (RKO, 1942), *Mexican Spitfire Sees a Ghost* (RKO, 1942), *Mexican Spitfire's Elephant* (RKO, 1942), *Ladies' Day* (RKO, 1943), *Mexican Spitfire's Blessed Event* (RKO, 1943), *Redhead From Manhattan* (Col., 1943).

VERA-ELLEN (Vera-Ellen Westmeyr Rohe) Born February 16, 1926, Cincinnati, Ohio. Married Robert Hightower (1945); divorced 1946. Married Victor Rothschild (1954).

Feature Films: *Wonder Man* (RKO, 1945), *The Kid From Brooklyn* (RKO, 1946), *Three Little Girls in Blue* (20th, 1946), *Carnival in Costa Rica* (20th, 1947), *Words and Music* (MGM, 1948), *Love Happy* (UA, 1949), *On the Town* (MGM, 1949), *Three Little Words* (MGM, 1950),

Tony Martin and Vera-Ellen in *Let's Be Happy*.

Happy Go Lovely (RKO, 1951), *The Belle of New York* (MGM, 1952), *Call Me Madam* (20th, 1953), *The Big Leaguer* (MGM, 1953), *White Christmas* (Par., 1954), *Let's Be Happy* (AA, 1957).

ROBERT WAGNER Born February 10, 1930, Detroit, Michigan. Married Natalie Wood (1957); divorced 1963. Married Marion Donen (1963), child: Katherine.

Robert Wagner and Steve McQueen in *The War Lover*.

Feature Films: *The Happy Years* (MGM, 1950), *Halls of Montezuma* (20th, 1950), *The Frogmen* (20th, 1951), *Let's Make It Legal* (20th, 1951), *With a Song in My Heart* (20th, 1952), *Stars and Stripes Forever* (20th, 1952), *What Price Glory* (20th, 1952), *The Silver Whip* (20th, 1953), *Titanic* (20th, 1953), *Beneath the 12-Mile Reef* (20th, 1953), *Prince Valiant* (20th, 1954), *Broken Lance* (20th, 1954), *White Feather* (20th, 1955), *A Kiss Before Dying* (UA, 1956), *The Mountain* (Par., 1956), *Between Heaven and Hell* (20th, 1956), *The True Story of Jesse James* (20th, 1957), *Stopover Tokyo* (20th, 1957), *The Hunters* (20th, 1958), *Mardi Gras* (20th, 1958), *In Love and War* (20th, 1958), *Say One for Me* (20th, 1959), *All the Fine Young Cannibals* (MGM, 1960), *Sail a Crooked Ship* (Col., 1961), *The Longest Day* (20th, 1962), *The War Lover* (Col., 1962), *The Condemned of Altona* (20th, 1963), *The Pink Panther* (UA, 1964), *Harper* (WB, 1966), *Banning* (Univ., 1967), *The Biggest Bundle of Them All* (MGM, 1968), *Don't Just Stand There* (Univ., 1968).

ROBERT WALKER (Robert Hudson Walker) Born October 13, 1914, Salt Lake City, Utah. Married Jennifer Jones (1939), children: Robert, Michael; divorced 1945. Married Barbara Ford (1948). Died August 28, 1951.

Feature Films: *Winter Carnival* (UA, 1939), *Bataan* (MGM, 1943), *Madame Curie* (MGM, 1943), *See Here, Private Hargrove* (MGM, 1944), *Since You Went Away* (UA, 1944), *Thirty Seconds Over Tokyo*

Henry Daniell and Robert Walker in *Song of Love*.

(MGM, 1944), *The Clock* (MGM, 1945), *Her Highness and the Bellboy* (MGM, 1945), *What Next, Corporal Hargrove?* (MGM, 1945), *The Sailor Takes a Wife* (MGM, 1945), *Till the Clouds Roll By* (MGM, 1946), *The Sea of Grass* (MGM, 1947), *The Beginning or the End* (MGM, 1947), *Song of Love* (MGM, 1947), *One Touch of Venus* (Univ., 1948), *Please Believe Me* (MGM, 1950), *The Skipper Surprised His Wife* (MGM, 1950), *Vengeance Valley* (MGM, 1951), *Strangers on a Train* (WB, 1951), *My Son, John* (Par., 1952).

Maurice Manson, Eli Wallach and Edward G. Robinson in *Seven Thieves.*

ELI WALLACH Born December 7, 1915, Brooklyn, New York. Married Anne Jackson (1948), children: Peter, Roberta, Katherine.

Feature Films: *Baby Doll* (WB, 1956), *The Lineup* (Col., 1958), *Seven Thieves* (20th, 1960), *The Magnificent Seven* (UA, 1960), *The Misfits* (UA, 1961), *Hemingway's Adventures of a Young Man* (20th, 1962), *How the West Was Won* (MGM, 1963), *The Victors* (Col., 1963), *Act One* (WB, 1963), *The Moon Spinners* (BV, 1964), *Kisses for My President* (WB, 1964), *Lord Jim* (Col., 1965), *Genghis Khan* (Col., 1965), *How to Steal a Million* (20th, 1966), *The Tiger Makes Out* (Col., 1967), *The Good, the Bad and the Ugly* (UA, 1967), *MacKenna's Gold* (Col., 1968), *A Lovely Way to Die* (Univ., 1968), *How to Save a Marriage— And Ruin Your Life* (Col., 1968).

LUCILE WATSON Born May 27, 1879, Ottawa, Canada. Married Rockcliffe Fellowes; divorced. Married Louis E. Shipman (1928); widowed 1933. Died June 24, 1962.

Feature Films: *What Every Woman Knows* (MGM, 1934), *The Bishop Misbehaves* (MGM, 1935), *A Woman Rebels* (RKO, 1936), *The Garden of Allah* (UA, 1936), *Three Smart Girls* (Univ., 1936), *The Young in Heart* (UA, 1938), *Sweethearts* (MGM, 1938), *Made for Each Other* (UA, 1939), *The Women* (MGM, 1939), *Florian* (MGM, 1940), *Waterloo Bridge* (MGM, 1940), *Mr. and Mrs. Smith* (RKO, 1941), *The Great Lie* (WB, 1941), *Rage in Heaven* (MGM, 1941), *Footsteps in the Dark*

Brian Aherne, Madge Evans and Lucile Watson in *What Every Woman Knows.*

(WB, 1941), *Model Wife* (Univ., 1941), *Watch on the Rhine* (WB, 1943), *Uncertain Glory* (WB, 1944), *Till We Meet Again* (Par., 1944), *The Thin Man Goes Home* (MGM, 1944), *My Reputation* (WB, 1946), *Tomorrow Is Forever* (RKO, 1946), *Song of the South* (RKO, 1946), *Never Say Goodbye* (WB, 1946), *The Razor's Edge* (20th, 1946), *Ivy* (Univ., 1947), *The Emperor Waltz* (Par., 1948), *Julia Misbehaves* (MGM, 1948), *That Wonderful Urge* (20th, 1948), *Little Women* (MGM, 1949), *Everybody Does It* (20th, 1949), *Let's Dance* (Par., 1950), *Harriet Craig* (Col., 1950), *My Forbidden Past* (RKO, 1951).

JOHN WAYNE (Marion Michael Morrison) Born May 26, 1907, Winterset, Iowa. Married Josephine Saenz (1933), children: Antonio, Melinda, Michael, Patrick; divorced 1944. Married Esperanza Baur (1946); divorced 1953. Married Pilar Pallette (1954), children: Aissa, Marisa, Ethan.

Barbara Stanwyck and John Wayne in *Baby Face.*

Sound Feature Films: *Salute* (Fox, 1929), *Men Without Women* (Fox, 1930), *Rough Romance* (Fox, 1930), *The Big Trail* (Fox, 1930), *Girls Demand Excitement* (Fox, 1931), *Three Girls Lost* (Fox, 1931), *Men Are Like That* (Col., 1931), *Range Feud* (Col., 1931), *Hurricane Express* (Mascot serial, 1932), *Shadow of the Eagle* (Mascot serial, 1932), *Maker of Men* (Col., 1932), *Two Fisted Law* (Col., 1932), *Texas Cyclone* (Col., 1932), *Lady and Gent* (Par., 1932), *Ride Him Cowboy* (WB, 1932), *The Big Stampede* (WB, 1932), *The Three Musketeers* (Mascot serial, 1933), *Haunted Gold* (WB, 1933), *Telegraph Trail* (WB, 1933), *His Private Secretary* (Showman's Pictures, 1933), *Central Airport* (WB, 1933), *Somewhere in Sonora* (WB, 1933), *The Life of Jimmy Dolan* (WB, 1933), *Baby Face* (WB, 1933), *The Man From Monterey* (WB, 1933), *Riders of Destiny* (Mon., 1933), *College Coach* (WB, 1933), *West of the Divide* (Mon., 1934), *Blue Steel* (Mon., 1934), *Lucky Texan* (Mon., 1934), *The Man From Utah* (Mon., 1934), *Randy Rides Alone* (Mon., 1934), *The Star Packer* (Mon., 1934), *The Trail Beyond* (Mon., 1934), *'Neath Arizona Skies* (Mon., 1934), *Texas Terror* (Mon., 1935), *The Lawless Frontier* (Mon., 1935), *Rainbow Valley* (Mon., 1935), *Paradise Canyon* (Mon., 1935), *The Dawn Rider* (Mon., 1935), *Westward Ho!* (Rep., 1935), *Desert Trail* (Mon., 1935), *The Lawless 90's* (Rep., 1936), *King of the Pecos* (Rep., 1936), *The Oregon Trail* (Rep., 1936), *Winds of the Wasteland* (Rep., 1936), *The Sea Spoilers* (Univ., 1936), *The Lonely Trail* (Rep., 1936), *Conflict* (Univ., 1936), *California Straight Ahead* (Univ., 1937), *I Cover the War* (Univ., 1937), *Idol of the Crowds* (Univ., 1937), *Adventure's End* (Univ., 1937), *Born to the West* (Par., 1938), *Pals of the Saddle* (Rep., 1938), *Overland Stage Raiders* (Rep., 1938), *Santa Fe Stampede* (Rep., 1938), *Red River Range* (Rep., 1938), *Stagecoach* (UA, 1939), *Night Riders* (Rep., 1939), *Three Texas Steers* (Rep., 1939), *Wyoming Outlaw* (Rep., 1939), *New Frontier* (Rep., 1939), *Allegheny Uprising* (RKO, 1939), *Dark Command* (Rep., 1940), *Three Faces West* (Rep., 1940), *The Long Voyage Home* (UA, 1940), *Seven Sinners* (Univ., 1940), *A Man Betrayed* (Rep., 1941), *The Lady From Louisiana* (Rep., 1941),

The Shepherd of the Hills (Par., 1941), *Lady for a Night* (Rep., 1941), *Reap the Wild Wind* (Par., 1942), *The Spoilers* (Univ., 1942), *In Old California* (Rep., 1942), *The Flying Tigers* (Rep., 1942), *Reunion* (MGM 1942), *Pittsburgh* (Univ., 1942), *A Lady Takes a Chance* (RKO, 1943), *In Old Oklahoma* (Rep., 1943), *The Fighting Seabees* (Rep., 1944), *Tall in the Saddle* (RKO, 1944), *Back to Bataan* (RKO, 1945), *Flame of Barbary Coast* (Rep., 1945), *Dakota* (Rep., 1945), *They Were Expendable* (MGM, 1945), *Without Reservations* (RKO, 1946), *Angel and the Badman* (Rep., 1947), *Tycoon* (RKO, 1947), *Fort Apache* (RKO, 1948), *Red River* (UA, 1948), *Three Godfathers* (MGM, 1948), *Wake of the Red Witch* (Rep., 1948), *The Fighting Kentuckian* (Rep., 1949), *She Wore a Yellow Ribbon* (RKO, 1949), *Sands of Iwo Jima* (Rep., 1949), *Rio Grande* (Rep., 1950), *Operation Pacific* (WB, 1951), *Flying Leathernecks* (RKO, 1951), *Big Jim McLain* (WB, 1952), *The Quiet Man* (Rep., 1952), *Trouble Along the Way* (WB, 1953), *Island in the Sky* (WB, 1953), *Hondo* (WB, 1953), *The High and the Mighty* (WB, 1954), *The Sea Chase* (WB, 1955), *Blood Alley* (WB, 1955), *The Conqueror* (RKO, 1956), *The Searchers* (WB, 1956), *Wings of Eagles* (MGM, 1957), *Jet Pilot* (Univ., 1957), *Legend of the Lost* (UA, 1957), *The Barbarian and the Geisha* (20th, 1958), *Rio Bravo* (WB, 1959), *The Horse Soldiers* (UA, 1959), *North to Alaska* (20th, 1960), *The Alamo* (UA, 1960), *The Comancheros* (20th, 1961), *The Man Who Shot Liberty Valance* (Par., 1962), *Hatari* (Par., 1962), *The Longest Day* (20th, 1962), *How the West Was Won* (MGM, 1963), *Donovan's Reef* (Par., 1963), *McLintock* (UA, 1963), *Circus World* (UA, 1964), *The Greatest Story Ever Told* (UA, 1965), *In Harm's Way* (Par., 1965), *The Sons of Katie Elder* (Par., 1965), *Cast a Giant Shadow* (UA, 1966), *El Dorado* (Par., 1967), *The War Wagon* (Univ., 1967), *The Green Berets* (WB-7 Arts, 1968).

MARJORIE WEAVER Born March 2, 1913, Grossville, Tennessee.

Marjorie Weaver, Jean Hersholt and Warner Baxter in *I'll Give a Million*.

Feature Films: *Transatlantic Merry-Go-Round* (UA, 1934), *China Clipper* (WB, 1936), *Big Business* (20th, 1937), *This is My Affair* (20th, 1937), *The Californian* (20th, 1937), *Life Begins in College* (20th, 1937), *Hot Water* (20th, 1937), *Second Honeymoon* (20th, 1937), *Sally, Irene and Mary* (20th, 1938), *Kentucky Moonshine* (20th, 1938), *I'll Give a Million* (20th, 1938), *Three Blind Mice* (20th, 1938), *Hold That Co-ed* (20th, 1938), *Young Mr. Lincoln* (20th, 1939), *Chicken Wagon Family* (20th, 1939), *The Honeymoon's Over* (20th, 1939), *The Cisco Kid and the Lady* (20th, 1940), *Shooting High* (20th, 1940), *Charlie Chan's Murder Cruise* (20th, 1940), *Maryland* (20th, 1940), *Murder Over New York* (20th, 1940), *Michael Shayne, Private Detective* (20th, 1940), *Murder Among Friends* (20th, 1941), *For Beauty's Sake* (20th, 1941), *Men At Large* (20th, 1941), *The Man*

Who Wouldn't Die (20th, 1942), *Just Off Broadway* (20th, 1942), *The Mad Martindales* (20th, 1942), *Let's Face It* (Par., 1943), *You Can't Ration Love* (Par., 1944), *Pardon My Rhythm* (Univ., 1944), *Shadow of Suspicion* (Mon., 1944), *The Great Alaskan Mystery* (Univ. serial, 1944), *Fashion Model* (Mon., 1945), *Leave It to Blondie* (Col., 1945).

CLIFTON WEBB (Webb Parmallee Hollenbeck) Born November 19, 1891, Indianapolis, Indiana. Died October 13, 1966.

Edmund Gwenn and Clifton Webb in *For Heaven's Sake*.

Sound Feature Films: *Laura* (20th, 1944), *The Dark Corner* (20th, 1946), *The Razor's Edge* (20th, 1946), *Sitting Pretty* (20th, 1948), *Mr. Belvedere Goes to College* (20th, 1949), *Cheaper by the Dozen* (20th, 1959), *For Heaven's Sake* (20th, 1950), *Mr. Belvedere Rings the Bell* (20th, 1951), *Elopement* (20th, 1951), *Dreamboat* (20th, 1952), *Stars and Stripes Forever* (20th, 1952), *Titanic* (20th, 1953), *Mister Scoutmaster* (20th, 1953), *Woman's World* (20th, 1954), *Three Coins in the Fountain* (20th, 1954), *The Man Who Never Was* (20th, 1956), *Boy on a Dolphin* (20th, 1957), *The Remarkable Mr. Pennypacker* (20th, 1959), *Holiday for Lovers* (20th, 1959), *Satan Never Sleeps* (20th, 1962).

JOHNNY WEISSMULLER Born June 2, 1907, Chicago, Illinois. Married Camille Louier; divorced. Married Bobbe Arnst; divorced 1932. Married Lupe Velez (1933); divorced 1938. Married Beryle Scott; divorced 1943. Married Allene Gates (1948), children: Wendy, John, Heidi; divorced 1962.

Feature Films: *Tarzan, the Ape Man* (MGM, 1932), *Tarzan and His*

Johnny Weissmuller, Maureen O'Sullivan, Paul Cavanagh and Neil Hamilton in *Tarzan and His Mate*.

Mate (MGM, 1934), *Tarzan Escapes* (MGM, 1936), *Tarzan Finds a Son* (MGM, 1939), *Tarzan's Secret Treasure* (MGM, 1941), *Tarzan's New York Adventure* (MGM, 1942), *Tarzan Triumphs* (RKO, 1943), *Stage Door Canteen* (UA, 1943), *Tarzan's Desert Mystery* (RKO, 1943), *Tarzan and the Amazons* (RKO, 1945), *Tarzan and the Leopard Women* (RKO, 1946), *Swamp Fire* (Par., 1946), *Tarzan and the Huntress* (RKO, 1947), *Tarzan and the Mermaids* (RKO, 1948), *Jungle Jim* (Col., 1948), *The Lost Tribe* (Col., 1949), *Captive Girl* (Col., 1950), *Mark of the Gorilla* (Col., 1950), *Pygmy Island* (Col., 1950), *Fury of the Congo* (Col., 1951), *Jungle Manhunt* (Col., 1951), *Jungle Jim and the Forbidden Land* (Col., 1952), *Voodoo Tiger* (Col., 1952), *Savage Mutiny* (Col., 1953), *Valley of the Headhunters* (Col., 1953), *Killer Ape* (Col., 1953), *Jungle Man-Eaters* (Col., 1954), *Cannibal Attack* (Col., 1954), *Jungle Moon Men* (Col., 1955), *Devil Goddess* (Col., 1955).

TUESDAY WELD (Susan Ker Weld) Born August 27, 1943, New York, New York. Married Claude Harz (1965).

Tuesday Weld and Mary Astor in *Return to Peyton Place*.

Feature Films: *Rock, Rock, Rock* (Vanguard, 1956), *The Wrong Man* (WB, 1956), *Rally 'Round the Flag, Boys!* (20th, 1958), *The Five Pennies* (Par., 1959), *Because They're Young* (Col., 1960), *High Time* (20th, 1960), *Sex Kittens Go to College* (AA, 1960), *The Private Lives of Adam and Eve* (Univ., 1960), *Return to Peyton Place* (20th, 1961), *Wild in the Country* (20th, 1961), *Bachelor Flat* (20th, 1961), *Soldier in the Rain* (AA, 1963), *I'll Take Sweden* (UA, 1965), *The Cincinnati Kid* (MGM, 1965), *Lord Love a Duck* (UA, 1966). *Pretty Poison* (20th, 1968), *She Let Him Continue* (20th, 1968).

ORSON WELLES (George Orson Welles) Born May 6, 1915, Kenosha, Wisconsin. Married Virginia Nicholson (1934), child: Christopher; divorced 1940. Married Rita Hayworth (1943), child: Rebecca; divorced 1947. Married Paola Mori (1956).

English-Language Feature Films: *Swiss Family Robinson* (narrator; RKO, 1940), *Citizen Kane* (RKO, 1941), *The Magnificent Ambersons*

Stephen Bekassy and Orson Welles in *Black Magic*.

(narrator; RKO, 1942), *Journey into Fear* (RKO, 1942), *Jane Eyre* (20th, 1944), *Follow the Boys* (Univ., 1944), *Tomorrow Is Forever* (RKO, 1946), *The Stranger* (RKO, 1946), *Duel in the Sun* (narrator; Selznick, 1946), *The Lady From Shanghai* (Col., 1948), *Macbeth* (Rep., 1948), *The Third Man* (Selznick, 1949), *Black Magic* (UA, 1949), *Prince of Foxes* (20th, 1949), *The Black Rose* (20th, 1950), *Return to Glennascaul* (British, 1951), *Trent's Last Case* (Rep., 1953), *Trouble in the Glen* (Rep., 1954), *Mr. Arkadin* ("Confidential Report"—WB, 1955), *Three Cases of Murder* (Associated Artists, 1955), *Othello* (UA, 1955), *Moby Dick* (WB, 1956), *Man in the Shadow* (Univ., 1957), *Touch of Evil* (Univ., 1958), *The Long, Hot Summer* (20th, 1958), *The Roots of Heaven* (20th, 1958), *High Journey* (narrator; Baylis, 1959), *South Seas Adventure* (narrator; Dudley, 1959), *Ferry to Hong Kong* (20th, 1959), *Compulsion* (20th, 1959), *A Crack in the Mirror* (20th, 1960), *Masters of the Congo Jungle* (narrator; 20th, 1960), *King of Kings* (narrator; MGM, 1961) *The Trial* (Gibraltar, 1962), *The V.I.P.'s* (MGM, 1963), *The Finest Hours* (narrator; Col., 1964), *Chimes at Midnight* ("Falstaff"—Counor, 1965), *Is Paris Burning?* (Par., 1966), *A Man for All Seasons* (Col., 1966), *Marco the Magnificent* (MGM, 1966), *Casino Royale* (Col., 1967), *The Sailor From Gibraltar* (Lopert, 1967), *I'll Never Forget What's 'is Name* (Rank, 1968), *House of Cards* (Univ., 1968). *Oedipus* (Univ., 1968).

MAE WEST Born August 17, 1892, Brooklyn, New York. Married Frank Wallace (1911); divorced 1943.

Mae West and Paul Cavanagh in *Goin' to Town*.

Feature Films: *Night After Night* (Par., 1932), *She Done Him Wrong* (Par., 1933), *I'm No Angel* (Par., 1933), *Belle of the Nineties* (Par., 1934), *Goin' to Town* (Par., 1935), *Klondike Annie* (Par., 1936), *Go West, Young Man* (Par., 1936), *Every Day's a Holiday* (Par., 1938), *My Little Chickadee* (Univ., 1940), *The Heat's On* (Col., 1943).

STUART WHITMAN (Stuart Maxwell Whitman) Born February 1, 1929, San Francisco, California. Married Patricia LaLonde (1952), children: Anthony, Michael, Linda, Scott; divorced 1966. Married Caroline Boubis (1966).

Feature Films: *When Worlds Collide* (Par., 1951), *The Day the Earth Stood Still* (20th, 1951), *Barbed Wire* (Col., 1952), *Appointment in Honduras* (RKO, 1953), *The All American* (Univ., 1953), *Rhapsody* (MGM, 1954), *Silver Lode* (RKO, 1954), *Brigadoon* (MGM, 1954), *Passion* (RKO, 1954), *King of the Carnival* (Rep. serial, 1955), *Diane* (MGM, 1955), *Seven Men From Now* (WB, 1956), *Crime of Passion* (UA, 1957), *War Drums* (UA, 1957), *Johnny Trouble* (WB, 1957), *Hell Bound* (UA, 1957), *The Girl in Black Stockings* (UA, 1957), *Bomb-*

Dennis Holmes, Stuart Whitman and Fabian in *Hound-Dog Man*.

ers B-52 (WB, 1957), *Darby's Rangers* (WB, 1958), *10 North Frederick* (20th, 1958), *China Doll* (UA, 1958), *The Decks Ran Red* (MGM, 1958), *These Thousand Hills* (20th, 1959), *The Sound and the Fury* (20th, 1959), *Hound-Dog Man* (20th, 1959), *The Story of Ruth* (20th, 1960), *Murder, Inc.* (20th, 1960), *The Fiercest Heart* (20th, 1961), *Francis of Assisi* (20th, 1961), *The Mark* (Continental Distributing, 1961), *The Comancheros* (20th, 1961), *Convicts 4* (AA, 1962), *The Longest Day* (20th, 1962), *Shock Treatment* (20th, 1964), *The Day and the Hour* (MGM, 1964), *Rio Conchos* (20th, 1964), *Signpost to Murder* (MGM, 1964), *Those Magnificent Men in Their Flying Machines* (20th, 1965), *Sands of the Kalahari* (Par., 1965), *An American Dream* (WB, 1966).

DAME MAY WHITTY Born June 19, 1865, London, England. Married Ben Webster (1891), child: Margaret; widowed 1946. Died May 29, 1948.

Dame May Whitty and Edward G. Robinson in *Flesh and Fantasy*.

Feature Films: *Night Must Fall* (MGM, 1937), *The Thirteenth Chair* (MGM, 1937), *Conquest* (MGM, 1937), *I Met My Love Again* (UA, 1938), *The Lady Vanishes* (Gaumont-British, 1938), *Raffles* (UA, 1940), *A Bill of Divorcement* (RKO, 1940), *One Night in Lisbon* (Par., 1941), *Suspicion* (RKO, 1941), *Mrs. Miniver* (MGM, 1942), *Thunder Birds* (20th, 1942), *Slightly Dangerous* (MGM, 1943), *Forever and a Day* (RKO, 1943), *Crash Dive* (20th, 1943), *The Constant Nymph* (WB, 1943), *Lassie, Come Home* (MGM, 1943), *Flesh and Fantasy* (Univ., 1943), *Madame Curie* (MGM, 1943), *Stage Door Canteen* (UA, 1943), *The White Cliffs of Dover* (MGM, 1944), *Gaslight* (MGM, 1944), *My Name Is Julia Ross* (Col., 1945), *Devotion* (WB, 1946), *This Time for Keeps* (MGM, 1947), *Green Dolphin Street* (MGM, 1947), *If Winter Comes* (MGM, 1947), *The Sign of the Ram* (Col., 1948).

Whit Bissell, Lisa Golm, Mary Wickes, Broderick Crawford and Gale Page in *Anna Lucasta*.

MARY WICKES (Mary Isabelle Wickenhauser) Born St. Louis, Missouri.

Feature Films: *The Man Who Came to Dinner* (WB, 1941), *The Mayor of 44th Street* (RKO, 1942), *Private Buckaroo* (Univ., 1942), *Now, Voyager* (WB, 1942), *Who Done It?* (Univ., 1942), *How's About It?* (Univ., 1943), *Rhythm of the Islands* (Univ., 1943), *Happy Land* (20th, 1943), *My Kingdom for a Cook* (Col., 1943), *Higher and Higher* (RKO, 1943), *June Bride* (WB, 1948), *The Decision of Christopher Blake* (WB, 1948), *Anna Lucasta* (Col., 1949), *The Petty Girl* (Col., 1950), *On Moonlight Bay* (WB, 1951), *I'll See You in My Dreams* (WB, 1951), *The Will Rogers Story* (WB, 1952), *Young Man With Ideas* (MGM, 1952), *By the Light of the Silvery Moon* (WB, 1953), *The Actress* (MGM, 1953), *Half a Hero* (MGM, 1953), *Destry* (Univ., 1954), *Good Morning, Miss Dove* (20th, 1955), *Dance With Me, Henry* (UA, 1956), *Don't Go Near the Water* (MGM, 1957), *It Happened to Jane* (Col., 1959), *Cimarron* (MGM, 1960), *The Sins of Rachel Cade* (WB, 1961), *The Music Man* (WB, 1962), *Who's Minding the Store?* (Par., 1963), *Fate Is the Hunter* (20th, 1964), *Dear Heart* (WB, 1964), *How to Murder Your Wife* (UA, 1965), *The Trouble With Angels* (Col., 1966), *Where Angels Go . . . Trouble Follows* (Col., 1968).

RICHARD WIDMARK Born December 26, 1914, Sunrise, Minnesota. Married Jean Hazelwood (1942), child: Anne.

Cecil Kellaway and Richard Widmark in *Down to the Sea in Ships*.

Feature Films: *Kiss of Death* (20th, 1947), *Road House* (20th, 1948), *Street With No Name* (20th, 1948), *Yellow Sky* (20th, 1949), *Down to the Sea in Ships* (20th, 1949), *Slattery's Hurricane* (20th, 1949), *Night and the City* (20th, 1950), *Panic in the Streets* (20th, 1950), *No Way Out*

(20th, 1950), *Halls of Montezuma* (20th, 1950), *The Frogmen* (20th, 1951), *O. Henry's Full House* (20th, 1952), *Don't Bother to Knock* (20th, 1952), *Red Skies of Montana* (20th, 1952), *My Pal Gus* (20th, 1952), *Destination Gobi* (20th, 1953), *Hell and High Water* (20th, 1954), *Broken Lance* (20th, 1954), *Garden of Evil* (20th, 1954), *A Prize of Gold* (Col., 1955), *The Cobweb* (MGM, 1955), *Backlash* (Univ., 1956), *Run for the Sun* (UA, 1956), *The Last Wagon* (20th, 1956), *Saint Joan* (UA, 1957), *Time Limit!* (UA, 1957), *The Law and Jake Wade* (MGM, 1958), *The Tunnel of Love* (MGM, 1958), *The Trap* (Par., 1959), *Warlock* (20th, 1959), *The Alamo* (UA, 1960), *The Secret Ways* (Univ., 1961), *Two Rode Together* (Col., 1961), *Judgment at Nuremberg* (UA, 1961), *How the West Was Won* (MGM, 1963), *Flight From Ashiya* (UA, 1964), *The Long Ships* (Col., 1964), *Cheyenne Autumn* (WB, 1964), *The Bedford Incident* (Col., 1965), *Alvarez Kelly* (Col., 1966), *The Way West* (UA, 1967), *Madigan* (Univ., 1968).

CORNEL WILDE Born October 13, 1915, New York, New York. Married Patricia Knight (1937), child: Wendy; divorced 1951. Married Jean Wallace (1951).

Cornel Wilde and Finlay Currie in *Treasure of the Golden Condor*.

Feature Films: *The Lady With Red Hair* (WB, 1940), *Kisses for Breakfast* (WB, 1941), *High Sierra* (WB, 1941), *Right to the Heart* (WB, 1941), *The Perfect Snob* (20th, 1942), *Life Begins at 8:30* (20th, 1942), *Manila Calling* (20th, 1942), *Wintertime* (20th, 1943), *Guest in the House* (UA, 1944), *A Thousand and One Nights* (Col., 1945), *A Song to Remember* (Col., 1945), *Leave Her to Heaven* (20th, 1945), *The Bandit of Sherwood Forest* (Col., 1946), *Centennial Summer* (20th, 1946), *The Homestretch* (20th, 1947), *Forever Amber* (20th, 1947), *It Had to Be You* (Col., 1947), *Roadhouse* (20th, 1948), *The Walls of Jericho* (20th, 1948), *Four Days Leave* (Film Classics, 1950), *Two Flags West* (20th, 1950), *At Sword's Point* (RKO, 1952), *The Greatest Show on Earth* (Par., 1952), *California Conquest* (Col., 1952), *The Treasure of The Golden Condor* (20th, 1953), *Main Street To Broadway* (MGM, 1953), *Saadia* (MGM, 1953), *Passion* (RKO, 1954), *Woman's World* (20th, 1954), *The Scarlet Coat* (MGM, 1955), *Storm Fear* (UA, 1955), *The Big Combo* (AA, 1955), *Star of India* (UA, 1956), *Hot Blood* (Col., 1956), *The Devil's Hairpin* (Par., 1957), *Omar Khayyam* (Par., 1957), *Beyond Mombasa* (Col., 1957), *Maracaibo* (Par., 1958), *The Edge of Eternity* (Col., 1959), *Constantine and the Cross* (Embassy, 1962), *The Sword of Lancelot* (Univ., 1963), *The Naked Prey* (Par., 1966), *Beach Red* (UA, 1967).

WARREN WILLIAM (Warren Krech) Born December 2, 1895, Aitkin, Minnesota. Died September 24, 1948.

Feature Films: *Expensive Women* (WB, 1931), *Honor of the Family* (WB, 1931), *Woman From Monte Carlo* (WB, 1932), *Under Eighteen* (WB, 1932), *The Mouthpiece* (WB, 1932), *Beauty and the Boss* (WB, 1932), *Dark Horse* (WB, 1932), *Skyscraper Souls* (WB, 1932), *Three on a Match* (WB, 1932), *The Match King* (WB, 1932),

Kay Francis and Warren William in *Dr. Monica*.

Employees' Entrance (WB, 1933), *Mind Reader* (WB, 1933), *Gold Diggers of 1933* (WB, 1933), *Lady for a Day* (Col., 1933), *Goodbye Again* (WB, 1933), *Bedside* (WB, 1934), *Smarty* (WB, 1934), *Dr. Monica* (WB, 1934), *Upper World* (WB, 1934), *Dragon Murder Case* (WB, 1934), *Cleopatra* (Par., 1934), *Case of the Howling Dog* (WB, 1934), *Imitation of Life* (Univ., 1934), *Outcast* (Par., 1937), *Midnight Madonna* (Par., 1937), *The Firefly* (MGM, 1937), *Madame X* (MGM, 1937), *Arsene Lupin Returns* (MGM, 1938), *The First Hundred Years* (MGM, 1938), *Wives Under Suspicion* (Univ., 1938), *The Lone Wolf Spy Hunt* (Col., 1939), *Gracie Allen Murder Case* (Par., 1939), *The Man in the Iron Mask* (UA, 1939), *Daytime Wife* (20th, 1939), *The Lone Wolf Strikes* (Col., 1940), *Lillian Russell* (20th, 1940), *The Lone Wolf Meets a Lady* (Col., 1940), *Arizona* (Col., 1940), *Trail of the Vigilantes* (Univ., 1940), *The Lone Wolf Takes a Chance* (Col., 1941), *The Lone Wolf Keeps a Date* (Col., 1941), *Wild Geese Calling* (20th, 1941), *The Wolf Man* (Univ., 1941), *One Dangerous Night* (Col., 1943), *Passport to Suez* (Col., 1943), *Strange Illusion* (PRC, 1945), *Fear* (Mon., 1946), *The Private Affairs of Bel Ami* (UA, 1947).

ESTHER WILLIAMS Born August 8, 1923, Los Angeles, California. Married Leonard Kovner (1940); divorced 1944. Married Benjamin Gage (1945), children: Benjamin, Kimball, Susan; divorced 1957. Married Fernando Lamas (1963).

Feature Films: *Andy Hardy's Double Life* (MGM, 1942), *A Guy Named*

Cliff Robertson and Esther Williams in *The Big Show*.

Joe (MGM, 1943), *Bathing Beauty* (MGM, 1944), *Thrill of a Romance* (MGM, 1945), *The Hoodlum Saint* (MGM, 1946), *Ziegfeld Follies of 1946* (MGM, 1946), *Easy to Wed* (MGM, 1946), *Till the Clouds Roll By* (MGM, 1946), *Fiesta* (MGM, 1947), *This Time for Keeps* (MGM, 1947), *On an Island With You* (MGM, 1948), *Take Me Out to the Ball Game* (MGM, 1949), *Neptune's Daughter* (MGM, 1949), *Duchess of Idaho* (MGM, 1950), *Pagan Love Song* (MGM, 1950), *Texas Carnival* (MGM, 1951), *Callaway Went Thataway* (MGM, 1951),* *Skirts Ahoy* (MGM, 1952), *Million Dollar Mermaid* (MGM, 1952), *Dangerous When Wet* (MGM, 1953), *Easy to Love* (MGM, 1953), *Jupiter's Darling* (MGM, 1955), *The Unguarded Moment* (Univ., 1956), *Raw Wind in Eden* (Univ., 1958), *The Big Show* (20th, 1961), *The Magic Fountain* (Agiula Films, 1961).

*Unbilled guest appearance

MARIE WINDSOR (Emily Marie Bertelson) Born December 11, 1922, Marysvale, Utah. Married Ted Steele (1947), annulled 1947. Married Jack Hupp (1954), child: Richard.

Forrest Tucker and Marie Windsor in *Hellfire*.

Feature Films: *All American Co-ed* (UA, 1941), *Call Out the Marines* (RKO, 1942), *Smart Alecks* (Mon., 1942), *Parachute Nurse* (Col., 1942), *The Big Street* (RKO, 1942), *George Washington Slept Here* (WB, 1942), *Three Hearts for Julia* (MGM, 1943), *Pilot No. 5* (MGM, 1943), *Let's Face It* (Par., 1943), *The Hucksters* (MGM, 1947), *Romance of Rosy Ridge* (MGM, 1947), *The Song of the Thin Man* (MGM, 1947), *The Unfinished Dance* (MGM, 1947), *On an Island With You* (MGM, 1948), *The Three Musketeers* (MGM, 1948), *The Kissing Bandit* (MGM, 1948), *Force of Evil* (MGM, 1949), *Outpost in Morocco* (UA, 1949), *The Beautiful Blonde From Bashful Bend* (20th, 1949), *The Fighting Kentuckian* (Rep., 1949), *Hellfire* (Rep., 1949), *Dakota Lil* (20th, 1950), *The Showdown* (Rep., 1950), *Frenchie* (Univ., 1950), *Double Deal* (RKO, 1950), *Little Big Horn* (Lip., 1951), *Hurricane Island* (Col., 1951), *Two Dollar Bettor* (Realart, 1951), *Japanese War Bride* (20th, 1952), *The Sniper* (Col., 1952), *The Narrow Margin* (RKO, 1952), *Outlaw Woman* (Lip., 1952), *The Jungle* (Lip., 1952), *The Tall Texan* (Lip., 1953), *Trouble Along the Way* (WB, 1953), *The City That Never Sleeps* (Rep., 1953), *So This Is Love* (WB, 1953), *The Eddie Cantor Story* (WB, 1953), *Cat Women of the Moon* (Astor, 1953), *Hell's Half Acre* (Rep., 1954), *The Bounty Hunter* (WB, 1954), *Silver Star* (Lip., 1954), *Abbott and Costello Meet the Mummy* (Univ., 1955), *No Man's Woman* (Rep., 1955), *Two Gun Lady* (Associated, 1955), *The Killing* (UA, 1956), *Swamp Women* (Woolner Bros., 1956), *The Unholy Wife* (Univ., 1957), *The Girl in Black Stockings* (UA, 1957), *The Story of Mankind* (WB, 1957), *The Parson and the Outlaw* (Col., 1957), *The Day of the Bad Man* (Univ., 1958), *Island Women* (UA, 1958), *Paradise Alley* (Sutton, 1962), *Critic's Choice* (WB, 1963), *The Day Mars Invaded Earth* (20th, 1963), *Mail Order Bride* (MGM, 1964), *Bedtime Story* (Univ., 1964), *Chamber of Horrors* (WB, 1966).

Farley Granger and Shelley Winters in *Behave Yourself!*

SHELLEY WINTERS (Shirley Schrift) Born August 18, 1922, St. Louis, Missouri. Married Mack Meyer (1943); divorced 1948. Married Vittorio Gassman (1952), child: Vittoria; divorced 1954. Married Anthony Franciosa (1957); divorced 1960.

English-Language Feature Films: *What a Woman!* (Col., 1943), *Nine Girls* (Col., 1944), *She's a Soldier, Too* (Col., 1944), *Sailor's Holiday* (Col., 1944), *Racket Man* (Col., 1944), *Knickerbocker Holiday* (UA, 1944), *Two Man Submarine* (Col., 1944), *Cover Girl* (Col., 1944), *Tonight and Every Night* (Col., 1945), *A Thousand and One Nights* (Col., 1945), *The Gangster* (AA, 1947), *Living in a Big Way* (MGM, 1947), *A Double Life* (Univ., 1948), *Larceny* (Univ., 1948), *Red River* (UA, 1948), *Cry of the City* (20th, 1948), *Take One False Step* (Univ., 1949), *The Great Gatsby* (Par., 1949), *Johnny Stool Pigeon* (Univ., 1949), *South Sea Sinner* (Univ., 1950), *Winchester '73* (Univ., 1950), *Frenchie* (Univ., 1950), *A Place in the Sun* (Par., 1951), *He Ran All the Way* (UA, 1951), *Behave Yourslf* (RKO, 1951), *The Raging Tide* (Univ., 1951), *Meet Danny Wilson* (Univ., 1951), *Phone Call From a Stranger* (20th, 1952), *Untamed Frontier* (Univ., 1952), *My Man and I* (MGM, 1952), *Saskatchewan* (Univ., 1954), *Tennessee Champ* (MGM, 1954), *Executive Suite* (MGM, 1954), *Playgirl* (Univ., 1954), *Mambo* (Par., 1955), *I Am a Camera* (DCA, 1955), *The Night of the Hunter* (UA, 1955), *The Big Knife* (UA, 1955), *I Died a Thousand Times* (WB, 1955), *The Treasure of Pancho Villa* (RKO, 1955), *Cash on Delivery* (RKO, 1956), *The Diary of Anne Frank* (20th, 1959), *Odds Against Tomorrow* (UA, 1959), *Let No Man Write My Epitaph* (Col., 1960), *The Young Savages* (UA, 1961), *Lolita* (MGM, 1962), *The Chapman Report* (WB, 1962), *The Balcony* (Continental, 1963), *Wives and Lovers* (Par., 1963), *A House Is Not a Home* (Embassy, 1964), *The Greatest Story Ever Told* (UA, 1965), *A Patch of Blue* (MGM, 1965), *Harper* (WB, 1966), *Alfie* (Par., 1966), *A Time of Indifference* (Continental, 1966), *Enter Laughing* (Col., 1967), *The Scalphunters* (UA, 1968), *Buona Sera, Mrs. Campbell* (Univ., 1968), *Wild in the Streets* (AIP, 1968).

JANE WITHERS Born April 12, 1926, Atlanta, Georgia. Married William Moss (1947), children: William, Wendy, Randy. divorced 1954. Married Kenneth Errair (1955), children: Kenneth, Kendall.

Jane Withers and Andrew Tombes in *The Holy Terror*.

Feature Films: *Handle With Care* (Fox, 1932), *Bright Eyes* (Fox, 1934), *Ginger* (Fox, 1935), *The Farmer Takes a Wife* (Fox, 1935), *This Is the Life* (Fox, 1935), *Paddy O' Day* (Fox, 1935), *Gentle Julia* (20th, 1936), *Little Miss Nobody* (20th, 1936), *Pepper* (20th, 1936), *Can This Be Dixie?* (20th, 1936), *The Holy Terror* (20th, 1937), *Angel's Holiday* (20th, 1937), *Wild and Woolly* (20th, 1937), *45 Fathers* (20th, 1937), *Checkers* (20th, 1937), *Rascals* (20th, 1938), *Keep Smiling* (20th, 1938), *Always in Trouble* (20th, 1938), *The Arizona Wildcat* (20th, 1938), *Boy Friend* (20th, 1939), *Pack Up Your Troubles* (20th, 1939), *Chicken Wagon Family* (20th, 1939), *Shooting High* (20th, 1940), *High School* (20th, 1940), *Youth Will Be Served* (20th, 1940), *Girl From Avenue A* (20th, 1940), *Golden Hoofs* (20th, 1941), *A Very Young Lady* (20th, 1941), *Her First Beau* (Col., 1941), *Small Town Deb* (20th, 1941), *Young America* (20th, 1942), *Johnny Doughboy* (Rep., 1942), *The Mad Martindales* (20th, 1942), *The North Star* (RKO, 1943), *My Best Gal* (Rep., 1944), *Faces in the Fog* (Rep., 1944), *Affairs of Geraldine* (Rep., 1946), *Danger Street* (Par., 1947), *Giant* (WB, 1956), *The Right Approach* (20th, 1961), *Captain Newman, M.D.* (Univ., 1963).

ANNA MAY WONG Born January 3, 1907, Los Angeles, California. Died February 3, 1961.

Eric Blore and Anna May Wong in *Island of Lost Men*.

English-Language Sound Feature Films: *Crimson City* (WB, 1928), *Piccadilly* (World Wide, 1929), *The Flame of Love* (British International 1930), *Daughter of the Dragon* (Par., 1931), *Shanghai Express* (Par., 1932), *A Study in Scarlet* (Fox-World Wide, 1933), *Tiger Bay* (Wyndham, 1933), *Limehouse Blues* (Par., 1934), *Chu Chin Chow* (Gaumont-British, 1934), *Java Head* (First Division, 1935), *Daughter of Shanghai* (Par., 1937), *Dangerous to Know* (Par., 1938), *When Were You Born?* (WB, 1938), *King of Chinatown* (Par., 1939), *Island of Lost Men* (Par., 1939), *Ellery Queen's Penthouse Mystery* (Col., 1941), *Bombs Over Burma* (PRC, 1942), *Lady From Chungking* (PRC, 1942), *Impact* (UA, 1949), *Portrait in Black* (Univ., 1960).

NATALIE WOOD (Natasha Gurdin) Born July 20, 1938, San Francisco, California. Married Robert Wagner (1957); divorced 1963.

Feature Films:
    as Natasha Gurdin *Happy Land* (20th, 1943).
    as Natalie Wood *Tomorrow Is Forever* (RKO, 1946), *The Bride Wore Boots* (Par., 1946), *The Miracle on 34th Street* (20th, 1947), *The Ghost and Mrs. Muir* (20th, 1947), *Driftwood* (Rep., 1947), *Scudda Hoo! Scudda Hay!* (20th, 1948), *Chicken Every Sunday* (20th, 1948), *The Green Promise* (RKO, 1949), *Father Was a Fullback* (20th, 1949), *Our Very Own* (RKO, 1950), *No Sad Songs for Me* (Col., 1950), *The Jackpot* (20th, 1950), *Never a Dull Moment* (RKO, 1950), *Dear Brat* (Par., 1951), *The Blue Veil* (RKO, 1951), *Just for You* (Par., 1952), *The Rose Bowl Story* (Mon., 1952), *The Star* (20th, 1953), *The Silver*

Robert Redford and Natalie Wood in *This Property is Condemned*.

Chalice (WB, 1954), *One Desire* (Univ., 1955), *Rebel Without a Cause* (WB, 1955), *The Searchers* (WB, 1956), *The Burning Hills* (WB, 1956), *A Cry in the Night* (WB, 1956), *The Girl He Left Behind* (WB, 1956), *Bombers B-52* (WB, 1957), *Marjorie Morningstar* (WB, 1958), *Kings Go Forth* (UA, 1958), *Cash McCall* (WB, 1959), *All the Fine Young Cannibals* (MGM, 1960), *Splendor in the Grass* (WB, 1961), *West Side Story* (UA, 1961), *Gypsy* (WB, 1962), *Love With the Proper Stranger* (Par., 1963), *Sex and the Single Girl* (WB, 1964), *The Great Race* (WB, 1965), *Inside Daisy Clover* (WB, 1965), *This Property Is Condemned* (Par., 1966), *Penelope* (MGM, 1966).

JOANNE WOODWARD (Joanne Gignilliat Woodward) Born February 27, 1930, Thomasville, Georgia. Married Paul Newman (1958), children: Elinore, Tessa, Cleo.

Claire Trevor and Joanne Woodward in *The Stripper*.

Feature Films: *Count Three and Pray* (Col., 1955), *A Kiss Before Dying* (UA, 1956), *The Three Faces of Eve* (20th, 1957), *No Down Payment* (20th, 1957), *The Long, Hot Summer* (20th, 1958), *Rally 'Round the Flag, Boys* (20th, 1958), *The Sound and the Fury* (20th, 1959), *The Fugitive Kind* (UA, 1959), *From the Terrace* (20th, 1960), *Paris Blues* (UA, 1961), *The Stripper* (20th, 1963), *A New Kind of Love* (Par., 1963), *Signpost to Murder* (MGM, 1964), *A Big Hand for the Little Lady* (WB, 1966), *A Fine Madness* (WB, 1966), *The Jest of God* (WB-7 Arts, 1968), *Rachel, Rachel* (WB-7 Arts, 1968).

MONTY WOOLLEY (Edgar Montillion Woolley) Born August 17, 1888, New York, New York. Died May 6, 1963.

Feature Films: *Live, Love and Learn* (MGM, 1937), *Nothing Sacred* (UA, 1937), *Arsene Lupin Returns* (MGM, 1938), *Girl of the Golden West* (MGM, 1938), *Everybody Sing* (MGM, 1938), *Three Comrades*

Monty Woolley, Ida Lupino and Cornel Wilde in *Life Begins at 8:30.*

(MGM, 1938), *Lord Jeff* (MGM, 1938), *Artists and Models Abroad* (Par., 1938), *Young Dr. Kildare* (MGM, 1938), *Vacation From Love* (MGM, 1938), *Never Say Die* (Par., 1939), *Midnight* (Par., 1939), *Zaza* (Par., 1939), *Man About Town* (Par., 1939), *Dancing Co-ed* (MGM, 1939), *The Man Who Came to Dinner* (WB, 1941), *The Pied Piper* (20th, 1942), *Life Begins at 8:30* (20th, 1942), *Holy Matrimony* (20th, 1943), *Since You Went Away* (UA, 1944), *Irish Eyes Are Smiling* (20th, 1944), *Molly and Me* (20th, 1945), *Night and Day* (WB, 1946), *The Bishop's Wife* (RKO, 1947), *Miss Tatlock's Millions* (Par., 1948), *As Young as You Feel* (20th, 1951), *Kismet* (MGM, 1955).

FAY WRAY Born September 10, 1907, Alberta, Canada. Married John Monk Saunders (1928), child: Susan; divorced 1939. Married Robert Riskin (1942), children: Robert, Vicky; widowed 1955.

Fay Wray and Robert Allen in *White Lies.*

Sound Feature Films: *Four Feathers* (Par., 1929), *Thunderbolt* (Par., 1929), *Pointed Heels* (Par., 1929), *Behind the Makeup* (Par., 1930), *Paramount on Parade* (Par., 1930), *The Texan* (Par., 1930), *The Border Legion* (Par., 1930), *The Sea God* (Par., 1930), *The Finger Points* (WB, 1931), *The Conquering Horde* (Par., 1931), *Not Exactly Gentlemen* (Fox, 1931), *Dirigible* (Col., 1931), *Captain Thunder* (WB, 1931), *The Lawyer's Secret* (Par., 1931), *The Unholy Garden* (UA, 1931), *Stowaway* (Univ., 1932), *Doctor X* (WB, 1932), *The Most Dangerous Game* (RKO, 1932), *Vampire Bat* (Majestic, 1933), *Mystery of the Wax Museum* (WB, 1933), *King Kong* (RKO, 1933), *Below the Sea* (Col., 1933), *Ann Carver's Profession* (Col., 1933), *The Woman I Stole* (Col., 1933), *The Big Brain* (RKO, 1933), *One Sunday Afternoon* (Par., 1933), *Shanghai Madness* (Fox, 1933), *The Bowery* (UA, 1933), *Master of Men* (Col., 1933), *Madame Spy* (Univ., 1943), *Once to Every Woman* (Col., 1934), *The Countess of Monte Cristo* (Univ., 1934), *Viva Villa!* (MGM, 1934), *The Affairs of Cellini* (UA, 1934), *Black Moon* (Col., 1934), *The Richest*

Girl in the World (RKO, 1934), *The Captain Hates the Sea* (Col., 1934), *Cheating Cheaters* (Univ., 1934), *Woman in the Dark* (RKO, 1934), *White Lies* (Col., 1934), *Bulldog Jack* (Gaumont-British, 1935), *Come Out of the Pantry* (UA, 1935), *Mills of the Gods* (Col., 1935), *The Clairvoyant* (Gaumont-British, 1935), *Roaming Lady* (Col., 1936), *When Knights Were Bold* (General Film Distributors, 1936), *They Met in a Taxi* (Col., 1936), *It Happened in Hollywood* (Col., 1937), *Once a Hero* (Col., 1937), *Murder in Greenwich Village* (Col., 1937), *The Jury's Secret* (Univ., 1938), *Smashing the Spy Ring* (Col., 1938), *Navy Secrets* (Mon., 1939), *Wildcat Bus* (RKO, 1940), *Adam Had Four Sons* (Col., 1941), *Melody for Three* (RKO, 1941), *Not a Ladies' Man* (Col., 1942), *Treasure of the Golden Condor* (20th, 1953), *Small Town Girl* (MGM, 1953), *The Cobweb* (MGM, 1955), *Queen Bee* (Col., 1955), *Hell on Frisco Bay* (WB, 1955), *Rock Pretty Baby* (Univ., 1957), *Crime of Passion* (UA, 1957), *Tammy and the Bachelor* (Univ., 1957), *Summer Love* (Univ., 1958), *Dragstrip Riot* (AIP, 1958).

TERESA WRIGHT (Muriel Teresa Wright) Born October 27, 1918, New York, New York. Married Niven Busch (1942), children: Niven, Mary; divorced 1952. Married Robert Anderson (1959).

Teresa Wright and David Niven in *Enchantment.*

Feature Films: *The Little Foxes* (RKO, 1941), *Mrs. Miniver* (MGM, 1942), *The Pride of the Yankees* (RKO, 1942), *Shadow of a Doubt* (Univ., 1943), *Casanova Brown* (RKO, 1944), *The Best Years of Our Lives* (RKO, 1946), *Pursued* (WB, 1947), *The Imperfect Lady* (Par., 1947), *The Trouble with Women* (Par., 1947), *Enchantment* (RKO, 1948), *The Capture* (RKO, 1950), *The Men* (UA, 1950), *Something to Live For* (Par., 1952), *California Conquest* (Col., 1952), *The Steel Trap* (20th, 1952), *Count the Hours* (RKO, 1953), *The Actress* (MGM, 1953), *Track of the Cat* (WB, 1954), *The Search for Bridey Murphy* (Par., 1956), *Escapade in Japan* (Univ., 1957). *The Restless Years* (Univ., 1958).

JANE WYATT Born August 10, 1911, Campgaw, New Jersey. Married Edgar Ward (1935), children: Christopher, Michael.

Ronald Colman and Jane Wyatt in *Lost Horizon.*

Feature Films: *One More River* (Univ., 1934), *Great Expectations* (Univ., 1934), *We're Only Human* (RKO, 1936), *Luckiest Girl in the World* (Univ., 1936), *Lost Horizon* (Col., 1937), *Girl From God's Country* (Rep., 1940), *Hurricane Smith* (Rep., 1941), *Weekend for Three* (RKO, 1941), *Kisses for Breakfast* (WB, 1941), *The Navy Comes Through* (RKO, 1942), *Army Surgeon* (RKO, 1942), *Buckskin Frontier* (UA, 1943), *The Kansan* (UA, 1943), *None But the Lonely Heart* (RKO, 1944), *Strange Conquest* (Univ., 1946), *The Bachelor's Daughters* (UA, 1946), *Boomerang* (20th. 1947), *Gentleman's Agreement* (20th, 1947), *Pitfall* (UA, 1948), *No Minor Vices* (MGM, 1948), *Bad Boy* (AA, 1949), *Canadian Pacific* (20th, 1949), *Task Force* (WB, 1949), *Our Very Own* (RKO, 1950), *House by the River* (Rep., 1950), *My Blue Heaven* (20th, 1950), *The Man Who Cheated Himself* (20th, 1950), *Criminal Lawyer* (Col., 1951), *Interlude* (Univ., 1957), *The Two Little Bears* (20th, 1961), *Never Too Late* (WB, 1965).

JANE WYMAN (Sarah Jane Fulks) Born January 4, 1914, St. Joseph, Missouri. Married Myron Futterman (1937); divorced 1938. Married Ronald Reagan (1940), children: Michael, Maureen; divorced 1948. Married Fred Karger (1952); divorced 1954. Remarried 1961.

Jane Wyman and Jack Carson in *Make Your Own Bed*.

Feature Films: *Gold Diggers of 1937* (WB, 1936), *My Man Godfrey* (Univ., 1936), *King of Burlesque* (20th, 1936), *Smart Blonde* (WB, 1936), *Stage Struck* (WB, 1936), *The King and the Chorus Girl* (WB, 1937), *Ready, Willing and Able* (WB, 1937), *Slim* (WB, 1937), *The Singing Marine* (WB, 1937), *Public Wedding* (WB, 1937), *Mr. Dodd Takes the Air* (WB, 1937), *The Spy Ring* (Univ., 1938), *He Couldn't Say No* (WB, 1938), *Wide Open Faces* (Col., 1938), *The Crowd Roars* (MGM, 1938), *Brother Rat* (WB, 1938), *Fools For Scandal* (WB, 1938), *Tailspin* (20th, 1939), *Private Detective* (WB, 1939), *The Kid From Kokomo* (WB, 1939), *Torchy Plays With Dynamite* (WB, 1939), *Kid Nightingale* (WB, 1939), *Brother Rat and a Baby* (WB, 1940), *An Angel From Texas* (WB, 1940), *Flight Angels* (WB, 1940), *My Love Came Back* (WB, 1940), *Tugboat Annie Sails Again* (WB, 1940), *Gambling on the High Seas* (WB, 1940), *Honeymoon for Three* (WB, 1941), *Bad Men of Missouri* (WB, 1941), *You're in the Army Now* (WB, 1941), *The Body Disappears* (WB, 1941), *Larceny, Inc.* (WB, 1942), *My Favorite Spy* (RKO, 1942), *Footlight Serenade* (20th, 1942), *Princess O'Rourke* (WB, 1943), *Make Your Own Bed* (WB, 1944), *Crime By Night* (WB, 1944), *The Doughgirls* (WB, 1944), *Hollywood Canteen* (WB, 1944), *The Lost Weekend* (Par., 1945), *One More Tomorrow* (WB, 1946), *Night and Day* (WB, 1946), *The Yearling* (MGM, 1946), *Cheyenne* (WB, 1947), *Magic Town* (RKO, 1947), *Johnny Belinda* (WB, 1948), *A Kiss in the Dark* (WB, 1949), *The Lady Takes a Sailor* (WB, 1949), *It's a Great Feeling* (WB, 1949), *Stage Fright* (WB, 1950), *The Glass Menagerie* (WB, 1950), *Three Guys Named Mike* (MGM, 1951), *Here Comes the Groom* (Par., 1951), *The Blue Veil* (RKO, 1951), *Starlift* (WB, 1951), *The Will Rogers Story* (WB, 1952), *Just for You* (Par., 1952), *Let's Do It Again* (WB, 1953), *So Big* (WB, 1953), *Magnificent*

Obsession (Univ., 1954), *Lucy Gallant* (Par., 1955), *All That Heaven Allows* (Univ., 1955), *Miracle in the Rain* (WB, 1956), *Holiday for Lovers* (20th, 1959), *Pollyanna* (BV, 1960), *Bon Voyage* (BV, 1962).

ED WYNN (Isaiah Edwin Leopold) Born November 9, 1886, Philadelphia, Pennsylvania. Married Hilda Keenan (1914), child: Keenan; divorced 1937. Married Frieda Mierse (1937); divorced 1939. Died June 19, 1966.

Effie Ellsler, Ed Wynn and Dorothy Mackill in *The Chief*.

Sound Feature Films: *Follow the Leader* (Par., 1930), *The Chief* (MGM, 1933), *Alice in Wonderland* (voice only; RKO, 1951), *The Great Man* (Univ., 1956), *Marjorie Morningstar* (WB, 1958), *The Diary of Anne Frank* (20th, 1959), *Cinderfella* (Par., 1960), *The Absent-Minded Professor* (BV, 1961), *Babes in Toyland* (BV, 1961), *Son of Flubber* (BV, 1963), *The Patsy* (Par., 1964), *Mary Poppins* (BV, 1965), *The Greatest Story Ever Told* (UA, 1965), *Dear Brigitte* (20th, 1965), *Those Calloways* (BV, 1965), *The Daydreamer* (voice only; Embassy, 1966), *The Gnome-Mobile* (BV, 1967).

KEENAN WYNN (Francis Xavier Aloysius Keenan Wynn) Born July 27, 1916, New York, New York. Married Eve Abbott (1939), children: Edmond, Tracy; divorced 1946. Married Betty Butler (1949); divorced 1953. Married Sharley Hudson (1954), children: Wynnie, Hilda.

Feature Films: *Somewhere I'll Find You* (MGM, 1942), *Northwest Rangers* (MGM, 1942), *For Me and My Gal* (MGM, 1942), *Lost Angel* (MGM, 1943), *See Here, Private Hargrove* (MGM, 1944), *Since You Went Away* (UA, 1944), *Marriage Is a Private Affair* (MGM, 1944), *Without Love* (MGM, 1945), *The Clock* (MGM, 1945), *Between Two Women* (MGM, 1945), *Weekend at the Waldorf* (MGM, 1945), *What Next, Corporal Hargrove?* (MGM, 1945), *Ziegfeld Follies of 1946* (MGM, 1946), *Easy to Wed* (MGM, 1946), *The Thrill of Brazil* (Col., 1946),

Keenan Wynn and Fred Essler in *What Next, Corporal Hargrove?*

No Leave, No Love (MGM, 1946), *The Cockeyed Miracle* (MGM, 1946), *The Hucksters* (MGM, 1947), *Song of the Thin Man* (MGM, 1947), *B.F.'s Daughter* (MGM, 1948), *The Three Musketeers* (MGM, 1948), *My Dear Secretary* (UA, 1948), *Neptune's Daughter* (MGM, 1949), *That Midnight Kiss* (MGM, 1949), *Love That Brute* (20th, 1950), *Annie Get Your Gun* (MGM, 1950), *Three Little Words* (MGM, 1950), *Royal Wedding* (MGM, 1951), *Angels in the Outfield* (MGM, 1951), *Texas Carnival* (MGM, 1951), *It's a Big Country* (MGM, 1951), *Phone Call From a Stranger* (20th, 1952), *The Belle of New York* (MGM, 1952), *Fearless Fagan* (MGM, 1952), *Sky Full of Moon* (MGM, 1952), *Desperate Search* (MGM, 1952), *Holiday for Sinners* (MGM, 1952), *Battle Circus* (MGM, 1953), *Code Two* (MGM, 1953), *All the Brothers Were Valiant* (MGM, 1953), *Kiss Me, Kate!* (MGM, 1953), *The Long, Long Trailer* (MGM, 1954), *Men of the Fighting Lady* (MGM, 1954), *Tennessee Champ* (MGM, 1954), *The Marauders* (MGM, 1955), *The Glass Slipper* (MGM, 1955), *Running Wild* (Univ., 1955), *Shack-out on 101* (AA, 1955), *The Man in the Gray Flannel Suit* (20th, 1956), *Johnny Concho* (UA, 1956), *The Naked Hills* (AA, 1956), *The Great Man* (Univ., 1956), *Joe Butterfly* (Univ., 1957), *The Fuzzy Pink Nightgown* (UA, 1957), *Don't Go Near the Water* (MGM, 1957), *The Deep Six* (WB, 1958), *A Time to Love and a Time to Die* (Univ., 1958), *The Perfect Furlough* (Univ., 1958), *A Hole in the Head* (UA, 1959), *That Kind of Woman* (Par., 1959), *The Crowded Sky* (WB, 1960), *The Absent-Minded Professor* (BV, 1961), *King of the Roaring 20's—The Story of Arnold Rothstein* (AA, 1961), *Pattern For Plunder* ("Operation Mermaid"—Herts Lion International, 1963), *Son of Flubber* (BV, 1963), *Man in the Middle* (20th, 1964), *Dr. Strangelove* (Col., 1964), *Honeymoon Hotel* (MGM, 1964), *Stage to Thunder Rock* (Par., 1964), *The Patsy* (Par., 1964), *Bikini Beach* (AIP, 1964), *The Americanization of Emily* (MGM, 1964), *Nightmare in the Sun* (Zodiac, 1965), *The Great Race* (WB, 1965), *Promise Her Anything* (Par., 1966), *Stagecoach* (20th, 1966), *Around the World Under the Sea* (MGM, 1966), *Night of the Grizzly* (Par., 1966), *Warning Shot* (Par., 1967), *Run Like a Thief* (Feature Film Corporation of America, 1967), *Welcome to Hard Times* (MGM, 1967), *The War Wagon* (Univ., 1967), *MacKenna's Gold* (Col., 1968), *Finian's Rainbow* (WB-7 Arts, 1968), *Blood Holiday* (Cinegai-Jolly, 1968).

Rock Hudson and Gig Young in *Strange Bedfellows*.

GIG YOUNG (Byron Ellsworth Barr) Born November 4, 1917, St. Cloud, Minnesota. Married Sheila Stapler; divorced. Married Sophie Rosenstein; widowed 1952. Married Elizabeth Montgomery (1956); divorced. Married Elaine Whitman (1963), child: Jennifer.

Feature Films:

as Byron Barr: *Misbehaving Husbands* (PRC, 1940), *Navy Blues* (WB, 1941), *One Foot in Heaven* (WB, 1941), *They Died With Their Boots On* (WB, 1941), *Sergeant York* (WB, 1941), *You're in the Army Now* (WB, 1941), *The Male Animal* (WB, 1942), *The Affairs of Susan* (Par., 1945).

as Gig Young: *Captains of the Clouds* (WB, 1942), *The Gay Sisters* (WB, 1942), *Air Force* (WB, 1943), *Old Acquaintance* (WB, 1943), *Escape Me Never* (WB, 1947), *The Woman in White* (WB, 1948), *Wake of the Red Witch* (Rep., 1948), *Lust for Gold* (Col., 1949), *Tell It to the Judge* (Col., 1949)., *Hunt the Man Down* (RKO, 1950), *Target Unknown* (Univ., 1951), *Only the Valiant* (WB, 1951), *Come Fill the Cup* (WB, 1951), *Slaughter Trail* (RKO, 1951), *Too Young to Kiss* (MGM, 1951), *Holiday for Sinners* (MGM, 1952), *You for Me* (MGM, 1952), *The Girl Who Had Everything* (MGM, 1953), *Arena* (MGM, 1953), *Torch Song* (MGM, 1953), *Young at Heart* (WB, 1954), *The Desperate Hours* (Par., 1955), *Desk Set* (20th, 1957), *Teacher's Pet* (Par., 1958), *The Tunnel of Love* (MGM, 1958), *Ask Any Girl* (MGM, 1959), *The Story on Page One* (20th, 1959), *That Touch of Mink* (Univ., 1962), *Kid Galahad* (UA, 1962), *Five Miles to Midnight* (UA, 1963), *For Love or Money* (Univ., 1963), *A Ticklish Affair* (MGM, 1964), *Strange Bedfellows* (Univ., 1964), *The Shuttered Room* (WB-7 Arts 1967).

LORETTA YOUNG (Gretchen Young) Born January 6, 1913, Salt Lake City, Utah. Married Grant Withers (1930); annulled 1931. Married Thomas Lewis (1940), children: Judy, Christopher, Peter.

Spencer Tracy, Loretta Young and Walter Connolly in *Man's Castle*.

Sound Feature Films: *The Forward Pass* (WB, 1929), *The Squall* (WB, 1929), *The Careless Age* (WB, 1929), *Fast Life* (WB, 1929), *Show of Shows* (WB, 1929), *Loose Ankles* (WB, 1930), *The Man From Blankley's* (WB, 1930), *The Second Floor Mystery* (WB, 1930), *Road to Paradise* (WB, 1930), *Kismet* (WB, 1930), *Truth About Youth* (WB, 1930), *The Devil to Pay* (UA, 1930), *Beau Ideal* (RKO, 1931), *Right of Way* (WB, 1931), *Three Girls Lost* (Fox, 1931), *Too Young to Marry* (WB, 1931), *Big Business Girl* (WB, 1931), *I Like Your Nerve* (WB, 1931), *Platinum Blonde* (Col., 1931), *The Ruling Voice* (WB, 1931), *Taxi* (WB, 1932), *The Hatchet Man* (WB, 1932), *Three Wise Girls* (Col., 1932), *Play Girl* (WB, 1932), *Zoo in Budapest* (Fox, 1933), *Week-End Marriage* (WB, 1932), *Life Begins* (WB, 1932), *They Call It Sin* (WB, 1932), *Employees' Entrance* (WB, 1933), *Grand Slam* (WB, 1933), *The Life of Jimmy Dolan* (WB, 1933), *Midnight Mary* (MGM, 1933), *Heroes for Sale* (WB, 1933), *The Devil's in Love* (Fox, 1933), *She Had to Say Yes* (WB, 1933), *Man's Castle* (Col., 1933), *House of Rothschild* (UA, 1934), *Bulldog Drummond Strikes Back* (UA, 1934), *Born to Be Bad* (UA, 1934), *Caravan* (Fox, 1934), *The White Parade* (Fox, 1934), *Clive of India* (UA, 1935), *Call of the Wild* (UA, 1935), *Shanghai* (Par., 1935), *The Crusades* (Par., 1935), *The Unguarded Hour* (MGM, 1936), *Private Number* (20th, 1936), *Ramona* (20th, 1936), *Ladies in Love* (20th, 1936), *Love Is News* (20th, 1937), *Cafe Metropole* (20th, 1937), *Love Under Fire* (20th, 1937), *Wife, Doctor and Nurse* (20th, 1937), *Second Honeymoon* (20th, 1937), *Four Men and a Prayer* (20th, 1938), *Three Blind Mice* (20th, 1938), *Suez* (20th, 1938), *Kentucky* (20th,

1938), *Wife, Husband and Friend* (20th, 1939), *The Story of Alexander Graham Bell* (20th, 1939), *Eternally Yours* (UA, 1939), *The Doctor Takes a Wife* (Col., 1940), *He Stayed for Breakfast* (Col., 1940), *The Lady From Cheyenne* (Univ., 1941), *The Men in Her Life* (Col., 1941), *Bedtime Story* (Col., 1941), *A Night to Remember* (Col., 1942), *China* (Par., 1943), *Ladies Courageous* (Univ., 1944), *And Now Tomorrow* (Par., 1944), *Along Came Jones* (RKO, 1945), *The Stranger* (RKO, 1946), *The Perfect Marriage* (Par., 1946), *The Farmer's Daughter* (RKO, 1947), *The Bishop's Wife* (RKO, 1947), *Rachel and the Stranger* (RKO, 1948), *The Accused* (Par., 1948), *Mother Is a Freshman* (20th, 1949), *Come to the Stable* (20th, 1949), *Key to the City* (MGM, 1950), *Cause for Alarm* (MGM, 1951), *Half Angel* (20th, 1951), *Paula* (Col., 1952), *Because of You* (Univ., 1952), *It Happens Every Thursday* (Univ., 1953).

Robert Young, Barbara Stanwyck and Hardie Albright in *Red Salute*.

ROBERT YOUNG Born February 22, 1907, Chicago, Illinois. Married Elizabeth Henderson (1933), children: Carol, Barbara, Elizabeth, Kathleen.

Feature Films: *Black Camel* (Fox, 1931), *The Sin of Madel on Claudet* (MGM, 1931), *Guilty Generation* (Col., 1931), *Hell Divers* (MGM, 1931), *Wet Parade* (MGM, 1932), *Strange Interlude* (MGM, 1932), *New Morals for Old* (MGM, 1932), *Unashamed* (MGM, 1932), *The Kid From Spain* (UA, 1932), *Today We Live* (MGM, 1933), *Hell Below* (MGM, 1933), *Men Must Fight* (MGM, 1933), *Tugboat Annie* (MGM, 1933), *Saturday's Millions* (Univ., 1933), *Right to Romance* (RKO, 1933), *House of Rothschild* (UA, 1934), *Carolina* (Fox, 1934), *Lazy River* (MGM, 1934), *Spitfire* (RKO, 1934), *Whom the Gods Destroy* (Col., 1934), *Paris Interlude* (MGM, 1934), *Death on the Diamond* (MGM, 1934), *The Band Plays On* (MGM, 1934), *West Point of the Air* (MGM, 1935), *Vagabond Lady* (MGM, 1935), *Calm Yourself* (MGM, 1935), *Red Salute* (UA, 1935), *The Bride Comes Home* (Par., 1935), *Remember Last Night?* (Univ., 1935), *Secret Agent* (Gaumont-British, 1936), *It's Love Again* (Gaumont-British, 1936), *Three Wise Guys* (MGM, 1936), *Sworn Enemy* (MGM, 1936), *The Bride Walks Out* (RKO, 1936), *The Longest Night* (MGM, 1936), *Stowaway* (20th, 1936), *Dangerous Number* (MGM, 1937), *I Met Him in Paris* (Par., 1937), *The Emperor's Candlesticks* (MGM, 193d), *Married Before Breakfast* (MGM, 1937), *The Bride Wore Red* (MGM, 1937), *Navy Blue and Gold* (MGM, 1937), *Paradise for Three* (MGM, 1938), *Josette* (20th, 1938), *The Toy Wife* (MGM, 1938), *Three Comrades* (MGM, 1938), *Rich Man—Poor Girl* (MGM, 1938), *The Shining Hour* (MGM, 1938), *Honolulu* (MGM, 1939), *Bridal Suite* (MGM, 1939), *Maisie* (MGM, 1939), *Miracles For Sale* (Col., 1939), *Florian* (MGM, 1940), *Northwest Passage* (MGM, 1940), *The Mortal Storm* (MGM, 1940), *Sporting Blood* (MGM, 1940), *Dr. Kildare's Crisis* (MGM, 1940), *The Trial of Mary Dugan* (MGM, 1941), *Western Union* (20th, 1941), *Lady Be Good* (MGM, 1941), *Married Bachelor* (MGM, 1941),

H.M. Pulham, Esq. (MGM, 1941), *Joe Smith, American* (MGM, 1942), *Cairo* (MGM, 1942), *Journey for Margaret* (MGM, 1942), *Slightly Dangerous* (MGM, 1943), *Claudia* (20th, 1943), *Sweet Rosie O'Grady* (20th, 1943), *The Canterville Ghost* (MGM, 1944), *Those Endearing Young Charms* (RKO, 1945), *The Enchanted Cottage* (RKO, 1945), *The Searching Wind* (Par., 1946), *Lady Luck* (RKO, 1946), *Claudia and David* (20th, 1946), *They Won't Believe Me* (RKO, 1947), *Crossfire* (RKO, 1947), *Relentless* (Col., 1948), *Sitting Pretty* (20th, 1948), *Adventure in Baltimore* (RKO, 1949), *Bride for Sale* (RKO, 1949), *That Forsyte Woman* (MGM, 1950), *And Baby Makes Three* (Col., 1950), *Goodbye, My Fancy* (WB, 1951), *The Second Woman* (UA, 1951), *On The Loose* (RKO, 1951), *The Half-Breed* (RKO, 1952), *Secret of the Incas* (Par., 1954).

ROLAND YOUNG Born November 11, 1887, London, England. Married Marjorie Kummer (1921); divorced 1940. Married Patience DuCroz (1948). Died June 5, 1953.

Roland Young and Joan Blondell in *Topper Returns*.

Feature Films: *Unholy Night* (MGM, 1929), *Her Private Life* (WB, 1929), *Wise Girl* (MGM, 1930), *The Bishop Murder Case* (MGM, 1930), *Madam Satan* (MGM, 1930), *New Moon* (MGM, 1930), *The Prodigal* (MGM, 1931), *Don't Bet on Women* (Fox, 1931), *Squaw Man* (MGM, 1931), *Annabelle's Affairs* (Fox, 1931), *The Guardsman* (MGM, 1931), *Pagan Lady* (Col., 1931), *Wedding Rehearsal* (London, 1932), *Lovers Courageous* (MGM, 1932), *A Woman Commands* (RKO, 1932), *One Hour With You* (Par., 1932), *This Is the Night* (Par., 1932), *Street of Women* (WB, 1932), *They Just Had to Get Married* (Univ., 1933), *A Lady's Profession* (Par., 1933), *Pleasure Cruise* (Fox, 1933), *Blind Adventure* (RKO, 1933), *His Double Life* (Par., 1933), *Here Is My Heart* (Par., 1934), *Ruggles of Red Gap* (MGM, 1935), *David Copperfield* (MGM, 1935), *The Unguarded Hour* (MGM, 1936), *One Rainy Afternoon* (UA, 1936), *Give Me Your Heart* (WB, 1936), *Call It a Day* (WB, 1937), *The Man Who Could Work Miracles* (UA, 1937), *Topper* (MGM, 1937), *Ali Baba Goes to Town* (20th, 1937), *Sailing Along* (Gaumont-British, 1938), *The Young in Heart* (UA, 1938), *Topper Takes a Trip* (UA, 1939), *Yes, My Darling Daughter* (WB, 1939), *The Night of Nights* (Par., 1939), *Here I Am, a Stranger* (20th, 1939), *He Married His Wife* (20th, 1940), *Irene* (RKO, 1940), *Star Dust* (20th, 1940), *Private Affairs* (Univ., 1940), *Dulcy* (MGM, 1940), *No, No, Nanette* (RKO, 1940), *The Philadelphia Story* (MGM, 1940), *Topper Returns* (UA, 1941), *The Flame of New Orleans* (Univ., 1941), *Two-Faced Woman* (MGM, 1941), *The Lady Has Plans* (Par., 1942), *They All Kissed the Bride* (Col., 1942), *Tales of Manhattan* (20th, 1942), *Forever and a Day* (RKO, 1943), *Standing Room Only* (Par., 1944), *And Then There Were None* (20th, 1945), *You Gotta Stay Happy* (Univ., 1948), *The Great Lover* (Par., 1949), *Bond Street* (Stratford, 1950), *Let's Dance* (Par., 1950), *St. Benny the Dip* (UA, 1951), *That Man From Tangier* (UA, 1953).

CHAPTER II

THE DIRECTORS

The Sullivans with Selena Royle, John Campbell, Edward Ryan, Trudy Marshall, Thomas Mitchell, James Cardwell, George Offerman, Jr., and John Alvin. *(Bacon)*

LLOYD BACON Born January 16, 1890; died November 15, 1955; *The Singing Fool*, 1928; *Honky Tonk*, 1929; *A Notorious Affair*, 1930; *Moby Dick*, 1930 (plus codirected with Michael Curtiz a separate German version, 1930); *Kept Husbands*, 1931; *Honor of the Family*, 1931; *You Said a Mouthful*, 1932; *42nd Street* (with Busby Berkeley), 1933; *Picture Snatcher*, 1933; *Mary Stevens, M.D.*, 1933; *Footlight Parade* (with Busby Berkeley), 1933; *Wonder Bar* (with Busby Berkeley), 1934; *He Was Her Man*, 1934; *Here Comes the Navy*, 1934; *Devil Dogs of the Air*, 1935; *In Caliente* (with Busby Berkeley), 1935; *Broadway Gondolier*, 1935; *The Irish in Us*, 1935; *Frisco Kid*, 1935; *Sons O' Guns*, 1936; *Cain and Mabel*, 1936; *Gold Diggers of 1937* (with Busby Berkeley), 1936; *Marked Woman*, 1937; *San Quentin*, 1937; *Submarine D-1*, 1937; *A Slight Case of Murder*, 1938; *Cowboy*

from Brooklyn, 1938; *Boy Meets Girl*, 1938; *Racket Busters*, 1938; *Wings of the Navy*, 1939; *The Oklahoma Kid*, 1939; *Indianapolis Speedway*, 1939; *Invisible Stripes*, 1939; *A Child Is Born*, 1940; *Three Cheers for the Irish*, 1940; *Brother Orchid*, 1940; *Knute Rockne, All American*, 1940; *Honeymoon for Three*, 1941; *Footsteps in the Dark*, 1941; *Affectionately Yours*, 1941; *Navy Blues*, 1941; *Larceny, Inc.*, 1942; *Wings for the Eagle*, 1942; *Action in the North Atlantic*, 1943; *The Sullivans*, 1944; *Sunday Dinner for a Soldier*, 1944; *I Wonder Who's Kissing Her Now*, 1947; *You Were Meant for Me*, 1948; *Give My Regards to Broadway*, 1948; *Don't Trust Your Husband*, or *An Innocent Affair*, 1948; *Mother Is a Freshman*, 1949; *It Happens Every Spring*, 1949; *Miss Grant Takes Richmond*, 1949; *Kill the Umpire*, 1950; *The Good Humor Man*, 1950; *The Fuller Brush Girl*, 1950; *Call Me Mister* (with Busby Berkeley), 1951; *The Frogmen*, 1951; *Golden Girl*, 1951; *The I Don't Care Girl*, 1953; *The Great Sioux Uprising*, 1953; *Walking My Baby Back Home*, 1953; *The French Line*, 1954; *She Couldn't Say No*, 1954.

Two Weeks With Love with Jane Powell, Ann Harding, Debbie Reynolds, Carleton Carpenter, Ricardo Montalban, Gary Gray, Phyllis Kirk and Tommy Rettig. *(Berkeley)*

BUSBY BERKELEY Born November 29, 1895; *Whoopee* (with Thornton Freeland), 1930; *Kiki* (with Samuel Taylor), 1931; *Palmy Days* (with Edward Sutherland), 1931; *Flying High* (with Charles Riesner), 1931; *Night World* (with Hobart Henley), 1932; *Bird of Paradise* (with King Vidor), 1932; *The Kid from Spain* (with Leo McCarey), 1932; *42nd Street* (with Lloyd Bacon), 1933; *Gold Diggers of 1933* (with Mervyn LeRoy), 1933; *She Had to Say Yes*, 1933; *Footlight Parade* (with Lloyd Bacon), 1933; *Roman Scandals* (with Frank Tuttle), 1933; *Wonder Bar* (with Lloyd Bacon), 1934; *Fashions of 1934* (with William Dieterle), 1934; *Twenty Million Sweethearts* (with Ray Enright), 1934; *Dames* (with Ray Enright), 1934; *Gold Diggers of 1935*, 1935; *Go Into Your Dance* (with Archie Mayo), 1935; *Bright Lights*, 1935; *In Caliente* (with Lloyd Bacon), 1935; *I Live for Love*, 1935; *Stars Over Broadway* (with William Keighley), 1935; *Stage Struck*, 1936; *Gold Diggers of 1937* (with Lloyd Bacon), 1936; *The Go-Getter*, 1937; *The Singing Marine* (with Ray Enright), 1937; *Varsity Show* (with William Keighley), 1937; *Hollywood Hotel*, 1937; *Men Are Such Fools*, 1938; *Gold Diggers in Paris* (with Ray Enright), 1938; *Garden of the Moon*, 1938; *Comet Over Broadway*, 1938; *They Made Me a Criminal*, 1939; *Broadway Serenade* (with Robert Z. Leonard), 1939; *Babes in Arms*, 1939; *Fast and Furious*, 1939; *Forty Little Mothers*, 1940; *Strike Up the Band*, 1940; *Blonde Inspiration*, 1941; *Ziegfeld Girl* (with Robert Z. Leonard), 1941; *Lady Be Good* (with Norman Z. McLeod), 1941; *Babes on Broadway*, 1941; *Born to Sing* (with Edward Ludwig), 1941; *For Me and My Gal*, 1942; *Girl Crazy* (with Norman Taurog), 1943; *The Gang's All Here*, 1943; *Cinderella Jones*, 1946; *Take Me Out to the Ball Game*, 1949; *Two Weeks With Love* (with Roy Rowland), 1950; *Call Me Mister* (with Lloyd Bacon), 1951; *Two Tickets to Broadway* (with James V. Kern), 1951; *Million Dollar Mermaid* (with Mervyn LeRoy), 1952; *Small Town Girl* (with Leslie Kardos), 1953; *Easy to Love* (with Charles Walters), 1953; *Rose Marie* (with Mervyn LeRoy), 1954; *Jumbo*, or *Billy Rose's Jumbo* (with Charles Walters), 1962.

FRANK CAPRA Born May 19, 1897; *Flight*, 1929; *Ladies of Leisure*, 1930; *Rain or Shine*, 1930; *Dirigible*, 1931; *Miracle Woman*, 1931; *Platinum Blonde*, 1931; *Forbidden*, 1932; *American Madness*, 1932; *The Bitter Tea of General Yen*, 1933; *Lady for a Day*, 1933; *It Happened One Night*, 1934; *Broadway Bill*, 1934; *Mr. Deeds Goes to Town*, 1936; *Lost Horizon*, 1937; *You Can't Take It With You*, 1938; *Mr. Smith Goes to Washington*, 1939; *Meet John Doe*, 1941; *Arsenic and Old Lace*, 1944; *It's a Wonderful Life*, 1946; *State of the Union*, 1948; *Riding High*, 1950; *Here Comes the Groom*, 1951; *A Hole in the Head*, 1959; *Pocketful of Miracles*, 1961.

Dirigible with Hobart Bosworth and Ralph Graves. *(Capra)*

ROGER CORMAN Born April 5, 1926; *The Monster From the Ocean Floor* (producer only), 1954; *The Fast and the Furious* (producer only), 1954; *Highway Dragnet* (producer only), 1954; *Five Guns West*, 1955; *Apache Woman*, 1955; *The Day the World Ended*, 1956; *Swamp Woman*, 1956; *Oklahoma Woman*, 1956; *Gunslinger*, 1956; *It Conquered the World*, 1956; *Not of This Earth*, 1957; *The Undead*, 1957; *She-Gods of*

The Raven with Boris Karloff and Peter Lorre. *(Corman)*

Shark Reef, 1957; *Naked Paradise*, 1957; *Attack of the Crab Monsters*, 1957; *Rock All Night*, 1957; *Teenage Doll*, 1957; *Carnival Rock*, 1957; *The Little Guy* (uncompleted), 1957; *Reception* (uncompleted), 1957; *Sorority Girl*, 1958; *Viking Women and the Sea Serpent*, 1958; *War of the Satellites*, 1958; *Machine Gun Kelly*, 1958; *Teenage Caveman*, 1958; *I, Mobster*, 1958; *Bucket of Blood*, 1959; *Cry Baby Killer*, 1959; *Wasp Woman*, 1959; *Ski Troop Attack*, 1960; *The Fall of the House of Usher*, 1960; *The Little Shop of Horrors*, 1960; *Last Woman on Earth*, 1960; *Creature from the Haunted Sea*, 1961; *Atlas*, 1961; *The Pit and the Pendulum*, 1961; *The Intruder*, 1961; *The Premature Burial*, 1962; *Tales of Terror*, 1962; *Tower of London*, 1962; *The Young Racers*, 1963; *The Raven*, 1963; *The Terror*, 1963; *X—The Man With the X-Ray Eyes*, 1963; *The Haunted Palace*, 1963; *The Secret Invasion*, 1964; *The Masque of the Red Death*, 1964; *The Tomb of Ligeia*, 1965; *The Wild Angels*, 1966; *The Saint Valentine's Day Massacre*, 1967; *The Trip*, 1967; *What's in It for Harry?*, 1968.

JOHN CROMWELL Born December 23, 1888; *The Dummy*, 1929; *The Mighty*, 1929; *The Dance of Life* (with Edward Sutherland), 1929; *Close Harmony* (with Edward Sutherland), 1929; *Street of Chance*, 1930; *Tom Sawyer*, 1930; *The Texan*, 1930; *For the Defense*, 1930; *Scandal Street*, 1931; *Rich Man's Folly*, 1931; *Vice Squad*, 1931; *Unfaithful*, 1931; *The World and the Flesh*, 1931; *Sweepings*, 1933; *The Silver Cord*, 1933; *Double Harness*, 1933; *Ann Vickers*, 1933; *Spitfire*, 1934; *This Man Is Mine*, 1934; *Of Human Bondage*, 1934; *The Fountain*, 1934; *Jalna*, 1935; *Village Tale*, 1935; *I Dream Too Much*, 1935; *Little Lord Fauntleroy*, 1936; *To Mary—With Love*, 1936; *Banjo on My Knee*, 1936; *The Prisoner of Zenda*, 1937; *Algiers*, 1938; *Made for Each Other*, 1939; *In Name Only*, 1939; *Abe Lincoln in Illinois*, 1940; *Victory*, 1940; *So Ends Our Night*, 1941; *Son of Fury*, 1942; *Since You Went Away*, 1944; *The Enchanted Cottage*, 1945; *Anna and the King of Siam*, 1946; *Dead Reckoning*, 1947; *Night Song*, 1947; *Caged*, 1950; *The Company She Keeps*, 1951; *The Racket*, 1951; *Hidden Fear*, 1957; *The Goddess*, 1958; *A Matter of Morals*, 1961.

Night Song with Ethel Barrymore and Merle Oberon. *(Cromwell)*

A Woman's Face with Conrad Veidt, Joan Crawford, Donald Meek and Connie Gilchrist. *(Cukor)*

GEORGE CUKOR Born July 7, 1899; *Grumpy* (with Cyril Gardner), 1930; *Virtuous Sin* (with Louis Gasnier), 1930 *The Royal Family of Broadway* (with Cyril Gardner), 1930; *Tarnished Lady*, 1931; *Girls About Town*, 1931; *One Hour With You* (with Ernst Lubitsch), 1932; *What Price Hollywood*, 1932; *A Bill of Divorcement*, 1932; *Rockabye*, 1932; *Our Betters*, 1933; *Dinner at Eight*, 1933; *Little Women*, 1933; *David Copperfield*, 1935; *Sylvia Scarlett*, 1935; *Romeo and Juliet*, 1936; *Camille*, 1936; *Holiday*, 1938; *Zaza*, 1939; *Gone With the Wind* (replaced by Sam Wood, then Victor Fleming), 1939; *The Women*, 1939; *Susan and God*, 1940; *The Philadelphia Story*, 1940; *A Woman's Face*, 1941; *Two-Faced Woman*, 1942; *Her Cardboard Lover*, 1942; *Keeper of the Flame*, 1942; *Gaslight*, 1944; *Winged Victory*, 1944; *Desire Me* (uncredited), 1947; *A Double Life*, 1947; *Edward, My Son*, 1948; *Adam's Rib*, 1949; *A Life of Her Own*, 1950; *Born Yesterday*, 1950; *The Model and the Marriage Broker*, 1951; *The Marrying Kind*, 1952; *Pat and Mike*, 1952; *The Actress*, 1953; *It Should Happen to You*, 1953; *A Star Is Born*, 1954; *Bhowani Junction*, 1956; *Les Girls*, 1957; *Wild Is the Wind*, 1957; *Heller in Pink Tights* (with Arthur Rosson), 1960; *Song Without End* (replaced the late Charles Vidor), 1959; *Let's Make Love*, 1960; *The Chapman Report*, 1962; *My Fair Lady* 1964; *The Nine-Tiger Man* (uncompleted), 1967.

MICHAEL CURTIZ Born December 24, 1888; died April 11, 1962; *The Glad Rag Doll*, 1929; *Madonna of Avenue A*, 1929; *The Gamblers*, 1929; *Hearts in Exile*, 1929; *Noah's Ark*, 1929; *Mammy*, 1930; *Under a Texas Moon*, 1930; *The Matrimonial Bed*, 1930; *A Soldier's Plaything*, 1930; *Bright Lights*, 1930; *River's End*, 1930; *God's Gift to Women*, 1931; *The Mad Genius*, 1931; *The Woman From Monte Carlo*, 1932; *The Strange Love of Molly Louvain*, 1932; *Alias the Doctor*, 1932; *Cabin in the Cotton* (with William Keighley), 1932; *Doctor X*, 1932; *20,000 Years in Sing Sing*, 1933; *The Mystery of the Wax Museum*, 1933; *The Keyhole*, 1933; *Private Detective 62*, 1933; *Goodbye Again*, 1933; *The Kennel Murder Case*, 1933; *Female*, 1933; *Mandalay*, 1934; *Jimmy the Gent*, 1934; *The Key*, 1934; *British Agent*, 1934; *Black Fury*, 1935;

I'll See You in My Dreams with Doris Day and Danny Thomas. *(Curtiz)*

The Case of the Curious Bride, 1935; *Captain Blood*, 1935; *Little Big Shot*, 1935; *Front Page Woman*, 1935; *The Walking Dead*, 1936; *The Charge of the Light Brigade*, 1936; *Stolen Holiday*, 1937; *Mountain Justice*, 1937; *Kid Galahad*, 1937; *The Perfect Specimen*, 1937; *Gold Is Where You Find It*, 1938; *Sons of Liberty*, 1938; *The Adventures of Robin Hood* (with William Keighley), 1938; *Four's a Crowd*, 1938; *Four Daughters*, 1938; *Angels With Dirty Faces*, 1938; *Dodge City*, 1939; *Daughters Courageous*, 1939; *The Private Lives of Elizabeth and Essex*, 1939; *Four Wives*, 1939; *Virginia City*, 1940; *The Sea Hawk*, 1940; *Santa Fe Trail*, 1940; *The Sea Wolf*, 1941; *Dive Bomber*, 1941; *Captains of the Clouds*, 1942; *Yankee Doodle Dandy*, 1942; *Casablanca*, 1942; *Mission to Moscow*, 1943; *This Is the army*, 1943; *Passage to Marseilles*, 1944; *Janie*, 1944; *Roughly Speaking*, 1945; *Mildred Pierce*, 1945; *Night and Day*, 1946; *Life With Father*, 1947; *The Unsuspected*, 1947; *Romance on the High Seas*, 1948; *My Dream Is Yours*, 1949; *Flamingo Road*, 1949; *The Lady Takes a Sailor*, 1949; *The Breaking Point*, 1950; *Bright Leaf*, 1950; *Young Man With a Horn*, 1950; *Force of Arms*, 1951; *Jim Thorpe, All American*, 1951; *I'll See You in My Dreams*, 1952; *The Story of Will Rogers*, 1952; *The Jazz Singer*, 1952; *Trouble Along the Way*, 1953; *The Boy From Oklahoma*, 1954; *The Egyptian*, 1954; *White Christmas*, 1954; *We're No Angels*, 1955; *The Vagabond King*, 1956; *The Scarlet Hour*, 1956; *The Best Things in Life Are Free*, 1956; *The Helen Morgan Story*, 1957; *King Creole*, 1958; *The Proud Rebel*, 1958; *The Hangman*, 1959; *The Man in the Net*, 1959; *A Breath of Scandal*, 1959; *The Adventures of Huckleberry Finn*, 1960; *Francis of Assisi*, 1961; *The Comancheros*, 1961;

DELMER DAVES Born July 24, 1904; *Destination Tokyo*, 1943; *The Very Thought of You*, 1944; *Hollywood Canteen*, 1944; *Pride of the Marines*, 1945; *This Love of Ours*, 1945; *The Red House*, 1947; *Dark Passage*, 1947; *To the Victor*, 1948; *A Kiss in the Dark*, 1949; *Task Force*, 1949; *Broken Arrow*, 1950; *Bird of Paradise*, 1951; *Return of the Texan*, 1952; *Treasure of the Golden Condor*, 1953; *Never Let Me Go*, 1953; *Demetrius and the Gladiators*, 1953; *Drumbeat*, 1954; *Jubal*, 1956; *The Last Wagon*, 1956; *3 : 10 to Yuma*, 1957; *Cowboy*, 1958; *Kings Go Forth*, 1958; *The Badlanders*, 1958; *The Hanging Tree*, 1959; *A Summer Place*, 1959; *Parrish*, 1961; *Susan Slade*, 1961; *Rome Adventure*, 1962; *Spencer's Mountain*, 1963; *Youngblood Hawke*, 1964; *The Battle of the Villa Fiorita*, 1965.

Drum Beat with Anthony Caruso, Marisa Pavan and Alan Ladd. *(Daves)*

CECIL B. DE MILLE Born August 12, 1881; died January 21, 1959; *The Godless Girl*, 1929; *Dynamite*, 1929; *Madame Satan*, 1930; *The Squaw Man*, 1931; *The Sign of the Cross*, 1932; *This Day and Age*, 1933; *Four Frightened People*, 1934; *Cleopatra*, 1934; *The Crusades*, 1935; *The Plainsman*, 1936; *The Buccaneer*, 1938; *Union Pacific*, 1939; *North West Mounted Police*, 1940; *Reap the Wild Wind*, 1942; *The Story of Dr. Wassell*, 1944; *Unconquered*, 1947; *Samson and Deliah*, 1949; *The Greatest Show on Earth*, 1952; *The Ten Commandments*, 1956; *The Buccaneer* (producer only), 1958.

209

Four Frightened People with Mary Boland, Claudette Colbert, Herbert Marshall, William Gargan and Leo Carrillo. *(DeMille)*

WILLIAM DIETERLE Born July 15, 1893, *Kismet* (separate German version), 1930; *The Last Flight*, 1931; *Her Majesty, Love*, 1931; *Man Wanted*, 1932; *Jewel Robbery*, 1932; *The Crash*, 1932; *Scarlet Dawn*, 1932; *Lawyer Man*, 1932; *Six Hours to Live*, 1932; *Grand Slam*, 1933; *From Headquarters*, 1933; *Fashions of 1934*, 1934; *Concealment*, 1934; *Firebird*, 1934; *Madame Du Barry*, 1934; *Fog Over Frisco*, 1934; *A Midsummer Night's Dream* (with Max Reinhardt), 1935; *Satan Met a Lady*, 1936; *The Story of Louis Pasteur*, 1935; *Dr. Socrates*, 1935; *The Great O'Malley*, 1936; *Another Dawn*, 1937; *The White Angel*, 1936; *The Life of Emile Zola*, 1937; *Blockade*, 1938; *Juarez*, 1939; *The Hunchback of Notre Dame*, 1939; *Dr. Ehrlich's Magic Bullet*, 1940; *A Dispatch from Reuters*, 1940; *All That Money Can Buy*, 1941; *Syncopation*, 1942; *Tennessee Johnson*, 1942; *Kismet*, 1944; *I'll Be Seeing You*, 1944; *Love Letters*, 1945; *This Love of Ours*, 1945; *The Searching Wind*, 1946; *Duel in the Sun* (with King Vidor), 1946; *A Portrait of Jennie*, 1948; *The Accused*, 1948; *Rope of Sand*, 1949; *Paid in Full* or *Bitter Victory*, 1949; *Volcano*, 1949; *September Affair*, 1950; *Dark City*, 1950; *Red Mountain*, 1951; *Peking Express*, 1951; *Turning Point*, 1952; *Boots Malone*, 1952; *Salome*, 1953; *Elephant Walk*, 1954; *Joseph and His Brethren* (unreleased), 1954; *Magic Fire*, 1956; *The Loves of Omar Khayyam*, 1957; *Friday the Thirteenth* (unreleased), 1957; *John Paul Jones*, 1959; *Dubrowsky* (shot initially in Italy), 1960.

Another Dawn with Kay Francis and Ian Hunter. *(Dieterle)*

EDWARD DMYTRYK Born August 4, 1908; *The Hawk*, 1935; *Television Spy*, 1939; *Emergency Squad*, 1940; *Golden Gloves*, 1940; *Mystery Sea Raider*, 1940; *Her First Romance*, 1940; *Secrets of the Lone Wolf*, 1941; *The Devil Commands*, 1941; *Under Age*, 1941; *Sweetheart of the Campus*, 1941; *The Blonde from Singapore*, 1941; *Confessions of Boston Blackie*, 1941; *Counter-Espionage*, 1942; *Seven Miles From Alcatraz*, 1942; *Hitler's Children*, 1943; *The Falcon Strikes Back*, 1943; *Captive Wild Woman*, 1943; *Behind the Rising Sun*, 1943; *Tender Comrade*, 1943; *Murder, My Sweet*, 1944; *Back to Bataan*, 1945; *Cornered*, 1945;

Till the End of Time, 1946; *Crossfire*, 1947; *So Well Remembered*, 1947; *Give Us This Day*, 1949; *The Hidden Room*, 1949; *Mutiny*, 1952; *The Sniper*, 1952; *Eight Iron Men*, 1952; *The Juggler*, 1953; *The Caine Mutiny*, 1954; *Broken Lance*, 1954; *The End of the Affair*, 1955; *Soldier of Fortune*, 1955; *The Left Hand of God*, 1955; *The Mountain*, 1956; *Raintree County*, 1957; *The Young Lions*, 1958; *Warlock*, 1959; *The Blue Angel*, 1959; *A Walk on the Wild Side*, 1962; *The Reluctant Saint*, 1962; *The Carpetbaggers*, 1964; *Mirage*, 1965; *Alvarez Kelly*, 1966; *Anzio*, 1968.

Mirage with Diane Baker and Gregory Peck. *(Dmytryk)*

ALAN DWAN Born April 3, 1885; *Frozen Justice*, 1929; *South Sea Rose*, 1929; *What a Widow*, 1930; *Man to Man*, 1930; *Chances*, 1931; *Wicked*, 1931; *While Paris Sleeps*, 1932; *Her First Affair*, 1933; *I Spy*, 1933; *Counsel's Opinion*, 1933; *The Morning After*, 1934; *Black Sheep*, or *Star for a Night*, 1935; *Navy Wife*, or *Beauty's Daughter*, 1935; *The Song and Dance Man*, 1936; *Human Cargo*, 1936; *High Tension*, 1936; *15 Maiden Lane*, 1936; *Woman Wise*, 1937; *That I May Live*, 1937; *One Mile From Heaven*, 1937; *Heidi*, 1937; *Rebecca of Sunnybrook Farm*, 1938; *Josette*, 1938; *Suez*, 1938; *The Three Musketeers*, 1939; *The Gorilla*, 1939; *Frontier Marshal*, 1939; *Sailor's Lady*, 1940; *Young People*, 1940; *Trail of the Vigilantes*, 1940; *Look Who's Laughing*, 1941; *Rise and Shine*, 1941; *Here We Go Again*, 1942; *Friendly Enemies*, 1942; *Around the World*, 1943; *Up in Mabel's Room*, 1944; *Abroad With Two Yanks*, 1944; *Brewster's Millions*, 1945; *Getting Gertie's Garter*, 1945; *Rendezvous With Annie*, 1946; *Calendar Girl*, 1947; *Northwest Outpost*, 1947; *Driftwood*, 1947; *The Inside Story*, 1948; *Angel in Exile* (with Philip Ford), 1948; *Sands of Iwo Jima*, 1949; *Surrender*, 1950; *Belle Le Grand*, 1951; *The Wild Blue Yonder*, 1951; *I Dream of Jeannie*, 1952; *Montana Belle* (shot in 1948), 1952; *The Woman They Almost Lynched*, 1953; *Sweethearts on Parade*, 1953; *Flight Nurse*, 1953; *Silver Lode*, 1954; *Passion*, 1954; *Cattle Queen of Montana*, 1954; *Escape to Burma*, 1955; *Pearl of the South Pacific*, 1955; *Tennessee's Partner*, 1955; *Slightly Scarlet*, 1956; *Hold Back the Night*, 1956; *The River's Edge*, 1957; *The Restless Breed*, 1957; *Enchanted Island*, 1958; *The Most Dangerous Man Alive* (shot in 1958), 1961.

Look Who's Laughing with Fibber McGee, Lucille Ball, Edgar Bergen and Molly McGee. *(Dwan)*

JOHN FORD Born February 1, 1895; *Black Watch*, 1929; *Salute*, 1929; *Men Without Women*, 1930; *Born Reckless*, 1930; *Up the River*, 1930; *The Seas Beneath*, 1931; *The Brat*, 1931; *Arrowsmith*, 1931; *Air Mail*, 1932; *Flesh*, 1932; *Pilgrimage*, 1933; *Doctor Bull*, 1933; *The Lost Patrol*, 1934; *The World Moves On*, 1934; *Judge Priest*, 1934; *The Whole Town's Talking*, 1935; *The Informer*, 1935; *Steamboat Round the Bend*, 1935; *The Prisoner of Shark Island*, 1936; *Mary of Scotland*, 1936; *The Plough and the Stars*, 1936; *Wee Willie Winkie*, 1937; *The Hurricane* (with Stuart Heisler), 1937; *Four Men and a Prayer*, 1938; *Submarine Patrol*, 1938; *Stagecoach*, 1939; *Young Mr. Lincoln*, 1939; *Drums Along the Mohawk*, 1939; *The Grapes of Wrath*, 1940; *The Long Voyage Home*, 1940; *Tobacco Road*, 1941; *How Green Was My Valley*, 1941; *They Were Expendable* (with Robert Montgomery), 1945; *My Darling Clementine*, 1946; *The Fugitive* (with Emilio Fernandez), 1947; *Fort Apache*, 1948; *Three Godfathers*, 1948; *Mighty Joe Young* (producer only), 1949; *Pinky* (replaced by Elia Kazan), 1949; *She Wore a Yellow Ribbon*, 1949; *When Willie Comes Marching Home*, 1950; *Wagonmaster*, 1950; *Rio Grande*, 1950; *What Price Glory*, 1952; *The Quiet Man*, 1952; *The Sun Shines Bright*, 1953; *Mogambo*, 1953; *Hondo*, 1953; *The Long Gray Line*, 1955; *Mister Roberts* (with Mervyn LeRoy), 1955; *The Searchers*, 1956; *The Wings of Eagles*, 1957; *The Rising of the Moon*, 1957; *The Last Hurrah*, 1958; *Gideon's Day*, 1959; *The Horse Soldiers*, 1959; *Sergeant Rutledge*, 1960; *The Alamo* (with John Wayne), 1960; *Two Rode Together*, 1961; *The Man Who Shot Liberty Valance*, 1961; *How the West Was Won*: "The Civil War" episode, 1962; *Donovan's Reef*, 1963; *Cheyenne Autumn*, 1964; *Young Cassidy* (replaced by Jack Cardiff), 1964, *7 Women*, 1965.

Rio Grande with John Wayne and Maureen O'Hara. *(Ford)*

JOHN FRANKENHEIMER Born February 19, 1930; *The Young Stranger*, 1957; *The Young Savages*, 1961; *All Fall Down*, 1962; *Bird Man of Alcatraz*, 1962; *The Manchurian Candidate*, 1962; *Seven Days in May*, 1964; *The Train* (replaced Arthur Penn, with Bernard Farrel), 1965, *Seconds*, 1966; *Grand Prix* (replaced John Sturges), 1967; *The Extraordinary Seaman*, 1968; *The Fixer*, 1968.

Seconds with Rock Hudson. *(Frankenheimer)*

TAY GARNETT Born 1905; *The Flying Fool*, 1929; *Oh Yeah!*, 1930; *Officer O'Brien*, 1930; *Her Man*, 1930; *Bad Company*, 1931; *Prestige*, 1932; *One Way Passage*, 1932; *Okay America*, 1932; *Destination Unknown*, 1933; *S.O.S. Iceberg*, 1933; *She Couldn't Take It*, 1935; *China Seas*, 1935; *Professional Soldier*, 1935; *Love Is News*, 1937; *Slave Ship*, 1937; *Stand-In*, 1937; *The Joy of Living*, 1938; *Trade Winds*, 1938; *Eternally Yours*, 1939; *Slightly Honorable*, 1940; *Seven Sinners*, 1940; *Cheers for Miss Bishop*, 1941; *Unexpected Uncle* (producer only), 1941), *Weekend for Three* (producer only), 1941; *My Favorite Spy*, 1942; *Bataan*, 1943; *The Cross of Lorraine*, 1943; *Mrs. Parkington*, 1944; *The Valley of Decision*, 1945; *The Postman Always Rings Twice*, 1946; *Wild Harvest*, 1947; *A Connecticut Yankee in King Arthur's Court*, 1949; *The Fireball*, 1950; *Cause for Alarm*, 1951; *Soldiers Three*, 1951; *One Minute to Zero*, 1952; *Main Street to Broadway*, 1953; *The Black Knight*, 1954; *Cinerama's Seven Wonders of the World*, India Sequence, 1956; *A Terrible Beauty*, or *The Night Fighters*, 1960; *Cattle King*, 1963.

Seven Sinners with John Wayne and Marlene Dietrich. *(Garnett)*

EDMUND GOULDING Born March 20, 1891; died December 24, 1959; *Paramount on Parade* (among various directors), 1930; *The Devil's Holiday*, 1930; *Reaching for the Moon*, 1931; *The Night Angel*, 1931; *Flesh*, 1932; *Grand Hotel*, 1932; *Blondie of the Follies*, 1932; *Riptide*, 1934; *The Flame Within*, 1935; *That Certain Woman*, 1937; *The Dawn Patrol*, 1938; *White Banners*, 1938; *Dark Victory*, 1939; *The Old Maid*, 1939; *We Are Not Alone*, 1939; *Till We Meet Again*,

The Flame Within with Henry Stephenson, Herbert Marshall and Ann Harding. *(Goulding)*

211

1940; *The Great Lie*, 1941; *Forever and a Day* (among various directors), 1943; *The Constant Nymph*, 1943; *Claudia*, 1943; *Of Human Bondage*, 1946; *The Razor's Edge*, 1946; *Nightmare Alley*, 1947; *Everybody Does It*, 1949; *Mister 880*, 1950; *We're Not Married*, 1952; *Down Among the Sheltering Palms* (completed 1951), 1953; *Teenage Rebel*, 1956; *Mardi Gras*, 1958.

HENRY HATHAWAY Born March 13, 1898; *Wild Horse Mesa*, 1933; *Heritage of the Desert*, 1933; *Under the Tonto Rim*, 1933; *Sunset Pass*, 1933; *Man of the Forest*, 1933; *To the Last Man*, or *Law of Vengeance*, 1933; *The Last Round-Up*, 1934; *Thundering Herd*, 1933; *The Witching Hour*, 1934; *Come On, Marines!*, 1934; *Now and Forever*, 1934; *Peter Ibbetson*, 1935; *Lives of a Bengal Lancer*, 1935; *The Trail of the Lonesome Pine*, 1936; *Go West, Young Man*, 1936; *Souls at Sea*, 1937; *Spawn of the North*, 1938; *The Real Glory*, 1939; *Johnny Apollo*, 1940; *Brigham Young—Frontiersman*, 1940; *The Shepherd of the Hills*, 1941; *Sundown*, 1941; *Ten Gentlemen From West Point*, 1942; *China Girl*, 1942; *Wing and a Prayer*, 1944; *Home in Indiana*, 1944; *Nob Hill*, 1945; *The House on 92nd Street*, 1945; *The Dark Corner*, 1946; *13 Rue Madeleine*. 1946; *Kiss of Death*, 1947; *Call Northside 777*, 1948; *Down to the Sea in Ships*, 1949; *The Black Rose*, 1949; *You're in the Navy Now*, 1951; *Rawhide*, 1951; *14 Hours*, 1951; *The Desert Fox*, 1951; *Diplomatic Courier*, 1952; *White Witch Doctor*, 1953; *Niagara*, 1953; *Prince Valiant*, 1954; *Garden of Evil*, 1954; *The Racers*, 1955; *The Bottom of the Bottle*, 1956; *23 Paces to Baker Street*, 1956; *Legend of the Lost*, 1957; *From Hell to Texas*, or *Man Hunt*, 1958; *Woman Obsessed*, 1959; *Seven Thieves*, 1960; *North to Alaska*, 1960; *How the West Was Won* (three to the five episodes; other two: John Ford and George Marshall), 1962; *Circus World*, 1964; *Of Human Bondage* (replaced Ken Hughes), 1964; *The Sons of Katie Elder*, 1965; *Nevada Smith*, 1966; *The Last Safari*, 1967.

Man's Favorite Sport? with Rock Hudson and Paula Prentiss. *(Hawks)*

Murder, 1930; *The Skin Game*, 1931; *Rich and Strange*, 1932; *Number Seventeen*, 1932; *Lord Camber's Ladies* (producer only), 1932; *Waltzes From Vienna*, 1933; *The Man Who Knew Too Much*, 1934; *The Thirty-Nine Steps*, 1935; *The Secret Agent*, 1936; *Sabotage*, 1936; *Young and Innocent*, 1937; *The Lady Vanishes*, 1938; *Jamaica Inn*, 1939; *Rebecca*, 1940; *Foreign Correspondent*, 1940; *Mr. and Mrs. Smith*, 1941; *Suspicion*, 1941; *Saboteur*, 1942; *Shadow of a Doubt*, 1943; *Lifeboat*, 1944; *Bon Voyage*, 1944; *Adventure Malgache*, 1944; *Spellbound*, 1945; *Notorious*, 1946; *The Paradine Case*, 1947; *Rope*, 1948; *Under Capricorn*, 1949; *Stage Fright*, 1950; *Strangers on a Train*, 1951; *I Confess*, 1953; *Dial M For Murder*, 1954; *Rear Window*, 1954; *To Catch a Thief*, 1955; *The Trouble With Harry*, 1955; *The Man Who Knew Too Much*, 1956; *The Wrong Man*, 1956; *Vertigo*, 1958; *North by Northwest*, 1959; *The Wreck of the Mary Deare* (replaced by Michael Anderson), 1959; *Psycho*, 1960; *The Birds*, 1963; *Marnie*, 1964; *Torn Curtain*, 1966.

China Girl with George Montgomery, Philip Ahn and Gene Tierney. *(Hathaway)*

Saboteur with Priscilla Lane, Robert Cummings and Otto Kruger. *(Hitchcock)*

HOWARD HAWKS Born May 30, 1896; *The Dawn Patrol*, 1930; *The Criminal Code*, 1931; *The Crowd Roars*, 1932; *Scarface, Shame of the Nation*, 1932; *Tiger Shark*, 1932; *Today We Live*, 1933; *Viva Villa!* (with Jack Conway), 1934; *Twentieth Century*, 1934; *Barbary Coast*, 1935; *Ceiling Zero*, 1936; *The Road to Glory*, 1936; *Come and Get It* (with William Wyler), 1936; *Bringing Up Baby*, 1938; *Only Angels Have Wings*, 1939; *His Girl Friday*, 1939; *The Outlaw* (with Howard Hughes; shot in 1943), 1946; *Sergeant York*, 1941; *Ball of Fire*, 1941; *Air Force*, 1943; *Corvette K-225* (producer only), 1943; *To Have and Have Not*, 1944; *The Big Sleep*, 1946; *Red River*, 1948; *A Song Is Born*, 1948; *I Was a Male War Bride*, 1949; *The Thing* (producer only), 1951; *The Big Sky*, 1952; *O. Henry's Full House:* "The Ransom of Red Chief" episode, 1952; *Monkey Business*, 1952; *Gentleman Prefer Blondes*, 1953; *Land of the Pharaohs*, 1955; *Rio Bravo*, 1959; *Hatari!*, 1962; *Man's Favorite Sport?*, 1963; *Red Line 7000*, 1965.

ALFRED HITCHCOCK Born August 13, 1899; *Blackmail*, 1929; *Elstree Calling*, two episodes, 1930; *Juno and the Paycock*, 1930;

JOHN HUSTON Born August 5, 1906; *The Maltese Falcon*, 1941; *In This Our Life*, 1942; *Across the Pacific*, 1942; *Report From the Aleutians*, 1943; *The Battle of San Pietro*, 1944; *Let There Be Light*, 1945; *The Stranger* (producer only, under Sam Spiegel), 1946; *The Treasure of Sierra Madre*, 1948; *Key Largo*, 1948; *We Were Strangers*, 1949; *The Asphalt Jungle*, 1950; *The Prowler* (producer only, under Sam Spiegel), 1951; *The Red Badge of Courage*, 1951; *The African Queen*, 1951; *Moulin Rouge*, 1952; *Beat the Devil*, 1953; *Moby Dick*, 1956; *Heaven Knows, Mr. Allison*, 1957; *A Farewell to Arms* (replaced by Charles Vidor), 1957; *The Barbarian and the Geisha*, 1958; *The Roots of Heaven*, 1958; *The Unforgiven*, 1960; *The Misfits*, 1960; *Freud, the Secret Passion*, 1962; *The List of Adrian Messenger*, 1963; *The Night of the Iguana*, 1964; *The Bible*, 1966; *Casino Royale* (David Niven footage only; 38 minutes), 1967; *Reflections in a Golden Eye*, 1967; *Sinful Davey*, 1968.

ELIA KAZAN Born September 7, 1909; *It's Up to You*, 1941; *A Tree Grows in Brooklyn*, 1945; *Sea of Grass*, 1947; *Boomerang*, 1947; *Gentle-*

The Maltese Falcon with Humphrey Bogart, Peter Lorre, Mary Astor and Sydney Greenstreet. *(Huston)*

man's Agreement, 1947; *Pinky*, 1949; *Panic in the Streets*, 1950; *A Streetcar Named Desire*, 1951; *Viva Zapata!*, 1952; *Man on a Tightrope*, 1953; *On the Waterfront*, 1954; *East of Eden*, 1955; *Baby Doll*, 1956; *A Face in the Crowd*, 1956; *Wild River*, 1960; *Splendor in the Grass*, 1961; *America America*, 1963.

Man on a Tightrope with Alex D'Arcy and Terry Moore. *(Kazan)*

HENRY KING Born January 24, 1896; *Hell's Harbor*, 1930; *Eyes of the World*, 1930; *Lightning*, 1930; *Merely Mary Ann*, 1931; *Over the Hill*, 1931; *The Woman in Room 13*, 1932; *State Fair*, 1933; *I Loved You Wednesday*, 1933; *Carolina*, 1934; *Marie Galante*, 1934; *One More Spring*, 1935; *Way Down East*, 1935; *The Country Doctor*, 1936; *Ramona*, 1936; *Lloyds of London*, 1936; *Seventh Heaven*, 1937; *In Old Chicago*, 1938; *Alexander's Ragtime Band*, 1938; *Jesse James*, 1939; *Stanley and Livingstone*, 1939; *Little Old New York*, 1940; *Maryland*, 1940; *Chad Hanna*, 1940; *A Yank in the R.A.F.*, 1941; *Remember the Day*, 1941; *The Black Swan*, 1942; *The Song of Bernadette*, 1943; *Wilson*, 1944; *A Bell for Adano*, 1945; *Margie*, 1946; *The Captain From Castile*, 1947; *Deep Waters*, 1948; *The Prince of Foxes*, 1949; *Twelve O'Clock High*, 1949; *The Gunfighter*, 1950; *I'd Climb the Highest Mountain*, 1951; *David and Bathsheba*, 1951; *Wait Till the Sun Shines, Nellie*, 1952; *O. Henry's Full House*: "The Gift of the Magi" episode, 1952; *The Snows of Kilimanjaro*, 1952; *King of the Khyber Rifles*, 1953; *Untamed*, 1955; *Love Is a Many-Splendored Thing*, 1955; *Carousel*, 1956; *The Sun Also Rises*, 1957; *The Old Man and the Sea* (replaced Fred Zinnemann; replaced by John Sturges), 1958; *The Bravados*, 1958; *This Earth Is Mine*, 1959; *Beloved Infidel*, 1959; *Tender Is the Night*, 1961.

Little Old New York with Henry Stephenson and Brenda Joyce. *(King)*

HENRY KOSTER Born May 1, 1905; *Three Smart Girls*, 1936; *One Hundred Men and a Girl*, 1937; *The Rage of Paris*, 1938; *First Love*, 1939; *Three Smart Girls Grow Up*, 1939; *It Started With Eve*, 1941; *Spring Parade*, 1940; *Between Us Girls*, 1942; *Music for Millions*, 1944; *Two Sisters From Boston*, 1946; *The Bishop's Wife*, 1947; *Luck of the Irish*, 1948; *Come to the Stable*, 1949; *The Inspector General*, 1949; *My Blue Heaven*, 1949; *Wabash Avenue*, 1950; *Harvey*, 1950; *No Highway in the Sky*, 1951; *Mr. Belvedere Rings the Bell*, 1951; *O. Henry's Full House*: "The Cop and the Anthem" episode, 1952; *Stars and Stripes Forever*, 1952; *My Cousin Rachel*, 1952: *The Robe*, 1953; *Desiree*, 1954; *A Man Called Peter*, 1955; *The Virgin Queen*, 1955; *Good Morning, Miss Dove*, 1955; *D-Day, The Sixth of June*, 1956; *The Power and the Prize*, 1956; *My Man Godfrey*, 1957; *Fraulein*, 1958; *The Naked Maja*, 1959; *The Story of Ruth*, 1960; *Flower Drum Song*, 1961; *Mr. Hobbs Takes a Vacation*, 1962; *Take Her, She's Mine*, 1963; *Dear Brigitte*, 1965; *The Singing Nun*, 1966.

My Blue Heaven with Dan Dailey, Betty Grable and Mitzi Gaynor. *(Koster)*

FRITZ LANG Born December 5, 1890, *Fury*, 1936; *You Only Live Once*, 1937; *You and Me*, 1938; *The Return of Frank James*, 1940; *Western Union*, 1941; *Man Hunt*, 1941; *Confirm or Deny* (replaced by Archie Mayo), 1941; *Moontide* (replaced by Archie Mayo), 1942; *Hangmen Also Die*, 1943; *The Ministry of Fear*, 1944; *The Woman in the Window*, 1944; *Scarlet Street*, 1945; *Cloak and Dagger*, 1946; *The Secret Beyond the Door*, 1948; *The House by the River*, 1950; *American Guerrilla in the Philippines*, 1950; *Rancho Notorious*, 1952; *Clash by Night*, 1952; *The Blue Gardenia*, 1953; *The Big Heat*, 1953; *Human Desire*, 1954; *Moonfleet*, 1955; *While the City Sleeps*, 1956; *Beyond a Reasonable Doubt*, 1956.

MITCHELL LEISEN Born October 6, 1899; *Cradle Song*, 1933; *Death Takes a Holiday*, 1934; *Murder at the Vanities*, 1934; *Behold My Wife*, 1935; *Four Hours to Kill*, 1935; *Hands Across the Table*, 1935; *13 Hours by Air*, 1936; *The Big Broadcast of 1937*, 1936; *Swing High, Swing Low*, 1937; *East Living*, 1937; *The Big Broadcast of 1938*, 1938;

The Ministry of Fear with Marjorie Reynolds and Ray Milland *(Lang)*

Artists and Models Abroad, 1938; *Midnight*, 1939; *Remember the Night*, 1940; *Arise, My Love*, 1940; *I Wanted Wings*, 1941; *Hold Back the Dawn*, 1941; *The Lady Is Willing*, 1942; *Take a Letter, Darling*, 1942; *No Time For Love*, 1943; *Lady in the Dark*, 1944; *Frenchman's Creek*, 1944; *Practically Yours*, 1944; *Kitty*, 1945; *Masquerade in Mexico*, 1945; *To Each His Own*, 1946; *Suddenly It's Spring*, 1947; *Golden Earrings*, 1947; *Dream Girl*, 1948; *Bride of Vengeance*, 1949; *Song of Surrender*, 1949; *No Man of Her Own*, 1950; *Captain Carey, U.S.A.*, 1950; *The Mating Season*, 1951; *Darling, How Could You!*, 1951; *Young Man with Ideas*, 1952; *Tonight We Sing*, 1953; *Bedevilled*, 1955; *The Girl Most Likely*, 1957; *Las Vegas by Night*, or *Here's Las Vegas*, 1963.

The Lady Is Willing with Marlene Dietrich and Sterling Holloway (man without flowers at window). *(Leisen)*

MERVYN LEROY Born October 15, 1900; *Dramatic School* (producer only), 1938; *Flying Romeos*, 1928; *Harold Teen*, 1928; *Naughty Baby*, 1929; *Hot Stuff*, 1929; *Broadway Daddy*, 1929; *Showgirl in Hollywood*, 1930; *Little Johnny Jones*, 1930; *Playing Around*, 1930; *Numbered Men*, 1930; *Top Speed*, 1930; *Little Caesar*, 1930; *Gentlemen's Fate*, 1931; *Five Star Final*, 1931; *Broad-Minded*, 1931; *Too Young to Marry*, 1931; *Local Boy Makes Good*, 1931; *Tonight or Never*, 1931; *Two Seconds*, 1932; *Heart of New York*, 1932; *Big City Blues*, 1932; *Three on a Match*, 1932; *I Am a Fugitive From a Chain Gang*, 1932; *High Pressure*, 1932; *Gold Diggers of 1933* (with Busby Berkeley), 1933; *Tugboat Annie*, 1933; *Elmer the Great*, 1933; *Hard to Handle*, 1933; *The World Changes*, 1933; *Heat Lightning*, 1934; *Sweet Adeline*, 1934; *Happiness Ahead*, 1934; *Hi, Nellie!*, 1934; *Page Miss Glory*, 1935; *Oil for the Lamps of China*, 1935; *I Found Stella Parish*, 1935; *Anthony Adverse*, 1936; *The King and the Chorus Girl*, 1937; *They Won't Forget*, 1937; *Fools for Scandal*, 1938; *A Day at the Circus* (producer only), 1939; *The Wizard of Oz* (producer only), 1939; *Escape*, 1940; *Waterloo Bridge*, 1940; *Blossoms in the Dust*, 1941; *Unholy Partners*, 1941; *Johnny Eager*, 1941; *Random Harvest*, 1942; *Madame Curie*, 1943; *Thirty Seconds Over Tokyo*, 1944; *Without Reservations*, 1946; *Homecoming*, 1948; *Little Women*, 1949; *In the Good Old Summertime*,

1949; *Any Number Can Play*, 1949; *East Side, West Side*, 1949; *Quo Vadis*, 1951; *Lovely to Look At* (with Vincente Minnelli), 1952; *Million Dollar Mermaid* (with Busby Berkeley), 1952; *Latin Lovers*, 1953: *Rose Marie* (with Busby Berkeley), 1954; *Strange Lady in Town*, 1955; *Mister Roberts* (with John Ford), 1955, *Toward the Unknown*, 1956; *The Bad Seed*, 1956; *No Time for Sergeants*, 1958; *Home Before Dark*, 1958; *The F.B.I. Story*, 1959; *Wake Me When It's Over*, 1960; *The Devil at Four O'Clock*, 1961; *A Majority of One*, 1962; *Gypsy*, 1962; *Mary, Mary*, 1963; *Moment to Moment*, 1965.

Latin Lovers with Lana Turner and Ricardo Montalban. *(LeRoy)*

ANATOLE LITVAK Born May 10, 1902; *The Woman I Love*, 1937; *Tovarich*, 1937; *The Amazing Dr. Clitterhouse*, 1938; *The Sisters*, 1938; *Confessions of a Nazi Spy*, 1939; *The Roaring Twenties* (replaced by Raoul Walsh), 1939; *Castle on the Hudson*, 1940; *All This, and Heaven Too*, 1940; *City for Conquest*, 1940; *Out of the Fog*, 1941; *One Foot in Heaven* (replaced by Irving Rapper), 1941; *Blues in the Night*, 1941; *This Above All*, 1942; "Why We Fight" series features: *The Nazis Strike*, 1942; *Divide and Conquer*, 1943; *The Battle of Russia*, 1943; *The Battle of China*, 1944; *War Comes to America* (with Frank Capra), 1945; *Operation Titanic*, 1943; *New Orleans* (replaced by Arthur Lubin), 1947; *The Long Night*, 1947; *Sorry, Wrong Number*, 1948; *The Snake Pit*, 1949; *Decision Before Dawn*, 1951; *Act of Love*, 1954; *The Deep Blue Sea*, 1955; *Anastasia*, 1956; *The Journey*, 1959; *Goodbye Again*, 1961; *Five Miles to Midnight*, 1963; *A Shot in the Dark* (replaced by Blake Edwards), 1964; *10:30 P.M. Summer* (producer only), 1966; *The Night of the Generals*, 1967.

The Journey with Yul Brynner and Deborah Kerr. *(Litvak)*

FRANK LLOYD Born February 2, 1889; died 1960; *Weary River*, 1929; *Drag*, 1929; *Young Nowheres*, 1929; *The Dark Streets*, 1929; *Son of the Gods*, 1930; *The Lash*, 1931; *East Lynne*, 1931; *Right of Way*, 1931; *Age for Love*, 1931; *Passport to Hell*, 1932; *Cavalcade*, 1933; *Berkeley Square*, 1933; *Hoopla*, 1933; *Servants' Entrance*, 1934; *Mutiny on the Bounty*, 1935; *A Tale of Two Cities*, 1935; *Under Two Flags*, 1936; *Maid of Salem*, 1937; *Wells Fargo*, 1937; *If I Were King*, 1938; *Rulers of the Sea*, 1939; *The Howards of Virginia* (producer only), 1940; *The Lady from Cheyenne*, 1941; *This Woman Is Mine*, 1941; *The Spoilers* (producer only), 1942; *Invisible Agent* (producer only), 1942; *Saboteur* (co-producer only), 1942; *Forever and a Day* (among various directors), 1943; *Blood on the Sun*, 1945; *Shanghai Story*, 1954; *The Last Command*, 1955.

If I Were King with Ronald Colman, Henry Wilcoxon, William Haade, Jean Fenwick, Sidney Toler, Stanley Ridges, Francis McDonald and Adrian Morris. *(Lloyd)*

LEO McCAREY Born October 30, 1894; *The Sophomore*, 1929; *Red Hot Rhythm*, 1929; *Wild Company*, 1930; *Let's Go Native*, 1930; *Part Time Wife*, 1930; *Indiscreet*, 1931; *The Kid From Spain* (with Busby Berkeley), 1932; *Duck Soup*, 1933; *Six of a Kind*, 1934; *Belle of the Nineties*, 1934; *Ruggles of Red Gap*, 1935; *The Milky Way*, 1936; *Make Way for Tomorrow*, 1937; *The Awful Truth*, 1937; *Love Affair*, 1939; *My Favorite Wife*, 1940; *Once Upon a Honeymoon*, 1942; *Going My Way*, 1944; *The Bells of St. Mary's*, 1945; *Good Sam*, 1948; *My Son John*, 1952; *An Affair to Remember*, 1957; *Rally 'Round the Flag, Boys!*, 1958; *Satan Never Sleeps*, 1961.

Satan Never Sleeps with William Holden, France Nuyen and Clifton Webb. *(McCarey)*

ROUBEN MAMOULIAN Born October 8, 1898; *Applause*, 1929; *City Streets*, 1931; *Dr. Jekyll and Mr. Hyde*, 1932; *Love Me Tonight*, 1932; *The Song of Songs*, 1933; *Queen Christina*, 1933; *We Live Again*, 1934; *Becky Sharp* (replaced Lowell Sherman, who died during shooting), 1935; *The Gay Desperado*, 1936; *High, Wide and Handsome*, 1937;

Golden Boy, 1939; *The Mark of Zorro*, 1940; *Blood and Sand*, 1941; *Rings on Her Fingers*, 1942; *Summer Holiday*, 1948; *The Wild Heart* (replaced Michael Powell, but uncredited), 1951; *Silk Stockings*, 1957; *Porgy and Bess* (replaced by Otto Preminger), 1959.

Rings on Her Fingers with Henry Fonda and Gene Tierney. *(Mamoulian)*

JOSEPH L. MANKIEWICZ Born February 11, 1909; *The Three Godfathers* (producer only), 1936; *Fury* (producer only), 1936; *The Gorgeous Hussy* (producer only), 1936; *Love on the Run* (producer only), 1936; *The Bride Wore Red* (producer only), 1937), *Double Wedding* (producer only), 1937); *Mannequin* (producer only), 1937; *Three Comrades* (producer only), 1938; *The Shopworn Angel* (producer only), 1938; ·*The Shining Hour* (producer only), 1938; *A Christmas Carol* (producer only), 1938; *The Adventures of Huckleberry Finn* (producer only), 1939; *Strange Cargo* (producer only), 1940; *The Philadelphia Story* (producer only), 1940; *The Wild Man of Borneo* (producer only), 1941); *The Feminine Touch* (producer only), 1941; *Woman of the Year* (producer only), 1942; *Cairo* (producer only), 1942; *Reunion in France* (producer only), 1942; *The Keys of the Kingdom* (producer only), 1944; *Dragonwyck*, 1946; *Somewhere in the Night*, 1946; *The Late George Apley*, 1947; *The Ghost and Mrs. Muir*, 1947; *Escape*, 1948; *A Letter to Three Wives*, 1949; *House of Strangers*, 1949; *No Way Out*, 1950; *All About Eve*, 1950; *People Will Talk*, 1951; *Five Fingers*, 1952; *Julius Caesar*, 1953; *The Barefoot Contessa*, 1954; *Guys and Dolls*, 1955; *The Quiet American*, 1958; *I Want to Live!* (co-producer only), 1958; *Suddenly, Last Summer*, 1959; *Cleopatra* (replaced various directors), 1963; *The Honey Pot*, 1967.

People Will Talk with Cary Grant and Jeanne Crain. *(Mankiewicz)*

ANTHONY MANN Born June 30, 1906; died April 29, 1967; *Dr. Broadway*, 1942; *Moonlight in Havana*, 1942; *Nobody's Darling*, 1943;

My Best Gal, 1944; *Strangers in the Night*, 1944; *The Great Flamarion*, 1945; *Two O'Clock Courage*, 1945; *Sing Your Way Home*, 1945; *Strange Impersonation*, 1946; *The Bamboo Blonde*, 1946; *Desperate*, 1947; *Railroaded*, 1947; *T-Men*, 1947; *Raw Deal*, 1948; *Reign of Terror*, 1949; *Follow Me Quietly*, 1949; *Border Incident*, 1949; *Side Street*, 1949; *Devil's Doorway*, 1950; *Winchester '73*, 1950; *The Furies*, 1950; *Quo Vadis* (as second-unit director under Mervyn LeRoy), 1951; *The Tall Target*, 1951; *Bend of the River*, 1952; *The Naked Spur*, 1953; *Thunder Bay*, 1953; *The Glenn Miller Story*, 1954; *The Far Country*, 1955; *Strategic Air Command*, 1955; *The Man From Laramie*, 1955; *The Last Frontier*, 1956; *Serenade*, 1956; *Men in War*, 1957; *The Tin Star*, 1957; *God's Little Acre*, 1957; *Man of the West*, 1958; *Spartacus* (replaced by Stanley Kubrick), 1960; *Cimarron*, 1960; *El Cid*, 1961; *The Fall of the Roman Empire*, 1964; *Heroes of Telemark*, 1965; *A Dandy in Aspic* (shot February 20, 1967 through Mann's death mid-shooting April 29, 1967; completed by Laurence Harvey, 1968).

Thunder Bay with James Stewart and Gilbert Roland. *(Mann)*

LEWIS MILESTONE Born September 30, 1895; *New York Nights*, 1929; *All Quiet on the Western Front*, 1930; *Hell's Angels* (with Howard Hughes), 1930; *The Front Page*, 1931; *Rain*, 1932; *Hallelujah, I'm a a Bum*, 1933; *The Captain Hates the Sea*, 1934; *Paris in the Spring*, 1935; *Anything Goes*, 1936; *The General Died at Dawn*, 1936; *Night of Nights*, 1939; *Of Mice and Men*, 1939; *Lucky Partners*, 1940; *My Life With Caroline*, 1941; *Edge of Darkness*, 1943; *North Star*, or *Armored Attack*, 1943; *The Purple Heart*, 1944; *A Walk in the Sun*, 1945; *The Strange Love of Martha Ivers*, 1946; *Guest in the House* (replaced John Brahm), 1945; *No Minor Vices*, 1948; *Arch of Triumph*, 1948; *The Red Pony*, 1949; *The Halls of Montezuma*, 1950; *Kangaroo*, 1952; *Les Miserables*, 1952; *Melba*, 1953; *They Who Dare*, 1954; *The Widow*, 1955; *King Kelly* (uncompleted), 1957; *Pork Chop Hill*, 1959; *Ocean's 11*, 1960; *Mutiny on the Bounty* (replaced Carol Reed), 1962; *PT-109* (replaced by Leslie H. Martinson), 1963; *The Dirty Game* (replaced by Terence Young, 1965), 1966.

Anything Goes with Charlie Ruggles, Bing Crosby and Ethel Merman. *(Milestone)*

VINCENTE MINNELLI Born February 28, 1906; *Cabin in the Sky*, 1943; *I Dood It*, 1943; *Meet Me in St. Louis*, 1944; *The Clock*, 1945; *Yolanda and the Thief*, 1945; *Ziegfeld Follies*, 1946; *Undercurrent*, 1946; *The Pirate*, 1948; *Madame Bovary*, 1949; *Father of the Bride*, 1950; *An American in Paris*, 1951; *Father's Little Dividend*, 1951; *The Bad and the Beautiful*, 1952; *Lovely to Look At* (with Mervyn LeRoy), 1952; *The Band Wagon*, 1953; *The Story of Three Loves*: "Mademoiselle" sketch, 1953; *The Long, Long Trailer*, 1953; *Brigadoon*, 1954; *The Cobweb*, 1955; *Kismet*, 1955; *Lust for Life*, 1956; *Tea and Sympathy*, 1956; *Designing Woman*, 1957; *The Seventh Sin* (replaced Ronald Neame), 1957; *Gigi*, 1958; *The Reluctant Debutante*, 1958; *Some Came Running*, 1958; *Home from the Hill*, 1960; *Bells are Ringing*, 1960; *The Four Horsemen of the Apocalypse*, 1962; *Two Weeks in Another Town*, 1962; *The Courtship of Eddie's Father*, 1963; *Goodbye Charlie*, 1964; *The Sandpiper*, 1965.

I Dood It with Red Skelton and Eleanor Powell. *(Minnelli)*

JEAN NEGULESCO Born February 29, 1900; *Kiss and Make Up*, 1934; *Crash Donovan*, 1936; *Singapore Woman*, 1941; *The Mask of Dimitrios*, 1944; *The Conspirators*, 1944; *Three Strangers*, 1946; *Nobody Lives Forever*, 1946; *Humoresque*, 1946; *Deep Valley*, 1947; *Johnny Belinda*, 1948; *Roadhouse*, 1948; *The Forbidden Street*, 1949; *Under My Skin*, 1950; *Three Came Home*, 1950; *The Mudlark*, 1950; *Take Care of My Little Girl*, 1951; *Phone Call From a Stranger*, 1952; *Lydia Bailey*, 1952; *Lure of the Wilderness*, 1952; *O. Henry's Full House*: "The Last Leaf" episode, 1952; *Titanic*, 1953; *Scandal at Scourie*, 1953; *How to Marry a Millionaire*, 1953; *Three Coins in the Fountain*, 1954; *Woman's World*, 1954; *Daddy Long Legs*, 1955; *The Rains of Ranchipur*, 1955; *Boy on a Dolphin*, 1957; *Dry Martini* (uncompleted), 1957; *The Gift of Love*, 1958; *A Certain Smile*, 1958; *Count Your Blessings*, 1959; *The Best of Everything*, 1959; *Jessica*, 1962; *The Pleasure Seekers*, 1964.

Scandal at Scourie with Greer Garson, Walter Pidgeon and Donna Corcoran. *(Negulesco)*

OTTO PREMINGER Born December 5, 1906; *Under Your Spell*, 1936; *Danger, Love at Work*, 1937; *Margin for Error*, 1943; *In the Meantime, Darling*, 1944; *Laura*, 1944; *A Royal Scandal*, 1945; *Fallen Angel*, 1945; *Centennial Summer*, 1946; *Forever Amber*, 1947; *Daisy Kenyon*, 1947; *That Lady in Ermine* (replaced Ernst Lubitsch), 1948; *The Fan*, 1949; *Whirlpool*, 1949; *Where the Sidewalk Ends*, 1950; *The Thirteenth Letter*, 1951; *Angel Face*, 1952; *The Moon Is Blue*, 1953; *River of No Return*, 1954; *Carmen Jones*, 1954; *The Court-Martial of Billy Mitchell*, 1955; *The Man with the Golden Arm*, 1955; *Saint Joan*, 1957; *Bonjour, Tristesse*, 1958; *Porgy and Bess* (replaced Rouben Mamoulian), 1959; *Anatomy of a Murder*, 1959; *Exodus*, 1960; *Advise and Consent*, 1962; *The Cardinal*, 1963; *In Harm's Way*, 1965; *Bunny Lake Is Missing*, 1965; *Hurry Sundown*, 1967.

Bunny Lake Is Missing with Clive Revill, Carol Lynley, Laurence Olivier and Keir Dullea. *(Preminger)*

MARK ROBSON Born December 4, 1913; *The Seventh Victim*, 1943; *Ghost Ship*, 1943; *Youth Runs Wild*, 1944; *Isle of the Dead*, 1945; *Bedlam*, 1946; *Roughshod*, 1949; *Champion*, 1949; *Home of the Brave*, 1949; *My Foolish Heart*, 1949; *Edge of Doom*, 1950; *Bright Victory*, 1951; *I Want You*, 1952; *Return to Paradise*, 1953; *Hell Below Zero*, 1954; *Phffft*, 1954; *The Bridges at Toko-Ri*, 1954; *A Prize of Gold*, 1955; *Trial*, 1955; *The Harder They Fall*, 1956; *The Little Hut*, 1957; *Peyton Place*, 1957; *The Inn of the Sixth Happiness*, 1958; *From the Terrace*, 1960; *Lisa* (producer only), 1962; *Nine Hours to Rama*, 1963; *The Prize*, 1963; *Von Ryan's Express*, 1965; *Lost Command*, 1966; *Valley of the Dolls*, 1967.

The Harder They Fall with Nehemiah Persoff, Humphrey Bogart, Jan Sterling and Rod Steiger. *(Robson)*

ROBERT ROSSEN Born May 16, 1908; died February 18, 1966; *Johnny O'Clock*, 1947; *Body and Soul*, 1947; *The Undercover Man* (producer only), 1949; *All the King's Men*, 1949; *No Sad Songs for Me* (producer only), 1950; *The Brave Bulls*, 1951; *Mambo*, 1955; *Alexander the Great*, 1956; *Island in the Sun*, 1957; *They Came to Cordura*, 1959; *The Hustler*, 1961; *Lilith*, 1964.

The Brave Bulls with Mel Ferrer, Eugene Iglesias (hand on gate). *(Rossen)*

GEORGE SEATON Born April 17, 1911; *Diamond Horseshoe* or *Billy Rose's Diamond Horseshoe*, 1945; *Junior Miss*, 1945; *The Shocking Miss Pilgrim*, 1947; *Miracle on 34th Street*, 1947; *Apartment for Peggy*, 1948; *Chicken Every Sunday*, 1949; *The Big Lift*, 1950; *For Heaven's Sake*, 1950; *Rhubarb* (producer only, with William Perlberg), 1951; *Aaron Slick from Punkin' Crick*, 1952; *Anything Can Happen*, 1952; *Somebody Loves Me*, 1952; *Little Boy Lost*, 1953; *The Bridges at Toko-Ri* (producer only, with William Perlberg), 1954; *The Country Girl*, 1955; *The Proud and the Profane*, 1956; *Williamsburg, Story of a Patriot*, 1957; *The Tin Star* (producer only, with William Perlberg), 1957; *Teacher's Pet*, 1958; *But Not for Me* (producer only, with William Perlberg), 1959; *The Rat Race* (producer only, with William Perlberg), 1960; *The Pleasure of His Company*, 1961; *The Counterfeit Traitor*, 1962; *The Hook*, 1963; *Twilight of Honor* (producer only, with William Perlberg), 1963; *36 Hours*, 1965.

The Shocking Miss Pilgrim with Dick Haymes and Betty Grable. *(Seaton)*

ROBERT SIODMAK Born August 8, 1900; *West Point Widow*, 1941; *Fly-By-Night*, 1942; *The Night Before the Divorce*, 1942; *My Heart Belongs to Daddy*, 1942; *Someone to Remember*, 1943; *Son of Dracula*, 1943; *Cobra Woman*, 1944; *Phantom Lady*, 1944; *Christmas Holiday*, 1944; *The Suspect*, 1945; *The Strange Affair of Uncle Harry*, 1945; *The Spiral Staircase*, 1946; *The Killers*, 1946; *The Dark Mirror*, 1946; *Time Out of Mind*, 1947; *Cry of the City*, 1948; *Criss Cross*, 1949; *The Great Sinner*, 1949; *The File on Thelma Jordan*, or *Thelma Jordan*, 1949; *Deported*, 1950; *The Whistle at Eaton Falls*, 1951; *The Crimson Pirate*, 1952; *Escape from East Berlin*, 1962; *Custer of the West*, 1967.

The Crimson Pirate with Eva Bartok and Burt Lancaster. *(Siodmak)*

GEORGE STEVENS Born December 18, 1904; *Cohens and Kellys in Trouble*, 1933; *Bachelor Bait*, 1934; *Kentucky Kernels*, 1934; *Laddie*, 1935; *The Nitwits*, 1935; *Alice Adams*, 1935; *Annie Oakley*, 1935; *Swing Time*, 1936; *Quality Street*, 1937; *A Damsel in Distress*, 1937; *Vivacious Lady*, 1938; *Gunga Din*, 1939; *Vigil in the Night*, 1940; *Penny Serenade*, 1941; *Woman of the Year*, 1942; *The Talk of the Town*, 1942; *The More the Merrier*, 1943; *I Remember Mama*, 1948; *A Place in the Sun*, 1951; *Shane*, 1953; *Giant*, 1956; *The Diary of Anne Frank*, 1959; *The Greatest Story Ever Told* (initially with David Lean), 1965; *The Stalking Moon*, 1968.

I Remember Mama with Irene Dunne, Rudy Vallee, Oscar Homolka and Steve Brown. *(Stevens)*

JOHN STURGES Born January 3, 1910; *Thunderbolt* (with William Wyler), 1945; *The Man Who Dared*, 1946; *Shadowed*, 1946; *Alias Mr. Twilight*, 1947; *For the Love of Rusty*, 1947; *Keeper of the Bees*, 1947; *Best Man Wins*, 1948; *Sign of the Ram*, 1948; *The Walking Hills*, 1949; *Mystery Street*, 1950; *The Capture*, 1950; *The Magnificent Yankee*, 1950; *Right Cross*, 1950; *Kind Lady*, 1951; *The People Against O'Hara*, 1951; *It's a Big Country:* "The Census Takers" sketch, 1951; *The Girl in White*, 1952; *Jeopardy*, 1953; *Escape from Fort Bravo*, 1953; *Bad Day*

The Scarlet Coat with Anne Francis and Cornel Wilde. *(Sturges)*

at Black Rock, 1954; *Underwater*, 1955; *The Scarlet Coat*, 1955; *Backlash*, 1956; *Gunfight at the O.K. Corral*, 1957; *The Obsessed* (uncompleted), 1957; *The Spirit of St. Louis* (replaced by Billy Wilder), 1957; *The Old Man and the Sea* (replaced various directors), 1958; *The Law and Jake Wade*, 1958; *Never So Few*, 1959; *Last Train from Gun Hill*, 1959; *The Magnificent Seven*, 1960; *By Love Possessed*, 1961; *Sergeants Three*, 1962; *A Girl Named Tamiko*, 1963; *The Great Escape*, 1963; *The Satan Bug*, 1965; *The Hallelujah Trail*, 1965; *Grand Prix* (replaced by John Frankenheimer), 1966; *Ice Station Zebra*, 1968.

NORMAN TAUROG Born February 23, 1899; *The Diplomats*, 1928; *The Farmer's Daughter*, 1928; *Lucky Boy*, 1929; *Sunny Skies*, 1930; *Hot Curves*, 1930; *Follow the Leader*, or *Manhattan Mary*, 1930; *Finn and Hattie* (with Norman Z. McLeod), 1931; *Skippy*, 1931; *Newly Rich*, 1931; *Huckleberry Finn*, 1931; *Sooky*, 1931; *Hold 'Em Jail*, 1932; *The Phantom President*, 1932; *If I Had a Million*, 1932; *A Bedtime Story*, 1933; *The Way to Love*, 1933; *We're Not Dressing*, 1934; *Mrs. Wiggs of the Cabbage Patch*, 1934; *College Rhythm*, 1934; *The Big Broadcast of 1936*, 1935; *Strike Me Pink*, 1936; *Rhythm on the Range*, 1936; *You Can't Have Everything*, 1937; *Mad About Music*, 1938; *The Adventures of Tom Sawyer*, 1938; *Boys Town*, 1938; *The Girl Downstairs*, 1938; *Lucky Night*, 1939; *Broadway Melody of 1940*, 1940; *Young Tom Edison*, 1940; *Little Nellie Kelly*, 1940; *Men of Boys' Town*, 1941; *Design for Scandal*, 1941; *A Yank at Eton*, 1942; *Presenting Lily Mars*, 1943; *Girl Crazy* (with Busby Berkeley), 1943; *The Hoodlum Saint*, 1946; *The Beginning, or the End*, 1947; *The Bride Goes Wild*, 1948; *Big City*, 1948; *Words and Music*, 1948; *That Midnight Kiss*, 1949; *Please Believe Me*, 1950; *The Toast of New Orleans*, 1950; *Mrs. O'Malley and Mr. Malone*, 1950; *Rich, Young and Pretty*, 1951; *Room for One More*, 1952; *Jumping Jacks*, 1952; *The Stooge*, 1952; *The Stars Are Singing*, 1953; *The Caddy*, 1953; *Living It Up*, 1954; *You're Never Too Young*, 1955; *The Birds and the Bees*, 1956; *Pardners*, 1956; *Bundle of Joy*, 1956; *The Fuzzy Pink Nightgown*, 1957; *Onionhead*, 1958; *Don't Give Up the Ship*, 1959; *Visit to a Small Planet*, 1960; *G. I. Blues*, 1960; *Blue Hawaii*, 1961; *Girls! Girls! Girls!*, 1962; *It Happened at the World's Fair*, 1963; *Palm Springs Weekend*, 1963; *Tickle Me*, 1965; *Sergeant Deadhead, the Astronut*, 1965; *Dr. Goldfoot and the Bikini Machine*, 1965; *Spinout*, 1966; *Double Trouble*, 1967; *Speedway*, 1967.

Please Believe Me with Robert Walker, Peter Lawford, Deborah Kerr and Mark Stevens. *(Taurog)*

JACQUES TOURNEUR Born November 12, 1904; *The Winning Ticket* (with Chuck Reisner), 1935; *A Tale of Two Cities* (with Jack Conway), 1935; *They All Come Out*, 1939; *Nick Carter, Master Detective*, 1939; *Phantom Raiders*, 1940; *Doctors Don't Tell*, 1941; *Cat People*, 1942; *I Walked With a Zombie*, 1943; *The Leopard Man*, 1943; *Days of Glory*, 1944; *Experiment Perilous*, 1944; *Canyon Passage*, 1946; *Out of the Past*, 1947; *Berlin Express*, 1948; *Easy Living*, 1949; *Stars in My Crown*, 1950; *The Flame and the Arrow*, 1950; *Circle of Danger*, 1951; *Anne of the Indies*, 1951; *Way of a Gaucho*, 1952; *Appointment in Honduras*, 1953; *Stranger on Horseback*, 1955; *Wichita*,

1955; *Great Day in the Morning*, 1956; *Nightfall*, 1956; *Night of the Demon*, 1957; *The Fearmakers*, 1958; *Timbuktu*, 1959; *The Giant of Marathon*, 1959; *The Comedy of Terrors*, 1963; *War Gods of the Deep*, 1965.

The Fearmakers with Veda Ann Borg and Dana Andrews. *(Tourneur)*

FRANK TUTTLE Born August 6, 1882; died 1963; *The Studio Murder Mystery*, 1929; *The Greene Murder Case*, 1929; *Sweetie*, 1929; *Only the Brave*, 1930; *The Benson Murder Case*, 1930; *Paramount on Parade* (among various directors), 1930; *True to the Navy*, 1930; *Love Among the Millionaires*, 1930; *Her Wedding Night*, 1930; *No Limit*, 1931; *It Pays to Advertise*, 1931; *This Is the Night*, 1932; *Big Broadcast*, 1932; *Roman Scandals* (with Busby Berkeley), 1933; *Ladies Should Listen*, 1934; *Springtime for Henry*, 1934; *The Glass Key*, 1935; *College Holiday*, 1936; *Waikiki Wedding*, 1937; *Dr. Rhythm*, 1938; *I Stole a Million*, 1939; *This Gun for Hire*, 1942; *Lucky Jordan*, 1942; *Hostages*, 1943; *The Hour Before Dawn*, 1944; *The Great John L.*, 1945; *Don Juan Quilligan*, 1945; *Suspense*, 1946; *Swell Guy*, 1946; *The Magic Face*, 1951; *Hell on Frisco Bay*, 1955.

The Glass Key with George Raft and Guinn "Big Boy" Williams. *(Tuttle)*

CHARLES VIDOR Born July 27, 1900; died June 5, 1959; *The Bridge*, 1931; *The Mask of Fu Manchu*, 1932; (*not* Charles Brabin, as appears in many sources); *Sensation Hunters*, 1933; *Double Door*, 1934; *Strangers All*, 1935; *The Arizonian*, 1935; *His Family Tree*, 1935; *Muss 'Em Up*, 1936; *A Doctor's Diary*, 1937; *The Great Gambini*, 1937; *She's No Lady*, 1937; *Romance of the Redwoods*, 1939; *Those High Grey Walls*, 1939; *My Son, My Son*, 1940; *The Lady in Question*, 1940; *New York Town*, 1941; *Ladies in Retirement*, 1941; *The Tuttles of Tahiti*, 1942; *The Desperadoes*, 1943; *Cover Girl*, 1944; *Together Again*, 1944; *A Song to Remember*, 1945; *Over 21*, 1945; *Gilda*, 1946; *The Guilt of Janet Ames*, 1947; *The Loves of Carmen*, 1948; *The Man From Colorado* (replaced by

Henry Levin), 1948; *It's a Big Country* (among various directors), 1951; *Hans Christian Andersen*, 1952; *Thunder in the East*, 1953; *Rhapsody*, 1954; *Love Me or Leave Me*, 1955; *The Swan*, 1956; *The Joker Is Wild*, 1957; *A Farewell to Arms* (replaced John Huston), 1957; *Song Without End* (died during shooting; completed by George Cukor), 1960.

Rhapsody with Vittorio Gassman and Elizabeth Taylor. *(Charles Vidor)*

KING VIDOR Born February 8, 1896; *Show People*, 1928; *The Political Flapper*, or *The Patsy*, 1928; *Hallelujah!*, 1929; *Not So Dumb*, 1930; *Billy the Kid*, 1930; *Street Scene*, 1931; *The Champ*, 1931; *Bird of Paradise* (with Busby Berkeley), 1932; *Cynara*, 1932; *The Stranger's Return*, 1933; *Our Daily Bread*, 1934; *The Wedding Night*, 1935; *So Red the Rose*, 1935; *The Texas Rangers*, 1936; *Stella Dallas*, 1937; *The Citadel*, 1938; *Northwest Passage*, 1940; *Comrade X*, 1940; *H. M. Pulham, Esq.*, 1941; *An American Romance*, 1944; *Duel in the Sun* (with William Dieterle), 1946; *On Our Merry Way* (with Leslie Fenton), 1948; *The Fountainhead*, 1949; *Beyond the Forest*, 1949; *Lightning Strikes Twice*, 1951; *Japanese War Bride*, 1952; *Ruby Gentry*, 1952; *Man Without a Star*, 1955; *War and Peace*, 1956; *Solomon and Sheba*, 1959.

Comrade X with Clark Gable and Hedy Lamarr. *(King Vidor)*

RAOUL WALSH Born March 11, 1892; *In Old Arizona* (with Irving Cummings), 1929; *The Cock-Eyed World*, 1929; *Hot for Paris*, 1929; *The Big Trail*, 1930; *The Man Who Came Back*, 1931; *Women of All Nations*, 1931; *The Yellow Ticket*, 1931; *Wild Girl*, 1932; *Me and My Gal*, 1932; *Sailor's Luck*, 1933; *The Bowery*, 1933; *Going Hollywood*, 1933; *Under Pressure*, 1935; *Baby Face Harrington*, 1935; *Every Night at Eight*, 1935; *Klondike Annie*, 1936; *Big Brown Eyes*, 1936; *Spendthrift*, 1936; *You're in the Army, Now!*, 1937; *When Thief Meets Thief*, 1937; *Artists and Models*, 1937; *Hitting a New High*, 1937; *College*

Swing, 1938; *Saint Louis Blues*, 1939; *The Roaring Twenties* (replaced Anatole Litvak), 1939; *Dark Command*, 1940; *They Drive by Night*, 1940; *High Sierra*, 1941; *The Strawberry Blonde*, 1941; *Manpower*, 1941; *They Died With Their Boots On*, 1941; *Desperate Journey*, 1942; *Gentleman Jim*, 1942; *Background to Danger*, 1943; *Northern Pursuit*, 1943; *Uncertain Glory*, 1944; *San Antonio* (with David Butler), 1945; *Objective Burma*, 1945; *Salty O'Rourke*, 1945; *The Horn Blows at Midnight*, 1945; *The Man I Love*, 1946; *Stallion Road* (with James V. Kern), 1947; *Pursued*, 1947; *Cheyenne*, 1947; *Silver River*, 1948; *Fighter Squadron*, 1948; *One Sunday Afternoon*, 1948; *Colorado Territory*, 1949; *White Heat*, 1949; *Along the Great Divide*, 1951; *Captain Horatio Hornblower*, 1951; *Distant Drums*, 1951; *Glory Alley*, 1952; *The World in His Arms*, 1952; *The Lawless Breed*, 1952; *Blackbeard the Pirate*, 1952; *Sea Devils*, 1953; *A Lion Is in the Streets*, 1953; *Gun Fury*, 1953; *Saskatchewan*, 1954; *Battle Cry*, 1955; *The Tall Men*, 1955; *The Revolt of Mamie Stover*, 1956; *The King and Four Queens*, 1956; *Band of Angels*, 1957; *The Naked and the Dead*, 1958; *The Sheriff of Fractured Jaw*, 1958; *A Private's Affair*, 1959; *Come September* (producer only), 1960; *Esther and the King*, 1960; *Marines, Let's Go!*, 1961; *A Distant Trumpet*, 1964.

Northern Pursuit with Errol Flynn (center). *(Walsh)*

ORSON WELLES Born April 6, 1915; *Citizen Kane*, 1941; *The Magnificent Ambersons*, 1942; *It's All True* (unreleased), 1942; *Journey into Fear* (with Norman Foster), 1942; *The Stranger*, 1946; *The Lady From Shanghai*, 1948; *Macbeth*, 1948; *Othello*, 1952; *Confidential Report*, or *Mr. Arkadin*, 1955; *Touch of Evil*, 1958; *The Trial*, 1962; *Chimes at Midnight*, 1965.

Macbeth with Orson Welles and Jeanette Nolan. *(Welles)*

WILLIAM WELLMAN Born February 29, 1896; *Chinatown Nights*, 1929; *The Man I Love*, 1929; *Woman Trap*, 1929; *Dangerous Paradise*, 1930; *Young Eagles*, 1930; *Maybe It's Love*, 1930; *The Steel Highway*, or *Other Men's Women*, 1930; *Public Enemy*, 1931; *The Star Witness*, 1931; *Night Nurse*, 1931; *Safe in Hell*, 1931; *The Conquerors*, 1932;

The Hatchet Man, 1932; *Love Is a Racket*, 1932; *So Big*, 1932; *The Purchase Price*, 1932; *Frisco Jenny*, 1933; *Central Airport*, 1933; *Lilly Turner*, 1933; *Wild Boys of the Road*, 1933; *College Coach*, 1933; *Heroes for Sale*, 1933; *Lady of the Night*, or *Midnight Mary*, 1933; *Looking for Trouble*, 1934; *Stingaree*, 1934; *The President Vanishes*, 1934; *Call of the Wild*, 1935; *Robin Hood of El Dorado*, 1936; *Small Town Girl*, 1936; *A Star Is Born*, 1937; *Nothing Sacred*, 1937; *Men With Wings*, 1938; *Beau Geste*, 1939; *The Light That Failed*, 1939; *Reaching for the Sun*, 1941; *Roxie Hart*, 1942; *The Great Man's Lady*, 1942; *Thunder Birds*, 1942; *Lady of Burlesque*, 1943; *The Ox-Bow Incident*, 1943; *Buffalo Bill*, 1944; *Air Ship Squadron #4*, 1944 (Service film later exhibited to public); *This Man's Navy*, 1945; *The Story of G.I. Joe*, 1945, *Gallant Journey*, 1946; *Magic Town*, 1947; *The Iron Curtain*, 1948; *Yellow Sky*, 1948; *Battleground*, 1949; *The Next Voice You Hear*, 1950; *The Happy Years* (completed in 1948), 1950; *It's a Big Country* (among various directors), 1951; *Across the Wide Missouri*, 1951; *Westward the Women*, 1951; *My Man and I*, 1952; *Island in the Sky*, 1953; *The High and the Mighty*, 1954; *Track of the Cat*, 1954; *Blood Alley*, 1955; *Goodbye, My Lady*, 1956; *Darby's Rangers*, 1958; *Lafayette Escadrille*, 1958.

Roxie Hart with George Montgomery and Ginger Rogers. *(Wellman)*

BILLY WILDER Born June 22, 1906; *The Major and the Minor*, 1942; *Five Graves to Cairo*, 1943; *Double Indemnity*, 1944; *The Lost Week-End*, 1945; *The Emperor Waltz*, 1948; *A Foreign Affair*, 1948; *Sunset Boulevard*, 1950; *The Big Carnival*, or *Ace in the Hole*, 1951; *Stalag 17*, 1953; *Sabrina*, 1954; *The Seven Year Itch*, 1955; *The Spirit of St. Louis* (replaced John Sturges), 1957; *Love in the Afternoon*, 1957; *Witness for the Prosecution*, 1957; *Some Like It Hot*, 1959; *The Apartment*, 1960; *One, Two, Three!*, 1961; *Irma La Douce*, 1963; *Kiss Me, Stupid*, 1964; *The Fortune Cookie*, 1966.

The Fortune Cookie with Jack Lemmon. *(Wilder)*

ROBERT WISE Born September 10, 1914; *The Curse of the Cat People* (with Gunther von Fritsch), 1944; *Mademoiselle Fifi*, 1944; *The Body Snatchers*, 1945; *The Game of Death*, 1945; *Criminal Court*, 1946; *Born to Kill*, 1947; *Mystery in Mexico*, 1948; *Blood on the Moon*, 1948; *The Set-Up*, 1949; *Three Secrets*, 1950; *Two Flags West*, 1950; *The House on Telegraph Hill*, 1951; *The Day the Earth Stood Still*, 1951; *Captive City*, 1952; *Something for the Birds*, 1952; *Destination Gobi*, 1953; *The Desert Rats*, 1953; *So Big*, 1953; *Executive Suite*, 1954; *Helen of Troy*, 1955; *Tribute to a Bad Man*, 1956; *Somebody Up There Likes Me*, 1956; *This Could Be the Night*, 1957; *Until They Sail*, 1957; *Bannon* (uncompleted), 1957; *Run Silent, Run Deep*, 1958; *I Want to Live!*, 1958; *Odds Against Tomorrow*, 1959; *West Side Story* (with Jerome Robbins), 1961; *Two for the Seesaw*, 1962; *The Haunting* 1963; *The Sound of Music*, 1965; *The Sand Pebbles*, 1966; *Star*, 1968.

The Day the Earth Stood Still with Lock Martin, Michael Rennie and Patricia Neal. *(Wise)*

WILLIAM WYLER Born July 1, 1902; *The Shakedown*, 1929; *The Love Trap*, 1929; *Come Across*, 1929; *Evidence*, 1929; *Hell's Heroes*, 1929; *The Storm*, 1930; *A House Divided*, 1932; *Tom Brown of Culver*, 1932; *Her First Mate*, 1933; *Counsellor at Law*, 1933; *Glamour*, 1934; *The Good Fairy*, 1935; *The Gay Deception*, 1935; *Come and Get It* (with Howard Hawks), 1936; *Dodsworth*, 1936; *These Three*, 1936; *Dead End*, 1937; *Jezebel*, 1938; *Wuthering Heights*, 1939; *The Western-er*, 1940; *The Letter*, 1940; *The Little Foxes*, 1941; *Mrs. Miniver*, 1942; *The Memphis Belle*, 1943 (this and the three films following were Service feature films later exhibited to the public); *The Fighting Lady*, 1944; *Glory for Me*, 1945; *Thunderbolt* (with John Sturges), 1945; *The Best Years of Our Lives*, 1946; *The Heiress*, 1949; *Detective Story*, 1951; *Carrie*, 1952; *Roman Holiday*, 1953; *The Desperate Hours*, 1955; *Friendly Persuasion*, 1956; *Thieves' Market* (uncompleted), 1957; *The Big Country*, 1958; *Ben-Hur*, 1959; *The Children's Hour*, 1962; *The Collector*, 1965; *How to Steal a Million*, 1966; *Funny Girl*, 1968.

Come and Get It with Walter Brennan, Edward Arnold and Frances Farmer. *(Wyler)*

FRED ZINNEMANN Born April 29, 1907; *Redes* (with Emilio Gomez Muriel), 1934; *Kid Glove Killer*, 1942; *Eyes in the Night*, 1942; *The Seventh Cross*, 1944; *Little Mr. Jim*, 1946; *My Brother Talks to Horses*, 1946; *The Search*, 1948; *Act of Violence*, 1948; *The Men*, 1950; *Teresa*, 1951; *High Noon*, 1952; *Member of the Wedding*, 1952; *From Here to Eternity*, 1953; *Oklahoma!*, 1955; *A Hatful of Rain*, 1957; *The Old Man and the Sea* (replaced by Henry King, then John Sturges), 1958; *The Nun's Story*, 1959; *The Sundowners*, 1960; *Behold a Pale Horse*, 1963; *Hawaii* (replaced by George Roy Hill), 1966; *A Man for All Seasons*, 1966.

Teresa with Pier Angeli. *(Zinnemann)*

CHAPTER III

THE PRODUCERS

No Sad Songs for Me with Wendell Corey and Margaret Sullavan.

(Adler)

BUDDY ADLER Born June 22, 1906; died July 12, 1960; *The Dark Past*, 1949; *A Woman of Distinction*, 1950; *No Sad Songs for Me*, 1950; *Saturday`s Hero*, 1951; *Last of the Comanches*, 1952; *Salome*, 1953; *From Here to Eternity*, 1953; *On the Waterfront*, 1954; *Violent Saturday*, 1955; *Soldier of Fortune*, 1955; *Love Is a Many-Splendored Thing*, 1955; *The Left Hand of God*, 1955; *House of Bamboo*, 1955; *The Lieutenant Wore Skirts*, 1956; *The Bottom of the Barrel*, 1956; *The Revolt of Mamie Stover*, 1956; *Bus Stop*, 1956; *Anastasia*, 1956; *Heaven Knows, Mr. Allison*, 1957; *A Hatful of Rain*, 1957; *South Pacific*, 1958; *The Inn of the Sixth Happiness*, 1958; *The Story of Ruth* (died after preparing production), 1960; *Cleopatra* (died after preparing production), 1963.

SAMUEL Z. ARKOFF Born June 12, 1918; *Voodoo Woman*, 1957; *Rock All Night*, 1957; *Dragstrip Girl*, 1957; *Invasion of the Saucer Men*, 1957; *Reform School Girl*, 1957; *Sorority Girl*, 1957; *Motorcycle Gang*, 1957; *How to Make a Monster*, 1958; *Suicide Battalion*, 1958; *Attack of the Puppet People*, 1958; *The Bonnie Parker Story*, 1958; *War of the Colossal Beast*, 1958; *Terror From the Year 5000*, 1958; *High School Hellcats*, 1958; *Paratroop Command*, 1959; *House of Usher*, 1960; *The Pit and the Pendulum*, 1961; *The Master of the World*, 1961; *Tales of Terror*, 1962; *Panic in Year Zero*, 1962; *The Premature Burial*, 1962; *The Comedy of Terrors*, 1963; *Beach Party*, 1964; *War Gods of the Deep*, 1965; *How to Stuff a Wild Bikini*, 1965; *Beach Blanket Bingo*, 1965; *Ski Party*, 1965; *Sergeant Deadhead, the Astronut*, 1965; *Die, Monster, Die!*, 1965; *Dr. Goldfoot and the Bikini Machine*, 1965; *The Big T-N-T Show*, 1966; *The Ghost in the Invisible Bikini*, 1966; *Fireball 500*, 1966; *Thunder Alley*, 1967; *Wild in the Streets*, 1967.

ROBERT ARTHUR Born November 1, 1909; *Buck Privates Come Home*, 1947; *The Wistful Widow of Wagon Gap*, 1947; *Are You With It?*, 1948; *Abbott and Costello Meet Frankenstein*, 1948; *Mexican Hayride*, 1948; *For the Love of Mary*, 1948; *Bagdad*, 1949; *The Big*

The Premature Burial with Richard Ney (center) and Ray Milland.

(Arkoff)

222

A Man Could Get Killed with James Garner, Anthony Franciosa and Roland Culver. *(Arthur)*

Heat (under Jerry Wald), 1953; *The Black Shield of Falworth*, 1954; *The Long Gray Line* (under Jerry Wald), 1955; *Pillars of the Sky*, 1955; *Kelly and Me*, 1957; *The Midnight Story*, 1957; *Man of a Thousand Faces*, 1957; *A Time to Love and a Time to Die*, 1958; *Flood Tide*, 1958; *The Perfect Furlough*, 1958; *Operation Petticoat*, 1959; *The Great Impostor*, 1961; *Come September*, 1961; *Lover Come Back*, 1962; *That Touch of Mink*, 1962; *The Spiral Road*, 1962; *For Love or Money*, 1963; *Captain Newman, M.D.*, 1963; *Father Goose*, 1964; *Bedtime Story*, 1964; *The Brass Bottle*, 1964; *Shenandoah*, 1965; *A Very Special Favor*, 1965; *A Man Could Get Killed*, 1966.

ROBERT BASSLER Born September 26, 1903; *My Gal Sal*, 1942; *The Black Swan*, 1942; *The Lodger*, 1944; *Hangover Square*, 1945; *Thunderhead, Son of Flicka*, 1945; *Smoky*, 1946; *The Homestretch*, 1947; *Thunder in the Valley*, 1947; *The Green Grass of Wyoming*, 1948; *The Snake Pit*, 1948; *Rope of Sand*, 1949; *Thieves' Highway*, 1949; *A Ticket to Tomahawk*, 1950; *The Halls of Montezuma*, 1950; *The House on Telegraph Hill*, 1951; *Kangaroo*, 1952; *Night Without Sleep*, 1952; *My Wife's Best Friend*, 1952; *Beneath the 12-Mile Reef*, 1953; *The Girl Next Door*, 1953; *Suddenly!*, 1954; *Gentlemen Marry Brunettes*, 1955; *Gunsight Ridge*, 1957; *Stranger at Soldier Springs* (uncompleted), 1957.

A Ticket to Tomahawk with Anne Baxter, Will Wright and Dan Dailey. *(Bassler)*

PANDRO S. BERMAN Born March 28, 1905; *Way Back Home*, 1932; *Ann Vickers*, 1933; *What Price Hollywood*, 1932; *The Gay Divorcee*, 1934; *Of Human Bondage*, 1934; *Roberta*, 1935; *Alice Adams*, 1935; *Top Hat*, 1935; *Mary of Scotland*, 1936; *Sylvia Scarlett*, 1936; *Winterset*, 1936; *Stage Door*, 1937; *A Damsel in Distress*, 1937; *Room Service*, 1938; *Vivacious Lady*, 1938; *The Flying Irishman*, 1939; *Gunga Din*, 1939; *Love Affair*, 1939; *The Hunchback of Notre Dame*, 1939; *The Story of Vernon and Irene Castle*, 1939; *Ziegfeld Girl*, 1941; *Honky Tonk*, 1941; *Dragon Seed*, 1944; *The Seventh Cross*, 1944; *National Velvet*, 1944; *The Picture of Dorian Gray*, 1945; *Undercurrent*, 1946; *Sea of Grass*, 1947; *Living in a Big Way*, 1947; *If Winter Comes*, 1947;

The Bribe, 1949; *The Three Musketeers*, 1948; *The Doctor and the Girl*, 1949; *Madame Bovary*, 1949; *Father of the Bride*, 1950; *Soldiers Three*, 1951; *Father's Little Dividend*, 1951; *The Light Touch*, 1951; *The Prisoner of Zenda*, 1952; *Lovely to Look At*, 1952; *Ivanhoe*, 1952; *The Knights of the Round Table*, 1953; *Battle Circus*, 1953; *All the Brothers Were Valiant*, 1953; *The Long, Long Trailer*, 1954; *The Blackboard Jungle*, 1955; *Quentin Durward*, 1955; *Bhowani Junction*, 1956; *Tea and Sympathy*, 1957; *Something of Value*, 1957; *Jailhouse Rock*, 1958; *The Brothers Karamazov*, 1958; *The Reluctant Debutante*, 1958; *All the Fine Young Cannibals*, 1960; *Butterfield 8*, 1960; *Sweet Bird of Youth*, 1962; *The Prize*, 1963; *Honeymoon Hotel*, 1964; *A Patch of Blue*, 1965.

If Winter Comes with Deborah Kerr and Walter Pidgeon. *(Berman)*

SAMUEL BISCHOFF Born August 11, 1890; *The Last Mile* (producer and director), 1932; *The Rich Are Always With Us*, 1932; *The Dark Horse*, 1932; *Three on a Match*, 1932; *The Big Shakedown*, 1934; *Front Page Woman*, 1935; *The Golden Arrow*, 1936; *The Charge of the Light Brigade*, 1936; *Kid Galahad*, 1937; *San Quentin*, 1937; *Swing Your Lady*, 1938; *Racket Busters*, 1938; *Angels With Dirty Faces*, 1938; *A Slight Case of Murder*, 1938; *The Oklahoma Kid*, 1939; *You Can't Get Away with Murder*, 1939; *The Roaring Twenties* (with Hal B. Wallis), 1939; *The Kid From Kokomo* (with Hal B. Wallis), 1939; *Castle on the Hudson*, 1940; *You'll Never Get Rich*, 1941; *Texas*, 1941; *A Night to Remember*, 1943; *None Shall Escape*, 1944; *A Thousand and One Nights*, 1945; *Best of the Bad Men*, 1948; *Pitfall*, 1948; *Mrs. Mike*. 1949; *Sealed Cargo*, 1951; *The Las Vegas Story*, 1952; *Macao*, 1952; *The Half-Breed*, 1952; *The System*, 1953; *South Sea Woman*, 1953; *The Bounty Hunter*, 1954; *A Bullet for Joey*, 1955; *The Phoenix City Story*, 1955; *Screaming Eagles*, 1956; *Operation Eichmann*, 1961; *King of the Roaring Twenties*, 1961; *The Strangler*, 1963.

Mrs. Mike with Evelyn Keyes, Dick Powell and J. M. Kerrigan. *(Bischoff)*

HENRY BLANKE Born December 30, 1901; *Female*, 1933; *Convention City*, 1933; *Bureau of Missing Persons*, 1933; *Fashions of 1934*, 1934; *The Story of Louis Pasteur*, 1935; *A Midsummer Night's Dream*, 1935; *Satan Met a Lady*, 1936; *The Petrified Forest*, 1936; *Green Pastures*, 1936; *The Life of Emile Zola*, 1937; *Jezebel* (under Hal B. Wallis), 1938; *Adventures of Robin Hood*, 1938; *Juarez* (under Hal B. Wallis), 1939; *The Old Maid* (under Hal B. Wallis), 1939; *The Sea Hawk*, 1940; *The Maltese Falcon* (under Hal B. Wallis), 1941; *The Great Lie* (under Hal B. Wallis), 1941; *Blues in the Night*, 1941; *Old Acquaintance*, 1943; *Edge of Darkness*, 1943; *The Mask of Dimitrios*, 1944; *Deception*, 1946; *Winter Meeting*, 1948; *June Bride*, 1948; *The Treasure of Sierra Madre*, 1948; *The Fountainhead*, 1949; *Beyond the Forest*, 1949; *Lightning Strikes Twice*, 1951; *Come Fill the Cup*, 1951; *The Iron Mistress*, 1952; *So Big*, 1953; *King Richard and the Crusaders*, 1954; *The McConnell Story*, 1955; *Sincerely Yours*, 1955; *Serenade*, 1956; *Too Much, Too Soon*, 1958; *Westbound*, 1959; *The Nun's Story*, 1959; *The Miracle*, 1959; *Cash McCall*, 1959; *Ice Palace*, 1960; *The Sins of Rachel Cade*, 1961; *Hell Is for Heroes*, 1962.

Cash McCall with James Garner and Natalie Wood. *(Blanke)*

JULIAN C. BLAUSTEIN Born May 30, 1913; *Broken Arrow*, 1950; *Mister 880*, 1950; *Half Angel*, 1950; *The Day the Earth Stood Still*, 1951; *Take Care of My Little Girl*, 1951; *Don't Bother to Knock*, 1952; *The Outcasts of Poker Flat*, 1952; *Desiree*, 1954; *The Racers*, 1955; *Storm Center*, 1956; *Guard of Honor* (uncompleted), 1957; *Bell, Book and Candle*, 1958; *The Wreck of the Mary Deare*, 1959; *Two Loves*, 1961; *The Four Horsemen of the Apocalypse*, 1962; *Khartoum*, 1966.

Mister 880 with Edmund Gwenn, Dorothy McGuire and Burt Lancaster. *(Blaustein)*

BENEDICT E. BOGEAUS Born c. 1910; *Shanghai Gesture*, 1941; *The Bridge of San Luis Rey*, 1944; *Dark Waters*, 1944; *Captain Kidd*, 1945; *Diary of a Chambermaid*, 1946; *Mr. Ace*, 1946; *The Macomber Affair*, 1947; *Christmas Eve*, 1947; *On Our Merry Way, or A Miracle*

Can Happen, 1948; *Lulu Belle*, 1948; *Girl From Manhattan*, 1948; *Johnny One Eye*, 1950; *My Outlaw Brother*, 1951; *One Big Affair*, 1952; *Count the Hours*, 1953; *Appointment in Honduras*, 1953; *Silver Lode*, 1954; *Passion*, 1954; *Cattle Queen of Montana*, 1954; *Escape to Burma*, 1955; *Pearl of the South Pacific*, 1955; *Tennessee's Partner*, 1955; *Slightly Scarlet*, 1956; *The River's Edge*, 1957; *Enchanted Island*, 1958; *From the Earth to the Moon*, 1958; *Jet Over the Atlantic*, 1959; *The Most Dangerous Man Alive*, 1958–1961.

Escape to Burma with Robert Ryan and Barbara Stanwyck. *(Bogeaus)*

CHARLES BRACKETT Born November 26, 1892; *Five Graves to Cairo*, 1943; *The Uninvited*, 1944; *The Lost Weekend*, 1945; *To Each His Own*, 1946; *The Emperor Waltz*, 1948; *A Foreign Affair*, 1948; *Miss Tatlock's Millions*, 1948; *Sunset Boulevard*, 1950; *The Mating Season*, 1951; *The Model and the Marriage Broker*, 1951; *Niagara*, 1953; *Titanic*, 1953; *Garden of Evil*, 1954; *Woman's World*, 1954; *The Girl in the Red Velvet Swing*, 1955; *The Virgin Queen*, 1955; *The King and I*, 1956; *D-Day, Sixth of June*, 1956; *Teenage Rebel*, 1956; *The Wayward Bus*, 1957; *The Gift of Love*, 1958; *Ten North Frederick*, 1958; *The Remarkable Mr. Pennypacker*, 1958; *Blue Denim*, 1959; *Journey to the Center of the Earth*, 1959; *High Time*, 1960; *State Fair*, 1962.

The Girl in the Red Velvet Swing with Ray Milland and Joan Collins. *(Brackett)*

SAMUEL BRONSTON *The Adventures of Martin Eden*, 1942; *Jack London*, 1943; *A Walk in the Sun*, 1945; *John Paul Jones*, 1959; *King of Kings*, 1961; *El Cid*, 1961; *55 Days at Peking*, 1963; *Circus World*, 1964; *The Fall of the Roman Empire*, 1964.

HARRY JOE BROWN Born September 22, 1893; *Madison Square Garden*, 1932; *Dangerous*, 1935; *Captain Blood*, 1935; *The Florentine Dagger*, 1935; *I Found Stella Parish*, 1935; *Ceiling Zero*, 1935; *Hearts Divided*, 1936; *The Great O'Malley*, 1937; *Alexander's Ragtime*

Jack London with Michael O'Shea. *(Bronston)*

Band (under Darryl F. Zanuck), 1938; *The Gorilla* (under Darryl F. Zanuck), 1939; *The Rains Came*, 1939; *Johnny Apollo*, 1940; *Down Argentine Way*, 1940; *Four Sons* (with Darryl F. Zanuck), 1940; *Young People*, 1940; *Moon Over Miami*, 1941; *Western Union*, 1941; *The Desperados*, 1943; *Sahara*, 1943; *Coroner Creek*, 1948; *The Untamed Breed*, 1948; *The Doolins of Oklahoma*, 1949; *Fortunes of Captain Blood*, 1950; *The Nevadan*, 1950; *Stage to Tucson*, 1950; *The Lady and the Bandit*, 1951; *Santa Fe*, 1951; *Man in the Saddle*, 1951; *Hangman's Knot*, 1952; *The Stranger Wore a Gun*, 1953; *Three Hours to Kill*, 1954; *Ten Wanted Men*, 1955; *A Lawless Street*, 1955; *Seventh Cavalry*, 1956; *The Guns of Fort Petticoat*, 1957; *The Tall T*, 1957; *Decision at Sundown*, 1957; *Screaming Mimi*, 1958; *Buchanan Rides Alone*, 1958; *Ride Lonesome*, 1959; *Comanche Station*, 1960; *The Son of Captain Blood*, 1963; *Duel at the Rio Grande*, 1964.

The Nevadan with Kate Drain Lawson (center) and Randolph Scott. *(Brown)*

MERIAN C. COOPER Born October 24, 1893; *The Four Feathers*, 1929; *The Phantom of Crestwood*, 1932; *King Kong*, 1933; *Lucky Devils*, 1933; *Morning Glory*, 1933; *Melody Cruise*, 1933; *Professional Sweetheart*, 1933; *Ann Vickers*, 1933; *Ace of Aces*, 1933; *Little Women*, 1933; *Flying Down to Rio*, 1933; *The Lost Patrol*, 1934; *She*, 1935; *The Last Days of Pompeii*, 1935; *The Toy Wife*, 1938; *The Jungle Book* (pre-production), 1942; *Eagle Squadron* (pre-production), 1942; *The Fugitive*, 1947; *Fort Apache*, 1948; *She Wore a Yellow Ribbon*, 1949; *Three Godfathers*, 1949; *Mighty Joe Young*, 1949; *Rio Grande*, 1950; *Wagonmaster*, 1950; *The Quiet Man*, 1952; *The Sun Shines Bright*, 1953; *This Is Cinerama*, 1952; *The Searchers*, 1956; *The Best of Cinerama*, 1963.

She with Nigel Bruce, Helen Mack and Randolph Scott. *(Cooper)*

JACK CUMMINGS *The Winning Ticket*, 1935; *Born to Dance*, 1936; *Broadway Melody of 1938*, 1937; *Honolulu*, 1939; *Broadway Melody of 1940*, 1940; *Go West*, 1940; *Ship Ahoy*, 1942; *I Dood It*, 1943; *Bathing Beauty*, 1944; *Romance of Rosy Ridge*, 1947; *Fiesta*, 1947; *Neptune's Daughter*, 1949; *The Stratton Story*, 1949; *Two Weeks With Love*, 1950; *Three Little Words*, 1950; *Excuse My Dust*, 1951; *Texas Carnival*, 1951; *Lovely to Look At*, 1952; *Sombrero*, 1953; *Give a Girl a Break*, 1953; *Kiss Me, Kate!*, 1953; *Seven Brides for Seven Brothers*, 1954; *The Last Time I Saw Paris*, 1954; *Many Rivers to Cross*, 1955; *Interrupted Melody*, 1955; *The Teahouse of the August Moon*, 1956; *The Blue Angel*, 1959; *Can Can*, 1960; *The Second Time Around*, 1961; *Bachelor Flat*, 1962; *Viva Las Vegas*, 1964.

Give a Girl a Break with Debbie Reynolds, Bob Fosse and Lurene Tuttle. *(Cummings)*

SAMUEL G. ENGEL Born December 29, 1904; *My Darling Clementine*, 1946; *Sitting Pretty*, 1948; *Deep Waters*, 1948; *The Street With No Name*, 1948; *Come to the Stable*, 1949; *Mr. Belvedere Goes to College*, 1949; *The Jackpot*, 1950; *Rawhide*, 1951; *Follow the Sun*, 1951; *Red Skies of Montana*, 1951; *The Frogmen*, 1952; *Belles on Their Toes*, 1953; *A Man Called Peter*, 1955; *Daddy Long Legs*, 1955; *Good Morning, Miss Dove*, 1956; *Bernadine*, 1957; *Boy on a Dolphin*, 1957; *The Story of Ruth*, 1960; *The Lion*, 1962.

Good Morning, Miss Dove with Robert Stack, Jennifer Jones and Biff Elliot. *(Engel)*

Private Lives with Reginald Denny and Norma Shearer. *(Franklin)*

SIDNEY FRANKLIN Born March 21, 1893.

Primarily a Director: *The Last of Mrs. Cheney*, 1929; *Devil May Care*, 1929; *The Lady of Scandal*, 1930; *A Lady's Morals*, or *Jenny Lind*, 1930; *The Guardsman*, 1931; *Smilin' Through*, 1932; *Reunion in Vienna*, 1933; *The Barretts of Wimpole Street*, 1934; *Private Lives*, 1934; *The Dark Angel*, 1935; *The Good Earth*, 1937; *Goodbye, Mr. Chips*, 1939.

Primarily a Producer: *On Borrowed Time*, 1939; *Waterloo Bridge*, 1939; *Mrs. Miniver*, 1942; *Random Harvest*, 1942; *Madame Curie*, 1943; *The White Cliffs of Dover*, 1944; *The Yearling*, 1946; *Homecoming*, 1948; *Command Decision*, 1948; *The Miniver Story*, 1950; *Young Bess*, 1953; *The Story of Three Loves*, 1953; *The Barretts of Wimpole Street* (producer and director), 1957.

ARTHUR FREED Born September 9, 1894; *The Wizard of Oz* (with Mervyn LeRoy), 1939; *Babes in Arms*, 1939; *Strike Up the Band*, 1940; *Little Nellie Kelly*, 1940; *Lady Be Good*, 1941; *Babes on Broadway*, 1941; *Panama Hattie*, 1942; *For Me and My Gal*, 1942; *Cabin in the Sky*, 1943; *Du Barry Was a Lady*, 1943; *Girl Crazy*, 1943; *Best Foot Forward*, 1943; *Meet Me in St. Louis*, 1944; *The Clock*, 1945; *Yolanda and the Thief*, 1945; *The Harvey Girls*, 1946; *Ziegfeld Follies*, 1946; *Till the Clouds Roll By*, 1946; *Good News*, 1947; *Summer Holiday*, 1948; *The Pirate*, 1948; *Easter Parade*, 1948; *Words and Music*, 1948; *Take Me Out to the Ball Game*, 1949; *The Barkleys of Broadway*, 1949; *Any Number Can Play*, 1949; *On the Town*, 1949; *Annie Get Your Gun*, 1950; *Crisis*, 1950; *Pagan Love Song*, 1950; *Royal Wedding*, 1951; *Show Boat*, 1951; *An American in Paris*, 1951; *Belle of New York*, 1952; *Singin' in the Rain*, 1952; *The Band Wagon*, 1953; *Brigadoon*, 1954; *It's Always Fair Weather*, 1955; *Kismet*, 1955; *Invitation to the Dance*, 1956; *Silk Stockings*, 1957; *Gigi*, 1958; *Bells Are Ringing*, 1960; *The Subterraneans*, 1960; *Light in the Piazza*, 1962.

Pagan Love Song with Charles Mauu, Rita Moreno, Howard Keel and Esther Williams. *(Freed)*

WILLIAM GOETZ Born March 24, 1903; *The Bowery*, 1933; *The Man From Laramie*, 1955; *Autumn Leaves*, 1956; *Sayonara*, 1957; *Me and the Colonel*, 1958; *They Came to Cordura*, 1959; *The Mountain Road*, 1960; *Song Without End*, 1960; *Cry for Happy*, 1961; *Assault on a Queen*, 1966.

Autumn Leaves with Cliff Robertson and Joan Crawford. *(Goetz)*

SAMUEL B. GOLDWYN Born August 27, 1884; *Bulldog Drummond*, 1929; *Condemned*, 1929; *Raffles*, 1930; *Whoopee*, 1930; *One Heavenly Night*, 1930; *The Devil to Pay*, 1930; *Street Scene*, 1931; *The Unholy Garden*, 1931; *Palmy Days*, 1931; *Tonight or Never*, 1931; *Arrowsmith*, 1931; *The Greeks Had a Word for Them*, 1932; *Cynara*, 1932; *The Kid From Spain*, 1932; *The Masquerader*, 1933; *Roman Scandals*, 1933; *Nana*, 1934; *We Live Again*, 1934; *Kid Millions*, 1934; *The Wedding Night*, 1935; *The Dark Angel*, 1935; *Barbary Coast*, 1935; *Splendor*, 1935; *Strike Me Pink*, 1936; *These Three*, 1936; *Dodsworth*, 1936; *Come and Get It*, 1936; *Beloved Enemy*, 1936; *Woman Chases Man*, 1937; *Hurricane*, 1937; *Stella Dallas*, 1937; *Dead End*, 1937; *The Adventures of Marco Polo*, 1938; *The Goldwyn Follies*, 1938; *The Cowboy and the Lady*, 1938; *The Real Glory*, 1939; *Wuthering Heights*, 1939; *They Shall Have Music*, 1939; *Raffles*, 1940; *The Westerner*, 1940; *The Little Foxes*, 1941; *Ball of Fire*, 1941; *The Pride of the Yankees*, 1942; *They Got Me Covered*, 1943; *The North Star*, or *Armored Attack*, 1943; *Up in Arms*, 1944; *The Princess and the Pirate*, 1944; *Wonder Man*, 1945; *The Kid From Brooklyn*, 1946; *The Best Years of Our Lives*, 1946; *The Secret Life of Walter Mitty*, 1947; *The Bishop's Wife*, 1947; *A Song is Born*, 1948; *Enchantment*, 1948; *Roseanna McCoy*, 1949; *My Foolish Heart*, 1949; *Our Very Own*, 1950; *Edge of Doom*, 1950; *I Want You*, 1951; *Hans Christian Andersen*, 1952; *Guys and Dolls*, 1955; *Porgy and Bess*, 1959.

JAMES EDMUND GRAINGER Born October 1, 1906; *A Holy Terror*, 1931; *Diamond Jim*, 1935; *Love Before Breakfast*, 1936; *Magnificent Brute*, 1936; *Sutter's Gold*, 1936; *The Road Back*, 1937; *The Road to*

Cynara with Kay Francis and Ronald Colman. *(Goldwyn)*

Reno, 1938; *The Crime of Dr. Hallet*, 1938; *The Jury's Secret*, 1938; *The Lady With Red Hair*, 1940; *Riders of the Purple Sage*, 1941; *International Squadron*, 1941; *Flying Tigers*, 1942; *The Fabulous Texan*, 1947; *Wake of the Red Witch*, 1948; *Sands of Iwo Jima*, 1949; *Flying Leathernecks*, 1951; *The Racket*, 1951; *One Minute to Zero*, 1952; *Blackbeard the Pirate*, 1952; *Split Second*, 1953; *Second Chance*, 1953; *Devil's Canyon*, 1953; *The French Line*, 1954; *The Treasure of Pancho Villa*, 1955; *Great Day in the Morning*, 1956; *Bundle of Joy*, 1956; *Ten Days in August* (uncompleted), 1957; *The Sheepman*, 1958; *Torpedo Run*, 1958; *Green Mansions*, 1959; *Never So Few*, 1959; *Home From the Hill*, 1960; *Cimarron*, 1960.

The French Line with Mary McCarty and Jane Russell. *(Grainger)*

HAROLD HECHT Born June 1, 1907; *The Flame and the Arrow*, 1950; *Ten Tall Men*, 1951; *The First Time*, 1952; *The Crimson Pirate*, 1952; *His Majesty O'Keefe*, 1953; *Apache*, 1954; *Vera Cruz*, 1954; *Marty*, 1955; *The Kentuckian*, 1955; *Trapeze*, 1956; *The Bachelor Party*, 1957; *Sweet Smell of Success*, 1957; *Tell It on the Drums* (uncompleted), 1957; *Run Silent, Run Deep*, 1958; *Separate Tables*, 1958; *The Devil's Disciple*, 1959; *The Unforgiven*, 1960; *The Young Savages*, 1961; *Taras Bulba*, 1962; *Bird Man of Alcatraz*, 1962; *Wild and Wonderful*, 1964; *Flight From Ashiya*, 1964; *Cat Ballou*, 1965; *The Way West*, 1967.

Marty with Ernest Borgnine and Esther Miniciotti. *(Hecht)*

MARK HELLINGER Born March 21, 1903; died December 21, 1947; *It All Came True* (under Hal B. Wallis), 1940; *Torrid Zone*, 1940; *Brother Orchid* (under Hal B. Wallis), 1940; *They Drive by Night* (under Hal B. Wallis), 1940; *High Sierra* (under Hal B. Wallis), 1941; *The Strawberry Blonde*, 1941; *Manpower* (with Hal B. Wallis), 1941; *Rise and Shine*, 1941; *Moontide*, 1942; *Thank Your Lucky Stars*, 1943; *The Horn Blows at Midnight*, 1945; *The Killers*, 1946; *The Two Mrs. Carrolls*, 1947; *Brute Force*, 1947; *The Naked City*, 1948.

Moontide with Jean Gabin and Ida Lupino. *(Hellinger)*

ARTHUR HORNBLOW, JR. Born March 15, 1893; *The Pursuit of Happiness*, 1934; *Mississippi*, 1935; *Ruggles of Red Gap*, 1935; *Wings in the Dark*, 1935; *The Princess Comes Across*, 1936; *Easy Living*, 1937; *Swing High, Swing Low*, 1937; *High, Wide and Handsome*, 1937; *Waikiki Wedding*, 1937; *Man About Town*, 1939; *Midnight*, 1939; *The Cat and the Canary*, 1939; *Arise, My Love*, 1940; *Nothing But the Truth*, 1941; *Hold Back the Dawn*, 1941; *I Wanted Wings*, 1941; *The Major and the Minor*, 1942; *The Heavenly Body*, 1943; *Gaslight*, 1944; *Weekend at the Waldorf*, 1945; *Desire Me*, 1947; *The Hucksters*, 1947; *Cass Timberlane*, 1947; *The Asphalt Jungle*, 1950; *Million Dollar Mermaid*, 1952; *Remains to Be Seen*, 1953; *Oklahoma!*, 1955; *Witness for the Prosecution*, 1957; *The War Lover*, 1962.

The Heavenly Body with William Powell, Hedy Lamarr and Connie Gilchrist. *(Hornblow)*

HOWARD HUGHES Born December 24, 1905; *Hell's Angels*, 1930; *The Front Page*, 1931; *Scarface*, 1932; *Sky Devils*, 1932; *The Outlaw* (Hughes personally replaced Howard Hawks as director around 1940), 1943—released 1946; *Vendetta* (directors Howard Hughes and Stuart Heisler replaced Max Ophüls), 1950; *Two Tickets to Broadway*, 1951; *The Racket*, 1951; *His Kind of Woman*, 1951; *Jet Pilot*, 1952, released 1957; *Double Dynamite*, 1952; *The Las Vegas Story*, 1952; *Montana Belle*, 1948, released 1952; *The French Line*, 1953; *Macao*, 1953; *Underwater*, 1955; *Son of Sinbad*, 1955.

ROSS HUNTER *A Guy, a Girl and a Gob*, 1945; *Take Me to Town*, 1953; *All I Desire*, 1953; *Tumbleweed*, 1953; *Taza, Son of Cochise*, 1954; *Magnificent Obsession*, 1954; *Naked Alibi*, 1954; *The Yellow Mountain*, 1954; *Captain Lightfoot*, 1955; *One Desire*, 1955; *All That Heaven Allows*, 1955; *The Spoilers*, 1955; *There's Always*

Macao with Robert Mitchum and Jane Russell. *(Hughes)*

Tomorrow, 1956; *Battle Hymn*, 1956; *Tammy and the Bachelor*, 1957; *Interlude*, 1957; *My Man Godfrey*, 1957; *This Happy Feeling*, 1958; *The Restless Years*, 1958; *Stranger in My Arms*, 1959; *Imitation of Life*, 1959; *Pillow Talk*, 1959; *Portrait in Black*, 1960; *Midnight Lace*, 1960; *Tammy, Tell Me True*, 1961; *Flower Drum Song*, 1961; *Back Street*, 1961; *If a Man Answers*, 1962; *The Thrill of It All*, 1963; *Tammy and the Doctor*, 1963; *The Chalk Garden*, 1964; *I'd Rather Be Rich*, 1964; *The Art of Love*, 1965; *Madame X*, 1966; *The Pad (and How to Use It)*, 1966; *Thoroughly Modern Millie*, 1967.

Stranger in My Arms with June Allyson, Charles Coburn and Mary Astor. *(Hunter)*

NUNNALLY JOHNSON Born December 5, 1897; *The Prisoner of Shark Island* (with Darryl F. Zanuck), 1936; *The Road to Glory* (with Darryl F. Zanuck), 1936; *The Grapes of Wrath* (with Darryl F. Zanuck), 1940; *The Pied Piper*, 1942; *Roxie Hart*, 1942; *The Moon Is Down*, 1943; *Holy Matrimony*, 1943; *The Woman in the Window*, 1944; *Casanova Brown*, 1944; *The Senator Was Indiscreet*, 1947; *Three Came Home*, 1950; *The Gunfighter*, 1950; *The Desert Fox*, 1951; *Phone Call From a Stranger*, 1952; *We're Not Married*, 1952; *My Cousin Rachel*, 1952; *How to Marry a Millionaire*, 1953; *The Black*

Oh Men! Oh Women! with Dan Dailey and Ginger Rogers. *(Johnson)*

Widow (producer and director), 1954; *How to Be Very, Very Popular* (producer and director), 1955; *The Three Faces of Eve* (producer and director), 1957; *Oh Men! Oh Women!* (producer and director), 1957; *The Man Who Understood Women* (producer and director), 1959.

SAM KATZMAN Born July 7, 1901; *Spotlight Serenade*, 1943; *Voodoo Man*, 1944; *Freddie Steps Out*, 1946; *Last of the Buccaneers*, 1950; *Purple Heart Diary*, 1951; *The Golden Hawk*, 1952; *California Conquest*, 1952; *Siren of Bagdad*, 1953; *Rock Around the Clock*, 1956; *Earth vs. the Flying Saucers*, 1956; *Rumble on the Docks*, 1956; *The Werewolf*, 1956; *Don't Knock the Rock*, 1957; *Utah Blaine*, 1957; *The Man Who Turned to Stone*, 1957; *Zombies of Mara-Tau*, 1957; *The Giant Claw*, 1957; *Calypso Heat Wave*, 1957; *The Night the World Exploded*, 1957; *The Tijuana Story*, 1957; *Escape From San Quentin*, 1957; *Crash Landing*, 1958; *Going Steady*, 1958; *The World Was His Jury*, 1958; *Life Begins at 17*, 1958; *The Last Blitzkrieg*, 1959; *Juke Box Rhythm*, 1959; *The Flying Fontaines*, 1959; *The Enemy General*, 1960; *The Wizard of Bagdad*, 1960; *The Pirates of Tortuga*, 1961; *Twist Around the Clock*, 1961; *The Wild Westerners*, 1962; *Don't Knock the Twist*, 1962; *Let's Twist Again*, 1961; *Hootenanny Hoot*, 1963; *Kissin' Cousins*, 1964; *Get Yourself a College Girl*, 1964; *Your Cheatin' Heart*, 1964; *Harum Scarum*, 1965; *When the Girls Meet the Boys*, 1965; *Hold On*, 1966; *Riot on the Sunset Strip*, 1967; *A Time to Sing*, 1968.

Your Cheatin' Heart with George Hamilton. *(Katzman)*

FRED KOHLMAR Born August 10, 1905; *The Lone Wolf Strikes*, 1940; *Take a Letter, Darling*, 1942; *The Glass Key*, 1942; *That Night in Rio*, 1945; *The Late George Apley*, 1947; *The Ghost and Mrs. Muir*, 1947; *Kiss of Death*, 1947; *You Were Meant for Me*, 1948; *When Willie Comes Marching Home*, 1950; *You're in the Navy Now*, 1951; *Elopement*, 1951; *Call Me Mister*, 1951; *It Should Happen to You*, 1953; *Phffft*, 1954; *Three Stripes in the Sun*, 1955; *My Sister Eileen*, 1955; *Picnic*, 1955; *The Solid Gold Cadillac*, 1956; *Full of Life*, 1957; *Pal Joey*, 1957; *The Great Sebastians* (uncompleted), 1957; *Lost Horizon* (remake uncompleted), 1957; *Gunman's Walk*, 1958; *The Last*

Dear Brigitte with John Williams, Glynis Johns and James Stewart. *(Kohlmar)*

Angry Man, 1959; *The Devil at Four O'Clock*, 1961; *The Notorious Landlady*, 1962; *Bye Bye Birdie*, 1963; *Dear Brigitte*, 1965; *How to Steal a Million*, 1966; *A Flea in Her Ear*, 1968.

STANLEY KRAMER Born September 29, 1913; *So Ends Our Night*, 1941; *The Moon and Sixpence*, 1942; *So This Is New York*, 1948; *Home of the Brave*, 1949; *Champion*, 1949; *The Men*, 1950; *Cyrano de Bergerac*, 1950; *High Noon*, 1952; *Death of a Salesman*, 1951; *The Sniper*, 1952; *The Happy Time*, 1952; *My Six Convicts*, 1952; *Member of the Wedding*, 1952; *The Wild One*, 1954; *The Caine Mutiny*, 1954; *Not as a Stranger* (producer and director), 1955; *The Pride and the Passion* (producer and director), 1957; *The Defiant Ones* (producer and director), 1958; *On the Beach* (producer and director), 1959; *Inherit the Wind* (producer and director), 1960; *Judgment at Nuremberg* (producer and director), 1961; *Pressure Point*, 1962; *A Child Is Waiting*, 1962; *It's a Mad, Mad, Mad, Mad World* (producer and director), 1963; *Invitation to a Gunfighter*, 1964; *Ship of Fools*, 1965; *Guess Who's Coming to Dinner* (also directed), 1967.

The Happy Time with Linda Christian, Louis Jourdan, Bobby Driscoll, Charles Boyer and Marsha Hunt. *(Kramer)*

CARL LAEMMLE, JR. Born April 28, 1908; *Show Boat*, 1929; *All Quiet on the Western Front*, 1930; *Bad Sister*, 1931; *The Spirit of Notre Dame*, 1931; *Frankenstein*, 1931; *Waterloo Bridge*, 1931; *Back Street*, 1932; *Once in a Lifetime*, 1932; *Air Mail*, 1932; *They Just Had to Get Married*, 1933; *Out All Night*, 1933; *Don't Bet on Love*, 1933; *Only Yesterday*, 1933; *By Candlelight*, 1934; *The Countess of Monte Cristo*, 1934; *Glamour*, 1934; *Little Man, What Now?*, 1934; *The Good Fairy*, 1935; *The Bride of Frankenstein*, 1935.

Out All Night with Slim Summerville, Billy Barty and ZaSu Pitts. *(Laemmle)*

SOL LESSER Born February 17, 1890; *Breaking the Ice*, 1938; *Tarzan the Fearless*, 1933; *Thunder Over Mexico* ("assembler"), 1933; *Peck's Bad Boy*, 1934; *The Dude Ranger*, 1934; *The Cowboy Millionaire*, 1935; *Hard Rock Harrigan*, 1935; *Thunder Mountain*, 1935; *O'Malley of the Mounted*, 1936; *Let's Sing Again*, 1936; *The Border Patrolman*, 1936; *King of the Royal Mounted*, 1936; *Wild Brian Kent*, 1936; *Rainbow on the River*, 1936; *The Californian*, 1937; *Make a Wish*, 1937; *Western Gold*, 1937; *Hawaii Calls*, 1938; *Peck's Bad Boy With the Circus*, 1938; *Tarzan's Revenge*, 1938; *Fisherman's Wharf*, 1939; *Way Down South*, 1939; *Everything's on Ice*, 1939; *Our Town*, 1940; *That Uncertain Feeling*, 1941; *The Tuttles of Tahiti*, 1942; *Tarzan Triumphs*, 1943; *Stage Door Canteen*, 1943; *Tarzan's Desert Mystery*, 1943; *Tarzan and the Leopard Woman*, 1946; *Tarzan and the Huntress*, 1947; *The Red House*, 1947; *Tarzan and the Mermaids*, 1948; *Tarzan's Magic Fountain*, 1949; *Tarzan's Peril*, 1951; *Kon-Tiki* ("assembler"), 1951; *Tarzan and the She-Devil*, 1953; *Vice Squad*, 1953; *Tarzan's Hidden Jungle*, 1955; *Tarzan and the Lost Safari*, 1957.

Peck's Bad Boy with Jackie Searl, Jackie Cooper and Gertrude Howard. *(Lesser)*

ROBERT LORD Born May 1, 1902; *Loose Ankles*, 1930; *Playing Around*, 1930; *The Flirting Widow*, 1930; *20,000 Years in Sing Sing*, 1933; *Fog Over Frisco*, 1934; *The Girl From Tenth Avenue*, 1935; *Oil for the Lamps of China*, 1935; *Black Legion*, 1936; *Tovarich* (under Hal B. Wallis), 1937; *Brother Rat*, 1938; *Dawn Patrol*, 1938; *The Amazing Dr. Clitterhouse*, 1938; *Dodge City*, 1939; *Confessions of a Nazi Spy*, 1939; *The Private Lives of Elizabeth and Essex* (under Hal B. Wallis), 1939; *The Letter* (under Hal B. Wallis), 1940; *High Wall*, 1947; *Knock on Any Door*, 1949; *Tokyo Joe*, 1949; *In a Lonely Place*, 1950; *Sirocco*, 1951; *The Family Secret*, 1951.

Oil for the Lamps of China with Josephine Hutchinson and Pat O'Brien. *(Lord)*

WALTER M. MIRISCH Born November 8, 1921; *Fall Guy*, 1947; *Bamba the Jungle Boy*, 1949; *The Hidden City*, 1950; *Bomba on Panther Island*, 1950; *The Lost Volcano*, 1950; *Country Fair*, 1950; *Elephant Stampede*, 1951; *Cavalry Scout*, 1951; *Flight to Mars*, 1951; *The Lion Hunters*, 1951; *The Maze*, 1953; *Wichita*, 1955; *The Warriors*, 1955; *The First Texan*, 1956; *The Oklahoman*, 1957; *The Tall Stranger*, 1957; *Man of the West*, 1958; *Fort Massacre*, 1958; *Cast a Long Shadow*, 1959; *The Gunfight at Dodge City*, 1959; *The Magnificent Seven*, 1960; *By Love Possessed*, 1961; *West Side Story*, 1961; *Town Without Pity*, 1961; *Two for the See-Saw*, 1962; *The Children's Hour*, 1962; *Kid Galahad*, 1962; *The Great Escape*, 1963; *Toys in the Attic*, 1963; *Stolen Hours*, 1963; *The Pink Panther*, 1964; *The Satan Bug*, 1965; *The Hallelujah Trail*, 1965; *A Rage to Live*, 1965; *Return From the Ashes*, 1965; *Hawaii*, 1966; *Cast a Giant Shadow*, 1966; *The Russians Are Coming, The Russians Are Coming*, 1966; *Return of the Seven*, 1966; *The Fortune Cookie*, 1966; *In the Heat of the Night*, 1967; *Fitzwilly*, 1967.

The Warriors with Yvonne Furneaux. *(Mirisch)*

ALAN J. PAKULA Born April 7, 1928; *Fear Strikes Out*, 1957; *To Kill a Mockingbird*, 1962; *Love With the Proper Stranger*, 1963; *Baby, the Rain Must Fall*, 1965; *Inside Daisy Clover*, 1965; *Up the Down Staircase*, 1967.

Baby, the Rain Must Fall with Kimberly Black, Lee Remick, Steve McQueen and Estelle Hemsley. *(Pakula)*

GEORGE PAL Born February 1, 1900; *The Great Rupert*, 1950; *Destination Moon*, 1950; *When Worlds Collide*, 1951; *Houdini*, 1953; *War of the Worlds*, 1953; *The Naked Jungle*, 1954; *The Conquest of Space*, 1955; *Captain Cook* (uncompleted), 1957; *tom thumb* (producer and director), 1958; *The Time Machine* (producer and director), 1960; *Atlantis, the Lost Continent* (producer and director, with Henry Levin), 1961; *The Wonderful World of the Brothers Grimm* (producer

The Time Machine with Yvette Mimieux and Rod Taylor. *(Pal)*

and director), 1962; *The Seven Faces of Dr. Lao* (producer and director), 1964.

JOE PASTERNAK Born September 17, 1901; *Three Smart Girls*, 1936; *One Hundred Men and a Girl*, 1937; *Mad About Music*, 1938; *Youth Takes a Fling*, 1938; *That Certain Age*, 1938; *Three Smart Girls Grow Up*, 1939; *The Under-Pup*, 1939; *Destry Rides Again*, 1939; *It's a Date*, 1940; *A Little Bit of Heaven*, 1940; *Seven Sinners*, 1940; *Nice Girl?*, 1941; *It Started With Eve*, 1941; *Flame of New Orleans*, 1941; *Seven Sweethearts*, 1942; *Presenting Lily Mars*, 1942; *Thousands Cheer*, 1943; *Song of Russia*, 1943; *Two Girls and a Sailor*, 1944; *Music for Millions*, 1944; *Anchors Aweigh*, 1945; *Her Highness and the Bellboy*, 1945; *Two Sisters from Boston*, 1946; *Holiday in Mexico*, 1946; *No Leave, No Love*, 1946; *Unfinished Dance*, 1947; *This Time for Keeps*, 1947; *Three Daring Daughters*, 1948; *The Kissing Bandit*, 1948; *On an Island With You*, 1948; *Luxury Liner*, 1948; *Big City*, 1948; *A Date With Judy*, 1948; *In the Good Old Summertime*, 1949; *That Midnight Kiss*, 1949; *Nancy Goes to Rio*, 1949; *The Duchess of Idaho*, 1950; *Summer Stock*, 1950; *The Toast of New Orleans*, 1950; *The Great Caruso*, 1951; *Rich, Young and Pretty*, 1951; *The Strip*, 1951; *Skirts Ahoy!*, 1952; *The Merry Widow*, 1952; *Because You're Mine*, 1952; *Small Town Girl*, 1953; *Latin Lovers*, 1953; *Easy to Love*, 1953; *The Flame and the Flesh*, 1954; *The Student Prince*, 1954; *Athena*, 1954; *Hit the Deck*, 1955; *Love Me or Leave Me*, 1955; *Meet Me in Las Vegas*, 1956; *The Opposite Sex*, 1956; *Ten Thousand Bedrooms*, 1957; *This Could Be the Night*, 1957; *Party Girl*, 1958; *Ask Any Girl*, 1959; *Please Don't Eat the Daisies*, 1960; *Where the Boys Are*, 1960; *The Horizontal Lieutenant*, 1961; *Billy Rose's Jumbo*, 1962; *The Courtship of Eddie's Father*, 1963; *A Ticklish Affair*, 1963; *Looking for Love*, 1964; *Girl Happy*, 1965; *Made in Paris*, 1966; *Spinout*, 1966; *Penelope*, 1966; *The Sweet Ride*, 1968.

Holiday in Mexico with Jose Iturbi, Jane Powell and Walter Pidgeon. *(Pasternak)*

WILLIAM PERLBERG Born October 22, 1899; *The King Steps Out*, 1936; *Golden Boy*, 1939; *Son of Fury*, 1942; *The Song of Bernadette*, 1943; *Miracle on 34th Street*, 1947; *Forever Amber* (with Darryl F. Zanuck), 1947; *The Shocking Miss Pilgrim*, 1947; *Escape*, 1948; *Apartment for Peggy*, 1948; *Forbidden Street*, 1949; *It Happens Every Spring*, 1949; *Slattery's Hurricane*, 1949; *For Heaven's Sake*, 1950; *The Big Lift*, 1950; *Wabash Avenue*, 1950; *I'll Get By*, 1950; *Rhubarb* (with George Seaton), 1951; *Anything Can Happen*, 1952; *Little Boy, Lost*, 1953; *The Bridges at Toko-Ri* (with George Seaton), 1954; *The Country Girl*, 1954; *The Proud and Profane*, 1956; *The Tin Star* (with George Seaton), 1957; *Teacher's Pet*, 1958; *But Not for Me* (with George Seaton), 1959; *The Rat Race* (with George Seaton), 1960; *The Pleasure of His Company*, 1961; *The Counterfeit Traitor*, 1962; *The Hook*, 1963; *Twilight of Honor* (with George Seaton), 1963; *36 Hours*, 1964; *Half a Sixpence*, 1967.

The Hook with Nehemiah Persoff (T-shirt), Robert Walker, Jr., Nick Adams and Kirk Douglas. *(Perlberg)*

AARON ROSENBERG Born August 26, 1912; *Johnny Stool Pigeon*, 1949; *Outside the Wall*, 1950; *Winchester '73*, 1950; *Air Cadet*, 1951; *Cattle Drive*, 1951; *The Iron Man*, 1951; *Here Come the Nelsons*, 1952; *Bend of the River*, 1952; *The World in His Arms*, 1952; *Red Ball Express*, 1952; *Gunsmoke*, 1953; *Thunder Bay*, 1953; *Man From the Alamo*, 1953; *All American*, 1953; *Wings of the Hawk*, 1953; *The Glenn Miller Story*, 1954; *Saskatchewan*, 1954; *The Far Country*, 1955; *Six Bridges to Cross*, 1955; *Man Without a Star*, 1955; *The Shrike*, 1955; *Foxfire*, 1955; *The Benny Goodman Story*, 1955; *To Hell and Back*, 1955; *Backlash*, 1956; *The World in My Corner*, 1956; *Walk the Proud Land*, 1956; *Four Girls in Town*, 1956; *Joe Butterfly*, 1957; *Night Passage*, 1957; *The Badlanders*, 1958; *Never Steal Anything Small*, 1959; *It Started With a Kiss*, 1959; *Go Naked in the World*, 1961; *Mutiny on the Bounty*, 1962; *Move Over, Darling*, 1963; *Fate Is the Hunter*, 1964; *Shock Treatment*, 1964; *The Saboteur, Code Name—Morituri*, 1965; *The Reward*, 1965; *Do Not Disturb*, 1965; *Smoky*, 1966; *Caprice*, 1967; *The Detective*, 1968.

Do Not Disturb with Rod Taylor and Doris Day. *(Rosenberg)*

VICTOR SAVILLE Born 1897.
Primarily a Director: *Sunshine Susie*, 1931; *Hindle Wakes*, 1931; *Michael and Mary*, 1932; *Love on Wheels*, 1932; *The Faithful Heart*, 1933; *The Good Companions*, 1933; *I Was a Spy*, 1934; *Friday the Thirteenth*, 1934; *Evensong*, 1934; *The Iron Duke*, or *Me and Marlborough*, 1934; *Evergreen*, 1935; *Loves of a Dictator*, 1935; *First a Girl*, 1935; *It's Love Again*, 1936; *Storm in a Teacup* (with Ian Dalrymple), 1937; *Dark Journey* (producer and director), 1937.
Primarily a Producer: *Action for Slander* (producer and director), 1938; *South Riding* (producer and director), 1938; *The Citadel*, 1938; *Goodbye, Mr. Chips*, 1939; *The Earl of Chicago*, 1940; *The Mortal Storm*, 1940; *Bitter Sweet*, 1940; *A Woman's Face*, 1941; *Dr. Jekyll and Mr. Hyde*, 1941; *Smilin' Through*, 1941; *The Chocolate Soldier*, 1941; *White Cargo*, 1942; *Keeper of the Flame*, 1942; *Forever and a Day* (director, among various others), 1943; *Above Suspicion*, 1943; *Tonight and Every Night* (producer and director), 1945; *The Green Years* (producer and director), 1946; *Green Dolphin Street* (producer and director), 1947; *If Winter Comes* (director), 1947; *The Conspirator* (director), 1949; *Kim* (producer and director), 1950; *Calling Bulldog Drummond* (producer and director), directed 1949, released 1951, 1951; *24 Hours of a Woman's Life* (director), 1952; *I, the Jury*, 1953; *Affair in Monte Carlo* (director), 1953; *The Long Wait* (director), 1954; *The Silver Chalice* (producer and director), 1954; *Kiss Me, Deadly*, 1955; *The Greengage Summer*, 1961.

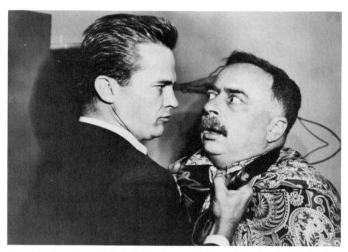

Kiss Me Deadly with Ralph Meeker and Silvio Minciotti. *(Saville)*

DORE SCHARY Born August 31, 1905; *Joe Smith, American*, 1942; *The War Against Mrs. Hadley*, 1942; *Journey for Margaret*, 1942; *Bataan*, 1943; *Lassie, Come Home*, 1943; *Lost Angel*, 1943; *I'll Be Seeing You*, 1944; *The Spiral Staircase*, 1946; *Till the End of Time*, 1946; *The Farmer's Daughter*, 1947; *Crossfire*, 1947; *The Bachelor and the Bobby-Soxer*, 1947; *Berlin Express*, 1948; *Mr. Blandings Builds His Dream House*, 1948; *The Set-Up*, 1949; *The Window*, 1949; *Battleground*, 1949; *The Next Voice You Hear*, 1950; *Go for Broke*, 1951; *It's a Big Country*, 1951; *Westward the Women*, 1951; *Washington*

Joe Smith, American with Marsha Hunt and Robert Young. *(Schary)*

Story, 1952; *Plymouth Adventure*, 1952; *Dream Wife*, 1953; *Take the High Ground*, 1953; *Bad Day at Black Rock*, 1954; *The Last Hunt*, 1956; *The Swan*, 1956; *Designing Woman*, 1957; *Lonelyhearts*, 1958; *Sunrise at Campobello*, 1960; *Act One* (producer and director), 1963.

SOL C. SIEGEL Born March 30, 1903; *Army Girl*, 1938; *Dark Command*, 1940; *Three Faces West*, 1940; *Among the Living*, 1941; *Hostages*, 1943; *Kiss and Tell*, 1945; *Blue Skies*, 1946; *Welcome Stranger*, 1947; *House of Strangers*, 1949; *A Letter to Three Wives*, 1948; *I Was a Male War Bride*, 1949; *Panic in the Streets*, 1950; *Fourteen Hours*, 1951; *Dream Boat*, 1952; *Deadline, U.S.A.*, 1952; *What Price Glory*, 1952; *Monkey Business*, 1952; *Call Me Madam*, 1953; *Gentlemen Prefer Blondes*, 1953; *Broken Lance*, 1954; *Three Coins in the Fountain*, 1954; *There's No Business Like Show Business*, 1954; *High Society*, 1956; *Man on Fire*, 1957; *Les Girls*, 1957; *Merry Andrew*, 1958; *Some Came Running*, 1958; *The World, the Flesh and the Devil*, 1959; *Home From the Hill*, 1960; *Walk, Don't Run*, 1966; *Alvarez Kelly*, 1966; *No Way to Treat a Lady*, 1968.

High Society with Grace Kelly, Frank Sinatra and Celeste Holm.
(*Siegel*)

DAVID O. SELZNICK Born May 10, 1902; died June 22, 1965; *What Price Hollywood*, 1932; *A Bill of Divorcement*, 1932; *The Animal Kingdom*, 1932; *Bird of Paradise*, 1932; *Our Betters*, 1933; *Topaze*, 1933; *Dinner at Eight*, 1933; *Night Flight*, 1933; *Dancing Lady*, 1933; *Little Women*, 1933; *Viva Villa!*, 1934; *Mahattan Melodrama*, 1934; *David Copperfield*, 1935; *Anna Karenina*, 1935; *A Tale of Two Cities*, 1935; *Little Lord Fauntleroy*, 1936; *The Garden of Allah*, 1936; *A Star Is Born*, 1937; *Nothing Sacred*, 1937; *The Prisoner of Zenda*, 1937; *The Adventures of Tom Sawyer*, 1938; *Intermezzo*, 1939; *Gone With the Wind*, 1939; *Rebecca*, 1940; *Claudia*, 1943; *Jane Eyre*, 1944; *The Keys of the Kingdom*, 1944; *Since You Went Away*, 1944; *I'll Be Seeing You*, 1944; *Spellbound*, 1945; *The Spiral Staircase*, 1946; *Notorious*, 1946; *Duel in the Sun*, 1946; *The Farmer's Daughter*, 1947; *The Bachelor and the Bobby-Soxer*, 1947; *The Paradine Case*, 1948; *Portrait of Jennie*, 1948; *The Third Man* (assisted Alexander Korda

Duel in the Sun with Lionel Barrymore and Harry Morgan.
(*Selznick*)

and Carol Reed), 1949; *The Wild Heart*, or *Gone to Earth*, 1952; *Stazione Termini* (financed only), 1953; *A Farewell to Arms*, 1957.

EDWARD SMALL Born February 1, 1891; *The Gorilla*, 1931; *I Cover the Waterfront*, 1933; *Palooka*, 1934; *The Count of Monte Cristo*, 1934; *Transatlantic Merry-Go-Round*, 1934; *Let 'em Have It*, 1935; *Red Salute*, 1935; *The Melody Lingers On*, 1935; *The Last of the Mohicans*, 1936; *Sea Devils*, 1937; *New Faces of 1937*, 1937; *Super Sleuth*, 1937; *The Toast of New York*, 1937; *The Duke of West Point*, 1938; *King of the Turf*, 1939; *The Man in the Iron Mask*, 1939; *My Son, My Son*, 1940; *South of Pago Pago*, 1940; *Kit Carson*, 1940; *The Son of Monte Cristo*, 1940; *International Lady*, 1941; *The Corsican Brothers*, 1941; *A Gentleman After Dark*, 1942; *Twin Beds*, 1942; *Miss Annie Rooney*, 1942; *Friendly Enemies*, 1942; *Up in Mabel's Room*, 1944; *Abroad With Two Yanks*, 1944; *Brewster's Millions*, 1945; *Getting Gertie's Garter*, 1945; *Temptation*, 1946; *The Return of Monte Cristo*, 1946; *T-Men*, 1947; *Red River*, 1948; *Scandal Sheet*, 1951; *Kansas City Confidential*, 1952; *Bandits of Corsica*, 1953; *Gun Belt*, 1953; *99 River Street*, 1953; *Steel Lady*, 1953; *Wicked Woman*, 1953; *Overland Pacific*, 1954; *Southwest Passage*, 1954; *Lone Gun*, 1954; *Down Three Dark Streets*, 1954; *Khyber Patrol*, 1954; *New York Confidential*, 1955; *The Naked Street*, 1955; *Top Gun*, 1955; *Witness for the Prosecution*, 1957; *Solomon and Sheba*, 1959; *Timbuktu*, 1959; *Jack, the Giant Killer*, 1962; *Diary of a Madman*, 1963; *Twice Told Tales*, 1963; *The Quick Gun*, 1964; *Apache Rifles*, 1964; *I'll Take Sweden*, 1965; *Frankie and Johnny*, 1966; *Boy, Did I Get a Wrong Number!*, 1966; *The Wicked Dreams of Paula Schultz*, 1968; *Hostile Witness*, 1968.

Palooka with Stuart Erwin and Marjorie Rambeau.   (*Small*)

HUNT STROMBERG Died 1968; *Our Blushing Brides*, 1930; *Guilty Hands*, 1931; *The Wet Parade*, 1932; *Letty Lynton*, 1932; *Red Dust*, 1932; *The White Sister*, 1933; *Penthouse*, 1933; *The Thin Man*, 1934; *Treasure Island*, 1934; *Hide-Out*, 1934; *The Painted Veil*, 1934; *Chained*, 1934; *Naughty Marietta*, 1935; *Ah, Wilderness*, 1935; *Rose Marie*, 1936; *Wife vs. Secretary*, 1936; *Small Town Girl*, 1936; *The Great Ziegfeld*, 1936; *After the Thin Man*, 1936; *Maytime*, 1937; *Night Must Fall*, 1937; *The Firefly*, 1937; *Sweethearts*, 1938; *Marie Antoinette*, 1938; *Idiot's Delight*, 1939; *The Women*, 1939; *Susan and God*, 1940; *Northwest Passage*, 1940; *Pride and Prejudice*, 1940; *They Met in Bombay*, 1941; *Shadow of the Thin Man*, 1941; *Lady of Burlesque*, 1943; *Guest in the House*, 1944; *The Strange Woman*, 1946; *Dishonored Lady*, 1947; *Lured*, 1947; *Too Late for Tears*, 1949.

WILLIAM C. THOMAS Born August 11, 1903; *Tokyo Rose*, 1945; *Follow That Woman*, 1945; *Scared Stiff*, 1945; *Hot Cargo*, 1946; *Swamp Fire*, 1946; *People Are Funny*, 1946; *Big Town*, 1947; *Fear in the Night*, 1947; *Danger Street*, 1947; *Jungle Flight*, 1947; *Seven Were Saved*, 1947; *I Cover the Big Town*, 1947; *Adventure Island*, 1947; *Big Town After Dark*, 1947; *Waterfront at Midnight*, 1948; *Speed to Spare*, 1948; *Shaggy*, 1948; *Mr. Reckless*, 1948; *Caged Fury*, 1948; *Big Town Scandal*, 1948; *Albuquerque*, 1948; *Disaster*, 1948; *Dynamite*, 1949; *El Paso*,

Idiot's Delight with Edward Arnold and Norma Shearer. *(Stromberg)*

1949; *Special Agent*, 1949; *Manhandled*, 1949; *Captain China*, 1949; *The Lawless*, 1950; *The Eagle and the Hawk*, 1950; *Crosswinds*, 1951; *Hong Kong*, 1951; *Blazing Forest*, 1952; *Carribbean*, 1952; *The Vanquished*, 1953; *Jamaica Run*, 1953; *Sangaree*, 1953; *Jivaro*, 1954; *Hell's Island*, 1955; *Run for Cover*, 1955; *Far Horizons*, 1955; *Lucy Gallant*, 1955; *Nightmare*, 1956; *The Big Caper*, 1957; *Bailout at 43,000*, 1957.

El Paso with John Payne, Gail Russell and Sterling Hayden. *(Thomas)*

JERRY WALD Born September 16, 1911; died July 13, 1962; *Navy Blues*, 1941; *All Through the Night*, 1942; *The Man Who Came to Dinner* (under Hal B. Wallis), 1942; *Larceny, Inc.*, 1942; *Juke Girl*, 1942; *Across the Pacific*, 1942; *Desperate Journey*, 1942; *George Washington Slept Here*, 1942; *Casablanca*, 1942; *The Hard Way*, 1942; *Air Force* (no screen credit), 1943; *Action in the North Atlantic*, 1943; *Background to Danger*, 1943; *Destination Tokyo*, 1943; *In Our Time*, 1944; *Shine On, Harvest Moon*, 1944; *The Very Thought of You*, 1944; *To Have and Have Not* (no screen credit), 1944; *Objective Burma*, 1945; *Pride of the Marines*, 1945; *Rhapsody in Blue*, 1945; *Humoresque*, 1946; *The Unfaithful*, 1947; *Possessed*, 1947; *Dark Passage*, 1947; *To the Victor*, 1948; *Key Largo*, 1948; *Johnny Belinda*, 1948; *One Sunday Afternoon*, 1948; *The Adventures of Don Juan*, 1948; *John Loves Mary*, 1949; *Flamingo Road*, 1949; *Look for the Silver Lining*, 1949; *Task Force*, 1949; *Always Leave Them Laughing*, 1949; *The Inspector General*, 1949; *Young Man With a Horn*, 1950; *Perfect Strangers*, 1950; *The Damned Don't Cry*, 1950; *Caged*, 1950; *The Breaking Point*, 1950; *The Glass Menagerie*, 1950; *Storm Warning*, 1951; *Behave Yourself* (this film and the three following were produced with Norman Krasna; Wald did the production work), 1951; *The Blue Veil*, 1951; *Clash by Night*, 1952; *The Lusty Men*, 1952; *From Here to Eternity*, 1953; *The Big Heat*, 1953; *Miss Sadie Thompson*, 1953; *The Caine Mutiny*, 1954; *Phffft*, 1954; *Cell 2455, Death Row* (Wald was the actual working producer), 1955; *The Queen Bee*, 1955; *Picnic*, 1955; *The Last Frontier*, 1955; *The Harder They Fall*, 1956; *Jubal*, 1956; *The Eddy Duchin Story*, 1956; *The Solid Gold Cadillac*, 1956; *You Can't Run Away from It*, 1956; *An Affair to Remember*, 1957; *No Down Payment*, 1957; *Kiss Them for Me*, 1957; *Peyton Place*,

1957; *The Hard-Hats* (uncompleted), 1957; *The Long Hot Summer*, 1958; *In Love and War*, 1958; *Mardi Gras*, 1958; *Beloved Infidel*, 1959; *The Sound and the Fury*, 1959; *Hound-Dog Man*, 1959; *The Best of Everything*, 1959; *The Story on Page One*, 1959; *Sons and Lovers*, 1960; *Let's Make Love*, 1960; *Hemingway's Adventures of a Young Man*, 1962; *The Stripper* (prepared the production and died before completion), 1963.

John Loves Mary with Ronald Reagan and Jack Carson. *(Wald)*

HAL B. WALLIS Born September 14, 1899; *Little Caesar*, 1930; *I Am a Fugitive From a Chain Gang*, 1932; *The Story of Louis Pasteur*, 1935; *A Midsummer Night's Dream*, 1935; *Green Pastures*, 1936; *The Life of Emile Zola*, 1936; *The Go-Getter*, 1937; *Marked Woman*, 1937; *Kid Galahad*, 1937; *That Certain Woman*, 1937; *It's Love I'm After*, 1937; *Tovarich* (with Robert Lord), 1937; *The Sisters*, 1938; *Jezebel* (with Henry Blanke), 1938; *The Adventures of Robin Hood*, 1938; *Invisible Stripes*, 1939; *Dark Victory*, 1939; *Juarez* (with Henry Blanke), 1939; *The Old Maid* (with Henry Blanke), 1939; *The Kid From Kokomo* (with Samuel Bischoff), 1939; *They Made Me a Criminal*, 1939; *The Roaring Twenties* (with Samuel Bischoff), 1939; *The Private Lives of Elizabeth and Essex* (with Robert Lord), 1939; *Virginia City*, 1940; *It All Came True* (with Mark Hellinger), 1940; *Brother Orchid* (with Mark Hellinger), 1940; *They Drive by Night* (with Mark Hellinger), 1940; *The Letter* (with Robert Lord), 1940; *City for Conquest*, 1940; *All This, and Heaven Too*, 1940; *The Sea Hawk*, 1941; *Footsteps in the Dark*, 1941; *Manpower* (with Mark Hellinger), 1941; *Sergeant York*, 1941; *The Maltese Falcon* (with Henry Blanke), 1941; *High Sierra* (with Mark Hellinger), 1941; *The Great Lie* (with Henry Blanke), 1941; *The Bride Came C.O.D.*, 1941; *One Foot in Heaven* (with Robert Lord), 1941; *The Man Who Came to Dinner* (with Jerry Wald), 1941; *Now, Voyager*, 1942; *In This Our Life*, 1942; *Desperate Journey*, 1942; *Casablanca*, 1942; *Yankee Doodle Dandy*, 1942; *Air Force*, 1943; *Watch on the Rhine*, 1943; *Passage to Marseille*, 1944; *The Affairs of Susan*, 1945; *Saratoga Trunk*, 1945; *Desert Fury*, 1947; *I Walk Alone*, 1947; *The Perfect Marriage*, 1947; *So Evil My Love*, 1948; *Sorry, Wrong Number*, 1948; *The Accused*, 1948; *My Friend Irma*, 1949; *Rope of Sand*, 1949; *Paid in Full*, 1949; *Thelma Jordan*, 1949; *September Affair*, 1950; *My Friend Irma Goes West*, 1950; *The Furies*, 1950; *Dark City*, 1950; *Red Mountain*, 1951; *That's My Boy*, 1951; *Sailor Beware*, 1951; *Peking Express*, 1951; *The Stooge*, 1952; *Jumping Jacks*, 1952; *Come Back, Little Sheba*, 1952; *Scared Stiff*, 1953; *Money From Home*, 1953; *About Mrs. Leslie*, 1954; *Three Ring Circus*, 1954; *Artists and Models*, 1955; *The Rose Tattoo*, 1955; *Hollywood or Bust*, 1956; *The Rainmaker*, 1956; *The Sad Sack*, 1957; *Gunfight at the O. K. Corral*, 1957; *Loving You*, 1957; *Wild Is the Wind*, 1957; *The Obsessed* (uncompleted), 1957; *Hot Spell*, 1958; *King Creole*, 1958; *Rock-A-Bye Baby*, 1958; *The Last Train From Gun Hill*, 1959; *Career*, 1959; *Don't Give Up the Ship*, 1960; *Visit to a Small Planet*, 1960; *G.I. Blues*, 1960; *All in a Night's Work*, 1961; *Summer and Smoke*, 1961; *Girls, Girls, Girls*, 1962; *A Girl Named Tamiko*, 1962; *Wives and Lovers*, 1963; *Fun in Acapulco*, 1963; *Becket*, 1964; *Roustabout*, 1964; *The Sons of Katie Elder*, 1965; *Boeing-Boeing*, 1965; *Paradise, Hawaiian Style*, 1966; *Barefoot in the Park*, 1967; *Easy Come, Easy Go*, 1967.

233

The Sisters with Bette Davis. *(Wallis)*

WALTER WANGER Born July 11, 1894; *The Cocoanuts*, 1929; *Washington Merry-Go-Round*, 1932; *The Bitter Tea of General Yen*, 1933; *Gabriel Over the White House*, 1933; *Another Language*, 1933; *Going Hollywood*, 1933; *Queen Christina*, 1933; *The President Vanishes*, 1934; *Private Worlds*, 1935; *Shanghai*, 1935; *Every Night at Eight*, 1935; *Mary Burns, Fugitive*, 1935; *The Trail of the Lonesome Pine*, 1936; *The Moon's Our Home*, 1936; *Big Brown Eyes*, 1936; *Palm Springs*, 1936; *Spendthrift*, 1936; *Fatal Lady*, 1936; *Sabotage*, 1936; *You Only Live Once*, 1937; *History Is Made at Night*, 1937; *Vogues of 1938*, 1937; *Stand-In*, 1937; *52nd Street*, 1937; *Blockade*, 1938; *Algiers*, 1938; *Trade Winds*, 1938; *Winter Carnival*, 1939; *Stagecoach*, 1939; *Eternally Yours*, 1939; *Slightly Honorable*, 1940; *The House Across the Bay*, 1940; *Foreign Correspondent*, 1940; *The Long Voyage Home*, 1940; *Sundown*, 1941; *Eagle Squadron*, 1942; *Arabian Nights*, 1942; *We've Never Been Licked*, 1943; *Gung Ho!*, 1943; *Ladies Courageous*, 1944; *Salome, Where She Danced*, 1945; *Scarlet Street*, 1945; *A Night in Paradise*, 1946; *Canyon Passage*, 1946; *Smash-up—the Story of a Woman*, 1947; *The Lost Moment*, 1947; *The Secret Beyond the Door*, 1948; *Tap Roots*, 1948; *Joan of Arc*, 1948; *Tulsa*, 1949; *Reign of Terror*, 1949; *The Reckless Moment*, 1949; *Aladdin and His Lamp*, 1952; *The Lady in the Iron Mask*, 1952; *Battle Zone*, 1952; *Kansas Pacific*, 1953; *Fort Vengeance*, 1953; *Riot in Cell Block 11*, 1954; *The Adventures of Hajji Baba*, 1954; *The Invasion of the Body Snatchers*, 1956; *The Quiet American*, 1958; *I Want to Live!*, 1958; *Cleopatra* (replaced by Darryl F. Zanuck), 1963.

A Night in Paradise with Merle Oberon and Turhan Bey. *(Wanger)*

LAWRENCE WEINGARTEN *Broadway Melody*, 1929; *Libeled Lady*, 1936; *A Day at the Races*, 1937; *I Love You Again*, 1940; *Escape*, 1940; *When Ladies Meet*, 1941; *Without Love*, 1945; *Adam's Rib*, 1949; *Invitation*, 1952; *Pat and Mike*, 1952; *The Actress*, 1953; *Rhap-*

sody, 1954; *The Tender Trap*, 1955; *I'll Cry Tomorrow*, 1955; *Don't Go Near the Water*, 1957; *Cat on a Hot Tin Roof*, 1958; *The Gazebo*, 1959; *Ada*, 1961; *The Honeymoon Machine*, 1961; *Period of Adjustment*, 1962; *The Unsinkable Molly Brown*, 1964; *Signpost to Murder*, 1965; *The Impossible Years*, 1968.

Invitation with Van Johnson and Dorothy McGuire. *(Weingarten)*

DARRYL F. ZANUCK Born September 5, 1902; *Noah's Ark*, 1929; *The Bowery*, 1933; *Moulin Rouge*, 1934; *The House of Rothschild*, 1934; *The Mighty Barnum*, 1934; *Cardinal Richelieu*, 1935; *Clive of India*, 1935; *Les Miserables*, 1935; *Prisoner of Shark Island*, (with Nunnally Johnson), 1936; *A Message to Garcia*, 1936; *Lloyds of London*, 1936; *One in a Million*, 1936; *The Road to Glory* (with Nunnally Johnson), 1936; *Wee Willie Winkie*, 1937; *Seventh Heaven*, 1937; *Alexander's Ragtime Band* (with Harry Joe Brown), 1938; *In Old Chicago*, 1938; *Suez*, 1938; *Kentucky*, 1938; *Four Men and a Prayer*, 1938; *Submarine Patrol*, 1938; *The Gorilla* (with Harry Joe Brown), 1939; *The Story of Alexander Graham Bell*, 1939; *Jesse James*, 1939; *Stanley and Livingston*, 1939; *The Rains Came*, 1939; *Young Mr. Lincoln*, 1939; *Drums Along the Mohawk*, 1939; *The Grapes of Wrath* (with Nunnally Johnson), 1940; *The Return of Frank James*, 1940; *The Mark of Zorro*, 1940; *Four Sons* (with Harry Joe Brown), 1940; *Tobacco Road*, 1941; *Western Union*, 1941; *How Green Was My Valley*, 1941; *Blood and Sand*, 1941; *A Yank in the R.A.F.*, 1941; *Son of Fury*, 1942; *This Above All*, 1942; *Winged Victory*, 1943; *The Purple Heart*, 1944; *Wilson*, 1944; *Anna and the King of Siam*, 1946; *The Razor's Edge*, 1946; *Dragonwyck*, 1946; *Forever Amber* (with William Perlberg), 1947; *Gentleman's Agreement*, 1947; *Pinky*, 1949; *Twelve O'Clock High*, 1949; *All About Eve*, 1950; *No Way Out*, 1950; *David and Bathsheba*, 1951; *People Will Talk*, 1951; *The Snows of Kilimanjaro*, 1952; *Viva Zapata!*, 1952; *The Egyptian*, 1954; *The Man*

Kentucky with Eddie "Rochester" Anderson, Walter Brennan, Loretta Young and Willard Robertson. *(Zanuck)*

in the Gray Flannel Suit, 1956; *Island in the Sun*, 1957; *The Sun Also Rises*, 1957; *Crime of the Century* (uncompleted), 1957; *Parris Island* (uncompleted), 1957; *The Roots of Heaven*, 1958; *Crack in the Mirror*, 1960; *Sanctuary*, 1961; *The Big Gamble*, 1961; *The Longest Day*, 1962; *The Chapman Report*, 1962; *Cleopatra* (replaced Walter Wanger), 1963; *The Visit*, 1964.

SAM ZIMBALIST Died November 4, 1958; *Tarzan Escapes*, 1936; *Married Before Breakfast*, 1937; *Navy Blue and Gold*, 1937; *The Crowd Roars*, 1938; *Tarzan Finds a Son*, 1939; *Boom Town*, 1940; *Tortilla Flat*, 1942; *Thirty Seconds Over Tokyo*, 1944; *Killer McCoy*, 1947; *Side Street*, 1949; *King Solomon's Mines*, 1950; *Too Young to Kiss*, 1951; *Quo Vadis*, 1951; *Mogambo*, 1953; *Beau Brummel*, 1954; *Tribute to a Bad Man*, 1956; *The Catered Affair*, 1956; *I Accuse!*, 1958; *Ben-Hur* (died during preparation), 1959.

(Zugsmith)

Platinum High School with Yvette Mimieux and Mickey Rooney.

ALBERT ZUGSMITH Born April 24, 1910; *Sword of Venus*, 1953; *Female on the Beach*, 1955; *The Square Jungle*, 1955; *Star in the Dust*, 1956; *Raw Edge*, 1956; *Red Sundown*, 1956; *Written on the Wind*, 1956; *The Tattered Dress*, 1957; *Slaughter on Tenth Avenue*, 1957; *The Incredible Shrinking Man*, 1957; *The Girl in the Kremlin*, 1957; *The Tarnished Angels*, 1957; *Man in the Shadow*, 1957; *Touch of Evil*, 1958; *The Female Animal*, 1958; *High School Confidential*, 1958; *The Beat Generation*, 1959; *The Big Operator*, 1959; *Girl's Town*, 1959; *Night of the Quarter Moon*, 1959; *Platinum High School*, 1960; *College Confidential*, 1960; *Sex Kittens Go to College*, 1960; *Dondi*, 1960; *The Private Lives of Adam and Eve*, 1960; *Confessions of an Opium Eater*, 1962; *Fanny Hill: Memoirs of a Woman of Pleasure*, 1965; *Movie Star American Style*, or *LSD I Hate You*, 1966; *The Chinese Room*, 1967; *The Ghost Riders*, 1967.

Side Street with Farley Granger and Jean Hagen. *(Zimbalist)*

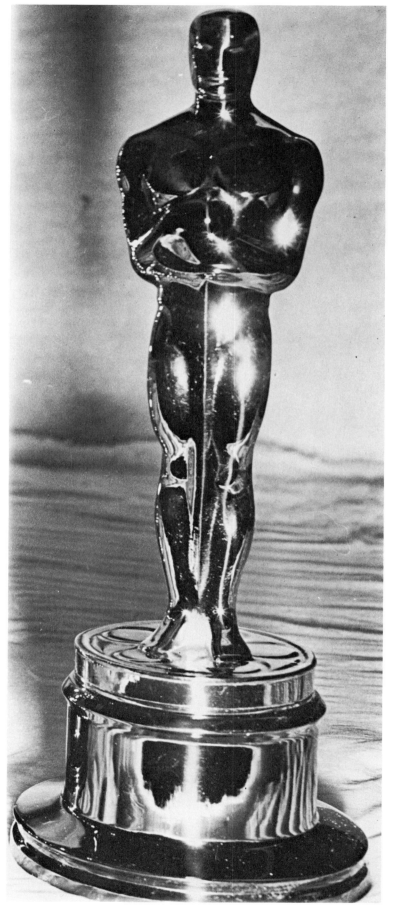

The Oscar

236

BIBLIOGRAPHY

Academy of Motion Picture Arts and Sciences, Research Council. *Motion Picture Sound Engineering.* New York: Van Nostrand, 1938.

Agee, James. *Agee on Film: Five Film Scripts.* Boston: Beacon, 1964.

Alicoate, Charles, ed. *Film Daily Year Book of Motion Pictures.* New York: *Film Daily* Annual.

Arliss, George. *My Ten Years in the Studios.* Boston: Little, Brown & Co., 1940.

Arnheim, Rudolf. *Film as Art.* Berkeley: University of California Press, 1957.

Bardeche, Maurice, and Brasillach, Robert. *The History of Motion Pictures.* New York: Norton, 1938.

Benoit-Levy, Jean. *The Art of the Motion Picture.* New York: Coward-McCann, 1946.

Bluestone, George. *Novels into Films.* Baltimore: Johns Hopkins Press, 1957.

Callenbach, Ernest. *Our Modern Art, the Movies.* Chicago: Center for Study of Liberal Education for Adults, 1955.

Catalog of Copyright Entries, cumulative series. Motion Pictures, 1912-1939. Washington, D. C.: Copyright Office, Library of Congress, 1951.

Catalog of Copyright Entries, cumulative series. Motion Pictures, 1940-1949. Washington, D. C.: Copyright Office, Library of Congress, 1953.

Catalog of Copyright Entries, cumulative series. Motion Pictures, 1950-1959. Washington, D. C.: Copyright Office, Library of Congress, 1963.

Catalog of Copyright Entries: Motion Pictures. Washington, D. C.: Copyright Office, Library of Congress. Semi-annual.

Ceram, C. W. *Archaeology of the Cinema.* New York: Harcourt, 1965.

Clason, W. E. *Dictionary of Cinema, Sound and Music.* New York: Van Nostrand, 1956.

Cogley, John. *Report on Blacklisting.* v. 1, Movies. New York: Fund for the Republic, 1956.

Conant, Michael. *Antitrust in the Motion Picture Industry.* Berkeley and Los Angeles: University of California Press, 1960.

Cooke, David C. *Behind the Scenes in Motion Pictures.* New York: Dodd, 1960.

Crowther, Bosley. *Hollywood Rajah: The Life and Times of Louis B. Mayer.* New York: Holt, 1960.

Crowther, Bosley. *Lion's Share: The Story of an Entertainment Empire.* New York: Dutton, 1957.

Dale, Edgar. *The Content of Motion Pictures.* New York: Macmillan, 1935.

Dale, Edgar, and Morrison, John. *Motion Picture Discrimination. An Annotated Bibliography.* Columbus, Ohio: Bureau of Educational Research, Ohio State University, 1951.

Dimmitt, Richard B. *A Title Guide to the Talkies: A Comprehensive Listing of 16,000 Feature-length Films from October 27, 1927, until December 1963.* 2 vols. New York: Scarecrow, 1965.

Dixon, Campbell, ed. *International Film Annual,* No. 1, 1957. New York: Doubleday.

Doyle, G. R. *Twenty-five Years of Films.* London: Mitre Press, 1936.

Everson, William K. *The American Movies.* New York: Atheneum, 1963.

Fenin, George N., and Everson, William K. *The Western: From Silents to Cinerama.* New York: Orion Press, 1962.

Field, Robert D. *The Art of Walt Disney.* New York: Macmillan, 1942.

Franklin, Harold B. *Sound Motion Pictures: From the Laboratory to Their Presentation.* New York: Doubleday, Doran & Co., 1929.

Fulton, A. R. *Motion Pictures: The Development of an Art from Silent Films to the Age of Television.* Norman: University of Oklahoma Press, 1960.

Goldwyn, Samuel. *Behind the Screen.* New York: Doran, 1923.

Green, Abel, and Laurie, Joe, Jr. *Show Biz, from Vaude to Video.* New York: Henry Holt & Co., 1951.

Griffith, Richard, and Mayer, Arthur. *The Movies.* New York: Simon and Schuster, 1957.

Hampton, Benjamin B. *A History of the Movies.* New York: Covici-Friede, 1931.

Handel, Leo A. *Hollywood Looks at Its Audience.* Urbana: University of Illinois Press, 1950.

Hays, Will H. *See and Hear: A Brief History of Motion Pictures and the Development of Sound.* New York: Motion Picture Producers and Distributors of America, 1929.

Holaday, Perry W., and Stoddard, George D. *Getting Ideas from the Movies.* New York: Macmillan, 1933.

Huaco, George A. *The Sociology of Film Art.* New York: Basic Books, 1965.

Hughes, Elinor. *Famous Stars of Filmdom.* Boston: L. C. Page & Co., 1932.

Inglis, Ruth A. *Freedom of the Movies: A Report on Self-regulation from the Commission on Freedom of the Press.* Chicago: University of Chicago Press, 1947.

International Film Guide. London: Tantivy Press. Annual.

Jacobs, Lewis. *The Rise of the American Film: A Critical History.* New York: Harcourt, Brace & Co., 1939.

Jacobs, Lewis, ed. *Introduction to the Art of the Movies: An Anthology of Ideas on the Nature of Movie Art.* New York: Noonday Press, 1960.

Kael, Pauline. *I Lost It at the Movies.* Boston: Atlantic-Little, 1965.

Kiesling, Barrett C. *Talking Pictures: How They Are Made, How to Appreciate Them.* New York: Johnson Pub. Co., 1937.

Knight, Arthur. *Liveliest Art: A Panoramic History of the Movies.* New York: Macmillan, 1957.

Lee, Norman. *Film Is Born: How 40 Film Fathers Bring a Modern Talking Picture into Being.* London: Jordan & Sons, 1945.

LeRoy, Mervyn. *It Takes More Than Talent,* as told to Alyce Canfield. New York: Alfred A. Knopf, 1953.

McAnany, Emile G. *The Film Viewer's Handbook.* Glen Rock: Paulist Press, 1965.

Mayer, Arthur. *Merely Colossal.* New York: Simon and Schuster, 1953.

Michael, Paul. *The Academy Awards: A Pictorial History.* Indianapolis: Bobbs-Merrill, 1964.

Michael, Paul. *Humphrey Bogart: The Man and His Films.* Indianapolis: Bobbs-Merrill, 1965.

Miller, Diane Disney. *The Story of Walt Disney.* New York: Holt, 1957.

New York City. Works Progress Administration. *The Film Index, a Bibliography.* New York: Museum of Modern Art Film Library, 1941.

Pitkin, Walter B., and Marston, William M. *The Art of Sound Pictures.* New York: Appleton, 1930.

Rideout, Eric H. *The American Film.* London: Mitre Press, 1937.

Sadoul, Georges. *Histoire Generale du Cinema.* 2 vols. Paris: Denocl., 1947. *1888-1949: A Pictorial Survey of World Cinema,* new enl. ed. London: Studio Publications, 1950.

Schary, Dore. *Case History of a Movie.* New York: Random House, 1950.

Schickel, Richard. *Movies: The History of an Art and an Institution.* New York: Basic Books, 1964.

Speed, F. M. *Movie Cavalcade: The Story of the Cinema, Its Stars, Studios and Producers.* London: Raven Books, 1944.

Talbot, Daniel, ed. and comp. *Film: An Anthology.* New York: Simon and Schuster, 1959.

Taylor, John R. *Cinema Eye, Cinema Ear: Some Key Film-Makers of the Sixties.* New York: Hill & Wang, 1964.

Thrasher, Frederic, ed. *Okay for Sound: How the Screen Found Its Voice.* New York: Duell, Sloan & Pearce, 1946.

Tyler, Parker. *Magic and Myth of the Movies.* New York: Henry Holt & Co., 1947.

Wagenknecht, Edward. *The Movies in the Age of Innocence.* Norman: University of Oklahoma Press, 1962.

Warshow, Robert. *The Immediate Experience: Movies, Comics, Theatre, and Other Aspects of Popular Culture.* Garden City: Doubleday, 1964.

Winchester's Screen Encyclopedia. London: Winchester Pub., 1948.

Zinsser, William K. *Seen Any Good Movies Lately?* New York: Doubleday, 1958.

Zukor, Adolph. *The Public Is Never Wrong: The Autobiography of Adolph Zukor,* with Dale Kramer. New York: G. P. Putnam's Sons, 1953.

NOTES AND COMMENTS

NOTES AND COMMENTS